PENGUIN CLASSICS

EARLY AMERICAN DRAMA

JEFFREY H. RICHARDS, associate professor of English at Old Dominion University, teaches early American literature and early through contemporary American drama. He is the author of *Theater Enough: American Culture and the Metaphor of the World Stage, 1607–1789* and *Mercy Otis Warren*.

48. *Tarentum.* Modern-day Taranto, in southern Italy.
49. *Chouse.* Cheat.
50. *Acheron.* Name for river crossed by souls into Hades and for Hades itself.
51. *Orcus.* Another term for the underworld or Hades.
52. *praetorium.* The tent or permanent dwelling of a general.

The Drunkard, by William Henry Smith

1. *Longfellow.* Henry Wadsworth (1807–1882); passage is from "The Light of Stars."
2. *affairs of men.* From William Shakespeare, *Julius Caesar*, act 4, scene 3. Brutus remarks, "There is a tide in the affairs of men / which, taken at the flood, leads on to fortune; / omitted, all the voyage of their life / Is bound in shallows and in miseries."
3. *scholar.* I do not know to whom Smith refers; however, Smith here is clearly taking credit for all but the story line, and in the literature is given credit as the author. As noted, Smith played Middleton in its Boston premiere.
4. *Intelligence Offices.* Something like employment agencies; intelligence suggests news of jobs.
5. *Bonus.* Good (Latin); Miss Spindle is a malapropist and probably means *Tempus*, time.
6. *foxed.* To fox is to fix a shoe or boot by adding a new upper portion.
7. *Polyhymnia.* The Greek muse of singing.
8. *Blue noses.* Puritans.
9. *Trapper.* The hero of James Fenimore Cooper's *Leatherstocking Tales,* Natty Bumppo, is called "the trapper" in *The Prairie* (1827).
10. *Chelsea.* Community north of Boston, near Chelsea Creek.
11. *Senna.* Cassia leaves, used medicinally as a laxative.
12. *horn.* Literally, a horn of an animal used for drinking, the term came simply to mean a glass or mug of ale or other alcoholic beverage.
13. *premunires.* Literally, to fortify (Latin); in English law, writs with various purposes, but including the enforcement of papal law in England. Cribbs is trying to scare William with legal mumbo jumbo.
14. *fieri facias.* Literally, cause to be made (Latin); in English common law, a judgment against a debtor that allows a creditor to collect out of the debtor's assets.
15. *prima faciae.* Literally, at first look (Latin); in law, meaning that no additional testimony is needed to establish credibility of evidence.

16. *William Wallace.* Scottish nationalist (c. 1270–1305) who led revolt against English authority in Scotland.

17. *Lucretia Borgia.* 1480–1519; member of prominent Italian political family and daughter of Pope Alexander VI, she was noted for charitable acts near the end of her life.

18. *general court.* Old term in Massachusetts for state legislature.

19. *non est inventus.* Literally, he was not found (Latin); in English law, what a sheriff says when he cannot locate a defendant.

20. *blue devils.* Depression; the blues.

21. *Five Points.* Notorious slum neighborhood in Manhattan.

22. *pornology.* Meaning unclear; Moody, *Dramas*, prints "pronology." *Porne* in Greek means harlot.

23. *Young Burke.* Master W. Burke, who played violin solo for the benefit of his brother Joseph, a child prodigy actor (billed as Master Burke, "The Irish Roscius") at the Tremont Theater, Boston, August 29, 1831.

24. *Ole Bull.* Norwegian violinist (1810–1880) who frequently toured United States. Smith probably saw both Bull and Burke.

25. *Col. Johnson* may be Richard Mentor Johnson (1780–1850), American soldier who, during the War of 1812, supposedly killed the Shawnee chieftain Tecumseh; he eventually became vice-president of the United States in 1837.

26. *Dr. Dodds.* John Bovee Dodds, American mesmerist and author of *The Philosophy of Electrical Psychology.*

27. *Tombs.* City jail in New York City.

28. *Home, Sweet Home.* Song by American expatriate actor and playwright John Howard Payne (1791–1852).

Fashion, by Anna Cora Mowatt

1. *Tennyson.* Quotation from Alfred Tennyson (1809–1892) poem "Lady Clara Vere de Vere" (1833).

2. *Costumes.* As printed in 1855 edition; many acting editions of plays from the period give this information, which I have generally omitted from other plays in the current volume.

3. *jenny-says-quoi.* One of Mrs. Tiffany's butcherings of French: *je ne sais quoi,* literally, I know not what, something inexpressible or special.

4. *comme il faut.* Proper.

5. *Princess Clementina.* Clémentine (1817–1907), daughter of Louis-Philippe, king of France from 1830 to 1848.

6. *abimé.* Overwhelmed; see another usage below.
7. *distingué.* Elegant.
8. *Sandwich Islands.* Hawaiian Islands, considered "primitive" in 1845.
9. *Wellington . . . d'Orsay.* Arthur Wellesley (1769–1852), first duke of Wellington, hero of Waterloo; Henry Peter Brougham (1778–1868), first baron Brougham and Vaux, champion of British Reform Bill in 1831; Alfred-Guillaume-Gabriel d'Orsay (1801–1852), French count and determiner of fashion in both the French and British capitals.
10. *Catteraugus.* County in southwestern New York state.
11. *voyture.* Voiture, vehicle; here, signifying carriage.
12. *rampant, couchant, passant.* Terms from heraldry that describe the animal postures on crests: (a) rearing on left hind leg with forelegs elevated; (b) lying down with head raised; (c) walking toward right with one foreleg raised.
13. *sal vous plait. S'il vous plaît,* if you please.
14. *bleeding.* Longtime treatment for a variety of ailments, including fever.
15. *Geneva.* City in western New York state, in Ontario County.
16. *Voila tout. Voilà tout,* that is all.
17. *recherché.* Exquisite.
18. *how ton. Haut ton,* high fashion.
19. *toot a fate. Tout à fait,* entirely.
20. *mal-ap-pro-pos. Mal à propos,* inappropriate, out of place; an allusion also to Mrs. Tiffany's stage predecessor, Mrs. Malaprop (whose name derives, of course, from the French expression) in Richard Brinsley Sheridan's *The Rivals.*
21. *bijou.* Gem.
22. *capital.* All the dialogue in act 3, scene 1 up to this point is marked in the 1855 edition as being omitted in the performance.
23. *Bung jure . . . Snobson? Bonjour, Comment vous portez-vous, Monsieur Snobson?* Good morning. How do you do, Mr. Snobson?
24. *Sassoyez vow. Asseyez-vous,* sit down.
25. *Perfide.* Traitor.
26. *Prend garde.* Watch out!
27. *Je vous salue, mes dames.* Your obedient servant, ladies.
28. *bon swear. Bonsoir,* good evening.
29. *bien etourdi . . . bon coeur.* He is a very thoughtless person, but he has a good heart.
30. *trompeur.* Impostor.
31. *sans doute.* Without fail.
32. *parole d'honneur.* Word of honor.
33. *parle bas.* Speak softly.
34. *bon gout.* Good taste.

35. *malgré moi*. Against my will.
36. *abimé*. Here, it means spoiled, in contrast with Mrs. Tiffany's earlier usage.

Uncle Tom's Cabin, by George L. Aiken

1. *Canada.* End point for escaped slaves. The passage of the Fugitive Slave Act of 1850 made capture of escaped slaves the law in all states, slave or free; thus no runaway slave could be safe unless purchased by sympathizers or gotten to Canada. In Stowe's novel, the Harrises are pursued all the way to Lake Erie before a boat gets them safely out of the United States.
2. *human bloodhounds.* Aiken uses the phrase from Stowe's novel, but the traveling Tom shows that followed Aiken had literal dogs following Eliza in the ice floe scene.
3. *Hannibal.* That is, noteworthy African. See notes to *The Gladiator*.
4. *daguerreotype.* Most popular photographic technique of the early 1850s for portraits. Named after the French inventor of the process, Louis Daguerre (1789–1851), daguerreotypy came to the United States in autumn of 1839. By the mid-1840s, several photographers had set up along Broadway in Manhattan; for little money, citizens could stroll in, sit in one of the upper-floor studios, and have a developed portrait in minutes. The better studios offered velvet-covered cases for the pictures. See also introduction to *The Octoroon*.
5. *traps.* Personal articles.
6. *professor.* Used by American Calvinists and others to signify one who professes the faith, the term was by the 1850s in wide use to signify college teacher.
7. *Jim Crow.* Refers to minstrel dance, "Jump Jim Crow," first popularized by Thomas D. Rice.
8. *brace of shakes.* Literally, a pair of moments; equivalent to something like "in just a second" or "in two shakes of a lamb's tail."
9. *mingled with fire.* Revelation 15:2: "And I saw it, as it were, a sea of glass mingled with fire, and them that had gotten the victory over the beast . . . standing on the sea of glass, having the harps of God" (KJV).
10. *bridegroom cometh.* Matthew 25:6, in the parable of the wise and foolish maidens.
11. *Spiritual Rappings.* Cultural phenomenon of the 1840s and early 1850s: people gathered together, often with a professional interpreter, to hear the tapping or voices of the dead.
12. *Yahoo.* Rube; from Jonathan Swift's *Gulliver's Travels*.

EARLY AMERICAN DRAMA

EDITED WITH

AN INTRODUCTION AND NOTES BY

JEFFREY H. RICHARDS

PENGUIN BOOKS

PENGUIN BOOKS
Published by the Penguin Group
Penguin Books USA Inc., 375 Hudson Street, New York, New York 10014, U.S.A.
Penguin Books Ltd, 27 Wrights Lane, London W8 5TZ, England
Penguin Books Australia Ltd, Ringwood, Victoria, Australia
Penguin Books Canada Ltd, 10 Alcorn Avenue,
Toronto, Ontario, Canada M4V 3B2
Penguin Books (N.Z.) Ltd, 182–190 Wairau Road,
Auckland 10, New Zealand

Penguin Books Ltd, Registered Offices:
Harmondsworth, Middlesex, England

First published in Penguin Books 1997

27 29 30 28 26

Copyright © Jeffrey H. Richards, 1997
All rights reserved

LIBRARY OF CONGRESS CATALOGING IN PUBLICATION DATA
Early American drama/edited with an introduction and notes by
Jeffrey H. Richards.
p. cm.
Includes bibliographical references (p.   ).
Contents: The contrast/by Royall Tyler—Andre/by William Dunlap—The Indian
princess/by James Nelson Barker—The gladiator/by Robert Montgomery Bird—
The drunkard/by William Henry Smith—Fashion/by Anna Cora Mowatt—Uncle
Tom's cabin/by George L. Aiken—The octoroon/by Dion Boucicault.
ISBN 0 14 04.3588 3
1. American drama—1783–1850. 2. American drama—19th century. 3. United
States—History—Drama. I. Richards, Jeffrey H.
PS631.E27 1997
812'.208—dc21 96–49410

Printed in the United States of America
Set in Sabon

ACKNOWLEDGMENTS

No one prepares a book alone. I wish to thank John Seelye for his faith at the start of this project and his comments at the end. My editor at Penguin, Michael Millman, has likewise encouraged me in the project through a commitment to get this book out and in a timely fashion. I am grateful to both. I also have not forgotten that Lawrence Avery pointed me toward early American drama a long time ago.

My debt to Elaine Dawson, word processor par excellence, is profound, especially in her ability to render clear copy from poorly printed and deteriorating original copies of these plays. One of my great fears —getting the texts right—turned out to be one of my great pleasures for the opportunity to work with Elaine.

I was also helped in both research and proofing stages by my able research assistant, Carolyn Gardner. The interlibrary loan office at Old Dominion University provided me with many difficult-to-obtain materials, while my colleagues in the English Department offered valuable comments when I presented some of the introductory material as a talk.

Doreen Alvarez Saar introduced me to the pleasures of the Clement Library when we both chanced to be in Ann Arbor, and I am grateful to her. Don Wilcox at the library was extremely helpful in finding materials for me. The passages that I quote in the introductions from manuscript letters by Lydia, W., and Henry Bird are used by kind permission of the William L. Clements Library. A conversation with Chip Walton while he was writing his fine thesis on Royall Tyler at the University of Colorado allowed me to clarify some issues regarding *The Contrast*.

Friends and family remain the vital forces behind all that I do. Everett and Katherine Emerson; Larry and Renee Earley; Tye, Wanda, Susannah, and Sam Hunter; Barbara Wildemuth and Gaylen Brubaker; John Morris; and Kent Peterson have all provided inspiration, as they have for years. My mother, Betty Richards; my sisters and their families—Suzanne, Amanda, Elizabeth, and Joe Uczen; Sally, Doug, Jake, and Emily Anderson—and my in-laws, Kenneth and Mary Sugioka, should all know they have a piece of this, somewhere. My one regret is the sudden loss of my brother-in-law Paul Uczen, a good man and a lover of books. I will miss all he might have said about these plays.

Gratitude grows the closer it gets to home. Thanks go to those who endure: my wife, Stephanie Sugioka; my son, Aaron Richards; and my daughter, Sarah Grace Richards.

CONTENTS

INTRODUCTION

Until recently, American drama before the Civil War was largely scorned by critics and historians as subliterary. There are many reasons for this, but none is stronger than prejudice—old prejudice against the American stage of the period, as well as its successor entertainments, film and television, for its lowbrow popularity; and another, more broad-based, against anything "melodramatic." Once merely a descriptive word for a stage entertainment with music, *melodrama* came to mean to a later era a play with excessively sentimental speeches; stereotyped characters; obvious, moralistic plot; and acting that bore no relation to actions and speech in "real life." By the early twentieth century, to call something "melodramatic" was to deride it as cheap and vulgar, popular at its most derogatory, and distinctly not worth any serious critical or historical discussion. Thus, whole centuries of American playwriting activity were abandoned by critics in the rush to embrace the new, and presumably nonmelodramatic, theater of O'Neill, Anderson, Williams, Miller, and Albee. Only recently have theater and literary scholars been able to take a fresh look at early American plays and inquire, if they were so bad, why so many people went to experience them.

The plays in this volume have been selected as examples of dramas by American writers that were performed in their time but also have texts that will still reward the careful reader. To appreciate them fully, however, one must first historicize them; in other words, make some attempt to imagine the social and theatrical conditions that made them possible. Antebellum drama was, primarily, popular culture, not the retreat of the elite. In recognizing our own responses to the popular culture of the present, we may be able to recover something of the expectations of audiences from the past. In this introduction, I intend first to provide a brief history of American drama before the Civil War and to lay out some of the problems and preconceptions facing audience and writer alike in the late eighteenth and early nineteenth centuries. At the same time, I will consider the difficulties facing modern readers in encountering these texts.

Playwrights and the Theater
in Early America: A Brief History

Although many histories, such as those by Quinn and Meserve, have
been written about the development of theater and the drama in
English-speaking America, its place in the culture has still not been explained fully. Early European settlers and explorers came from societies
that made theater a significant element of public experience. The major
colonial powers—Spain, France, and England—were establishing their
authority in the New World at the same time that their national dramas
were growing in importance. Lope de Vega, Corneille, and Shakespeare
were creating some of the greatest plays in the history of the West while
colonists were busy exploring new territory, cutting down forests, or
crushing Indian resistance. That is to say, the very shaping of the ideology of conquest was in some ways tied to a theatrical view of life, the
notion of the *theatrum mundi* or world as a stage. As people like Captain John Smith saw the New World as a theater on which to play their
roles in history, theatergoers in Madrid, Paris, and London viewed
the stage as a world in miniature, a microcosm. Ironically, at least in
English-controlled territory, actual playhouses or theatrical performances were few or absent altogether. Thus it seems that before there
were theaters in America, there was theatrical thinking (Richards, *Theater*, 61–84).
    The first play known to have been performed in English-speaking
America was *The Bear and the Cub* (or as it was written down in the
court records, *Ye Bare and Ye Cubb*), acted in a tavern in Pungoteague,
on the Eastern Shore of Virginia, in 1665 (Meserve, *Emerging*, 16). No
theater building is known until the early 1700s, when it seems that
Williamsburg, Virginia, and New York City built or converted buildings
to theater use (McNamara; Young). By the late 1740s, professional actors from England via Jamaica—Walter Murray and Thomas Kean's
Company of Comedians from Virginia—began to play in American cities. The Hallam family of actors arrived in Virginia directly from England in 1752 and played brief seasons in a number of cities (Wright,
31–33; Highfill). At the time of the Revolution, New York, Philadelphia,
Williamsburg, and Charleston had active theater seasons, and by the
turn of the century, many other cities, including Boston, Baltimore,
Richmond, Norfolk, Wilmington, and Savannah, had buildings to accommodate plays—and patrons to view them. With the movement west,
further theaters came to Mobile, Cincinnati, Louisville, and St. Louis.

With the advent of the Civil War, plays were being acted throughout the East and Midwest and as far west as San Francisco. In brief, the theater went from a few scattered sites and performances to become the dominant cultural medium of the United States.

From the beginning, attitudes toward theater were varied and contradictory. The early adventurers in Virginia were people steeped in Elizabethan and Jacobean cultural attitudes; Captain Smith not only used stage language in his writing, but also fought a running battle in London with those who would mock his American exploits on the stage. Yet, in a sermon preached to colonists embarking for Virginia, one cleric, William Crashaw, told them to keep out "the players" if they wanted to have a successful enterprise. Although, in general, attitudes in the Anglican-dominated South were less rigid about what constituted legitimate entertainment, and southern cities were more sympathetic to theater than many in the North, wealthy landowners like William Byrd II still had to feed their desire for playgoing by living in London for long stretches. No one found that operating a theater in the South would produce much in the way of fame, profit, or locally written drama during the 1700s.

In the North, New York was an early home to actors and theatrical entertainments. By the 1730s, there must have been sufficient interest in playgoing among Manhattanites that immigrants sought jobs as actors. Young Elizabeth Ashbridge, who would later gain fame for her spiritual autobiography, arrived in New York in 1732 from Ireland and tried her hand at acting before eventually turning to preaching in her adopted religious community, the Society of Friends. In fact, another congenial home to theater was the Quaker city, Philadelphia, which had the honor of producing the first tragedy known to have been written by an American, *The Prince of Parthia* (1759) by Thomas Godfrey, Jr. The production of Godfrey's play in 1767 would be a good yardstick of how the theater would operate later. Originally on the bill was another homegrown play, a comedy by Thomas Forrest called *The Disappointment*, but its slang-laden, ethnically inscribed dialogue and its satiric bite caused the managers to fear reprisals. They opted for the safe, turgid drama of events and people far removed from midcentury Philadelphia. Even in the eighteenth century, the dread of lost revenues would often be the standard by which plays and entertainments would be written and produced.

Yet, Philadelphia, too, like nearly all cities where theatrical entertainments appeared in the 1700s and early 1800s, had many people who resisted the planting of theater at all, often on religious grounds.

The most vehement opposition to the institutionalizing of theater came from Massachusetts. English Calvinism early set itself in opposition to the theater for several reasons, but two are noteworthy: the first is that theaters drew criminals (and experience with pickpockets and prostitutes in the theaters south of the Thames in England showed this criticism had its merits); the second asserted that acting was merely a form of hypocrisy, a pretending to be someone a person was not, and therefore only encouraged youth to imitate bad behavior. The latter criticism proved to be the more lasting one. Dancing masters, displays of sword prowess, and anything that smacked of frivolous entertainment were proscribed by civil authorities under sway of the old Puritan beliefs. Not until 1794 would Boston have its first professional theater season.

But it was not only Puritans who objected to the stage. When Lewis Hallam and David Douglass brought professional troupes to American shores, they encountered some hostility in nearly every venue. This led to the practice of turning plays into "lectures," whereby scenes from *Othello*, for instance, could be passed off as a lecture on jealousy. During the Revolutionary War, Washington, a great supporter of the theater who sometimes used plays like Joseph Addison's *Cato* to encourage morale, had to bow to the will of the Continental Congress when it banned plays in patriot-controlled territory in 1778 (Rankin; Brown). Thereafter, only those places the British occupied could hold plays; and since New York was the one American city of note held by the British for the entirety of the war, it was the only venue in the new republic that was fully prepared after the war to launch ambitious new seasons. Consequently, the supporters of a revived theater in other places had to counter not only the continued religious antagonism to theater but also a political-cultural one: theater was the province of our late enemy, the British. Therefore, to admit it as a legitimate entertainment would be to sink the new country into corruption and frivolity when the work of nation-building had only just begun. The challenge for potential actors, playwrights, managers, and spectators was how to create an institution that could provide plays yet satisfy the moral and cultural criticisms leveled at the stage.

Even before mounting plays on the stage was a real possibility, many writers used dramatic form. In some respects, closet or tacit drama had been a part even of Puritan literary culture. The English Calvinist John Foxe had written religious plays for university production in the mid-1500s, before Puritan cultural critics like Philip Stubbes in *The Anatomie of Abuses* (1583) began to denounce the stage. Yet, we see that American Puritans still read plays—Samuel Sewall relaxed with a drama by Dryden, for instance, and Increase Mather owned volumes by classical playwrights (Richards, *Theater*, 101–93). By the 1700s, plays became vehicles for political commentary or satire. The royal governor of New York, Robert Hunter, penned a satiric play, *Androborus* (1714), that took swipes at his political enemies. An opponent of Massachusetts governor Jonathan Belcher in 1732 circulated a play that condemned Belcher's method of coming to power and painted the governor as a designing villain who uses dishonesty to get his post (Robert E. Moody). That same strategy would be used by America's first female playwright, Mercy Otis Warren. In a series of three linked satiric dramas, *The Adulateur* (1772), *The Defeat* (1773), and *The Group* (1775), Warren would excoriate the regime of a later Massachusetts royal governor, Thomas Hutchinson, and his Tory cronies (Richards, *Warren*, 84–120). Some of America's early closet playwrights took the high road, seeking for heroes or tragically noble figures. Robert Rogers's *Ponteach* (1766) was the first English-language play by someone resident in America to feature a Native character as the focus (Meserve, *Emerging*, 53–55). Other playwrights looked to the American Revolution for material. Battles at Lexington and Concord, at Bunker Hill, and at Quebec lie behind dramas by John Leacock (*The Fall of British Tyranny*) and Hugh Henry Brackenridge (*The Battle of Bunkers-Hill* and *The Death of General Montgomery*). But closet drama was not limited to supporters of the Revolution. Such Tory vehicles as Jonathan Sewall's *A Cure for the Spleen* or the anonymous *The Battle of Brooklyn* were used to roast the Whiggish patriots. These political plays were written not for the actual playhouse but, as Leacock suggests, the stage of the world on which the real-life events referred to were being acted. American authors would have to wait for the war's conclusion before the small stage would be available as a space on which to display their work (Richards, *Theater*, 247–51).

Later playwrights, who were more likely to get their works on stage, followed the lead of these pioneers in looking to American history for material. One of the plays in this volume, William Dunlap's *André* (1798), proved that an author could have some success on stage with a serious examination of the complexities of a historical moment—in this case, the capture and execution of the popular British officer John André, in 1780. In that sense, then, the closet and satiric dramatists of the eighteenth century paved the way for those who would have real theaters to write for.

With the reopening of theaters after the Revolution and the demand for new buildings, American writers saw the possibilities of a local theatrical tradition. Even so, it was a battle for recognition that would take many decades. The postwar theater managers did not rush out to demand new American works; instead, they trotted out the old prewar favorites, or imported new hits from London. Shakespeare, Sheridan, Farquhar, and O'Keeffe were far more likely to be shown than anything American. Not surprisingly, then, enterprising American playwrights had to confront the realities of audiences and managers. The politics of America may have been new for the world, but the theatrical forms would remain thoroughly tried, if not always true.

When a soldier-lawyer-poet named Royall Tyler came to New York in March 1787, he sized up the situation with a practical eye. Playing at the John Street Theater, a prewar stage that had been reopened in 1786, were two British plays: the main feature was Richard Brinsley Sheridan's *The School for Scandal*, a comedy of manners; the light piece was called *The Poor Soldier*, by John O'Keeffe, starring the popular comic actor Thomas Wignell. Whether Tyler had been working on a play before he came to town is not entirely clear, but, at any rate, the manuscript he presented to the John Street managers was formally speaking a combination of the bill he had seen plus several other plays that had been performed by the Old American Company. His play *The Contrast* was a comedy of manners with a farcical role, the Yankee Jonathan, that matched the skills of Wignell, who took the part; cobbled together from what was currently popular, the play was accepted in time to be mounted in April. As a play, there was nothing in Tyler's work to challenge the sensibilities of the audience.

Nevertheless, the production of this comedy, the first by an American to be presented at a professional theater, marks a key moment in American dramatic history. As the playwright himself announces through a poetic prologue, the audience will not find the usual subject, the lords and ladies of London. Rather, it is "native themes" that he portrays. Set in New York among a well-to-do class of postwar Americans with too much time on their hands, *The Contrast* could make comic hay out of the American desire for fashion and luxuries and mores from Europe. Through the noble, if somewhat dull, characters of Colonel Manly and Maria, Tyler points toward an American virtue that at once resists corruption from Europe without rejecting entirely the cultural inheritance of the Old World. Negotiating between complete capitulation to the Anglophiles in the audience—New York, we recall, was occupied by the British during the whole of the war—and total denunciation of the perversions of the stage, Tyler steers a middle course that in essence says, Theater is good for America as long as it affirms virtue. The old demand that theater be didactic if it be admitted at all had not yet died away.

If the English comedy of manners provided Tyler with a model, another imported form, the "melo-drame," would prove wildly popular for nearly a century on American stages. Originating in France as a play with music to accompany dialogue, melodrama acquired its combination of extravagant plot and large gestures in the French Revolution. In his essay "Melodrama, Body, Revolution," Peter Brooks has argued that beginning with Boutet de Monvel's *Les victimes cloîtrées* (1791), the combination of revolutionary fervor and the drama created a form that was in its origins of and for the people. Both moral and democratic, melodrama was a suitable dramatic type for people who sought some verification of their desires. Made popular in France through the numerous plays of Guilbert de Pixérécourt and brought to England in November 1802 through Thomas Holcroft's loose adaptation of Pixérécourt's *Coelina ou l'Enfant du mystère*, melodrama quickly crossed the Atlantic. Holcroft's play *A Tale of Mystery*, classified as "A Melo-Drame in Two Acts," appeared on the New York stage by early 1803, reaching Charleston later that year and Richmond in 1804. One of the first American productions to use the French expression for a play with music was Philadelphian James Nelson Barker's *The Indian Princess* (1808). Barker called his play an "Operatic Melo-drame," one of the many hybrid plays that approximate what we might now call light opera. Part comic stereotyping, part romantic love story, part historical high drama, *The Indian Princess* not only propelled melodrama along on its sure path, but also inaugurated a taste for Indian plays.

One of those Indian plays, *Metamora, or The Last of the Wampanoags* (1829), was written for a competition held by the rising American actor Edwin Forrest. Seeking vehicles for his star status, Forrest sought to encourage local writers to provide him with new material, which he appropriated from the authors upon payment of prize money. While people like John Augustus Stone, the author of *Metamora*, or another Forrest prizewinner, Robert Montgomery Bird, often struggled financially, the man of the people, Forrest, made thousands of dollars from his portrayal of the tragic Indian chief or Bird's Roman gladiator. Forrest's acting—muscular, loud, sometimes criticized as "rant"—brought him wildly enthusiastic partisans, especially among the mechanic classes and the street denizens of lower Manhattan, the b'hoys. Though Forrest usually acted in Shakespeare, his prize plays, and other stock dramas of the time, his audience might also see on the same bill with their hero other plays with lesser-known actors—farces, sketches about firemen, or, beginning in the 1840s, black-faced white performers in minstrel shows. In any event, Forrest tapped into a well of enthusiasm for theater the likes of which we might only see now at rock concerts and athletic events.

This new popularity of the stage meant larger theaters, with capacities in the low thousands. From narrow boxlike theaters in the eighteenth century, architects began to design and managers to build larger, wider structures with a proscenium stage, wide pit, and three tiers of box seats and gallery. Pricing for theaters was fairly uniform, with gallery seats the cheapest, often at 25 cents, pit seats going for 50 cents, and the boxes up to $1.00 per seat. By the 1830s and 1840s, classes of patrons emerged in the decorum of seating. Single men, unmarried women with escorts, and critics sat in the seats in front of the stage, the pit. Apprentices, servants, slaves, and others of lower income inhabited the gallery in the rear of the theater, with some cities restricting gallery seating further in sections by race. The fashionable set held the first tier of boxes lining the sides of the house; respectable middling families sat in the second tier; and the third tier, ironically, given the moralism of many of the plays, welcomed prostitutes and their clients. Indeed, the third tier had its own special entryway that allowed the streetwalkers early access, well before the plays began—and convenient exit, as the women took their customers to local boardinghouses or hotels for assignations during the show (Johnson). Thus, parents could take young people to the theater and ignore, in Victorian fashion, the selling of bodies going on just above their heads.

To be sure, despite the success of plays featuring American themes and subjects, the early-nineteenth-century stage still presented large numbers of costume dramas about the long ago and the far away. Retread versions of Pixérécourt melodramas, or new melodramatically tinged tragedies, like the hits from the British writer Edward Bulwer-Lytton (*The Lady of Lyons, Richelieu*), continued to prove popular with audiences and actors alike. One could find buried in Bird's *The Gladiator* a language of radical democracy or see in Mowatt's *Fashion* a gentle tweak at the parvenu class, but for the most part, American playwrights stayed clear of engaging controversial subjects of the day head-on.

By the 1840s, however, some subjects were becoming unavoidable. One of those was temperance. After rather modest beginnings before 1820, by the mid-1830s, several societies made stopping the public thirst for alcohol their priority. Appeals to fear of drunken immigrants were coupled with the dread of domestic instability in the middling classes brought about by alcohol abuse. Temperance preachers and organizations galvanized millions of Americans into forswearing the evils of drink or, as the act of repudiation was known, "taking the pledge." When the actor-manager W. H. Smith saw that temperance played big with the same class of people who came to his theaters in Boston, he knew he had hit material on his hands. Indeed, after a fitful beginning, his drama *The Drunkard* launched a minor industry—the temperance play. Even so, the play itself was not politically very controversial. No one with a public reputation to maintain was in favor of drunkenness. Although topical, *The Drunkard* and its sister plays did not really confront a radicalizing theme.

All that changed when the stage took up the problem of slavery. One of the first authors to sensationalize slavery was black autobiographer, novelist, and playwright William Wells Brown. Having in an earlier book given Harriet Beecher Stowe the idea for a slave woman crossing an ice floe to freedom, Brown published a novel, *Clotel* (1853), that implicated Thomas Jefferson in the fathering of a child by a black slave. In 1858, his play, the first to be published by an African American, *The Escape; or, A Leap for Freedom. A Drama in Five Acts*, appeared in Boston. Unfortunately, because the white-dominated theater of the time was not receptive to original work by black writers, other authors had already claimed the slavery field. Neither the novelty of its being written by an African American nor its subject was enough to earn the play more than a short run.

The real confrontation with slavery in the popular mind began with the publication of Stowe's novel *Uncle Tom's Cabin* (1852). With a rhetoric at once evangelical, satirical, and sentimental, Stowe's text ripped through the American reading public—in the words of David Crockett's "A Pretty Predicament"—"like a pint of whiskey among forty men." That a work which forced Americans to face up to slavery and the Fugitive Slave Act could generate huge sales was not lost on playwrights. Even before the novel was finished (it was first published serially), playwrights were already at work on stage versions. One of the most successful and most faithful to Stowe's text was George L. Aiken's play; with a run of over three hundred nights, *Uncle Tom's Cabin* stimulated playhouse owners and actors alike to see that topicality could pay off.

Other playwrights than Aiken could see gold in American issues. The Irish playwright Dion Boucicault, with a string of London successes behind him, came to New York in 1853 to try his luck in the United States. With *The Poor of New York* (1857), an Englished and Americanized version of the French urban melodrama *Les Pauvres de Paris* (1856), by Eugène Nus and Edouard Brisebarre, Boucicault hit his stride. Combining the usual domestic plot with an exposé of urban poverty, adding a thrilling sequence of scenes that culminates in a spectacular fire of a rooming house in Manhattan, and bringing on those city favorites, the firemen, Boucicault showed his skill at adaptation to American circumstances.

Boucicault again absorbed the topical when he mounted his own slave melodrama, *The Octoroon*, in 1859. With a splendid cast that included his wife, Agnes Robertson, and the future star of *Rip Van Winkle*, Joseph Jefferson, as well as himself, Boucicault borrowed elements from *Uncle Tom's Cabin*, minstrel shows, and his earlier pyrotechnic hit to fashion a story about a doomed young woman. One-eighth African by blood, the character Zoe came to embody one of the stock figures in literature by this time, the tragic mulatta. As tensions concerning slavery had grown to the rabid pitch of the late 1850s, Boucicault knew his play would be controversial. As a man of the theater, however, he also knew that he could not afford to alienate one-half of his audience—and New York had a large number of proslavery inhabitants and visitors in its borders. As Jefferson later described it, the play tried to please both abolitionist and antiabolitionist adherents, but in fact was "noncommittal" (214).

Thus, even in embracing the topical, antebellum American playwrights refused by and large to make their plays vehicles for political position or ideological commitment. No longer just an amateur activity, theater in America was business—big business. The kind of overt partisanship seen in the Revolutionary closet dramas could not be maintained on stage even a few years after the war. Fear of customer defection led to a consumer-driven dramatic culture. In a world swirling with contentious political rhetoric, financial panics, and controversies of all kinds, the mainstream stage saw its bread buttered in appealing to the subpolitical, "universal," desire among theater patrons to laugh or cry—to be entertained.

Reading Early American Drama

While the early American theater may not have taken the lead in facing the difficult subjects of the day, its documents and history provide a rich source of insight into American culture then and now. For twenty-first-century readers of plays from the period before 1860, however, access to the nuances and signification of elements in the texts may not be easy. When plays from the period are revived, they are often played in a camp style. I recall from my own childhood, through cartoons like "Dudley Do-Right of the Mounties" and television shows like *Fractured Flickers*, how gestures and plots associated with melodrama (which silent films carried on to a large degree) were routinely held up to ridicule. Over years of exposure to that kind of mockery, we come to assume that audiences from the late 1700s or 1800s were simpletons, with no aesthetic sensibility, and that actors were no better than clowns, without method or ability other than that connected to exaggeration. As for the playwrights, their work for decades was considered too awful, or too unintentionally funny, to be rated as literature. Yet, at the same time, we admire the poetry and fiction of people like Poe, Hawthorne, Melville, Whitman, and James—all habitués, at one period or another in their lives, of the stages that mounted the plays in this volume.

In fact, one of the points I wish to make is that to understand the rest of American literature, one has to understand its drama and theater. Of all entertainments, theater was perhaps the closest to a universal experience for most Americans. Plays and players were everywhere, from the cities to the towns and villages to frontier saloons. Though both men traveled widely and appeared before audiences over much of the United States, Edwin Forrest was far better known to the public than Ralph Waldo Emerson. When a transplanted New England woman wrote to her friend in Massachusetts in 1839, she felt that her new home of Mobile, Alabama, was, in the eyes of many, a "*barbarous country*," but all that would change next week: "[W]e are to have Forrest and it is the first time he ever played in Mobile, the inhabitants are preparing for quite a sensation" (Lydia). Emerson could cause a stir at Harvard Divinity School and send Poe into a froth, but as for exciting bright and culturally active people like Lydia, Edwin Forrest would be much more likely in 1839 to carry the day.

Actors

Long before the star system reigned in Hollywood, it dominated the American theater. If Forrest was the first of the big American stars, imported actors had played that role much earlier. As we noted above with Royall Tyler, playwrights learned to write with stars in mind. *The Contrast* can be said to feature the best-developed stage Yankee character to date, Jonathan, but Jonathan's particular dimensions take their shape from the comic gifts of the actor for whom the role was designed, Thomas Wignell. While we as readers may be tempted to see Jonathan as low relief in a comedy of upper-class manners, contemporary audiences mostly remembered Jonathan when they thought of the play later. Short, pugnacious on stage, and well known, Wignell could exploit his comic persona fully in the figure of the naïve waiter to Colonel Manly. Tyler even assigned the rights of the play to Wignell, and after its first New York appearance in 1787, it was Wignell's play.

But we also need to remember that Wignell was British by birth. In other words, in the late-eighteenth-century theater, characters that we might view as quintessentially American might be acted by persons whose commitment to America was more monetary than anything else. There are always ironies in any theater when actors play roles nothing like themselves, but at a time when nationalist sympathies were tender, the casting of a Brit to play Jonathan, a "true-blue son of liberty," has special resonance. For many American theatergoers, "lately played in London" meant "worth going to see." And while one might expect during the colonial period that the first professionals would be immigrants or visitors, as was the case, this trend does not stop with independence. Charles Mathews, another comic actor, also perfected a Yankee persona that he played to great applause both in the United States and in England during the 1820s (Hodge, 60–77). George Frederick Cooke, Edmund Kean, Charles Kemble, Fanny Kemble, Junius Brutus Booth, John Durang, Ellen Tree, and William Macready are some of the actors from the British Isles or other parts of Europe who came to conquer the seemingly provincial stages of America. Some stayed to form family dynasties, as with Booth. Others fled for their lives, as Macready did after his rivalry with Forrest led to the bloody Astor Place Riot in New York in 1849. Thus, even in the 1830s and 1840s, when American actors were getting a foothold on fame, foreign plays and actors still carried the cachet of quality for American audiences.

Not surprisingly, some American theater people saw travel in the other direction as the key to fame. John Howard Payne, an actor and playwright whose first drama, *Julia*, was performed when he was not yet fifteen, journeyed to England and stayed for many years, writing plays that appealed to British taste. Like his contemporary, friend, and sometime collaborator, the prose writer Washington Irving (who likewise gained fame first overseas, then reimported it to his native country), Payne designed his texts with English audiences in mind. In Payne's case, that meant English actors as well. Thus, we have the situation of an American writer constructing a play, *Charles the Second, or The Merry Monarch* (1824), for the London theater, from where it could be brought to New York a few months later and presented as having been successful overseas. But for a rising generation of American playwrights, Payne's could only be a transitional strategy (Meserve, *Emerging*, 280–90).

It was Forrest who would provide a catalyst for a more peculiarly American style of drama. Meanwhile, he was also a star, in competition with British leading actors for the large purses that awaited the successful. Behind the curtain, the balance of power in the 1830s favored the star actor, whose name alone was a draw, and, often secondarily, the manager, who controlled the purse strings. The whole style of acting in the period put the star always in the limelight or gaslight. Much of a production relied on the star's ability to achieve *points*. Those points were certain gestures or enunciations of certain words or phrases that would gain the most applause. Indeed, stars were used to being applauded in the middle of a scene, not just at intermission and the end of the play. To score a point, the actor would move to center front stage, speak lines or emote directly to the audience, and in essence form a bond with the customers more than with the player's colleagues on the stage (Booth, 125). These points were part of the actor's *business* —that is, the peculiarities of playing a role, often inherited from other successful interpreters of the same role. The power of the star, the insistence that a play have several opportunities for points, and the inclusion of other actor-inspired stage business put the writer of the play into eclipse.

But the playwright was not the only person of the theater left out in the cold when the house receipts were tallied. The star system worked terribly to the disadvantage of the subordinate actors. Most urban theaters had house casts who filled all but the leading roles. The stars traveled about, coming into town to play Virginius, for example, while the local cast would round out the parts. Often, the house cast was uneven in quality, and plays were edited by actors or managers to feature the star at the expense of the others onstage. The idea of ensemble acting was rarely used. Thus, the star, especially if egocentric, would virtually ignore the rest of the cast; instead, he or she would face the audience and intone or emote or gesticulate, leaving the others in a rear tableau as if they were no more than props. What seem to us now as flat characterizations in the minor roles of nineteenth-century dramas are so by design, to enable the star literally to stand out from the crowd.

If the house cast was often overshadowed by the star, the remainder of the corps were plunged into a dingy obscurity. Every large theater had, in addition to its regulars, who took named parts, a group of *supernumeraries*, who took the anonymous roles of "citizens, soldiers, etc." Paid only a minimum wage, the "supers" were often forced to take additional employment backstage as carpenters, scene painters, seamstresses, and the like. Despite their loyalty to the theatrical life, and no doubt the hopes of some to graduate to the house cast, the supernumeraries most probably lived in grinding poverty, made the more apparent by contrast to the splendid style in which the stars traveled.

Also forced to endure wretched conditions was another theatrical underclass, the ballet girls. These young women would be used in the airy productions, the pantomimes and light entertainments designed to alleviate any gloom that the main play might inspire. If a major play called for fairies or sprites, the manager would ask his or her corps de ballet to fill those roles. The women who danced in the corps not only struggled against poverty, but also exposed themselves to a variety of dangers. Often hoisted by ropes and wires in simulated flight, ballet girls could be caught in the machinery or burned by gas lamps, even killed in doing their part. At the same time, they suffered more than other actors in general a reputation for sexual profligacy. In George Lippard's novel *The Quaker City* (1845), one cynical member of a private men's club devoted to sensual pleasures speaks loosely about ballet girls and actresses he can blackmail into having sex. Lippard's readers would understand the characterization of Buzby Poodle not only as an exploiter but also as one who traffics in the kind of flesh peddling tied to the low reputation of this class of theatrical personage.

The particular problems faced by the young women in the ballet corps reflect difficulties faced by actresses in general on the early American stage. Although they had been allowed on stage in England since the reopening of the theaters in the Restoration (1660) and were never formally banned from American stages, women—like the theater in general—often had to struggle for a good reputation. Even to the end of the period covered by this volume, the position of women was never so secure that an actress could assume her professional expertise would be enough to wipe away entirely the prejudices held by the public against women in the theater.

One way to counter the prejudice was for actresses to use only their married title and their husbands' names. Frequently, actresses were married to actors; in the playbill, one would see "Mr. G. C. Germon" in the list of male characters at the top and "Mrs. G. C. Germon" in the list of female characters below. This obliteration of name served the purpose of keeping the married actress above suspicion of looseness, for her life's interests would be seen as absorbed in the figure of her husband. For unmarried women, the situation was potentially more pre-carious, as we have seen with the ballet girls. However, this was often overcome by the creation of the *ingenue*, the childlike woman whose innocence was so palpable to the audience that the "Miss" in front of her name in the cast list could only connote unassailable purity. The persona projected by the silent film actress Lillian Gish is directly con-nected to a long history on the nineteenth-century stage of such female roles.

Not all actresses were bound by this narrow definition. One of the great actresses of the period was Charlotte Cushman, a versatile and powerful performer who could play heroines and *breeches* parts—cross-dressed as Hamlet or some other male character. But Cushman's inter-national fame, financial reward, and ability to choose roles were more the exception than the rule. More typical of the lot of the actress was Eliza Arnold, a touring professional at the turn of the century. Slight of build, with a passable, sweet singing voice—in other words, projecting that image of girlish innocence so cultivated by the insecure stage of the time—Eliza proved a favorite in many of the cities her company visited. The itinerant life, however, forced a woman to have to choose an actor or other theatrical person as a spouse, for reasons of travel, money—she could offer no dowry to a marriage—and reputation. In Eliza Ar-nold's case, she settled for a David Poe, a strolling player like herself but with less acting ability. After he disappeared, fleeing catcalls and domestic responsibilities, she was left in charge of her two children. Vulnerable to sickness and exhaustion, Eliza Poe died during a tour in Richmond—an event probably watched by her two-year-old son, Edgar—one more casualty to an often grueling and unforgiving profes-sion (Shockley; Silverman).

Even so, some women worked to expand possibilities for their sex on stage. Anna Cora Mowatt, fresh from her success as a playwright, launched a career as an actress in 1845 from financial necessity. Al-though she, like her predecessor Eliza Arnold Poe, projected the image of the slight and sweet young woman, she brought to the profession her social position and an ability to articulate what sort of role it was proper for a woman to play. Her greatest success was her first role, as Pauline Deschappelles in Bulwer-Lytton's *The Lady of Lyons*, which she played with dignity, modesty, and naturalistic restraint. While the vehicles available for women often called for fainting, shrieking, or hand-wringing passivity, Mowatt in her acting sought to redirect the audi-ence's attention to a woman's real strength rather than playacted

weakness. If dramas to suit her style did not come readily from playwrights, she at least paved the way for a differing conception of woman
on stage in later generations of actors and writers.

It is important to recognize that when playwrights set out to pen
works that could be acted, they were bound by the reigning ideas of
what images actors and actresses should project; the personalities of the
popular actors of the period; and a complex system of hiring in theaters
that defined actors by type. Thus, a stock company would hire actors
to fit these types, as listed by Dion Boucicault:

> A leading man, leading juvenile man, heavy man [who played
> villains], first old man, first low comedian, walking gentleman,
> second old man and utility, second low comedian and character
> actor, second walking gentleman and utility, leading woman, lead-
> ing juvenile woman, heavy woman, first old woman, first cham-
> bermaid, walking lady, second old woman and utility, second
> chambermaid and character actress, second walking lady and util-
> ity walking lady. (Booth, 126)

This is not the end of it, but one can see how restrictive such a scheme
would have been for actors and playwrights alike. For the actor, one
could get a position not by being "a good actor" but by suitability to
fill a vacancy in, say, a "walking lady" role—someone attractive enough
to be the friend to the leading lady but one who would not steal her
thunder or tears. For playwrights, then, construction of the drama must
be forged to meet casting realities. Thus we cannot realistically expect
from dramas in the period covered by this collection to find more than
one or two developed characters in each play—acting companies would
not have had the personnel or the personalities to allow such a thing.

Managers and Audiences

The American theatrical system functioned in ways very similar to
its English counterpart. There was really no "artistic" director—rarely
was the term *director* used. Instead, power was vested in star actors, in
managers, and in the audience. Theater owners did not necessarily involve themselves with actual production; that was left to the lessee, the
manager. Sometimes the manager was also an actor; but the basic responsibilities assumed by the manager would now be parceled out to
several people. In *Theatre in the Victorian Age*, what Michael Booth
describes for the British theatrical manager of the period applies as well
to the American:

He chose actors and cast them in each play; he selected key administrative, backstage and front-of-house staff. He was responsible for the weekly salary bill for all personnel before and behind the curtain. . . . He decided which plays were to be performed and scheduled them, frequently cutting and rearranging the texts to suit the exigencies of production and the acting capabilities of his company. He usually superintended rehearsals, and if he were an actor performed leading roles in a part of the repertory. A myriad of major and minor matters, both artistic and administrative, occupied his attention. He read plays, dealt with rejected authors, interviewed acting applicants, kept an eye on the door-keepers and the box-office staff, machinery, and auditorium. (28–29)

Depending on seniority in the business and degree of financial backing, the manager could be little more than a conduit for stars or a petty tyrant. At any rate, the manager was above all a person of business, whose job was to run a profitable enterprise and, by extension, please the customer.

When assessing the theater of the nineteenth century, historians have often looked for someone or something to *blame* for it. Actors, managers, and audiences all receive their share of the debit. Certainly, the theater was guided by market forces; without patrons or sponsors, those responsible for mounting plays had to acknowledge the taste of the day. For the scrupulous manager, this need to keep an eye on the bottom line while at the same time trying to promote the development of the drama in America led to difficult choices. The great managers of the time—William Wood, William Henry Smith, Francis Courtney Wemyss—were, in fact, sensitive to the artistic dilemma that an art governed by appeal to mass taste implied.

In a letter of advice to a newer counterpart, a seasoned manager in 1830 expressed the problem thus:

It is evident that the predilection for the Drama has declined in this country, and that Theatrical taste is getting exceedingly bad. The former is doubtless owing to the scarcity of *stock* talent at any one establishment, consequent upon the *undue increase* of Theatres, and the latter (the bad taste) is attributable to the frequent introduction of pieces "full of sound and fury, signifying nothing" to please those who are fond only of "inexplicable dumb show and noise," and who in consequence of the present low price of admission to the Theatres form much the largest portion of an audience.

For this manager, the question came down to the theater's role in the creation of taste. Are theaters only passive instruments, feeding an "*existing* taste" that is demonstrably low? Or ought the stage be elevating that taste, seeing the appeal to "*vulgar*" taste as only "*temporary*"?

His response to his own questions—too long to be printed or even summarized in its entirety here—shows at least one future direction for the theater: while providing such entertainments as keep customers coming to the playhouse, the manager must cultivate a new audience "whose taste is yet to be formed . . . the young of the middling orders of society." In other words, while the present demands the broadest possible appeal, the future looks to the rising bourgeoisie, the new middle class, to keep the theater afloat. The manager's advice to his counterpart hinges on the principle that it is "much more difficult . . . to satisfy an individual of refinement with a low representation than it is to please a genially vulgar man with a chaste performance" (W.). As Bruce McConachie explains in *Melodramatic Formations*, audience power during the period 1820 to 1870 gradually shifts from the "gallery gods," as the cheap-seat occupants were called, to those who were willing to pay more to make the theater a shrine to their own rising socioeconomic status. That change in taste and power of audiences from broadly popular to more narrowly middle class would by the end of the Civil War have been nearly complete.

In the meantime, however, the letter-writing manager makes clear who *he* thinks has power: the lowbrow audience (Levine). While managers may have felt obliged to provide British productions because they carried the cachet of having been popular in London, they also had to meet the taste for variety. With frequent changes of bill the norm in the earlier part of the period, managers were by necessity forced to consider American products (Grimsted, 144–45). Perhaps it is fair to say that popular demand inspired managers to provide both the latest hit from London (which was often a translated version of the latest hit from Paris) and a steady diet of sketches, pantomimes, and plays by American authors. The real tension was not so much British versus American plays as between a manager's accepting audience taste or trying to influence or alter it by playhouse policy and practice.

Construction of Plays

Although writers and critics alike deplored the taste of their own time, the plays of the period often reflect a consistent aesthetic with common features. One important dimension of play construction during the period was the *scenery*. Tyler's *The Contrast* was staged in New York with only a few props—chairs, a table—and *flats*, painted scenery that could be slid into place from the sides or *wings*, or with a background painting. As a comedy of manners, the play focuses on character interaction, soliloquies, and comic business associated with Jonathan. Later plays demanded increasingly complex stage materials—which often took audience interest away from character and dialogue. Machines that raised or lowered characters to show flight; more sophisticated use of trap doors, as in Boucicault's famous lateral trap used in the ghost scene of *The Corsican Brothers*; construction of hills or mountains; water effects, including the ice floe in *Uncle Tom's Cabin*; and, finally, safer and more elaborate pyrotechnics, as in the burning of the ship in *The Octoroon*—all of these technical developments worked to shape what playwrights would or could do in the construction of their plays.

Music is a second component of almost all productions during this period. In *The Contrast*, Maria sings the well-known air about the noble Indian Alknomook, and, of course, in *The Indian Princess*, nearly every major character sings a song or duet. But the common use of music in ordinary plays, especially after 1800, was to heighten mood, introduce character, or otherwise add to the sensual effects of the production. The use of mood music in modern films is directly traceable to the stage practice, developed in France in the late 1700s, of layering scenes with music that underscored what was happening or being said, not as accompaniment for song. Silent films continued the tradition of having a live orchestra or organist interpret the visuals; indeed, the power generated by a well-crafted silent film and a seriously rendered live musical score indicates for us how superfluous the dialogue must have been for many of the more spectacular productions of the nineteenth-century stage. Thus, as we read the texts written for the early American theater, we need to imagine other sounds than the voices of actors.

Even though playwrights wrote for a theater that demanded increasingly elaborate visual and aural effects in production, a third element, *dialogue*, was still the stuff around which the best plays were constructed. As many authors discovered, however, their texts were often chopped into unrecognizable bits during the reading rehearsals or were altered *ad libitum* by actors who had some business to work or points to gain by going outside the text. Even Shakespeare's dramas suffered the indignities of butchered dialogue for the sake of acting or scenic effect. Given the realities of production, playwrights constructed dialogue frequently as *declamation* rather than interaction. This style suited the star actor's need to intone to the audience, but it also matched the reigning notion that plays gained seriousness by being Romanized. The opening of Bird's *The Gladiator* shows the style. Phasarius speaks three long passages, ostensibly to his interlocutor Ænomaiis, but really to us, to set the scene. Ænomaiis's lines are little more than a prompt to his longer-winded companion, but no one in the audience expects anything different. When the hero, Spartacus, enters chained later in act 1, and apparently talks to Lentulus and Bracchius, the latter says, "Observe him.—He mutters to himself." Particularly in tragic or highly melodramatic plays, we can expect many of the major speeches spoken as if the character is unaware that other figures inhabit the same stage space.

In plays with more contemporary settings or with comic scenes, the dialogue often involves the kinds of jokes popularized in the twentieth century by people like Abbott and Costello or those still heard in sitcoms. Indeed, the vaudeville traditions of straight man and jester go back to the minstrel shows and well before. In *The Contrast*, for instance, Jessamy, the servant imitator of his rake master, Dimple, plays straight man to the naïve Jonathan, feeding him setup lines for Jonathan's famous misinterpretations of meeting the prostitute, courting Jenny, and attending the play. In a later social comedy, Mowatt's *Fashion*, much of the dialogue plays into Mrs. Tiffany's malaprop French, with bad puns and tortured expressions in abundance. As in Tyler's play, she has a servant imitator, in this case, the clever but befuddled black servant Zeke (rechristened Adolph), who also provides the sort of linguistic humor found in the minstrel shows. Those latter productions, originally a semicircle of white men in blackface, developed a style of comic dialogue whereby the straight man, the *interlocutor*, would create opportunities for the *end men*, called Tambo and Bones, to tell jokes or mispronounce something. Both *Uncle Tom's Cabin* and *The Octoroon* owe some of their comic dialogue to the minstrel shows. Occasionally, playwrights will use quick repartee, as in the comic *stichomythia* between Charlotte and Letitia in *The Contrast*. But, overall, the dominant comic dialogue style in American drama is based on use of slang, folk speech, mispronunciation, and double entendre.

A fourth element is *plot*. The same basic considerations for comedies or tragedies still apply to plays in those forms. In the comedies of manners, vice is corrected or nonviolently expelled, virtue rewarded through marriage or other affirmation of a social institution. In tragedies, the protagonist falls after reaching past what ordinary people would attempt. But in melodrama, which often incorporates elements from both tragedies and comedies, plotting moves differently from either of the others. Closely resembling the Jacobean tragicomedies, melodramas develop stock situations that can have either dark or light resolutions. The basic plot involves a young woman exposed to danger by some compromising action involving an important male figure in her life, a father, brother, or husband. Into the vacuum created when the male is absent, weakened, or indisposed steps another male with designs on the woman, her fortune or status, or her use as a pawn to gain revenge on the other man. Frequently, a second good man enters as a guardian figure who prevents danger to the woman until such time as the protagonist male can recover himself and take an active role in the woman's salvation. In the light plot, the villain is thwarted, then expelled or corrected and brought back into the community, before anyone is seriously hurt. In the dark plot, the woman or the heroic male is killed or brought to mortal ruin before the forces of moral rightness assert their dominance. In almost no case is the villain allowed to prevail, though sometimes he—or occasionally she—gets away with something close to murder without full punishment for the crime. In both plots, though, the difference between melodrama and straight comedy or tragedy is that the protagonists are often monochromatic characters, without significant self-questioning (Smith).

In plotting a play for the stage, writers must be cognizant of how an audience will follow plot. Frequently, especially in melodrama, an object like a letter often gets passed from character to character, full of meaning, if only its truth will be exposed to public view. In teaching this drama, I refer to such an object as a *telltale artifact*—a thing that tells a story when it can be interpreted by the right people. In Dunlap's play, a cockade torn from Bland's helmet is restored later, saying much about Bland's change of position. *The Octoroon* has two such artifacts: the bank document from England and the photographic plate. A cruder use of the telltale artifact is the incriminating—or liberating—document that shows someone has inherited the money needed to pay the mortgage but, because it has been stolen by the villain, does not arrive in the hands of the one for whom it would do good until the play's end. In an influential English melodrama, Douglas Jerrold's *Black-Eyed Susan*, a document found on the body of the drowned villain prevents an honest sailor from being hanged and serves as a version of deus ex machina, the interposing agency that turns tragedy into "Saved!"

Such use of the telltale artifact seems to us now to typify the artificiality of nineteenth-century theater. Yet this kind of plotting resonated with writers of all stripes, including those who used theatrical language against itself. Herman Melville, for instance, borrows the plot of *Black-Eyed Susan* in his novella, *Billy Budd*, but deliberately rejects the use of the saving artifact at the end. While the device is not original with American dramatists—one finds it in Shakespeare, for instance, with the handkerchief in *Othello*—the reliance on a visual object to carry the plot becomes a hallmark of much of this theater, especially after 1800. One only need think of the Chinese lantern in *A Streetcar Named Desire* or constantly refilled booze glasses in *Who's Afraid of Virginia Woolf?*—or, better, the imaginary telegram—to realize how persistent the telltale artifact has remained.

A fifth element to consider is *character*. As one can see by Boucicault's list of acting company roles, characters in plays during the period tended to fit snugly into types. Characters rarely develop in the way we are accustomed to in the modern theater, and nuances of psychology get overlooked for large-scale changes. Most characters stay the same from beginning to end. Villains are rotten at the start and remain rotten throughout, sometimes undergoing a radical transformation in the very last scene that only makes more apparent how little such characters truly resist type. Good people also stay primarily good but often must undergo a transformation through others' perceptions. Maria in *The Contrast* is considered a prude by her friends, but in the end, her devotion to her heart and her essential filial loyalty receive their just reward; the changes that occur happen in the eyes of her father and Charlotte, not within Maria herself.

Some characters go outside type long enough to be interesting for that fact. Edward Middleton, in his phase as a hard-core alcoholic, displays a mania one does not often see in the protagonist. Spartacus, both noble and savage—one could say the same for Metamora—embraces dimensions that cover the spectrum from villainy to heroism. Or, in *Fashion*, the French maid, Millinette, both schemes to deceive her employers and is a victim of the false count's scheming. One of the more problematic characters in that play, Tiffany, commits forgery in the name of domestic felicity, but is saved in the eyes of the audience by himself being the object of a more hateful crime, blackmail. Thus, while in the main, goodness or wickedness appears rooted in the character before the action occurs onstage, a number of authors try strategies which affirm that essential doctrine of the early theater and complicate it at the same time.

If good and bad provide one ready distinction between characters, male and female offer another. The rigid social rules that divided men and women in real life were also practiced on stage, although not necessarily in ways that mirrored "nature." A quick glance at cast lists shows that fewer female than male characters appear on stage, though in spectacles or other light performances, the boards could be filled with ballet girls. Men are gentlemen, businessmen, farmers, firemen, lawyers, or sharpers of all sorts. They also are lovers and husbands—often faltering ones—or fathers, either sentimental or severe. Women are ladies and maids, virgins and dowagers. Wives and lovers are loyal and accept abuse from whatever source as part of the package; daughters never waver in support of incompetent or clumsy fathers. Men can stray from virtue—Middleton abandons hearth and home for drink—but women as a rule cannot. Charlotte in *The Contrast* flirts, but eventually she learns what Maria knows: "Reputation is the life of woman." Pocahontas gets involved in amorous badinage with Rolfe in *The Indian Princess*, but her innocence to its erotic meaning keeps her from losing her reputation with the audience. The female protagonist's faithfulness to a male in her life, along with a telltale artifact, is often the thread that ties together the erratic and cobbled plots of the time.

Often—strangely often—mothers have no presence at all. The absent mother motif makes up one of the curiosities of the early stage. If Mother is mentioned, she is spoken of as dead. Even mothers who do appear on stage frequently have no real presence; Marie St. Clare virtually abandons little Eva in *Uncle Tom's Cabin* in order to indulge her neurasthenia. Since so many plays, particularly melodramas, build plots around a vulnerable young female, an author's depriving the depicted society of mothers enhances the heroine's vulnerability and forces men to serve as protectors as well as robbers of virtue. In essence, without mothers or other stable female support, stage women have no choice in relations but to bond to men.

For readers of our own time, the ethnic characters may cause the most objection. In the language of the stage, the Dutch, Jewish, Swedish, Irish, Indian, and African-American characters who show up in plays of the time are *stock* figures, types that elicit a predetermined set of responses without being allowed to display any subjectivity. We often call the images, or caricatures, they present *stereotypes*; and, unfortunately, the stage creations may have influenced the development of narrow cultural perceptions of actual people. Ethnicity, like gender, is for the nineteenth-century theater a marker, a shorthand access to character that most writers use to avoid spending the time on development of individuals. But it also seems that the audience wanted types.

In the case of black characters, the interpretation of such figures is highly problematic. There were African-American actors in the early 1800s, but they usually had to play in segregated companies or leave the country altogether. The great Ira Aldridge (1805–1867), whose talent was first noticed by the traveling English actor Edmund Kean, was forced to debut his Othello in London and remain abroad to continue his career. Thus, when we read in an American play that a black character enters the scene—Pete in *The Octoroon*, Adolph/Zeke in *Fashion*—we need to imagine a white actor coming on in blackface in order to understand the conditions of first production.

The dialect assigned to black characters grows more from stage tradition, passed on from white actor to white playwright, than from the actual speech of living African-American people. True, some white actors observed blacks in real life and adopted mannerisms they thought would work on stage. Thomas Dartmouth Rice, the creator of the "Jim Crow" blackface character and one of the originators of the minstrel show, allegedly picked up his act from imitating a crippled black stableboy. But Rice's shtick did not have to pass any test of authenticity, only that of entertainment. When Jim Crow proved hugely successful at the box office, Rice inspired other imitators—imitators of Rice, that is—to develop the comic burned-cork types in minstrel shows. These in turn influenced the depiction of the black character in plays, the figure known as the "stage darky." Only after the Civil War would African Americans themselves launch minstrel companies, but until well into the 1930s, with radio shows like *Amos 'n' Andy* or films like *The Jazz Singer*, whites still appropriated the aural and visual representations of black people.

Even so, some playwrights push the limit of stereotype and suggest complexity where an audience expects a single dimension. The servant in *Fashion* plays the fool, speaking in malapropisms that are made comic through dialect; on the other hand, Anna Cora Mowatt puts Zeke in the context of a family of white parvenu fools and suggests that he has a much better grasp of the situation than his employer, Mrs. Tiffany. He knows he plays a role; Mrs. Tiffany imagines she is the real article. Uncle Tom, whose character—or a version of it—inspired the modern epithet used by African Americans against other blacks for accommodation to whites, was in his time a subversive figure. His thorough goodness challenges ownership of virtue, and his stoical defiance of Legree has its origins in the Romanized tragedies of noble suffering.

The most complex black characters tend to be found in plays that feature the *tragic mulatta* (Roberts). Represented as a light-skinned black woman, the tragic mulatta finds herself caught in a political and personal identity crisis. Cassie in *Uncle Tom's Cabin* and Zoe in *The Octoroon* represent objects of desire for white men, but their refined manners and speech put them on a par with the virtuous white maidens who populate romances. Their unassailable goodness makes them pitiable to a middling audience, but their stage blackness explains why contemporary spectators would not expect them to realize their dreams or ideals. In both aforementioned plays, the situation is made tragic by slavery; the threat or reality of being consumed in the horrors of perpetual bondage touches white audiences most profoundly when a white actress, only slightly darkened by makeup, plays a woman of virtue about to be or actually compromised by the mere fact of having some African blood. The message is, of course, ambiguous. Does one who has more than just a "drop" of non-Caucasian blood then more deserve her awful fate? Or can we read into the Zoes and Cassies the humanity of all ethnically African people? In any case, one thing is clear: the tragic mulatta represents the country at large, at war with itself over a racial divide.

Among other ethnic types represented on the early stage, two more predominate. One, the Indian, proved a popular character on the American stage. In James Nelson Barker's *The Indian Princess*, we see almost the whole range of Native representations, from the scheming, villainous savages Grimosco and Miami, to the sometimes noble Powhatan, to the virtuous princess, Pocahontas. As with black characters, Indians are played by white actors in tawny makeup; but in some cities, theater audiences might also have seen actual Native Americans in exhibitions, performing dances. In the latter performance, the authenticity of the Indians, presented as a kind of spectacle, would have been the draw; in the fictional plays, the validation of cultural preconceptions—not the reality of living people—would be the hook. Sometimes, a portrayal of an Indian could be subversive. Forrest's Metamora raised hackles in Georgia at a time when the Cherokee were being expelled in a white land grab. But, more often than not, the Indian is perfunctory, like Wahnotee in *The Octoroon*, reduced to little more than wielding a hatchet and saying "Ugh."

The other popular ethnic type on the boards is the stage Irishman. Nostalgic, buffoonish, and frequently alcoholic, the Irish character serves almost always in a comic role. Larry in *The Indian Princess* moons for his lady love with an occasional Gaelic lament, but no one would read his feeling of loss as something to pity. Audiences came to expect the kind of character popularized by Barney Williams, an Irish-born American actor who starred in such 1840s brogue vehicles as *The Irish Tutor, The Bashful Irishman,* and *The Limerick Boy* (Meserve, "Barney"). Unlike black and Indian plays, Irish dramas and character types were often written or played by people from Ireland or of Irish descent. Dion Boucicault, who as an actor relished a hammy brogue role, did much as a playwright to flesh out Irish types in hits like *The Colleen Bawn* and *The Shaughraun.* Other Irish or Irish-American actors like Tyrone Power in the 1830s or James O'Neill later in the century gave prominence to flesh-and-blood Irishmen on stage. But the persistence of the stereotype, or the complex interplay among Irish characters, Irish acting style, and actual Irish-American life, can be seen well into this century, as in the play by James O'Neill's son Eugene, *Long Day's Journey into Night* (1940).

Theory and Criticism

Late-eighteenth- and early-nineteenth-century drama in general, and melodrama in particular, represent rich areas of investigation awaiting readers who can suspend a quick dismissal of this theater. While there is a considerable body of information on many American playwrights and actors from the antebellum period, the amount of critical and theoretical work, although growing, is comparatively small. Many early histories of the American stage are flawed by misinformation or have limited utility by being confined to a narrow historical window. One of the important tasks is to rehistoricize these plays, examining them not simply in terms of this followed that on the New York stage but also in terms of cultural and socioeconomic forces at work; of audience composition and response; living and working conditions for actors and playwrights; and interplay among other forms of cultural expression and the theater.

What are the cultural conditions that foster melodrama? Peter Brooks, whose work underlies many recent studies of the form, traces a history that begins in the French Revolution. Citing Charles Nodier's assessment (in his 1841 introduction to the plays of Pixérécourt) that "Melodrama was the morality of the Revolution," Brooks notes these implications: "that it is inherently a democratic form, in which the humble of the earth stand up to overbearing tyrants and express home truths, about the value of the good heart, the sanctity of the domestic hearth, the essential moral equality of all and the fraternity of the virtuous, and win through to see villainy punished and virtue rewarded, in spectacular fashion, in the last act" ("Melodrama," 16). By extension to the American scene, then, melodrama serves an audience essentially uninterested in shades of meaning or ambiguities of interpretation. A clear system of values coupled with an inclusiveness—something for the bootblacks in the gallery and those with polished shoes in the boxes— makes melodrama the medium of the masses, energetic, sometimes chaotic, spectacular, definite.

Nonetheless, ambiguities abound in rethinking such a form. Is melodrama an expression of democratic sympathies? Many of the plays themselves depict aristocratic societies; the two social comedies in this collection both feature New York families whose wealth or social station puts them beyond the means of many in the audience. Other plays, imported and American-authored, show stock European hierarchies, where nobility is figured by status, not necessarily by action. Playwrights such as George Henry Boker, a Philadelphia banker and genteel man of letters, sought to redirect the stage away from democratic America by penning dramas of European court life. His most famous work, *Francesca da Rimini* (1855), draws on Dante and Shakespeare, not Dunlap and Boucicault. Nevertheless, despite the popularity of costume dramas, theater audiences did not clamor for the kind of appeal to the elite (and to the ages) Boker hoped to make. One finds, then, contradictory evidence of a pandering to pretensions for elevated class status and a deliberate courting of working-class participation in the shaping of entertainment.

Another level of inquiry that could prove fruitful is myth and psychological criticism. Myth criticism, which came to prominence in the 1960s and 1970s, examines texts for their participation in the development or transmission of mythologies centered in the American space. Barker's *The Indian Princess* is the first play to feature Pocahontas, but hardly the last; the persistence of Pocahontas as a mythological rather than a historical personage can be seen still in the Disney animated feature of 1995. Looking at Barker's Pocahontas in light of other versions both before and after his, on stage and in other media, allows us to examine the text of his drama as part of a larger cultural desire to use the Indian princess to express the country's sense of itself.

Seeing these plays as expressions of desire also links them to the psychological. Whether pursuing the myth-related archetypes of Jungian analysis, or the Oedipally driven forces in Freudian and Lacanian thinking, we might well query the attraction of types for the theatergoing public. The stock characters and plots, to moderns the very problem with melodrama, become in psychological critiques the stuff of fascination and confrontation with a drama of the subconscious. As Brooks remarks, following Foucault, the extremity of situation in melodrama amounts to a presentation of the "hystericized body"; conversely, psychoanalysis itself, a product of late-nineteenth-century European urban culture, looks to be another form of melodrama ("Melodrama," 22). Examined in this light, characters cease to be viewed as deficient imitations of surface reality but instead come to be taken as representations of contending forces within the psyche. Dunlap's Washington and André, although based on historical persons, function more as constructs of fatherhood and sacrificial child than as characters in a reenactment of a scene from the Revolutionary War.

Another useful vehicle for criticism of this theater is feminist and gender criticism. In many cases, critics must first reconstruct the historical reality of women in the theater. While an actress on stage plied her trade, enacting the virtuous maiden and supplicating a villain, in the upper boxes of large urban theaters other women were trying to entice men to have sex with them at nearby rooming houses. Both the actress and the prostitute were attempting to make a living; but the oppositions of stage fantasy and third-tier reality create a critical wedge with which to pry apart texts and examine the constructions of femaleness in them. Or one might simply ask, What are the relations between the plots and social situations depicted on stage and the actual playing out in drawing rooms and bedrooms of the gender politics of American society (Halttunen)? Another avenue was suggested above in the discussion of character, pursuing the traces of the absent mother.

Queer theory, African-American criticism, and postcolonial studies all suggest methodologies for seeking out other traces as well. While such writers as Melville, Whitman, and Dickinson are under scrutiny for elements of the homoerotic, plays from the period would seem to be a more resistant body of work. After all, the plots of American dramas frequently resolve themselves through heterosexual marriage. Still, through various stage traditions, including cross-dressing and breeches parts, investigators might be able to detect traces of suppressed and subversive desire. Indeed, the presence, even the absence, of other marginalized groups, particularly blacks, may also inspire acts of recovery through reading the traces, as postcolonial theory suggests. In *The Contrast*, there is no Negro character among the dramatis personae, but nonetheless a person figured as black, Hannah, enters the dialogue of Charlotte. In a few lines, Tyler hints at several prevailing cultural understandings and depictions of female black servants—"though a black, she is a wench that was never caught in a lie in her life"—that might lead to pursuit not only of white perceptions or even of Hannah the absent yet speaking character but also of an actual African-American servant woman in the North in the 1780s.

Although there are many other critical approaches one could adopt, I want to mention one more: intertextuality. If in the texts of plays we find traces of living persons, but not their full figuration, so it is in other texts, dramatic and nondramatic, that one can discover traces of the plays of the period. Cooper, Poe, Hawthorne, Melville, and Whitman are only a few of the writers of the time who betray their attendance at the theater in their work. Rather than say that Melville's work has many references to Shakespeare, one might rather examine what performances, what histrionic tics of what particular actors of Shakespeare, make their way into his fiction? The process moves back and forth. Hawthorne attended the Boston theater with some frequency as a young man; *The Scarlet Letter* is filled with stage metaphors and constructions that would reflect back to a reading audience not a seventeenth-century scaffold but a nineteenth-century stage. Later still, his novel was turned into plays, including one by Gabriel Harrison, who was a friend of Poe, then a drama critic in New York; a follower and biographer of Forrest, the leading actor of the time; and photographer of Whitman, the lover of the grand theatrical gesture. In short, the culture of the time is saturated with references to and depictions of the early theater and its personalities. Studying the plays in this volume and other texts from the period can open windows not only to the stage and to dramatic literature but also to American culture as a whole.

Jeffrey H. Richards

SUGGESTIONS
FOR FURTHER READING

Anthologies

Clark, Barrett H., ed. *America's Lost Plays*. 20 vols. 1940; Bloomington: Indiana University Press, 1965.

Halline, Allen Gates, ed. *American Plays*. New York: American Book, 1935.

Hatch, James V., ed. *Black Theater, U.S.A.: Forty-five Plays by Black Americans, 1847–1974*. New York: Free Press, 1974.

Kritzer, Amelia Howe, ed. *Plays by Early American Women, 1775–1850*. Ann Arbor: University of Michigan Press, 1995.

Moody, Richard, ed. *Dramas from the American Theatre, 1762–1909*. Cleveland: World, 1966. Contains excellent bibliographies.

Moses, Montrose J., ed. *Representative Plays by American Dramatists*. 3 vols. 1925; New York: Benjamin Blom, 1964.

Quinn, Arthur Hobson, ed. *Representative American Plays from 1767 to the Present Day*. 7th ed. New York: Appleton-Century-Crofts, 1957.

Watt, Stephen, and Gary A. Richardson, eds. *American Drama: Colonial to Contemporary*. Fort Worth: Harcourt Brace, 1995.

History and Criticism

Agnew, Jean-Christophe. *Worlds Apart: The Market and the Theater in Anglo-American Thought, 1550–1750*. Cambridge: Cambridge University Press, 1986.

Bank, Rosemarie K. *Theatre Culture in America, 1825–1860*. Cambridge: Cambridge University Press, 1997.

Barish, Jonas. *The Antitheatrical Prejudice*. Berkeley: University of California Press, 1981.

Booth, Michael R. *Theatre in the Victorian Age*. Cambridge: Cambridge University Press, 1991.

Brooks, Peter. "Melodrama, Body, Revolution." In *Melodrama: Stage Picture Screen*, edited by Jacky Bratton, Jim Cook, and Christine Gledhill, 11–24. London: British Film Institute, 1994.

———. *The Melodramatic Imagination: Balzac, Henry James, Melo-*

drama, and the Mode of Excess. 1976; New Haven: Yale University Press, 1995.

Brown, Jared. *The Theatre in America During the Revolution.* Cambridge: Cambridge University Press, 1995.

Clapp, William W., Jr. *A Record of the Boston Stage.* 1853; New York: Greenwood, 1969.

Grimsted, David. *Melodrama Unveiled: American Theater and Culture, 1800–1850.* Chicago: University of Chicago Press, 1968.

Halttunen, Karen. *Confidence Men and Painted Women: A Study of Middle-Class Culture in America, 1830–1870.* New Haven: Yale University Press, 1982.

Havens, Daniel F. *The Columbian Muse of Comedy: The Development of a Native Tradition in Early Social Comedy, 1787–1845.* Carbondale: Southern Illinois University Press, 1973.

Highfill, Philip, Jr. "The British Background of the American Hallams." *Theatre Survey* 11 (1970): 1–35.

Hill, Errol. *The Jamaican Stage, 1655–1900: Profile of a Colonial Theatre.* Amherst: University of Massachusetts Press, 1992.

Hixon, Don L., and Don A. Hennessee. *Nineteenth-Century American Drama: A Finding Guide.* Metuchen, N.J.: Scarecrow, 1977.

Hodge, Francis. *Yankee Theatre: The Image of America on the Stage, 1825–1850.* Austin: University of Texas Press, 1964.

Jefferson, Joseph. *The Autobiography of Joseph Jefferson.* New York: Century, 1890.

Johnson, Claudia D. "That Guilty Third Tier: Prostitution in Nineteenth-Century American Theater." In *Victorian America,* edited by Daniel Walker Howe, 111–20. Philadelphia: University of Pennsylvania Press, 1976.

Levine, Lawrence W. *Highbrow/Lowbrow: The Emergence of Cultural Hierarchy in America.* Cambridge: Harvard University Press, 1988.

Lydia. Letter to Elizabeth D. Whiton, 13 Feb. 1839. William L. Clements Library, University of Michigan. Cited with permission.

McConachie, Bruce. *Melodramatic Formations: American Theatre & Society, 1820–1870.* Iowa City: University of Iowa Press, 1992.

McNamara, Brooks. *The American Playhouse in the Eighteenth Century.* Cambridge: Harvard University Press, 1969.

Mason, Jeffrey D. *Melodrama and the Myth of America.* Bloomington: Indiana University Press, 1993.

Meserve, Walter J. "Barney Williams: A Genuine American Paddy." In *Studies in Theatre and Drama: Essays in Honor of Hubert C. Heff-*

ner, edited by Oscar G. Brockett, 158–76. The Hague: Mouton, 1972.

———. *An Emerging Entertainment: The Drama of the American People to 1828.* Bloomington: Indiana University Press, 1977.

———. *Herald of Promise: The Drama of the American People During the Age of Jackson, 1829–1849.* New York: Greenwood, 1986.

Moody, Richard. *America Takes the Stage: Romanticism in American Drama and Theatre, 1750–1900.* Bloomington: Indiana University Press, 1955.

Moody, Robert E., ed. "Boston's First Play." *Proceedings of the Massachusetts Historical Society* 92 (1980): 117–39.

Odell, George C. D. *Annals of the New York Stage.* 15 vols. New York: Columbia University Press, 1927–1949.

Porter, Susan L. *With an Air Debonair: Musical Theatre in America, 1785–1815.* Washington, D.C.: Smithsonian Institution Press, 1991.

Quinn, Arthur H. *A History of the American Drama from the Beginning to the Civil War.* 1923; New York: Appleton-Century-Crofts, 1943.

Rahill, Frank. *The World of Melodrama.* University Park: Pennsylvania State University Press, 1967.

Rankin, Hugh F. *The Theatre of Colonial America.* Chapel Hill: University of North Carolina Press, 1965.

Richards, Jeffrey H. *Mercy Otis Warren.* New York: Twayne, 1995.

———. *Theater Enough: American Culture and the Metaphor of the World Stage, 1607–1789.* Durham: Duke University Press, 1991.

Richardson, Gary A. *American Drama from the Colonial Period through World War I: A Critical History.* New York: Twayne, 1993.

Roberts, Diane. *The Myth of Aunt Jemima: Representations of Race and Region.* New York: Routledge, 1994.

Rourke, Constance. "The Rise of Theatricals." In *The Roots of American Culture and Other Essays*, edited by Van Wyck Brooks, 60–160. New York: Harcourt, Brace, 1942.

Shockley, Martin Staples. *The Richmond Stage, 1784–1812.* Charlottesville: University Press of Virginia, 1977.

Silverman, Kenneth. *Edgar A. Poe: Mournful and Never-ending Remembrance.* New York: HarperCollins, 1991.

Smith, James L. *Melodrama.* London: Methuen, 1973.

Vaughan, Jack A. *Early American Dramatists from the Beginnings to 1900.* New York: Ungar, 1981.

W. Letter to Mr. Lamb, 14 Nov. 1830. William L. Clements Library, University of Michigan.

Wilmeth, Don B., and Tice L. Miller, eds. *Cambridge Guide to American Theatre*. Cambridge: Cambridge University Press, 1993.

Wright, Richardson. *Revels in Jamaica, 1682–1838*. 1937; New York: Blom, 1969.

Young, William C. *Famous American Playhouses, 1716–1899*. Chicago: American Library Association, 1973.

A NOTE ON THE TEXTS

The text of *The Contrast* used in this edition is a somewhat modernized version of the 1790 Philadelphia Prichard & Hall printing. Most modern reprintings have completely updated the archaic and sometimes idiosyncratic punctuation of the first edition; I have followed those practices to a point, but I have left in more of Tyler's original dashes and some other punctuation where a clear reading of the text is at issue. Spelling is largely that of the 1790 edition, with the main exceptions being that such words as "every thing" are closed up and misspelled names (Johnson for Jonson) are corrected. In addition, I have omitted the single quotation marks that indicated deleted portions of speeches in actual production.

The text used for *André* is that of *André: A Tragedy in Five Acts* (New York: T. & J. Swords, 1798). Spelling in the original has been maintained, except for a few archaisms ("gulph") that might prove distracting. I have made some minor format changes and have included scene numbers in brackets; Dunlap did not include such numbers.

The text of *The Indian Princess* is based on the 1808 Philadelphia edition. Following the lead of Montrose Moses, I have regularized stage direction format; for the most part, I have preserved Barker's spelling, except where it is inconsistent, the one notable exception being "potatoe."

The text of *The Gladiator* used here is essentially that established by Clement E. Foust in his *Life and Dramatic Works of Robert Montgomery Bird* (New York: Knickerbocker, 1919), 301–440. Foust used an autograph manuscript in the University of Pennsylvania library that had also been read and marked by Edwin Forrest. I have included the sections marked by Forrest, apparently listing production cuts and marked them as Foust has, with < > marks. I have made minor changes where an obvious punctuation error occurs and to format, but not wording, of stage directions.

The text of *The Drunkard* is based on the 1847 version published by Samuel French. As with other plays in this collection, I have corrected obvious errors, omitted or clarified some directions (e.g., "crossing, and going, l." becomes "going"), and made other slight changes for consistency.

The text of *Fashion* I have used is the one in Anna Cora Mowatt, *Plays*, new and revised edition (Boston: Ticknor and Fields, 1855), with only minor changes to spelling, punctuation, and format of stage directions.

For *Uncle Tom's Cabin*, I've followed the French's Standard Drama acting edition, no. 217: *Uncle Tom's Cabin; or, Life among the Lowly* (New York: Samuel French, 1858?). Spelling is that in the original, except where inconsistencies or errors are obvious; stage directions have been slightly reformatted. One important difference between this and another known version will be noted in the Explanatory and Textual Notes section.

For the text of *The Octoroon*, I have used a "printed, not published" version from 1861 or 1862 and have made the usual minor changes.

EARLY AMERICAN DRAMA

THE CONTRAST (1787)

ROYALL TYLER

The first successful American dramatist, Royall Tyler (1757–1826), is also typical among early American playwrights in devoting to the drama only a small part of his life. Born in Boston, a city that would not legalize theater until the 1790s, young Tyler had no opportunity to apprentice to a practicing writer for the stage or even see professional actors. As a college student at Harvard, he participated in illicit theatricals with his classmates, complete with guards posted to warn of coming proctors, but with the intervention of the Revolution, further opportunities for such rash behavior would be few. He wrote poems and studied law and hoped by that combination to earn the good graces of one of his countrywomen, Nabby Adams, daughter of John Adams, the future president. And while he made progress with the daughter, his reputation in some circles as a frivolous youth damned Tyler in the father's eyes. Tyler would later marry Mary Hunt Palmer, by whom he had nine sons and two daughters.

Moving to Vermont in the 1790s, Tyler carved out a law career that culminated with his service on the Vermont Supreme Court. At the same time, however, he continued his literary pursuits, writing a novel, *The Algerine Captive* (1797), and several satirical prose pieces, often in collaboration with essayist and poet Joseph Dennie. After losing his judgeship in 1813, Tyler went on a long downward path, with his last several years spent in poverty and physical pain. He did manage to write several religious plays during this period, but he suffered greatly from the cancer that eventually killed him in 1826.

Although Tyler had some reputation in his own time as both jurist and literary man, his small fame now rests largely on the play he wrote in 1787. In the Revolution, Tyler participated in only one battle, Sullivan's failed attack on British positions in Newport, Rhode Island. After the war, during a conflict between the new state government and angry citizens in western Massachusetts, lawyer Tyler became Major Tyler, served as an aide-de-camp to Benjamin Lincoln on the government side, and actually pursued the rebel chieftain, Daniel Shays. Sent eventually to New York to appeal to that state for cooperation in apprehending Shays and his men, Tyler at last could attend the theater openly.

The theater that Tyler visited in March of 1787 was the John Street

Theatre in what is now Lower Manhattan. The story of *The Contrast*
has as much to do with that theater as it does with the nationalist
themes raised by the play. The John Street Theatre was reopened in
December 1785 by members of the American Company of Comedians,
soon to rechristen themselves the Old American Company. Founded by
Lewis Hallam, Sr., and his family in 1752, when they sailed to Virginia
from London, the troupe had merged with another company headed up
by David Douglass, a printer-turned-actor from Jamaica, who had married Hallam's widow. Playing in Philadelphia and New York, among
other cities, the Hallam-Douglass group was the premier professional
company in America and probably did more than any other single force
to bring about acceptance of the stage in English North America. Forced
to leave by the Anglo-American conflict and a 1774 edict from the Continental Congress restricting plays, the players went largely to Jamaica
—controlled during the Revolution by the British—although Lewis
Hallam, Jr., tried his hand back in England with a coolly received
Hamlet.

During and after the war, the company crystallized in the West Indies
around a core group: the younger Hallam's co-manager, an English-
born and -trained actor named John Henry; Thomas Wignell, a skilled
low comedian; Owen Morris and Mrs. Morris; Joseph Harper and his
wife; and Maria Storer. As Richardson Wright outlines, for seasons in
Montego Bay in 1784 and 1785, Henry, Wignell, the Harpers, and the
Morrises appeared in such plays as Richard Brinsley Sheridan's *School
for Scandal* and John O'Keeffe's light opera, *The Poor Soldier*. Of this
group, the most noteworthy figures were Henry, Wignell, and Mrs.
Morris.

By 1787, the company continued to play what had become staples
of their repertoire, including *School for Scandal* and *The Poor Soldier*.
By the time Royall Tyler saw the troupe, he would have had a good
sense of who could do what. His play, a comedy of manners in the style
of Sheridan, could make use of the large, engaging John Henry (who
had studied elocution under Sheridan's father and who arranged for the
first authorized publication of *School* in 1786) as Colonel Manly; the
"tall, imposing, well-formed person" and "transcendent genius" of Mrs.
Morris as Charlotte; and the small, vigorous, and very funny Wignell
as Jonathan. With Hallam as Dimple, the attractive Mrs. Harper as
Maria, Mr. Morris and Mr. Harper as Van Rough and Jessamy respectively, and a newcomer, the apparently American-born Miss Tuke (an
alcoholic whose imbibing grew more pronounced when she became
Mrs. Hallam), as Jenny, the casting was complete.

Tyler's essential problem was how to write a play for a country without much of a theatrical tradition. On the one hand, the theater was highly suspect as an institution, undergoing severe attack in the press as a corrupting force in an infant republic; theater, in the sense of the playhouse stage, was identifiably British, not American. On the other hand, Tyler and others wanted to have in America the same arts celebrated in Europe, not simply as imitations but as forms that could take their own local stamp and still rise to greatness. This division in American opinion meant he would have to placate two opposing points of view. The virulent paper war in Massachusetts between protheater advocates like Harrison Gray Otis and antitheater revolutionists like Samuel Adams was only a larger form of battles fought in other American cities, including a city that only a few years ago had been occupied by the late enemy.

His solution, imperfect though it may be, was to work a double satire. Through Charlotte and straight man Manly, Tyler skewers the social theatricality of the "*bon ton*," the wealthy, young, fashion-conscious New Yorkers whose interest in pleasure far exceeds their commitment to a cause. Charlotte's speech about what people do at the theater—everything except give the actors their serious attention—illustrates the danger to society of a theater that only functions as entertainment, a noisy excuse for patrons to exhibit their bodies, not their virtues, in public. One of the play's chief ironies, then, is to use the theater against itself, to deconstruct its practices so as to nullify their power to corrupt the audience watching *The Contrast*.

The other satire makes fun of those who know nothing about the theater except what they hear from their frontier parson. From Tyler's perspective, the attacks on the theater were often launched by people who had no experience with a real stage. The ultranaïve Jonathan, who imagines pretty young women to be universally innocent and a playhouse—which he, as a good Vermont Calvinist, would never enter—to be someone's house rigged up with a curtain, takes everything at face value. He cannot square his pleasurable experience watching Wignell (and thus himself) play the Irish character Darby in *The Poor Soldier* with the news that he had been in "the devil's drawing room." No one in the audience wants to identify with that level of ignorance, but of course Jonathan's basic good intentions are redeemed in his loyalty to Colonel Manly.

The Chesterfield-quoting Dimple would seem to make an easy target for satire, the extreme example of the Europeanized American who despises his country's pathetic attempts in the arts. He's also a seducer and a gold digger, one whose concept of the "main chance" is indulging in as much amoral, even immoral, pleasure as possible. Dimple may in fact speak for some in the audience who in their worldliness despise the provinciality of Americans. Strangely, however, he has more in common with Jonathan than he would want to admit. Dimple reveals having very little knowledge of theater, for all its importance to his set. He turns his back to the stage and says of being in a New York theater, "I was tortured there once." The "unpolished, untraveled" Manly, by contrast, understands satire, plays, and the function of drama in a republic: laughter is good, as long as it is a corrective to vice and a stimulant to virtue. In the end, it is Manly who beseeches the audience for applause, asking not only for a benison on the performance, but an affirmation of homespun American manners both in life and—importantly for the playwright—on stage as well.

The Contrast has its place in theater history as the first full-length comic play by an American to be performed by a professional company. It was also the first hit, measured in the terms of the time. After four performances in New York in April and May of 1787, the play traveled with the company to Philadelphia and Baltimore that same year, and by 1804 had been performed again in the aforementioned cities, as well as in Boston, Charleston, Alexandria, Richmond, Spanish Town (Jamaica), and a host of smaller towns, often in unauthorized productions. Erroneously billed sometimes as the first American play, *The Contrast* earned notoriety both for its patriotism and its stage Yankee, Jonathan. The play is filled with topical references and witticisms, not to mention layers of satire that are not always easy to peel off. Criticized for its plot, its similarity to Sheridan, and its sometimes stiff lines, *The Contrast* is nevertheless the most important play by an American in the eighteenth century. In fact, it may be the most important American drama before 1900, one that looks at contemporary American mores, language, politics, and culture—including the theater itself—and sees them as ripe material for an often sprightly, smart-alecky, still actable play.

SELECTED BIBLIOGRAPHY

Brown, Helen Tyler. Introduction. *The Contrast.* 1920; New York: AMS, 1970, xxiii–xxxviii.
Carson, Ada Lou, and Herbert L. Carson. *Royall Tyler.* Boston: Twayne, 1979.

Review of *The Contrast* [performance]. *The Daily Advertiser* (New York), April 18, 1787.

Review of *The Contrast* [text]. *The Universal Asylum and Columbian Magazine* (Philadelphia) 5 (August 1790): 117–20. Portion reprinted in *The Dawning of American Drama: American Dramatic Criticism, 1746–1915*, edited by Jürgen C. Wolter, 32–33. Westport, Conn.: Greenwood, 1993.

Evelev, John. "*The Contrast*: The Problem of Theatricality and Political and Social Crisis in Postrevolutionary America." *Early American Literture* 31 (1996): 74–97.

Havens, Daniel F. "Enter Jonathan." In *The Columbian Muse of Comedy: The Development of a Native Tradition in Early American Social Comedy, 1787–1845*, 8–51. Carbondale: Southern Illinois University Press, 1973.

Meserve, Walter J. *An Emerging Entertainment: The Drama of the American People to 1828*, 95–102. Bloomington: Indiana University Press, 1977.

Nethercot, Arthur H. "The Dramatic Background of Royall Tyler's *The Contrast*." *American Literature* 12 (1941): 435–46.

Pressman, Richard S. "Class Positioning and Shays' Rebellion: Resolving the Contradictions of *The Contrast*." *Early American Literature* 21 (1986): 87–102. See also corrections to this article in Pressman, Letter to the Editor, *Early American Literature* 22 (1987): 230.

Richards, Jeffrey H. "Play and Earnest on the Postwar Stage." *Theater Enough: American Culture and the Metaphor of the World Stage, 1607–1789*, 265–79. Durham: Duke University Press, 1991.

Richardson, Gary A. "Royall Tyler and Nationalistic Comedy." In *American Drama from the Colonial Period through World War I: A Critical History*, 47–52. New York: Twayne, 1993.

Rinehart, Lucy. "A Nation's 'Noble Spectacle': Royall Tyler's *The Contrast* as Metatheatrical Commentary." *American Drama* 3.2 (1994): 29–52.

Seibert, Donald T., Jr. "Royall Tyler's 'Bold Example': *The Contrast* and the English Comedy of Manners." *Early American Literature* 13 (1978): 3–11.

Silverman, Kenneth. *A Cultural History of the Revolution*. 1976; New York: Columbia University Press, 1987, 536–67.

Stein, Roger B. "Royall Tyler and the Question of Our Speech." *New England Quarterly* 38 (1965): 454–74.

Tanselle, G. Thomas. *Royall Tyler*. Cambridge: Harvard University Press, 1967.

Tyler, Royall. *Four Plays*, edited by Arthur Wallace Peace and George Floyd Newbrough. *America's Lost Plays*. Vol. 15. 1940; Bloomington: Indiana University Press, 1965.

Wright, Richardson. *Revels in Jamaica, 1682–1838*. 1937; New York: Blom, 1969, 193–226, 275.

THE

CONTRAST,

A

COMEDY;

IN FIVE ACTS:

WRITTEN BY A
CITIZEN OF THE UNITED STATES;

Performed with Applause at the Theatres in NEW-YORK,
PHILADELPHIA, and MARYLAND;

AND PUBLISHED *(under an Assignment of the Copy-Righ*
THOMAS WIGNELL.

───◆◆◆───

Primus ego in patriam
Aonio—deduxi vertice Musas.

VIRGIL

(Imitated.)

First on our shores I try THALIA's powers,
And bid the *laughing, useful* Maid be ours.

───◆◆◆───

PHILADELPHIA:

FROM THE PRESS OF PRICHARD & HALL, IN MARKET STREET;
BETWEEN SECOND AND FRONT STREETS.

─────

M.DCC.XC.

PROLOGUE[1]

WRITTEN BY A YOUNG GENTLEMAN OF NEW-YORK,
AND SPOKEN BY MR. WIGNELL[2]

EXULT, each patriot heart!—this night is shewn
A piece, which we may fairly call our own;
Where the proud titles of "My Lord! Your Grace!"
To humble *Mr.* and plain *Sir* give place.
Our Author pictures not from foreign climes
The fashions or the follies of the times;
But has confin'd the subject of his work
To the gay scenes—the circles of New-York.
On native themes his Muse displays her pow'rs;
If ours the faults, the virtues too are ours.
Why should our thoughts to distant countries roam,
When each refinement may be found at home?
Who travels now to ape the rich or great,
To deck an equipage and roll in state;
To court the graces, or to dance with ease,
Or by hypocrisy to strive to please?
Our free-born ancestors such arts despis'd;
Genuine sincerity alone they priz'd;
Their minds, with honest emulation fir'd;
To solid good—not ornament—aspir'd;
Or, if ambition rous'd a bolder flame,
Stern virtue throve, where indolence was shame.

But modern youths, with imitative sense,
Deem taste in dress the proof of excellence;
And spurn the meanness of your homespun arts,
Since homespun habits would obscure their parts;
Whilst all, which aims at splendour and parade,
Must come from Europe, *and be ready made.*
Strange! we should thus our native worth disclaim,
And check the progress of our rising fame.
Yet *one*, whilst imitation bears the sway,
Aspires to nobler heights, and points the way.
Be rous'd, my friends! his bold example view;
Let your own Bards be proud to copy *you!*

7

Should rigid critics reprobate our play,
At least the patriotic heart will say,
"Glorious our fall, since in a noble cause.
The bold *attempt alone* demands applause."
Still may the wisdom of the Comic Muse
Exalt your merits, or your faults accuse.
But think not, 't is her aim to be severe;—
We all are mortals, and as mortals err.
If candour pleases, we are truly blest;
Vice trembles, when compell'd to stand confess'd.
Let not light Censure on your faults offend,
Which aims not to expose them, but amend.
Thus does our Author to your candour trust;
Conscious, the *free* are generous, as just.

CHARACTERS

COL. MANLY
DIMPLE
VAN ROUGH
JESSAMY
JONATHAN

CHARLOTTE
MARIA
LETITIA
JENNY

SERVANTS

SCENE, *NEW-YORK*

THE CONTRAST

ACT I

SCENE 1: *An Apartment at* CHARLOTTE'S. CHARLOTTE *and* LETITIA *discovered.*

LETITIA: And so, Charlotte, you really think the pocket-hoop unbecoming.

CHARLOTTE: No, I don't say so. It may be very becoming to saunter round the house of a rainy day; to visit my grand-mamma, or to go to Quakers' meeting: but to swim in a minuet, with the eyes of fifty well-dressed beaux upon me, to trip it in the Mall, or walk on the battery,[3] give me the luxurious, jaunty, flowing, bell-hoop. It would have delighted you to have seen me the last evening, my charming girl! I was dangling o'er the battery with Billy Dimple; a knot of young fellows were upon the platform; as I passed them I faultered with one of the most bewitching false steps you ever saw, and then recovered myself with such a pretty confusion, flirting my hoop to discover a jet black shoe and brilliant buckle. Gad! how my little heart thrilled to hear the confused raptures of—*"Demme, Jack, what a delicate foot!"* *"Ha! General, what a well-turn'd——"*

LETITIA: Fie! fie! Charlotte [*stopping her mouth*], I protest you are quite a libertine.

CHARLOTTE: Why, my dear little prude, are we not all such libertines? Do you think, when I sat tortured two hours under the hands of my friseur,[4] and an hour more at my toilet, that I had any thoughts of my aunt Susan, or my cousin Betsey? though they are both allowed to be critical judges of dress.

LETITIA: Why, who should we dress to please, but those who are judges of its merit?

CHARLOTTE: Why, a creature who does not know *Buffon*[5] from *Souflée*—Man!—my Letitia—Man! for whom we dress, walk, dance, talk, lisp, languish, and smile. Does not the grave Spectator[6] assure us that even our much be praised diffidence, modesty, and blushes are all directed to make ourselves good wives and mothers as fast as we can? Why, I'll undertake with one flirt of this hoop to bring more beaux to my feet in one week than the grave Maria, and her sentimental circle, can do, by sighing sentiment till their hairs are grey.

9

LETITIA: Well, I won't argue with you; you always out-talk me; let us change the subject. I hear that Mr. Dimple and Maria are soon to be married.

CHARLOTTE: You hear true. I was consulted in the choice of the wedding clothes. She is to be married in a delicate white sattin, and has a monstrous pretty brocaded lutestring for the second day. It would have done you good to have seen with what an affected indifference the dear sentimentalist turned over a thousand pretty things, just as if her heart did not palpitate with her approaching happiness, and at last made her choice and arranged her dress with such apathy as if she did not know that plain white sattin and a simple blond lace would shew her clear skin and dark hair to the greatest advantage.

LETITIA: But they say her indifference to dress, and even to the gentleman himself, is not entirely affected.

CHARLOTTE: How?

LETITIA: It is whispered that if Maria gives her hand to Mr. Dimple, it will be without her heart.

CHARLOTTE: Though the giving [of] the heart is one of the last of all laughable considerations in the marriage of a girl of spirit, yet I should like to hear what antiquated notions the dear little piece of old-fashioned prudery has got in her head.

LETITIA: Why, you know that old Mr. John-Richard-Robert-Jacob-Isaac-Abraham-Cornelius Van Dumpling, Billy Dimple's father (for he has thought fit to soften his name, as well as manners, during his English tour), was the most intimate friend of Maria's father. The old folks, about a year before Mr. Van Dumpling's death, proposed this match: the young folks were accordingly introduced, and told they must love one another. Billy was then a good-natured, decent-dressing young fellow, with a little dash of the coxcomb, such as our young fellows of fortune usually have. At this time, I really believe she thought she loved him; and had they then been married, I doubt not they might have jogged on, to the end of the chapter, a good kind of a sing-song lack-a-daysaical life, as other honest married folks do.

CHARLOTTE: Why did they not then marry?

LETITIA: Upon the death of his father, Billy went to England to see the world and rub off a little of the patroon rust. During his absence, Maria, like a good girl, to keep herself constant to her *nown true-love*, avoided company, and betook herself, for her amusement, to her books, and her dear Billy's letters. But, alas! how many ways has the mischievous demon of inconstancy of stealing into a woman's heart! Her love was destroyed by the very means she took to support it.

CHARLOTTE: How?—Oh! I have it—some likely young beau found the way to her study.

LETITIA: Be patient, Charlotte—your head so runs upon beaux. Why, she read Sir Charles Grandison, Clarissa Harlow, Shenstone, and the Sentimental Journey;[7] and between whiles, as I said, Billy's letters. But, as her taste improved, her love declined. The contrast was so striking betwixt the good sense of her books and the flimsiness of her love-letters, that she discovered she had unthinkingly engaged her hand without her heart; and then the whole transaction, managed by the old folks, now appeared so unsentimental, and looked so like bargaining for a bale of goods, that she found she ought to have rejected, according to every rule of romance, even the man of her choice, if imposed upon her in that manner. Clary Harlow would have scorned such a match.

CHARLOTTE: Well, how was it on Mr. Dimple's return? Did he meet a more favourable reception than his letters?

LETITIA: Much the same. She spoke of him with respect abroad, and with contempt in her closet. She watched his conduct and conversation, and found that he had by travelling acquired the wickedness of Lovelace[8] without his wit, and the politeness of Sir Charles Grandison without his generosity. The ruddy youth, who washed his face at the cistern every morning, and swore and looked eternal love and constancy, was now metamorphosed into a flippant, palid, polite beau, who devotes the morning to his toilet, reads a few pages of Chesterfield's letters,[9] and then minces out, to put the infamous principles in practice upon every woman he meets.

CHARLOTTE: But, if she is so apt at conjuring up these sentimental bugbears, why does she not discard him at once?

LETITIA: Why, she thinks her word too sacred to be trifled with. Besides, her father, who has a great respect for the memory of his deceased friend, is ever telling her how he shall renew his years in their union, and repeating the dying injunctions of old Van Dumpling.

CHARLOTTE: A mighty pretty story! And so you would make me believe that the sensible Maria would give up Dumpling manor, and the all-accomplished Dimple as a husband, for the absurd, ridiculous reason, forsooth, because she despises and abhors him. Just as if a lady could not be privileged to spend a man's fortune, ride in his carriage, be called after his name, and call him her *nown dear lovee* when she wants money, without loving and respecting the great he-creature. Oh! my dear girl, you are a monstrous prude.

LETITIA: I don't say what I would do; I only intimate how I suppose she wishes to act.

CHARLOTTE: No, no, no! A fig for sentiment. If she breaks, or wishes to break, with Mr. Dimple, depend upon it, she has some other man in her eye. A woman rarely discards one lover until she is sure of another.—Letitia little thinks what a clue I have to Dimple's conduct. The generous man submits to render himself disgusting to Maria, in order that she may leave him at liberty to address me. I must change the subject. [*Aside, and rings a bell.*]

[*Enter* SERVANT.]

Frank, order the horses to.——Talking of marriage—did you hear that Sally Bloomsbury is going to be married next week to Mr. Indigo, the rich Carolinian?

LETITIA: Sally Bloomsbury married!—Why, she is not yet in her teens.

CHARLOTTE: I do not know how that is, but, you may depend upon it, 'tis a done affair. I have it from the best authority. There is my aunt Wyerley's Hannah. (You know Hannah; though a black, she is a wench that was never caught in a lie in her life.) Now, Hannah has a brother who courts Sarah, Mrs. Catgut the milliner's girl, and she told Hannah's brother, and Hannah, who, as I said before, is a girl of undoubted veracity, told it directly to me, that Mrs. Catgut was making a new cap for Miss Bloomsbury, which, as it was very dressy, it is very probable is designed for a wedding cap: now, as she is to be married, who can it be but to Mr. Indigo? Why, there is no other gentleman that visits at her papa's.

LETITIA: Say not a word more, Charlotte. Your intelligence is so direct and well grounded, it is almost a pity that it is not a piece of scandal.

CHARLOTTE: Oh! I am the pink of prudence. Though I cannot charge myself with ever having discredited a tea-party by my silence, yet I take care never to report anything of my acquaintance, especially if it is to their credit,—*discredit*, I mean,—until I have searched to the bottom of it. It is true, there is infinite pleasure in this charitable pursuit. Oh! how delicious to go and condole with the friends of some backsliding sister, or to retire with some old dowager or maiden aunt of the family, who love scandal so well that they cannot forbear gratifying their appetite at the expense of the reputation of their nearest relations! And then to return full fraught with a rich collection

of circumstances, to retail to the next circle of our acquaintance under the strongest injunctions of secrecy,—ha, ha, ha!—interlarding
the melancholy tale with so many doleful shakes of the head, and
more doleful "Ah! who would have thought it! so amiable, so prudent a young lady, as we all thought her, what a monstrous pity!
well, I have nothing to charge myself with; I acted the part of a
friend, I warned her of the principles of that rake, I told her what
would be the consequence; I told her so, I told her so."—Ha, ha, ha!

LETITIA: Ha, ha, ha! Well, but Charlotte, you don't tell me what you
think of Miss Bloomsbury's match.

CHARLOTTE: Think! why I think it is probable she cried for a plaything,
and they have given her a husband. Well, well, well, the puling chit
shall not be deprived of her plaything: 'tis only exchanging London
dolls for American babies.—Apropos, of babies, have you heard
what Mrs. Affable's high-flying notions of delicacy have come to?

LETITIA: Who, she that was Miss Lovely?

CHARLOTTE: The same; she married Bob Affable of Schenectady. Don't
you remember?

[*Enter* SERVANT.]

SERVANT: Madam, the carriage is ready.

LETITIA: Shall we go to the stores first, or visiting?

CHARLOTTE: I should think it rather too early to visit, especially Mrs.
Prim; you know she is so particular.

LETITIA: Well, but what of Mrs. Affable?

CHARLOTTE: Oh, I'll tell you as we go; come, come, let us hasten. I
hear Mrs. Catgut has some of the prettiest caps arrived you ever saw.
I shall die if I have not the first sight of them.   [*Exeunt*].

SCENE 2: *A Room in* VAN ROUGH'S *House*. MARIA *sitting disconsolate
at a Table, with Books, &c.*

SONG[10]

I

The sun sets in night, and the stars shun the day;
But glory remains when their lights fade away!
Begin, ye tormentors! your threats are in vain,
For the son of Alknomook shall never complain.

II

Remember the arrows he shot from his bow;
Remember your chiefs by his hatchet laid low:
Why so slow?—do you wait till I shrink from the pain?
No—the son of Alknomook will never complain.

III

Remember the wood where in ambush we lay,
And the scalps which we bore from your nation away:
Now the flame rises fast, you exult in my pain;
But the son of Alknomook can never complain.

IV

I go to the land where my father is gone;
His ghost shall rejoice in the fame of his son:
Death comes like a friend, he relieves me from pain;
And thy son, Oh Alknomook! has scorn'd to complain.

There is something in this song which ever calls forth my affections.
The manly virtue of courage, that fortitude which steels the heart
against the keenest misfortunes, which interweaves the laurel of glory
amidst the instruments of torture and death, displays something so noble, so exalted, that in despite of the prejudices of education I cannot
but admire it, even in a savage. The prepossession which our sex is
supposed to entertain for the character of a soldier is, I know, a standing
piece of raillery among the wits. A cockade,[11] a lapell'd coat, and a
feather, they will tell you, are irresistible by a female heart. Let it be
so.—Who is it that considers the helpless situation of our sex, that does
not see that we each moment stand in need of a protector, and that a
brave one too? Formed of the more delicate materials of nature, en-
dowed only with the softer passions, incapable, from our ignorance of
the world, to guard against the wiles of mankind, our security for happiness often depends upon their generosity and courage.—Alas! how
little of the former do we find. How inconsistent! that man should be
leagued to destroy that honour upon which solely rests his respect and
esteem. Ten thousand temptations allure us, ten thousand passions betray us; yet the smallest deviation from the path of rectitude is followed
by the contempt and insult of man, and the more remorseless pity of
woman; years of penitence and tears cannot wash away the stain, nor

a life of virtue obliterate its remembrance. Reputation is the life of woman; yet courage to protect it is masculine and disgusting; and the only safe asylum a woman of delicacy can find is in the arms of a man of honour. How naturally, then, should we love the brave and the generous; how gratefully should we bless the arm raised for our protection, when nerv'd by virtue and directed by honour! Heaven grant that the man with whom I may be connected—may be connected!—Whither has my imagination transported me—whither does it now lead me— Am I not indissolubly engaged, by every obligation of honour which my own consent and my father's approbation can give, to a man who can never share my affections, and whom a few days hence it will be criminal for me to disapprove—to disapprove! would to heaven that were all—to despise. For, can the most frivolous manners, actuated by the most depraved heart, meet, or merit, anything but contempt from every woman of delicacy and sentiment?   [VAN ROUGH *without*. Mary!] Ha! my father's voice—Sir!——

          [*Enter* VAN ROUGH.]

VAN ROUGH: What, Mary, always singing doleful ditties, and moping over these plaguy books.

MARIA: I hope, Sir, that it is not criminal to improve my mind with books, or to divert my melancholy with singing, at my leisure hours.

VAN ROUGH: Why, I don't know that, child; I don't know that. They us'd to say, when I was a young man, that if a woman knew how to make a pudding, and to keep herself out of fire and water, she knew enough for a wife. Now, what good have these books done you? have they not made you melancholy? as you call it. Pray, what right has a girl of your age to be in the dumps? haven't you everything your heart can wish; an't you going to be married to a young man of great fortune; an't you going to have the quit-rent[12] of twenty miles square?

MARIA: One-hundredth part of the land, and a lease for life of the heart of a man I could love, would satisfy me.

VAN ROUGH: Pho, pho, pho! child; nonsense, downright nonsense, child. This comes of your reading your story-books; your Charles Grandisons, your Sentimental Journals, and your Robinson Crusoes, and such other trumpery. No, no, no! child, it is money makes the mare go; keep your eye upon the main chance, Mary.

MARIA: Marriage, Sir, is, indeed, a very serious affair.

VAN ROUGH: You are right, child; you are right. I am sure I found it so, to my cost.

MARIA: I mean, Sir, that as marriage is a portion for life, and so intimately involves our happiness, we cannot be too considerate in the choice of our companion.

VAN ROUGH: Right, child; very right. A young woman should be very sober when she is making her choice, but when she has once made it, as you have done, I don't see why she should not be as merry as a grig; I am sure she has reason enough to be so. Solomon says that "there is a time to laugh, and a time to weep." Now, a time for a young woman to laugh is when she has made sure of a good rich husband. Now, a time to cry, according to you, Mary, is when she is making choice of him; but *I* should think that a young woman's time to cry was when she despaired of *getting* one.—Why, there was your mother, now: to be sure, when I popp'd the question to her she did look a little silly; but when she had once looked down on her apron-strings, as all modest young women us'd to do, and drawled out ye-s, she was as brisk and as merry as a bee.

MARIA: My honoured mother, Sir, had no motive to melancholy; she married the man of her choice.

VAN ROUGH: The man of her choice! And pray, Mary, an't you going to marry the man of your choice—what trumpery notion is this? It is these vile books [*throwing them away*]. I'd have you to know, Mary, if you won't make young Van Dumpling the man of *your* choice, you shall marry him as the man of *my* choice.

MARIA: You terrify me, Sir. Indeed, Sir, I am all submission. My will is yours.

VAN ROUGH: Why, that is the way your mother us'd to talk. "My will is yours, my dear Mr. Van Rough, my will is yours"; but she took special care to have her own way, though, for all that.

MARIA: Do not reflect upon my mother's memory, Sir——

VAN ROUGH: Why not, Mary, why not? She kept me from speaking my mind all her *life*, and do you think she shall henpeck me now she is *dead* too? Come, come; don't go sniveling; be a good girl, and mind the main chance. I'll see you well settled in the world.

MARIA: I do not doubt your love, Sir, and it is my duty to obey you. I will endeavour to make my duty and inclination go hand in hand.

VAN ROUGH: Well, well, Mary; do you be a good girl, mind the main chance, and never mind inclination. Why, do you know that I have been down in the cellar this very morning to examine a pipe of Madeira[13] which I purchased the week you were born, and mean to tap on your wedding day?—That pipe cost me fifty pounds sterling. It was well worth sixty pounds; but I over-reach'd Ben Bulkhead, the supercargo. I'll tell you the whole story. You must know that——

[*Enter* SERVANT.]

SERVANT: Sir, Mr. Transfer, the broker, is below.   [*Exit.*]
VAN ROUGH: Well, Mary, I must go.—Remember, and be a good girl, and mind the main chance.   [*Exit.*]
MARIA [*alone*]: How deplorable is my situation! How distressing for a daughter to find her heart militating with her filial duty! I know my father loves me tenderly; why then do I reluctantly obey him? Heaven knows! with what reluctance I should oppose the will of a parent, or set an example of filial disobedience; at a parent's command, I could wed awkwardness and deformity. Were the heart of my husband good, I would so magnify his good qualities with the eye of conjugal affection, that the defects of his person and manners should be lost in the emanation of his virtues. At a father's command, I could embrace poverty. Were the poor man my husband, I would learn resignation to my lot; I would enliven our frugal meal with good humour, and chase away misfortune from our cottage with a smile. At a father's command, I could almost submit to what every female heart knows to be the most mortifying, to marry a weak man, and blush at my husband's folly in every company I visited. But to marry a depraved wretch, whose only virtue is a polished exterior; who is actuated by the unmanly ambition of conquering the defenceless; whose heart, insensible to the emotions of patriotism, dilates at the plaudits of every unthinking girl; whose laurels are the sighs and tears of the miserable victims of his specious behaviour.—Can he, who has no regard for the peace and happiness of other families, ever have a due regard for the peace and happiness of his own? Would to heaven that my father were not so hasty in his temper! Surely, if I were to state my reasons for declining this match, he would not compel me to marry a man, whom, though my lips may solemnly promise to honour, I find my heart must ever despise.

[*Exit.*]

END OF ACT I

ACT II

SCENE 1

[*Enter* CHARLOTTE *and* LETITIA.]

CHARLOTTE [*at entering*]: Betty, take those things out of the carriage and carry them to my chamber; see that you don't tumble them. My dear, I protest, I think it was the homeliest of the whole. I declare I was almost tempted to return and change it.

LETITIA: Why would you take it?

CHARLOTTE: Didn't Mrs. Catgut say it was the most fashionable?

LETITIA: But, my dear, it will never fit becomingly on you.

CHARLOTTE: I know that; but did not you hear Mrs. Catgut say it was fashionable?

LETITIA: Did you see that sweet airy cap with the white sprig?

CHARLOTTE: Yes, and I longed to take it; but, my dear, what could I do? Did not Mrs. Catgut say it was the most fashionable; and if I had not taken it, was not that awkward gawky, Sally Slender, ready to purchase it immediately?

LETITIA: Did you observe how she tumbled over the things at the next shop, and then went off without purchasing anything, nor even thanking the poor man for his trouble? But, of all the awkward creatures, did you see Miss Blouze endeavouring to thrust her unmerciful arm into those small kid gloves?

CHARLOTTE: Ha, ha, ha, ha!

LETITIA: Then did you take notice with what an affected warmth of friendship she and Miss Wasp met? when all their acquaintance know how much pleasure they take in abusing each other in every company.

CHARLOTTE: Lud! Letitia, is that so extraordinary? Why, my dear, I hope you are not going to turn sentimentalist.—Scandal, you know, is but amusing ourselves with the faults, foibles, follies, and reputations of our friends;—indeed, I don't know why we should have friends, if we are not at liberty to make use of them. But no person is so ignorant of the world as to suppose, because I amuse myself with a lady's faults, that I am obliged to quarrel with her person every time we meet: believe me, my dear, we should have very few acquaintance at that rate.

[SERVANT *enters and delivers a letter to* CHARLOTTE, *and*——]

[*Exit*].

CHARLOTTE: You'll excuse me, my dear. [*Opens and reads to herself.*]

LETITIA: Oh, quite excusable.

CHARLOTTE: As I hope to be married, my brother Henry is in the city.

LETITIA: What, your brother, Colonel Manly?

CHARLOTTE: Yes, my dear; the only brother I have in the world.

LETITIA: Was he never in this city?

CHARLOTTE: Never nearer than Harlem Heights,[14] where he lay with his regiment.

LETITIA: What sort of a being is this brother of yours? If he is as chatty, as pretty, as sprightly as you, half the belles in the city will be pulling caps for him.

CHARLOTTE: My brother is the very counterpart and reverse of me: I am gay, he is grave; I am airy, he is solid; I am ever selecting the most pleasing objects for my laughter, he has a tear for every pitiful one. And thus, whilst he is plucking the briars and thorns from the path of the unfortunate, I am strewing my own path with roses.

LETITIA: My sweet friend, not quite so poetical, and a little more particular.

CHARLOTTE: Hands off, Letitia. I feel the rage of simile upon me; I can't talk to you in any other way. My brother has a heart replete with the noblest sentiments, but then, it is like—it is like—Oh! you provoking girl, you have deranged all my ideas—it is like—Oh! I have it—his heart is like an old maiden lady's bandbox; it contains many costly things, arranged with the most scrupulous nicety, yet the misfortune is that they are too delicate, costly, and antiquated for common use.

LETITIA: By what I can pick out of your flowery description, your brother is no beau.

CHARLOTTE: No, indeed; he makes no pretension to the character. He'd ride, or rather fly, an hundred miles to relieve a distressed object, or to do a gallant act in the service of his country; but should you drop your fan or bouquet in his presence, it is ten to one that some beau at the farther end of the room would have the honour of presenting it to you before he had observed that it fell. I'll tell you one of his antiquated, anti-gallant notions. He said once in my presence, in a room full of company—would you believe it?—in a large circle of ladies, that the best evidence a gentleman could give a young lady of his respect and affection was to endeavour in a friendly manner to rectify her foibles. I protest I was crimson to the eyes, upon reflecting that I was known as his sister.

LETITIA: Insupportable creature! tell a lady of her faults! If he is so grave, I fear I have no chance of captivating him.

CHARLOTTE: His conversation is like a rich, old-fashioned brocade—it will stand alone; every sentence is a sentiment. Now you may judge what a time I had with him, in my twelve months' visit to my father. He read me such lectures, out of pure brotherly affection, against the extremes of fashion, dress, flirting, and coquetry, and all the other dear things which he knows I doat upon, that I protest his conversation made me as melancholy as if I had been at church; and heaven knows, though I never prayed to go there but on one occasion, yet I would have exchanged his conversation for a psalm and a sermon. Church is rather melancholy, to be sure; but then I can ogle the beaux, and be regaled with "here endeth the first lesson," but his brotherly *here*, you would think had no end. You captivate him! Why, my dear, he would as soon fall in love with a box of Italian flowers. There is Maria, now, if she were not engaged, she might do something.—Oh! how I should like to see that pair of pensorosos[15] together, looking as grave as two sailors' wives of a stormy night, with a flow of sentiment meandering through their conversation like purling streams in modern poetry.

LETITIA: Oh! my dear fanciful——

CHARLOTTE: Hush! I hear some person coming through the entry.

[*Enter* SERVANT.]

SERVANT: Madam, there's a gentleman below who calls himself Colonel Manly; do you chuse to be at home?

CHARLOTTE: Shew him in. [*Exit* SERVANT.] Now for a sober face.

[*Enter* COLONEL MANLY.]

MANLY: My dear Charlotte, I am happy that I once more enfold you within the arms of fraternal affection. I know you are going to ask (amiable impatience!) how our parents do,—the venerable pair transmit you their blessing by me. They totter on the verge of a well-spent life, and wish only to see their children settled in the world, to depart in peace.

CHARLOTTE: I am very happy to hear that they are well. [*Coolly.*] Brother, will you give me leave to introduce you to our uncle's ward, one of my most intimate friends.

MANLY [*saluting* LETITIA]: I ought to regard your friends as my own.

CHARLOTTE: Come, Letitia, do give us a little dash of your vivacity; my brother is so sentimental and so grave, that I protest he'll give us the vapours.

MANLY: Though sentiment and gravity, I know, are banished [from] the polite world, yet I hoped they might find some countenance in the meeting of such near connections as brother and sister.

CHARLOTTE: Positively, brother, if you go one step further in this strain, you will set me crying, and that, you know, would spoil my eyes; and then I should never get the husband which our good papa and mamma have so kindly wished me—never be established in the world.

MANLY: Forgive me, my sister—I am no enemy to mirth; I love your sprightliness; and I hope it will one day enliven the hours of some worthy man; but when I mention the respectable authors of my existence—the cherishers and protectors of my helpless infancy, whose hearts glow with such fondness and attachment that they would willingly lay down their lives for my welfare—you will excuse me if I am so unfashionable as to speak of them with some degree of respect and reverence.

CHARLOTTE: Well, well, brother; if you won't be gay, we'll not differ; I will be as grave as you wish. [Affects gravity.] And so, brother, you have come to the city to exchange some of your commutation notes[16] for a little pleasure?

MANLY: Indeed you are mistaken; my errand is not of amusement, but business; and as I neither drink nor game, my expenses will be so trivial, I shall have no occasion to sell my notes.

CHARLOTTE: Then you won't have occasion to do a very good thing. Why, there was the Vermont General—he came down some time since, sold all his musty notes at one stroke, and then laid the cash out in trinkets for his dear Fanny. I want a dozen pretty things myself; have you got the notes with you?

MANLY: I shall be ever willing to contribute, as far as it is in my power, to adorn or in any way to please my sister; yet I hope I shall never be obliged for this to sell my notes. I may be romantic, but I preserve them as a sacred deposit. Their full amount is justly due to me, but as embarrassments, the natural consequences of a long war, disable my country from supporting its credit, I shall wait with patience until it is rich enough to discharge them. If that is not in my day, they shall be transmitted as an honourable certificate to posterity, that I have humbly imitated our illustrious WASHINGTON, in having exposed my health and life in the service of my country, without reaping any other reward than the glory of conquering in so arduous a contest.

CHARLOTTE: Well said heroics. Why, my dear Henry, you have such a lofty way of saying things, that I protest I almost tremble at the thought of introducing you to the polite circles in the city. The belles would think you were a player run mad, with your head filled with old scraps of tragedy; and as to the beaux, they might admire, because they would not understand you. But, however, I must, I believe, venture to introduce you to two or three ladies of my acquaintance.

LETITIA: And that will make him acquainted with thirty or forty beaux.

CHARLOTTE: Oh! brother, you don't know what a fund of happiness you have in store.

MANLY: I fear, sister, I have not refinement sufficient to enjoy it.

CHARLOTTE: Oh! you cannot fail being pleased.

LETITIA: Our ladies are so delicate and dressy.

CHARLOTTE: And our beaux so dressy and delicate.

LETITIA: Our ladies chat and flirt so agreeably.

CHARLOTTE: And our beaux simper and bow so gracefully.

LETITIA: With their hair so trim and neat.

CHARLOTTE: And their faces so soft and sleek.

LETITIA: Their buckles so tonish and bright.

CHARLOTTE: And their hands so slender and white.

LETITIA: I vow, Charlotte, we are quite poetical.

CHARLOTTE: And then, brother, the faces of the beaux are of such a lily-white hue! None of that horrid robustness of constitution, that vulgar corn-fed glow of health, which can only serve to alarm an unmarried lady with apprehensions, and prove a melancholy memento to a married one, that she can never hope for the happiness of being a widow. I will say this to the credit of our city beaux, that such is the delicacy of their complexion, dress, and address, that, even had I no reliance upon the honour of the dear Adonises, I would trust myself in any possible situation with them, without the least apprehensions of rudeness.

MANLY: Sister Charlotte!

CHARLOTTE: Now, now, now, brother [*interrupting him*], now don't go to spoil my mirth with a dash of your gravity; I am so glad to see you, I am in tip-top spirits. Oh! that you could be with us at a little snug party. There is Billy Simper, Jack Chaffé, and Colonel Van Titter, Miss Promonade, and the two Miss Tambours, sometimes make a party, with some other ladies, in a side-box at the play. Everything is conducted with such decorum. First we bow round to the company in general, then to each one in particular, then we have so many inquiries after each other's health, and we are so happy to meet each other, and it is so many ages since we last had that pleasure, and if a married lady is in company, we have such a sweet dissertation upon her son Bobby's chin-cough; then the curtain rises, then our sensibility is all awake, and then, by the mere force of apprehension, we torture some harmless expression into a double meaning, which the poor author never dreamt of, and then we have recourse to our fans, and then we blush, and then the gentlemen jog one another, peep under the fan, and make the prettiest remarks; and then we giggle and they simper, and they giggle and we simper, and then the curtain drops, and then for nuts and oranges, and then we bow, and it's pray, Ma'am, take it, and pray, Sir, keep it, and oh! not for the world, Sir; and then the curtain rises again, and then we blush and giggle and simper and bow all over again. Oh! the sentimental charms of a side-box conversation! [*All laugh.*]

MANLY: Well, sister, I join heartily with you in the laugh; for, in my opinion, it is as justifiable to laugh at folly as it is reprehensible to ridicule misfortune.

CHARLOTTE: Well, but, brother, positively I can't introduce you in these clothes: why, your coat looks as if it were calculated for the vulgar purpose of keeping yourself comfortable.

MANLY: This coat was my regimental coat in the late war. The public tumults of our state have induced me to buckle on the sword in support of that government which I once fought to establish. I can only say, sister, that there was a time when this coat was respectable, and some people even thought that those men who had endured so many winter campaigns in the service of their country, without bread, clothing, or pay, at least deserved that the poverty of their appearance should not be ridiculed.

CHARLOTTE: We agree in opinion entirely, brother, though it would not have done for me to have said it: it is the coat makes the man respectable. In the time of the war, when we were almost frightened to death, why, your coat was respectable, that is, fashionable; now another kind of coat is fashionable, that is, respectable. And pray direct the taylor to make yours the height of the fashion.

MANLY: Though it is of little consequence to me of what shape my coat is, yet, as to the height of the fashion, there you will please to excuse me, sister. You know my sentiments on that subject. I have often lamented the advantage which the French have over us in that particular. In Paris, the fashions have their dawnings, their routine, and declensions, and depend as much upon the caprice of the day as in other countries; but there every lady assumes a right to deviate from the general *ton* as far as will be of advantage to her own appearance. In America, the cry is, what is the fashion? and we follow it, indiscriminately, because it is so.

CHARLOTTE: Therefore it is, that when large hoops are in fashion, we often see many a plump girl lost in the immensity of a hoop-petticoat, whose want of height and *en-bon-point*[17] would never have been remarked in any other dress. When the high head-dress is the mode, how then do we see a lofty cushion, with a profusion of gauze, feathers, and ribband, supported by a face no bigger than an apple! whilst a broad full-faced lady, who really would have appeared tolerably handsome in a large head-dress, looks with her smart chapeau as masculine as a soldier.

MANLY: But remember, my dear sister, and I wish all my fair countrywomen would recollect, that the only excuse a young lady can have for going extravagantly into a fashion is because it makes her look extravagantly handsome.—Ladies, I must wish you a good morning.

CHARLOTTE: But, brother, you are going to make home with us.

MANLY: Indeed I cannot. I have seen my uncle and explained that matter.

CHARLOTTE: Come and dine with us, then. We have a family dinner about half-past four o'clock.

MANLY: I am engaged to dine with the Spanish ambassador. I was introduced to him by an old brother officer; and instead of freezing me with a cold card of compliment to dine with him ten days hence, he, with the true old Castilian frankness, in a friendly manner, asked me to dine with him to-day—an honour I could not refuse. Sister, adieu—Madam, your most obedient——   [*Exit.*]

CHARLOTTE: I will wait upon you to the door, brother; I have something particular to say to you.   [*Exit.*]

LETITIA [*alone*]: What a pair!—She the pink of flirtation, he the essence of everything that is *outré* and gloomy.—I think I have completely deceived Charlotte by my manner of speaking of Mr. Dimple; she's too much the friend of Maria to be confided in. He is certainly rendering himself disagreeable to Maria, in order to break with her and proffer his hand to me. This is what the delicate fellow hinted in our last conversation.   [*Exit.*]

SCENE 2: *The Mall.*

[*Enter* JESSAMY.]

JESSAMY: Positively this Mall is a very pretty place. I hope the cits[18] won't ruin it by repairs. To be sure, it won't do to speak of in the same day with Ranelagh or Vauxhall;[19] however, it's a fine place for a young fellow to display his person to advantage. Indeed, nothing is lost here; the girls have taste, and I am very happy to find they have adopted the elegant London fashion of looking back, after a genteel fellow like me has passed them.—Ah! who comes here? This, by his awkwardness, must be the Yankee colonel's servant. I'll accost him.

[*Enter* JONATHAN.]

Votre très-humble serviteur, Monsieur.[20] I understand Colonel Manly, the Yankee officer, has the honour of your services.

JONATHAN: Sir!——

JESSAMY: I say, Sir, I understand that Colonel Manly has the honour of having you for a servant.

JONATHAN: Servant! Sir, do you take me for a neger,—I am Colonel Manly's waiter.

JESSAMY: A true Yankee distinction, egad, without a difference. Why, Sir, do you not perform all the offices of a servant? do you not even blacken his boots?

JONATHAN: Yes; I do grease them a bit sometimes; but I am a true blue son of liberty, for all that. Father said I should come as Colonel Manly's waiter, to see the world, and all that; but no man shall master me: my father has as good a farm as the colonel.

JESSAMY: Well, Sir, we will not quarrel about terms upon the eve of an acquaintance from which I promise myself so much satisfaction;— therefore, sans ceremonie[21]——

JONATHAN: What?——

JESSAMY: I say I am extremely happy to see Colonel Manly's waiter.

JONATHAN: Well, and I vow, too, I am pretty considerably glad to see you—but what the dogs need of all this outlandish lingo? Who may you be, Sir, if I may be so bold?

JESSAMY: I have the honour to be Mr. Dimple's servant, or, if you please, waiter. We lodge under the same roof, and should be glad of the honour of your acquaintance.

JONATHAN: You a waiter! by the living jingo, you look so topping, I took you for one of the agents to Congress.

JESSAMY: The brute has discernment, notwithstanding his appearance. —Give me leave to say I wonder then at your familiarity.

JONATHAN: Why, as to the matter of that, Mr. ——; pray, what's your name?

JESSAMY: Jessamy, at your service.

JONATHAN: Why, I swear we don't make any great matter of distinction in our state between quality and other folks.

JESSAMY: This is, indeed, a levelling principle.—I hope, Mr. Jonathan, you have not taken part with the insurgents.

JONATHAN: Why, since General Shays[22] has sneaked off and given us the bag to hold, I don't care to give my opinion; but you'll promise not to tell—put your ear this way—you won't tell?—I vow I did think the sturgeons were right.

JESSAMY: I thought, Mr. Jonathan, you Massachusetts-men always argued with a gun in your hand.—Why didn't you join them?

JONATHAN: Why, the colonel is one of those folks called the Shin— Shin[23]—dang it all, I can't speak them lignum vitae[24] words—you know who I mean—there is a company of them—they wear a china goose at their button-hole—a kind of gilt thing.—Now the colonel told father and brother,—you must know there are, let me see— there is Elnathan, Silas, and Barnabas, Tabitha—no, no, she's a she —tarnation, now I have it—there's Elnathan, Silas, Barnabas, Jonathan, that's I—seven of us, six went into the wars, and I staid at home to take care of mother. Colonel said that it was a burning shame for the true blue Bunker Hill sons of liberty, who had fought Governor Hutchinson, Lord North, and the Devil,[25] to have any hand in kicking up a cursed dust against a government which we had, every mother's son of us, a hand in making.

JESSAMY: Bravo!—Well, have you been abroad in the city since your arrival? What have you seen that is curious and entertaining?

JONATHAN: Oh! I have seen a power of fine sights. I went to see two marble-stone men and a leaden horse that stands out in doors in all weathers; and when I came where they was, one had got no head, and t'other wern't there. They said as how the leaden man was a damn'd tory, and that he took wit in his anger and rode off in the time of the troubles.

JESSAMY: But this was not the end of your excursion.

JONATHAN: Oh, no; I went to a place they call Holy Ground. Now I counted this was a place where folks go to meeting; so I put my hymn-book in my pocket, and walked softly and grave as a minister; and when I came there, the dogs a bit of a meeting-house could I see. At last I spied a young gentle-woman standing by one of the seats which they have here at the doors. I took her to be the deacon's daughter, and she looked so kind, and so obliging, that I thought I would go and ask her the way to lecture, and—would you think it?—she called me dear, and sweeting, and honey, just as if we were married: by the living jingo, I had a month's mind to buss her.

JESSAMY: Well, but how did it end?

JONATHAN: Why, as I was standing talking with her, a parcel of sailor men and boys got round me, the snarl-headed curs fell a-kicking and cursing of me at such a tarnal rate, that I vow I was glad to take to my heels and split home, right off, tail on end, like a stream of chalk.

JESSAMY: Why, my dear friend, you are not acquainted with the city; that girl you saw was a——[*Whispers.*]

JONATHAN: Mercy on my soul! was that young woman a harlot!— Well! if this is New-York Holy Ground, what must the Holy-day Ground be!

JESSAMY: Well, you should not judge of the city too rashly. We have a number of elegant, fine girls here that make a man's leisure hours pass very agreeably. I would esteem it an honour to announce you to some of them.—Gad! that announce is a select word; I wonder where I picked it up.

JONATHAN: I don't want to know them.

JESSAMY: Come, come, my dear friend, I see that I must assume the honour of being the director of your amusements. Nature has given us passions, and youth and opportunity stimulate to gratify them. It is no shame, my dear Blueskin,²⁶ for a man to amuse himself with a little gallantry.

JONATHAN: Girl huntry! I don't altogether understand. I never played at that game. I know how to play hunt the squirrel, but I can't play anything with the girls; I am as good as married.

JESSAMY: Vulgar, horrid brute! Married, and above a hundred miles from his wife, and thinks that an objection to his making love to every woman he meets! He never can have read, no, he never can have been in a room with a volume of the divine Chesterfield.—So you are married?

JONATHAN: No, I don't say so; I said I was as good as married, a kind of promise.

JESSAMY: As good as married!——

JONATHAN: Why, yes; there's Tabitha Wymen, the deacon's daughter,

at home; she and I have been courting a great while, and folks say
as how we are to be married; and so I broke a piece of money with
her when we parted, and she promised not to spark it with Solomon
Dyer while I am gone. You wou'dn't have me false to my true-love,
would you?

JESSAMY: May be you have another reason for constancy; possibly the
young lady has a fortune? Ha! Mr. Jonathan, the solid charms: the
chains of love are never so binding as when the links are made of
gold.

JONATHAN: Why, as to fortune, I must needs say her father is pretty
dumb rich; he went representative for our town last year. He will
give her—let me see—four times seven is—seven times four—nought
and carry one;—he will give her twenty acres of land—somewhat
rocky though—a Bible, and a cow.

JESSAMY: Twenty acres of rock, a Bible, and a cow! Why, my dear Mr.
Jonathan, we have servant-maids, or, as you would more elegantly
express it, waitresses, in this city, who collect more in one year from
their mistresses' cast clothes.

JONATHAN: You don't say so!——

JESSAMY: Yes, and I'll introduce you to one of them. There is a little
lump of flesh and delicacy that lives at next door, waitress to Miss
Maria; we often see her on the stoop.

JONATHAN: But are you sure she would be courted by me?

JESSAMY: Never doubt it; remember a faint heart never—blisters on my
tongue—I was going to be guilty of a vile proverb; flat against the
authority of Chesterfield.—I say there can be no doubt that the bril-
liancy of your merit will secure you a favourable reception.

JONATHAN: Well, but what must I say to her?

JESSAMY: Say to her! why, my dear friend, though I admire your profound knowledge on every other subject, yet, you will pardon my
saying that your want of opportunity has made the female heart
escape the poignancy of your penetration. Say to her! Why, when a
man goes a-courting, and hopes for success, he must begin with doing, and not saying.

JONATHAN: Well, what must I do?

JESSAMY: Why, when you are introduced you must make five or six
elegant bows.

JONATHAN: Six elegant bows! I understand that; six, you say?
Well——

JESSAMY: Then you must press and kiss her hand; then press and kiss, and so on to her lips and cheeks; then talk as much as you can about hearts, darts, flames, nectar and ambrosia—the more incoherent the better.

JONATHAN: Well, but suppose she should be angry with I?

JESSAMY: Why, if she should pretend—please to observe, Mr. Jonathan—if she should pretend to be offended, you must—— But I'll tell you how my master acted in such a case: He was seated by a young lady of eighteen upon a sofa, plucking with a wanton hand the blooming sweets of youth and beauty. When the lady thought it necessary to check his ardour, she called up a frown upon her lovely face, so irresistibly alluring, that it would have warmed the frozen bosom of age; remember, said she, putting her delicate arm upon his, remember your character and my honour. My master instantly dropped upon his knees, with eyes swimming with love, cheeks glowing with desire, and in the gentlest modulation of voice he said: My dear Caroline, in a few months our hands will be indissolubly united at the altar; our hearts I feel are already so; the favours you now grant as evidence of your affection are favours indeed; yet, when the ceremony is once past, what will now be received with rapture will then be attributed to duty.

JONATHAN: Well, and what was the consequence?

JESSAMY: The consequence!—Ah! forgive me, my dear friend, but you New-England gentlemen have such a laudable curiosity of seeing the bottom of everything;—why, to be honest, I confess I saw the blooming cherub of a consequence smiling in its angelic mother's arms, about ten months afterwards.

JONATHAN: Well, if I follow all your plans, make them six bows, and all that, shall I have such little cherubim consequences?

JESSAMY: Undoubtedly.—What are you musing upon?

JONATHAN: You say you'll certainly make me acquainted?—Why, I was thinking then how I should contrive to pass this broken piece of silver—won't it buy a sugar-dram?[27]

JESSAMY: What is that, the love-token from the deacon's daughter?— You come on bravely. But I must hasten to my master. Adieu, my dear friend.

JONATHAN: Stay, Mr. Jessamy—must I buss her when I am introduced to her?

JESSAMY: I told you, you must kiss her.

JONATHAN: Well, but must I buss her?

JESSAMY: Why kiss and buss, and buss and kiss, is all one.

JONATHAN: Oh! my dear friend, though you have a profound knowledge of all, a pugnency of tribulation, you don't know everything.
[*Exit.*]

JESSAMY [*alone*]: Well, certainly I improve; my master could not have
insinuated himself with more address into the heart of a man he
despised. Now will this blundering dog sicken Jenny with his nau-
seous pawings, until she flies into my arms for very ease. How sweet
will the contrast be between the blundering Jonathan and the courtly
and accomplished Jessamy!

END OF ACT II

ACT III

SCENE 1: DIMPLE'S *Room.* DIMPLE *discovered at a Toilet, Reading.*

DIMPLE: "Women have in general but one object, which is their beauty."
Very true, my lord; positively very true. "Nature has hardly formed
a woman ugly enough to be insensible to flattery upon her person."
Extremely just, my lord; every day's delightful experience confirms
this. "If her face is so shocking that she must, in some degree, be
conscious of it, her figure and air, she thinks, make ample amends
for it." The sallow Miss Wan is a proof of this. Upon my telling the
distasteful wretch, the other day, that her countenance spoke the
pensive language of sentiment, and that Lady Wortley Montagu[28]
declared that if the ladies were arrayed in the garb of innocence, the
face would be the last part which would be admired, as Monsieur
Milton[29] expresses it, she grinn'd horribly a ghastly smile. "If her
figure is deformed, she thinks her face counterbalances it."

[*Enter* JESSAMY *with letters.*]

Where got you these, Jessamy?

JESSAMY: Sir, the English packet is arrived.

DIMPLE [*opens and reads a letter enclosing notes*].
"Sir,
"I have drawn bills on you in favour of Messrs. Van Cash and Co.
as per margin. I have taken up your note to Col. Piquet, and discharged your debts to my Lord Lurcher and Sir Harry Rook. I herewith enclose you copies of the bills, which I have no doubt will be

immediately honoured. On failure, I shall empower some lawyer in your country to recover the amounts.

"I am, Sir,

"Your most humble servant,

"JOHN HAZARD."

Now, did not my lord expressly say that it was unbecoming a well-bred man to be in a passion, I confess I should be ruffled. [*Reads.*] "There is no accident so unfortunate, which a wise man may not turn to his advantage; nor any accident so fortunate, which a fool will not turn to his disadvantage." True, my lord; but how advantage can be derived from this I can't see. Chesterfield himself, who made, however, the worst practice of the most excellent precepts, was never in so embarrassing a situation. I love the person of Charlotte, and it is necessary I should command the fortune of Letitia. As to Maria! —I doubt not by my *sang-froid*[30] behaviour I shall compel her to decline the match; but the blame must not fall upon me. A prudent man, as my lord says, should take all the credit of a good action to himself, and throw the discredit of a bad one upon others. I must break with Maria, marry Letitia, and as for Charlotte—why, Charlotte must be a companion to my wife.—Here, Jessamy!

[*Enter* JESSAMY. DIMPLE *folds and seals two letters.*]

DIMPLE: Here, Jessamy, take this letter to my love. [*Gives one.*]

JESSAMY: To which of your honour's loves?—Oh! [*reading*] to Miss Letitia, your honour's rich love.

DIMPLE: And this [*delivers another*] to Miss Charlotte Manly. See that you deliver them privately.

JESSAMY: Yes, your honour. [*Going.*]

DIMPLE: Jessamy, who are these strange lodgers that came to the house last night?

JESSAMY: Why, the master is a Yankee colonel; I have not seen much of him; but the man is the most unpolished animal your honour ever disgraced your eyes by looking upon. I have had one of the most *outré*[31] conversations with him!—He really has a most prodigious effect upon my risibility.

DIMPLE: I ought, according to every rule of Chesterfield, to wait on him and insinuate myself into his good graces.——Jessamy, wait on the colonel with my compliments, and if he is disengaged I will do myself the honour of paying him my respects.—Some ignorant, unpolished boor——

[JESSAMY *goes off and returns.*]

JESSAMY: Sir, the colonel is gone out, and Jonathan his servant says that
he is gone to stretch his legs upon the Mall.—Stretch his legs! what
an indelicacy of diction!

DIMPLE: Very well. Reach me my hat and sword. I'll accost him there,
in my way to Letitia's, as by accident; pretend to be struck with his
person and address, and endeavour to steal into his confidence. Jessamy, I have no business for you at present.

JESSAMY [*taking up the book*]: My master and I obtain our knowledge
from the same source;—though, gad! I think myself much the prettier
fellow of the two. [*Surveying himself in the glass.*] That was a brilliant thought, to insinuate that I folded my master's letters for him;
the folding is so neat, that it does honour to the operator. I once
intended to have insinuated that I wrote his letters too; but that was
before I saw them; it won't do now: no honour there, positively.—
"Nothing looks more vulgar, [*reading affectedly*] ordinary, and illib-
eral than ugly, uneven, and ragged nails; the ends of which should
be kept even and clean, not tipped with black, and cut in small segments of circles."—Segments of circles! surely my lord did not consider that he wrote for the beaux. Segments of circles! what a crabbed
term! Now I dare answer that my master, with all his learning, does
not know that this means, according to the present mode, to let the
nails grow long, and then cut them off even at top. [*Laughing without.*] Ha! that's Jenny's titter. I protest I despair of ever teaching that
girl to laugh; she has something so execrably natural in her laugh,
that I declare it absolutely discomposes my nerves. How came she
into our House! [*Calls.*] Jenny!

[*Enter* JENNY.]

Prythee, Jenny, don't spoil your fine face with laughing.

JENNY: Why, mustn't I laugh, Mr. Jessamy?

JESSAMY: You may smile; but, as my lord says, nothing can authorise a
laugh.

JENNY: Well, but I can't help laughing.—Have you seen him, Mr. Jessamy? ha, ha, ha!

JESSAMY: Seen whom?

JENNY: Why, Jonathan, the New-England colonel's servant. Do you
know he was at the play last night, and the stupid creature don't
know where he has been. He would not go to a play for the world;
he thinks it was a show, as he calls it.

JESSAMY: As ignorant and unpolished as he is, do you know, Miss Jenny, that I propose to introduce him to the honour of your acquaintance?

JENNY: Introduce him to me! for what?

JESSAMY: Why, my lovely girl, that you may take him under your protection, as Madame Rambouillet[32] did young Stanhope; that you may, by your plastic hand, mould this uncouth cub into a gentleman. He is to make love to you.

JENNY: Make love to me!——

JESSAMY: Yes, Mistress Jenny, make love to you; and, I doubt not, when he shall become *domesticated* in your kitchen, that this boor, under your auspices, will soon become *un amiable petit Jonathan.*[33]

JENNY: I must say, Mr. Jessamy, if he copies after me, he will be vastly, monstrously polite.

JESSAMY: Stay here, one moment, and I will call him.—Jonathan!—Mr. Jonathan!—[*Calls.*]

JONATHAN [*within*]: Holla! there.—[*Enters.*] You promise to stand by me—six bows you say. [*Bows.*]

JESSAMY: Mrs. Jenny, I have the honour of presenting Mr. Jonathan, Colonel Manly's waiter, to you. I am extremely happy that I have it in my power to make two worthy people acquainted with each other's merit.

JENNY: So, Mr. Jonathan, I hear you were at the play last night.

JONATHAN: At the play! why, did you think I went to the devil's drawing-room?

JENNY: The devil's drawing-room!

JONATHAN: Yes; why an't cards and dice the devil's device, and the play-house the shop where the devil hangs out the vanities of the world upon the tenter-hooks of temptation? I believe you have not heard how they were acting the old boy one night, and the wicked one came among them sure enough, and went right off in a storm, and carried one quarter of the play-house with him. Oh! no, no, no! you won't catch me at a play-house, I warrant you.

JENNY: Well, Mr. Jonathan, though I don't scruple your veracity, I have some reasons for believing you were there: pray, where were you about six o'clock?

JONATHAN: Why, I went to see one Mr. Morrison, the *hocus pocus* man; they said as how he could eat a case knife.

JENNY: Well, and how did you find the place?

JONATHAN: As I was going about here and there, to and again, to find it, I saw a great crowd of folks going into a long entry[34] that had lanterns over the door; so I asked a man whether that was not the place where they played *hocus pocus?* He was a very civil, kind man, though he did speak like the Hessians; he lifted up his eyes and said, "They play *hocus pocus* tricks enough there, Got knows, mine friend."

JENNY: Well—

JONATHAN: So I went right in, and they shewed me away, clean up to the garret, just like meeting-house gallery. And so I saw a power of topping folks, all sitting round in little cabbins, "just like father's corn-cribs"; and then there was such a squeaking with the fiddles, and such a tarnal blaze with the lights, my head was near turned. At last the people that sat near me set up such a hissing—hiss—like so many mad cats; and then they went thump, thump, thump, just like our Peleg threshing wheat, and stampt away, just like the nation; and called out for one Mr. Langolee,—I suppose he helps act the tricks.

JENNY: Well, and what did you do all this time?

JONATHAN: Gor, I—I liked the fun, and so I thumpt away, and hiss'd as lustily as the best of 'em. One sailor-looking man that sat by me, seeing me stamp, and knowing I was a cute fellow, because I could make a roaring noise, clapt me on the shoulder and said, "You are a d——d hearty cock, smite my timbers!" I told him so I was, but I thought he need not swear so, and make use of such naughty words.

JESSAMY: The savage!—Well, and did you see the man with his tricks?

JONATHAN: Why, I vow, as I was looking out for him, they lifted up a great green cloth and let us look right into the next neighbour's house. Have you a good many houses in New-York made so in that'ere way?

JENNY: Not many; but did you see the family?

JONATHAN: Yes, swamp it; I see'd the family.

JENNY: Well, and how did you like them?

JONATHAN: Why, I vow they were pretty much like other families;— there was a poor, good-natured, curse of a husband, and a sad rantipole of a wife.

JENNY: But did you see no other folks?

JONATHAN: Yes. There was one youngster; they called him Mr. Joseph; he talked as sober and as pious as a minister; but, like some ministers that I know, he was a sly tike in his heart for all that. He was going to ask a young woman to spark it with him, and—the Lord have mercy on my soul!—she was another man's wife.

JESSAMY: The Wabash!

JENNY: And did you see any more folks?

JONATHAN: Why, they came on as thick as mustard. For my part, I thought the house was haunted. There was a soldier fellow, who talked about his row de dow, dow, and courted a young woman; but, of all the cute folk I saw, I liked one little fellow—

JENNY: Aye! who was he?

JONATHAN: Why, he had red hair, and a little round plump face like mine, only not altogether so handsome. His name was—Darby;— that was his baptizing name; his other name I forgot. Oh! it was Wig—Wag—Wag-all, Darby Wag-all;—pray, do you know him?— I should like to take a sling with him, or a drap of cyder with a pepper-pod in it, to make it warm and comfortable.

JENNY: I can't say I have that pleasure.

JONATHAN: I wish you did; he is a cute fellow. But there was one thing I didn't like in that Mr. Darby; and that was, he was afraid of some of them 'ere shooting irons, such as your troopers wear on training days. Now, I'm a true born Yankee American son of liberty, and I never was afraid of a gun yet in all my life.

JENNY: Well, Mr. Jonathan, you were certainly at the play-house.

JONATHAN: I at the play-house!—Why didn't I see the play then?

JENNY: Why, the people you saw were players.

JONATHAN: Mercy on my soul! did I see the wicked players?—Mayhap that 'ere Darby that I liked so was the old serpent himself, and had his cloven foot in his pocket. Why, I vow, now I come to think on't, the candles seemed to burn blue, and I am sure where I sat it smelt tarnally of brimstone.

JESSAMY: Well, Mr. Jonathan, from your account, which I confess is very accurate, you must have been at the play-house.

JONATHAN: Why, I vow, I began to smell a rat. When I came away, I went to the man for my money again; you want your money? says he; yes, says I; for what? says he; why, says I, no man shall jocky me out of my money; I paid my money to see sights, and the dogs a bit of a sight have I seen, unless you call listening to people's private business a sight. Why, says he, it is the School for Scandalization.— The School for Scandalization!—Oh! ho! no wonder you New-York folks are so cute at it, when you go to school to learn it; and so I jogged off.

JESSAMY: My dear Jenny, my master's business drags me from you; would to heaven I knew no other servitude than to your charms.

JONATHAN: Well, but don't go; you won't leave me so——

JESSAMY: Excuse me.—Remember the cash. [Aside to him, and—Exit.]

JENNY: Mr. Jonathan, won't you please to sit down? Mr. Jessamy tells
me you wanted to have some conversation with me. [*Having brought
forward two chairs, they sit.*]

JONATHAN: Ma'am!——

JENNY: Sir!——

JONATHAN: Ma'am!——

JENNY: Pray, how do you like the city, Sir?

JONATHAN: Ma'am!——

JENNY: I say, Sir, how do you like New-York?

JONATHAN: Ma'am!——

JENNY: The stupid creature! but I must pass some little time with him,
if it is only to endeavour to learn whether it was his master that
made such an abrupt entrance into our house, and my young mistress's heart, this morning. [*Aside.*] As you don't seem to like to talk,
Mr. Jonathan—do you sing?

JONATHAN: Gor, I—I am glad she asked that, for I forgot what Mr.
Jessamy bid me say, and I dare as well be hanged as act what he bid
me do, I'm so ashamed. [*Aside.*] Yes, Ma'am, I can sing—I can sing
Mear, Old Hundred, and Bangor.

JENNY: Oh! I don't mean psalm tunes. Have you no little song to please
the ladies, such as Roslin Castle, or the Maid of the Mill?[35]

JONATHAN: Why, all my tunes go to meeting tunes, save one, and I
count you won't altogether like that 'ere.

JENNY: What is it called?

JONATHAN: I am sure you have heard folks talk about it; it is called
Yankee Doodle.

JENNY: Oh! it is the tune I am fond of; and if I know anything of my
mistress, she would be glad to dance to it. Pray, sing!

JONATHAN [*sings*]:

> Father and I went up to camp,
> Along with Captain Goodwin;
> And there we saw the men and boys,
> As thick as hasty-pudding.
> > Yankee doodle do, &c.

> And there we saw a swamping gun,
> Big as log of maple,
> On a little deuced cart,
> A load for father's cattle.
> > Yankee doodle do, &c.

And every time they fired it off
It took a horn of powder,
It made a noise—like father's gun,
Only a nation louder.
                    Yankee doodle do, &c.

There was a man in our town,
His name was——

No, no, that won't do. Now, if I was with Tabitha Wymen and
Jemima Cawley down at father Chase's, I shouldn't mind singing this
all out before them—you would be affronted if I was to sing that,
though that's a lucky thought; if you should be affronted, I have
something dang'd cute, which Jessamy told me to say to you.

JENNY: Is that all! I assure you I like it of all things.

JONATHAN: No, no; I can sing more; some other time, when you and I
are better acquainted, I'll sing the whole of it—no, no—that's a fib
—I can't sing but a hundred and ninety verses; our Tabitha at home
can sing it all.—— [Sings.]

Marblehead's a rocky place,
And Cape-Cod is sandy;
Charlestown is burnt down,
Boston is the dandy.
                    Yankee doodle, doodle do, &c.

I vow, my own town song has put me into such topping spirits that
I believe I'll begin to do a little, as Jessamy says we must when we
go a-courting.—[Runs and kisses her.] Burning rivers! cooling
flames! red-hot roses! pig-nuts! hasty-pudding and ambrosia!

JENNY: What means this freedom? you insulting wretch. [Strikes him.]

JONATHAN: Are you affronted?

JENNY: Affronted! with what looks shall I express my anger?

JONATHAN: Looks! why as to the matter of looks, you look as cross as
a witch.

JENNY: Have you no feeling for the delicacy of my sex?

JONATHAN: Feeling! Gor, I—I feel the delicacy of your sex pretty
smartly [rubbing his cheek], though, I vow, I thought when you city
ladies courted and married, and all that, you put feeling out of the
question. But I want to know whether you are really affronted, or
only pretend to be so? 'Cause, if you are certainly right down af-

fronted, I am at the end of my tether; Jessamy didn't tell me what to say to you.

JENNY: Pretend to be affronted!

JONATHAN: Aye aye, if you only pretend, you shall hear how I'll go to work to make cherubim consequences. [*Runs up to her.*]

JENNY: Begone, you brute!

JONATHAN: That looks like mad; but I won't lose my speech. My dearest Jenny—your name is Jenny, I think?—My dearest Jenny, though I have the highest esteem for the sweet favours you have just now granted me—Gor, that's a fib, though; but Jessamy says it is not wicked to tell lies to the women. [*Aside.*] I say, though I have the highest esteem for the favours you have just now granted me, yet you will consider that, as soon as the dissolvable knot is tied, they will no longer be favours, but only matters of duty and matters of course.

JENNY: Marry you! you audacious monster! get out of my sight, or, rather, let me fly from you. [*Exit hastily.*]

JONATHAN: Gor! she's gone off in a swinging passion, before I had time to think of consequences. If this is the way with your city ladies, give me the twenty acres of rock, the Bible, the cow, and Tabitha, and a little peaceable bundling.[36]

SCENE 2: *The Mall.*

[*Enter* MANLY.]

MANLY: It must be so, Montagu![37] and it is not all the tribe of Mandevilles[38] shall convince me that a nation, to become great, must first become dissipated. Luxury is surely the bane of a nation: Luxury! which enervates both soul and body, by opening a thousand new sources of enjoyment, opens, also, a thousand new sources of contention and want: Luxury! which renders people weak at home, and accessible to bribery, corruption, and force from abroad. When the Grecian states knew no other tools than the axe and the saw, the Grecians were a great, a free, and a happy people. The kings of Greece devoted their lives to the service of their country, and her senators knew no other superiority over their fellow-citizens than a glorious pre-eminence in danger and virtue. They exhibited to the world a noble spectacle,—a number of independent states united by a similarity of language, sentiment, manners, common interest, and common consent in one grand mutual league of protection.—And, thus united, long might they have continued the cherishers of arts and sciences, the protectors of the oppressed, the scourge of tyrants, and the safe asylum of liberty. But when foreign gold, and still more pernicious foreign luxury, had crept among them, they sapped the vitals of their virtue. The virtues of their ancestors were only found in their writings. Envy and suspicion, the vices of little minds, possessed them. The various states engendered jealousies of each other; and, more unfortunately, growing jealous of their great federal council, the Amphictyons,[39] they forgot that their common safety had existed, and would exist, in giving them an honourable extensive prerogative. The common good was lost in the pursuit of private interest; and that people who, by uniting, might have stood against the world in arms, by dividing, crumbled into ruin:—their name is now only known in the page of the historian, and what they once were is all we have left to admire. Oh! that America! Oh! that my country, would, in this her day, learn the things which belong to her peace!

[*Enter* DIMPLE.]

DIMPLE: You are Colonel Manly, I presume?

MANLY: At your service, Sir.

DIMPLE: My name is Dimple, Sir. I have the honour to be a lodger in the same house with you, and, hearing you were in the Mall, came hither to take the liberty of joining you.

MANLY: You are very obliging, Sir.

DIMPLE: As I understand you are a stranger here, Sir, I have taken the liberty to introduce myself to your acquaintance, as possibly I may have it in my power to point out some things in this city worthy your notice.

MANLY: An attention to strangers is worthy a liberal mind, and must ever be gratefully received. But to a soldier, who has no fixed abode, such attentions are particularly pleasing.

DIMPLE: Sir, there is no character so respectable as that of a soldier. And, indeed, when we reflect how much we owe to those brave men who have suffered so much in the service of their country, and secured to us those inestimable blessings that we now enjoy, our liberty and independence, they demand every attention which gratitude can pay. For my own part, I never meet an officer, but I embrace him as my friend, nor a private in distress, but I insensibly extend my charity to him.——I have hit the Bumkin off very tolerably. [*Aside.*]

MANLY: Give me your hand, Sir! I do not proffer this hand to everybody; but you steal into my heart. I hope I am as insensible to flattery as most men; but I declare (it may be my weak side) that I never hear the name of soldier mentioned with respect, but I experience a thrill of pleasure which I never feel on any other occasion.

DIMPLE: Will you give me leave, my dear Colonel, to confer an obligation on myself, by shewing you some civilities during your stay here, and giving a similar opportunity to some of my friends?

MANLY: Sir, I thank you; but I believe my stay in this city will be very short.

DIMPLE: I can introduce you to some men of excellent sense, in whose company you will esteem yourself happy; and, by way of amusement, to some fine girls, who will listen to your soft things with pleasure.

MANLY: Sir, I should be proud of the honour of being acquainted with those gentlemen;—but, as for the ladies, I don't understand you.

DIMPLE: Why, Sir, I need not tell you, that when a young gentleman is alone with a young lady he must say some soft things to her fair cheek—indeed, the lady will expect it. To be sure, there is not much pleasure when a man of the world and a finished coquette meet, who perfectly know each other; but how delicious is it to excite the emotions of joy, hope, expectation, and delight in the bosom of a lovely girl who believes every tittle of what you say to be serious!

MANLY: Serious, Sir! In my opinion, the man who, under pretensions of marriage, can plant thorns in the bosom of an innocent, unsuspecting girl is more detestable than a common robber, in the same proportion as private violence is more despicable than open force, and money of less value than happiness.

DIMPLE: How he awes me by the superiority of his sentiments. [*Aside.*] As you say, Sir, a gentleman should be cautious how he mentions marriage.

MANLY: Cautious, Sir! No person more approves of an intercourse between the sexes than I do. Female conversation softens our manners, whilst our discourse, from the superiority of our literary advantages, improves their minds. But, in our young country, where there is no such thing as gallantry, when a gentleman speaks of love to a lady, whether he mentions marriage or not, she ought to conclude either that he meant to insult her or that his intentions are the most serious and honourable. How mean, how cruel, is it, by a thousand tender assiduities, to win the affections of an amiable girl, and, though you leave her virtue unspotted, to betray her into the appearance of so many tender partialities, that every man of delicacy would suppress his inclination towards her, by supposing her heart engaged! Can any man, for the trivial gratification of his leisure hours, affect the happiness of a whole life! His not having spoken of marriage may add to his perfidy, but can be no excuse for his conduct.

DIMPLE: Sir, I admire your sentiments;—they are mine. The light observations that fell from me were only a principle of the tongue; they came not from the heart—my practice has ever disapproved these principles.

MANLY: I believe you, Sir. I should with reluctance suppose that those pernicious sentiments could find admittance into the heart of a gentleman.

DIMPLE: I am now, Sir, going to visit a family, where, if you please, I will have the honour of introducing you. Mr. Manly's ward, Miss Letitia, is a young lady of immense fortune; and his niece, Miss Charlotte Manly, is a young lady of great sprightliness and beauty.

MANLY: That gentleman, Sir, is my uncle, and Miss Manly my sister.

DIMPLE: The devil she is! [Aside.] Miss Manly your sister, Sir? I rejoice to hear it, and feel a double pleasure in being known to you.——
Plague on him! I wish he was at Boston again, with all my soul. [Aside.]

MANLY: Come, Sir, will you go?

DIMPLE: I will follow you in a moment, Sir. [Exit MANLY.] Plague on it! this is unlucky. A fighting brother is a cursed appendage to a fine girl. Egad! I just stopped in time; had he not discovered himself, in two minutes more I should have told him how well I was with his sister. Indeed, I cannot see the satisfaction of an intrigue, if one can't have the pleasure of communicating it to our friends. [Exit.]

END OF ACT III

ACT IV

SCENE 1: CHARLOTTE'S *Apartment.*

[CHARLOTTE *leading in* MARIA.]

CHARLOTTE: This is so kind, my sweet friend, to come to see me at this moment. I declare, if I were going to be married in a few days, as you are, I should scarce have found time to visit my friends.

MARIA: Do you think, then, that there is an impropriety in it?—How should you dispose of your time?

CHARLOTTE: Why, I should be shut up in my chamber; and my head would so run upon—upon—upon the solemn ceremony that I was to pass through!—I declare, it would take me above two hours merely to learn that little monosyllable—Yes. Ah! my dear, your sentimental imagination does not conceive what that little tiny word implies.

MARIA: Spare me your raillery, my sweet friend; I should love your agreeable vivacity at any other time.

CHARLOTTE: Why, this is the very time to amuse you. You grieve me to see you look so unhappy.

MARIA: Have I not reason to look so?

CHARLOTTE: What new grief distresses you?

MARIA: Oh! how sweet it is, when the heart is borne down with misfortune, to recline and repose on the bosom of friendship! Heaven knows that, although it is improper for a young lady to praise a gentleman, yet I have ever concealed Mr. Dimple's foibles, and spoke of him as one whose reputation I expected would be linked with mine; but his late conduct towards me has turned my coolness into contempt. He behaves as if he meant to insult and disgust me; whilst my father, in the last conversation on the subject of our marriage, spoke of it as a matter which lay near his heart, and in which he would not bear contradiction.

CHARLOTTE: This works well: oh! the generous Dimple. I'll endeavour to excite her to discharge him. [Aside.] But, my dear friend, your happiness depends on yourself:—Why don't you discard him? Though the match has been of long standing, I would not be forced to make myself miserable: no parent in the world should oblige me to marry the man I did not like.

MARIA: Oh! my dear, you never lived with your parents, and do not know what influence a father's frowns have upon a daughter's heart. Besides, what have I to alledge against Mr. Dimple, to justify myself to the world? He carries himself so smoothly, that every one would impute the blame to me, and call me capricious.

CHARLOTTE: And call her capricious! Did ever such an objection start into the heart of woman? For my part, I wish I had fifty lovers to discard, for no other reason than because I did not fancy them. My dear Maria, you will forgive me; I know your candour and confidence in me; but I have at times, I confess, been led to suppose that some other gentleman was the cause of your aversion to Mr. Dimple.

MARIA: No, my sweet friend, you may be assured, that though I have seen many gentlemen I could prefer to Mr. Dimple, yet I never saw one that I thought I could give my hand to, until this morning.

CHARLOTTE: This morning!

MARIA: Yes;—one of the strangest accidents in the world. The odious Dimple, after disgusting me with his conversation, had just left me, when a gentleman, who, it seems, boards in the same house with him, saw him coming out of our door, and, the houses looking very much alike, he came into our house instead of his lodgings; nor did he discover his mistake until he got into the parlour, where I was; he then bowed so gracefully, made such a genteel apology, and looked so manly and noble!——

CHARLOTTE: I see some folks, though it is so great an impropriety, can praise a gentleman, when he happens to be the man of their fancy. [Aside.]

MARIA: I don't know how it was,—I hope he did not think me indelicate,—but I asked him, I believe, to sit down, or pointed to a chair. He sat down, and, instead of having recourse to observations upon the weather, or hackneyed criticisms upon the theatre, he entered readily into a conversation worthy a man of sense to speak, and a lady of delicacy and sentiment to hear. He was not strictly handsome, but he spoke the language of sentiment, and his eyes looked tenderness and honour.

CHARLOTTE: Oh! [eagerly] you sentimental, grave girls, when your hearts are once touched, beat us rattles a bar's length. And so you are quite in love with this he-angel?

MARIA: In love with him! How can you rattle so, Charlotte? am I not going to be miserable? [Sighs.] In love with a gentleman I never saw but one hour in my life, and don't know his name! No; I only wished that the man I shall marry may look, and talk, and act, just like him. Besides, my dear, he is a married man.

CHARLOTTE: Why, that was good-natured—he told you so, I suppose, in mere charity, to prevent your falling in love with him?

MARIA: He didn't tell me so; [peevishly] he looked as if he was married.

CHARLOTTE: How, my dear; did he look sheepish?

MARIA: I am sure he has a susceptible heart, and the ladies of his acquaintance must be very stupid not to——

CHARLOTTE: Hush! I hear some person coming.

[Enter LETITIA.]

LETITIA: My dear Maria, I am happy to see you. Lud! what a pity it is that you have purchased your wedding clothes.

MARIA: I think so. [*Sighing.*]

LETITIA: Why, my dear, there is the sweetest parcel of silks come over you ever saw! Nancy Brilliant has a full suit come; she sent over her measure, and it fits her to a hair; it is immensely dressy, and made for a court-hoop. I thought they said the large hoops were going out of fashion.

CHARLOTTE: Did you see the hat? Is it a fact that the deep laces round the border is still the fashion? DIMPLE [*within*]: Upon my honour, Sir.

MARIA: Ha! Dimple's voice! My dear, I must take leave of you. There are some things necessary to be done at our house. Can't I go through the other room?

[*Enter* DIMPLE *and* MANLY.]

DIMPLE: Ladies, your most obedient.

CHARLOTTE: Miss Van Rough, shall I present my brother Henry to you? Colonel Manly, Maria,—Miss Van Rough, brother.

MARIA: Her brother! [*Turns and sees* MANLY.] Oh! my heart! the very gentleman I have been praising.

MANLY: The same amiable girl I saw this morning!

CHARLOTTE: Why, you look as if you were acquainted.

MANLY: I unintentionally intruded into this lady's presence this morning, for which she was so good as to promise me her forgiveness.

CHARLOTTE: Oh! ho! is that the case! Have these two penserosos been together? Were they Henry's eyes that looked so tenderly? [*Aside.*] And so you promised to pardon him? and could you be so good-natured? have you really forgiven him? I beg you would do it for my sake [*whispering loud to* MARIA]. But, my dear, as you are in such haste, it would be cruel to detain you; I can show you the way through the other room.

MARIA: Spare me, my sprightly friend.

MANLY: The lady does not, I hope, intend to deprive us of the pleasure of her company so soon.

CHARLOTTE: She has only a mantua-maker who waits for her at home. But, as I am to give my opinion of the dress, I think she cannot go yet. We were talking of the fashions when you came in, but I suppose the subject must be changed to something of more importance now.—Mr. Dimple, will you favour us with an account of the public entertainments?

DIMPLE: Why, really, Miss Manly, you could not have asked me a question more *mal-apropos*. For my part, I must confess that, to a man who has travelled, there is nothing that is worthy the name of amusement to be found in this city.

CHARLOTTE: Except visiting the ladies.

DIMPLE: Pardon me, Madam; that is the avocation of a man of taste. But for amusement, I positively know of nothing that can be called so, unless you dignify with that title the hopping once a fortnight to the sound of two or three squeaking fiddles, and the clattering of the old tavern windows, or sitting to see the miserable mummers, whom you call actors, murder comedy and make a farce of tragedy.

MANLY: Do you never attend the theatre, Sir?

DIMPLE: I was tortured there once.

CHARLOTTE: Pray, Mr. Dimple, was it a tragedy or a comedy?

DIMPLE: Faith, Madam, I cannot tell; for I sat with my back to the stage all the time, admiring a much better actress than any there—a lady who played the fine woman to perfection; though, by the laugh of the horrid creatures round me, I suppose it was comedy. Yet, on second thoughts, it might be some hero in a tragedy, dying so comically as to set the whole house in an uproar.—Colonel, I presume you have been in Europe?

MANLY: Indeed, Sir, I was never ten leagues from the continent.

DIMPLE: Believe me, Colonel, you have an immense pleasure to come; and when you shall have seen the brilliant exhibitions of Europe, you will learn to despise the amusements of this country as much as I do.

MANLY: Therefore I do not wish to see them; for I can never esteem that knowledge valuable which tends to give me a distaste for my native country.

DIMPLE: Well, Colonel, though you have not travelled, you have read.

MANLY: I have, a little; and by it have discovered that there is a laudable partiality which ignorant, untravelled men entertain for everything that belongs to their native country. I call it laudable; it injures no one; adds to their own happiness; and, when extended, becomes the noble principle of patriotism. Travelled gentlemen rise superior, in their own opinion, to this; but if the contempt which they contract for their country is the most valuable acquisition of their travels, I am far from thinking that their time and money are well spent.

MARIA: What noble sentiments!

CHARLOTTE: Let my brother set out where he will in the fields of conversation, he is sure to end his tour in the temple of gravity.

MANLY: Forgive me, my sister. I love my country; it has its foibles undoubtedly;—some foreigners will with pleasure remark them—but such remarks fall very ungracefully from the lips of her citizens.

DIMPLE: You are perfectly in the right, Colonel—America has her faults.

MANLY: Yes, Sir; and we, her children, should blush for them in private, and endeavour, as individuals, to reform them. But, if our country has its errors in common with other countries, I am proud to say America—I mean the United States—has displayed virtues and achievements which modern nations may admire, but of which they have seldom set us the example.

CHARLOTTE: But, brother, we must introduce you to some of our gay folks, and let you see the city, such as it is. Mr. Dimple is known to almost every family in town; he will doubtless take a pleasure in introducing you?

DIMPLE: I shall esteem every service I can render your brother an honour.

MANLY: I fear the business I am upon will take up all my time, and my family will be anxious to hear from me.

MARIA: His family! But what is it to me that he is married! [*Aside.*] Pray, how did you leave your lady, Sir?

CHARLOTTE: My brother is not married [*observing her anxiety*]; it is only an odd way he has of expressing himself.—Pray, brother, is this business, which you make your continual excuse, a secret?

MANLY: No, sister; I came hither to solicit the honourable Congress, that a number of my brave old soldiers may be put upon the pension-list, who were, at first, not judged to be so materially wounded as to need the public assistance. My sister says true [*to* MARIA].—I call my late soldiers my family. Those who were not in the field in the late glorious contest, and those who were, have their respective merits; but, I confess, my old brother-soldiers are dearer to me than the former description. Friendships made in adversity are lasting; our countrymen may forget us, but that is no reason why we should forget one another. But I must leave you; my time of engagement approaches.

CHARLOTTE: Well, but, brother, if you will go, will you please to conduct my fair friend home? You live in the same street——I was to have gone with her myself—[*aside.*] A lucky thought.

MARIA: I am obliged to your sister, Sir, and was just intending to go. [*Going.*]

MANLY: I shall attend her with pleasure.

[*Exit with* MARIA, *followed by* DIMPLE *and* CHARLOTTE.]

MARIA: Now, pray, don't betray me to your brother.

CHARLOTTE [*just as she sees him make a motion to take his leave*]: One word with you, brother, if you please. [*Follows them out. Manent,* DIMPLE *and* LETITIA.]

DIMPLE: You received the billet I sent you, I presume?

LETITIA: Hush!—Yes.

DIMPLE: When shall I pay my respects to you?

LETITIA: At eight I shall be unengaged.

[*Reenter* CHARLOTTE.]

DIMPLE: Did my lovely angel receive my billet? [*To* CHARLOTTE.]

CHARLOTTE: Yes.

DIMPLE: What hour shall I expect with impatience?

CHARLOTTE: At eight I shall be at home unengaged.

DIMPLE: Unfortunate! I have a horrid engagement of business at that hour. Can't you finish your visit earlier and let six be the happy hour?

CHARLOTTE: You know your influence over me.   [*Exeunt severally.*]

SCENE 2: VAN ROUGH'S *House.*

VAN ROUGH [*alone*]: It cannot possibly be true! The son of my old friend can't have acted so unadvisedly. Seventeen thousand pounds! in bills! Mr. Transfer must have been mistaken. He always appeared so prudent, and talked so well upon money matters, and even assured me that he intended to change his dress for a suit of clothes which would not cost so much, and look more substantial, as soon as he married. No, no, no! it can't be; it cannot be. But, however, I must look out sharp. I did not care what his principles or his actions were, so long as he minded the main chance. Seventeen thousand pounds! If he had lost it in trade, why the best men may have ill-luck; but to game it away, as Transfer says—why, at this rate, his whole estate may go in one night, and, what is ten times worse, mine into the bargain. No, no; Mary is right. Leave women to look out in these matters; for all they look as if they didn't know a journal from a ledger, when their interest is concerned they know what's what; they mind the main chance as well as the best of us. I wonder Mary did not tell me she knew of his spending his money so foolishly. Seventeen thousand pounds! Why, if my daughter was standing up to be married, I would forbid the banns, if I found it was to a man who did not mind the main chance.—Hush! I hear somebody coming. 'Tis Mary's voice; a man with her too! I shouldn't be surprised if this should be the other string to her bow. Aye, aye, let them alone; women understand the main chance.—Though, i'faith, I'll listen a little. [*Retires into a closet.*]

[MANLY *leading in* MARIA.]

MANLY: I hope you will excuse my speaking upon so important a subject so abruptly; but, the moment I entered your room, you struck me as the lady whom I had long loved in imagination, and never hoped to see.

MARIA: Indeed, Sir, I have been led to hear more upon this subject than I ought.

MANLY: Do you, then, disapprove my suit, Madam, or the abruptness of my introducing it? If the latter, my peculiar situation, being obliged to leave the city in a few days, will, I hope, be my excuse; if the former, I will retire, for I am sure I would not give a moment's inquietude to her whom I could devote my life to please. I am not so indelicate as to seek your immediate approbation; permit me only to be near you, and by a thousand tender assiduities to endeavour to excite a grateful return.

MARIA: I have a father, whom I would die to make happy; he will disapprove——

MANLY: Do you think me so ungenerous as to seek a place in your esteem without his consent? You must—you ever ought to consider that man as unworthy of you who seeks an interest in your heart contrary to a father's approbation. A young lady should reflect that the loss of a lover may be supplied, but nothing can compensate for the loss of a parent's affection. Yet, why do you suppose your father would disapprove? In our country, the affections are not sacrificed to riches or family aggrandizement: should you approve, my family is decent, and my rank honourable.

MARIA: You distress me, Sir.

MANLY: Then I will sincerely beg your excuse for obtruding so disagreeable a subject, and retire. [*Going.*]

MARIA: Stay, Sir! your generosity and good opinion of me deserve a return; but why must I declare what, for these few hours, I have scarce suffered myself to think?—I am——

MANLY: What?——

MARIA: Engaged, Sir;—and, in a few days to be married to the gentleman you saw at your sister's.

MANLY: Engaged to be married! And I have been basely invading the rights of another? Why have you permitted this? Is this the return for the partiality I declared for you?

MARIA: You distress me, Sir. What would you have me say? You are too generous to wish the truth. Ought I to say that I dared not suffer myself to think of my engagement, and that I am going to give my hand without my heart? Would you have me confess a partiality for you? If so, your triumph is compleat, and can be only more so when days of misery with the man I cannot love will make me think of him whom I could prefer.

MANLY [*after a pause*]: We are both unhappy; but it is your duty to obey your parent—mine to obey my honour. Let us, therefore, both follow the path of rectitude; and of this we may be assured, that if we are not happy, we shall, at least, deserve to be so. Adieu! I dare not trust myself longer with you.   [*Exeunt severally.*]

END OF ACT IV

ACT V

SCENE 1: DIMPLE'S *Lodgings.*

[JESSAMY *meeting* JONATHAN.]

JESSAMY: Well, Mr. Jonathan, what success with the fair?

JONATHAN: Why, such a tarnal cross tike you never saw! You would have counted she had lived upon crab-apples and vinegar for a fortnight. But what the rattle makes you look so tarnation glum?

JESSAMY: I was thinking, Mr. Jonathan, what could be the reason of her carrying herself so coolly to you.

JONATHAN: Coolly, do you call it? Why, I vow, she was fire-hot angry: may be it was because I buss'd her.

JESSAMY: No, no, Mr. Jonathan; there must be some other cause; I never yet knew a lady angry at being kissed.

JONATHAN: Well, if it is not the young woman's bashfulness, I vow I can't conceive why she shouldn't like me.

JESSAMY: May be it is because you have not the Graces, Mr. Jonathan.

JONATHAN: Grace! Why, does the young woman expect I must be converted before I court her?

JESSAMY: I mean graces of person: for instance, my lord tells us that we must cut off our nails even at the top, in small segments of circles—though you won't understand that; in the next place, you must regulate your laugh.

JONATHAN: Maple-log seize it! don't I laugh natural?

JESSAMY: That's the very fault, Mr. Jonathan. Besides, you absolutely misplace it. I was told by a friend of mine that you laughed outright at the play the other night, when you ought only to have tittered.

JONATHAN: Gor! I—what does one go to see fun for if they can't laugh?

JESSAMY: You may laugh; but you must laugh by rule.

JONATHAN: Swamp it—laugh by rule! Well, I should like that tarnally.

JESSAMY: Why, you know, Mr. Jonathan, that to dance, a lady to play with her fan, or a gentleman with his cane, and all other natural motions, are regulated by art. My master has composed an immensely pretty gamut,[40] by which any lady or gentleman, with a few years' close application, may learn to laugh as gracefully as if they were born and bred to it.

JONATHAN: Mercy on my soul! A gamut for laughing—just like fa, la, sol?

JESSAMY: Yes. It comprises every possible display of jocularity, from an *affettuoso* smile to a *piano* titter, or full chorus *fortissimo*[41] ha, ha, ha! My master employs his leisure hours in marking out the plays, like a cathedral chanting-book, that the ignorant may know where to laugh; and that pit, box, and gallery may keep time together, and not have a snigger in one part of the house, a broad grin in the other, and a d——d grum look in the third. How delightful to see the audience all smile together, then look on their books, then twist their mouths into an agreeable simper, then altogether shake the house with a general ha, ha, ha! loud as a full chorus of Handel's[42] at an Abbey commemoration.

JONATHAN: Ha, ha, ha! that's dang'd cute, I swear.

JESSAMY: The gentlemen, you see, will laugh the tenor; the ladies will play the counter-tenor; the beaux will squeak the treble; and our jolly friends in the gallery a thorough base, ho, ho, ho!

JONATHAN: Well, can't you let me see that gamut?

JESSAMY: Oh! yes, Mr. Jonathan; here it is. [*Takes out a book.*] Oh! no, this is only a titter with its variations. Ah, here it is. [*Takes out another.*] Now, you must know, Mr. Jonathan, this is a piece written by Ben Jonson,[43] which I have set to my master's gamut. The places where you must smile, look grave, or laugh outright, are marked below the line. Now look over me. "There was a certain man"— now you must smile.

JONATHAN: Well, read it again; I warrant I'll mind my eye.

JESSAMY: "There was a certain man, who had a sad scolding wife,"— now you must laugh.

JONATHAN: Tarnation! That's no laughing matter though.

JESSAMY: "And she lay sick a-dying";—now you must titter.

JONATHAN: What, snigger when the good woman's a-dying! Gor, I——

JESSAMY: Yes, the notes say you must—"and she asked her husband leave to make a will,"—now you must begin to look grave; "and her husband said"——

JONATHAN: Ay, what did her husband say? Something dang'd cute, I reckon.

JESSAMY: "And her husband said, you have had your will all your life-time, and would you have it after you are dead, too?"

JONATHAN: Ho, ho, ho! There the old man was even with her; he was up to the notch—ha, ha, ha!

JESSAMY: But, Mr. Jonathan, you must not laugh so. Why you ought to have tittered *piano*, and you have laughed *fortissimo*. Look here; you see these marks, A, B, C, and so on; these are the references to the other part of the book. Let us turn to it, and you will see the directions how to manage the muscles. This [*turns over*] was note D you blundered at.—"You must purse the mouth into a smile, then titter, discovering the lower part of the three front upper teeth."

JONATHAN: How? read it again.

JESSAMY: "There was a certain man"—very well!—"who had a sad scolding wife,"—why don't you laugh?

JONATHAN: Now, that scolding wife sticks in my gizzard so pluckily that I can't laugh for the blood and nowns of me. Let me look grave here, and I'll laugh your belly full, where the old creature's a-dying.

JESSAMY: "And she asked her husband"—[*Bell rings.*] My master's bell! he's returned, I fear.—Here, Mr. Jonathan, take this gamut; and I make no doubt but with a few years' close application, you may be able to smile gracefully.   [*Exeunt severally.*]

SCENE 2: CHARLOTTE'S *Apartment*.

[*Enter* MANLY.]

MANLY: What, no one at home? How unfortunate to meet the only lady my heart was ever moved by, to find her engaged to another, and confessing her partiality for me! Yet engaged to a man who, by her intimation, and his libertine conversation with me, I fear, does not merit her. Aye! there's the sting; for, were I assured that Maria was happy, my heart is not so selfish but that it would dilate in knowing

it, even though it were with another. But to know she is unhappy!
—I must drive these thoughts from me. Charlotte has some books;
and this is what I believe she calls her little library. [*Enters a closet.*]

[*Enter* DIMPLE *leading* LETITIA.]

LETITIA: And will you pretend to say now, Mr. Dimple, that you propose to break with Maria? Are not the banns published? Are not the
clothes purchased? Are not the friends invited? In short, is it not a
done affair?

DIMPLE: Believe me, my dear Letitia, I would not marry her.

LETITIA: Why have you not broke with her before this, as you all along
deluded me by saying you would?

DIMPLE: Because I was in hopes she would, ere this, have broke
with me.

LETITIA: You could not expect it.

DIMPLE: Nay, but be calm a moment; 'twas from my regard to you that
I did not discard her.

LETITIA: Regard to me!

DIMPLE: Yes; I have done everything in my power to break with her,
but the foolish girl is so fond of me that nothing can accomplish it.
Besides, how can I offer her my hand when my heart is indissolubly
engaged to you?

LETITIA: There may be reason in this; but why so attentive to Miss
Manly?

DIMPLE: Attentive to Miss Manly! For heaven's sake, if you have no
better opinion of my constancy, pay not so ill a compliment to my
taste.

LETITIA: Did I not see you whisper her to-day?

DIMPLE: Possibly I might—but something of so very trifling a nature
that I have already forgot what it was.

LETITIA: I believe she has not forgot it.

DIMPLE: My dear creature, how can you for a moment suppose I should
have any serious thoughts of that trifling, gay, flighty coquette, that
disagreeable——

[*Enter* CHARLOTTE.]

My dear Miss Manly, I rejoice to see you; there is a charm in your
conversation that always marks your entrance into company as
fortunate.

LETITIA: Where have you been, my dear?

CHARLOTTE: Why, I have been about to twenty shops, turning over pretty things, and so have left twenty visits unpaid. I wish you would step into the carriage and whisk round, make my apology, and leave my cards where our friends are not at home; that, you know, will serve as a visit. Come, do go.

LETITIA: So anxious to get me out! but I'll watch you. [*Aside.*] Oh! yes, I'll go; I want a little exercise. Positively [DIMPLE *offering to accompany her*], Mr. Dimple, you shall not go; why, half my visits are cake and caudle[44] visits; it won't do, you know, for you to go.

[*Exit, but returns to the door in the back scene and listens.*]

DIMPLE: This attachment of your brother to Maria is fortunate.

CHARLOTTE: How did you come to the knowledge of it?

DIMPLE: I read it in their eyes.

CHARLOTTE: And I had it from her mouth. It would have amused you to have seen her! She, that thought it so great an impropriety to praise a gentleman that she could not bring out one word in your favour, found a redundancy to praise him.

DIMPLE: I have done everything in my power to assist his passion there: your delicacy, my dearest girl, would be shocked at half the instances of neglect and misbehaviour.

CHARLOTTE: I don't know how I should bear neglect; but Mr. Dimple must misbehave himself indeed, to forfeit my good opinion.

DIMPLE: Your good opinion, my angel, is the pride and pleasure of my heart; and if the most respectful tenderness for you, and an utter indifference for all your sex besides, can make me worthy of your esteem, I shall richly merit it.

CHARLOTTE: All my sex besides, Mr. Dimple!—you forgot your tête-à-tête with Letitia.

DIMPLE: How can you, my lovely angel, cast a thought on that insipid, wry-mouthed, ugly creature!

CHARLOTTE: But her fortune may have charms?

DIMPLE: Not to a heart like mine. The man, who has been blessed with the good opinion of my Charlotte, must despise the allurements of fortune.

CHARLOTTE: I am satisfied.

DIMPLE: Let us think no more on the odious subject, but devote the present hour to happiness.

CHARLOTTE: Can I be happy, when I see the man I prefer going to be married to another?

DIMPLE: Have I not already satisfied my charming angel, that I can never think of marrying the puling Maria? But, even if it were so, could that be any bar to our happiness? for, as the poet sings,

"Love, free as air, at sight of human ties,
Spreads his light wings, and in a moment flies."[45]

Come then, my charming angel! why delay our bliss? The present moment is ours; the next is in the hand of fate. [*Kissing her.*]

CHARLOTTE: Begone, Sir! By your delusions you had almost lulled my honour asleep.

DIMPLE: Let me lull the demon to sleep again with kisses. [*He struggles with her; she screams.*]

[*Enter* MANLY.]

MANLY: Turn, villain! and defend yourself.——[*Draws.*]

[VAN ROUGH *enters and beats down their swords.*]

VAN ROUGH: Is the devil in you? are you going to murder one another? [*Holding* DIMPLE.]

DIMPLE: Hold him, hold him,—I can command my passion.

[*Enter* JONATHAN.]

JONATHAN: What the rattle ails you? Is the old one in you? Let the colonel alone, can't you? I feel chock-full of fight,—do you want to kill the colonel?

MANLY: Be still, Jonathan; the gentleman does not want to hurt me.

JONATHAN: Gor! I—I wish he did; I'd shew him Yankee boys play, pretty quick.—Don't you see you have frightened the young woman into the *hystrikes?*

VAN ROUGH: Pray, some of you explain this; what has been the occasion of all this racket?

MANLY: That gentleman can explain it to you; it will be a very diverting story for an intended father-in-law to hear.

VAN ROUGH: How was this matter, Mr. Van Dumpling?

DIMPLE: Sir,—upon my honour,—all I know is, that I was talking to this young lady, and this gentleman broke in on us in a very extraordinary manner.

VAN ROUGH: Why, all this is nothing to the purpose; can you explain it Miss? [*To* CHARLOTTE.]

[*Enter* LETITIA *through the back scene.*]

LETITIA: I can explain it to that gentleman's confusion. Though long betrothed to your daughter [*to* VAN ROUGH], yet, allured by my fortune, it seems (with shame do I speak it) he has privately paid his addresses to me. I was drawn in to listen to him by his assuring me that the match was made by his father without his consent, and that he proposed to break with Maria, whether he married me or not. But, whatever were his intentions respecting your daughter, Sir, even to me he was false; for he has repeated the same story, with some cruel reflections upon my person, to Miss Manly.

JONATHAN: What a tarnal curse!

LETITIA: Nor is this all, Miss Manly. When he was with me this very morning, he made the same ungenerous reflections upon the weakness of your mind as he has so recently done upon the defects of my person.

JONATHAN: What a tarnal curse and damn, too!

DIMPLE: Ha! since I have lost Letitia, I believe I had as good make it up with Maria.—Mr. Van Rough, at present I cannot enter into particulars; but, I believe, I can explain everything to your satisfaction in private.

VAN ROUGH: There is another matter, Mr. Van Dumpling, which I would have you explain. Pray, Sir, have Messrs. Van Cash & Co. presented you those bills for acceptance?

DIMPLE: The deuce! Has he heard of those bills! Nay, then, all's up with Maria, too; but an affair of this sort can never prejudice me among the ladies; they will rather long to know what the dear creature possesses to make him so agreeable. [Aside.] Sir, you'll hear from me. [To MANLY.]

MANLY: And you from me, Sir——

DIMPLE: Sir, you wear a sword——

MANLY: Yes, Sir. This sword was presented to me by that brave Gallic hero, the Marquis DE LA FAYETTE.[46] I have drawn it in the service of my country, and in private life, on the only occasion where a man is justified in drawing his sword, in defence of a lady's honour. I have fought too many battles in the service of my country to dread the imputation of cowardice. Death from a man of honour would be a glory you do not merit; you shall live to bear the insult of man and the contempt of that sex whose general smiles afforded you all your happiness.

DIMPLE: You won't meet me, Sir? Then I'll post you for a coward.

MANLY: I'll venture that, Sir. The reputation of my life does not depend upon the breath of a Mr. Dimple. I would have you to know, however, Sir, that I have a cane to chastise the insolence of a scoundrel, and a sword and the good laws of my country to protect me from the attempts of an assassin——

DIMPLE: Mighty well! Very fine, indeed! Ladies and gentleman, I take
my leave; and you will please to observe in the case of my deportment
the contrast between a gentleman who has read Chesterfield and
received the polish of Europe and an unpolished, untravelled
American.   [*Exit.*]

[*Enter* MARIA.]

MARIA: Is he indeed gone?——
LETITIA: I hope never to return.
VAN ROUGH: I am glad I heard of those bills; though it's plaguy unlucky;
I hoped to see Mary married before I died.
MANLY: Will you permit a gentleman, Sir, to offer himself as a suitor
to your daughter? Though a stranger to you, he is not altogether so
to her, or unknown in this city. You may find a son-in-law of more
fortune, but you can never meet with one who is richer in love for
her, or respect for you.
VAN ROUGH: Why, Mary, you have not let this gentleman make love
to you without my leave?
MANLY: I did not say, Sir——
MARIA: Say, Sir!——I—the gentleman, to be sure, met me accidentally.
VAN ROUGH: Ha, ha, ha! Mark me, Mary; young folks think old folks
to be fools; but old folks know young folks to be fools. Why, I knew
all about this affair. This was only a cunning way I had to bring it
about. Hark ye! I was in the closet when you and he were at our
house. [*Turns to the company.*] I heard that little baggage say she
loved her old father, and would die to make him happy! Oh! how I
loved the little baggage!—And you talked very prudently, young
man. I have inquired into your character, and find you to be a man
of punctuality and mind the main chance. And so, as you love Mary
and Mary loves you, you shall have my consent immediately to be
married. I'll settle my fortune on you, and go and live with you the
remainder of my life.
MANLY: Sir, I hope——
VAN ROUGH: Come, come, no fine speeches; mind the main chance,
young man, and you and I shall always agree.
LETITIA: I sincerely wish you joy [*advancing to* MARIA]; and hope your
pardon for my conduct.
MARIA: I thank you for your congratulations, and hope we shall at once
forget the wretch who has given us so much disquiet, and the trouble
that he has occasioned.
CHARLOTTE: And I, my dear Maria,—how shall I look up to you for

forgiveness? I, who, in the practice of the meanest arts, have violated the most sacred rights of friendship? I never can forgive myself, or hope charity from the world; but, I confess, I have much to hope from such a brother; and I am happy that I may soon say, such a sister.

MARIA: My dear, you distress me; you have all my love.

MANLY: And mine.

CHARLOTTE: If repentance can entitle me forgiveness, I have already much merit; for I despise the littleness of my past conduct. I now find that the heart of any worthy man cannot be gained by invidious attacks upon the rights and characters of others;—by countenancing the addresses of a thousand;—or that the finest assemblage of features, the greatest taste in dress, the genteelest address, or the most brilliant wit, cannot eventually secure a coquette from contempt and ridicule.

MANLY: And I have learned that probity, virtue, honour, though they should not have received the polish of Europe, will secure to an honest American the good graces of his fair countrywomen, and I hope, the applause of THE PUBLIC.

THE END

ANDRÉ *(1798)*

WILLIAM DUNLAP

Nearly a century after the death of William Dunlap (1766–1839), the literary historian Fred Lewis Pattee summed up the playwright's modern significance:

> An important figure he was in the period, the father of the American stage-drama, our first professional playwright, yet time has rendered him in our day little more than a name. Even the organization of his admirers into a club . . . has not rescued from oblivion much more than his mere name. He lives more in the literary influence he was able to exert upon his times, an influence in those pioneer days not small.

Despite the reclamation of many early American writers since Pattee wrote, what held for Dunlap's reputation in 1935 has not changed significantly in the several decades since. He remains recognized as a historically key figure, but basically is not read.

Yet, in his time, Dunlap was a pivotal figure in the development of a post-Revolutionary culture. Born in Perth Amboy, New Jersey, only nine years before the battles of Lexington and Concord, Dunlap was too young to fight during the war. His father, a loyalist, relocated to New York City to be near the occupying British army. In addition, an accident cost young Dunlap the use of his right eye. In 1784, he went to England to study painting under another loyalist, the American-born artist Benjamin West. After his return to the United States, he was inspired by the example of Royall Tyler to write a play, *The Modest Soldier*, in 1787. His drama was not mounted, but Dunlap befriended members of the Old American Company anyway. His next effort, *The Father; or, American Shandyism*, appeared on the boards in New York in 1789. Although he continued to paint portraits and miniatures, he became increasingly engrossed with the theater. By the time he came to write *André*, Dunlap was the most prolific of American stage authors, turning out original plays on foreign themes; after *André*, he earned success with several translations and adaptations of foreign works, particularly those of the German August von Kotzebue. He was also manager of the John Street Theatre and, later, the New Park Theatre, and a member of literary and cultural circles.

Following the Revolution, as we have noted in our discussion of Tyler, American attitudes toward the stage were mixed. Indeed, there was a large discrepancy between popular entertainments, particularly the often exuberant patriotic celebrations and spectacles, and the offerings of the "legitimate" theater. During the war, high-minded Whig authors wrote closet plays about unfolding events, but it was not until 1797 that an entire drama was produced in an American theater that dealt with an event of historic consequence. That was John Daly Burk's *Bunker-Hill*, a play that continued to be represented on American stages until the middle of the nineteenth century. Perhaps Dunlap hoped to cash in on the popularity of recent history as a stage subject by himself turning to a war he missed, the American Revolution. At any rate, he claims to have had the idea for such a play for several years before he finished *André*.

Whatever his motivations, Dunlap found out soon enough that portraying American history before an audience for whom it was still a fresh memory was not all kudos and profit. True, the first performance of *André*, on March 30, 1798, netted receipts of $817, "a temporary relief" to the cash-strapped manager and author, and "was received with warm applause." But as Dunlap continues in his *History of the American Theatre*, one gesture in the play brought hissing—the throwing down of the cockade by the American officer Bland, played by the British-born actor Thomas Abthorpe Cooper. After the play was over, this seemingly antipatriotic bit of stage business—exaggerated in its severity by Cooper's Englishness—inspired such heated discussion that some partisans wanted the play withdrawn. Dunlap altered the text slightly, inserting a brief scene in which Bland picks up the cockade and reinserts it in his cap. This allowed the play to be continued, although not without problems. Cooper, wanting the role of M'Donald and jealous of John Hodgkinson, who played André, spent little time learning his lines, and in a scene where Bland cries out to his friend, "Oh André," the actor kept up a string of "Oh André"s and punctuated them with "Damn the prompter!" and "What's next, Hodgkinson?" A performance on the early stage was often not a perfectly honed operation.

Whatever the material difficulties in getting a good production, the incidents described above illustrate one of the fundamental critical problems facing a reader and spectator of the play: decoding what Dunlap means when he says that André is the hero. This is less a topical issue than it was in Dunlap's day, but, to some extent, the problem of the

hero in *André* is a mirror of the difficulties faced by supporters of the
theater in the 1790s. As we know, Dunlap spent the war years in occupied New York. Any plays he saw there during the years between
1776 and 1783 would have been exhibited under the auspices of—
indeed, often performed by—the officer corps of the British military.
One of its leading figures was, in fact, John André, a young, handsome,
artistically accomplished major who not only was General Clinton's aide
but also was a favorite of the ladies. André could act, produce, even
paint scenery.

André's demise came abruptly when he was captured by three American militiamen. He had been visiting the American post at West Point,
commanded by General Benedict Arnold. André had been sent to ne-
gotiate both the secret transfer of the fort from American to British
control and Arnold's switch of allegiance. The British officer might have
been released with a pass had he not, under Arnold's urging, disguised
himself. The American commander, George Washington, hearing of André's capture, had him tried for espionage, and upon his conviction,
refused all entreaties from New Yorkers and from other Americans who
were attracted to the young officer. Despite his own pleas to be shot,
André was hanged on October 2, 1780—the same method of execution
meted upon the patriot spy, Nathan Hale, four years before. The death
of André was for many Americans, Whig and Tory, a blot on Washington's record.

Thus, to put on a play about André—one that also featured Washington as the "General"—not only reopened a sore subject concerning
still-living participants in the event, but it also brought up the whole
question of the purpose of an American theater. For the British occu-
piers, theater's place was to entertain, to lighten spirits during wartime.
For the American patriots, theater was just that institution which illus-
trated the frivolity of British mores, and, of course, it had been banned
in American territory in 1778. Dunlap, son of a loyalist in New York,
student of an émigré loyalist in London, found as an American citizen
of 1798 that matters of national identity could not easily be enacted on
a stage. Certainly, the changes he made to the actual facts—bringing in
Honora, for instance, when the real Honora Sneyd, as Norman Philbrick points out, had been André's mistress in England and was dead
before André was captured—expose how much he wanted sympathy
for his British character.

In addition, as Jay Fliegelman makes clear, the André story is one
more in a series of events that beg a kind of Oedipal reading of the
attachments and conflicts of sons and fathers. If for the patriots King

George III became the father to be "killed" in order for a nation to be independent, then, in this play, Washington becomes a father—the father of his country, after all—whose "son" Bland is in essence ritually sacrificed through the death of Bland's friend André and the potential death of Bland's literal father in retaliation. At any rate, the play gives André a largely sympathetic role, even though he is the enemy; by the same token, Washington is made to seem severe. A staunchly Whig reader of the play might, in the closet, applaud the General's stoic resolve; but a spectator at the play—one who remembered with fondness the theatrical seasons in New York during the war—might direct sympathies to the sentimental and heroic actor-officer whose death history demands. Far more than *The Contrast*, Dunlap's *André* exposes cultural rifts in the new republic that would last for decades.

André played three nights in New York, with attendance falling off the last two, then was published in April 1798 with an introduction by Dunlap and documents supporting the historical accuracy of the play. Giving up for the time being on serious dramas about recent history, Dunlap kept his focus on translation and adaptations of foreign works. Finally, in an 1803 revision that Robert H. Canary has labeled "criminal," he plucked a few scenes from *André* and attached them to a more overtly patriotic vehicle, *The Glory of Columbia—Her Yeomanry!*, which became a July fourth staple for years afterward. Yet, *André* is the more serious, more ambitious, more dangerous play, one that opens to the readers of our time the unhealed wounds of the new republic.

SELECTED BIBLIOGRAPHY

Canary, Robert H. *William Dunlap*. New York: Twayne, 1970.

Coad, Oral S. *William Dunlap: A Study of His Life and Works and of His Place in Contemporary Culture*. New York: Dunlap Society, 1917.

Dickson, Harold E. *Arts of the Young Republic: The Age of William Dunlap*. Chapel Hill: University of North Carolina Press, 1968.

Dunlap, William. *Diary*, edited by Dorothy C. Barck. 3 vols. New York: New York Historical Society, 1930.

———. *History of the American Theatre*. 2 vols. 1832; London: Bentley, 1833, vol. 2:20–22.

———. *Plays*, edited by Oral S. Coad. *America's Lost Plays*, Vol. 2. 1940; Bloomington: Indiana University Press, 1965.

Fliegelman, Jay. *Prodigals and Pilgrims: The American Revolution Against Patriarchal Authority*, 216–19. Cambridge: Cambridge University Press, 1982.

Grimsted, David. *Melodrama Unveiled: American Theater and Culture, 1800–1850*, 1–21. Chicago: University of Chicago Press, 1968.

Hodgkinson, John. *A Narrative of His Connection with the Old American Company*. New York, 1797.

Johnson, Claudia. "William Dunlap," *Dictionary of Literary Biography*. Vol. 37. See also *DLB*, vols. 30, 59.

Jost, Francois. "German and French Themes in Early American Drama." *JGE: The Journal of General Education* 28.3 (1976): 190–222.

Meserve, Walter J. *An Emerging Entertainment: The Drama of the American People to 1828*, 102–15. Bloomington: Indiana University Press, 1977.

Moody, Richard. Introduction to *André. Dramas from the American Theatre, 1762–1909*, 87–93. Cleveland: World, 1966.

Moramarco, Fred. "The Early Drama Criticism of William Dunlap." *American Literature* 40 (1968): 9–14.

Pattee, Fred Lewis. *The First Century of American Literature, 1770–1870.* 1935; New York: Cooper Square, 1966, 232–35.

Paulding, James Kirk. "Dramatic Literature." *The American Quarterly Review* (Philadelphia) 8.15 (September 1830): 134–61. Portion reprinted in *The Dawning of American Drama: American Dramatic Criticism, 1746–1915*, edited by Jürgen C. Wolter, 87–89. Westport, Conn.: Greenwood, 1993.

Philbrick, Norman. "The Spy as Hero: An Examination of *André* by William Dunlap." *Studies in Theatre and Drama: Essays in Honor of Hubert C. Heffner*, edited by Oscar G. Brockett, 97–119. The Hague: Mouton, 1972. The best article on *André*.

Richards, Jeffrey H. "A Theater Just Erected: America at War." *Theater Enough: American Culture and the Metaphor of the World Stage, 1607–1789*, 247–64. Durham: Duke University Press, 1991. Historical *André* in context.

Richardson, Gary. *American Drama from the Colonial Period through World War I: A Critical History*, 52–60. New York: Twayne, 1993.

Zipes, Jack. "Dunlap, Kotzebue, and the Shaping of American Theater: A Reevaluation from a Marxist Perspective." *Early American Literature* 8 (1974): 272–89.

ANDRÉ;

A *TRAGEDY*, IN FIVE ACTS:

AS PERFORMED BY THE OLD AMERICAN COMPANY,
NEW-YORK, MARCH 30, 1798.

TO WHICH ARE ADDED

AUTHENTIC DOCUMENTS

RESPECTING

MAJOR ANDRÉ;

CONSISTING OF

LETTERS TO MISS SEWARD,

THE

COW CHACE,

PROCEEDINGS OF THE COURT MARTIAL, &c.

———◆———

NEW-YORK:

Printed by T. & J. SWORDS, No. 99 Pearl-Street
—1798—

PREFACE

More than nine years ago the Author made choice of the death of Major André as the subject of a Tragedy, and part of what is now offered to the public was written at that time. Many circumstances discouraged him from finishing his Play, and among them must be reckoned a prevailing opinion that recent events are unfit subjects for tragedy. These discouragements have at length all given way to his desire of bringing a story on the Stage so eminently fitted, in his opinion, to excite interest in the breasts of an American audience.

In exhibiting a stage representation of a real transaction, the particulars of which are fresh in the minds of many of the audience, an author has this peculiar difficulty to struggle with, that those who know the events expect to see them *all* recorded; and any deviation from what they remember to be fact, appears to them as a fault in the poet; they are disappointed, their expectations are not fulfilled, and the writer is more or less condemned, not considering the difference between the poet and the historian, or not knowing that what is intended to be exhibited is a free poetical picture, not an exact historical portrait.

Still further difficulties has the Tragedy of André to surmount, difficulties independent of its own demerits, in its way to public favor. The subject necessarily involves political questions; but the Author presumes that he owes no apology to any one for having shewn himself an American. The friends of Major André (and it appears that all who knew him were his friends) will look with a jealous eye on the Poem, whose principal incident is the sad catastrophe which his misconduct, in submitting to be an instrument in a transaction of treachery and deceit, justly brought upon him: but these friends have no cause of offence; the Author has adorned the poetical character of André with every virtue; he has made him his Hero; to do which, he was under the necessity of making him condemn his own conduct, in the one dreadfully unfortunate action of his life. To shew the effects which Major André's excellent qualities had upon the minds of men, the Author has drawn a generous and amiable youth, so blinded by his love for the accomplished Briton, as to consider his country, and the great commander of her armies, as in the commission of such horrid injustice, that he, in the anguish of his soul, disclaims the service. In this it appears, since the first representation, that the Author has gone near to offend the veterans of the American army who were present on the first night, and who not knowing the sequel of the action, felt much disposed to condemn him: but

surely they must remember the diversity of opinion which agitated the
minds of men at the time, on the question of the propriety of putting
André to death; and when they add the circumstances of André's having
saved the life of this youth, and gained his ardent friendship, they will
be inclined to mingle with their disapprobation, a sentiment of pity, and
excuse, perhaps commend, the Poet, who has represented the action
without sanctioning it by his approbation.

As a sequel to the affair of the cockade, the Author has added the
following lines, which the reader is requested to insert, page 55, between
the 5th and 15th lines instead of the lines he will find there, which were
printed before the piece was represented.[1]—

BLAND: Noble M'Donald, truth and honor's champion!
   Yet think not strange that my intemperance wrong'd thee:
   Good as thou art! for, would'st thou, can'st thou, think it?
   My tongue, unbridled, hath the same offence,
   With action violent, and boisterous tone,
   Hurl'd on that glorious man, whose pious labors
   Shield from every ill his grateful country!
   That man, whom friends to adoration love,
   And enemies revere.—Yes, M'Donald,
   Even in the presence of the first of men
   Did I abjure the service of my country,
   And reft my helmet of that glorious badge
   Which graces even the brow of Washington.
   How shall I see him more!—
M'DONALD: Alive himself to every generous impulse,
   He hath excus'd the impetuous warmth of youth,
   In expectation that thy fiery soul,
   Chasten'd by time and reason, will receive
   The stamp indelible of godlike virtue.
   To me, in trust, he gave this badge disclaim'd,
   With power, when thou should'st see thy wrongful error,
   From him, to reinstate it in thy helm,
   And thee in his high favor. [*Gives the cockade.*]
BLAND [*takes the cockade and replaces it*]: Shall I speak my thoughts
    of thee and him?
   No:—let my actions henceforth shew what thou
   And he have made me. Ne'er shall my helmet
   Lack again its proudest, noblest ornament,

Until my country knows the rest of peace,
Or Bland the peace of death!   [*Exit.*]

This alteration, as well as the whole performance, on the second
night, met the warm approbation of the audience.

To the performers the Author takes this opportunity of returning his
thanks for their exertions in his behalf; perfectly convinced, that on this,
as on former occasions, the members of the Old American Company[2]
have anxiously striven to oblige him.

If this Play is successful, it will be a proof that recent events may be
so managed in tragedy as to command popular attention; if it is unsuc-
cessful, the question must remain undetermined until some more powerful writer shall again make the experiment. The Poem is now
submitted to the ordeal of closet examination, with the Author's respectful assurance to every reader, that as it is not his interest, so it has
not been his intention to offend any; but, on the contrary, to impress,
through the medium of a pleasing stage exhibition, the sublime lessons
of Truth and Justice upon the minds of his countrymen.

                                                        W. DUNLAP.

New-York, April 4th, 1798.

PROLOGUE

SPOKEN BY MR. MARTIN,[1]

A Native Bard, a native scene displays,
And claims your candor for his daring lays:
Daring, so soon, in mimic scenes to shew,
What each remembers as a real woe.
Who has forgot when gallant ANDRÉ died?
A name by Fate to Sorrow's self allied.
Who has forgot, when o'er the untimely bier,
Contending armies paus'd, to drop a tear.

Our Poet builds upon a fact tonight;
Yet claims, in building, every Poet's right;
To choose, embellish, lop, or add, or blend,
Fiction with truth, as best may suit his end;
Which, he avows, is pleasure to impart,
And move the passions but to mend the heart.

O, may no party-spirit blast his views,
Or turn to ill the meanings of the Muse:
She sings of wrongs long past, Men as they
    were,
To instruct, without reproach, the Men that
    are;
Then judge the Story by the genius shown,
And praise, or damn, it, for its worth alone.

CHARACTERS

GENERAL, *dress, American staff uniform, blue, faced with buff, large gold epaulets, cocked hat, with the black and white cockade, indicating the union with France, buff waistcoat and breeches, boots.*
M'DONALD, *a man of forty years of age, uniform nearly the same of the first.*
SEWARD, *a man of thirty years of age, staff uniform.*
ANDRÉ, *a man of twenty-nine years of age, full British uniform after the first scene.*

BLAND, *a youthful but military figure, in the uniform of a Captain of horse—dress, a short blue coat, faced with red, and trimmed with gold lace, two small epaulets, a white waistcoat, leather breeches, boots and spurs; over the coat, crossing the chest from the right shoulder, a broad buff belt, to which is suspended a manageable hussar sword; a horseman's helmet on the head, decorated as usual, and the union cockade affixed.*

MELVILLE, *a man of middle age, and grave deportment; his dress a Captain's uniform when on duty; a blue coat, with red facings, gold epaulet, white waistcoat and breeches, boots and cocked hat, with the union cockade.*

BRITISH OFFICER.

AMERICAN OFFICER.

CHILDREN.

AMERICAN SERGEANT.

AMERICAN OFFICERS AND SOLDIERS, &c.

MRS. BLAND.

HONORA.

SCENE, *the Village of Tappan,*[4] *Encampment, and adjoining Country. Time, ten hours.*[4]

ANDRÉ

ACT I

SCENE 1, *a Wood seen by starlight; an Encampment at a distance appearing between the trees.*

[*Enter* MELVILLE.]

MELVILLE: The solemn hour, "when night and morning meet,"
    Mysterious time, to superstition dear,
    And superstition's guides, now passes by;
    Deathlike in solitude. The sentinels,
    In drowsy tones, from post to post, send on
    The signal of the passing hour. "All's well,"
    Sounds through the camp. Alas! all is not well;
    Else, why stand I, a man, the friend of man,
    At midnight's depth, deck'd in this murderous guise,
    The habiliment of death, the badge of dire,
    Necessitous coercion. 'T is not well.
    —In vain the enlighten'd friends of suffering man
    Point out, of war, the folly, guilt, and madness.
    Still, age succeeds to age, and war to war;
    And man, the murderer, marshalls out his hosts
    In all the gaiety of festive pomp,
    To spread around him death and desolation.
    How long! how long!——
    —Methinks I hear the tread of feet this way.
    My meditating mood may work me woe. [*Draws.*]
    Stand, whoso'er thou art, Answer. Who's there?

    [*Enter* BLAND.]

BLAND: A friend.
MELVILLE: Advance and give the countersign.
BLAND: Hudson.
MELVILLE: What, Bland!
BLAND: Melville, my friend, you *here?*
MELVILLE: And *well*, my brave young friend. But why do you,
    At this dead hour of night, approach the camp,
    On foot, and thus alone?

BLAND: I have but now
  Dismounted; and, from yon sequester'd cot,
  Whose lonely taper through the crannied wall
  Sheds its faint beams, and twinkles midst the trees,
  Have I, adventurous, grop'd my darksome way.
  My servant, and my horses, spent with toil,
  There wait till morn.

MELVILLE: Why waited not yourself?

BLAND: Anxious to know the truth of those reports
  Which, from the many mouths of busy Fame,
  Still, as I pass'd, struck varying on my ear,
  Each making th' other void. Nor does delay
  The color of my hasteful business suit.
  I bring dispatches for our great Commander;
  And hasted hither with design to wait
  His rising, or awake him with the sun.

MELVILLE: You will not need the last, for the blest sun
  Ne'er rises on his slumbers; by the dawn
  We see him mounted gaily in the field,
  Or find him wrapt in meditation deep,
  Planning the welfare of our war-worn land.

BLAND: Prosper, kind heaven! and recompense his cares.

MELVILLE: You're from the South, if I presume right?

BLAND: I am; and, Melville, I am fraught with news.
  The South⁵ teems with events; convulsing ones:
  The Briton, there, plays at no mimic war;
  With gallant face he moves, and gallantly is met.
  Brave spirits, rous'd by glory, throng our camp;
  The hardy hunter, skill'd to fell the deer,
  Or start the sluggish bear from covert rude;
  And not a clown that comes, but from his youth
  Is trained to pour from far the leaden death,
  To climb the steep, to struggle with the stream,
  To labor firmly under scorching skies,
  And bear, unshrinking, winter's roughest blast.
  This, and that heaven-inspir'd enthusiasm
  Which ever animates the patriot's breast,
  Shall far outweigh the lack of discipline.

MELVILLE: Justice is ours; what shall prevail against her?

BLAND: But as I past along, many strange tales,
  And monstrous rumours, have my ears assail'd:

That Arnold[6] had prov'd false; but he was ta'en,
And hung, or to be hung—I know not what.
Another told, that all our army, with their
Much lov'd Chief, sold and betray'd, were captur'd.
But, as I nearer drew, at yonder cot,
'Twas said, that Arnold, traitor like, had fled;
And that a Briton, tried and prov'd a spy,
Was, on this day, as such, to suffer death.

MELVILLE: As you drew near, plain truth advanced to meet you.
    'Tis even as you heard, my brave young friend.
    Never had people on a single throw
    More interest at stake; when he, who held
    For us the die, prov'd false, and play'd us foul.
    But for a circumstance of that nice kind,
    Of cause so microscopic, that the tongues
    Of inattentive men call it the effect
    Of chance, we must have lost the glorious game.

BLAND: Blest, blest be heaven! whatever was the cause!

MELVILLE: The blow ere this had fallen that would have bruis'd
    The tender plant which we have striven to rear,
    Crush'd to the dust, no more to bless this soil.

BLAND: What warded off the blow?

MELVILLE: The brave young man, who this day dies, was seiz'd
    Within our bounds, in rustic garb disguis'd.
    He offer'd bribes to tempt the band that seiz'd him;
    But the rough farmer,[7] for his country arm'd,
    That soil defending which his ploughshare turn'd,
    Those laws, his father chose, and he approv'd,
    Cannot, as mercenary soldiers may,
    Be brib'd to sell the public-weal for gold.

BLAND: 'Tis well. Just heaven! O grant that thus may fall
    All those who seek to bring this land to woe!
    All those, who, or by open force, or dark
    And secret machinations, seek to shake
    The Tree of Liberty, or stop its growth,
    In any soil where thou hast pleas'd to plant it.

MELVILLE: Yet not a heart but pities and would save him;
    For all confirm that he is brave and virtuous;
    Known, but till now, the darling child of Honor.

BLAND [contemptuously]: And how is call'd this—honorable spy?

MELVILLE: André's his name.

BLAND [*much agitated*]:   André!
MELVILLE: Aye, Major André.
BLAND: André!—O no, my friend, you're sure deceiv'd—
   I'll pawn my life, my ever sacred fame,
   My General's favor, or a soldier's honor,
   That gallant André never yet put on
   The guise of falsehood. O, it cannot be!
MELVILLE: How might I be deceiv'd? I've heard him, seen him,
   And what I tell, I tell from well-prov'd knowledge;
   No second tale-bearer, who heard the news.
BLAND: Pardon me, Melville. O, that well-known name,
   So link'd with circumstances infamous!—
   My friend must pardon me. Thou wilt not blame
   When I shall tell what cause I have to love him:
   What cause to think him nothing more the pupil
   Of Honor stern, than sweet Humanity.
   Rememberest thou, when cover'd o'er with wounds,
   And left upon the field, I fell the prey
   Of Britain? To a loathsome prison-ship
   Confin'd, soon had I sunk, victim of death,
   A death of aggravated miseries;
   But, by benevolence urg'd, this best of men,
   This gallant youth, then favor'd, high in power,
   Sought out the pit obscene of foul disease,
   Where I, and many a suffering soldier lay,
   And, like an angel, seeking good for man,
   Restor'd us light, and partial liberty.
   Me he mark'd out his own. He nurst and cur'd,
   He lov'd and made his friend. I liv'd by him,
   And in my heart he liv'd, till, when exchang'd,
   Duty and honor call'd me from my friend.—
   Judge how my heart is tortur'd.—Gracious heaven!
   Thus, thus to meet him on the brink of death—
   A death so infamous! Heav'n grant my prayer. [*Kneels.*]
   That I may save him, O, inspire my heart
   With thoughts, my tongue with words that move to pity! [*Rises.*]
   Quick, Melville, shew me where my André lies.
MELVILLE: Good wishes go with you.
BLAND: I'll save my friend.   [*Exeunt.*]

SCENE [2], *the Encampment, by starlight.*

[*Enter the* GENERAL, M'DONALD, *and* SEWARD.]

GENERAL[8]: 'Tis well. Each sentinel upon his post
  Stands firm, and meets me at the bayonet's point;
  While in his tent the weary soldier lies,
  The sweet reward of wholesome toil enjoying;
  Resting secure as erst within his cot
  He careless slept, his rural labor o'er;
  Ere Britons dar'd to violate those laws,
  Those boasted laws by which themselves are govern'd,
  And strove to make their fellow-subjects slaves.
SEWARD: They know to whom they owe their present safety.
GENERAL: I hope they know that to themselves they owe it:
  To that good discipline which they observe,
  The discipline of men to order train'd,
  Who know its value, and in whom 'tis virtue;
  To that prompt hardihood with which they meet
  Or toil or danger, poverty or death.
  Mankind who know not whence that spirit springs,
  Which holds at bay all Britain's boasted power,
  Gaze on their deeds astonish'd. See the youth
  Start from his plough, and straightway play the hero;
  Unmurmuring bear such toils as veterans shun;
  Rest all content upon the dampsome earth;
  Follow undaunted to the deathful charge;
  Or, when occasion asks, lead to the breach,
  Fearless of all the unusual din of war,
  His former peaceful mates. O patriotism!
  Thou wond'rous principle of god-like action!
  Wherever liberty is found, there reigns
  The love of country. Now the self-same spirit
  Which fill'd the breast of great Leonidas,[9]
  Swells in the hearts of thousands on these plains,
  Thousands who never heard the hero's tale.
  'Tis this alone which saves thee, O my country!
  And, till that spirit flies these western shores,
  No power on earth shall crush thee!
SEWARD: 'Tis wond'rous!
  The men of other climes from this shall see

How easy 'tis to shake oppression off;
How all resistless is an union'd people;
And hence, from our success (which, by my soul,
I feel as much secur'd, as though our foes
Were now within their floating prisons hous'd,
And their proud prows all pointing to the east),
Shall other nations break their galling fetters,
And re-assume the dignity of man.

M'DONALD: Are other nations in that happy state,
That, having broke Coercion's iron yoke,
They can submit to Order's gentle voice,
And walk on earth self-ruled? I much do fear it.
As to ourselves, in truth, I nothing see,
In all the wond'rous deeds which we perform,
But plain effects from causes full as plain.
Rises not man for ever 'gainst oppression?
It is the law of life; he can't avoid it.
But when the love of property unites
With sense of injuries past, and dread of future,
Is it then wonderful, that he should brave
A lesser evil to avoid a greater?

GENERAL [*sportively*]: 'Tis hard, quite hard, we may not please
      ourselves,
By our great deeds ascribing to our virtue.

SEWARD: M'Donald never spares to lash our pride.

M'DONALD: In truth I know of nought to make you proud.
   I think there's none within the camp that draws
   With better will his sword than does M'Donald.
   I have a home to guard. My son is—butcher'd—

SEWARD: Hast thou no nobler motives for thy arms
   Than love of property, and thirst of vengeance?

M'DONALD: Yes, my good Seward, and yet nothing wond'rous.
   I love this country for the sake of man.
   My parents, and I thank them, cross'd the seas,
   And made me native of fair Nature's world,
   With room to grow and thrive in. I have thriven;
   And feel my mind unshackled, free, expanding,
   Grasping, with ken unbounded, mighty thoughts,
   At which, if chance my mother had, good dame,
   In Scotia,[10] our revered parent soil,
   Given me to see the day, I should have shrunk

Affrighted. Now, I see in this new world
A resting spot for man, if he can stand
Firm in his place, while Europe howls around him,
And all unsettled as the thoughts of vice,
Each nation in its turn threats him with feeble malice.
One trial, now, we prove; and I have met it.

GENERAL: And met it like a man, my brave M'Donald.

M'DONALD: I hope so; and I hope my every act
Has been the offspring of deliberate judgment;
Yet, feeling second reason's cool resolves.
O! I could hate, if I did not more pity,
These bands of mercenary Europeans,
So wanting in the common sense of nature,
As, without shame, to sell themselves for pelf,
To aid the cause of darkness, murder man—
Without inquiry murder, and yet call
Their trade the trade of honor—high-soul'd honor—
Yet honor shall accord in act with falsehood.
O that proud man should e'er descend to play
The tempter's part, and lure men to their ruin!
Deceit and honor badly pair together.

SEWARD: You have much shew of reason; yet, methinks
What you suggest of one, whom fickle Fortune,
In her changeling mood, hath hurl'd, unpitying,
From her topmost height to lowest misery,
Tastes not of charity. André, I mean.

M'DONALD: I mean him, too; sunk by misdeed, not fortune.
Fortune and chance. O, most convenient words!
Man runs the wild career of blind ambition,
Plunges in vice, takes falsehood for his buoy,
And when he feels the waves of ruin o'er him,
Curses, in "good set terms," poor Lady Fortune.

GENERAL [sportively to SEWARD]: His mood is all untoward; let us
    leave him.
Tho' he may think that he is bound to rail,
We are not bound to hear him. [To M'DONALD.] Grant you that?

M'DONALD: O, freely, freely! you I never rail on.

GENERAL: No thanks for that; you've courtesy for office.

M'DONALD: You slander me.

GENERAL: Slander that would not wound.
    Worthy M'Donald, though it suits full well

The virtuous man to frown on all misdeeds;
Yet ever keep in mind that man is frail;
His tide of passion struggling still with Reason's
Fair and favorable gale, and adverse
Driving his unstable Bark, upon the
Rocks of error. Should he sink thus shipwreck'd,
Sure it is not Virtue's voice that triumphs
In his ruin. I must seek rest. Adieu!

[Exeunt GENERAL and SEWARD.]

M'DONALD: Both good and great thou art: first among men:
By nature, or by early habit, grac'd
With that blest quality which gives due force
To every faculty, and keeps the mind
In healthful equipoise, ready for action;
Invaluable temperance—by all
To be acquired, yet scarcely known to any.   [*Exit.*]

END OF ACT I

ACT II

SCENE 1, *a Prison.* ANDRÉ *discovered in a pensive posture, sitting at a table; a book by him and candles: his dress neglected, his hair dishevelled: he rises and comes forward.*

ANDRÉ: Kind heaven be thank'd for that I stand alone
In this sad hour of life's brief pilgrimage!
Single in misery; no one else involving,
In grief, in shame, and ruin. 'Tis my comfort.
Thou, my thrice honor'd sire, in peace went'st down
Unto the tomb, nor knew to blush, nor knew
A pang for me! And thou, revered matron,
Could'st bless thy child, and yield thy breath in peace!
No wife shall weep, no child lament, my loss.
Thus may I consolation find in what
Was once my woe. I little thought to joy
In not possessing, as I erst possest,
Thy love, Honora! André's death, perhaps,
May cause a cloud pass o'er thy lovely face;
The pearly tear may steal from either eye;
For thou mayest feel a transient pang, nor wrong

A husband's rights: more than a transient pang
O mayest thou never feel! The morn draws nigh
To light me to my shame. Frail nature shrinks.—
And *is* death then so fearful? I have brav'd
Him, fearless, in the field, and steel'd my breast
Against his thousand horrors; but his cool,
His sure approach, requires a fortitude
Which nought but conscious rectitude can give. [*Retires, and sits leaning.*]

[*Enter* BLAND, *unperceived by* ANDRÉ.]

BLAND: And is that André! O how chang'd! Alas!
Where is that martial fire, that generous warmth,
Which glow'd his manly countenance throughout,
And gave to every look, to every act,
The tone of high chivalrous animation?—
André, my friend! look up.

ANDRÉ: Who calls *me* friend?

BLAND: Young Arthur Bland.

ANDRÉ [*rising*]:   That name sounds like a friend's. [*With emotion.*]
I have inquir'd for thee—wish'd much to see thee—
I prithee take no note of these fool's tears—
My heart was full—and seeing thee—

BLAND [*embracing him*]: O, André!—
I have but now arrived from the south—
Nor heard—till now—of this—I cannot speak.
Is this a place?—O, thus to find my friend!

ANDRÉ: Still dost thou call me friend? I, who dared act
Against my reason, my declared opinion;
Against my conscience, and a soldier's fame?
Oft in the generous heat of glowing youth,
Oft have I said how fully I despis'd
All bribery base, all treacherous tricks in war;
Rather my blood should bathe these hostile shores,
And have it said, "he died a gallant soldier,"
Than with my country's gold encourage treason,
And thereby purchase gratitude and fame.

BLAND: Still mayest thou say it, for thy heart's the same.

ANDRÉ: Still is my heart the same: still may I say it:
But now my deeds will rise against my words;

And should I dare to talk of honest truth,
Frank undissembling probity and faith,
Memory would crimson o'er my burning cheek,
And actions retrospected choke the tale.
Still is my heart the same. But there has past
A day, an hour—which ne'er can be recall'd!
Unhappy man! tho' all thy life pass pure;
Mark'd by benevolence thy every deed;
The out-spread map, which shows the way thou'st trod,
Without one devious track, or doubtful line;
It all avails thee naught, if in one hour,
One hapless hour, thy feet are led astray;—
Thy happy deeds, all blotted from remembrance;
Cancel'd the record of thy former good.
Is it not hard, my friend? Is 't not unjust?
BLAND: Not every record cancel'd—O, there are hearts,
   Where Virtue's image, when 'tis once engrav'd,
   Can never know erasure.
ANDRÉ: Generous Bland! [*Takes his hand.*]
   The hour draws nigh which ends my life's sad story.
   I should be firm—
BLAND: By heaven thou shalt not die!
   Thou dost not sure deserve it. Betray'd, perhaps—
   Condemn'd without due circumstance made known?
   Thou didst not mean to tempt our officers?
   Betray our yeoman soldiers to destruction?
   Silent. Nay, then 'twas from a duteous wish
   To serve the cause thou wast in honor bound—
ANDRÉ: Kind is my Bland, who is to his generous heart,
   Still finds excuses for his erring friend.
   Attentive hear and judge me.—
   Pleas'd with the honors daily shower'd upon me,
   I glow'd with martial heat, my name to raise
   Above the vulgar herd, who live to die,
   And die to be forgotten. Thus I stood,
   When, avarice or ambition Arnold tempted,
   His country, fame, and honor to betray;
   Linking his name to infamy eternal.
   In confidence it was to me propos'd,
   To plan with him the means which should ensure
   Thy country's downfall. Nothing then I saw

But confidential favor in the service,
My country's glory, and my mounting fame;
Forgot my former purity of thought,
And high-ton'd honor's scruples disregarded.
BLAND: It was thy duty so to serve thy country.
ANDRÉ: Nay, nay; be cautious ever to admit
That duty can beget dissimulation.
On ground, unoccupied by either part,
Neutral esteem'd, I landed, and was met.
But ere my conference was with Arnold clos'd,
The day began to dawn: I then was told
That till the night I must my safety seek
In close concealment. Within your posts convey'd,
I found myself involv'd in unthought dangers.
Night came. I sought the vessel which had borne
Me to the fatal spot; but she was gone.
Retreat that way cut off, again I sought
Concealment with the traitors of your army.
Arnold now granted passes, and I doff'd
My martial garb, and put on curs'd disguise!
Thus in a peasant's form I pass'd your posts;
And when, as I conceiv'd, my danger o'er,
Was stopt and seiz'd by some returning scouts.
So did ambition lead me, step by step,
To treat with traitors, and encourage treason;
And then, bewilder'd in the guilty scene,
To quit my martial designating badges,
Deny my name, and sink into the spy.[11]
BLAND: Thou didst no more than was a soldier's duty,
To serve the part on which he drew his sword.
Thou shalt not die for this. Straight will I fly—
I surely shall prevail—
ANDRÉ: It is in vain.
All has been tried. Each friendly argument—
BLAND: All has not yet been tried. The powerful voice
Of friendship, in thy cause, has not been heard.
My General favors *me*, and loves my father—
My gallant father! Would that he were here!
But he, perhaps, now wants an André's care,
To cheer his hours—perhaps, now languishes
Amidst those horrors whence thou sav'd'st his son!

The present moment claims my thought. André—
I fly to save thee!—

ANDRÉ: Bland, it is in vain.
But, hold—there is a service thou may'st do me.

BLAND: Speak it.

ANDRÉ: O, think, and as a soldier think,
How I must die—The *manner* of my death—
Like the base ruffian, or the midnight thief,
Ta'en in the act of stealing from the poor,
To be turn'd off the felon's—murderer's cart,
A mid-air spectacle to gaping clowns;—
To run a short, an envied course of glory,
And end it on a gibbet.¹²——

BLAND: Damnation!!

ANDRÉ: Such is my doom. O! have the manner changed,
And of mere death I'll think not. Dost thou think—?
Perhaps thou canst gain *that*——?

BLAND [*almost in a phrenzy*]:   Thou shalt not die!

ANDRÉ: Let me, O! let me die a soldier's death,
While friendly clouds of smoke shroud from all eyes
My last convulsive pangs, and I'm content.

BLAND [*with increasing emotion*]: Thou shalt not die! Curse on the
   laws of war!—
If worth like thine must thus be sacrificed,
To policy so cruel and unjust,
I will forswear my country and her service:
I'll hie me to the Briton, and with fire,
And sword, and every instrument of death
Or devastation, join in the work of war!
What, shall worth weight for nought? I will avenge thee!

ANDRÉ: Hold, hold, my friend; thy country's woes are full.
What! wouldst thou make me cause another traitor?
No more of this; and, if I die, believe me,
Thy country for my death incurs no blame.
Restrain thy ardor—but ceaselessly intreat,
That André may at least die as he lived,
A soldier.

BLAND: By heaven thou shalt not die!—

BLAND [*rushes off:* ANDRÉ *looks after him with an expression of love
   and gratitude, then retires up the stage. Scene closes.*]

SCENE [2], *the* GENERAL'S *Quarters.*

[*Enter* M'DONALD *and* SEWARD, *in conversation.*]

[M'DONALD [*coming forward*]: Three thousand miles the Atlan-
tic wave rolls on,
Which bathed Columbia's shores, ere, on the strand
Of Europe, or of Afric, their continents,
Or sea-girt isles, it chafes.—
SEWARD: O! would to heaven
That in mid-way between these sever'd worlds,
Rose barriers, all impassable to man,
Cutting off intercourse, till either side
Had lost all memory of the other.
M'DONALD: What spur now goads thy warm imagination?
SEWARD: Then might, perhaps, one land on earth be found,
Free from th' extremes of poverty and riches;
Where ne'er a scepter'd tyrant should be known,
Or tyrant lordling, curses of creation;—
Where the faint shrieks of woe-exhausted age,
Raving, in feeble madness, o'er the corse
Of a polluted daughter, stained by lust
Of viand-pamper'd luxury, might ne'er be heard;—
Where the blasted form of much abused
Beauty, by villainy seduced, by knowledge
All unguarded, might ne'er be view'd, flitting
Obscene, 'tween lamp and lamp, i' th' midnight street
Of all defiling city; where the child——
M'DONALD: Hold! Shroud thy raven imagination!
Torture not me with images so curst!
SEWARD: Soon shall our foes, inglorious, fly these shores.
Peace shall again return. Then Europe's ports
Shall pour a herd upon us, far more fell
Than those, her mercenary sons, who, now,
Threaten our sore chastisement.
M'DONALD: Prophet of ill,
From Europe shall enriching commerce flow,
And many an ill attendant; but from thence
Shall likewise flow blest Science. Europe's knowledge,
By sharp experience bought, we should appropriate;

Striving thus to leap from that simplicity,
With ignorance curst, to that simplicity,
By knowledge blest; unknown the gulf between.
SEWARD: Mere theoretic dreaming!
M'DONALD: Blest wisdom
Seems, from out the chaos of the social world,
Where good and ill, in strange commixture, float,
To rise, by strong necessity, impell'd;
Starting, like Love divine, from womb of Night,
Illuming all, to order all reducing;
And shewing, by its bright and noontide blaze,
That happiness alone proceeds from justice.
SEWARD: Dreams, dreams! Man can know nought but ill on earth.
M'DONALD: I'll to my bed, for I have watch'd all night;
And may my sleep give pleasing repetition
Of these my waking dreams! Virtue's incentives.   [Exit.]
SEWARD: Folly's chimeras rather: guides to error.

[Enter BLAND, preceded by a SERGEANT.]

SERGEANT: Pacquets for the General.
BLAND: Seward, my friend!
SEWARD: Captain! I'm glad to see the hue of health
Sit on a visage from the sallow south.
BLAND: The lustihood of youth hath yet defied
The parching sun, and chilling dew of even.
The General—Seward—?
SEWARD: I will lead you to him.
BLAND: Seward, I must make bold. Leave us together,
When occasion offers. 'Twill be friendly.
SEWARD: I will not cross your purpose.   [Exeunt.]

SCENE [3], a Chamber.

[Enter MRS. BLAND.]

MRS. BLAND: Yes, ever be this day a festival
In my domestic calendar. This morn
Will see my husband free. Even now, perhaps,
Ere yet Aurora flies the eastern hills,
Shunning the sultry sun, my Bland embarks.

Already, on the Hudson's dancing wave,
He chides the sluggish rowers, or supplicates
For gales propitious; that his eager arms
May clasp his wife, may bless his little ones.
O! how the tide of joy makes my heart bound,
Glowing with high and ardent expectation!

[*Enter two* CHILDREN.]

1ST CHILD: Here we are, Mama, up, and dress'd already.

MRS. BLAND: And why were ye so early?

1ST CHILD: Why, did not you tell us that Papa was to be home to-day?

MRS. BLAND: I said, perhaps.

2ND CHILD [*disappointed*]: Perhaps!

1ST CHILD: I don't like perhaps's.

2ND CHILD: No, nor I neither; nor "may be so's."

MRS. BLAND: We make not certainties, my pretty loves;
I do not like "perhaps's" more than you do.

2ND CHILD: Oh! don't say so, Mama! for I'm sure hardly ever ask you anything but you answer me with "may be so,"—"perhaps,"—or "very likely."—"Mama, shall I go to the camp to-morrow, and see the General?" "May be so, my dear." Hang "may be so," say I.

MRS. BLAND: Well said, Sir Pertness.

1ST CHILD: But I am sure, Mama, you said, that, to-day, Papa would have his liberty.

MRS. BLAND: So, your dear father, by his letters, told me.

2ND CHILD: Why, then, I *am sure* he will be here to-day. When he can come *to us*, I'm sure he will not stay among those strange Englishmen and Hessians. I often wish'd that I had wings to fly, for then I would soon be with him.

MRS. BLAND: Dear boy!

[*Enter* SERVANT, *and gives a letter to* MRS. BLAND.]

SERVANT: An express, madam, from New-York to Headquarters, in passing, delivered this.

2ND CHILD: Papa's coming home to-day, John.

[*Exeunt* SERVANT *and* CHILDREN.]

MRS. BLAND: What fears assail me! Oh! I did not want
A letter now! [*She reads in great agitation, exclaiming, while her eyes are fixed on the paper.*]

My husband! doom'd to die! Retaliation! [*She looks forward with
    wildness, consternation and horror.*]
To die, if André dies! *He* dies to-day!—
My husband to be murdered! And to-day!
To-day, if André dies! Retaliation!
O curst contrivance!—Madness relieve me!
Burst, burst, my brain!—Yet—André is not dead:
My husband lives. [*Looks at the letter.*] "One man has power."
I fly to save the father of my children! [*Rushes out.*]

END OF ACT II

ACT III

SCENE [1], *the* GENERAL'S *Quarters.*

[*The* GENERAL *and* BLAND *come forward.*]

GENERAL [*papers in his hand*]: Captain, you are noted here with
    honorable
    Praises. Depend upon that countenance
    From me, which you have prov'd yourself so richly
    Meriting. Both for your father's virtues.
    And your own, your country owes you honor—
    The sole return the poor can make for service.
BLAND: If from my country ought I've merited,
    Or gain'd the approbation of her champion,
    At any other time, I should not dare,
    Presumptuously, to shew my sense of it;
    But now, my tongue, all shameless, dares to name
    The boon, the precious recompense, I wish,
    Which, granted, pays all service, past or future,
    O'erpays the utmost I can e'er achieve.
GENERAL: Brief, my young friend, briefly, your purpose.
BLAND: If I have done my duty as a soldier;
    If I have brav'd all dangers for my country;
    If my brave father has deserved ought;
    Call all to mind—and cancel all—but grant
    My one request—mine, and humanity's.
GENERAL: Be less profuse of words, and name your wish;

If fit, its fitness is the best assurance
That not in vain you sue; but, if unjust,
Thy merits, nor the merits of thy race,
Cannot its nature alter, nor my mind,
From its determined opposition change.
BLAND: You hold the fate of my most lov'd of friends;
  As gallant soldier as e'er faced a foe,
  Bless'd with each polish'd gift of social life,
  And every virtue of humanity.
  To me, a savior from the pit of death,
  To me, and many more my countrymen.
  Oh! could my words portray him what he is;
  Bring to your mind the blessings of his deeds,
  While thro' the fever-heated, loathsome holds,
  Of floating hunks, dungeons obscene, where ne'er
  The dewy breeze of morn, or evening's coolness,
  Breath'd on our parching skins, he pass'd along,
  Diffusing blessings; still his power exerting,
  To alleviate the woes which ruthless war,
  Perhaps, thro' dire necessity, heap'd on us;
  Surely, the scene would move you to forget
  His late intent—(tho' only serving then,
  As duty prompted)—and turn the rigour
  Of War's iron law from him, the best of men,
  Meant only for the worst.
GENERAL: Captain, no more.
BLAND: If André lives, the prisoner finds a friend;
  Else helpless and forlorn——
  All men will bless the act, and bless thee for it.
GENERAL: Think'st thou thy country would not curse the man,
  Who, by a clemency ill-tim'd, ill-judg'd,
  Encourag'd treason? That *pride* encourag'd,
  Which, by denying us the rights of nations,
  Hath caus'd those ills which thou hast now portray'd?
  Our prisoners, brave and generous peasantry,
  As rebels have been treated, not as men.
  'Tis mine, brave yeomen, to assert your rights;
  'Tis mine to teach the foe, that, though array'd
  In rude simplicity, ye, yet, are men,
  And rank among the foremost. Oft their scouts,
  The very refuse of the English arms,

Unquestion'd, have our countrymen consign'd
To death, when captur'd, mocking their agonies.
BLAND: Curse them! [*Checking himself.*] Yet let not censure fall on
    André.
O, there are Englishmen as brave, as good,
As ever land on earth might call its own;
And gallant André is among the best!
GENERAL: Since they have hurl'd war on us, we must shew
That by the laws of war we will abide;
And have the power to bring their acts for trial,
To that tribunal, eminent 'mongst men,
Erected by the policy of nations,
To stem the flood of ills, which else fell war
Would pour, uncheck'd, upon the sickening world,
Sweeping away all trace of civil life.
BLAND: To pardon him would not encourage ill.
His case is singular; his station high;
His qualities admired; his virtues lov'd.
GENERAL: No more, my good young friend: it is in vain.
The men entrusted with they country's rights
Have weigh'd, attentive, every circumstance.
An individual's virtue is, by them,
As highly prized as it can be by thee.
I know the virtues of this man, and love them.
But the destiny of millions, millions
Yet unborn, depends upon the rigour
Of this moment. The haughty Briton laughs
To scorn our armies and our councils. Mercy,
Humanity, call loudly, that we make
Our now despised power be felt, vindictive.
Millions demand the death of this young man.
My injur'd country, he his forfeit life
Must yield, to shield thy lacerated breast
From torture. [*To* BLAND.] Thy merits are not overlook'd.
Promotion shall immediately attend thee.
BLAND [*with contemptuous irony*]: Pardon me, sir, I never shall de-
    serve it.
[*With increasing heat.*] The country that forgets to reverence virtue:
That makes no difference 'twixt the sordid wretch,
Who, for reward, risks treason's penalty,
And him unfortunate, whose duteous service

Is, by mere accident, so chang'd in form,
As to assume guilt's semblance, I serve not:
Scorn to serve. I have a soldier's honor,
But 'tis in union with a freeman's judgment,
And when I act, both prompt. Thus from my helm
I tear, what once I proudly thought, the badge
Of virtuous fellowship. [*Tears the cockade from his helmet.*] My
    sword I keep. [*Puts on his helmet.*]
Would, André, thou hadst never put thine off!
Then hadst thou through opposers' hearts made way
To liberty, or bravely pierc'd thine own!   [*Exit.*]
GENERAL: Rash, headstrong, maddening boy!
Had not this action past without a witness,
Duty would ask that thou shouldst rue thy folly—
But, for the motive, be the deed forgotten.   [*Exit.*]

SCENE [2], *a Village. At a distance some tents. In front muskets, drums,
and other indications of soldiers' quarters.*

[*Enter* MRS. BLAND *and* CHILDREN, *attended by* MELVILLE.]

MELVILLE: The General's doors to you are ever open.
    But why, my worthy friend, this agitation?
    Our Colonel, your husband——
MRS. BLAND [*in tears, gives him the letter*]: Read, Melville.
1ST CHILD: Do not cry, Mama, for I'm sure if Papa said he would
    come home to-day he will come yet: for he always does what he
    says he will.
MRS. BLAND: He cannot come, dear love; they will not let him.
2ND CHILD: Why, then, they told him lies. O, fie upon them!
MELVILLE [*returning the letter*]: Fear nothing, Madam, 'tis an empty
    threat:
    A trick of policy. They dare not do it.
MRS. BLAND: Alas! alas! what dares not power to do?
    What art of reasoning, or what magic words,
    Can still the storm of fears these lines have rais'd?
    The wife's, the mother's fears? Ye innocents,
    Unconscious on the brink of what a perilous
    Precipice ye stand, unknowing that to-day
    Ye are cast down the gulf, poor babes, ye weep
    From sympathy. Children of sorrow, nurst,

Nurtur'd, midst camps and arms; unknowing man,
But as man's fell destroyer; must ye now,
To crown your piteous fate, be fatherless?
O, lead me, lead me to him! Let me kneel,
Let these, my children, kneel, till André, pardon'd,
Ensures to me a husband, them a father.

MELVILLE: Madam, duty forbids further attendance.
I am on guard to-day. But see your son;
To him I leave your guidance. Good wishes
Prosper you!   [*Exit* MELVILLE.]

        [*Enter* BLAND.]

MRS. BLAND: My Arthur, O my Arthur!
BLAND: My mother! [*Embracing her.*]
MRS. BLAND: My son, I have been wishing
        For you——[*Burst into tears, unable to proceed.*]
BLAND: But whence this grief, these tears, my mother?
    Why are these little cheeks bedew'd with sorrow? [*He kisses the
        children, who exclaim,* Brother, brother!]
    Have I done ought to cause a mother's sadness?
MRS. BLAND: No, my brave boy! I oft have fear'd, but never
    Sorrow'd for thee.
BLAND: High praise!—Then bless me, Madam;
    For I have pass'd through many a bustling scene
    Since I have seen a father or a mother.
MRS. BLAND: Bless thee, my boy! O bless him, bless him, Heaven!
    Render him worthy to support these babes!
    So soon, perhaps, all fatherless—dependent.—
BLAND: What mean'st thou, madam? Why these tears?
MRS. BLAND: Thy father——
BLAND: A prisoner of war—I long have known it—
    But made so without blemish to his honor,
    And soon exchang'd, returns unto his friends,
    To guard these little ones, and point and lead,
    To virtue and to glory.
MRS. BLAND: Never, never!
    His life, a sacrifice to André's *manes*,[13]
    Must soon be offer'd. Even now, endungeon'd,
    Like a vile felon, on the earth he lies,
    His death expecting. André's execution

Gives signal for the murder of thy father—
André now dies!!——

BLAND [*despairingly*]: My father and my friend!!

MRS. BLAND: There is but one on earth can save my husband—
But one can pardon André.

BLAND: Haste, my mother!
Thou wilt prevail. Take with thee in each hand
An unoffending child of him thou weep'st.
Save—save them both! This way—haste—lean on me.   [*Exeunt.*]

SCENE [3], *the* GENERAL'S *Quarters.*

[*Enter the* GENERAL *and* M'DONALD.]

GENERAL: *Here* have I intimation from the foe,
That still they deem the spy we have condemn'd,
Merely a captive; by the laws of arms
From death protected; and retaliation,
As they term it, threaten, if we our purpose hold.
Bland is the victim they have singled out,
Hoping his threaten'd death will André save.

M'DONALD: If I were Bland I boldly might advise
My General how to act. Free, and in safety,
I will now suppose my counsel needless.

[*Enter an* AMERICAN OFFICER.]

OFFICER: Another flag hath from the foe arriv'd,
And craves admittance.

GENERAL: Conduct it hither.   [*Exit* OFFICER.]
Let us, unwearied hear, unbias'd judge,
Whate'er against our martial court's decision,
Our enemies can bring.

[*Enter* BRITISH OFFICER, *conducted by the* AMERICAN OFFICER.]

GENERAL: You are welcome, sir.
What further says Sir Henry?[14]

BRITISH OFFICER: This from him.
He calls on you to think what weighty woes
You now are busy bringing on your country.

He bids me say, that, if your sentence reach
The prisoner's life (prisoner of arms he deems him,
And no spy), on him alone it falls not.
He bids me loud proclaim it, and declare,
If this brave officer, by cruel mockery
Of war's stern law, and justice's feign'd pretence,
Be murder'd; the sequel of our strife, bloody,
Unsparing and remorseless, *you* will make.
Think of the many captives in our power.
Already one is mark'd; for André mark'd;—
And when his death, unparallel'd in war,
The signal gives, then Colonel Bland must die.

GENERAL: 'Tis well, sir; bear this message in return.
Sir Henry Clinton knows the laws of arms:
He is a soldier, and, I think, a brave one.
The prisoners he retains he must account for.
Perhaps the reckoning's near. I, likewise, am
A soldier; entrusted by my country.
What I shall judge most for that country's good,
That shall I do. When doubtful, I consult
My country's friends; never her enemies.
In André's case there are no doubts: 'tis clear:
Sir Henry Clinton knows it.

BRITISH OFFICER: Weigh consequences.

GENERAL: In strict regard to consequence I act;
And much should doubt to call that action right,
However specious, whose apparent end
Was misery to man. That brave officer
Whose death you threaten, for himself drew not
His sword—his country's wrongs arous'd his mind;
Her good alone his aim; and if his fall
Can further fire that country to resistance,
He will, with smiles, yield up his glorious life,
And count his death a gain; and tho' Columbians
Will lament his fall, they will lament in blood. [GENERAL *walks up
    the stage.*]

M'DONALD: Hear this! hear this, mankind!

BRITISH OFFICER: Thus am I answered?

    [*Enter a* SERGEANT *with a letter.*]

SERGEANT: Express from Colonel Bland. [*Delivers it and exit.*]

GENERAL: With your permission. [*Opens it.*]

BRITISH OFFICER: Your pleasure, sir. It may my mission further.

M'DONALD: O, Bland! my countryman, surely I know thee!

GENERAL: 'Tis short: I will put form aside, and read it. [*Reads.*] "Excuse me, my Commander, for having a moment doubted your virtue: but you love me. If you waver, let this confirm you. My wife and children, to you and my country. Do *your* duty." Report this to your General.

BRITISH OFFICER: I shall, sir. [*Bows, and exit with* AMERICAN OFFICER.]

GENERAL: O, Bland! my countryman! [*Exit with emotion.*]

M'DONALD: Triumph of virtue!
Like him and thee, still be Americans.
Then, tho' all-powerful Europe league against us,
And pour in arms her legions on our shores;
Who is so dull would doubt their shameful flight?
Who doubt our safety, and our glorious triumph?

SCENE [4], *the Prison.*

[*Enter* BLAND.]

BLAND: Lingering, I come to crush the bud of hope
My breath has, flattering, to existence warm'd.
Hard is the task to friendship! hard to say,
To the lov'd object there remains no hope,
No consolation for thee; thou *must* die;
The worst of deaths; no circumstance abated.

[*Enter* ANDRÉ *in his uniform, and dress'd.*]

ANDRÉ: Is there that state on earth which friendship cannot cheer?

BLAND: Little *I* bring to cheer thee, André.

ANDRÉ: I understand. 'Tis well. 'Twill soon be past.
Yet, 'twas not much I ask'd. A soldier's death.
A trifling change of form.

BLAND: Of that I spoke not.
By vehemence of passion hurried on,
I pleaded for thy precious life alone;
The which denied, my indignation barr'd

All further parley. But strong solicitation
Now is urg'd to gain the wish'd-for favor.

ANDRÉ: What is 't o'clock?

BLAND: 'Tis past the stroke of nine.

ANDRÉ: Why, then 'tis almost o'er. But to be hung—
Is there no way to escape that infamy?
What then *is* infamy?—no matter—no matter.

BLAND: Our General hath received another flag.

ANDRÉ: Soliciting for me?

BLAND: On thy behalf.

ANDRÉ: I have been ever favor'd.

BLAND: Threat'nings, now;
No more solicitations. Harsh, indeed,
The import of the message: harsh, indeed.

ANDRÉ: I am sorry for it. Would that I were dead,
And all was well with those I leave behind.

BLAND: Such a threat! Is it not enough, just heaven,
That I must lose this man? Yet there was left
One for my soul to rest on. But, to know
That the same blow deprives them both of life—

ANDRÉ: What mean'st thou, Bland? Surely my General
Threats not retaliation. In vengeance,
Dooms not some better man to die for me?

BLAND: The best of men.

ANDRÉ: Thou hast a father, captive—
I dare not ask—

BLAND: That father dies for thee.

ANDRÉ: Gracious heaven! how woes are heap'd upon me!
What! cannot one, so trifling in life's scene,
Fall, without drawing such a ponderous ruin?
Leave me, my friend, awhile—I yet have life—
A little space of life—let me exert it
To prevent injustice:—From death to save
Thy father, thee to save from utter desolation.

BLAND: What mean'st thou, André?

ANDRÉ: Seek thou the messenger
Who brought this threat. I will my last entreaty
Send by him. My General, sure, will grant it.

BLAND: To the last thyself!

ANDRÉ: If, at this moment,
When the pangs of death already touch me,

Firmly my mind against injustice strives,
And the last impulse to my vital powers
Is given by anxious wishes to redeem
My fellowmen from pain; surely my end,
Howe'er accomplish'd, is *not* infamous.   [*Exit.*]

END OF ACT III

ACT IV

SCENE [1], *the Encampment.*

[*Enter* M'DONALD *and* BLAND.]

BLAND: It doth in truth appear, that as a—spy—
    Detested word!—brave André must be view'd.
    His sentence he confesses strictly just.
    Yet sure a deed of mercy, from *thy* hand,
    Could never lead to ill. By such an act,
    The stern and blood-stain'd brow of War
    Would be disarm'd of half its gorgon horrors;
    More humanized customs be induced;
    And all the race of civilized man
    Be blest in the example. Be it thy suit:
    'Twill well become thy character and station.
M'DONALD: Trust me, young friend, I am alone the judge
    Of what becomes my character and station:
    And having judg'd that this young Briton's death,
    Even 'though attended by thy father's murder,
    Is necessary, in these times accurs'd,
    When every thought of man is ting'd with blood,
    I will not stir my finger to redeem them.
    Nay, much I wonder, Bland, having so oft
    The reasons for this necessary rigour
    Enforced upon thee, thou wilt still persist
    In vain solicitations. Imitate
    Thy father!
BLAND: My father knew not André.
    I know his value; owe to him my life;

And, gratitude, that first, that best of virtues,—
Without the which man sinks beneath the brute,—
Binds me in ties indissoluble to him.
M'DONALD: That man-created virtue blinds thy reason.
Man owes to man all love; when exercised,
He does no more than duty. Gratitude,
That selfish rule of action, which commands
That we our preference make of men,
Not for their worth, but that they did *us* service,
Misleading reason, casting in the way
Of justice stumbling blocks, cannot be virtue.
BLAND: Detested sophistry!—'Twas André sav'd me!
M'DONALD: He sav'd thy life, and thou art grateful for it.
How self intrudes, delusive, on man's thoughts!
He sav'd thy life, yet strove to damn thy country;
Doom'd millions to the haughty Briton's yoke;
The best, and foremost in the cause of virtue,
To death, by sword, by prison, or the halter:
His sacrifice now stands the only bar
Between the wanton cruelties of war,
And our much-suffering soldiers: yet, when weigh'd
With gratitude, for that he sav'd *thy* life,
These things prove gossamer, and balance air:—
Perversion monstrous of man's moral sense!
BLAND: Rather perversion monstrous of all good,
Is thy accurs'd, detestable opinion.
Cold-blooded reasoners, such as thee, would blast
All warm affection; asunder sever
Every social tie of humanized man.
Curst be thy sophisms! cunningly contriv'd
The callous coldness of thy heart to cover,
And screen thee from the brave man's detestation.
M'DONALD: Boy, boy!
BLAND: Thou knowest that André's not a spy.
M'DONALD: I know him one. Thou hast acknowledg'd it.
BLAND: Thou liest!
M'DONALD: Shame on thy ruffian tongue! how passion
Mars thee! I pity thee! Thou canst not harm,
By words intemperate, a virtuous man.
I pity thee! for passion sometimes sways
My older frame, through former uncheck'd habit:

But when I see the havoc which it makes
In others, I can shun the snare accurst,
And nothing feel but pity.

BLAND [*indignantly*]:   Pity me! [*Approaches him, and speaks in
an under voice.*]
    Thou canst be cool, yet, trust me, *passion* sways thee.
    Fear does not *warm* the blood, yet 't is a *passion*.
    Hast thou no feeling? I have call'd thee liar!

M'DONALD: If thou could'st make me one, I then might grieve.

BLAND: Thy coolness goes to freezing: thou'rt a coward.

M'DONALD: Thou knowest thou tell'st a falsehood.

BLAND: Thou shalt know
    None with impunity speaks thus of me.
    That to rouse thy courage. [*Touches him gently, with his open
    hand, in crossing him.* M'DONALD *looks at him unmoved.*] Dost
    thou not yet feel?

M'DONALD: For *thee* I feel. And tho' another's acts
    Cast no dishonor on the worthy man,
    I still feel for thy father. Yet, remember,
    I may not, haply, ever be thus guarded;
    I may not always the distinction make,
    However just, between the blow intended
    To provoke, and one that's meant to injure.

BLAND: Hast thou no sense of honor?

M'DONALD: Truly, yes:
    For I am honor's votary. Honor, with me,
    Is worth: 'tis truth; 'tis virtue; 'tis a thing,
    So high pre-eminent, that a boy's breath,
    Or brute's, or madman's blow, can never reach it.
    My honor is so much, so truly mine,
    That none hath power to wound it, save myself.

BLAND: I will proclaim thee through the camp a coward.

M'DONALD: Think better of it! Proclaim not thine own shame.

BLAND: I'll brand thee—Damnation!   [*Exit.*]

M'DONALD: O, passion, passion!
    A man who values fame, far more than life;
    A brave young man; in many things a good;
    Utters vile falsehood; adds injury to insult;
    Striving with blood to seal such foul injustice;
    And all from impulse of unbridled feeling.—[*Pause.*]
    Here comes the mother of this headstrong boy,

Severely rack'd—What shall allay her torture?
For common consolation, *here*, is insult.

[*Enter* MRS. BLAND *and* CHILDREN.]

MRS. BLAND: O, my good friend!
M'DONALD [*taking her hand*]:   I know thy cause of sorrow.
    Art thou now from our Commander?
MRS. BLAND [*drying her tears, and assuming dignity*]: I am.
    But vain is my entreaty. All unmov'd
    He hears my words, he sees my desperate sorrow.
    Fain would I blame his conduct—but I cannot.
    Strictly examin'd, with intent to mark
    The error which so fatal proves to *me*,
    My scrutiny but ends in admiration.
    Thus when the prophet from the Hills of Moab,[15]
    Look'd down upon the chosen race of heaven,
    With fell intent to curse; ere yet he spake,
    Truth all resistless, emanation bright
    From great Adonai, fill'd his froward mind,
    And chang'd the curses of his heart to blessings.
M'DONALD: Thou payest high praise to virtue. Whither now?—
MRS. BLAND: I still must hover round this spot until
    My doom is known.
M'DONALD: Then to my quarters, lady,
    There shall my mate give comfort and refreshment:
    One of your sex can best your sorrows soothe.   [*Exeunt.*]

SCENE [2], *the Prison.*

[*Enter* BLAND.]

BLAND: Where'er I look cold desolation meets me.
    My father—André—and self-condemnation!
    Why seek I André now? Am *I* a man,
    To soothe the sorrows of a suffering friend?
    The weather-cock of passion! fool inebriate!
    Who could with ruffian hand strive to provoke
    Hoar wisdom to intemperance! who could lie!
    Aye, swagger, lie, and brag!—Liar! Damnation!!
    O, let me steal away and hide my head,

Nor view a man, condemn'd to harshest death,
Whose words and actions, when by mine compar'd,
Show white as innocence, and bright as truth.
I now would shun him; but that his shorten'd
Thread of life, gives me no line to play with.
He comes, with smiles, and all the air of triumph;
While *I* am sinking with remorse and shame:
Yet *he* is doom'd to death, and *I* am free!

[*Enter* ANDRÉ.]

ANDRÉ: Welcome, my Bland! Cheerly, a welcome hither!
I feel assurance that my last request
Will not be slighted. Safely thy father
Shall return to thee. [*Holding out a paper.*] See what employment
For a dying man. Take thou these verses;
And, after my decease, send them to her
Whose name is woven in them; whose image
Hath control'd my destiny. Such tokens
Are rather out of date. Fashions
There are in love as in all else; they change
As variously. A gallant Knight, erewhile,
Of Coeur de Lion's[16] day, would, dying, send
His heart home to its mistress; degenerate
Soldier I, send but some blotted paper.
BLAND: If 'twould not damp thy present cheerfulness,
I would require the meaning of thy words.
I ne'er till now did hear of André's mistress.
ANDRÉ: Mine is a story of that common kind,
So often told, with scanty variation,
That the pall'd ear loaths the repeated tale.
Each young romancer chooses for his theme
The woes of youthful hearts, by the cold hand
Of frosty Age, arm'd with parental power,
Asunder torn. But I long since have ceas'd
To mourn; well satisfied that she I love,
Happy in holy union with another,
Shares not my wayward fortunes. Nor would I
Now these tokens send, remembrance to awaken,
But that I know her happy: and the happy
Can think on misery and share it not.

BLAND [*agitated*]: Some one approaches.

ANDRÉ: Why, 'tis near the time.
   But tell me, Bland, say—is the manner chang'd?

BLAND: I hope it—but I yet have no assurance.

ANDRÉ: Well, well!

HONORA[17] [*without*]: I must see him.

ANDRÉ: Whose voice was that?
   My senses!—Do I dream—? [*Leans on* BLAND.]

   [*Enter* HONORA.]

HONORA: Where is he?

ANDRÉ: 'Tis she!! [*Starts from*
   BLAND *and advances towards* HONORA; *she rushes into his arms.*]

HONORA: It is enough! He lives, and *I* shall save him. [*She faints in
   the arms of* ANDRÉ.]

ANDRÉ: She sinks—assist me, Bland! O, save her, save her! [*Places her
   in a chair, and looks tenderly on her.*]
   Yet, why should she awake from that sweet sleep!
   Why should she open her eyes—[*wildly*]—to see me hung!
   What does she here? Stand off—[*tenderly*]—and let her die.
   How pale she looks! how worn that tender frame!—
   She has known sorrow! Who could injure her?

BLAND: She revives—André—soft, bend her forward. [ANDRÉ *kneels
   and supports her.*]

HONORA: André—!

ANDRÉ: Lov'd excellence!

HONORA: Yes, it is André! [*Rises and looks at him.*]
   No more deceived by visionary forms,
   By him supported—[*Leans on him.*]

ANDRÉ: Why is this?
   Thou dost look pale, Honora—sick and wan—
   Languid thy fainting limbs—

HONORA: All will be well.
   But was it kind to leave me as thou did'st—?
   So rashly to desert thy vow-link'd wife?—

ANDRÉ: When made another's both by vows and laws—

HONORA [*quitting his support*]: What meanest thou?

ANDRÉ: Did'st thou not marry him?

HONORA: Marry!

ANDRÉ: Did'st thou not give thy hand away
  From me?
HONORA: O, never, never!
ANDRÉ: Not married?
HONORA: To none but thee, and but in will to thee.
ANDRÉ: O, blind, blind wretch!—Thy father told me——
HONORA: Thou wast deceived. They hurried me away,
  Spreading false rumours to remove thy love—
  [*Tenderly.*] Thou didst too soon believe them.
ANDRÉ: Thy father—
  How could I but believe Honora's father?
  And he did tell me so. I reverenced age,
  Yet knew, age was not virtue. I believed
  His snowy locks, and yet they did deceive me!
  I have destroy'd myself and thee!—Alas!
  Ill-fated maid! why didst thou not forget me?
  Hast thou rude seas and hostile shores explor'd
  For this? To see my death? Witness my shame?
HONORA: I come to bless thee, André; and shall do it.
  I bear such offers from thy kind Commander,
  As must prevail to save thee. Thus the daughter
  May repair the ills her cruel sire inflicted.
  My father, dying, gave me cause to think
  That arts were us'd to drive thee from thy home;
  But what those arts I knew not. An heiress left,
  Of years mature, with power and liberty,
  I straight resolv'd to seek thee o'er the seas.
  A long-known friend who came to join her lord,
  Yielded protection and lov'd fellowship.—
  Indeed, when I did hear of thy estate
  It almost kill'd me:—I was weak before—
ANDRÉ: 'Tis I have murder'd thee!—
HONORA: All shall be well.
  Thy General heard of me, and instant form'd
  The plan of this my visit. I am strong,
  Compar'd with what I was. Hope strengthens me:
  Nay, even solicitude supports me now:
  And when thou shalt be safe, *thou* wilt support me.
ANDRÉ: Support thee!—O heaven! What!—And *must* I die?
  Die!—and leave her *thus*—suffering—unprotected!—

[*Enter* MELVILLE *and* GUARD.]

MELVILLE: I am sorry that my duty should require
   Service, at which my heart revolts; but, Sir,
   Our soldiers wait in arms. All is prepar'd—
HONORA: To death!—Impossible! Has my delay,
   Then, murder'd him?—A momentary respite—
MELVILLE: Lady, I have no power.
BLAND: Melville, my friend,
   This lady bears dispatches of high import,
   Touching this business:—should they arrive too late——
HONORA: For pity's sake, and heaven's, conduct me to him;
   And wait the issue of our conference.
   Oh, 'twould be murder of the blackest dye,
   Sin execrable, not to break thy orders—
   Inhuman, thou art not.
MELVILLE: Lady, thou say'st true;
   For rather would I lose my rank in arms,
   And stand cashier'd for lack of discipline,
   Than, gain 'mongst military men all praise,
   Wanting the touch of sweet humanity.
HONORA: Thou grantest my request?
MELVILLE: Lady, I do.
   Retire! [SOLDIERS *go out.*]
BLAND: I know not what excuse, to martial men,
   Thou can'st advance for this; but to thy heart
   Thou wilt need none, good Melville.
ANDRÉ: O, Honora!
HONORA: Cheer up, I feel assur'd. Hope wings my flight,
   To bring thee tidings of much joy to come.
            [*Exit* HONORA, *with* BLAND *and* MELVILLE.]
ANDRÉ: Eternal blessings on thee, matchless woman!—
   If death now comes, he finds the veriest coward
   That e'er he dealt withal. I cannot think
   Of dying. Void of fortitude, each thought
   Clings to the world—the world that holds Honora!   [*Exit.*]

END OF ACT IV

ACT V

SCENE [1], *the Encampment.*

[*Enter* BLAND.]

BLAND: Suspense—uncertainty—man's bane and solace!
  How racking now to me! My mother comes.
  Forgive me, O, my father! if in this war,
  This wasting conflict of my wildering passions,
  Memory of thee holds here a second place!
  M'Donald comes with her. I would not meet him:
  Yet I *will* do it. Summon up some courage—
  Confess my fault, and gain, if not *his* love,
  At least the approbation of *my* judgment.

[*Enter* MRS. BLAND *and* CHILDREN, *with* M'DONALD.]

BLAND: Say, Madam, is there no change of counsel,
  Or new determination?
MRS. BLAND: *Nought new,* my son.
  The tale of misery is told unheard.
  The widow's and the orphan's sighs
  Fly up, unnoted by the eye of man,
  And mingle, undistinguish'd, with the winds.
  My friend [*to* M'DONALD], attend thy duties. I must away.
2ND CHILD: You need not cry, Mama, the General will do it, I am
  sure; for I saw him cry. He turn'd away his head from you, but I
  saw it.
MRS. BLAND: Poor thing! come let us home and weep. Alas!
  I can no more, for war hath made men rocks.
                        [*Exeunt* MRS. BLAND *and* CHILDREN.]
BLAND: Colonel, I used thee ill this morning.
M'DONALD: No!
  Thyself thou used'st most vilely, I remember.
BLAND: Myself sustained the injury, most true;
  But the intent of what I said and did
  Was ill to thee alone: I'm sorry for it.
  Seest thou these blushes? They proceed from warmth
  As honest as the heart of man e'er felt;—
  But not with shame unmingled, while I force
  This tongue, debased, to own, it slander'd thee,

And utter'd—I could curse it—utter'd falsehood.
Howe'er misled by passion, still my mind
Retains that sense of honest rectitude
Which makes the memory of an evil deed
A troublesome companion. I was wrong.

M'DONALD: Why, now this glads me; for thou *now* art right.
O, may thy tongue, henceforward, utter nought
But Truth's sweet precepts, in fair Virtue's cause!
Give me thy hand. [*Takes his hand.*] Ne'er may it grasp a sword
But in defense of justice.

BLAND: Yet, erewhile,
A few short hours scarce past, when this vile hand
Attempted on *thee* insult; and was raised
Against thy honor; ready to be raised
Against thy life. If this my deep remorse—

M'DONALD: No more, no more. 'Tis past. Remember it
But as thou would'st the action of another,
By thy enlighten'd judgment much condemn'd;
And serving as a beacon in the storms
Thy passions yet may raise. Remorse is vice:
Guard thee against its influence debasing.
Say to thyself, "I *am* not what I *was;*
I am not *now* the instrument of vice;
I'm changed; I am a man; Virtue's firm friend;
Sever'd for ever from my former self;
No link, but in remembrance salutary."

BLAND: How[18] all men tower above me!

M'DONALD: Nay, not so.
Above what once thou wast, some few do rise;
None above what thou art.

BLAND: It shall be so.

M'DONALD: It is so.

BLAND: Then to prove it.
For I must yet a trial undergo,
That will require a consciousness of virtue.   [*Exit.*]

M'DONALD: O, what a temper doth in man reside!
How capable of yet unthought perfection!   [*Exit.*]

SCENE [2], *the* GENERAL'S *Quarters.*

[*Enter* GENERAL *and* SEWARD.]

GENERAL: Ask her, my friend, to send by thee her pacquets.

[*Exit* SEWARD.]

O, what keen struggles must I undergo!
Unbless'd estate! to have the power to pardon;
The court's stern sentence to remit;—give life;—
Feel the strong wish to use such blessed power;
Yet know that circumstances strong as fate
Forbid to obey the impulse. O, I feel
That man should never shed the blood of man.

[*Enter* SEWARD.]

SEWARD: Nought can the lovely suitor satisfy,
But conference with thee, and much I fear
Refusal would cause madness.
GENERAL: Yet to admit,
To hear, be tortur'd, and refuse at last—
SEWARD: Sure never man such spectacle of sorrow
Saw before. Motionless the rough-hewn soldiers
Silent view her, or walk aside and weep.
GENERAL [*after a pause*]: Admit her. [SEWARD *goes out.*] O, for the art,
the precious art,
To reconcile the sufferer to his sorrows!

[HONORA *rushes in, and throws herself wildly on her knees before him; he endeavors to raise her.*]

HONORA: Nay, nay, here is my place, or here, or lower,
Unless thou grant'st his life. All forms away!
Thus will I clasp thy knees, thus cling to thee.—
I am his wife—'tis I have ruin'd him—
O save him! Give him to me! Let us cross
The mighty seas, far, far—ne'er to offend again.—[*The* GENERAL *turns away, and hides his eyes with his hand.*[19]]

[*Enter* SEWARD *and an* OFFICER.]

GENERAL: Seward, support her—my heart is torn in twain.

[HONORA, *as if exhausted, suffers herself to be raised, and leans on* SEWARD.]

OFFICER: This moment, sir, a messenger arrived
   With well confirm'd and mournful information,
   That gallant Hastings, by the lawless scouts
   Of Britain taken, after cruel mockery
   With show of trial and condemnation,
   On the next tree was hung.
HONORA [*wildly*]:   O, it is false!
GENERAL: Why, why, my country, did I hesitate?   [*Exit.*]

   [HONORA *sinks, faints, and is borne off by* SEWARD *and* OFFICER.]

SCENE [3], *the Prison.*

   [ANDRÉ *meeting* BLAND.]

ANDRÉ: How speeds Honora? [*Pause.*] Art thou silent, Bland?
   Why, then I know my task. The mind of man,
   If not by vice debas'd, debilitated,
   Or by disease of body quite unton'd,
   Hath o'er its thoughts a power—energy divine!
   Of fortitude the source and every virtue—
   A godlike power, which e'en o'er circumstance
   Its sov'reignty exerts. Now, from my thoughts,
   Honora! Yet she is left alone—expos'd—
BLAND: O, André, spurn me, strike me to the earth;
   For what a wretch am I, in André's mind,
   That he can think he leaves his love alone,
   And I retaining life!
ANDRÉ: Forgive me, Bland,
   My thoughts glanc'd not on thee. Imagination
   Pictur'd only, then, her orphan state, helpless;
   Her weak and grief-exhausted frame. Alas!
   This blow will kill her!
BLAND [*kneeling*]:   Here do I myself
   Devote, my fortune consecrate, to thee,
   To thy remembrance, and Honora's service!—
ANDRÉ: Enough! Let me not see her more—nor think of her—
   Farewell! farewell, sweet image! Now for death.
BLAND: Yet that you should'st the felon's fate fulfill—
   Damnation! my blood boils. Indignation

Makes the current of my life course wildly
Through its round, and maddens each emotion.

ANDRÉ: Come, come, it matters not.

BLAND: I do remember,
When a boy, at school, in our allotted tasks,
We, by our puny acts, strove to portray
The giant thoughts of Otway. I was Pierre.[20]—
O, thou art Pierre's reality! a soldier,
On whose manly brow sits fortitude enamour'd!
A Mars, abhorring vice, yet doom'd to die
A death of infamy; thy corse expos'd
To vulgar gaze—halter'd—distorted—Oh!! [*Pauses, and then adds
in a low, hollow voice.*]
Pierre had a friend to save him from such shame—
And so hast thou.

ANDRÉ: No more, as thou dost love me.

BLAND: I have a sword, and arm, that never fail'd me.

ANDRÉ: Bland, such an act would justly thee involve,
And leave that helpless one thou sworest to guard,
Expos'd to every ill. O! think not of it.

BLAND: If thou wilt not my aid—take it thyself. [*Draws and offers his
sword.*]

ANDRÉ: No, men will say that cowardice did urge me.
In my mind's weakness, I did wish to shun
That mode of death which error represented
Infamous: Now let me rise superior;
And with a fortitude too true to start
From mere appearances, show your country,
That she, in me, destroys a man who might
Have liv'd to virtue.

BLAND [*sheathing his sword*]: I will not think more of it;
I was again the sport of erring passion.

ANDRÉ: Go thou and guide Honora from this spot.

HONORA [*entering*]: Who shall oppose his wife? I will have way!
They, cruel, would have kept me from thee, André.
Say, am I not thy wife? *Wilt* thou deny me?
Indeed I am not dress'd in bridal trim.
But I have travell'd far:—rough was the road—
Rugged and rough—that must excuse my dress.
[*Seeing* ANDRÉ'S *distress.*] Thou art not glad to see me.

ANDRÉ: Break my heart!
HONORA: Indeed, I feel not much in spirits. I wept but now.

[*Enter* MELVILLE *and* GUARD.]

BLAND [*to* MELVILLE]: Say nothing.
ANDRÉ: I am ready.
HONORA [*seeing the* GUARD]:   Are *they* here?
  Here again!—The *same*—but they shall not harm me—
  I am with *thee*, my André—I am safe—
  And *thou* are safe with me. Is it not so? [*Clinging to him.*]

[*Enter* MRS. BLAND]

MRS. BLAND: Where is this lovely victim?
BLAND: Thanks, my mother.
MRS. BLAND: M'Donald sent me hither. My woes are past.
  Thy father, by the foe releas'd, already
  Is in safety. This be forgotten now;
  And every thought be turn'd to this sad scene.
  Come, lady, home with me.
HONORA: Go home with thee?
  Art thou my André's mother? We will home
  And rest, for thou art weary—very weary. [*Leans on* MRS. BLAND.]

  [ANDRÉ *retires to the* GUARD, *and goes off with them, looking on
  her to the last, and with an action of extreme tenderness takes
  leave of her.* MELVILLE *and* BLAND *accompany him.*]

HONORA: Now we will go. Come, love! Where is he?
  All gone!—I do remember—I awake—
  They have him. Murder! Help! O, save him! save him!

  [HONORA *attempts to follow, but falls.* MRS. BLAND *kneels to
  assist her. Scene closes.*]

SCENE [4], *the Encampment. Procession to the execution of* ANDRÉ.

[*First enter Pioneers—Detachment of Infantry—Military Band of Music—Infantry. The Music having passed off, enter* ANDRÉ *between* MEL-
VILLE *and* AMERICAN OFFICER; *they sorrowful, he cheerfully conversing
as he passes over the stage.*]

ANDRÉ: It may in me be merely prejudice,
  The effect of young-opinion deep engraved

Upon the tender mind by care parental;
But I must think your country has mistook
Her interests. Believe me, but for this I should
Not willingly have drawn a sword against her. [*They bow their
    heads in silence.*]
Opinion must, nay ought, to sway our actions;
Therefore—

[*Having crossed the stage, he goes out as still conversing with
them. Another detachment of Infantry, with muffled and craped
drums, close the procession: as soon as they are off—*]

[*Scene draws and discovers the distant view of the Encampment.*]

[*Procession enters in the same order as before, proceeds up the
stage, and goes off on the opposite side.*]

[*Enter* M'DONALD, *leading* BLAND, *who looks wildly back.*]

BLAND: I dare not *thee* resist. Yet why, O, why
    Thus hurry me away—?—
M'DONALD: Would'st thou behold——
BLAND: Oh, name it not!
M'DONALD: Or would'st thou, by thy looks
    And gestures wild, o'erthrow that manly calmness
    Which, or assum'd or felt, so well becomes thy friend?
BLAND: What means that cannon's sound?
M'DONALD [*after a pause*]:   Signal of death
    Appointed. André, thy friend, is now no more!
BLAND: Farewell, farewell, brave spirit! O, let my countrymen,
    Henceforward, when the cruelties of war
    Arise in their remembrance; when their ready
    Speech would pour forth torrents in their foe's dispraise,
    Think on this act accurst, and lock complaint in silence. [BLAND
        throws himself on the earth.]
M'DONALD: Such are the dictates of the heart, not head.
    O, may the children of Columbia still
    Be taught by every teacher of mankind,
    Each circumstance of calculative gain,
    Or wounded pride, which prompted our oppressors;
    May every child be taught to lisp the tale:
    And may, in times to come, no foreign force,
    No European influence, tempt to misstate,

Or awe the tongue of eloquence to silence.
Still may our children's children deep abhor
The motives, doubly deep detest the actors;
Ever remembering, that the race who plan'd,
Who acquiesced, or did the deeds abhor'd,
Has pass'd from off the earth; and, in its stead,
Stand men who challenge love or detestation
But from their proper, individual deeds.
Never let memory of the sire's offence
Descend upon the son.

CURTAIN DROPS

THE INDIAN PRINCESS *(1808)*

JAMES NELSON BARKER

As one of the early theatrical centers in English America, Philadelphia nurtured several incipient playwrights. One, James Nelson Barker (1784–1858), the son of a mayor of that city, is the most important of the first generation to come to prominence after 1800. Over his career, Barker wrote ten plays or adaptations, as well as dramatic criticism. Like most playwrights of his time, he had other jobs, many of them political, including mayor of Philadelphia and controller of the United States Treasury in the Van Buren administration. In other words, as a playwright, Barker was an amateur. Nevertheless, he, like many American followers of Shakespeare, understood that history made for good theater and mined not only European history but that of his own country.

Barker's first staged play (he had written drafts of at least three others, all lost or destroyed, before this), *Tears and Smiles*, was a social comedy acted at the Chestnut Street theater in Philadelphia, March 4, 1807. With a crudely drawn stage Yankee and the by-now familiar social-class contrasts already shaped by Tyler, it was the sort of derivative play that one finds throughout nineteenth-century drama. Modern politics informed his next effort, *The Embargo; or, What News?* (1808), but with his third play, *The Indian Princess*, Barker had found his vocabulary. Two other important plays, *Marmion; or, The Battle of Flodden Field* (1812), and *Superstition* (performed in 1824, but probably written well before this), also turn to historical materials. While the former borrows from Walter Scott and Raphael Holinshed, in the latter, Barker explores the problem of witchcraft persecution in New England and the extremism of popular prejudice. What Walter J. Meserve considers his best-written play, *Superstition*, was also Barker's last.

If *Superstition* is a moderately well crafted drama and meant to be serious, then *The Indian Princess* is something else again, full of subplots, songs, and sexual humor. Written first as a play, then, at the urging of composer John Bray, as a light opera or "melo-drame," *The Indian Princess* is the first *stage* drama that survives in its entirety to feature Native American characters. As such, it is also the first representation on stage of Pocahontas, at least as she comes to us through Barker's chief source, Captain John Smith's *Generall Historie of Vir-*

ginia (1624). While *The Indian Princess* never achieved the success of *The Contrast*, it did move from Philadelphia, where the initial run was cut short by the unpopularity of one of the actors, to New York, Charleston, Richmond, and Baltimore. It was also staged in London in 1820, making the play the first by an American to premiere in the United States before being performed in an English theater. From the perspective of dramatic history, *The Indian Princess* is an important play.

Nevertheless, few scholars have looked very seriously at it; no doubt its very loose construction and its heavy borrowing from Shakespearean comedies have prevented readers from seeking too far. However, the play has many suggestive threads that interweave the fabric of romantic love plots and adulterated history. *The Indian Princess* presents its story in ideologically shaped images of the history of white settlement, white-red relations, and the future of the American state in what is intended as a pleasing, popular package. Drawing on a rhetoric of imperial justification—or, as Francis Jennings calls it, "the cant of conquest"—the play affirms for its audience the rightness of white conquest and the transplantation theme whereby America inherits the greatness of Europe. Captain Smith stands above the fray, asserting white privilege but at the same time looking for alliances with Indians who accept European superiority. While such characters as Robin and Nima, Rolfe and Pocahontas, and others involved in love plots worry about their lovers, disguise their bodies or intentions, and otherwise engage in unbusiness-like behavior, Smith calls the mission to its purpose, speaks the prophesy of coming glory, and emerges as the play's ideological hero. Barker's play serves as an early affirmation of Smith's original text and reads it romantically as a work of historical justification.

We should not confuse *The Indian Princess*, however, with what Smith's book actually says. *The Generall Historie*, for all its propaganda value as a vehicle for Smith's possible return to the New World, does not dabble in frivolity. There are no women to speak of in Smith's chapters on Virginia, with the exception of a "masque" of Native women—described in the play by Walter as a way of teasing Alice—and Pocahontas. Even for the latter, there is little in the history that suggests a romantic reading of the famous scene in which Smith is saved by Pocahontas. As Robert S. Tilton reminds us, Barker's play belongs to another history, that of the romanticizing and sexualizing of Pocahontas that converts her from the child of Smith's history into the adult—if naïve and sexually available—woman in the nineteenth- and twentieth-century interpretations. The Walt Disney animated feature is only one in a long series of interpretations of the Pocahontas legend, which has a beginning point with *The Indian Princess*.

Although Barker violates history with impunity, adding white women, an Irishman, and flamingos to Smith's landscape, we may find his interpretation of Native Americans to be the most troublesome. In Smith's *Generall Historie*, the supreme chief, Powhatan, is a wily and powerful figure, skilled in rhetoric and ability to make war; he rarely is seen in weakness, even when Smith bests him. In the play, however, Powhatan is a sentimentalized father, a precursor of the loving but inept Rip Van Winkle of Joseph Jefferson's play more than half a century after Barker. Barker's Powhatan is easily misled by a shaman, Grimosco (who does not appear in Smith's text), and must go to war against another tribe, the Susquehannocks, whom Smith portrays as large of stature but friendly, and who live outside Powhatan's territory. The villain, a precursor of James Fenimore Cooper's Magua, is Miami, a character who does not appear in Smith but whose name evokes a tribe that had engineered a massacre of American soldiers in 1791. The Susquehannock prince desires Pocahontas and shows off his value by proclaiming his prowess in the hunt. Pocahontas, however, who in a moment of pity has forsworn hunting, prefers the European love style; indeed, she has to learn what love is through Rolfe. Once having tasted the possibility of romantic-erotic attachment, Pocahontas can never return without loss and regret to the "savage" ways of her Indian suitor. The play ends, then, with a justification of white assimilation and obliteration of Native characteristics. The only good Indian, the play announces, is a whitened, acculturated one. The savage must die or retreat before European might or else face the erotic conversion of Native women into love objects and symbols of European possession of the land.

In reading the play, we must remain aware throughout that this is a musical, a genre, as Susan L. Porter describes, that held great interest for American audiences. Almost all performances during this period, whether containing songs or not, were accompanied by music. Much of that music has been lost, but we are fortunate to have John Bray's score available to us. The effect of some of the lyrics is to trivialize characters, particularly the Native warriors. Other lyrics seem incidental to the main action. In the third scene of act 5, Walter sings a song of Smith's exploits among the Turks, described not in *The Generall Historie* but in Smith's autobiography, *The True Travels* (1630). However, we see that Smith is tied to several women in that story, protecting females who have harbored the captain after his ritual defeat of three Turkish warriors and his escape from Turkish captivity. Not only is Pocahontas then part of a long train of such women, but we also are made aware that Smith has been sexual in the past—just not this time with the young Indian woman. Thus, even the songs, as silly as some of them appear, serve a purpose in the formation of an image of Smith's potency and restraint and of the same characteristics in American colonization.

The Indian Princess looks forward to a number of plays that would remain popular on stage for the next half century. Such dramas as Metamora (1829), by John Augustus Stone, the Pocahontas (1830) of George Washington Parke Custis, and Nick of the Woods (1838), by Louisa Medina, would feature Native characters prominently and play to the Eastern audience fascination with Indians. By the end of our period, in John Brougham's spoof of Indian plays, Po-ca-hon-tas (1855), or Dion Boucicault's The Octoroon (1859), the Native once given some nobility in the earlier plays has become a figure of humor or a one-dimensional, one-syllable savage. Barker deserves credit for inaugurating the trend toward representing Native Americans on stage, but deserves blame as well for shaping a tradition that diminished the possibilities of Native subjecthood in the drama. Far from seeing this or the other plays as portraying real Indians, we are better served by taking The Indian Princess as a register of white preconceptions, prejudices, and fears about the people whom American civilization was rapidly displacing.

SELECTED BIBLIOGRAPHY

Barker, James Nelson. "The Drama." Philadelphia Democratic Press, December 18, 1816–February 19, 1817. Eleven articles.
———. Superstition. In American Plays, edited by Allan Gates Halline, 124–51. New York: American Book, 1935. See also Halline's introduction to Barker, 119–23.
Bray, John. The Indian Princess, or, La Belle Savauge . . . The Music. Philadelphia 1808. Facsimile reprint, with text of play, in Earlier American Music, edited by H. Wiley Hitchcock, Vol. 11. New York: Da Capo, 1972.
Crowley, John W. "James Nelson Barker in Perspective." Educational Theatre Journal 24 (1972): 363–69.
Dunlap, William. History of the American Theatre. 2 vols. 1832; London: Bentley, 1833, vol. 2:308–16.
Federal Music Society Opera Company. The Indian Princess sound recording. New World Records NW 232, 1978.
Jennings, Francis. The Invasion of America: Indians, Colonialism, and the Cant of Conquest. Chapel Hill: University of North Carolina Press, 1975.

Jones, Eugene. *Native Americans as Shown on the Stage, 1753–1916*, 50–53. Metuchen, N.J.: Scarecrow, 1988.

Mason, Jeffrey D. "*Metamora* (1829) and the 'Indian' Question." In *Melodrama and the Myth of America*, 23–59. Bloomington: Indiana University Press, 1993. New-historicist treatment of related play.

Meserve, Walter J. *An Emerging Entertainment: The Drama of the American People to 1828*, 177–84, 259–63. Bloomington: Indiana University Press, 1977.

Musser, Paul H. *James Nelson Barker*. Philadelphia: University of Pennsylvania Press, 1929. Includes text of *Tears and Smiles*.

Pearce, Roy Harvey. *The Savages of America: A Study of the Indians and the Idea of Civilization*. Rev. ed., 173–74. Baltimore: Johns Hopkins University Press, 1965.

Porter, Susan L. *With an Air Debonair: Musical Theatre in America, 1785–1815*. Washington, D.C.: Smithsonian Institution Press, 1991. Background.

Richards, Jeffrey H. "Prospero in Virginia: The Example of Captain John Smith." *Theater Enough: American Culture and the Metaphor of the World Stage, 1607–1789*, 85–98. Durham: Duke University Press, 1991. Smith and theater.

Richardson, Gary A. *American Drama from the Colonial Period through World War I: A Critical History*, 60–68. New York: Twayne, 1993.

Sears, Priscilla. *A Pillar of Fire to Follow: American Indian Dramas, 1808–1859*. Bowling Green: Bowling Green University Popular Press, 1982. *IP* discussed throughout.

Smith, John. *The Complete Works of Captain John Smith*, edited Philip Barbour. 3 vols. Chapel Hill: University of North Carolina Press, 1986.

Tilton, Robert S. *Pocahontas: The Evolution of an American Narrative*. New York: Cambridge University Press, 1994. Background and brief mention of *IP*.

Wilmeth, Don B. "Noble or Ruthless Savage? The American Indian on Stage and in the Drama." *Journal of American Drama and Theatre* 1 (Spring 1989): 39–78.

THE

INDIAN PRINCESS

OR,

LA BELLE SAUVAGE.

AN OPERATIC MELO-DRAME.

IN THREE ACTS.

PERFORMED AT THE THEATRES PHILADELPHIA AND
BALTIMORE.

———◆———

BY J.N. BARKER.

———◆———

FIRST ACTED APRIL 6, 1808.

———

PHILADELPHIA.

PRINTED BY T. & G. PALMER,
FOR G. E. BLAKE, NO. 1, SOUTH THIRD-STREET.

———

1808.

PREFACE

While I am proud to acknowledge my grateful sense of those flattering marks of liberal kindness with which my dramatic entrée has been greeted by an indulgent audience, I feel so fully conscious of the very humble merit of this little piece, that perhaps nothing but the peculiar circumstances under which it was acted should have induced me to publish it. In sending it to the press I am perfectly apprized of the probability that it goes only to add one more to the list of those unfortunate children of the American drama, who, in the brief space that lies between their birth and death, are doomed to wander, without house or home, unknown and unregarded, or who, if heeded at all, are only picked up by some critic beadle to receive the usual treatment of vagrants. Indeed, were I disposed to draw comfort from the misfortunes of others, I might make myself happy with the reflection, that however my vagabond might deserve the lash, it would receive no more punishment than those who deserved none at all; for the gentlemen castigators seldom take the pains to distinguish Innocence from Guilt, but most liberally bestow their stripes on all poor wanderers who are unhappily of American parentage. Far, however, from rejoicing at this circumstance, I sincerely deplore it. In all ages, and in every country, even the sturdiest offspring of genius have felt the necessity and received the aid of a protecting hand of favour to support and guide their first trembling and devious footsteps; it is not, therefore, wonderful, that here, where every art is yet but in its infancy, the youthful exertions of dramatic poetry, unaided and unsupported, should fail, and that its imbecile efforts should for ever cease with the failure; that chilled by total neglect, or chid with undeserved severity; depressed by ridicule, starved by envy, and stricken to the earth by malevolence, the poor orphan, heartless and spirit-broken, should pine away a short and sickly life. I am not, I believe, quite coxcomb enough to advance the most distant hint that the child of my brain deserves a better fate; that it may meet with it I might, however, be indulged in hoping, under the profession that the hope proceeds from considerations distinct from either it or myself. Dramatic genius, with genius of every other kind, is assuredly native of our soil, and there wants but the wholesome and kindly breath of favour to invigourate its delicate frame, and bid it rapidly arise from its cradle to blooming maturity. But alas! poor weak ones! what a climate are ye doomed to draw your first breath in! the teeming press has scarcely ceased groaning at your delivery, ere you are suffocated with the stagnant atmosphere of entire apathy, or swept out of existence by the hurricane of unsparing, indiscriminating censure!

Good reader, I begin to suspect that I have held you long enough by the button. Yet, maugre my terror of being tiresome, and in despite of my clear anticipation of the severe puns which will be made in this punning city, on my *childish* preface, I must push my allusion a little further, to deprecate the wrath of the critics, and arouse the sympathies of the ladies. Then, O ye sage censors! ye goody gossips at poetic births! I vehemently importune ye to be convinced, that for my bantling I desire neither rattle nor bells; neither the lullaby of praise, nor the pap of patronage, nor the hobby-horse of honour. 'Tis a plain-palated, home-bred, and I may add independent urchin, who laughs at sugar plums, and from its little heart disdains gilded gingerbread. If you like it—so; if not—why so; yet, without being mischievous, it would fain be amusing; therefore, if its gambols be pleasant, and your gravities permit, laugh; if not, e'en turn aside your heads, and let the wanton youngling laugh by itself. If it speak like a sensible child, prithee, pat its cheek, and say so; but if it be ridiculous when it would be serious, smile, and permit the foolish attempt to pass. But do not, O goody critic, apply the birch, because its unpractised tongue cannot lisp the language of Shakespeare, nor be very much enraged, if you find it has to creep before it can possibly walk.

To your bosoms, ladies, sweet ladies! the little stranger flies with confidence for protection; shield it, I pray you, from the iron rod of rigour, and scold it yourselves, as much as you will, for on *your* smooth and polished brows it can never read wrinkled cruelty; the mild anger of *your* eyes will not blast it like the fierce scowl of the critic; the chidings of *your* voice will be soothing music to it, and it will discover the dimple of kindness in your very frowns. Caresses it does not ask; its modesty would shrink from that it thought it deserved not; but if its faults be infantile, its punishment should be gentle, and from you, dear ladies, correction would be as thrillingly sweet as that the little *Jean Jacques* received from the fair hand of Mademoiselle Lambercier.[1]

THE AUTHOR

ADVERTISEMENT

The principal materials that form this dramatic trifle are extracted from the General History of Virginia, written by Captain Smith,[2] and printed London, folio, 1624; and as close an adherence to historic truth has been preserved as dramatic rules would allow of. The music[3] was furnished by Mr. John Bray, of the New Theatre.

DRAMATIS PERSONAE

EUROPEANS.

DELAWAR
CAPTAIN SMITH
LIEUTENANT ROLFE
PERCY
WALTER
LARRY
ROBIN
TALMAN

GERALDINE
KATE
ALICE

SOLDIERS *and* ADVENTURERS.

VIRGINIANS.

POWHATAN, *king*
NANTAQUAS, *his son*
MIAMI, *a prince*
GRIMOSCO, *a priest*

POCAHONTAS, *the princess*
NIMA, *her attendant*

WARRIORS *and* INDIAN GIRLS.

SCENE, *Virginia.*

THE INDIAN PRINCESS

ACT I

SCENE 1: *Powhatan River;⁴ wild and picturesque. Ships appear. Barges approach the shore, from which land* SMITH, ROLFE, PERCY, WALTER, LARRY, ROBIN, ALICE, &c.

CHORUS.

Jolly comrades, raise the glee,
Chorus it right cheerily;
For the tempest's roar is heard no more,
And gaily we tread the wish'd-for shore:
   Then raise the glee merrily,
   Chorus it cheerily,
For past are the perils of the blust'ring sea.

SMITH: Once more, my bold associates, welcome. Mark
  What cheery aspects look upon our landing:
  The face of Nature dimples o'er with smiles,
  The heav'ns are cloudless, whiles the princely sun,
  As glad to greet us in his fair domain,
  Gives us gay salutation—
LARRY: [*To* WALTER.] By St. Patrick
  His fiery majesty does give warm welcome.
  Arrah! His gracious smiles are melting—
WALTER: Plague!
  He burthens us with favours till we sweat.
SMITH: What think ye, Percy, Rolfe, have we not found
  Sir Walter Raleigh⁵ faithful in his tale?
  Is't not a goodly land? Along the bay,
  How gay and lovely lie its skirting shores,
  Fring'd with the summer's rich embroidery!
PERCY: Believe me, sir, I ne'er beheld that spot
  Where Nature holds more sweet varieties.
SMITH: The gale was kind that blew us hitherward.
  This noble bay were undiscover'd still,
  Had not that storm arose propitious,
  And, like the ever kindly breath of heav'n,

Which sometimes rides upon the tempest's wing,
Driv'n us to happiest destinies, e'en then
When most we fear'd destruction from the blast.

ROLFE: Let our dull, sluggish countrymen at home
Still creep around their little isle of fogs,
Drink its dank vapours, and then hang themselves.
In this free atmosphere and ample range
The bosom can dilate, the pulses play,
And man, erect, can walk a manly round.

ROBIN: [*Aside.*] Ay, and be scalp'd and roasted by the Indians.

SMITH: Now, gallant cavalier adventurers,
On this our landing spot we'll rear a town
Shall bear our good king's name to after-time,
And yours along with it; for ye are men
Well worth the handing down; whose paged names
Will not disgrace posterity to read:
Men born for acts of hardihood and valour,
Whose stirring spirits scorn'd to lie inert,
Base atoms in the mass of population
That rots in stagnant Europe. Ye are men
Who a high wealth and fame will bravely win,
And wear full worthily. I still shall be
The foremost in all troubles, toil, and danger,
Your leader and your captain, nought exacting
Save strict obedience to the watchful care
Which points to your own good: be wary then,
And let not any mutinous hand unravel
Our close knit compact. Union is its strength:
Be that remember'd ever. Gallant gentlemen,
We have a noble stage, on which to act
A noble drama; let us then sustain
Our sev'ral parts with credit and with honour.
Now, sturdy comrades, cheerly to our tasks!

[*Exeunt* SMITH, ROLFE, *&c.*]

SCENE 2: *A grove.*

[*Enter* WALTER *and* LARRY.[6]]

LARRY: Now by the black eyes of my Katy, but that master of yours
and captain of mine is a prince!

WALTER: Tut, you hav'n't seen an inch yet of the whole hero. Had you followed him as I have, from a knee-high urchin, you'd confess that there never was soldier fit to cry comrade to him. O! 'twould have made your blood frisk in your veins to have seen him in Turkey and Tartary,[7] when he made the clumsy infidels dance to the music of his broad sword!

LARRY: Troth now, the mussulmans[8] may have been mightily amused by the caper; but for my part I should modestly prefer skipping to the simple jig of an Irish bag-pipe.

WALTER: Then he had the prettiest mode of forming their manners—

LARRY: Arrah, how might that be?

WALTER: For example: whenever they were so ill-bred as to appear with their turbans on before him, he uses me this keen argument to convince them they shewed discourtesy. He whips me out his sword, and knocks their turbans off—

LARRY: Knocks their turbans off?

WALTER: Ay, egad, and their heads to boot.

LARRY: A dev'lish cutting way of reasoning indeed; that argument cou'dn't be answered asily.

WALTER: Devil a tongue ever wagg'd in replication, Larry.—Ah! my fairy of felicity—my mouthful of melody—my wife—

[*Enter* ALICE.]

Well, Alice, we are now in the wilds of Virginia, and, tell me truly, doesn't repent following me over the ocean, wench? wilt be content in these wild woods, with only a little husband, and a great deal of love, pretty Alice?

ALICE: Can you ask that? are not all places alike if you are with me, Walter?

SONG.—ALICE.

In this wild wood will I range;
    Listen, listen, dear!
Nor sigh for towns so fine, to change
    This forest drear.
Toils and dangers I'll despise,
    Never, never weary;
And be, while love is in thine eyes,
    Ever cheery.

> Ah! what to me were cities gay;
>> Listen, listen, dear!
> If from me thou wert away,
>> Alas! how drear!
> Oh! still o'er sea, o'er land I'll rove,
>> Never, never weary;
> And follow on where leads my love,
>> Ever cheery.

LARRY: Och! the creature!

WALTER: Let my lips tell thee what my tongue cannot. [*Kiss.*]

LARRY: Aye, do, do stop her mellifluous mouth; for the little nightingale warbles so like my Kate, she makes me sigh for Ballinomoné; ah! just so would the constant creature carol all day about, roving through the seas and over the woods.

[*Enter* ROBIN.]

ROBIN: Master Walter, the captain is a going to explore the country, and you must along.

WALTER: That's our fine captain, always stirring.

ROBIN: Plague on his industry! would you think it, we are all incontinently to fall a chopping down trees, and building our own houses, like the beavers.

LARRY: Well, sure, that's the fashionable mode of paying rent in this country.

ALICE: O, Walter, these merciless savages! I sha'n't be merry till you return—

ROBIN: I warrant ye, mistress Alice—Lord love you I shall be here.

WALTER: Cheerly, girl; our captain will make the red rogues scamper like so many dun deer. Savages, quotha! at sight of him, their copper skins will turn pale as silver, with the very alchemy of fear. Come, a few kisses, en passant,[9] and then away! cheerly, my dainty Alice.

[*Exeunt* WALTER *and* ALICE.]

ROBIN: Ay, go your ways, master Walter, and when you are gone—

LARRY: What then! I suppose you'll be after talking nonsense to his wife. But if ever I catch you saying your silly things—

ROBIN: Mum, Lord love you, how can you think it? But hark ye, master Larry, in this same drama that our captain spoke of, you and I act parts, do we not?

LARRY: Arrah, to be sure, we are men of parts.

ROBIN: Shall I tell you in earnest what we play in this merry comedy?

LARRY: Be doing it.

ROBIN: Then we play the parts of two fools, look you, to part with all at home, and come to these savage parts, where, Heaven shield us, our heads may be parted from our bodies. Think what a catastrophe, master Larry!

LARRY: So the merry comedy ends a doleful tragedy, and exit fool in the character of a hero! That's glory, sirrah, a very feather in our cap.

ROBIN: A light gain to weigh against the heavy loss of one's head. Feather quotha! what use of a plumed hat without a head to wear it withal?

LARRY: Tut, man, our captain will lead us through all dangers.

ROBIN: Will he? an' he catch me following him through these same dangers—

LARRY: Och, you spalpeen! I mean he'll lead us out of peril.

ROBIN: Thank him for nothing; for I've predetermined, look you, not to be led into peril. Oh, master Larry, what a plague had I to do to leave my snug cot and my brown lass, to follow master Rolfe to this devil of a country, where there's never a girl nor a house!

LARRY: Out, you driveller! didn't I leave as neat a black-ey'd girl, and as pretty a prolific potato-patch all in tears—

ROBIN: Your potato-patch in tears! that's a bull, master Larry—

LARRY: You're a calf, master Robin. Wasn't it raining? Och, I shall never forget it; the thunder rolling, and her tongue a-going, and her tears and the rain; och, bother, but it was a dismal morning!

SONG.—LARRY.

I.

Och! dismal and dark was the day, to be sure,
When Larry took leave of sweet Katy Maclure;
And clouds dark as pitch hung just like a black lace
O'er the sweet face of Heav'n and my Katy's sweet face.
Then, while the wind blow'd, and she sigh'd might and main,
Drops from the black skies
Fell—and from her black eyes;
Och! how I was soak'd with her tears—and the rain.

[Speaks.] And then she gave me this beautiful keep-sake [shows a pair of scissors], which if ever I part with, may a tailor clip me in two with his big shears. Och! when Katy took you in hand, how nicely did you snip and snap my bushy, carroty locks; and now you're cutting the hairs of my heart to pieces, you tieves you—

[*Sings.*] Och! Hubbaboo—Gramachree—Hone![10]

II.

When I went in the garden, each bush seem'd to sigh
Because I was going—and nod me good-bye;
Each stem hung its head, drooping bent like a bow,
With the weight of the water—or else of its woe;
And while sorrow, or wind, laid some flat on the ground,
Drops of rain, or of grief,
Fell from every leaf,
Till I thought in a big show'r of tears I was drown'd.

[*Speaks.*] And then each bush and leaf seem'd to sigh, and say, "don't forget us, Larry." I won't, said I.—"But arrah, take something for remembrance," said they; and then I dug up this neat jewel [*shows a potato*]; you're a little withered to be sure, but if ever I forget your respectable family, or your delightful dwelling place—may I never again see any of your beautiful brothers and plump sisters!—Och! my darling, if you had come hot from the hand of Katy, how my mouth would have watered at ye; now, you divil, you bring the water into my eyes.

[*Sings.*] Och! Hubbaboo—Gramachree—Hone!   [*Exeunt.*]

SCENE 3: *Werocomoco, the royal village of* POWHATAN.[11] INDIAN GIRLS *arranging ornaments for a bridal dress. Music.*

NIMA: Let us make haste, my companions, to finish the dress of the bride; to-day the prince Miami returns with our hunters from the chase; to-morrow he will bear away our princess to his own nation.

[*Enter* POCAHONTAS[12] *from the wood, with bow and arrow, and a flamingo (red bird). Music as she enters.*]

PRINCESS: See, Nima, a flamingo.[13]

[INDIAN GIRLS *crowd around, and admire the bird.*]

PRINCESS: O Nima! I will use my bow no longer; I go out to the wood, and my heart is light; but while my arrow flies, I sorrow; and when the bird drops through the branches, tears come into mine eyes. I will no longer use my bow.

[*Distant hunting-horn. Music. They place themselves in attitudes of listening. Hunting-horn nearer.*]

NIMA: 'Tis Miami and our hunters. Princess, why are your looks sad?
PRINCESS: O Nima! the prince comes to bear me far from my father and my brother. I must quit for ever the companions and the woods that are dear to me. Nima, the Susquehannocks[14] are a powerful nation, and my father would have them for his friends. He gives his daughter to their prince, but his daughter trembles to look upon the fierce Miami.

[*Music.* HUNTERS *seen winding down the hills; they are met by the women of the village;* MIAMI *approaches* POCAHONTAS, *and his attendants lay skins at her feet.*]

MIAMI: Princess, behold the spoils I bring thee. Our hunters are laden with the deer and the soft furred beaver. But Miami scorned such prey: I watched for the mighty buffalo and the shaggy bear; my club felled them to the ground, and I tore their skins from their backs. The fierce carcajou[15] had wound himself around the tree, ready to dart upon the hunter; but the hunter's eyes were not closed, and the carcajou quivered on the point of my spear. I heard the wolf howl as he looked at the moon, and the beams that feel upon his upturned face shewed my tomahawk the spot it was to enter. I marked where the panther had crouched, and, before he could spring, my arrow went into his heart. Behold the spoils the Susquehannock brings thee!
PRINCESS: Susquehannock, thou'rt a mighty hunter. Powhatan shall praise thee for his daughter. But why returns not my brother with thee?
MIAMI: Nantaquas still finds pleasure in the hunt, but the soul of Miami grew weary of being away from Werocomoco, for there dwelt the daughter of Powhatan.
PRINCESS: Let us go to my father.

[*Music. Exeunt* PRINCESS *and* MIAMI *into palace, followed by* NIMA *and train; the others into their several cabins.*]

SCENE 4: *A Forest.*

[SMITH *enters, bewildered in its mazes. Music, expressive of his situation.*]

SMITH: 'Tis all in vain! no clue to guide my steps. [*Music.*]
　By this the explorers have return'd despairing,
　And left their forward leader to his fate.
　The rashness is well punish'd, that, alone.
　Would brave the entangling mazes of these wilds.
　The night comes on, and soon these gloomy woods
　Will echo to the yell of savage beasts,
　And savage men more merciless. Alas!
　And am I, after all my golden dreams
　Of laurel'd glory, doom'd in wilds to fall,
　Ignobly and obscure, the prey of brutes? [*Music.*]
　Fie on these coward thoughts! this trusty sword,
　That made the Turk and Tartar crouch beneath me,
　Will stead me well, e'en in this wilderness. [*Music.*]
　O glory! thou who led'st me fearless on,
　Where death stalk'd grimly over slaughter'd heaps,
　Or drank the drowning shrieks of shipwreck'd wretches,
　Swell high the bosom of thy votary! [*Music.*]   [*Exit* SMITH.]

[*Music. A party of* INDIANS *enter, as following* SMITH, *and steal cautiously after him. The* INDIANS *yell within. Music, hurried. Re-enter* SMITH, *engaged with the* INDIANS; *several fall. Exeunt, fighting, and enter from the opposite side the* PRINCE NANTAQUAS,[16] *who views with wonder the prowess of* SMITH; *when the music has ceased he speaks.*]

PRINCE: Sure 'tis our war-god, Aresqui[17] himself, who lays our chiefs low! Now they stop; he fights no longer; he stands terrible as the panther, which the fearful hunter dares not approach. Stranger, brave stranger, Nantaquas must know thee! [*Music.*]

[*He rushes out, and re-enters with* SMITH.]

PRINCE: Art thou not then a God?
SMITH: As thou art, warrior, but a man.
PRINCE: Then art thou a man like a God; thou shalt be the brother of Nantaquas. Stranger, my father is king of the country, and many nations obey him: will thou be the friend of the great Powhatan?

SMITH: Freely, prince; I left my own country to be the red man's friend.

PRINCE: Wonderful man, where is thy country?

SMITH: It lies far beyond the wide water.

PRINCE: Is there then a world beyond the wide water? I thought only the sun had been there: thou comest then from behind the sun?

SMITH: Not so, prince.

PRINCE: Listen to me. Thy country lies beyond the wide water, and from it do mine eyes behold the sun rise each morning.

SMITH: Prince, to your sight he seems to rise from thence, but your eyes are deceived, they reach not over the wilderness of waters.

PRINCE: Where sleeps the sun then?

SMITH: The sun never sleeps. When you see him sink behind the mountains, he goes to give light to other countries, where darkness flies before him, as it does here, when you behold him rise in the east: thus he chases Night for ever round the world.

PRINCE: Tell me, wise stranger, how came you from your country across the wide water? when our canoes venture but a little from the shore, the waves never fail to swallow them up.

SMITH: Prince, the Great Spirit is the friend of the white men, and they have arts which the red men know not.

PRINCE: My brother, will you teach the red men?

SMITH: I come to do it. My king is a king of a mighty nation; he is great and good: go, said he, go and make the red men wise and happy.

[*During the latter part of the dialogue, the* INDIANS *had crept in, still approaching till they had almost surrounded* SMITH. *A burst of savage music. They seize and bear him off, the* PRINCE *in vain endeavouring to prevent it.*]

PRINCE: Hold! the white man is the brother of your prince; hold, coward warriors! [*He rushes out.*]

SCENE 5: *Powhatan River, as the first scene.*

[*Enter* LARRY.]

LARRY: Now do I begin to suspect, what, to be sure, I've been certain of a long time, that master Robin's a little bit of a big rogue. I just now observed him with my friend Walter's wife. Arrah! here they come. By your leave, fair dealing, I'll play the eavesdropper behind this tree. [*Retires behind a tree.*]

[*Enter* ALICE, *followed by* ROBIN.]

ROBIN: But, mistress Alice, pretty Alice.

ALICE: Ugly Robin, I'll not hear a syllable.

ROBIN: But plague, prithee, Alice, why so coy?

[*Enter* WALTER; *observing them, stops.*]

ALICE: Master Robin, if you follow me about any longer with your fooleries, my Walter shall know of it.

ROBIN: A fig for Walter! is he to be mentioned the same day with the dapper Robin? can Walter make sonnets and madrigals, and set them, and sing them? besides, the Indians have eat him by this, I hope.

WALTER: Oh, the rascal!

ROBIN: Come, pretty one, quite alone, no one near, even that blundering Irishman away.

LARRY: O you spalpeen![18] I'll blunder on you anon.

ROBIN: Shall we, Alice, shall we?

QUARTETTO.

ROBIN:	Mistress Alice, say,
	Walter's far away,
	Pretty Alice!
	Nay, now—prithee, pray,
	Shall we, Alice? hey!
	Mistress Alice?
ALICE:	Master Robin, nay—
	Prithee, go your way,
	Saucy Robin!
	If you longer stay,
	You may rue the day,
	Master Robin.
WALTER: [*Aside.*]	True my Alice is.
LARRY: [*Aside.*]	Wat shall know of this.
ROBIN: [*Struggling.*]	Pretty Alice!
WALTER: [*Aside.*]	What a rascal 'tis!
LARRY: [*Aside.*]	He'll kill poor Rob, I wish!
ROBIN: [*Struggling.*]	Mistress Alice,
	Let me taste the bliss—[*Attempts to kiss her.*]
ALICE:	Taste the bliss of this [*Slaps his face.*],
	Saucy Robin!
WALTER: [*Advancing.*]	Oh, what wond'rous bliss!

LARRY: [*Advancing.*]   How d'ye like the kiss?
ALICE:
WALTER: }
LARRY: }   Master Robin?

[ROBIN *steals off.*]

WALTER: Jackanapes!
LARRY: Aye, hop off, cock robin! Blood and thunder now, that such a
   sparrow should try to turn hawk, and pounce on your little pullet
   here.
ALICE: Welcome, my bonny Walter.
WALTER: A sweet kiss, Alice, to season my bitter tidings. Our captain's
   lost.
LARRY: }
ALICE: }   Lost!
WALTER: You shall hear. A league or two below this, we entered a
   charming stream, that seemed to glide through a fairy land of fertil-
   ity. I must know more of this, said our captain. Await my return
   here. So bidding us moor the pinnace in a broad basin, where the
   Indian's arrows could reach us from neither side, away he went,
   alone in his boat, to explore the river to its head.
LARRY: Gallant soul!
WALTER: What devil prompted us to disobey his command I know not,
   but scarce was he out of sight, when we landed; and mark the end
   on't: up from their ambuscado started full three hundred black
   fiends, with a yell that might have appalled Lucifer, and whiz came
   a cloud of arrows about our ears. Three tall fellows of ours fell:
   Cassen, Emery, and Robinson.[19] Our lieutenant, with Percy and myself, fought our way to the water side, where, leaving our canoe as
   a trophy to the victors, we plunged in, and, after swimming, dodging,
   and diving like ducks,[20] regained the pinnace that we had left like
   geese.
ALICE: Heaven be praised, you are safe; but our poor captain—
WALTER: Aye; the day passed and he returned not; we came back for a
   reinforcement, and to-morrow we find him, or perish.
ALICE: Perish!—
WALTER: Aye; shame seize the poltroon who wou'dn't perish in such a
   cause; wou'dn't you, Larry?
LARRY: By Saint Patrick, it's the thing I would do, and hould my head
   the higher for it all the days of my life after.
WALTER: But see, our lieutenant and master Percy.

[*Enter* ROLFE *and* PERCY.]

ROLFE: Good Walter, look to the barge, see it be ready
  By earliest dawn.
WALTER: I shall, sir.
ROLFE: And be careful,
  This misadventure be not buzz'd abroad,
  Where 't may breed mutiny and mischief. Say
  We've left the captain waiting our return,
  Safe with the other three; meantime, choose out
  Some certain trusty fellows, who will swear
  Bravely to find their captain or their death.
WALTER: I'll hasten, sir, about it.
LARRY: Good lieutenant,
  Shall I along?
ROLFE: In truth, brave Irishman,
  We cannot have a better. Pretty Alice,
  Will you again lose Walter for a time?
ALICE: I would I were a man, sir, then, most willingly I'd lose myself
  to do our captain service.
ROLFE: An Amazon!
WALTER: Oh, 'tis a valiant dove.
LARRY: But come; Heaven and Saint Patrick prosper us.
                        [*Exeunt* WALTER, LARRY, ALICE.]
ROLFE: Now, my sad friend, cannot e'en this arouse you?
  Still bending with the weight of shoulder'd Cupid?
  Fie! throw away that bauble, love, my friend:
  That glist'ning toy of listless laziness,
  Fit only for green girls and growing boys
  T' amuse themselves withal. Can an inconstant,
  A fickle changeling, move a man like Percy?
PERCY: Cold youth, how can you speak of that you feel not?
  You never lov'd.
ROLFE: Hum! yes, in mine own way;
  Marry, 'twas not with signs and folded arms;
  For mirth I sought in it, not misery.
  Sir, I have ambled through all love's gradations
  Most jollily, and seriously the whilst.
  I have sworn oaths of love on my knee, yet laugh'd not;
  Complaints and chidings heard, but heeded not;

Kiss'd the cheek clear from tear-drops, and yet wept not;
Listen'd to vows of truth, which I believed not;
And after have been jilted—
PERCY: Well!
ROLFE: And car'd not.
PERCY: Call you this loving?
ROLFE: Ay, and wisely loving.
    Not, sir, to have the current of one's blood
    Froz'n with a frown, and molten with a smile;
    Make ebb and flood under a lady Luna,
    Liker the moon in changing than in chasteness.
    'Tis not to be a courier, posting up
    To the seventh Heav'n, or down to the gloomy centre,
    On the fool's errand of a wanton—pshaw!
    Women! they're made of whimsies and caprice,
    So variant and so wild, that, ty'd to a God,
    They'd dally with the devil for a change.—
    Rather than wed a European dame,
    I'd take a squaw o' the woods, and get papooses.
PERCY: If Cupid burn thee not for heresy,
    Love is no longer catholic religion.
ROLFE: An' if he do, I'll die a sturdy martyr.
    And to the last preach to thee, pagan Percy,
    Till I have made a convert. Answer me,
    Is not this idol of they heathen worship
    That sent thee hither a despairing pilgrim;
    Thy goddess, Geraldine, is she not false?
PERCY: Most false!
ROLFE: For shame, then; cease adoring her;
    Untwine the twisted cable of your arms,
    Heave from your freighted bosom all its charge,
    In one full sigh, and puff it strongly from you;
    Then, raising your earth-reading eyes to Heaven,
    Laud your kind stars you were not married to her,
    And so forget her.
PERCY: Ah! my worthy Rolfe,
    'Tis not the hand of infant Resolution
    Can pluck this rooted passion from my heart:
    Yet what I can I will; by heaven! I will.
ROLFE: Why, cheerly said; the baby Resolution
    Will grow apace; time will work wonders in him.

PERCY: Did she not, after interchange of vows—
  But let the false one go, I will forget her.
  Your hand, my friend; now will I act the man.
ROLFE: Faith, I have seen thee do't, and burn'd with shame,
  That he who so could fight should ever sigh.
PERCY: Think'st thou our captain lives?
ROLFE: Tush! he must live;
  He was not born to perish so. Believe 't,
  He'll hold these dingy devils at the bay,
  Till we come up and succour him.
PERCY: And yet
  A single arm against a host—alas!
  I fear me he has fallen.
ROLFE: Then never fell
  A nobler soul, more valiant, or more worthy,
  Or fit to govern men. If he be gone,
  Heaven save our tottering colony from falling!
  But see, th' adventurers from their daily toil.

[*Enter* ADVENTURERS, WALTER, LARRY, ROBIN, ALICE, *&c.*]

WALTER: Now, gentleman labourers, a lusty roundelay after the toils of
  the day; and then to a sound sleep, in houses of our own building.

Roundelay CHORUS.

  Now crimson sinks the setting sun,
  And our tasks are fairly done.
  Jolly comrades, home to bed,
  Taste the sweets by labour shed;
  Let his poppy seal your eyes,
  Till another day arise,
  For our tasks are fairly done,
  As crimson sinks the setting sun.

ACT II

SCENE 1: *Inside the palace at Werocomoco.* POWHATAN *in state,*
GRIMOSCO, *&c., his wives, and warriors, ranged on each side. Music.*

POWHATAN: My people, strange beings have appeared among us; they
  come from the bosom of the waters, amid fire and thunder; one of them
  has our war-god delivered into our hands: behold the white being!

[*Music.* SMITH *is brought in; his appearance excites universal wonder;* POCAHONTAS *expresses peculiar admiration.*]

POCAHONTAS: O Nima! is it not a God!

POWHATAN: Miami, though thy years are few, thou art experienced as age; give us thy voice of counsel.

MIAMI: Brothers, this stranger is of a fearful race of beings; their barren hunting grounds lie beneath the world, and they have risen, in monstrous canoes, through the great water, to spoil and ravish from us our fruitful inheritance. Brothers, this stranger must die; six of our brethren have fall'n by his hand. Before we lay their bones in the narrow house, we must avenge them: their unappeased spirits will not go to rest beyond the mountains; they cry out for the stranger's blood.

NANTAQUAS: Warriors, listen to my words; listen, my father, while your son tells the deeds of the brave white man. I saw him when 300 of our fiercest chiefs formed the war-ring around him. But he defied their arms; he held lightning in his hand. Wherever his arm fell, there sunk a warrior: as the tall tree falls, blasted and riven, to the earth, when the angry Spirit darts his fires through the forest. I thought him a God; my feet grew to the ground; I could not move!

POCAHONTAS: Nima, dost thou hear the words of my brother?

NANTAQUAS: The battle ceased, for courage left the bosom of our warriors; their arrows rested in their quivers; their bowstrings no longer sounded; the tired chieftains leaned on their war-clubs, and gazed at the terrible stranger, whom they dared not approach. Give an ear to me, king: 'twas then I held out the hand of peace to him, and he became my brother; he forgot his arms, for he trusted to his brother; he was discoursing wonders to his friend, when our chiefs rushed upon him, and bore him away. But oh! my father, he must not die; for he is not a war captive; I promised that the chain of friendship should be bright between us. Chieftains, your prince must not falsify his word; father, your son must not be a liar!

POCAHONTAS: Listen, warriors; listen, father; the white man is my brother's brother!

GRIMOSCO:[21] King! when last night our village shook with the loud noise, it was the Great Spirit who talk'd to his priest; my mouth shall speak his commands: King, we must destroy the strangers, for they are not our God's children; we must take their scalps, and wash our hands in the white man's blood, for he is an enemy to the Great Spirit.

NANTAQUAS: O priest, thou hast dreamed a false dream; Miami, thou tellest the tale that is not. Hearken, my father, to my true words! the white man is beloved by the Great Spirit; his king is like you, my father, good and great; and he comes from a land beyond the wide water, to make us wise and happy!

[POWHATAN *deliberates. Music.*]

POWHATAN: Stranger, thou must prepare for death. Six of our brethren fell by thy hand. Thou must die.

POCAHONTAS: Father, O father!

SMITH: Had not your people first beset me, king,
I would have prov'd a friend and brother to them;
Arts I'd have taught, that should have made them gods,
And gifts would I have given to your people,
Richer than red men ever yet beheld.
Think not I fear to die. Lead to the block.
The soul of the white warrior shall shrink not.
Prepare the stake! amidst your fiercest tortures,
You'll find its fiery pains as nobly scorned,
As when the red man sings aloud his death-song.

POCAHONTAS: Oh! shall that brave man die!

[*Music. The* KING *motions with his hand, and* SMITH *is led to the block.*]

MIAMI: [*To executioners.*] Warriors, when the third signal strikes, sink your tomahawks in his head.

POCAHONTAS: Oh, do not, warriors, do not! Father, incline your heart to mercy; he will win your battles, he will vanquish your enemies! [*First signal.*] Brother, speak! save your brother! Warriors, are you brave? preserve the brave man! [*Second signal.*] Miami, priest, sing the song of peace; ah! strike not, hold! mercy!

[*Music. The third signal is struck, the hatchets are lifted up: when the* PRINCESS, *shrieking, runs distractedly to the block, and presses* SMITH'S *head to her bosom.*]

White man, thou shalt not die; or I will die with thee!

[*Music. She leads* SMITH *to the throne, and kneels.*]

My father, dost thou love thy daughter? listen to her voice: look upon her tears: they ask for mercy to the captive. Is thy child dear to thee, my father? Thy child will die with the white man.

[*Plaintive music. She bows her head to his feet.* POWHATAN, *after some deliberation, looking on his daughter with tenderness, presents her with a string of white wampum.* POCAHONTAS, *with the wildest expression of joy, rushes forward with* SMITH, *presenting the beads of peace.*]

Captive! thou art free![22]—

[*Music. General joy is diffused*—MIAMI *and* GRIMOSCO *only appear discontented. The prince* NANTAQUAS *congratulates* SMITH. *The* PRINCESS *shows the most extravagant emotions of rapture.*]

SMITH: O woman! angel sex! where'er thou art,
   Still art thou heavenly. The rudest clime
   Robs not they glowing bosom of its nature.
   Thrice blessed lady, take a captive's thanks! [*He bows upon her hand.*]
POCAHONTAS: My brother!—

[*Music.* SMITH *expresses his gratitude.*]

NANTAQUAS: Father, hear the design that fills my breast. I will go among the white men; I will learn their arts; and my people shall be made wise and happy.
POCAHONTAS: I too will accompany my brother.
MIAMI: Princess!—
POCAHONTAS: Away, cruel Miami; you would have murdered my brother!—
POWHATAN: Go, my son; take thy warriors, and go with the white men. Daughter, I cannot lose thee from mine eyes; accompany thy brother but a little on his way. Stranger, depart in peace; I entrust my son to thy friendship.
SMITH: Gracious sir,
   He shall return with honours and with wonders;
   My beauteous sister! noble brother, come!

[*Music. Exeunt, on one side,* SMITH, PRINCESS, NANTAQUAS, NIMA, *and train. On the other,* KING, PRIEST, MIAMI, &c. *The two latter express angry discontent.*]

SCENE 2: *A forest.*

[*Enter* PERCY, ROLFE]

ROLFE: So far indeed 'tis fruitless, yet we'll on.
PERCY: Ay, to the death.
ROLFE: Brave Percy, come, confess
   You have forgot your love.
PERCY: Why, faith, not quite;
   Despite of me, it sometimes through my mind
   Flits like a dark cloud o'er a summer sky;
   But passes off like that, and leaves me cloudless.
   I can't forget that she was sweet as spring;
   Fair as the day.
ROLFE: Ay, ay, like April weather;
   Sweet, fair, and faithless.
PERCY: True, alas! like April!

SONG.—PERCY.

   Fair Geraldine each charm of spring possest,
      Her cheek glow'd with the rose and lily's strife;
   Her breath was perfume, and each winter'd breast
      Felt that her sunny eyes beam'd light and life.

   Alas! that in a form of blooming May,
      The mind should April's changeful liv'ry wear!
   Yet ah! like April, smiling to betray,
      Is Geraldine, as false as she is fair!

ROLFE: Beshrew the little gipsy! let us on. [*Exeunt* PERCY, ROLFE.]

[*Enter* LARRY, WALTER, ROBIN, *&c.*]

LARRY: Go no further? Och! you hen-hearted cock robin!
ROBIN: But, master Larry—
WALTER: Prithee, thou evergreen aspen leaf, thou non-intermittent ague!
   why didst along with us?
ROBIN: Why, you know, my master Rolfe desired it; and then you were
   always railing out on me for chicken-heartedness. I came to shew ye
   I had valour.
WALTER: But forgetting to bring it with thee, thou wouldst now back
   for it; well, in the name of Mars, go; return for thy valour, Robin.

ROBIN: What! alone?

LARRY: Arrah! then stay here till it comes to you, and then follow us.

ROBIN: Stay here! O Lord, methinks I feel an arrow sticking in my gizzard already! Hark ye, my sweet master, let us sing.

LARRY: Sing?

ROBIN: Sing; I'm always valiant when I sing. Beseech you, let us chaunt the glee that I dish'd up for us three.

LARRY: It has a spice of your cowardly cookery in it.

WALTER: But since 'tis a provocative to Robin's valour—

LARRY: Go to: give a lusty hem, and fall on.

Glee.

> We three, adventurers be,
> Just come from our own country;
> We have cross'd thrice a thousand ma,
> Without a penny of money.
>
> We three, good fellows be,
> Who wou'd run like the devil from Indians three;
> We never admir'd their bowmandry;
> Oh, give us whole skins for our money.
>
> We three, merry men be,
> Who gaily will chaunt our ancient glee,
> Though a lass or a glass, in this wild country,
> Can't be had, or for love, or for money.

LARRY: Well, how do you feel?

ROBIN: As courageous as, as a—

LARRY: As a wren, little Robin. Are you sure, now, you won't be after fancying every deer that skips by you a divil, and every bush a bear?

ROBIN: I defy the devil; but hav'n't you heard, my masters, how the savages go a hunting, drest out in deer-skin? How could you put one in mind, master Larry? O Lord! that I should come a captain-hunting! the only game we put up is deer that carry scalping knives! or if we beat the bush to start a bold commander, up bolts a bloody bear!

[WALTER *and* LARRY *exchange significant nods.*]

LARRY: To be sure we're in a parlous case. The forest laws are dev'lish
    severe here: an they catch us trespassing upon their hunting ground,
    we shall pay a neat poll-tax: nothing less than our heads will serve.
ROBIN: Our heads?
WALTER: Yes, faith! they'll soon collect their capitation.
    They wear men's heads, sir, hanging at the breast,
    Instead of jewels; and at either ear,
    Most commonly, a child's, by way of ear-drop.
ROBIN: Oh! curse their finery! jewels, heads, O Lord!
LARRY: Pshaw man! don't fear. Perhaps they'll only burn us.
    What a delicate roasted Robin you wou'd make!
    Troth! they'd so lick their lips!
ROBIN: A roasted robin!—
WALTER: Tut! if they only burn us, 'twill be brave.
    Robin shall make our death-songs.
ROBIN: Death-songs, oh! [ROBIN *stands motionless with fear.*]
LARRY: By the good looking right eye of Saint Patrick,
    There's Rolfe and Percy, with a tribe of Indians. [*Looking out.*]
ROBIN: Indians! they're pris'ners, and we—we're dead men! [*While*
    WALTER *and* LARRY *exeunt,* ROBIN *gets up into a tree.*]
    O Walter, Larry! ha! what gone, all gone!
    Poor Robin, what is to become of thee?

    [*Enter* SMITH, POCAHONTAS, NANTAQUAS, PERCY, ROLFE, NIMA,
    and INDIANS, LARRY, *and* WALTER.]

SMITH: At hazard of her own dear life she saved me.
    E'en the warm friendship of the prince had fail'd,
    And death, inevitable death, hung over me.
    Oh, had you seen her fly, like Pity's herald,
    To stay the uplifted hatchet in its flight;
    Or heard her, as with cherub voice she pled,
    Like Heav'n's own angel-advocate, for mercy.
POCAHONTAS: My brother, speak not so. [*Bashfully.*]
ROLFE: What gentleness!
    What sweet simplicity! what angel softness!

    [ROLFE *goes to her. She, timidly, but with evident pleasure, re-
    ceives his attentions. During this scene the* PRINCESS *discovers the
    first advances of love in a heart of perfect simplicity.* SMITH, &c.,
    converse apart.*]

ROBIN: [*In the tree.*] Egad! there's never a head hanging to their ears; and their ears hang to their heads, for all the world as if they were christians; I'll venture down among them. [*Getting down.*]

NIMA: Ah! [*Bends her bow, and is about to shoot at him.*]

LARRY: Arrah! my little dark Diana, choose noble game, that's only little Robin.

ROBIN: Ay, bless you, I'm only little Robin. [*Jumps down.*]

[NIMA *examines him curiously, but fearfully.*]

ROBIN: Gad, she's taken with my figure; ah! there it is now; a personable fellow shall have his wench any where. Yes, she's admiring my figure. Well, my dusky dear, how could you like such a man as I am?

NIMA: Are you a man?

ROBIN: I'll convince you of it some day. Hark ye, my dear. [*Attempts to whisper.*]

NIMA: Ah! don't bite.

ROBIN: Bite! what do you take me for?

NIMA: A raccoon.

ROBIN: A raccoon! Why so?

NIMA: You run up the tree. [*Motions as if climbing.*]

LARRY: Well said, my little pagan Pythagoras!—Ha! ha!

ROBIN: Hum! [*Retires disconcerted.*]

[ROLFE *and* PERCY *come forward.*]

ROLFE: Tell me, in sooth, didst ever mark such sweetness!
Such winning—such bewitching gentleness!

PERCY: What, caught, my flighty friend, love-lim'd[23] at last?
O Cupid, Cupid! thou'rt a skilful birder.
Although thou spread thy net, i' the wilderness,
Or shoot thy bird-bolt from an Indian bow,
Or place thy light in savage ladies' eyes,
Or pipe thy call in savage ladies' voices,
Alas! each tow'ring tenant of the air
Must fall heart pierc'd—or stoop, at thy command,
To sigh his sad notes in thy cage, O Cupid!

ROLFE: A truce; a truce! O friend, her guiltless breast
Seems Love's pavilion, where, in gentle sleep,
The unrous'd boy has rested. O my Percy!
Could I but wake the slumb'rer—

PERCY: Nay, i' faith,
   Take courage; thou hast given the alarm:
   Methinks the drowsy god gets up apace.

ROLFE: Say'st thou?

SMITH: Come, gentlemen, we'll toward the town.

NANTAQUAS: My sister, you will now return to our father.

PRINCESS: Return, my brother?

NANTAQUAS: Our father lives but while you are near him. Go, my sister, make him happy with the knowledge of his son's happiness.
   Farewell, my sister! [*The* PRINCESS *appears dejected.*]

SMITH: Once more, my guardian angel, let me thank thee. [*Kissing
her hand.*]
   Ere long we will return to thee, with presents
   Well worth a princess' and a king's acceptance.
   Meantime, dear lady, tell the good Powhatan
   We'll show the prince such grace and entertainment,
   As shall befit our brother and his son.
   Adieu, sweet sister.

     [*Music. They take leave of the* PRINCESS; *she remains silently de-
     jected; her eyes anxiously follow* ROLFE, *who lingers behind, and
     is the last to take leave.*]

PRINCESS: Stranger, wilt thou too come to Werocomoco?

ROLFE: Dost thou wish it, lady?

PRINCESS: [*Eagerly.*] O yes!

ROLFE: And why, lovely lady?

PRINCESS: My eyes are pleased to see thee, and my ears to hear thee,
   stranger.

ROLFE: And did not the others who were here also please thy sight and
   hearing?

PRINCESS: Oh! they were all goodly; but—their eyes looked not like
   thine; their voices sounded not like thine; and their speeches were
   not like thy speeches, stranger.

ROLFE: Enchanting simplicity! But why call me stranger? Captain Smith
   thou callest brother. Call me so too.

PRINCESS: Ah, no!

ROLFE: Then thou thinkest not of me as thou dost of him? [*She shakes
her head and sighs.*] Is Captain Smith dear to thee?

PRINCESS: Oh yes! very dear; [ROLFE *is uneasy*] and Nantaquas too:
   they are my brothers;—but—that name is not thine—thou art—

ROLFE: What, lovely lady?

PRINCESS: I know not; I feel the name thou art, but I cannot speak it.

ROLFE: I am thy lover, dear princess.

PRINCESS: Yes, thou art my lover. But why call me princess?

ROLFE: Dear lady, thou art a king's daughter.

PRINCESS: And if I were not, what wouldst thou call me?

ROLFE: Oh! if thou wert a beggar's, I would call thee love!

PRINCESS: I know not what a beggar is; but oh! I would I were a beggar's daughter, so thou wouldst call me love. Ah! do not longer call me king's daughter. If thou feelst the name as I do, call me as I call thee: thou shalt be *my* lover; I will be *thy* lover.

ROLFE: Enchanting, lovely creature! [*Kisses her ardently.*]

PRINCESS: Lover, thou hast made my cheek to burn, and my heart to beat! Mark it.

ROLFE: Dear innocence! [*Putting his hand to her heart.*]

PRINCESS: Lover, why is it so? To-day before my heart beat, and mine eyes were full of tears; but then my white brother was in danger. Thou art not in danger, and yet behold—[*Wipes a tear from her eye.*] Besides, then, my heart hurt me, but now! Oh, now!—Lover, why is it so? [*Leaning on him with innocent confidence.*]

ROLFE: Angel of purity! thou didst to-day feel pity; and now—Oh, rapturous task to teach thee the difference!—now, thou dost feel love.

PRINCESS: Love!

ROLFE: Love: the noblest, the sweetest passion that could swell thy angel bosom.

PRINCESS: Oh! I feel that 'tis very sweet. Lover, with thy lips thou didst make me feel it. My lips shall teach thee sweet love. [*Kisses him, and artlessly looks up in his face; placing her hand upon his heart.*] Does thy heart beat?

ROLFE: Beat! O heaven!—

[ROBIN, *who had been with* NIMA, *comes forward.*]

ROBIN: Gad! we must end our amours, or we shall be left. Sir, my master, hadn't we better—

ROLFE: Booby! idiot!

[*Enter* WALTER.]

WALTER: Sir, lieutenant, the captain awaits your coming up.

ROLFE: I'll follow on the instant.

PRINCESS: Thou wilt not go?

ROLFE: But for a time, love.

PRINCESS: I do not wish thee to leave me.

ROLFE: I must, love; but I will return.

PRINCESS: Soon—very soon?

ROLFE: Very—very soon.

PRINCESS: I am not pleased now—and yet my heart beats. Oh, lover!

ROLFE: My angel! there shall not a sun rise and set, ere I am with thee. Adieu! thy own heavenly innocence be thy safeguard. Farewell, sweet love!

[*Music. He embraces her and exit, followed by* ROBIN *and* WALTER. PRINCESS *looks after him. A pause.*]

PRINCESS: O Nima!

NIMA: Princess, white men are pow-wows. The white man put his lips here, and I felt something—here—[*Putting her hand to her heart.*]

PRINCESS: O lover!

[*She runs to the place whence* ROLFE *went out, and gazes after him. Music. Enter from opposite side,* MIAMI.]

MIAMI: [*Sternly.*] Princess!

PRINCESS: [*Turning.*] Ah!

MIAMI: Miami has followed thy steps. Thou art the friend of the white men.

PRINCESS: Yes, for they are good and godlike.

MIAMI: Mine eyes beheld the pale youth part from you; your arms were entwined, your lips were together! [*Struggling with jealousy.*]

PRINCESS: He is my lover; I am his lover. [*Still looking after* ROLFE.]

MIAMI: [*Stamps with anger.*] Hear me! In what do the red yield to the white men? and who among the red men is like Miami? While I was yet a child, did the dart which my breath blew through my sarbacan[24] ever fail to pierce the eye of the bird? What youth dared, like Miami, to leap from the precipice, and drag the struggling bear from the foaming torrent? Is there a hunter—is there a warrior—skilful and brave as Miami? Come to my cabin, and see the scalps and the skins that adorn it. They are the trophies of the Susquehannock!

PRINCESS: Man, mine eyes will never behold thy trophies. They are not pleased to look on thee. [*Averting her eyes with disgust.*]

MIAMI: Ha! [*Pause—he resumes in a softened tone.*] Princess, I have crossed many woods and waters, that I might bear the daughter of Powhatan to my nation. Shall my people cry out, with scorn, "behold! our prince returns without his bride?" In what is the pale youth above the red Miami?

PRINCESS: Thine eyes are as the panther's; thy voice like the voice of the wolf. Thou shouldst make my heart beat with joy; and I tremble before thee. O no! Powhatan shall give me to my lover. I will be my lover's bride!

[*Music.* MIAMI *stamps furiously; his actions betray the most savage rage of jealousy; he rushes to seize the* PRINCESS, *but, recollecting that her attendants are by, he goes out in an agony, by his gestures menacing revenge. The* PRINCESS *exit on the opposite side, followed by train.*]

SCENE 3: *Werocomoco. Music.*

[*Enter from the palace* POWHATAN *and* GRIMOSCO; *met by the* PRINCESS, *who runs to her father.*]

POWHATAN: My daughter!

PRINCESS: O father! the furious Miami!

POWHATAN: What of the prince?

PRINCESS: Father, my father! do not let the fierce prince bear me to his cruel nation!

POWHATAN: How!

PRINCESS: By the spirit of my mother, I implore my father. Oh! if thou deliver me to the Susquehannock, think not thine eyes shall ever again behold me; the first kind stream that crosses our path shall be the end of my journey; my soul shall seek the soul of the mother that loved me, far beyond the mountains.

POWHATAN: Daughter, mention not thy mother!

PRINCESS: Her shade will pity her unhappy child, and I shall be at rest in her bosom. [*Weeping.*]

POWHATAN: Rest in my bosom, my child! [*She starts with joyful emotion.*] Thou shalt not go from thy father.

PRINCESS: Father; dear father! [*Seizing his hand.*]

[*Music. An* INDIAN *enters, bearing a red hatchet.*]

INDIAN: King!

POWHATAN: Thou art of the train of the Susquehannock: speak.

INDIAN: My prince demands his bride.

[*The* PRINCESS *clings fearfully to the* KING.]

POWHATAN: Tell thy prince, my daughter will not leave her father.

INDIAN: Will Powhatan forget his promise to Miami?

POWHATAN: Powhatan will not forget his promise to her mother; and he vowed, while the angel of death hovered over her, that the eye of tender care should never be averted from her darling daughter. `

INDIAN: Shall not then my prince receive his bride?

POWHATAN: The daughter of Powhatan—never.

INDIAN: Take then his defiance. [*Music. He presents the red hatchet.*]

POWHATAN: The red hatchet! 'Tis well. Grimosco, summon our warriors.

GRIMOSCO: O king! might I—

POWHATAN: Speak not. Tell our chiefs to assemble; and show them the war-signal. [*Exit* GRIMOSCO.] Go, tell your master, the great Powhatan will soon meet him, terrible as the minister of vengeance. [*Exit* INDIAN.] The chiefs approach. My child, retire from this war scene.

PRINCESS: O dear parent! thine age should have been passed in the shade of peace; and do I bring my father to the bloody war-path?

POWHATAN: Not so; the young prince has often dared my power, and merited my vengeance; he shall now feel both.

PRINCESS: Alas! his nation is numerous and warlike.

POWHATAN: Fear not, my child; we will call the valiant Nantaquas from his brothers; the brave English too will join us.

PRINCESS: Ah! then is thy safety and success certain.

[*Exit into palace, followed by* NIMA, *&c.*]

[*Music. Enter* GRIMOSCO *and* WARRIORS.]

POWHATAN: Brave chieftains! need I remind you of the victories you have gained; the scalps you have borne from your enemies? Chieftains, another victory must be won; more trophies from your foes must deck your cabins; the insolent Miami has braved your king, and defied him with the crimson tomahawk. Warriors! we will not bury it till his nation is extinct. Ere we tread the war-path, raise to our god Aresqui the song of battle, then march to triumph and to glory.

Song to Aresqui.

Aresqui! Aresqui!
Lo! thy sons for war prepare!
Snakes adorn each painted head,
While the cheek of flaming red
Gives the eye its ghastly glare.
Aresqui! Aresqui!
Through the war-path lead aright,
Lo! we're ready for the fight.

WAR SONG.

FIRST INDIAN: See the cautious warrior creeping!
SECOND INDIAN: See the tree-hid warrior peeping!
FIRST INDIAN: Mark! Mark!
              Their track is here; now breathless go!
SECOND INDIAN: Hark! Hark!
              The branches rustle—'tis the foe!
CHORUS: Now we bid the arrow fly—
              Now we raise the hatchet high.
              Where is urg'd the deadly dart,
              There is pierced a chieftain's heart;
              Where the war-club swift descends,
              A hero's race of glory ends!
FIRST INDIAN: In vain the warrior flies—
              From his brow the scalp we tear.
SECOND INDIAN: Or home the captiv'd price,
              A stake-devoted victim, bear.
FIRST AND SECOND INDIAN: The victors advance—
              And while amidst the curling blaze,
              Our foe his death-song tries to raise—
              Dance the warriors' dance. [*War-dance.*]
GRAND CHORUS: Aresqui! Aresqui!
              Through the war-path lead aright—
              Lo! we're ready for the fight. [*March to battle.*]

ACT III

SCENE 1: *Jamestown—built.* WALTER *and* ALICE.

WALTER: One mouthful more. [*Kiss.*] Oh! after a long lent of absence,
    what a charming relish is a kiss, served from the lips of a pretty wife,
    to a hungry husband.

ALICE: And, believe me, I banquet at the high festival of return with
    equal pleasure. But what has made your absence so tedious, prithee?

WALTER: Marry, girl, thus it was: when we had given the enemies of
    our ally, Powhatan, defeature, and sent the rough Miami in chains
    to Werocomoco, our captain dispatches his lieutenant, Rolfe, to sup-
    ply his place, here, in the town; and leading us to the water's edge,
    and leaping into the pinnace, away went we on a voyage of discov-
    ery.[25] Some thousand miles we sailed, and many strange nations dis-

covered; and for our exploits, if posterity reward us not, there is no
faith in history.

ALICE: And what were your exploits?

WALTER: Rare ones, egad!
We took the devil, Okee,[26] prisoner.

ALICE: And have you brought him hither?

WALTER: No: his vot'ries
Redeem'd him with some score or two of deer-skins.
Then we've made thirty kings our tributaries:
Such sturdy rogues, that each could easily
Fillip[27] a buffalo to death with 's finger.

ALICE: But have you got their treasures?

WALTER: All, my girl.
Imperial robes of raccoon, crowns of feather;
Besides the riches of their sev'ral kingdoms—
A full boat load of corn.

ALICE: Oh, wonderful!

WALTER: Ay, is it not? But, best of all, I've kiss'd
The little finger of a mighty queen.
Sweet soul! among the court'sies of her court,
She gave us a Virginian mascarado.[28]

ALICE: Dost recollect the fashion of it?

WALTER: Oh!
Were I to live till Time were in his dotage,
'Twould never from mine eyes. Imagine first,
The scene, a gloomy wood; the time, midnight;
Her squawship's maids of honour were the masquers;
Their masks were wolves' heads curiously set on,
And, bating a small difference of hue,
Their dress e'en such as madam Eve had on
Or ere she eat the apple.

ALICE: Pshaw!

WALTER: These dresses,
All o'er perform'd with the self-same pomado
Which our fine dames at home buy of old Bruin,
Glisten'd most gorgeously unto the moon.
Thus, each a firebrand brandishing aloft,
Rush'd they all forth, with shouts and frantic yells,
In dance grotesque and diabolical,
Madder than mad Bacchantes.[29]

ALICE: O the powers!

WALTER: When they had finished the divertisement
    A beauteous Wolf-head came to me—
ALICE: To you?
WALTER: And lit me with her pine-knot torch to bedward,
    Where, as the custom of the court it was,
    The beauteous Wolf-head blew the flambeau out,
    And then—
ALICE: Well!
WALTER: Then, the light being out, you know,
    To all that follow'd I was in the dark.
    Now you look grave. In faith I went to sleep.
    Could a grim wolf rival my gentle lamb?
    No, truly, girl: though in this wilderness
    The trees hang full of divers colour'd fruit,
    From orange-tawny to sloe-black, egad,
    They'll hang until they rot or ere I pluck them,
    While I've my melting, rosy nonpareil. [*Kiss.*]
ALICE: Oh! you're a Judas!
WALTER: Then am I a Jew!

[*Enter* SMITH, PERCY, NANTAQUAS, LARRY, *&c.*]

SMITH: Yet, prince, accept at least my ardent thanks:
    A thousand times told over, they would fail
    To pay what you and your dear sister claim.
    Through my long absence from my people here,
    You have sustain'd their feebleness.
NANTAQUAS: O brother,
    To you, the conqueror of our father's foes;
    To you, the sun which from our darken'd minds
    Has chas'd the clouds of error, what can we
    Not to remain your debtors?
SMITH: Gen'rous soul!
    Your friendship is my pride. But who knows aught
    Of our young Rolfe?
PERCY: This morning, sir, I hear,
    An hour ere our arrival, the lieutenant
    Accompanied the princess to her father's.
SMITH: Methinks our laughing friend has found at last
    The power of sparkling eyes. What say you, prince,
    To a brave, worthy soldier for your brother?
NANTAQUAS: Were I to choose, I'd put all other by

To make his path-way clear unto my sister.
But come, sir, shall we to my father's banquet?
One of my train I've sent to give him tidings
Of your long-wish'd for coming.
SMITH: Gentle prince,
You greet my fresh return with welcome summons,
And I obey it cheerfully. Good Walter,
And, worthy sir [*to* LARRY], be it your care
To play the queen bee here, and keep the swarm
Still gathering busily. Look to it well:
Our new-raised hive must hold no drones within it.
Now, forward, sirs, to Werocomoco.

> [*Exeunt* SMITH, PRINCE, PERCY, *&c.*]

> [*Manent* WALTER *and* LARRY.]

WALTER: So, my compeer in honour, we must hold
The staff of sway between us.
LARRY: Arrah, man,
If we hould it between us, any rogue
Shall run clean off before it knocks him down,
While at each end we tug for mastery.
WALTER: Tush, man! we'll strike in unison.
LARRY: Go to—
WALTER: And first, let's to the forest—the young sparks
In silken doublets there are felling trees,
Poor, gentle masters, with their soft palms blister'd;
And, while they chop and chop, they swear and swear,
Drowning with oaths the echo of their axe.
LARRY: Are they so hot in choler?
WALTER: Ay.
LARRY: We'll cool 'em;
And pour cold patience down their silken sleeves.
WALTER: Cold patience!
LARRY: In the shape of water, honey.
WALTER: A notable discovery; come away!
LARRY: Ha! isn't that a sail?
WALTER: A sail! a fleet! [*Looking toward the river.*]

> [*Enter* TALMAN.]

TALMAN: We have discovered nine tall ships.
LARRY: Discovered!

Away, you rogue, we have discovered them,
With nature's telescopes. Run—scud—begone—
Down to the river! Och, St. Pat, I thank you!

[*Go toward river. Huzza within. Music expresses joyful bustle.
Scene closes.*]

SCENE 2: *A grove.*

[*Enter* ROBIN *and* NIMA.]

ROBIN: Ay, bless you, I knew I should creep into your heart at last, my
little dusky divinity.
NIMA: Divinity! what's that?
ROBIN: Divinity—it's a—O, it's a pretty title that we lords of the creation bestow upon our playthings. But hist! here they come. Now is
it a knotty point to be argued, whether this parting doth most affect
the mistress and master, or the maid and man. Let Cupid be umpire,
and steal the scales of Justice to weigh our heavy sighs. [*Retire.*]

[*Enter* ROLFE *and* POCAHONTAS.]

PRINCESS: Nay, let me on—
ROLFE: No further, gentle love;
The rugged way has wearied you already.
PRINCESS: Feels the wood pigeon weariness, who flies,
Mated with her beloved? Ah! lover, no.
ROLFE: Sweet! in this grove we will exchange adieus;
My steps should point straight onward; were thou with me,
Thy voice would bid me quit the forward path
At every pace, or fix my side-long look,
Spell-bound, upon thy beauties.
PRINCESS: Ah! you love not
The wild-wood prattle of the Indian maid,
As once you did.
ROLFE: By heaven! my thirsty ear,
Could ever drink its liquid melody.
Oh! I could talk with thee, till hasty night,
Ere yet the sentinel day had done his watch;
Veil'd like a spy, should steal on printless feet,
To listen to our parley! Dearest love!
My captain has arrived, and I do know,
When honour and when duty call upon me,

Thou wouldst not have me chid for tardiness.
But, ere the matin of to-morrow's lark,
Do echo from the roof of nature's temple,
Sweetest, expect me.
PRINCESS: Wilt thou surely come?
ROLFE: To win thee from thy father will I come;
And my commander's voice shall join with mine,
To woo Powhatan to resign his treasure.
PRINCESS: Go then, but ah! forget not—
ROLFE: I'll forget
All else, to think on thee!
PRINCESS: Thou art my life!
I lived not till I saw thee, love; and now,
I live not in thine absence. Long, O! long
I was the savage child of savage Nature;
And when her flowers sprang up, while each green bough
Sang with the passing west wind's rustling breath;
When her warm visitor, flush'd Summer, came,
Or Autumn strew'd her yellow leaves around,
Or the shrill north wind pip'd his mournful music,
I saw the changing brow of my wild mother
With neither love nor dread. But now, O! now,
I could entreat her for eternal smiles,
So thou might'st range through groves of loveliest flowers,
Where never Winter, with his icy lip,
Should dare to press thy cheek.
ROLFE: My sweet enthusiast!
PRINCESS: O! 'tis from thee that I have drawn my being:
Thou'st ta'en me from the path of savage error,
Blood-stain'd and rude, where rove my countrymen,
And taught me heavenly truths, and fill'd my heart
With sentiments sublime, and sweet, and social.
Oft has my winged spirit, following thine,
Cours'd the bright day-beam, and the star of night,
And every rolling planet of the sky,
Around their circling orbits. O, my love!
Guided by thee, has not my daring soul,
O'ertopt the far-off mountains of the east,
Where, as our fathers' fable, shad'wy hunters
Pursue the deer, or clasp the melting maid,
'Mid ever blooming spring? Thence, soaring high

From the deep vale of legendary fiction,
Hast thou not heaven-ward turn'd my dazzled sight,
Where sing the spirits of the blessed good
Around the bright throne of the Holy One?
This thou hast done; and ah! what couldst thou more,
Belov'd preceptor, but direct that ray,
Which beams from Heaven to animate existence,
And bid my swelling bosom beat with love!
ROLFE: O, my dear scholar!
PRINCESS: Prithee, chide me, love:
My idle prattle holds thee from thy purpose.
ROLFE: O! speak more music! and I'll listen to it,
Like stilly midnight to sweet Philomel.[30]
PRINCESS: Nay, now begone; for thou must go: ah! fly,
The sooner to return—
ROLFE: Thus, then, adieu! [*Embrace.*]
But, ere the face of morn blush rosy red,
To see the dew-besprent, cold virgin ground
Stain'd by licentious step; O, long before
The foot of th' earliest furred forrester,
Do mark its imprint on morn's misty sheet,
With sweet good morrow will I wake my love.
PRINCESS: To bliss thou'lt wake me, for I sleep till then
Only with sorrow's poppy on my lids.

[*Music. Embrace; and exit* ROLFE, *followed by* ROBIN; PRINCESS
looks around despondingly.]

But now, how gay and beauteous was this grove!
Sure ev'ning's shadows have enshrouded it,
And 'tis the screaming bird of night I hear,
Not the melodious mock-bird. Ah! fond girl!
'Tis o'er thy soul the gloomy curtain hangs;
'Tis in thy heart the rough-toned raven sings.
O, lover! haste to my benighted breast;
Come like the glorious sun, and bring me day!

SONG.

When the midnight of absence the day-scene pervading
    Distils its chill dew o'er the bosom of love,
Oh, how fast then the gay tints of nature are fading!

How harsh seems the music of joy in the grove!
While the tender flow'r droops till return of the light,
Steep'd in tear drops that fall from the eye of the night.
But Oh! when the lov'd-one appears,
Like the sun a bright day to impart,
To kiss off those envious tears,
To give a new warmth to the heart;
Soon the flow'ret seeming dead
Raises up its blushing head,
Glows again the breast of love,
Laughs again the joyful grove;
While once more the mock-bird's throat
Trolls the sweetly various note.
But ah! when dark absence the day-scene pervading
Distils its chill dew o'er the bosom of love,
O! fast then the gay tints of nature are fading!
O! harsh seems the music of joy in the grove!
And the tender flow'r droops till return of the light,
Steep'd in tear drops that fall from the eye of the night.

PRINCESS: Look, Nima, surely I behold our captive,
    The prince Miami, and our cruel priest.
NIMA: Lady, 'tis they; and now they move this way.
PRINCESS: How earnest are their gestures; ah! my Nima,
    When souls like theirs mingle in secret council,
    Stern murder's voice alone is listen'd to.
    Miami too at large—O! trembling heart,
    Most sad are thy forebodings; they are here—
    Haste, Nima; let us veil us from their view. [*They retire.*]

    [*Enter* MIAMI *and* GRIMOSCO.]

GRIMOSCO: Be satisfied; I cannot fail—hither the king will soon come.
    This deep shade have I chosen for our place of meeting. Hush! he
    comes. Retire, and judge if Grimosco have vainly boasted—away!
    [MIAMI *retires.*]

    [*Enter* POWHATAN.]

POWHATAN: Now, priest, I attend the summons of thy voice.
GRIMOSCO: So you consult your safety, for 'tis the voice of warning.
POWHATAN: Of what would you warn me?
GRIMOSCO: Danger.

POWHATAN: From whom?

GRIMOSCO: Your enemies.

POWHATAN: Old man, these have I conquered.

GRIMOSCO: The English still exist.

POWHATAN: The English!

GRIMOSCO: The nobler beast of the forest issues boldly from his den, and the spear of the powerful pierces his heart. The deadly adder lurks in his covert till the unwary footstep approach him.

POWHATAN: I see no adder near me.

GRIMOSCO: No, for thine eyes rest only on the flowers under which he glides.

POWHATAN: Away, thy sight is dimmed by the shadows of age.

GRIMOSCO: King, for forty winters hast thou heard the voice of counsel from my lips, and never did its sound deceive thee; never did my tongue raise the war cry, and the foe appeared not. Be warned then to beware the white man. He has fixed his serpent eye upon you, and, like the charmed bird, you flutter each moment nearer to the jaw of death.

POWHATAN: How, Grimosco?

GRIMOSCO: Do you want proof of the white man's hatred to the red? Follow him along the bay; count the kings he has conquered, and the nations that his sword has made extinct.

POWHATAN: Like a warrior he subdued them, for the chain of friendship bound them not to each other. The white man is brave as Aresqui; and can the brave be treacherous?

GRIMOSCO: Like the red feather of the flamingo is craft, the brightest plume that graces the warrior's brow. Are not your people brave? Yet does the friendly tree shield them while the hatchet is thrown. Who doubts the courage of Powhatan? Yet has the eye of darkness seen Powhatan steal to the surprise of the foe.

POWHATAN: Ha! priest, thy words are true. I will be satisfied. Even now I received a swift messenger from my son: to-day he will conduct the English to my banquet. I will demand of him if he be the friend of Powhatan.

GRIMOSCO: Yes; but demand it of him as thou drawest thy reeking hatchet from his cleft head. [KING starts.] The despoilers of our land must die!

POWHATAN: What red man can give his eye-ball the glare of defiance when the white chief is nigh? He who stood alone amidst seven hundred foes, and, while he spurned their king to the ground, dared them to shoot their arrows; who will say to him, "White man, I am thine enemy?" No one. My chiefs would be children before him.

GRIMOSCO: The valour of thy chiefs may slumber, but the craft of thy priest shall watch. When the English sit at that banquet from which they shall never rise; when their eyes read nothing but friendship in thy looks, there shall hang a hatchet over each victim head, which, at the silent signal of Grimosco—

POWHATAN: Forbear, counsellor of death! Powhatan cannot betray those who have vanquished his enemies; who are his friends, his brothers.

GRIMOSCO: Impious! Can the enemies of your God be your friends? Can the children of another parent be your brethren? You are deaf to the counsellor: 'tis your priest now speaks. I have heard the angry voice of the Spirit you have offended; offended by your mercy to his enemies. Dreadful was his voice; fearful were his words. Avert his wrath, or thou art condemned; and the white men are the ministers of his vengeance.

POWHATAN: Priest!

GRIMOSCO: From the face of the waters will he send them, in mighty tribes, and our shores will scarce give space for their footsteps. Powhatan will fly before them; his beloved child, his wives, all that is dear to him, he will leave behind. Powhatan will fly; but whither? which of his tributary kings will shelter him? Not one. Already they cry, "Powhatan is ruled by the white; we will no longer be the slaves of a slave!"

POWHATAN: Ha!

GRIMOSCO: Despoiled of his crown, Powhatan will be hunted from the land of his ancestors. To strange woods will the fugitive be pursued by the Spirit whom he has angered—

POWHATAN: O dreadful!

GRIMOSCO: And at last, when the angel of death obeys his call of anguish, whither will go his condemned soul? Not to the fair forests, where his brave fathers are. O! never will Powhatan clasp the dear ones who have gone before him. His exiled, solitary spirit will forever howl on the barren heath where the wings of darkness rest. No ray of hope shall visit him; eternal will be his night of despair.

POWHATAN: Forbear, forbear! O, priest, teach me to avert the dreadful doom.

GRIMOSCO: Let the white men be slaughtered.

POWHATAN: The angry Spirit shall be appeased. Come.   [*Exit.*]

GRIMOSCO: Thy priest will follow thee.

[*Enter* MIAMI.]

MIAMI: Excellent Grimosco! Thy breath, priest, is a deadly pestilence, and hosts fall before it. Yet—still is Miami a captive.

GRIMOSCO: Fear not. Before Powhatan reach Werocomoco thou shalt be free. Come.

MIAMI: Oh, my soul hungers for the banquet; for then shall Miami feast on the heart of his rival!   [*Exeunt with savage triumph.*]

> [*Music. The* PRINCESS *rushes forward, terror depicted in her face. After running alternately to each side, and stopping undetermined and bewildered, speaks.*]

PRINCESS: O whither shall I fly? what course pursue?
At Werocomoco, my phrenzied looks
Would sure betray me. What if hence I haste?
I may o'ertake my lover, or encounter
My brother and his friends. Away, my Nima!   [*Exit* NIMA.]
O holy Spirit! thou whom my dear lover
Has taught me to adore and think most merciful,
Wing with thy lightning's speed my flying feet! [*Music.*]
          [*Exit* PRINCESS.]

SCENE 3: *Near Jamestown.*

[*Enter* LARRY, *and* KATE *as a page.*]

LARRY: Nine ships, five hundred men, and a lord governor! Och! Saint Patrick's blessing be upon them; they'll make this land flow with buttermilk like green Erin. What say you, master page, isn't this a nice neat patch to plant potatoes—I mean, to plant a nation in?

KATE: There's but one better.

LARRY: And which might that be?

KATE: E'en little green Erin that you spoke of.

LARRY: And were you ever—och, give me your fist—were you ever in Ireland?

KATE: It's there I was born—

LARRY: I saw its bloom on your cheek.

KATE: And bred.

LARRY: I saw it in your manners.

KATE: O, your servant, sir. [*Bows.*] And there, too, I fell in love.

LARRY: And, by the powers, so did I; and if a man don't fall into one of the beautiful bogs that Cupid has digged there, faith he may stand

without tumbling, though he runs over all the world beside. Och, the
creatures, I can see them now—

KATE: Such sparkling eyes—

LARRY: Rosy cheeks—

KATE: Pouting lips—

LARRY: Tinder hearts! Och, sweet Ireland!

KATE: Ay, it was there that I fixed my affections after all my wanderings.

SONG—KATE.

Young Edward, through many a distant place,
  Had wandering pass'd, a thoughtless ranger;
And, cheer'd by a smile from beauty's face,
  Had laugh'd at the frowning face of danger.
    Fearless Ned,
    Careless Ned,
  Never with foreign dames was a stranger;
    And huff,
    Bluff,
  He laugh'd at the frowning face of danger.

But journeying on to his native place,
  Through Ballinamoné pass'd the stranger;
Where, fix'd by the charms of Katy's face,
  He swore he'd no longer be a ranger,
    Pretty Kate,
    Witty Kate,
  Vow'd that no time could ever change her;
    And kiss,
    Bliss—
  O, she hugg'd to her heart the welcome stranger.

LARRY: How's that? Ballinamoné, Kate, did you say, Kate?

KATE: Ay, Katy Maclure; as neat a little wanton tit—

LARRY: My wife a wanton tit!—Hark ye, master Whipper-snapper, do
you pretend—

KATE: Pretend! No, faith, sir, I scorn to *pretend,* sir; I am above boasting
of ladies' favours, unless I receive 'em. Pretend, quotha!

LARRY: Fire and faggots! Favours!—

KATE: You seem to know the girl, mister—a—

LARRY: Know her! she's my wife.

KATE: Your wife! Ridiculous! I thought, by your pother, that she had been *your friend's wife*, or your mistress. Hark ye, mister—a— cuckoo—

LARRY: Cuckoo!

KATE: Your ear. Your wife loved me as she did herself.

LARRY: She did?

KATE: Couldn't live without me; all day we were together.

LARRY: You were!

KATE: As I'm a cavalier; and all night—we lay—

LARRY: How?

KATE: How! why, close as two twin potatoes; in the same bed, egad!

LARRY: Tunder and turf! I'll split you from the coxcomb to the—

KATE: Aye, do split the twin potato asunder, do. [*Discovers herself.*]

LARRY: It is—no—what! Och, is it nobody but yourself? O, my darling!—[*Catches her in his arms.*] And so—But how did you?— And where—and what—O, boderation! [*Kisses.*] And how d' ye do? and how's your mother? and the pigs and praties,³¹ and—kiss me, Kate. [*Kiss.*]

KATE: So; now may I speak?

LARRY: Ay, do be telling me—but stop every now and then, that I may point your story with a grammatical kiss.

KATE: Oh, hang it! you'll be for putting nothing but periods to my discourse.

LARRY: Faith, and I should be for counting—[*kisses*]—four.—Arrah! there, then; I've done with that sentence.

KATE: You remember what caused me to stay behind, when you embarked for America?

LARRY: Ay, 'twas because of your old sick mother. And how does the good lady? [KATE *weeps.*] Ah! well, Heaven rest her soul—Cheerly, cheerly. To be sure, I can't give *you* a mother; but I tell you what I'll do, I'll give your children one; and that's the same thing, you know. So, kiss me, Kate. Cheerly.

KATE: One day, as I sat desolate in my cottage, a carriage broke down near it, from which a young lady was thrown with great violence. My humble cabin received her, and I attended her till she was able to resume her journey.

LARRY: My kind Kate!

KATE: The sweet young lady promised me her protection, and pressed me to go with her. So, having no mother—nor Larry to take care of—

LARRY: You let the pigs and praties take care of themselves.

KATE: I placed an honest, poor neighbour in my cottage, and followed the fortunes of my mistress—and—O Larry, such an angel!

LARRY: But where is she?

KATE: Here, in Virginia.

LARRY: Here?

KATE: Ay, but that's a secret.

LARRY: Oh! is it so? that's the reason then you won't tell it me.

[GERALDINE, *as a page, and* WALTER *appear behind.*]

KATE: That's she.

LARRY: Where?

KATE: There.

LARRY: Bother! I see no one but a silken cloaked spark, and our Wat; devil a petticoat!

KATE: That spark is my mistress.

LARRY: Be asy. Are you sure you ar'n't his mistress?

KATE: Tut, now you've got the twin potatoes in your head.

LARRY: Twins they must be, if any, for faith I hav'n't had a *single* potato in my head this many a long day. But come, my Kate, tell me how you and your mistress happened to jump into—

KATE: Step aside then.

LARRY: Have with you, my dapper page. [*They retire.*]

[GERALDINE *and* WALTER *advance.*]

GERALDINE: You know this Percy, then?

WALTER: Know him! Oh, yes!
He makes this wild wood, here, a past'ral grove.
He is a love-lorn shepherd; an Orlando,[32]
Carving love-rhymes and cyphers on the trees,
And warbling dying ditties of a lady
He calls false Geraldine.

GERALDINE: O my dear Percy!
How has one sad mistake marr'd both our joys! [*Aside.*]

WALTER: Yet, though a shepherd, he can wield a sword
As easy as a crook.

GERALDINE: Oh! he is brave.

WALTER: As Julius Caesar, sir, or Hercules;
Or any other hero that you will,
Except our captain.

GERALDINE: Is your captain, then,
Without his peer?

WALTER: Ay, marry is he, sir,
  Sans equal in this world. I've follow'd him
  Half o'er the globe, and seen him do such deeds!
  His shield is blazon'd with three Turkish heads.
GERALDINE: Well, sir.
WALTER: And I, boy, saw him win the arms;
  Oh, 'twas the bravest act!
GERALDINE: Prithee, recount it.
WALTER: It was at Regal, close beleaguer'd then
  By the duke of Sigismund[33] of Transylvania,
  Our captain's general. One day, from the gate
  There issued a gigantic mussulman,
  And threw his gauntlet down upon the ground,
  Daring our christian knights to single combat.
  It was our captain, sir, pick'd up the glove,
  And scarce the trump had sounded to the onset,
  When the Turk Turbisha[34] had lost his head.
  His brother, fierce Grualdo, enter'd next,
  But left the lists sans life or turban too.
  Last came black Bonamolgro, and he paid
  The same dear forfeit for the same attempt.
  And now my master, like a gallant knight,
  His sabre studded o'er with ruby gems,
  Prick'd on his prancing courser round the field,
  In vain inviting fresh assailants; while
  The beauteous dames of Regal, who, in throngs
  Lean'd o'er the rampart to behold the tourney,
  Threw show'rs of scarfs and favours from the wall,
  And wav'd their hands, and bid swift Mercuries
  Post from their eyes with messages of love;
  While manly modesty and graceful duty
  Wav'd on his snowy plume, and, as he rode,
  Bow'd down his casque unto the saddle bow.
GERALDINE: It was a deed of valour, and you've dress'd it
  In well-beseeming terms. And yet, methinks,
  I wonder at the ladies' strange delight;
  And think the spectacle might better suit
  An audience of warriors than of women.
  I'm sure I should have shudder'd—that is, sir,
  If I were woman.

WALTER: Cry your mercy, page;
   Were you a woman, you would love the brave.
   You're yet but boy; you'll know the truth of this,
   When father Time writes man upon your chin.
GERALDINE: No doubt I shall, sir, when I get a beard.
WALTER: My master, boy, has made it crystal clear:
   Be but a Mars, and you shall have your Venus.

Song—WALTER.

   Captain Smith is a man of might,
   In Venus' soft wars or in Mars' bloody fight:
   For of widow, or wife, or of damsel bright,
           A bold blade, you know, is all the dandy.

           One day his sword he drew,
           And a score of Turks he slew;
               When done his toil,
               He snatch'd the spoil,
               And, as a part,
               The gentle heart
           Of the lovely lady Tragabizandy.[35]

   Captain Smith trod the Tartar land;
   While before him, in terror, fled the turban'd band,
   With his good broad-sword, that he whirl'd in his hand,
           To a three-tail'd bashaw[36] he gave a pat—a.

           The bashaw, in alarm,
           Turn'd tails, and fled his arm.
               But face to face,
               With lovely grace,
               In all her charms,
               Rush'd to his arms
           The beautiful lady Calamata.[37]

   Captain Smith, from the foaming seas,
   From pirates, and shipwreck, and miseries,
   In a French lady's arms found a haven of ease;
           Her name—pshaw! from memory quite gone 't has.

>   And on this savage shore,
>   Where his faulchion[38] stream'd with gore,
>   His noble heart
>   The savage dart
>   Had quiver'd through;
>   But swifter flew
>   To his heart the pretty princess Pocahontas.

[Exit WALTER.]

[Enter KATE.]

GERALDINE: Now, brother page—
KATE: Dear mistress, I have found
   My faithful Larry.
GERALDINE: Happy girl! and I
   Hope soon to meet my heart's dear lord, my Percy.
   Hist! the lord governor—
KATE: He little thinks
   Who is the page he loves so—
GERALDINE: Silence.
KATE: Mum.

[Enter DELAWAR,[39] WALTER, LARRY, &c.]

DELAWAR: Each noble act of his that you recite
   Challenge all my wonder and applause.
   Your captain is a brave one; and I long
   To press the hero's hand. But look, my friends,
   What female's this, who, like the swift Camilla,[40]
   On airy step flies hitherward?
WALTER: My lord,
   This is the lovely princess you have heard of;
   Our infant colony's best patroness;
   Nay, sir, its foster-mother.
DELAWAR: Mark how wild—

   [Music. The PRINCESS enters, with wild anxiety in her looks;
   searches eagerly around for SMITH and ROLFE.]

DELAWAR: Whom do you look for, lady?
PRINCESS: They are gone!
   Gone to be slaughter'd!
WALTER: If you seek our captain,
   He has departed for your father's banquet.

PRINCESS: Then they have met, and they will both be lost,
    My lover and my friend. O! faithless path,
    That led me from my lover! Strangers, fly!
    If you're the white man's friends—
DELAWAR: Lady, we are.
PRINCESS: Then fly to save them from destruction!
DELAWAR: How?
PRINCESS: Inquire not; speak not; treachery and death
    Await them at the banquet.
DELAWAR: Haste, my friends,
    Give order for immediate departure.
PRINCESS: E'en now, perhaps, they bleed! O lover! brother! Fly,
    strangers, fly!

    [*Music. Drum beats; a bustle; scene closes.*]

SCENE 4: *At* Werocomoco; *banquet.* SMITH, ROLFE, PERCY, NANTAQUAS, POWHATAN, &c., *seated.* GRIMOSCO, MIAMI, *and a number of* INDIANS *attending.*

POWHATAN: White warriors, this is the feast of peace, and yet you wear your arms. Will not my friends lay by their warlike weapons? They fright our fearful people.
SMITH: Our swords are part of our apparel, king;
    Nor need your people fear them. They shall rest
    Peaceful within their scabbards, if Powhatan
    Call them not forth, with voice of enmity.
POWHATAN: O that can never be! feast then in peace,
    Children and friends—[*Leaves his place and comes forward to*
        GRIMOSCO.]
    O priest! my soul is afraid it will be stained with dishonour.
GRIMOSCO: Away! the Great Spirit commands you. Resume your seat; hold the white men in discourse; I will but thrice wave my hand, and your foes are dead. [KING *resumes his seat.*] [*To* MIAMI.] Now, prince, has the hour of vengeance arrived.
POWHATAN: [*With a faltering voice.*] Think not, white men, that Powhatan wants the knowledge to prize your friendship. Powhatan has seen three generations pass away; and his locks of age do not float upon the temples of folly.

[GRIMOSCO *waves his hand: the* INDIANS *steal behind the* EN-GLISH, MIAMI *behind* ROLFE. KING *proceeds.*]

If a leaf but fall in the forest, my people cry out with terror, "hark! the white warrior comes!" Chief, thou art terrible as an enemy, and Powhatan knows the value of thy friendship.

[GRIMOSCO *waves his hand again; the* INDIANS *seize their toma-hawks, and prepare to strike.* KING *goes on.*]

Think not, therefore, Powhatan can attempt to deceive thee—

[*The* KING'S *voice trembles; he stops, unable to proceed. The* IN-DIANS' *eyes are fixed on* GRIMOSCO, *waiting for the last signal. At this moment the* PRINCESS *rushes in.*]

PRINCESS: Treachery to the white men!

[*At the same instant, drum and trumpet without. Music. The* EN-GLISH *seize the uplifted arms of the* INDIANS, *and form a tableau, as enter* DELAWAR *and his party. After the music, the* SOLDIERS *take charge of the* INDIANS. POCAHONTAS *flies to the arms of* ROLFE.]

NANTAQUAS: Oh father! [POWHATAN *is transfixed with confusion.*]
SMITH: Wretched king! what fiend could urge you?
POWHATAN: Shame ties the tongue of Powhatan. Ask of that fiend-like priest, how, to please the angry Spirit, I was to massacre my friends.
SMITH: Holy Religion! still beneath the veil
Of sacred piety what crimes lie hid!
Bear hence that monster. Thou ferocious prince—
MIAMI: Miami's tortures shall not feast your eyes! [*Stabbing himself.*]
SMITH: Rash youth, thou mightst have liv'd—
MIAMI: Liv'd! man, look there! [*Pointing to* ROLFE *and* PRINCESS. *He is borne off.*]
POWHATAN: Oh, if the false Powhatan might—
SMITH: No more.
Wiser than thou have been the dupes of priesthood.
Your hand. The father of this gen'rous pair
I cannot choose but love. My noble lord,
I pray you pardon my scant courtesy
And sluggish duty, which so tardy-paced
Do greet your new arrival—
DELAWAR: Valiant captain!

Virtue-ennobled sir, a hero's heart
Will make mine proud by its most near acquaintance. [*Embrace.*]
SMITH: Your coming was most opportune, my lord.
One moment more—
DELAWAR: Nay, not to us the praise.
Behold the brilliant star that led us on.
SMITH: Oh! blest is still its kindly influence!
Could a rough soldier play the courtier, lady,
His practis'd tongue might grace thy various goodness,
With proper phrase of thanks; but oh! reward thee!
Heaven only can—
PRINCESS: And has, my brother. See!
I have its richest gift. [*Turning to* ROLFE.]
ROLFE: My dearest love!
SMITH: Her brother, sir, and worthy of that name.

[*Introduces* NANTAQUAS *to* DELAWAR; PERCY *and* GERALDINE,
who had been conversing, advance.]

PERCY: You tell me wonders.
GERALDINE: But not miracles.
Being near the uncle, sir, I knew the lady.
PERCY: And was I then deceived?
GERALDINE: What, gentle Percy!
Young man, 'twas not well done, in idle pique,
To wound the heart that lov'd you.
PERCY: O sir! speak!
My Geraldine, your niece, is she not married?
DELAWAR: Nor like to be, poor wench, but to her grave,
If mourning for false lovers break maids' hearts.
PERCY: Was she then true? O madman! idiot!
To let the feeble breath of empty rumour
Drive me from heavenly happiness!
DELAWAR: Poor girl!
She fain would have embark'd with me.
PERCY: Ah, sir!
Why did she not?
DELAWAR: Marry, sir, I forbade her:
The rough voyage would have shook her slender health
To dissolution.
GERALDINE: Pardon, sir; not so—
DELAWAR: How now, pert page?

GERALDINE: For here she is, my lord.
    And the rough voyage has giv'n her a new life.
PERCY: My Geraldine!
DELAWAR: My niece! O, brazenface!
    Approach me not; fly from your uncle's anger;
    Fly to your husband's arms for shelter, hussy!

        [GERALDINE *flies to* PERCY'S *embrace.*]

PERCY: Oh! speechless transport! mute let me infold thee!
DELAWAR: [*To* KATE.] And you, my little spark, perhaps, your cloak
    Covers another duteous niece—or daughter.
    Speak lady: for I see that title writ
    In crimson characters upon your cheek.
    Art of my blood?
LARRY: No, sir, she's of my flesh;
    Flesh of my flesh, my lord. Now, arrah, Kate,
    Don't blush. This goodly company all knows
    My flesh may wear the breeches, without scandal.
WALTER: Listen not, Alice, to his sophistry.
    Sir, if our good wives learn this argument,
    They'll logically pluck away our—
ALICE: Tut:
    Fear ye not that; for when a woman would,
    She'll draw them on without a rule of reason.
DELAWAR: Methinks 'tis pairing time among the turtles.
    Who have we here?

        [ROBIN *and* NIMA *come forward.*]

ROBIN: A pair of pigeons, sir; or rather a robin and a dove. A wild
    thing, sir, that I caught in the wood here. But when I have clipt her
    wings, and tamed her, I hope (without offence to this good company)
    that we shall bill without biting more than our neighbours.
SMITH: Joy to ye, gentle lovers; joy to all;
    A goodly circle, and a fair. Methinks
    Wild Nature smooths apace her savage frown,
    Moulding her features to a social smile.
    Now flies my hope-wing'd fancy o'er the gulf
    That lies between us and the aftertime,
    When this fine portion of the globe shall teem
    With civiliz'd society; when arts,
    And industry, and elegance shall reign,

As the shrill war-cry of the savage man
Yields to the jocund shepherd's roundelay.
Oh, enviable country! thus disjoin'd
From old licentious Europe! may'st thou rise,
Free from those bonds which fraud and superstition
In barbarous ages have enchain'd *her* with;
Bidding the antique world with wonder view
A great, yet virtuous empire in the west!

Finale.

Freedom, on the western shore
  Float thy banner o'er the brave;
Plenty, here thy blessings pour;
  Peace, thy olive sceptre wave!

PERCY, WALTER, &c.: Fire-eyed Valour, guard the land;
 Here uprear thy fearless crest;
PRINCESS, KATE, ALICE, &c.: Love, diffuse thy influence bland
 O'er the regions of the west.
CHORUS, *Freedom, &c.*
LARRY: Hither, lassie, frank and pretty,
     Come and live without formality,
    Thou, in English christen'd Pity,
     But call'd, in Irish, Hospitality.
CHORUS, *Freedom, &c.*

THE END

THE GLADIATOR *(1831)*
ROBERT MONTGOMERY BIRD

Although known to specialists now as an early writer of frontier novels, Robert Montgomery Bird (1806–1854) was at one time looked upon as a potential leader in the development of a new American drama. Born in New Castle, Delaware, and trained as a physician, Bird settled in Philadelphia, a literary center. Forgoing his vocation for a calling, Bird turned to writing and developed an ambitious program whereby he would produce something in almost every major genre. Among his early works were several dramatic comedies, including *The City Looking Glass* (1828), and tragedies, among them *The Cowled Lover* (1827). Many of these works were fragments, and none of his plays was published in his lifetime.

Following a trip to Kentucky and a visit to Mammoth Cave—travels he would draw upon for his most famous novel, *Nick of the Woods* (1837)—Bird turned his energies to playwriting. The impetus was a contest held by Edwin Forrest, Bird's precise contemporary but already a well-known actor, the most famous American-born actor of his day. Forrest advertised a yearly competition to provide him with original plays that featured heroic central characters. The winner of the first contest was John Augustus Stone, another Philadelphian, whose *Metamora, or The Last of the Wampanoags* (1829) gave Forrest one of his most popular vehicles.

Bird captured the prize the following year with a classical play entitled *Pelopidas*, the story of an exiled Theban who wrests his home city from Spartan control. Forrest never produced the play, however, probably because Pelopidas does not dominate the action in the way that, say, Metamora does in Stone's play. Instead, Bird wrote another classical drama to substitute; *The Gladiator* took the 1831 prize and was rushed into production. It proved to be a major vehicle for Forrest, for the role of Spartacus was perfectly conceived to meet the actor's strengths. Bird's brother Henry advised him that the new play deserved the author's attention much more than *Pelopidas:* "Stick to the Gladiator: it is not only a captivating but popular name, and a character altogether more suited to Forrest's Roman figure & actions." Thus, long before movies were made to fit Hollywood stars, plays were crafted with the deliberate intention of putting a stage star in the most flattering light.

The story of *The Gladiator* is then twofold: that of the life of Spartacus, the leader of a slave revolt against Rome; and that of the actor, Forrest, who played the role over a thousand times in his career. For the first, Bird drew on a number of classical and contemporary sources for his story of the Third Servile War (73–71 B.C.). As Curtis Dahl lists them, "Bird read Livy, Florus, Eutropius, Velleius Paterculus, and Appian, as well as the modern historians Ferguson and Hooks. . . . He also looked up articles on Spartacus in *Blackwood's Magazine*." Since he already knew Plutarch, the source of *Pelopidas,* Bird had a thorough grounding in the history and legend of the period.

The play begins with a dark assessment of Rome and its politics by Phasarius, a Thracian gladiator and slave. The previous dictator of Rome, Lucius Cornelius Sulla (or Sylla), is dead; so is his rival, the popular leader Gaius Marius. Other Roman leaders are busy punishing rebels in the Empire: Quintus Caecilius Metellus is chasing Quintus Sertorius in Spain; Lucius Licinius Lucullus is battling a longtime enemy to Rome, Mithridates VI, king of the Asia Minor country of Pontus; and Julius Caesar, who had also worn the popular banner against the oligarchic Sulla, is busy with pirates in the Mediterranean islands. For Phasarius, the sum of these enterprises tells him that no one cares about freedom or the lives of people in Rome itself. The leader of the city, after all, is Marcus Licinius Crassus, a wealthy praetor who achieved his power through slave dealing and buying up fire-damaged houses for very little then reselling them at a profit.

Into this corrupt world comes the slave Spartacus, a gladiator of Capua who has been brought to Rome by Lentulus. Crassus and others figure to make money on the prowess of this muscular fighter, but Spartacus has no loyalty to Rome; he, after all, is a captive and at first assumes his wife and child have been dispatched. When they also show up among the captives, he feels he has something to fight for—his and their freedom. Spartacus and Phasarius, the local champion, are forced to fight; discovering they are brothers, they unite rather than fight each other to the death. Both having anticipated a propitious moment, Spartacus shouts "Freedom!" and the war is on.

Such a hero—loud, dynamic, athletic, and antiaristocratic—suited Forrest's image of himself perfectly. Forrest's seat of strength was among the b'hoys of New York, the working-class young men of the city who were drawn to the actor's roles of oppressed men of the people. He projected the image of the man's man, "one of the roughs," as Walt Whitman called himself. Whitman, in fact, was drawn to Bird's drama: "it is a play, this *Gladiator,* calculated to make the hearts of the masses well responsively to all those nobler manlier aspirations in behalf of mortal freedom!" But even Whitman found limits to Forrest's method, especially as it was imitated by others, specifically "the loud mouthed ranting style." With an imposing physique, great booming voice, and some genuine understanding of what worked on stage, Forrest—if not his imitators—could generally pull it off. When he toured Great Britain for the first time, he opened not with Shakespeare but with Bird's *Gladiator*. No one accused Forrest of subtlety, but even English audiences and critics would grant him the power of his representation.

The question remains, then, why a story about a gladiator would have resonance with American audiences of the nineteenth century. Clearly, people saw in Spartacus the type of the American democrat, the oppressed underdog who through thirst for individual freedom and love of family risks all in taking on a tyrannical government. Thus, Forrest, having already cultivated through his legion of supporters a reputation as the people's actor, could meld his own stage personality with that of the character he portrayed and voice the popular desires of Americans for the promises of the Revolution. Indeed, it would have been easy enough to see *The Gladiator* as about the Revolution, with Britain as Rome and the colonials as slaves.

But the matter of its immediate social relevance is complicated. In 1831, the only "slaves" in America were African in origin. That same year, a Virginia slave named Nat Turner organized a violent uprising in Southampton County that resulted in many white deaths before he and his men were captured and executed. For Walt Whitman fifteen years later, there was little question of the play's abolitionist tendencies. Whether the playwright intended such things, however, is not as clear. In his *Secret Records*, a diary he kept at the time, Bird shows that he understood the inflammatory potential of his play, especially if it were produced in the South. As Dahl reads it, however, Bird's prophecy of a mass slave revolt is predicated on a belief that African Americans will be violent and ruthless, not noble Thracians with "Roman" manners. Nevertheless, the play enunciates precisely the issues that faced freedom fighters in the 1830s, including the method of splitting slave family units through separate sales. Even if Bird or Forrest could not have made the complete leap to portraying black slaves in revolt, they did combine to produce a play that articulates the very longings we now recognize that African-American slaves themselves maintained. Some adventurous director might still produce this play, set it on a plantation, and the point would be made.

In other ways, though, *The Gladiator* is fully of its period. Senona, the wife of Spartacus, is a version of Nahmeokee, the all-sacrificing spouse of Metamora in Stone's play—a drama, by the way, rewritten by Bird for Forrest. There is, of course, a virgin in danger, Julia, the niece of Crassus. She lacks a protective mother figure, as most young women in melodrama do, and depends on the honor of some man to protect her from the dishonor that might be brought by another man. As Bruce McConachie notes, this drama, like other heroic Forrest plays, includes romantic devices with its ostensibly Jacksonian politics; not only is there love interest, but Spartacus also pastoralizes his lost home of Thrace. Such romanticizing, as Richard Moody has made clear, is a dominant tendency of drama in this period.

The Rome portrayed here, like the public America of Bird's day, is a man's world, where matters of honor and freedom are dealt with in terms of male combat and provocative talk. Nevertheless, Rome ends up standing for many, often contradictory things in the theater. For Forrest, the figure of the gladiator represented his own pugnacious striving to be The Star, the unbested champion of the boards. His chief rival was the British actor William Macready, whose more subtle style Forrest saw as European effeminacy on display. Forrest, while attending a performance by Macready in Scotland, actually hissed his rival; later, in New York, provocative actions by Forrest's supporters while Macready was acting there led to the infamous Astor Place Riot. It was as if Forrest could never quite shake the gladiator from his system.

For Bird, Rome meant classical greatness, poetry in drama, an ennobling trope by which to elevate the theater of his day. This notion was pursued by many of the Philadelphia writers, including George Henry Boker. But for Boker, the Roman ideal was antidemocratic, an assertion of an elite aesthetic over popular entertainment. Bird, whatever his desires for greatness, did not divorce his practice from trying at some level to please the people.

In the end, Forrest and Bird, for a while staunch friends and traveling companions, broke up their relationship over Forrest's alleged refusal to pay Bird what he owed him. After his *Broker of Bogota* won another Forrest competition in 1834, Bird gave up the stage, another high-minded victim of the competitive practices of the nineteenth-century American theater. Forrest's career, by contrast, lasted forty years past the premiere of *The Gladiator,* by fame and fortune enriched manyfold over the paltry sums he paid his most important personal dramatist, Robert Montgomery Bird.

SELECTED BIBLIOGRAPHY

Bird, Henry. Letter to Robert Montgomery Bird. December 31, 1830. Diedrich Collection. William L. Clements Library, Ann Arbor.

Bird, Robert Montgomery. *Plays*, edited by Edward H. O'Neill. *America's Lost Plays*. Vol. 12. 1940; Bloomington: Indiana University Press, 1965.

Dahl, Curtis. *Robert Montgomery Bird*. New York: Twayne, 1963. Best bibliography on Bird, with good chapter on *The Gladiator*.

Foust, Clement E. *The Life and Dramatic Works of Robert Montgomery Bird*. New York: Knickerbocker, 1919. Includes texts of *Pelopidas*, *The Gladiator*, *Oralloosa*, and *The Broker of Bogota*.

Grimsted, David. *Melodrama Unveiled: American Theater and Culture, 1800–1850*, 167–70. Chicago: University of Chicago Press, 1968.

Halline, Allan Gates. Introduction to *The Gladiator*. *American Plays*, edited by Allan Gates Halline, 155–59. New York: American Book, 1935.

Harris, Richard. "A Young Dramatist's Diary: *The Secret Records* of R. M. Bird." *University of Pennsylvania Chronicle* 25 (1959): 8–24.

McConachie, Bruce A. *Melodramatic Formations: American Theatre and Society, 1820–1870*, 97–117 passim. Iowa City: University of Iowa Press, 1992.

Meserve, Walter J. *Heralds of Promise: The Drama of the American People During the Age of Jackson, 1829–1849*, 58–66. New York: Greenwood, 1986.

Moody, Richard. *America Takes the Stage: Romanticism in American Drama and Theatre, 1750–1900*, 193–97. Bloomington: Indiana University Press, 1955.

———. Introduction to *The Gladiator*. In *Dramas from the American Theatre, 1762–1909*, edited by Richard Moody, 229–40. Cleveland: World, 1966.

Moses, Montrose J. *The Fabulous Forrest: The Record of an American Actor*. 1929; New York: Benjamin Blom, 1969, 101–10, 142–47.

Richardson, Gary A. "Robert Montgomery Bird: Romantic Drama in the Age of Jackson." *American Drama from the Colonial Period through World War I: A Critical History*, 74–80. New York: Twayne, 1993.

Thompson, C. S. "Life of Robert Montgomery Bird: Written by His Wife, Mary Mayer Bird . . . with Selections from Bird's Correspondence." *University of Pennsylvania Library Chronicle* 12 (1944): 71–120; 13 (1945): 1–94.

Whitman, Walt. "*The Gladiator*—Mr. Forrest—Acting." *Brooklyn Eagle*, December 26, 1846. Reprinted in *The American Theatre as Seen by Its Critics, 1752–1934*, edited by Montrose J. Moses and John Mason Brown. 1934; New York: Cooper Square, 1967, 69–70.

THE GLADIATOR

A TRAGEDY

IN FIVE ACTS

PHILADELPHIA, APRIL, 1831

PERSONS REPRESENTED

MARCUS LICINIUS CRASSUS, *a Roman Praetor.*
LUCIUS GELLIUS, *a Consul.*
SCROPHA, *a Quaestor.*
JOVIUS, *a Centurion.*
MUMMIUS, *lieutenant to* CRASSUS.
BATIATUS LENTULUS, *a Capuan Lanista, or master of gladiators.*
BRACCHIUS, *a Roman Lanista.*
FLORUS, *son of* B. LENTULUS.
SPARTACUS, *a Thracian [Gladiator].*
PHASARIUS, *his brother [Gladiator].*
ÆNOMAIIS, *a Gaul [Gladiator].*
CRIXUS, *a German [Gladiator].*
   and others [Gladiators].
A *boy, son of* SPARTACUS.
JULIA, *niece of* CRASSUS.
SENONA, *wife of* SPARTACUS.
Citizens, soldiers, etc.

SCENE *Rome, and parts of Italy. Time,* B.C. 73

THE GLADIATOR

ACT I

SCENE 1: *Rome. The street before* BRACCHIUS'S *house.*

[*Enter* PHASARIUS, ÆNOMAIIS, *and other gladiators.*]

PHASARIUS: There never was a properer moment. I look around me on the Roman flocks, that are deserted by their watchdogs and shepherds, and my fingers itch to be at their throats. Rome has sent forth her generals to conquer the world, and left nothing but her name for the protection of her citizens. Where now is that warlike, arrogant, and envious coxcomb, Pompey? Quarreling,—he and that old brawler, Metellus,—in Spain, with the rebel, Sartorious: Lucullus, the Spoiler? Chasing the braggart, Mithridates, over his Pontic mountains: and Marcus, his brother? Killing the rest of my countrymen, the furies speed him! That restless boy, young Caesar? Among the islands, crucifying the pirates. Marius dead, Sylla rotting.[1]—There is not a man in Rome, that Rome could now look to for service.

ÆNOMAIIS: The praetor, Crassus.[2]

PHASARIUS: The miserable rich man, the patrician monger, that, by traffic in human flesh, has turned a patrimony of an hundred talents into an hundred thousand! If there be any virtue in the love of wealth, then is the praetor a most virtuous man; for he loves it better than he loves the gods. And if he be great and magnanimous, who coins his gold from the sinews of his bondsmen, set me down Crassus as the beloved of all greatness. 'Sblood, brother sworder, what were such a counter of silver in the iron wars? Get me up a rebellion, and you shall see this great man brained by the least of his merchandise.

ÆNOMAIIS: Well, I should like to be at the killing of some dozen such tyrants.

PHASARIUS: Why should you not? Some thousands like ourselves
Most scurvy fellows, that have been trained, like dogs
To tear each other for their masters' pleasure,
Shed blood, cut throats, and do such mortal mischiefs
As men love best to work upon their foes,—
Of these there are some thousands in this realm,
Have the same wish with us, to turn their swords
Upon their masters. And, 'tis natural,

173

That wish, and reasonable, very reasonable.
I am tired of slaying bondmen like myself,
I am sick of it. That day the Roman knight,
To win the smile of the rich quaestor's[3] daughter,
In the arena sprung, and volunteered
To kill a gladiator,[4] and did find
His liver spitted, like a thing of naught,
Upon my weapon,—since that day I tasted
Of Roman blood, I have had no desire
To kill poor slaves—I've longed for naught but Romans!

ÆNOMAIIS: Well, we can die, and kill some, ere we die.

PHASARIUS: Ay, marry, some dozens;
And should those wretches be but moved to join us,
We might, for dozens, count us glorious thousands.

ÆNOMAIIS: Well, we are all agreed to this. We are thirty. But how
Shall we get weapons?

PHASARIUS: Set our dens afire,
And force the armoury.

ÆNOMAIIS: Our master, Bracchius,
Has a sharp watch to that.

PHASARIUS: In half an hour,
We are at our morning's practice. Now, thou knowest,
To keep me in good heart, he humours me
Most fulsomely. I have won him some great wagers,
So I am worth his fooling. I will urge him,
For this day's play, instead of laths, to give us
True brands, for keener practice, that we may
Show nobler for him at the praetor's games.

ÆNOMAIIS: <He knows, indeed, 'tis needful we have ready,
For these same games, the best of skill:> I've heard
That Lentulus the Capuan[5] brings a troop
Of excellent swordsmen on that day.

PHASARIUS: What, excellent?
Did I not beat his boaster?—Excellent?

ÆNOMAIIS: 'Tis rumoured so.

PHASARIUS: By Jove, we will put off
This thing a day! I have seen no excellence
In weapons for a month.

ÆNOMAIIS: Why need you see it?

PHASARIUS: Nay, if he have a man to meet a man,
I must be in the arena: No desertion,

When there's a peril to be dared and ended!
Faith, I will have a bout, if it but be
To make Rome talk. You shall see, Ænomaiis,
If he be matched with me in the Thracian combat,
How I will use that trick my brother taught me,
When first I flashed a weapon.

ÆNOMAIIS: I doubt not,
You will maintain your reputation.

PHASARIUS: Faith,
I'll hear once more this Roman acclamation,
Ere it be changed to curses.

ÆNOMAIIS: See! Our master—

PHASARIUS: Well, get you gone.

ÆNOMAIIS: Forget not for the weapons.

PHASARIUS: Ay, ay—after the shows.

                    [*Exit* ÆNOMAIIS *and the* GLADIATORS.]

    [*Enter* BRACCHIUS.]

BRACCHIUS: How now, Phasarius; what did these cutthroats here?
    Idling, Sirrah?

PHASARIUS: No; they were moralizing over their scars, and asking what
    they had got by 'em.

BRACCHIUS: Do the rogues think themselves soldiers, that their cuts
    should be worth anything but showing?

PHASARIUS: No. But some of them hope to be made freemen one day,
    when they are no longer fit for the arena.

BRACCHIUS: Fellow, thou knowest I love thee, and will enfranchise
    thee.

PHASARIUS: Yes,—when my eye is dimmed, my arm stiffened, my heart
    chilled, my head gray: I look for redemption no sooner. I am a lusty,
    serviceable rogue yet. Why should you free me now?

BRACCHIUS: Sirrah, are you insolent? I will have the centupondium to
    your heels, and the lash to your shoulders.

PHASARIUS: Which will make me fight the better at the praetor's games,
    hah! Which of us is the lunatic?

BRACCHIUS: What, you knave!

PHASARIUS: Thou art my master; but I know, thou wouldst as soon set
    me free, as scourge me. Both would destroy thy subsistence, and one
    thy life; in either case, I would fight no more. And if thou wert to
    touch me lawfully with the thong, thou knowest, I would unlawfully
    murder thee.

BRACCHIUS: You shall be crucified![6]

PHASARIUS: Then shall the crows pick forty thousand crowns from my bones; for so much are these muscles worth.

BRACCHIUS: Out upon you, villain! It is my favour has made thee so insolent.

PHASARIUS: It is my knowledge of my own price, and not thy favour, which is more perilous than thine anger. Pr'ythee, threaten me no more; or I shall grow peaceable, and spoil thy fortune.

BRACCHIUS: You have sworn never to decline the combat.

PHASARIUS: Ay; so I have. But I have found no one regards a slave's oath; and why now should the slave? It is my humour, and not my oath, makes me a shedder of blood. But the humour may change.

BRACCHIUS: Well, thou art a most impudent talker; it is eternal Saturnalia[7] with thee. But I forgive thee, and will do thee more kindness than I have done already.

PHASARIUS: Which is to say, you have some new jeopardy to put my neck in. You have some gladiator of fame you would have me fight, is it not?

BRACCHIUS: Ay, if rumour be worth the noting. Crassus has hired the gladiators from Capua; and, 'tis said, Lentulus will bring with them a man that will cut the coxcomb from thy pate, and utterly annihilate thee.

PHASARIUS: They say so? Annihilate me?

BRACCHIUS: Faith, 'tis so reckoned, and strong wagers are making against you.

PHASARIUS: Hah? Against me? Annihilate me! If he have a head of adamant and a breast of brass, he may do it, but if his scull be common bone, and his skin no thicker than bullhide—Mehercle! Let me see this Cyclops.

BRACCHIUS: Now, by Jupiter, I love thy spirit.

PHASARIUS: Has he no name? No country? No voucher of triumphs? Marry, for a mushroom, a thing that was yesterday unknown, his credit is a jot too arrogant; and, as I am a Thracian, and feel the blood of the warlike god, the father of Thrace, still tingle in my fingers, I will make my iron acquainted with his ribs.—Out upon him,—Annihilate me!

BRACCHIUS: Come, thou art his better; but he is noted enough to make thy triumph the more glorious. Put thyself in the meanwhile to practice. But who comes here? What, Lentulus of Capua?

[*Enter* LENTULUS.]

By mine honesty, I am glad to see thee. Bringest thou any new cut-throats? What man, here is my Mars of gladiators, my most un-matched and unmatchable, Phasarius the Thracian. Look how hasty the knave looks! Hast anything fit to be slashed by such a fellow?

LENTULUS: Nay, I know not. 'Tis a most gallant villain. <Slew he not six at the shows given by Gellius the consul?

BRACCHIUS: Yes, by Mars; and would have made eel's meat of the sev-enth, but that the people grew pitiful and pointed their thumbs.—I could have cuffed 'em, senators and all.—He had him on his hip, his body bent round him thus, his fist to his poll, his dagger to his throat. By Mars, 'twas the noblest sight I had seen for a month: and yet when he looked to them for the doom, the pitiful things cried Nay —I could have cuffed 'em!>

LENTULUS: But is he thy best man?

BRACCHIUS: The best in Rome. I have a Gaul too; but he is not his equal. I would thou hadst a match for either. Crassus will pay: the best gladiator in the land were no loss, if killed in his service.

LENTULUS: I have brought some indifferent good fellows: and one of them, I think, I would wager against your unmatchable.

BRACCHIUS: Hearest thou that, Phasarius? Get in and practice.

[*Exit* PHASARIUS.]

LENTULUS: But he will not take the gladiator's oaths.

BRACCHIUS: What, is he slave or felon?

LENTULUS: A slave that I bought of the quaestor just returned from the army of Thrace;[8] a shepherd, I think, they told me, and leader of a horde of his savage countrymen. I bought him on the faith of the fame he brought with him, of being the most desperate, unconquer-able, and, indeed, skilful barbarian in the province. <Thou hast not forgot Caius Clypeus,[9] the centurion, that fought in the shows at the funeral of Sylla?

BRACCHIUS: He was accounted on that day the second swordsman in Rome.

LENTULUS: His bones, with those of two of his followers, are rotting on the banks of the Strymon.[10] The three attacked the valiant savage, my bondman; and by Jupiter, without other help than fortune and extraordinary prowess, he slew them all.

BRACCHIUS: Hercules! he has magic weapons!> But how was he taken?

LENTULUS: Betrayed by his follower, while he slept; and yet he had vengeance on his betrayer, for he dashed his brains out upon a rock.

BRACCHIUS: Excellent! Dash his brains out! He is a Titan. I would have given a dozen common slaves to have seen him do that thing!

LENTULUS: But he will not swear.

BRACCHIUS: Come, thou knowest not the nature of these fellows. Didst thou speak him kindly?

LENTULUS: Ay: but I had better have talked softly to a hyena: he did but scowl at me. Faith, he will sit you by the day, looking at his chains, or the wall; and if one has a word from him, it is commonly a question. How many leagues he is away from Thrace.

BRACCHIUS: Didst thou tell him of the honours of a gladiator?

LENTULUS: Ay; and he asked if cutting throats was the most honourable occupation in Rome?

BRACCHIUS: By Mars, thou shouldst have scourged him.

LENTULUS: I did.

BRACCHIUS: And how wrought it?

LENTULUS: I think the knave had killed me, when I struck him,—ay, even with his manacled fist,—but that he was felled by the staff of my freedman. I should have hanged him, but was loath to lose so bold a varlet. Wherefore I had him scourged again, and faith he took it as passively as a stone. But it will not make him swear.

BRACCHIUS: Didst thou vow to the gods to hang him up like a dog, if he were so obstinate?

LENTULUS: I had a halter put to his neck; but then he laughed, and thanked his barbarous gods for such indulgence.

BRACCHIUS: Nay, this is a madman.

LENTULUS: I had the fetters taken from his arm, and sent one to attack him with a weapon. But although I laid a sword by him, he would not use it; yet he struck the assailant with his fist, and felled him as one would a wall with a battering ram. But then he was angry. Another time, he sat still, and let the slave wound him, unresisting.

BRACCHIUS: Moody caitiff! Thou hadst better drown him.—Look thou—Mine eyes are dim—I have brought a troop of women and children—Thracians too—and I think those be they coming yonder.

LENTULUS: Thou art mistaken. Those are mine own cutthroats, and the wild Thracian among them.

BRACCHIUS: Why didst thou bring him to Rome?

LENTULUS: In a last hope to urge him to the oath. Look, is he not a most warlike and promising fellow?

[Enter SPARTACUS,[11] chained, and FLORUS with the CAPUAN GLADIATORS.]

BRACCHIUS: A Hercules, a Mars! What, thou rogue, why dost thou droop thus? Why art thou so sullen and obstinate? No words? What, can'st thou not speak?—Fetch me a scourge hither—I'll find thee a tongue.

LENTULUS: Come, sirrah, look up, speak, show thyself.

SPARTACUS: Is it a thousand leagues away to Thrace?

LENTULUS: What, thou fool, wilt thou always be harping on Thrace? 'Tis so far away, thou wilt never see it more.

SPARTACUS: Never.

LENTULUS: Why I say, never. Why wilt thou be so mad as to think of it?

SPARTACUS: Have Romans father, and wives, and children?

BRACCHIUS: Truly! Thou art a Thracian; what is thy name?

SPARTACUS: Misery.

LENTULUS: Thou seest!

BRACCHIUS: Faith, thou hast scourged him too much; thou has broke his heart. Come, sirrah, dost thou love thy country?

SPARTACUS: I have none,—I am a slave. I was bought; I say, I was bought. Do you doubt it? That man scourges me; *thou* didst threaten me with stripes; every Roman I look upon, speaks to me of scourging. Nay they may: I was bought.

LENTULUS: Thou seest, Bracchius! This is the manner of his obstinacy.

BRACCHIUS: Nay, I see more than thou thinkest. I can move him yet.— Observe him.—He mutters to himself.

SPARTACUS: Is not this Rome? The great city?

BRACCHIUS: Ay; and thou shouldst thank the gods they have suffered thee to see it, before thou diest.—

SPARTACUS: I heard of it, when I was a boy among the hills, piping to my father's flocks. They said, that spoke of it, it was the queen of cities, the metropolis of the world. My heart grew big within me, to hear of its greatness. I thought those men who could make it so, were greater than men; they were gods.

LENTULUS: And are they not, sirrah?—

SPARTACUS: How many palaces, that look like the habitations of divinities, are here about me! Here are marble mountains, that have been hewn down and shaped anew, for men to dwell among. Gold, and silver, and purple, and a million of men thronging the pillared hills!

BRACCHIUS: And what thinkest thou, now thou hast seen it?

SPARTACUS: That,—if Romans had not been fiends, Rome had never been great! Whence came this greatness, but from the miseries of subjugated nations? How many myriads of happy people—people that had not wronged Rome, for they knew not Rome—how many myriads of these were slain like the beasts of the field, that Rome might fatten upon their blood, and become *great*? Look ye,

Roman,—there is not a palace upon these hills that cost not the lives of a thousand innocent men; there is no deed of greatness ye can boast, but it was achieved upon the ruin of a nation; there is no joy ye can feel, but its ingredients are blood and tears.

LENTULUS: Now marry, villain, thou wert bought not to prate, but to fight.

SPARTACUS: I will not fight. I will contend with mine enemy, when there is strife between us; and if that enemy be one of these same fiends, a Roman, I will give him advantage of weapon and place; he shall take a helmet and buckler; while I, with my head bare, my breast naked, and nothing in my hand but my shepherd's staff, will beat him to my feet and slay him. But I will not slay a man for the diversion of Romans.

BRACCHIUS: Thou canst boast, barbarian! If thou canst do this, what brought thee to Rome, a captive?

SPARTACUS: Treachery! I was friendless, sick, famished. My enemies came in numbers. They were like the rats of Egypt, that will not come near the crocodile while he is awake: they attacked me sleeping. Had they found me with a weapon in my hands, Gods! I had not now been a thing for Romans to scourge.

BRACCHIUS: Fellow, I love thee. What is thy name?

SPARTACUS: What matters it?

BRACCHIUS: Wilt thou be free?

SPARTACUS: Free!

BRACCHIUS: Take the oaths of a gladiator, and kill me a score of lusty fellows—

SPARTACUS: A score! kill a score of men? in cold blood? and for the diversion of Rome's rabble? I will not.

BRACCHIUS: By Mars, then you shall be sent to man young Caesar's galleys, and be whipped daily.

LENTULUS: Fight me half a score, and, by Jupiter, I will send thee back to thy wife.

SPARTACUS: My wife!—The last thing that mine eyes looked on,
When my steps turned from Thrace, it was my cottage,
A hideous ruin; the Roman fires had scorched it;
No wife sat sobbing by the wreck; no child
Wept on the sward; not even the watchdog howled;
There was no life there.—Well, why should I talk?
'Tis better they are perished.

LENTULUS: This is despair:
The slave is reckless.—

SPARTACUS: O ye heavens! That sight
  Withered my heart; I was a man no more.
  I had been happy too!—Had ye spared them,
  Then spoke of freedom, you should have had my blood,
  For beastly ransome: All integrity
  And pride of heart I would have sold for it.
BRACCHIUS: Sirrah, there are more wives in Thrace.
LENTULUS: Lo now!
  He'll speak no more.—You, Bracchius, have more skill
  To move these obstinates. You shall buy him of me.
BRACCHIUS: And hang him! Marry, not I. He is a madman.
  I have some better merchandise here now,
  Not warlike, but as gainful.

     [Enter SENONA, with a child, and other slaves.]

                 Thou seest these creatures:
  Here are some Thracians too.—The moody villain!
  He should be hanged.—The Thracian women are
  Most excellent spinners. Buy a brace of them
  For your wife. I care not for so many.
LENTULUS: This woman
  That weeps so, she with the brat,—is she a Thracian?
BRACCHIUS: Hark ye, mistress, answer—are you of Thrace?
  She might swear it by her silence; for these savages
  Are always obstinate at the first. You like her?
  Well, out of my friendship now, I'll almost give her to you.
  Three thousand drachmas—
LENTULUS: Three thousand furies!
BRACCHIUS: Ay, with the boy too—'Tis a lusty imp.
LENTULUS: Three thousand sesterces;[12] and that's too much.
BRACCHIUS: Jove! talk of sesterces? This cub is worth it! [BRACCHIUS
  handling the child roughly.]
SENONA: Ah, hurt him not.
SPARTACUS: Hah!
LENTULUS: Three thousand sesterces.
SPARTACUS: Did my ears mock me?
BRACCHIUS: Well then sesterces,
  For the woman alone.
SENONA: You will not part us?
SPARTACUS: Hah!

Gods, pity me! Does the grave give back the dead?
Senona!
SENONA: Hah! Hah! My husband!
BRACCHIUS: What's the matter?
LENTULUS: A bargain—
BRACCHIUS: What, his wife? Six thousand drachmas.
No more sesterces!—Caitiff, is this thy wife?—[To SPARTACUS.]
SPARTACUS: And my miserable boy too.
Exposed in the street to sell!
BRACCHIUS: By Jove, I have you.
Six thousand drachmas.
SPARTACUS: Why didst thou not die?—
Villains, do you put them up for sale, like beasts?
Look at them: they are human.
LENTULUS: Silence, rogue.—
SPARTACUS: I will not silence. I will ransome them,
What way you will, with life or blood.—
BRACCHIUS: By Jove,
I will not sell her. Into the house, get in.—
Take her along.
SPARTACUS: You shall not—I will brain that man
That lays his hand upon her.
BRACCHIUS: Kill the villain.—
SPARTACUS: Man, master!—See, I am at your feet, and call you,
Of mine own will, *My Master!*—I will serve you
Better than slave e'er served;—grant me this prayer,
And hire my blood out. Buy—yes, that's the word;
It does not choke me—buy her, buy the boy;
Keep us together—
BRACCHIUS: Six thousand drachmas—
SPARTACUS: I will earn them,
Though they were doubled.
LENTULUS: Will you fight?
SPARTACUS: And die.
LENTULUS: Die! Then my gold is lost.
SPARTACUS: I will not die.—
Buy them, buy them.
LENTULUS: And you will swear?
SPARTACUS: I will,—
To be a cutthroat and a murderer.—
Whate'er you will,—so you will buy them.

LENTULUS: Unbind him.

BRACCHIUS: Six thousand—

LENTULUS: Three. Remember, Bracchius,
If you prevent his fighting, your own profit
Suffers as well as mine.

BRACCHIUS: Five thousand then.

LENTULUS: Nay, pr'ythee, four.

BRACCHIUS: Well, out of friendship,
It shall be four.—But, faith, my Gaul shall kill him.

LENTULUS: We shall see. I'll wager even, and no less
Than the purchase money.—

SPARTACUS: Come dry your eyes, Senona.
We are slaves: Why should slaves weep?

SENONA: O, dear my husband,
Though I ne'er thought to have the joy to meet you
Again, in this dark world, I scarce feel joy—
I think, my heart is burst.

SPARTACUS: Come, be of better cheer:—
Art thou not now amid the gorgeous piles
Of the potential and the far-famed Rome?

SENONA: But Oh, the hills of our own native land!
The brooks and forests—

SPARTACUS: Ah! no more, no more:
Think of them not.—

SENONA: Where we fed sheep, and laughed
To think there could be sorrow in the world;
The bright, clear rivers, even that washed the walls
Of our burned cottage—

SPARTACUS: No more, no more, no more.
Are there not hills and brooks in Italy,
Fairer than ours? Content you, girl.

SENONA: Alas,
This boy must be a Roman, and a slave.

SPARTACUS: By heaven, he shall not! Free as rock-hatched eagles,
Thy boy was born, and so shall live and die!—
We wear our fetters only for a time—
Romans are not all like these men. We'll see
Our home yet. We are slaves but for a time.—
I need not ask thee for my mother, girl:
I know this thing has slain her. Her heart cracked,
When they bore off my brother.

LENTULUS: With the Gaul then:
  And if he beat him, as I think he will,
  Then shall he battle with your best.—Now, sirrah.
SPARTACUS: Hah!
SENONA: Husband!
SPARTACUS: Well, it is not chains alone
  That makes the slave. What will my master have?
LENTULUS: I'll have thee exercise thine arm in practice.
  Thou wilt have brave men to contend with.
SPARTACUS: Well,
  I will do so: but speak it not before my wife.
LENTULUS: Get thee along. Florus, conduct them to
  Their lodgings. See this Thracian exercised.   [Exeunt.]

END OF ACT I

ACT II

SCENE 1: A room in CRASSUS'S house.

[Enter CRASSUS, JOVIUS, an ARTIFICER, and a SLAVE.]

CRASSUS: To the full letter of the law. What, use
  My excellent slave in thy most gainful craft,
  And groan at the reckoning? By Jupiter,
  Thou shalt his hire pay to the utmost sesterce,
  Or have a quittance writ upon thy back.
  Breed I then servants for the good of knaves?
  Find me the money, or I'll have thee whipped.
  Begone. [Exit ARTIFICER.] I built not up my fortunes thus,
  By taking sighs for coin: had I done so,
  Foul breath had ruined me. How should I then
  Have borne the hard expenses of these games.
  The uproarious voters clamour for?
JOVIUS: What! True.
  Wealth is the key to office, here in Rome,—
  Or is the lock that best secures it.
CRASSUS: Sirrah,
  Thou dost not mean, the officers bribe the people?
JOVIUS: I had sooner lug old Cerberus[13] by the ears,

Than do aught to our citizens, but praise 'em.
But, in your gracious ears,—our sovereign Romans
Are something bauble-brained; and, like to children,
Pass qualmish by their needful medicines,
To snatch at sugary playthings. What do they
In their elections? Faith, I have observed,
They ask not if their candidate have honour,
Or honesty, or proper qualities;
But, with an eager grin, *What is his wealth?*
If thus and thus—*Then he can give us shows
And feasts; and therefore is the proper man.*
An excellent mode of judging!

CRASSUS: Ancient comrade,
At me thou point'st now.

JOVIUS: Not irreverently:
I question of the people; and, I think,
They loved great Marius more for his rich feasts,
Than his rich victories. Sooth, when angry Sylla
Swept them, like dogs, out of his bloody path,
And made their hearts sore, they forgot their fury.
When once they had looked upon his fighting lions.

CRASSUS: Hence, thou inferrest, they have chose me praetor,
Being rich enough to purchase them diversions!
But I have done them service in the wars,
And, out of gratitude—But no more of that.—
They shall be pleased: the games go bravely on.
The Capuan hath brought me a new sworder.—
Sirrah, go bid my niece here. [*Exit* SLAVE.] This Capuan hath
A son most insolent and troublesome.

[*Enter* FLORUS.]

What, Sirrah, again? Hast thou not had thy answer?
<Kill me these flies that being lean themselves,
Swarm after fatness.> Why art thou this fool,
To covet my rich niece?

FLORUS: I seek not riches.

CRASSUS: Pah! Will poor lovers sing eternally
The self-same song? They seek not riches! Jove,
Why pass they then all poverty, where their choice
Might find a wider compass?

FLORUS: Excellent praetor,
   Give me the maid, and keep her lands thyself.
CRASSUS: Sirrah, thou know'st, the girl abhors thee. Look,
   She has the blood of nobles in her veins,
   Distilling purely through a thousand years;
   And thine comes grossly from a German slave's,
   That was thy grandsire.
FLORUS: Worth and deserving toil can raise me up,
   Even from my poverty, to wealth and honours.
   And these shall do it.
CRASSUS: Get thee away then
   To warring Pompey, and, with thy soiled sword,
   Carve out clean honours; not forgetting, whilst
   Thy right hand grasps the enemy's throat, to thrust
   The left into his purse: For what is honour,
   With empty pockets, in this thievish world?
   Honour is men's consideration: men
   Consider none, but those can profit them.
   Therefore, if thou'lt be quick
   In gaining honour, use thy right hand rather
   For gathering gold than killing—or rather use them both:
   Make much, and thou shalt be most honourable.
JOVIUS: Thou hearest, Florus? This is the truer wisdom.
   I've fought for honour some good thirty years,—
   <Courting her with such madman freaks, as leaping,
   First man, upon an arm'd wall in the storm;
   Saving a comrade's life (some dozen of 'em,)
   Out of the jaws of death; contesting singly
   With scores, in divers places.> But being foolish,
   In my hot haste for slaughter, I forgot
   To look for spoil; and lo, the consequence!
   I bear the vine-branch,[14] and am only honoured
   As a gray-haired centurion.
CRASSUS: Get thee gone.
   When thou art worthy, ask her, and no sooner.   [*Exit* FLORUS.]
   A most mad, insolent boy, and honest son
   Of a breeder of cutthroats! Would some knave would hang him.
   He has the damsel's heart too. See, she comes.—
   Is the litter ready?

        [*Enter* JULIA.]

JULIA: It cannot be, dear uncle,
  You will send me to the country?
CRASSUS: It cannot be!
  What, chuff, it cannot be? In faith, it can be,
  And, instantly, it shall be.—Into the country,
  To weep and meditate. I am ashamed
  You have so poor a spirit as to love
  This base-born Capuan, whose whole wealth you might,
  Piled up in coin, base on a puny drachma.
JULIA: Ah! When did love e'er think of drachmas, uncle?
  <You would have me, when a lover moans, demand him,
  Could he coin gold, as easily as sighs;
  Or when he wept, ask if his pockets had
  As many talents as his eyes had tears.
  Then should he change his manner, and where he might
  Have wooed me with soft words, assault me with
  A schedule of his properties; instead
  Of flattering, boast me of his lands; his vows
  Change into oaths of, lord, how rich he was.
  How could I say him nay?>
CRASSUS: A milksop boy,
  That has done nothing in the world but breathe,—
  Has won no name or fortune. Why should such
  A natural expletive. <a sack of breath,>
  Aspire to wealth or woman? When he proves him
  Worth his existence, then let him aspire.
  Till then thou shalt be hid from his presumption,
  Even in Campania.[15]
JULIA: Oh, but not today.
  Tomorrow, or the next day, when the games are done.
  I must see them: 'twould kill me, not to look
  Once more upon the fighting gladiators.
CRASSUS: Pho!
  Thou a green girl, and talk of gladiators!
  My youth was pass'd in battles, and I am not
  Unused to blood; but my flesh always creeps,
  To see these cold-blood slaughters.
JULIA: So does mine,
  Ugh! My heart stops with terror, and my eyes
  Seem parting from their sockets; my brain reels,
  While I look on; and while I look, each time,

I swear I ne'er will look again. But when
They battle boldly, and the people shout,
And the poor creatures look so fearless,—frowning,
Not groaning, when they are hurt.—Indeed 'tis noble!
<And though they fright me, always make me weep,
I have to see them. These are your own shows:>
Oh, I must see them.

JOVIUS: This is a brave maiden.
<You should look on a battle—two great armies,
Perhaps a hundred thousand men apiece:
Fighting as staunchly as so many wolves,
Throttling and stabbing, dying in multitudes,—
A chaos of death:—Even such a one as that
(My own first fight) at Aqua Sextia,[16]
Against the Ambrones, where a hundred thousand
Of the barbarians fell.

JULIA: An hundred thousand!

JOVIUS: Was it not glorious?

JULIA: Horrid!

JOVIUS: Horrid! Humph,
Still woman.—But these were barbarians.

JULIA: Were they not men?

JOVIUS: Why yes, a sort of men.
They had legs and arms, noses and eyes like men,
They bled like men; but, being barbarians,
Of not much matter of account as men.

JULIA: That makes a difference. But an hundred thousand
Was many to kill, even of barbarians.

CRASSUS: Come, you're a goose, you know not what you say.

JULIA: O but these gladiators! My friend, Caloeia,
Told me that famous one, Phasarius,
Would fight today. He is a handsome rogue,
And kills a man the prettiest in the world.>

CRASSUS: You shall not see him.

JULIA: Dear my uncle.

CRASSUS: You came
Into this city, modest and obedient;
Now you have learnt to cog, cajole and cozen;
And, in the teeth of my authority,
Give private hopes to this low Capuan;
And, while mine eyes are tied upon the games,

Would—But I'll balk your hoped for interviews.
The litter waits you at the door. Farewell.
This good old man, who once was my tried client,
Shall have you in charge. Now no more opposition.
Farewell. Be wise, and love none but the worthy.   [*Exeunt.*]

SCENE 2: *A court before* LENTULUS'S *house.*

[*Enter* FLORUS *with* SPARTACUS, CRIXUS,[17] *and other gladiators.*]

FLORUS: You have played well, and beaten Crixus fairly.
　Carry this skilfulness to the arena.
　And you shall win great honour.
SPARTACUS: Great degradation.
　No matter: I am sworn to be a caitiff.
　Where have you placed my wife? It was conditioned,
　You should not part us.
FLORUS: She is lodged hard by:
　After the combat, you shall see her.—Come,
　Play me a bout here with Soturius.
　I'll fetch you foils.
SPARTACUS: I'll play no more: I was not sworn to that.
FLORUS: You cannot go too well prepared.
SPARTACUS: Even as I stand,
　Awkward or skilful, doomed to die or kill,
　So will I go.—I'll train no more for murder.
FLORUS: Well, as you will.
SPARTACUS: Will it not be enough,
　If I disarm or worst my enemy?
　May I not spare him?
FLORUS: Not unless the people
　Grant you permission. <When you have him at
　Your mercy, look to the spectators then.
　If they consent, they will their thumbs raise—thus:
　Then you shall spare. But if their hands be clenched,
　And the thumbs hid, then must you slay.>
SPARTACUS: Well, well;
　I understand.
FLORUS: Breathe yourselves here awhile,
　Then follow to the armoury.   [*Exit.*]

SPARTACUS: Good brother,
Have you yet fought I' th' Amphitheatre?
CRIXUS: Ay.
SPARTACUS: And killed
Your adversary?
CRIXUS: Ay. Each one of us
Has won some reputation.
SPARTACUS: Reputation!
Call you this reputation?
This is the bulldog's reputation:
He and the gladiator only need
The voice o' the master, to set on to mischief.—
Love you your masters?
CRIXUS: No.
SPARTACUS: Or of your own wishes
Go ye to perish?
CRIXUS: No; but being slaves,
We care not much for life; and think it better
To die upon the arena, than the cross.
SPARTACUS: If ye care not for life, why die ye not
Rather like men, than dogs?
CRIXUS: What mean you?
SPARTACUS: Were it not better
To turn upon your masters, and so die,
Killing them that oppress you, rather than fall,
Killing your brother wretches?
CRIXUS: True, it were.
Put arms into our hands, unlock our dungeons,
And set us out among the citizens;
Then ask this question.
SPARTACUS: Do you say this? By heaven,
This spirit joys me.—Fight ye all today?
CRIXUS: We are so ordered.
SPARTACUS: How many do you number?
CRIXUS: Fifty.
SPARTACUS: Fifty? How many hath this Roman,
This villain Bracchius?
CRIXUS: Some five and thirty.
SPARTACUS: And fight they all?
CRIXUS: Some forty pairs today.
SPARTACUS: O heaven, what, forty?

CRIXUS: And ere the shows are done,
  Two hundred pairs.
SPARTACUS: Two hundred pairs!—Four hundred
  Arm'd slaves, that hate their masters!
CRIXUS: On the third day,
  All that survive, will fight in general battle.
SPARTACUS: In general battle!—If Senona now,
  And the young infant were in Thrace.—Alas,
  To peril them.—
CRIXUS: What say'st thou, Thracian?
SPARTACUS: Nothing;
  At least, not much.—Are there now troops in Rome?
CRIXUS: Four legions of Praetorian Guards;[18] and now
  Each legion counts five thousand.
SPARTACUS: 'Twill not do.
CRIXUS: What will not do?
SPARTACUS: I'll tell you by and by:
  'Tis worth your ear.—But let us now go arm,
  Then to the Arena, to begin the work
  Of slavish murder.—We are gladiators.   [Exeunt.]

SCENE 3: *The Arena of an Amphitheatre, behind which are many citizens.*
CRASSUS *seated with his Lictors,* MUMMIUS, LENTULUS, BRACCHIUS,
FLORUS, *and many officers,—Aediles, Conquistitores,*[19] *etc.*

CRASSUS: Let our good friends, the citizens, be seated.
  We purpose to delight their humours with
  The bravest gladiators of this realm.—
  What say'st thou, Capuan? Why tell me, thou
  Hast brought me some brave cutthroats, to be pitched,
  Through the first hours, in single combat, with
  The best slaves of our Bracchius.
LENTULUS: Even so,
  Most noble praetor; and, with the consent
  Of your appointed officers, we first
  Will bring a lusty Thracian, who, although
  Yet unadventured in the Arena, bears
  A name of valour.
CRASSUS: Let him before us.   [*Exit* FLORUS.]
  Had Thracians, by their firesides, fought as fiercely

As now they fight upon the Roman sand,
The cranes o' the Strymon still had been their sentries.

[*Reenter* FLORUS, *with* SPARTACUS, *as a gladiator.*]

Is this the man? A very capital knave;
Yet, or I err, of but a little spirit.
Where is the fiery confidence, should flash
From his bold eyes? the keen and tameless spirit,
Should brace his strong limbs to activity?

LENTULUS: Driveller, arouse thee!—Let not his gloom condemn him:
He is most wayward, but, in truth, right valiant.
What, sirrah, shake off these clouds, and do thy homage
To the most noble praetor. Bend thy knee.

SPARTACUS: Did I swear that? Kneel *thou,* whose servile soul
Was given for crouching. I am here to fight!

CRASSUS: This is some madman!

LENTULUS: A barbarian,
Bred in a savage roughness.

SPARTACUS: Well, I am here,
Among these beasts of Rome, a spectacle.
This is the temple, where they mock the Gods
With human butchery,—Most grand and glorious
Of structure and device!—It should have been a cave,
Some foul and midnight pit, or den of bones,
Where murder best might veil himself from sight.—
Women and children, too, to see men die,
And clap their hands at every stab! This is
The boastful excellence of Rome! I thank the Gods
There are Barbarians.

CRASSUS: Now by Jupiter,
The rogue speaks well—But Romans must be pleased—
Sirrah,—[*Comes down center.*]

SPARTACUS: Roman!

CRASSUS: Most impudently bold.
I did mistake him. Prepare thyself.

SPARTACUS: I am ready,
As ready to die, as thou to see me die.
Where is the opponent? Of what nation comes
The man that I must kill?

CRASSUS: What matters it?

SPARTACUS: Much, very much. Bring me some base ally
   Of Roman rapine, or, if ye can, a Roman:—
   I will not grieve to slay him.
CRASSUS: Faith, I like
   This fearless taunting, and will sound it further.
   Thy foe shall be a Spaniard.
SPARTACUS: Alas, I should
   Bethink me of his country, as of mine,
   Ruined and harried by our common foe;
   His kinsmen slain, his wife and children sold,
   And nothing left of all his country's greatness,
   Save groans and curses on the conquerors.
CRASSUS: A Carthaginian.
SPARTACUS: What, a Carthaginian?
   A relic of that noble tribe, that ne'er
   Would call Rome friend, and perished rather than
   Become Rome's vassal? I could not fight with him:
   We should drop swords, and recollect together,
   As brothers, how the Punic steel had smote,
   Of yore, to Rome's chill'd heart; yea, how Rome quaked,
   How shook her proud sons, when the African[20]
   Burst from the sea, like to its mightiest surge,
   Swept your vain shores, and swallow'd up your armies!
   How, when his weapons, gored with consular blood,
   Waved o'er your towns, your bucklered boasters fled,
   Or shook, like aguish boys, and wept and prayed:—
   Yea, feared to die, and wept and prayed.
LENTULUS: <Peace, villain.>
CRASSUS: Strike him not, Lentulus. The prattler knows
   There's scarce a man of the Punic stock left living,
   To boast of these mishaps.—Thy adversary
   Is a brave Gaul.
SPARTACUS: Why there again! The name
   Speaks of Rome's shame. Name but a Gaul, and I
   Bethink me of the Tiber running blood,
   His tributaries choked with knightly corses;
   Of Rome in ashes, and of Brennus[21] laughing
   At the starved cravens in the Capitol.
CRASSUS: Sirrah, no more.
   Be but thy sword as biting as thy tongue,

And I'll assure thee victory.—Bring in
The Gaul. Use thy best skill, if skill thou hast,
Or I'll not lay an obolus[22] on thy life.—

[*A* GALLIC GLADIATOR *is brought in.*]

Clear the Arena. [*Ascends chair again.*]
SPARTACUS: I will fight with him;
But give me to spare his life.
CRASSUS: That privilege
Rests with the people. Remember thy oath.—Sound, trumpets. [*A
  flourish.*]
SPARTACUS: Brother—
CRASSUS: No words; but do thy best. <He'll spit thee.>

[*They fight. The* GAUL *is disarmed, and thrown on his knees.*
SPARTACUS *looks to the people.*]

Thine oath! Strike, <villain!> Hah! [SPARTACUS *kills the* GAUL.]
                                        Why that was bravely done.
SPARTACUS: Well, I have done it. Let me go hence.
CRASSUS: Not so.—
Most nobly fought!
SPARTACUS: Alas, alas, poor slave!—
CRASSUS: Bring me another. [*The body is taken away.*]
SPARTACUS: I will fight no more.
CRASSUS: Sirrah!
SPARTACUS: I have heart enough to die, but not to kill.
CRASSUS: Why 'twas most capitally done! Remember
Thy oath.
SPARTACUS: I care not. I will fight no more.
CRASSUS: Thou shalt have freedom. Nay, I'll ransome for thee,
Thy wife and boy.
SPARTACUS: Wilt thou?
CRASSUS: By Mars, I will.
Fight through these games; and thou and they shall be
Sent back to Thrace.
SPARTACUS: Shall we see Thrace again?—
Let him come on; yes, though it sick my soul,—
Let him come on.
CRASSUS: Bring in the Thracian!   [*Exit* BRACCHIUS.]
SPARTACUS: Thracian?
I will not fight a Thracian! 'Tis my countryman!

CRASSUS: Nay, but thou shalt, and kill him too; or thou
    And they, are slaves eternally.
SPARTACUS: O heaven!
    Bring me a Spaniard, German, Carthaginian,
    Another Gaul, a Greek—any but Thracian.
CRASSUS: None
    But this same Thracian is thy match; and truly
    If thou slay him, there will remain no other
    Worthy of thee. Thou shalt be quickly free.
SPARTACUS: I will fight two—three—so they be not Thracians.
CRASSUS: The Thracian, or eternal bondage; bondage
    For wife and child too.
SPARTACUS: Wilt thou swear to free us?
    Fight with a Thracian!—Wilt thou *swear* to free us?
CRASSUS: Bring hither the *Vindicta*:[23] With this rod,
    If thou escape this man, the praetor frees thee.

     [*Reenter* BRACCHIUS, *with* PHASARIUS.]

    This is thy foe.
PHASARIUS: [*Aside.*] What, do I dream?
SPARTACUS: Alas,
    Thou art a Thracian and my countryman,
    And yet we meet as deadly foes. Forgive me.
PHASARIUS: [*Aside.*] This is no fantasy!
CRASSUS: Observe them, Bracchius:
    Thy boaster hesitates.
PHASARIUS: Thou art a Thracian?
SPARTACUS: Would thou wert not.
PHASARIUS: Of the Ciconian tribe—
    A son of blue-waved Hebrus?[24]
SPARTACUS: Such I am.
    And comest thou too of the same race? and set
    Against thy brother?
PHASARIUS: Brother, indeed!
    Thy name is Spartacus.
SPARTACUS: Where learn't you that?
    Freemen have heard it, but not slaves.
PHASARIUS: How fares thy father?
SPARTACUS: Didst thou know him?—Dead—
    I cannot fight thee.
PHASARIUS: Hadst thou not a brother?—

CRASSUS: Why prate these cutthroats? Come, prepare, prepare—
SPARTACUS: A young, brave heart, whose steps I taught to dare
. The crags and chasms and roaring cataracts
   Of his own native hills, till he was freer
   Among them than the eagles. What art thou,
   That seem'st to know him? I would be angry with thee:
   These words make me look on thee as a friend.
PHASARIUS: Seem I not like Phasarius?
SPARTACUS: What, thou?
   A mailed warrior like a singing boy?—
   The Romans slew him.
PHASARIUS: They enslaved him—Brother,
   Changed as I am, and from a harmless boy,
   Turned to a rough destroyer, still am I
   The selfsame fool that once thou called'st brother.
SPARTACUS: Thou mock'st me. Thou!
PHASARIUS: My father, Menalon—
SPARTACUS: Thy father, Menalon?
PHASARIUS: My mother—
SPARTACUS: Ay, thy mother?
PHASARIUS: Laödice.
SPARTACUS: My brother!
CRASSUS: What mean these rogues, that they have dropped their
      swords,
   And faln, like friends, about each other's necks?
   What ho, ye slaves, give o'er this timeless juggling:
   Take up your swords, and look ye to the signal.
SPARTACUS: I do believe the gods have given me o'er
   To some new madness: First, I find in Rome,
   Where naught I looked for but despair, my wife
   And then my brother!
<CRASSUS: Villains!
SPARTACUS: But I am sorry
   To find thee here, Phasarius.>
LENTULUS: <Whining miscreant,>
   Why mark'st thou not the praetor?
CRASSUS: <Rogues, prepare.>
   Let the trumpet sound.
SPARTACUS: Bring me my adversary.
CRASSUS: Thou hast him there.

SPARTACUS: What he? This is my brother.
  You would not have me fight with him!
CRASSUS: His brother!
PHASARIUS: 'Tis true, most excellent praetor.
CRASSUS: Now, by Hercules.
  This is too strange for truth.
LENTULUS: Ye cogging[25] rogues,
  Think ye to balk us thus?
<BRACCHIUS: Conspiracy!
  Shameful collusion! Out on you, Phasarius,
  You're not afeard now? Out, ye cheating villain.>
PHASARIUS: Hear me, good praetor—
CRASSUS: <Rogues>, prepare yourselves,
  This is a most evident knavery, to 'scape
  From one another.—Brothers indeed!—Prepare;
  Take up your arms.
SPARTACUS: Foul Roman—
CRASSUS: Bring me in
  The guarding cohort: [An OFFICER goes out.] I'll have them cut to
    pieces,
  If they refuse the battle.—Brothers indeed!
SPARTACUS: Thou hard, unnatural man—
PHASARIUS: Patience, brother—
SPARTACUS: Let them come in—We are armed.—
CRASSUS: Most strange and insolent contumacy!
PHASARIUS: [Aside.] 'Tis something sudden—and in Rome!—Peace
  brother.—
SPARTACUS: We will resist them, armed as we are.
  Can we not die?
PHASARIUS: Most worthy praetor, pardon.
  Grant us a word together, and we are ready.
CRASSUS: Fine knavery! I did almost suspect
  You cutthroat for a coward—that 'twas skill alone
  Gave him his courage, which he fear'd to try
  With that more skilful savage. For the barbarian,
  His soul is made of contrariety.
PHASARIUS: [Apart to SPARTACUS.] I know them all—This thing was
    hatch'd before.—
  They wait without,
  Circled by cohorts, but all arm'd for combat.

Let me but raise the cry of *Freedom* to them,
And each man strikes his Roman to the earth.
SPARTACUS: The slaves of Lentulus—they will strike too:
Let us but reach them, and they rise with us.—
PHASARIUS: One moment, princely praetor.
CRASSUS: Not an instant.
What, shall our shows wait on the time and pleasure
Of our base bondmen? Sound the trumpets there—
What, treachery, ho! Call in the soldiers!—
PHASARIUS: Freedom
For gladiators!
SPARTACUS: Death to all their masters!—
CRASSUS: Treachery!—
SPARTACUS: Death to the Roman fiends, that make their mirth
Out of the groans of bleeding misery!
Ho, slaves, arise! it is your hour to kill!
Kill and spare not—For wrath and liberty!—
Freedom for bondmen—freedom and revenge!

[*Shouts and trumpets—The guards and gladiators rush and engage in combat, as the curtain falls.*]

END OF ACT II

ACT III

SCENE 1:[26] *A room in* CRASSUS'S *house.*

[*Enter* CRASSUS, JOVIUS, LENTULUS, BRACCHIUS, MUMMIUS.]

‹CRASSUS: Incredible! What, fight a consular army?
Or look one in the face?
JOVIUS: So says the courier.
'Tis sworn, that half the slaves of Italy
Are flocking to his banner.
CRASSUS: Fight a consul!
Fight Cneus Lentulus!
JOVIUS: 'Tis not so much
To one who has already beat a proconsul.

You'll not doubt that? nor that these madman slaves,
Led by this whirlwind slayer—

LENTULUS: My precious Thracian!—

JOVIUS: Have vanquished severally, and in pitched battles,
Three praetors of the provinces.

CRASSUS: Shame upon them!
Sneers for their lives, contempt for epitaphs!
Beaten by slaves!—I warrant me, by mine—
Two thousand costly and ungrateful villains:—
I'll hang them, every man.—Beaten by slaves,
Cross, starving, unarmed slaves!

JOVIUS: Not now unarmed.
Each rogue has got a Roman harness on,
Filched from the carcass of a Roman veteran.
Not starving neither, whilst every day they sack
Some camp or city—pouncing sudden down,
Like vultures, from their hills upon our troops.

CRASSUS: Scandalous, scandalous! Slaves, wretched slaves,
Led by a slave too!

LENTULUS: Still my precious Thracian!

CRASSUS: A scurvy gladiator, with no brains;
An ignorant savage.—

JOVIUS: Come, give the rogue his due:
He has more brains than all our generals,
For he has beaten them; that's a soldier's proof.
This Spartacus, so late a bondman, has
A soul for master; though a shepherd bred,
He has fought battles, ay, and led men too,—
Some mountain malcontents in his own land,—
'Gainst Roman conquerors; and, by the faith
Of honesty, for honest I will be,
In courage, strategem, resource, exploits,
He shows a good commander. He has formed,
Out of this slavish, ragged scum, an army;
Arms it and feeds it at his foeman's cost,
Recruits it in his foeman's territory;
Which foe is renowned Rome, resistless Rome,
Rome the great head and empress of the world!
Is he not then a general?

CRASSUS: I grant you,
The rogue is not a common one; but still

A slave. And much it shames me that the senate
Finds me no worthier enemy; whom to conquer,
Wins neither spoil nor honour.

JOVIUS: No spoil indeed,
Unless you count their arms and bodies such;
But honour enough to him that beats the vanquished
Of some half score commanders: There's your honour!
Come, stir these centuries: My old bones are aching
For one more battering, ere they fall to dust.
The reprobates must be put down, that's certain,
And by yourself, or Pompey.>

CRASSUS: Now the gods rest him!
Is there no trouble can befall the state,
But men must cry for Pompey? As if Rome
Had whelped no other fit to do her service.
<Still is it Pompey, great and valiant Pompey,
Must all our state thorns conjure into laurels.—
Well, Crassus is not Pompey, but may serve
For the besom.

JOVIUS: What, a besom?

CRASSUS: Ay, to sweep away
This filthy blush out of Rome's cheek.>—These varlets,
These fooled *lanistae*, that have trained slaves up
To fight their masters, shall to camp with me,
And of the evils they have caused, partake.

LENTULUS: I am willing.
I'll kill my Thracian, though he be a general.

BRACCHIUS: It matters not how soon I am knock'd o' the head.
I have not now a gladiator left.—
The rogues have ruined me.

CRASSUS: Where is thy son?
This knave shall march too. Have you brought the woman,
The wife o' the Thracian, here to Rome?

LENTULUS: I have sent for her.
My son has gone into Campania.

CRASSUS: What, to Campania? Now by Jupiter,
This fool will set me mad.

LENTULUS: I know not that.
He went with the band of youthful volunteers,
To the camp of Gellius,[27] the consul.

JOVIUS: Bravely done.
   That was in memory of our counselling.
   But now for action. <You remember, praetor,
   This consul prays immediate succours, being
   But ill provided, should the Gladiator,
   In contest with his colleague, prove victorious,
   As there is ground to fear; for Lentulus,[28]
   At the last word, was at extremities.
   Being deprived too by the angry senate
   Of their authority, their mutinous troops
   But scurvily obey them.> Should the rebels
   Come near your country-seat—
CRASSUS: No more of that:
   The consul shall protect her.—Presently
   Bring me six legions; which, being added to
   The consular troops and the knights volunteers,
   We'll have appointed to this service. Then
   There shall be knocks enough, I promise you.
   See that these people follow, and all men
   Whose slaves have joined the rebels. It is reason,
   The rogues should kill no masters but their own.   [*Exeunt.*]

SCENE 2: *A Plain in Campania, after the battle. Some corses lying about.*
March of trumpets.

   [*Enter, sumptuously armed,* SPARTACUS, PHASARIUS, CRIXUS,
   ÆNOMAIIS, *and attendants.*]

SPARTACUS: So, we are victors, conquerors again.
   The hotbrained boasters, that in mockery thought
   To ape the angry Scythian, and subdue us
   With whips, instead of warlike instruments,
   Lie hush'd and gory; and, despite the claim
   Of their high honours and nobility,
   There is no slave too base to tread upon them.
   There he's a Consul.—I have known that word
   Fright men more than the name of gorgeous kings.
   Say to barbaric States, *A Consul comes,*
   A Roman Consul, and their preparation
   Of war or welcome, speaks a demigod.

And yet lies he on the opprobrious earth,
A palmy Consul, by a slave's hand slain,
No nobler than his horse—a thing to
Glut the starved hyena's maw.[29]

PHASARIUS: Ay—and there's another
Must lie beside him.

SPARTACUS: Speak you of Gellius?

PHASARIUS: Ay, marry. I'll fight now nothing less than consuls.
There is another of them, and I say,
Another battle and another victory.

CRIXUS: 'Tis but to will, and we have won it.

SPARTACUS: Ay;
But not today. Our medly bands have earned
Their armour, and are weary.—'Tis full six leagues
To Gellius' camp.

CRIXUS: My Germans will not fear it.

SPARTACUS: It cannot be, and must not.

CRIXUS: Must not, Spartacus!

SPARTACUS: Ay, man, I say so: this thing must not be.
When ye were few, with one consent, ye chose me
Your leader, with each man an oath to yield
To me sole guidance. This was little honour,
To be the chief of fourscore fugitives,
And none would have it, save myself. I took it,
And ye have prospered. Under my authority,
In a few days your ranks have been swell'd up
To fearful thousands; and from a band of slaves,
Skulking in caves, you have become an army
Can fight a Roman Consul. This is proof,
I have deserved obedience; and therefore,
I still command it.

CRIXUS: And my countrymen
Myself have made their leader; and they bid me
Lead them to Gellius.

SPARTACUS: We are but one army,
With but one object, howsoe'er our ranks
Are filled with various nations. We are slaves,
All of us slaves, contesting for our freedom;
And so far free, that we have arms and kill;
No further. We have yet to cut our way
Out of this tyrant empire; which to do,

We must destroy more armies, that are gathering
To hem us in. We do not fight for conquest,
But conquer for our liberties; and they
Are lost by rashness. Let us rest our troops,
And think of Gellius on the morrow.
CRIXUS: Today, today,
Ere he have rallied this fight's fugitives.
SPARTACUS: The thousands that are crowding to our lines
Will, by the dawn, have trebled all his gain.
CRIXUS: I will beat him with the Germans alone.
SPARTACUS: You shall not;
I am your general, and forbid you.
CRIXUS: Thracian,
I was a slave, but am not now.
PHASARIUS: Brother Crixus,
On second thoughts, 'tis better put this off,
According as the general commands.
CRIXUS: I am sole leader of my countrymen.
PHASARIUS: Sirrah, thou art a mutineer.—
SPARTACUS: Peace, brother.—
PHASARIUS: Defy the general! If one beggar's rogue
Of all his Germans dare to leave the lines,
I'll have him spitted like a cur.
SPARTACUS: Peace, brother.
Contention will harm worse than this partition.
German, thou hast thy wish: depart in peace,
But without hope of succour, if the Roman
Prevail above thee.
PHASARIUS: Pray the gods he do!
<And thwack them till they are skinless, all. Base rascals
And mutineers!>
SPARTACUS: Take all thy countrymen,
Or all that wish to follow thee.   [*Exit* CRIXUS.]
PHASARIUS: Rank mutiny!
Why did you let him go?
SPARTACUS: To teach him, brother,
Him and some others of our lieutenants,
(For we are growing mad upon success,)
An humbling lesson. A defeat were now
Better than victory; and, in his Germans,
We best can bear it.

PHASARIUS: Let them go, and hang;
  They are all villainous hotheads, and presumptuous
  Beyond all tolerance. And, to punish them,
  They shall not share with us the fame and spoil
  Of the sack'd city.
SPARTACUS: Brother, I think thou art
  Almost as madbrained as the rest.
PHASARIUS: I have
  A kind of ardour, that, for aught I know,
  May be a lunacy. But this is clear:
  Rome is a city; cities may be sack'd;
  So Rome may be.
SPARTACUS: A city, that the world
  Looks frighted at, even in her sleep of peace,
  As gazers look at sleeping lions. I told
  This German fool, we did not fight for conquest,
  But for a passport to our several homes.
  What care we then to waste our vigour on
  The gates of fortressed cities?
PHASARIUS: But this city—
SPARTACUS: Is as impregnable as the storm-arm'd sea.
  Why should we talk of it? Great Mithridates,
  Though populous Asia followed at his back,
  Should, were his frothy hopes to point at it,
  Be laughed at for a kingly maniac.
  What should be said of us, the mushroom warriors
  Of Roman dunghills, should our arrogance
  Mad us so far? I think, we do not fight
  To make the world talk?
PHASARIUS: I would have you do so;
  Fight now for glory; let ambition raise you
  Among the deathless, now while fate invites you.
  Rome has no greatness, but is now employed
  In foreign climes: You have well tried yourself;
  And consuls vanish, when your trumpet sounds.
  March on the city, and there swear to die,
  Or live its master, and you are its master.
  Think, brother, think what glorious fame were ours,
  As lasting as the eternal world, should we,
  The upturned dregs of servitude, destroy,

As, by the inviting fates! We may destroy,
This lair of lions, this den of conquerors,
This womb of heroes, whose boastings fright the earth,
And whose ambition (—look, Ambition!)—chains it!
<SPARTACUS: This is a wild and most preposterous hope.
Even the fierce Hannibal, with veteran troops,
And all the towns of Italy at his feet,
Save this alone, here paused his hopes.
PHASARIUS: Hope thou
T' excel the vaunted African, and dare
Beyond his daring. Hast thou not a heart
Bigger than his, that, with a herd of slaves,
Hast wrought as much as all his veterans?
Smiles heaven upon thee less, which, in an hour,
Has, from a dungeon, raised thee to an army,
Still growing, still victorious? Do this deed,
And live for ever.>
SPARTACUS: Well, well, I'll think of it.
Perhaps Senona's there:—Ah, would to heaven, Phasarius.
I were with her now and my smiling boy,
In Thrace again, beside our mountain cot,[30]
Or in those vales, where babbling Hebrus tumbles
Along his golden sands; and dreamt no more
Of sacks and battles.
PHASARIUS: Whilst this city stands,
This ne'er can be; for just so long our country
Remains a Roman province. Tear it down,
And you enfranchise Thrace, and half the world.
SPARTACUS: We'll think of this again, when we are stronger,
And when we have Senona sent to us.
Meanwhile we must the final effort make
To ransome her. <Did you secure a guide,
To lead us through the mountains? I have seen
The camp most strongly guarded, and fear not
To trust it with the trusty Ænomaiis.
When the tired troops have slept an hour, I'll order
To bring them after us, to see indeed
How we may end, what Crixus may begin,
Disastrously for him, on Gellius,
In the confusion of the Consul's triumph.>

Pick me an hundred of our swiftest horses,
And have them presently in wait for me.
I shall fight better, when I know, each blow
Strikes a protection for my family.   [*Exeunt.*]

SCENE 3: *A room in* CRASSUS'S *Villa.*

[*Enter* JULIA *and* FLORUS.]

JULIA: I am glad to see thee. This terrific din
Of the near battle made a sparrow of me.
I was afeard to breathe, <lest I should swallow
Some of your horrid missiles; for I ran
Unto the housetop, to look on the fight.
But the moon was more coward than myself,
And hid her pale face in a cloud: so nothing
I saw. But I could hear the brazen trumps,
The conchs and cornets, the shouts and yells of fury,
The clang of arms, and whistling in the air
Of stones and arrows. But, come tell me now,
My general, have you killed a foe tonight?
FLORUS: And won a civic crown, by saving a friend.
JULIA: That's good; I am glad to hear it.>
FLORUS: But I am sorry
To find you here among these fears and perils.
I would you were in Rome.
JULIA: There is no peril.
Have you not beaten these wild gladiators?
A shepherd flying from his pastures, told me,
That Gellius had the victory, and had taken
Or killed the insurgent, bloody Spartacus.
FLORUS: I know not that. 'Tis true, that we have beaten
A band of mad rogues, that assaulted us;
And 'tis believed, their general, Spartacus,
Is dead upon our trenches; for whose body
Search is now made. But one poor prisoner,
<I think, the only one whose life was spared,>
Declared these troops to be but a small band
Of mutinous runagates,[31] that had left their leader,
Being thereto moved by their late victory
Over the consul Lentulus.

JULIA: What, Florus!
  A victory over Lentulus?
FLORUS: 'Tis even so:
  His army has been vanquished, himself slain
  By the late bondman. And those, who give faith
  To the assurance of our prisoner,
  Fear for *our* consul, should the Thracian march,
  After his mutineers, upon us now;
  Our camp being all a confused festival
  Of drunken triumph,—half our soldiers scattered
  In search of spoil and fugitives.—
SPARTACUS [*within*]:   Guard the doors:
  Let none go out.
FLORUS: What voice is that? By heaven,
  We are betrayed!

    [*Enter* SPARTACUS, PHASARIUS, *and others.* ÆNOMAIIS.]

SPARTACUS: <Sold, lost, and dead!>—Look to the maiden.
  <What, flourishing fool,> drop thy sword's point, or die.
FLORUS: A thousand times, ere thou, malicious rebel,
  Touch this endangered lady.
SPARTACUS: Straw, I say! [*He disarms* FLORUS.]
  Know I not this boy's face?[32]
FLORUS: I think thou should'st.
  Spare thou the lady, rich will be her ransome.
  And for myself, I know, thy deadly fury
  Grants never quarter.
SPARTACUS: By the stripes not yet
  Fled from mine outraged limbs, thou art the son
  Of Lentulus the scourger!
PHASARIUS: Ay, the same.
  Let him atone his rascal father's sins:
  Scourge him to death.
FLORUS: Give me a soldier's death:
  Let me die by the sword. I never scourged thee.
SPARTACUS: Thou! Miserable boy!
FLORUS: And well thou knowest,
  Thou fierce and fiendish man, this tongue of mine
  Was oft thy intercessor.
SPARTACUS: I do know,
  One of thy blood did give me to the scourge—

Me, a free son of a free sire, and imaged
After the semblance of the Only Master—
Gave me to thongs and whips, as a poor beast,
Till I became one. This I know; know thou,
From that shamed hour, when first my body writhed
Under the merciless lash, I did devote
The scourger and his household to the furies,
To quick and murderous death. And thinkest thou,
Thy whining kindness took away a pang?
Thou art the Roman's son, and thou shalt die.

FLORUS: Let it be so—

SPARTACUS: It shall be so. Thou seest,
Command and dignities have not wiped out
The memory of wrongs; and Roman blood,
Running in rivers ever at my feet,
Sates not the thirst for more!—Take him away;
Scourge him to death.

JULIA: [To SPARTACUS.] Thou horrible monster, spare him,
And name whate'er thou wilt for ransome.

SPARTACUS: Ransome!
Drachmas for stripes!

FLORUS: Beseech him not, fair Julia.
Think of thyself, or let me think for thee.

JULIA: He never did thee hurt.

SPARTACUS: Let her be ta'en away.

FLORUS: Let her be ransomed, and for thine own wife.

SPARTACUS: Ay, so I will: 'twas e'en for that I took her.

FLORUS: Then may'st thou instantly exchange them.—

SPARTACUS: How!

FLORUS: Thy wife is in the consul's camp—

SPARTACUS: In the consul's camp?

FLORUS: There driven by the fright of her conductors.
And thou may'st instant ransome her.—

SPARTACUS: Ha, ha!
Now does Jove smile. What, ransome her? Ay, ransome;
But with the steel:—I can almost forgive thee,
For this good news.—Praetor, I have thee now
In the same trap thou set'dst for me!—What, sirrah,
Ye have beaten my refractory lieutenant,
The German Crixus?

FLORUS: Ay, I thank the gods.

SPARTACUS: And so do I; it wins me victory,
 And puts the second consul in my hands.—
 Asistheus, see these captives safely guarded.—
 Brother, the troops must now be nigh upon us.—
 Take thou the Thracian cohorts, and in secret
 Steal to the heights that overhang his rear,
 Posting a strong guard on the river. Let none 'scape,
 And let none live. Myself will force the camp,
 And drive the rioting fools upon your swords.—
 I say, spare none.

PHASARIUS: 'Twere much too troublesome
 To imitate them, and build crucifixes
 For the prisoners.

SPARTACUS: Let not a moment's rashness
 Bring us a limping victory. Stand fast
 Upon your post, and every rogue is dead.—
 Roman, thou shalt see how I'll ransome her!   [*Exeunt.*]

SCENE 4: *The Tent of* GELLIUS, *the Consul* GELLIUS *discovered, with* SCROPHA, SENONA, *and her child, and attendants.*

GELLIUS: There is no doubt, this foolish German lies.
 'Twas the main body of the rebels surely.
 No mere detachment would have impudence
 To march upon a consul. Now this victory,
 Which, on the morn, I'll follow up, will change
 The tone o' the angry senate, and restore me
 To my full rank, and, what is better, send
 The scheming Crassus empty-handed back.
 This is a man should fight in the Velabrum,[33]
 Among the cheating mongers, and not bring
 His brains of a broker to a glorious camp.
 This woman here, the wife o' the Gladiator,
 That cutthroat caitiff—

SENONA: Why dost thou slander him?
 Has he not fought a consul?

GELLIUS: Pr'ythee, be silent.
 He's a brave rebel, and will be renowned.—
 Now, as I said, with this same woman here,

The Greek-brained Crassus did design some trick,
Some scurvy plot upon the Gladiator—[*Alarums.*]
SCROPHA:[34] Hark!
GELLIUS: A device of the rejoicing drunkards.—
This thing meant Crassus, this—
SCROPHA: The clang increases! [*A great
    shout is heard.*]
GELLIUS: The knaves are noisy.—

[*Enter a* CENTURION, *wounded.*]

CENTURION: Fly for your lives! The camp is forced—
GELLIUS: What camp?
CENTURION: Your own. The Gladiators are upon us:
We are surprised, and all is lost.   [*Exit.*]
GELLIUS: My armour!
What ho, my armour!   [*Exeunt all but* SENONA *and child.*]

[*Enter* SPARTACUS, ÆNOMAÏS, *and Gladiators.*]

SPARTACUS: Victory! Ha! ha!
Romans are sheep—search every tent—ah! Jove!
I have found ye wife, aye, and have ransomed ye.
What, did you think I had deserted you?
Look, I have found you in a noble hour:
When last we met I was a slave: and now
In a Consul's camp I stand a conqueror![35]

CURTAIN

END OF ACT III

ACT IV

SCENE 1:[36] *The Camp of* CRASSUS.

[*Enter* CRASSUS, MUMMIUS,[37] JOVIUS, LENTULUS, BRACCHIUS, *and
    attendants.*]

CRASSUS: And Gellius beaten too? both consuls beaten?
This is some demigod that hath ta'en man's shape,

To whip us for our sins.—Both consuls beaten?
I would I had those Macedonian legions.
JOVIUS: Have them thou shalt; ay, and the Spanish too:
   The senate, in their terror, (for the victories
   Of this great savage now add fright to shame,)
   Did Pompey and Lucullus, with their troops,
   Instant embark for Rome.
CRASSUS: Why should they send
   For Pompey too?—Perhaps it may be better.—
   See that the fugitives from the consular camps
   Be decimated, and so punished. The cowards should
   Be slain by duplates rather than by tithes:[38]
   I'll make example of them.—Jovius,
   Lay not this consul near my villa? I would not
   My niece should come to harm; and it is horrid
   To think her in the hands of the barbarians.
JOVIUS: I am sorry, praetor—
CRASSUS: What, man, is it so?
JOVIUS: A herdsman, fled that night from the estate,
   Just on the eve of battle, saw the house
   Beset by numerous slaves.—
CRASSUS: The gods be with her.
   I loved her well.—Sirrah, where is that woman,
   I bade thee bring me?
LENTULUS: Not yet reached the camp,
   But on the road.
CRASSUS: Let her be hastened hither.
   I did intend to use her as a check
   On the uxorious chief. Now shall she ransome
   My Julia from him.—Where lies the enemy?
JOVIUS: He is advancing on us.
CRASSUS: What, advancing?
JOVIUS: With countless multitudes at his heels.—
CRASSUS: What! come,
   Intrench, intrench.
JOVIUS: Rather march out to meet him.
   Shall it be said, that Crassus, the lieutenant
   Of valiant Sylla, hid behind a trench,
   When bondmen menaced him?
CRASSUS: Shall it be said,
   Crassus, the praetor, like a hair-brained[39] fool,

Helped these same bondmen to a victory?
Spear me those cowards; and intrench, I say.—
What, sirrah?

[*Enter a* MESSENGER, *who speaks with* JOVIUS.]

JOVIUS: Happy tidings! Marcus Lucullus
 Hath landed his army at Brundisium;[40]—
CRASSUS: The gods be thank'd.—
JOVIUS: And legion'd Pompey too
 At Ostia.[41]
CRASSUS: Still thanks. Let messengers
Be sent o' the instant to both generals,
Praying them, as they love the gods and Rome,
Their march to hasten.   [*Exit Messenger.*]
               Good centurion,
I will employ thee in a difficult office,
Wherein thou may'st the state and me do service.
JOVIUS: Let it be honest then and soldier-like.
CRASSUS: So it shall be. I'll have thee an ambassador
To this mad Thracian, to propose a ransome
For my unhappy niece, if niece I have;
Or to exchange for her his wife and brat,
Now in our hands. If she be living, have her
At any ransome; stick not at the sum.—
And hark ye, use your eyes and wisdom well.
Look me out, as a soldier, what 'twould profit
A soldier to have known; and if thou find'st
A man among his officers to be bribed
To any treason may advantage us,
Make him what gain thou wilt.—But see thou bring
My Julia with thee.—If thou find'st a man,
That may be bought, at any price, to murder
The Thracian, buy him for that act.
JOVIUS: Not I:
No foul and dastard blow i' the back.
CRASSUS: Ay, none
For honest enemies; but felon foes
E'en crush feloniously.—Away: heaven speed thee.
Kill we the chief, and I will end the war,
Ere Pompey comes to share with me the honour.   [*Exeunt.*]>

SCENE 1: *The Camp of* SPARTACUS.

[*Enter* SENONA, JULIA, FLORUS, *and* ÆNOMAIIS.]

SENONA: Weep not, poor lady.—
JULIA: Why bid'st thou me not weep?
  Hadst thou no tears, when thou didst find thyself
  The slave of strangers? Yes, thou hadst, although
  In bond of the merciful, who were never used
  To aught but gentleness with woman. Yet me,
  The lily-cradled daughter of great nobles,
  Brought to the slavish[42] thrall of slaves, exposed
  To all their brutal cruelty, thou bid'st
  To weep no more.
SENONA: It is thy fright, that conjures
  These shapes of danger. Thou art here as safe
  As woman may be in a troubled camp.
  Thou art no slave; but, I am sure, art held
  To timely ransome. Pray be comforted:—
  I know, thou art safe.
JULIA: I have, I know, that safety
  That may be found in den of wolves or bears.—
  Would I had died or e'er my fate had thrust me
  Among these dreadful murderers.
SENONA: They are such
  To none my husband favours.
JULIA: Is not he
  As fierce and pitiless as the rest, who seeks
  To venge his wrongs upon the innocent?
  He that has madly doomed that hapless captive
  His father's crime in blood to expiate?
SENONA: He has not doomed him; nay, if he said so,
  It was in wrath; and he will pardon him.
  The heart that throbs beneath his bloody mail,
  Can melt to pity quickly as thine own.
  I think, he'll free him; for thyself, I know,
  Thou art protected.
JULIA: Am I from his brother,
  The insolent Phasarius?—Heard I not
  What claim that villain made to me? Alas,
  Thou art a woman, and can pity me.

SENONA: Thine ears deceived thee; did they not, Ænomaiis?

ÆNOMAIIS: I think so, lady.

SENONA: Did not this argument
Point to some claim of war?

ÆNOMAIIS: A bold proposal
Made by Phasarius, by the chief denied:
This was their argument.

    [*Enter* SPARTACUS.]

JULIA: Alas, behold
How frowns the angry fury on his face!
Bodes this no ill to Florus or to me?

SENONA: What is the matter, husband, that you look
So sad and heavy?

SPARTACUS: Sad and heavy, am I?—
[*Aside.*] And shall I, for this face of snow provoke
A threatening ruin? Out of foolish pity
For one that loves me not, drive from my heart,
The heart that loves me well?

SENONA: What say'st thou, Spartacus?

SPARTACUS: [*Aside.*] To save her girlish body from the shame,
Her baby bosom from the pang,—to rescue
From a short dream of sorrow, one young fool
Out of the million millions of the mourning,
Kill mine own coming glory and the hopes
Of a wrong'd world?

SENONA: I fear me, thou art angry.

SPARTACUS: Hark ye, my girl—that fool that trembles yonder—

SENONA: I pity her.

SPARTACUS: Dost thou indeed? And art thou
Assured she is worth thy pity? Were the world
A jot the worse, were she removed from it?

SENONA: Alas, you will not harm her? She has indeed
A kind and foolish heart.

SPARTACUS: Has she indeed?
Well, she shall to her father.

SENONA: She has none.

SPARTACUS: What, wife, an orphan? Now the incensed heaven
Smite my hard heart! A poor and feeble child
Left struggling fatherless in the world, and I
Consent to wrong her!

SENONA: What is't you say?
SPARTACUS: Not I,
Though forty thousand unjust brothers storm'd.—
One day mine own child will be fatherless.—
We'll ransome her.
SENONA: I'm glad to hear you say so.
SPARTACUS: [To JULIA.] What, foolish maid, why dost thou weep?
    Come, smile,
I'll send thee to the praetor—and the boy too.—
I think 'twould break her heart to kill him.—

    [Enter PHASARIUS.]

                                    Brother—
Brother, I hope thou hast forgot this folly.
PHASARIUS: I claim the captive.
SPARTACUS: Thou shalt have a thousand;
But not these twain.
PHASARIUS: I care not for the boy.
The girl is mine,—captured by mine own hands;
Therefore mine own.
FLORUS: Base caitiff!
SPARTACUS: Sirrah, begone.—
PHASARIUS: Deny me her, and, by the fates, thou art
No longer brother of mine. 'Twas I that helped thee
To this high station; and the troops thou rulest,
Are but my lending; for that hour I leave thee,
They leave thee to.
SPARTACUS: Come,—look me in the face,
And let me see how bad desires have changed thee.
PHASARIUS: I claim the captive.
SPARTACUS: Set thine eye upon her:
Lo you, she weeps, and she is fatherless.
Thou wouldst not harm an orphan? What, I say,
Art thou, whom I have carried in my arms
To mountain-tops, to worship the great God,
Art thou a man to plot a wrong and sorrow
(And thou a man!) against a feeble orphan?
Wilt thou now ask her?
PHASARIUS: Ay.
SPARTACUS: Thou art a changeling!
My father ne'er begot so base a heart.—

Brother, I do conjure thee, for I love thee,
Forget this thing.

PHASARIUS: Farewell.

SPARTACUS: Thou wilt not go?

PHASARIUS: Ay, by great Jove, I will. Play thou the tyrant
On those that follow thee.

SPARTACUS: My younger brother:—
Nay, I'll not call thee such,—but a hot fool
And heartless enemy.—

PHASARIUS: Call what thou wilt:
I am a man not to be mock'd and wrong'd,
Nor flouted in my counsels. I did ask you,
Now that you had the wind of the fooled praetor,
Now when rich Rome is emptied by her levies,
Now when the eager troops cry all, *for Rome,*
To march upon it, ere the joining armies
Of Pompey and Lucullus should prevent you.
This I did ask, and this you did deny.
Though, by a former promise, pledged thereto.

SPARTACUS: I promised not.

PHASARIUS: By heaven, you did—*when stronger.*
This you refuse; and when, forgiving this,
I ask my captive, you deny me her,
With many a sharp and contumelious word,
Such as is fitter for a dog than me.

SPARTACUS: Forgive me, if my anger used such shame;
I knew not what I said.

PHASARIUS: March then to Rome.

SPARTACUS: It cannot be. We should but set us down
Under her walls, where the three generals,
Ere we could force the gates, would hedge us in.
We cannot stand against them all even here;
But, when in Sicily, are invincible.

PHASARIUS: Rome, or the captive: no more Sicily.

SPARTACUS: To Sicily:
There, by the ocean fenced, rouse up and gather
The remnants of those tribes by Rome destroyed,
Invited to their vengeance. Then will come,
Arm'd with retributive and murderous hate,
The sons of fiery Afric,—Carthaginians
Out of their caves, Numidians from their deserts;

The Gaul, the Spaniard, the Sardinian;
The hordes of Thessaly, Thrace, and Macedon,
And swarming Asia;—all at last assembled
In vengeful union 'gainst this hell of Rome.
Then may we crush, but now we crush ourselves.
Let us to Sicily.

PHASARIUS: Those that will. Farewell.

SPARTACUS: Will you desert me?

PHASARIUS: I did think thee meant
For the most godlike enterprise of earth:
Thou fail'st. Farewell; protect thyself.

SPARTACUS: Mad boy.
Remember Crixus.

PHASARIUS: And his thousand Germans!
I go with Gauls and Thracians, and fifty thousand.
A Roman girl was worth this coil!—Farewell:
Learn to be juster.   [Exit.]

SPARTACUS: Gone! Alas, alas,
Am I unjust? I did not think my brother
Could e'er desert me.

ÆNOMAIIS: Spartacus—

SPARTACUS: Ænomaiis,
Dost thou remain? Why dost thou stay with me?

ÆNOMAIIS: For that I know thee wiser than thy brother.
I will stand, fight, or die with thee. But look;
If thou speak not, the army to a man,
Will follow this young madman.

SPARTACUS: Mad and ungrateful all! Will none remain?

SENONA: Beseech you, speak with them, my honoured husband.

SPARTACUS: And he endanger'd thee too! By the heavens,
I'll ne'er forgive him.—Nay, to your couch.
I'll speak with them. They will not all desert me.   [Exeunt.]

SCENE 2: The Camp of CRASSUS. Enter CRASSUS and LENTULUS.

CRASSUS: Thy son was kill'd then? I am sorry for him.
I heard, he bore him soldier-like, and I,
Upon this promise, did intend him favour.

LENTULUS: I know not that he certainly was killed;
But, I thank Jove, he did not fly his post.

[*Enter* BRACCHIUS.]

CRASSUS: What of the enemy? does he still approach?
BRACCHIUS: No, he is flying.
LENTULUS: Flying! thou art mad.
BRACCHIUS: That may be, for my slaves have ruined me.
  Why should brains stick where gold will not?
CRASSUS: Come, sirrah,
  What didst thou mean by saying the foe fled?
  <How flies he?
BRACCHIUS: As a hound, that having coursed
  A sinking brock,[43] upon a sudden turns,
  To chase a noble stag.—Ourselves the badger,
  And Rome the worthier quarry.
CRASSUS: Tedious fool,>
  What dost thou mean?
BRACCHIUS: That the fierce Gladiators
  Instead of dinging[44] us, as seemed designed,
  Are now upon the highway to the city.
CRASSUS: To Rome?
BRACCHIUS: Yes, flying to Rome.
CRASSUS: Presumptuous fools!
  <Now may we build a forest of crucifixes.
  Did the men cast away their picks, and arm.>
  We'll after them.
BRACCHIUS: I think there's some division
  Among the leaders; for the herds afoot,
  March in disorder.
CRASSUS: Separated! Jove,
  I thank thee for this boon.—Another Crixus!
  To arms, I say. Send out the cavalry,
  <To gain their flanks and front, letting them get
  Beyond the leader's camp.>—This is a triumph.—
  To arms, I say.   [*Exeunt.*]

SCENE 3: *The Camp of* SPARTACUS.

[*Enter* SPARTACUS *and* ÆNOMAIIS.]

SPARTACUS: Seven thousand true? A handful, but enough,
  Being staunch and prudent, for the enterprise.—

Desert me! Well, well, well.—Among the hills
Are many paths that may be safely trod;
Whereby we'll gain the sea, and so pass o'er
To safer Sicily.—Perhaps I spoke
Too roughly,—but no matter.—Did you send
To hire the shipping of those pirates? Well.—
And all prepared to march at nightfall?—Ænomaiis,
Do you not think they'll beat him?

ÆNOMAIIS: I doubt it not;
Phasarius being a soldier, but no leader.

<SPARTACUS: An excellent leader, but that he is rash.

ÆNOMAIIS: That is the misery. He will fight you hotly
An army of lions; but a troop of foxes
May easily beat him. Now the praetor's brain
Is all o' the fox's colour.>

SPARTACUS: Well, I care not:
We will to Rhegium.[45]—Think you, Ænomaiis,
I might not, while the praetor steals upon him,
Steal on the praetor, and so save the army?
What say'st thou?

ÆNOMAIIS: Hang them, no. This brings Lucullus
On our seven thousand. Let the mutineers
Look to themselves.

SPARTACUS: Right, very right, right, Ænomaiis.
Let them look to themselves. He did desert me;
My father's son deserted me, and left me
Circled by foes. I say, 'tis very right.
<He shall no help from me; not though they beat him
An hundred times; no, no, no help from me.>

ÆNOMAIIS: Lo you, a messenger!

SPARTACUS: From Phasarius!—
Perhaps he is sorry.—

    [*Enter* JOVIUS.]

ÆNOMAIIS: Chief, an embassy
From Crassus.

SPARTACUS: And what would Crassus with the Gladiator,
The poor base slave, and fugitive, Spartacus?
Speak, Roman: wherefore does thy master send
Thy gray hairs to the cutthroat's camp?

JOVIUS: Brave rebel,—

SPARTACUS: Why that's a better name than a rogue or bondman,
But, in this camp, I am call'd general.
JOVIUS: Brave general; for, though a rogue and bondman,
As you have said, I'll still allow you general,
As he that beats a consul surely is,—
SPARTACUS: Say two,—two consuls; and to that e'en add
A proconsul, three praetors, and some generals.
JOVIUS: Why 'tis no more than true.—Are you a Thracian?
SPARTACUS: Ay.
JOVIUS: There is something in the air of Thrace
Breeds valour up as rank as grass. 'Tis pity
You are a barbarian.
SPARTACUS: Wherefore?
JOVIUS: Had you been born
A Roman, you had won by this a triumph.
SPARTACUS: I thank the gods I am barbarian;
For I can better teach the grace-begot
And heaven-supported masters of the earth,
How a mere dweller of a desert rock
Can bow their crown'd heads to his chariot wheels.
Man is heaven's work, and beggar's brats may 'herit
A soul to mount them up the steeps of fortune,
With regal necks to be their steeping-blocks.—
But come, what is thy message?
JOVIUS: Julia, niece
Of the praetor, is thy captive.
SPARTACUS: Ay.
JOVIUS: For whom
Is offered in exchange thy wife, Senona,
And thy young boy.
SPARTACUS: Tell thou the praetor, Roman,
The Thracian's wife is ransomed.
JOVIUS: How is that?
SPARTACUS: What ho, Senona!

[SENONA *appears with the child at a tent door.*]

                        Lo, she stands before you,
Ransomed, and by the steel, from out the camp
Of slaughtered Gellius.   [*Exit* SENONA.]
JOVIUS: This is sorcery!—
But name a ransome for the general's niece.

SPARTACUS: Have I not now the praetor on the hip?
   He would, in his extremity, have made
   My wife his buckler of defence; perhaps
   Have doomed her to the scourge! But this is Roman.
   Now the barbarian is instructed. Look,
   I hold the praetor by the heart; and he
   Shall feel how tightly grip barbarian fingers.
JOVIUS: Men do not war on women. Name her ransome.
SPARTACUS: Men do not war on women! Look you:
   One day I clomb upon the ridgy top
   Of the cloud-piercing Haemus, where, among
   The eagles and the thunders, from that height,
   I look'd upon the world—or, far as where,
   Wrestling with storms, the gloomy Euxine chafed
   On his recoiling shores; and where dim Adria
   In her blue bosom quenched the fiery sphere.
   Between those surges lay a land, might once
   Have served for paradise, but Rome had made it
   A Tartarus.[46]—In my green youth I look'd
   From the same frosty peak, where now I stood,
   And then beheld the glory of those lands,
   Where peace was tinkling on the shepherd's bell
   And singing with the reapers; <or beneath
   The shade of thatch eaves, smiled with grey old men,
   And with their children laughed along the green.>
   Since that glad day, Rome's conquerors had past
   With withering armies there, and all was changed:
   Peace had departed; howling war was there,
   Cheered on by Roman hunters: then, methought,
   Even as I looked upon the altered scene,
   Groans echoed through the valleys, through which ran
   Rivers of blood, like smoking Phlegethons;[47]
   Fires flashed from burning villages, and famine
   Shriek'd in the empty cornfields. Women and children,
   Robb'd of their sires and husbands, left to starve—
   These were the dwellers of the land!—Say'st thou
   Rome wars not then on women?
JOVIUS: This is not to the matter.
SPARTACUS: Now, by Jove,
   It is. These things do Romans. But the earth
   Is sick of conquerors. There is not a man,

Not Roman, but is Rome's extremest foe;
And such am I, sworn from that hour I saw
These sights of horror, while the gods support me,
To wreak on Rome such havock as Rome wreaks,
Carnage and devastation, wo and ruin.
Why should I ransome, when I swear to slay?—
Begone: this is my answer!
<JOVIUS: With your leave
This prattling scares no Romans; and these threats
Come weakly from a chief of mutineers.
SPARTACUS: Of mutineers?
JOVIUS: Ay, marry, 'tis well known,
Your cutthroats have deserted you. Content you,
Crassus will punish the foul traitors.
SPARTACUS: Crassus!
JOVIUS: Ay, Crassus.—Hercules, how men will talk!
Wreak wo on Rome!—I tell you, your lieutenant
Will hang upon a cross before the morrow.
So name your ransome, while 'tis offered you.
SPARTACUS: Begone, I say.   [Exit JOVIUS.]
                        Alas, my Ænomaiis,
Should we not strike now? Now while we might fall
Upon their rear, and take them by surprise?
ÆNOMAIIS: Let them be punished, castigated well,
And they'll return to wisdom and obedience.
SPARTACUS: Right, right. Let them be punished, hack'd to the bones:
This will speak better than my words. Prepare
For Rhegium. He'll return to us tomorrow.   [Exeunt.]>

END OF ACT IV

ACT V

SCENE 1: *The Peninsula of Rhegium. The Camp of the Gladiators.*

[*Enter* SPARTACUS *and* ÆNOMAIIS.]

SPARTACUS: Routed and cut to pieces!—Said I not?
Did I not tell them?—Utterly destroyed!
Scattered like chaff!—Now by the eternal fates,

They did provoke high heaven, deserting me.—
How many slain?

ÆNOMAIIS: Indeed it is not known.

SPARTACUS: Many, I'm glad; I should be very glad:
Did I not lead them ever on to victory?
And did they not forsake me? Wretched fools,
This was my vengeance, yea, my best of vengeance,
To leave them to themselves, that Roman praetors
Might whip them for me. Art thou not rejoiced?
Art thou not, Ænomaiis, glad of this?
Glad, very glad?

<ÆNOMAIIS: I shall be, when I see
Half of them back again.

SPARTACUS: I'll decimate them:
Even as the Romans punish, so I'll punish.—
Ruin me all these grand and glorious hopes?
Nay they were certainties.—An excellent army,
That might have fought with Pompey, broke and ruined
By their mad mutiny! An excellent army——

ÆNOMAIIS: Indeed, an excellent.

SPARTACUS: Foolish, Ænomaiis,
Why did'st thou stay me, when I would have saved them?

ÆNOMAIIS: Had this been well? Had their ingratitude
Deserved it of thee?

SPARTACUS: Ay, ingratitude.
Did I oppress them? Did I tyrannise?>

ÆNOMAIIS: 'Tis rumoured that Phasarius fell.

SPARTACUS: My brother,
My foolish brother—why did he part from me?—
Nay, I'll not mourn him.

ÆNOMAIIS: This evil news must now
Hasten our embarkation. The pirate ships
Already are launching from the shore.

SPARTACUS: Why now
You are too fast. Bid them be beached again.—
<Alas, that foolish boy! We'll rest awhile,
And see what fugitives may come to us.>
Art sure Phasarius was slain?—the pride
Of his dead mother's heart; and, I do know,
Though prone to anger, of a loving spirit.—
We'll rest awhile here on this promontory.

ÆNOMAIIS: Each moment has a peril. For these pirates
   They are most treacherous hounds, and may set sail
   Without us; and the praetor, thou know'st well,
   Is trenching us in on this peninsula.
SPARTACUS: What care I for the praetor and his trenches?
   <This is a boy's trick, and a boy might meet it.>
   Trenches to stop a Thracian!—Look you now
   What drooping slave is that? By all the gods,
   It is my brother!—But I'll not be glad.
   Lo you, how humbled, spiritless he looks!
   Where are his troops?

    [*Enter* PHASARIUS.]

                  Sirrah, why comest thou here?
   Didst thou not part from me, and take mine army?
   Did'st thou not teach my followers mutiny,
   And lead them to destruction? Thou whipp'd fool,
   Why comest thou here?
PHASARIUS: To ask thy pardon, and to die.
SPARTACUS: Couldst thou not die with those thou led'st to death,
   That men, who after should have called thee madman,
   Might not have called thee craven?
PHASARIUS: I am no craven;
   A wretch, I grant you, but no craven.
SPARTACUS: Where are thy troops? that throng'd and valiant army
   Thou stol'dst from me?
PHASARIUS: With Pluto. Why demand me?
   I am alone of all.
SPARTACUS: Most wretched man,
   Thou hast murder'd fifty thousand men, destroyed
   Thy brother and thy country, and all hope
   Of the earth's disenthralment.
PHASARIUS: I have ruined
   My brother, that's enough.
SPARTACUS: Ay, look, behold;
   But yestermorn, I was a conqueror,
   On the high verge and pinnacle of renown;
   Today a skulking, trembling, despised man,
   Thrust in a pit. Whose traitorous hand was it,
   Pluck'd me from my high seat, and sunk so low?
   Who did this thing, this foul, felonious thing?

PHASARIUS: Myself, that was thy brother.

SPARTACUS: Ay, that was!

PHASARIUS: Why shouldst thou stab me with thy words? O brother,
    Strike me with thy sharp sword, but speak no more.
    Give me to punishment, or drive me forth
    To die by Romans; but upbraid no more.

SPARTACUS: Shall I forgive him? Look, he is penitent.

ÆNOMAIIS: But he has lost them all.

SPARTACUS: Ay, so he has.—
    Ask'st thou for pardon, when thou hast slain all?
    Away! thou didst discard me from thy heart:
    I banish thee from mine.

PHASARIUS: It is but just.
    Why should I live, when I have ruined thee?
    I should have died before. Farewell.

SPARTACUS: Come back:
    I will forgive thee: nay, I have.—O brother,
    Why didst thou do this wrong? But I'll forget it.—
    Let the ships now be launched, now, Ænomaiis;
    Now cross to Sicily.   [*Exit* ÆNOMAIIS.]
                  With these fifty thousand—
    But I've forgot it.—What, were all destroyed?

PHASARIUS: All, all.

SPARTACUS: A disciplined army!—But no matter.—
    All slain upon the field?

PHASARIUS: Six thousand wretches
    Yielded them prisoners to the praetor.

SPARTACUS: Well,
    He took six thousand prisoners. These will now
    Suffer a double wretchedness.

PHASARIUS: Never fear it:
    They will not.

SPARTACUS: How is that, Phasarius?
    Did not the praetor, in his proclamations,
    Threat us with bondmen's deaths by crucifixion?

PHASARIUS: And he will keep his word—nay, he has kept it.

SPARTACUS: What!

PHASARIUS: Are men beasts, that life should count no more
    Than a beast's sob?

SPARTACUS: Thou fill'st my soul with terror.
    Are they condemned? All?

PHASARIUS: Executed.
SPARTACUS: Horror!
   Six thousand men, and crucified!
PHASARIUS: Crucified.
   I saw a sight last night, that turned my brain,
   And set my comrade mad. The Roman highway
   Is, each side, lined with crosses, and on each cross
   Is nailed a gladiator.—Well, 'twas night,
   When, with a single follower, I did creep
   Through the trenched army to that road, and saw
   The executed multitude uplifted
   Upon the horrid engines. Many lived:
   Some moaned and writhed in stupid agony;
   Some howled, and prayed for death, and cursed the gods;
   Some turned to lunatics, and laughed at horror;
   And some with fierce and hellish strength, had torn
   Their arms free from the beams, and so had died,
   Grasping, headlong, at air. And, oh the yells,
   That rose upon the gusty sighs of night,
   And babbled hideously along the skies,
   As *they* were fill'd with murder!
SPARTACUS: Say no more:
   This is too dreadful for man's ear. I swear
   For this to make Rome howl. What, Ænomaiis.

   [*Reenter* ÆNOMAIIS.]

   Are the ships all afloat?
ÆNOMAIIS: And gone.
SPARTACUS: What, gone?
ÆNOMAIIS: These same perfidious pirates, with their hire,
   Have set their sails, and fled.
SPARTACUS: The ocean god
   Meet them with hurricanes, sink their ships, and feed
   Sea monsters with their corses!
ÆNOMAIIS: All is finished.
   This is the fruit of mercy for deserters.
SPARTACUS: Be that forgot.
ÆNOMAIIS: What now remains for us,
   But to sit down and die?
SPARTACUS: I'll tell thee, what:
   To fight the praetor.

ÆNOMAIIS: Though his troops outnumber
   Ten times our own!
SPARTACUS: Ay; our despair will make us
   Each ten times stronger than his foe. Fill up
   This schoolboy ditch with disregarded plunder,
   And when the watchdogs sleep, like wolves, steal on them
   And take them by the throat. I have no fear,
   But we shall find a pathway through their camp.
   Then to Tarentum;[48] there we'll find us ships.
   Or, if that fail, with a despairing fury,
   Turn upon Rome, and perish there.

   [*Enter* SENONA, *with the child.*]

                         What now?
   Com'st thou to mourn o'er our mishaps, Senona?
   Be not dismayed: I'll find thee safety yet.
SENONA: Thou wouldst conceal these newer perils from me;
   But well I know, that every hour now brings
   A menacing cloud about thee.
SPARTACUS: Clouds, ay, clouds:
   A cloud is on my path, but my ambition
   Has glory in't: as travellers who stand
   On mountains, view upon some neighbouring peak,
   Among the mists, a figure of themselves,
   Traced in sublimer characters; so I
   Here see the vapory image of myself,
   Distant and dim, but giantlike—I'll make
   These perils glories.
SENONA: And the ships have left thee?
SPARTACUS: Thou art a soldier's wife, and wilt not tremble
   To share his danger. Look, through yonder camp
   Our path lies.
SENONA: I will walk it by thy side.
SPARTACUS: Not so; for though unharmed by steel, the sight
   Of the near fray would kill thee. I have discovered
   A path almost unguarded; where, whilst I
   Assault the Roman in his sleep, thyself
   And my war-cradled boy, with my Phasarius
   To guard thee, shall in safety pass, and join me
   After the battle.

SENONA: Why not lead your army
  By that unguarded path?
SPARTACUS: Trust me, dear wife,
  I'll make it such for thee, but cannot have it
  Safe for an army. The surprised distraction
  Of the attack will call the guards away.
  This is the safest.
SENONA: Let me go with thee.
  I do not fear the horrors of the storm.
SPARTACUS: It cannot be. What, brother—
PHASARIUS: Let some one else
  Be made her guard; while I, in fight, find vengeance,
  And reparation of my faults.
SPARTACUS: Wilt thou
  Refuse me this, Phasarius?
PHASARIUS: Am not I
  A rash and witless fool? Trust not to me
  What thou so valuest.
SENONA: I beseech you, hear him.
  Let me not leave you, Spartacus: my heart
  Is full of dismal and of ominous fear,
  If I do leave you now, I leave for ever.
  If I must die, let me die where thou art.
SPARTACUS: Why talk'st thou now of death? I say, I'll make
  This path most safe for thee. How could I fight,
  Or play the leader in a bloody storm,
  With thy pale visage ever in my eye?
PHASARIUS: I do beseech you, make me not her guard.
SPARTACUS: It must be so. And hear me now, Phasarius;
  I put into thy hands more than my soul:—
  See, my dear wife, and here my innocent boy.—
  These are the very jewels of my heart.
  Protect them for me. Be not rash; steal softly,
  With the small faithful troop I'll send with thee,
  Through glens and woods; and when the alarm is sounded,
  March fast but wisely. For thy life, and mine,
  Avoid all contest, shouldst thou meet a foe;
  Nay, though thou know'st thou hast advantage, fight not.
  Join me, with these in safety, and assure me
  No man has drawn his sword.—And now farewell.

Farewell, Senona: I pray you do not speak.—
Thou art very safe. Farewell.

[*Exeunt* SENONA, *child, and* PHASARIUS.]

ÆNOMAIIS: He is too rash.

SPARTACUS: Rash, had I given him a command in battle;
But will not be with them.—Rouse up the troops,
Fill up the ditch with baggage, as I told thee.—
<I'll see that all be schooled for this assault.>   [*Exeunt.*]

SCENE 2: *Before the tent of* CRASSUS.

[*Enter* CRASSUS, MUMMIUS, JOVIUS, LENTULUS, *and* BRACCHIUS.]

CRASSUS: Now I lament me, on this overthrow
Of the chief army of the enemy,
I prayed for Pompey and Lucullus. If
I end not instant, by another blow,
The war I have so maimed, comes me a colleague
To chouse[49] me of my triumphs.

JOVIUS: You must be quick then.
The dawn will show you Pompey by your side;
Or rather, dashing with a Roman scorn,
Amongst the ruffians you have trapp'd.

CRASSUS: I think,
Ourselves may do it.—And this hell-dog holds
The girl to doom?

JOVIUS: He says, he is instructed
By your fore-thought intentions with his spouse.

CRASSUS: But dost thou think he'll slay her?

JOVIUS: Not while he
May purchase mercy with her.

CRASSUS: Shall I take her
Out of his camp by force? or send thee back,
To offer mercy and receive submission?

JOVIUS: Propose him life and liberty, and make him
A Roman citizen.

CRASSUS: What, a rebel slave!

JOVIUS: In these rough, rotten times, we do not scruple
To raise our rogues to honour. Why then blush,
To anoint a slave, that's capable and honest?

The genius of this Thracian, had it been
In honourable trust display'd, had quell'd
A score of barbarous nations; and *may* yet,
Make but the man a Roman.

CRASSUS: We will make him
A captive first.—Were my poor Julia free!—[*Loud alarums.*]
What is the matter?

JOVIUS: The rats are out! By Jove,
The slaves have pass'd the trenches, and assault us!

CRASSUS: Thou art mad! They dare not—What, to arms, to arms!
Nay, if they will, let them into the camp,
But let not out.—To arms, to arms!   [*Exeunt.*]

SCENE 3: *Another part of the Roman Camp.*

[*Enter* CRASSUS, JOVIUS, MUMMIUS, *and* LENTULUS.]

CRASSUS: Mischiefs and plagues, and slavish stripes disgrace
These shameless cowards! What, ope their ranks, and give
A path to these few madmen! Let them scape us!

JOVIUS: Nay, they are gone, that's certain,—but will drop
Into the jaws of Pompey.

CRASSUS: Bid the legions
Follow them.

JOVIUS: When the day breaks; but not now.

CRASSUS: Shall I let Pompey take them, and have Rome
Laugh at my shame? Have Pompey join the scorners,
And mock me too? Hie thee away, good Jovius;
Follow the Thracian; offer pardon, freedom,
Whate'er thou wilt. Do but delay his march:
Let him not come near Pompey—Quick, away!   [*Exeunt.*]

SCENE 4: *The Camp of* SPARTACUS, *among the hills.*

[*Enter* SPARTACUS *and* ÆNOMAIIS.]

SPARTACUS: Was not this well? When desperate men contest,
The brave will fly from them. To fight for life,
Fights surest for a victory. Fought we well?
I would not give these seven thousand poor rogues,
For a whole herd of angry Gauls. We'll win
The highway to Tarentum yet.—Lieutenant,
Should they not now be here?

ÆNOMAIIS: Who?
SPARTACUS: Who! Phasarius
   And his care-chosen guard—my brother and my wife.
ÆNOMAIIS: They tread a rough and tangled path.
SPARTACUS: 'Tis true;
   And finding there more guards than I had word of,
   Their caution journeys them the slower. I
   Am almost grieved, I brought them not with me.—
   How fare the captives? Bring me to Tarentum,
   I'll send that girl unransomed to the praetor.—
   Would they were here!—Bring in the prisoner,
   And find how march the coming generals.

   [BRACCHIUS *is brought in, guarded.*]

ÆNOMAIIS: This fellow was the master of thy brother.
   Question him, and then hang him, for a baser,
   More heartless master never yet struck slave.
SPARTACUS: I am sick of blood.—Is not the sun yet up?
   If they be seen—but I'll not think of that.—
   Be not afeard: hadst thou been worth a blow,
   I had not spared thee. Speak, and truly speak,
   Or thou shalt fat the kites: When looks the praetor
   For Pompey and his Spanish troops?
BRACCHIUS: He looks
   Not for, but at him.
SPARTACUS: Wretch.
BRACCHIUS: And so may'st thou,
   Yonder among the heights upon thy left.
SPARTACUS: Wretch, if thou mock me, I will strike thee dead.
   Know I now well the praetor's craft? These eagles
   That spread their golden pinions on the hills,
   Were wing'd by Crassus thither, to affright me.
   Are they not Crassus's standards? Own me that,
   Or look tonight to sup in Acheron.[50]
BRACCHIUS: To sup on earth, then, I'll agree to this;
   But I shall lie.
SPARTACUS: Rogue, answer me again:
   Are those troops Pompey's?
BRACCHIUS: Ay.
SPARTACUS: The gods forbid!
   They are in motion too! Now I begin

To feel my desolation, and despair.
What, Ænomaiis, send me out a scout
To view those hill-perched foes, and quick prepare
The army for the march. And my poor wife!
Why did I trust her with Phasarius?
<Send out a cunning guide to hunt the path.>   [*Exit* ÆNOMAIIS.]
Roman, if thou speak false, I'll have thee slain.—
Where rests Lucullus?
BRACCHIUS: In no place he rests,
Save nightly on the highroad from Tarentum.
<SPARTACUS: Villain, thou liest! The gods have not so left me.
I say, thou speak'st not true.
BRACCHIUS: Well, I speak false;
But notwithstanding, he is on that road.—
These are the bloodiest cutthroats!—>
SPARTACUS: Now, out on me,
My heart is full of fear. The praetor on my rear,
Lucullus, Pompey on my front and left,
And naught but howling seas upon my right!
Seven thousand men against an hundred thousand!
If Crassus love the girl—He fears disgrace—
'Tis not infeasible—unless, alas,
My wife, perchance, be faln into his hands;
Then can the maiden buy me naught but her.

[*Reenter* ÆNOMAIIS, *with* JOVIUS.]

ÆNOMAIIS: The Roman praetor
Sends thee again an envoy.
SPARTACUS: Speak, centurion;
What word sends Crassus?
JOVIUS: For the Roman lady,
A princely ransome; for thyself, an offer
Of mercy, pardon, Roman denization,
And martial honour and command; provided—
SPARTACUS: Ay, provided!
JOVIUS: Thou instantly, ere Pompey leave the hills,
Surrender up these malefactious slaves
To whips and crosses. Therefore, most valiant Thracian,
Put by the frenzy, that would fight against

Three circling armies, and accept this boon
Generous and great.

SPARTACUS: I am unfortunate,
Thou know'st that well; but not being Roman yet,
I scorn the foul condition, that makes me
To my true friends a traitor. Give them freedom,
And they lay down their arms; but talk of crosses,
And they have yet the arms that cut a path
Through the proud praetor's camp.

JOVIUS: Why shouldst thou care,
Thou, who hast such a Roman soul, for these
Vile runagate rogues, who, at an opportunity,
Thee would betray as freely as their masters?
Let them be hanged, and be thou made a Roman.
Perhaps thy word may save the least offending;
But let the scum be punished.

SPARTACUS: They shall die,
Like soldiers, on the field, or live in freedom.
But hearken, Roman:
I know the praetor, that he loves his niece,
But honour more; I know, if Pompey strike
At me one blow, the honour all is his,
And nothing left for Crassus, but comparison
Betwixt what Pompey does, and what *he* could not.
He will not then have Pompey strike me, and
He would have back his niece. While I lie here
On this impregnable and forted hill,
Pompey approaches and sits down beside him.
Now he'll consent himself to lose the honour
O' the hunted gladiator's overthrow,
So Pompey wins it not.

JOVIUS: That may be true,
For Crassus loves not Pompey. But on that
What project found you?

SPARTACUS: This: Let him but wish,
While I steal darkly to Tarentum, there
T' embark my army.

JOVIUS: Hah!

SPARTACUS: I'll find a way
To cozen Pompey and pass by Lucullus,

Provided he not follow at my heels.
Gage me but this, and he shall have his niece
Ransomed back; deny me, and by Pluto,
Pompey alone shall gain the laurel.

JOVIUS: Jove!
This is a mad proposal. Help you fly!
Will you surrender, or be cut to pieces?

SPARTACUS: Bring forth the captives.

[JULIA and FLORUS are brought in.]

                              Lo, I'll march tonight:
If Crassus follow me, the girl shall die.

JOVIUS: Art thou a savage?

SPARTACUS: Ay; or if you will,
A beast, whose nature not being fierce, the hunters
Have toil'd and goaded into fury. Nature
Makes fewer rogues, than misery. But yesterday,
I had saved that maiden's blood, at cost of mine;
Now, with a cool ferocity, I doom her
To perish like a thing abhorred, when'er
The praetor bids me.

JULIA: Out, alas, alas!
Didst thou not swear thou wouldst not harm my life?
Thou didst, unto thy wife.

SPARTACUS: Well, speak not of it.—
She is surely taken.—Roman, listen to me:
South of thy camp there liest a secret path,
Where, for a certain reason, I did send
A party, to escape the fears of conflict.
Have they been captured?

JOVIUS: I know not, but think so.
Who were they?

SPARTACUS: Well, they are not taken then?

JOVIUS: I'll not say that. A double guard was sent,
Under your one time master, Lentulus,
Last night, to watch that path.

SPARTACUS: I have some prisoners
I would exchange for them—Look, all but her.

JOVIUS: But who were these?

SPARTACUS: Some women and children. Yes,
Some helpless fools, not fit to look on battle.—
Not that I care for them; but I'll exchange them.

JOVIUS: Some women and children?

SPARTACUS: Sirrah, wilt thou have it?
Why 'twas my wife then, and my child. If they
Be captured, I'll exchange them for my captives.
Crassus shall have his niece too. Nay, I'll send her,
Without the exchange, provided Crassus swear
To give them freedom, and send back to Thrace.
Let him swear this: let them to Thrace, I say,—
Let them be safe, and I can die.—[*Alarums.*]

ÆNOMAIIS: Look, general!
We are attacked!

SPARTACUS: By heavens, a troop of horse
Rushing against our hill! Why these are madmen?—
Soft you, they chase some mounted fugitive;
Nay, he has cleared them—Look, man, look! O gods,
Do I not know him?—

JOVIUS: For this proposed exchange—

SPARTACUS: Look, look! 'Tis he! They are lost!

ÆNOMAIIS: His horse has fallen.
He is bloody too.

SPARTACUS: But where are they?

[*Enter* PHASARIUS, *wounded.*]

What, brother, brother,
Speak, speak.—Where are they? Ah!

PHASARIUS: My brother!

SPARTACUS: Speak!
Dost thou not know me? By thy soul, I charge thee,
Speak to me; tell me of my love, my boy!
Where hast thou left them?

PHASARIUS: Strike me to the heart.
I have robbed thee, brother, of much more than life,
And all the blood these gaping wounds have left,
Will not repay thee.

SPARTACUS: Art thou mad?
I ask thee of my wife, my boy, my loves!
And thou dost prate to me of wounds and blood!—
Speak!

PHASARIUS: I can better speak than thou canst hear.—
    Why madest thou me their escort? Why, O fool!
    Thou should'st have known that I would quickly lead them
    Through the first perils that invited me;
    And where a Roman throat was to be cut,
    Would drag them to the hideous spectacle.
SPARTACUS: But thou did'st bear them off! Come, say it, brother;
    Thou wert imprudent, but still kind and true.
    I'll not be angry—come, I know thou wert worsted,
    Thy troops cut off—but thou hast saved them, brother!
PHASARIUS: I would have done it, let my wounds speak for me.
SPARTACUS: They are captives then? O traitor!—my poor wife,
    And my blithe boy!
PHASARIUS: The troops were cut to pieces;
    The boy—
SPARTACUS: What of him?
PHASARIUS: Cried for mercy to
    A Roman soldier—
SPARTACUS: Who spared him!
PHASARIUS: Struck him to the earth.
SPARTACUS: God!—And his mother?
PHASARIUS: She sprang upon the throat of the black monster—
    Ask me no more—I faint.
SPARTACUS: My wife! my wife!
    Let furies lash thee into consciousness.
    My wife, I say! She sprang upon his throat;
    What then?
PHASARIUS: He slew her—but I clove him to the nave.
    I could not save, but with my best avenged. [*Falls.*]
SPARTACUS: There are no gods in heaven;
    Pity has fled, and human rage reigns there.—
    Wretch, doth the earth still hold thee? Murderer,
    Most traitorous, foul, unnatural murderer,
    If the warm blood of thy thrice-martyred victims
    Reach not thy soul, and strike it dead within thee,
    My sword shall sacrifice thee to their fury.—
ÆNOMAIIS: Hold, hold! Thou wilt not strike him? Look, he dies!

    [PHASARIUS *dies.*]

SPARTACUS: What, is he dead? All dead? and I alone
    Upon the flinty earth? No wife, no child,

[No brother]. All slain by Romans? Yes, by Romans.—Look,
I will have vengeance, fierce and bloody vengeance,
Upon the praetor's blood, upon the praetor's.—
Thou grey and hoary wretch,—for being Roman,
A wretch thou art—I'll send back to the praetor
His niece a corse, and thou shalt carry her.—
What ho, my Guards!

    [*Enter Guards.*]

JOVIUS: Savage fiend, forbear;
  Shed not the blood o' the innocent.
SPARTACUS: <Foolish man,>
  Was not Senona's innocent, and my child's?
  Did they e'er harm a Roman?—Blood for blood,
  And life for life, and vengeance on the praetor!
FLORUS: Unhappy Spartacus, mar not thy glory
  With this unnatural and unjust deed.
  Let my head fall for hers.
SPARTACUS: Thy head *and* hers—
  <Fools, ye are Romans, and shall die.
JOVIUS: Forbear—>
SPARTACUS: Take them away—
JULIA: Now may the heavens forgive thee.
SPARTACUS: Off, foolish girl; there is no pity left:
  My heart now thirsts for blood, and blood will have.
JULIA: I have your promise—
SPARTACUS: Breath, that I revoke.
JULIA: I have Senona's; pity me for her,
  For she did love me; pity for your child,
  Whom I have nestled in my arms, till it
  Did love me too, and thou, whilst looking on,
  Didst swear no harm should ever reach to me.
  Yes, for thy babe and wife, thou didst swear this;
  And while thou think'st of them, thou canst not kill me.
SPARTACUS: Well, thou art saved.
JOVIUS: Wilt thou, unlucky chief,
  Now claim the praetor's mercy? Let thy people
  Return to bonds, and have their lives.
SPARTACUS: These twain
  Shall go with you; the rest is for my vengeance.
  To show thee that the Thracian still defies,—

Even in his hour of misery and despair,—
Still cries for vengeance, still derides the mercy
Of the accursed Roman, thou shalt see
I court his fury.—Hang this Roman cutthroat
Upon a cross, and set it where the Romans
May see him perish.

[BRACCHIUS *is taken out; and the body of* PHASARIUS.]

JOVIUS: This will steel all hearts,
And change all pity into murderous hate.
SPARTACUS: It is for that I hang him to the tree:
There shall no life be spared in fight today.
Look—let the grooms there kill my horse.—'Tis done:
There shall no flight be known; nothing but death.
Begone, centurion and prisoners. Begone or perish.
<FLORUS: I thought thee cruel, but I find thee kind.
Spare that man, and accept the praetor's pardon.
SPARTACUS: Begone, thou foolish boy, while yet thou may'st.
JULIA: Shall I not thank thee, Thracian, for my life?
SPARTACUS: Begone, or die,—and all the hearted griefs,
That rack more bitterly than death, go with you,
And reach your abhorred country: May the gods,
Who have seen Rome fill the earth with wo and death,
Bring worse than wo and death on Rome; light up
The fires of civil war and anarchy,
Curse her with kings, imperial torturers;
And while these rend her bowels, bring the hosts
Of Northern savages, to slay, and feed
Upon her festering fatness; till the earth,
Shall know, as it has known no land so great,
No land so curst as miserable Rome!—
Begone, or perish.>   [*Exeunt* JOVIUS, JULIA *and* FLORUS.]
                    Let the troops array.
And all that would not die upon the cross,
Slaying their horses, to the plain descend,
And die in battle.
>ÆNOMAIIS: You will not fight today?
SPARTACUS: This day, this hour, this minute, fight and die.
Why should we struggle longer, in this dream
Of life, which is a mocking lunacy,
With ever sunshine playing far ahead,

But thunderbolts about us? Fight I say.
There is no Orcus⁵¹ blacker than the hell
That life breeds in the heart.>

ÆNOMAIIS: Alas, dear general,
You are not fit for battle.

SPARTACUS: Fit to make
The Roman mothers howl.—Spare not one life;
Bad blood, and laugh; and if ye meet a woman
Hiding her babe in her scared bosom, slay her,
Nay both.—O Ænomaiis, but to think
How lone I stand now on this pitiless earth!—
Had I not parted with them!—O ye heavens,
Could ye look on and see the merciless steel
Struck at their sinless hearts?

<ÆNOMAIIS: Alas, alas,
Give not this way to grief.

SPARTACUS: ·   I will not, brother;
My grief is blackened into scowling vengeance.>

ÆNOMAIIS: Pray you, come to your tent.

SPARTACUS: To tents no more;
I couch no more but on the corse-strewn plain,—
Draw out the troops—I say, upon the ground,
Pillow'd on death; thus shall my slumbers be.
Come, battle, battle.   [*Exeunt.*]

SCENE 5: *The Camp of* CRASSUS.

[*Enter* CRASSUS, MUMMIUS, JOVIUS, LENTULUS, FLORUS, *etc.*
Alarums.]

CRASSUS: Thus ends rebellious rage in lunacy;
Despair hath set the gladiator mad.
Look, how with wild and impotent wrath, he rushes
Upon our ready spearmen!—Lentulus,
I am sorry thou didst slay his family.

LENTULUS: Nay, 'twas not I. Perhaps, *I* am not sorry;
They were my slaves, punish'd as fugitives.

CRASSUS: Detach the third rank and the cavalry,
On all sides to surround them. Take them prisoner;
This soldier death befits them not. Ten thousand
Greek drachmae to the man that brings alive
The leader Spartacus.   [*Exit* LENTULUS.]

<JOVIUS: That ne'er will be.
   He slew his horse, and thus rejecting flight,
   His life devoted to the infernal gods.
CRASSUS: A valiant madman!—Had he held my girl—
   Nay, but I should have storm'd his mountain camp.
   Look, moves not Pompey from the hills? What, friends,
   Shall we stand staring at this handful [of] foes,
   Till Pompey comes to help us? To the front,
   Away, to the front!   [*Exeunt.*]>

SCENE 6: *Another part of the same.*

[*Enter* SPARTACUS, ÆNOMAIIS, *and others.*]

SPARTACUS: Leave slaying in the ranks, and rush with me
   Even to the forum and praetorium,[52]
   To strike the officers.
<ÆNOMAIIS: See, the troops of Pompey,
   Are following on our rear!
SPARTACUS: What care I for the rear? I see alone
   The inviting vengeance beck'ning to the front,
   Where flows the blood that Rome may bitterest mourn.
   Let me beside the praetor. Mark, no prisoners;
   Kill, kill, kill all! There's nothing now but blood
   Can give me joy. Now can I tell how gore
   Inspires the thirsty tiger, and gives strength
   Unto the fainting wolf.—No prisoners!
   On to the general!>

[*Enter* LENTULUS, *with others.*]

LENTULUS: Lo, the bloody chief!
   Now yield thee, villain.
SPARTACUS: Murder-spotted fiend,
   Thou led'st the band that slew my wife and boy!
   Kill, kill, kill all! [*He kills* LENTULUS, *and exit with the rest
   fighting.*]

SCENE 7: *The praetorium.*

[*Enter* CRASSUS, JOVIUS, JULIA, *etc.*]

CRASSUS: Get thee away; thou wilt be slain.
JULIA: I fear not:
   Let me look on the battle, and perhaps
   Return the gift of life to Spartacus.

CRASSUS: Pr'y'thee, retire. This man has won more honour,
    Than even the braggart Pompey; for all ages
    Shall own there needed two united armies
    To quell him, yea, two Roman armies.
    What now? Why fliest thou?

    [*Enter* FLORUS.]

FLORUS: He has broken through
    The second rank. Give me more troops, and fresh,
    To venge my father's death.
CRASSUS: Nay, tarry here,
    And mark, how like the timbers of a ship,
    Crushed in the mighty seas, the sundered wrecks
    Of this rebellion vanish from our eyes.
SPARTACUS: [*Within.*] On to the general!
CRASSUS: What is that cry?
    This is a victory, but Pompey shares it.—
    What rout is this here at our tents? By heaven,
    My guards are reeling in confusion!—Lo,
    What man is this, unbuckler'd and unhelm'd,
    Gored with a thousand deaths, that waves so wildly
    A broken weapon?

    [*Enter* SPARTACUS, *wounded, etc.*]

SPARTACUS: All is lost; but cry
    Victory! On: I'll reach the general.
CRASSUS: Smite him! 'tis Spartacus.

    [SPARTACUS *is wounded by several.*]

SPARTACUS: Hah! Victory!
    Crassus, thou diest! I know thee very well.—
    Romans are straws.—No prisoners.—Naught but blood.
    Why should there be night now?—[*He falls.*]
JULIA: O dear uncle, strike not.
    Let him be spared.—He gave me life.—Alas,
    He dies, he dies!
SPARTACUS: Well—never heed the tempest—
    There are green valleys in our mountains yet.—
    Set forth the sails.—We'll be in Thrace anon.—[*Dies.*]

<CRASSUS: Thy bark is wreck'd, but nobly did she buffet
  These waves of war, and grandly lies at last,
  A stranded ruin on this fatal shore.
  Let him have burial; not as a base bondman,
  But as a chief enfranchised and ennobled.
  If we denied him honour while he lived,
  Justice shall carve it on his monument.>

  [*Dead March, etc. Curtain.*]

                         THE END

THE DRUNKARD (1844)

WILLIAM HENRY SMITH

Although American dramatists had broached topical issues in plays before 1840, few works for the early stage confronted social problems head-on. Criticism of slavery would have its day beginning with *Uncle Tom's Cabin*, but one of the first serious social ailments to be addressed directly was alcoholism. By the first third of the nineteenth century, Americans were truly a guzzling people, inhabiting what W. J. Rorabaugh has called "the alcoholic republic." As Jeffrey Mason has shown, *The Drunkard*, by William H. Smith (1806–1872), appeared at a time when the temperance movement was in full swing. After restrained beginnings with the Massachusetts Society for the Suppression of Intemperance, temperance groups that sprang up later, like the American Tract Society, the American Temperance Union, and the Washingtonians, rallied millions of citizens behind a popular cause. By 1844, most urban-dwelling Americans would have been familiar with the temperance issue, the pledge of abstinence, and the threats to family harmony that alcoholism engendered. Sermons, public meetings, speeches, sensational or pietistic tracts were the means by which temperance advocates appealed to the fallen—or, more likely, to those who had not yet plunged into moral decay. The only mass medium yet to be tapped fully was the stage.

Smith's play, first presented on February 12, 1844 at Moses Kimball's Boston Museum theater, obviously met its audience's expectations, becoming the first American drama to have a run of one hundred performances. Smith himself played Edward Middleton, the college-educated landowner who falls prey to the evils of drink. Born on December 4, 1806, in Montgomeryshire, Wales, Smith (originally named Sedley) left home at age fourteen to become an actor. By summer of 1827, the young actor was in Philadelphia, playing the role of Jeremy Diddler in James Kenney's *Raising the Wind*. From 1828 on, Smith was involved in the Boston stage both as actor and stage manager, in which latter capacity, claims William Clapp, he had "no equal in the city." In the same year that Smith moved from Philadelphia, one of the first plays to treat drunkenness noncomically, Douglas Jerrold's *Fifteen Years of a Drunkard's Life*, played in London. Smith may have used his own problems with the bottle as the basis for the play—his appearance as Middleton, apparently, had the force of someone who was publicly confessing to having been afflicted by alcoholism himself—but he was working a dramatic area that had already been exploited with success overseas.

The tremendous popularity the play enjoyed in Boston led to its being staged by P. T. Barnum (among other managers) in New York in 1850. Crowds came to see not only a "moral lecture" but also often intemperate acting, especially when poor Middleton (played at Barnum's by C. W. "Drunkard" Clarke) gets delirium tremens. Although not the very first temperance play to be staged, *The Drunkard* inaugurated a fashion for similar plays. The bibliography by Don L. Hixon and Don A. Hennessee identifies over one hundred temperance dramas printed during the nineteenth century, most of them appearing after Smith's. Appealing to domestic sensibilities and the increased concerns among middle classes about a growing immigrant class, crime, and social decay, Smith seems to have recognized that on this issue, at least, the worries of the people could be translated into compelling entertainment.

Bruce McConachie speaks of *The Drunkard* as a "moral reform drama." Such a play usually features a "man of principle" (in this case, the afflicted but not entirely debased Middleton); a grasping villain (lawyer Cribbs); but curiously no "woman of principle," that is, no female character who initiates reform action (Middleton's wife, Mary, suffers stoically). The implications of the plot, where an appeal to Middleton's rational self-interest by the philanthropist Arden Rencelaw is all that is needed to turn him around, go beyond sentimental appeals to hearth and home. McConachie argues that plays such as *The Drunkard* "prepared Americans to accept an undemocratic social order, based not on charismatic leadership, as in Forrest's melodramas, but on rational respectability in a liberal economy." That is, only those characters who have the capacity to reason well—by implication, the educated middle class—can have the wherewithal to resist at last the serpent of inebriated despair.

In a similar vein, Mason sees Smith's play as having the effect of an extended sermon. It is, he says, an "exegetical representation," an argument for temperance converted into the language of the stage. But at the same time, the play was not really designed so much to sway audiences, perhaps, as to confirm their newly won beliefs. In either event, argues Mason, in a play like *The Drunkard,* "the primary purpose is to galvanize the audience into accepting the message acting upon it; the aesthetic of performance is only a by-product."

Despite its connections to moral reforms in general or the temperance movement in particular, Smith's *play* is just that—a play fully in the melodramatic tradition. Contrary to Mason's assertion, the "aesthetic of performance" seems to have been very much at the center of the playwright-manager's construction, for the design of the drama comes not so much from the pulpit as from the theater. Figures recognizable from transatlantic dramas—the virtuous woman, the scheming villain, the loyal sidekick, the hero in trouble—people the stage. The only significant difference is the topicality. By its sentimental appeal, its use of tableau and telltale artifact, its resolution through accident framed as purposeful good fortune, *The Drunkard* reminds us of so many other plays as to be fully within the theatrical mainstream. Smith may have wanted secondarily to save drunks, but he knew a good piece of theater when he had it.

Thus, far from being primarily an "exegetical representation," as Mason would have it, *The Drunkard* is, in fact, one more highly entertaining, feverish, conventional dramatic exhibition. Some of the resonances within the play, however, show peculiarities of theme that individualize the conjunction of temperance and melodrama. For instance, at the very outset, the clearly demarked and nearly monolithic villain, Cribbs, cites as part of his reason for revenge upon Middleton that Edward's father, having caught him in an "atrocious act," later pardoned and "pitied" him. For Cribbs, pity amounts to contempt, a reinforcement of Middleton's status as one of the landed elite. Cribbs aspires to the material prosperity of Middleton, but lacks the social position. As a lawyer, Cribbs *on stage* plays to a discourse that denominates the lawyer as vulgarly open in his desires, lower-class in sensibility, and capable of duping the trusting members of the higher social and economic orders. Thus, the ultimate revenge would be to place Middleton in a place where he could be pitied; and this Cribbs achieves, at least in a clever fiction, when, during Middleton's deep slide into pariah status, Cribbs tells him that his wife is doing fine, has a lively circle of friends, and "pities" him. For Middleton, such pity can only plant the seed, later almost enacted, of suicide. Thus, the difference between good and bad is not in reacting unfavorably to pity but in method: one seeks oblivion, the other revenge.

Sex and violence also make their way into the domestic drama, but often as dark hints rather than fully displayed themes. In Act 1, Scene 2, Cribbs accuses Middleton of wanting to keep Mary Wilson in the cottage on his land for purposes of illicit sex: "Traps for wild fowl; mother and daughter grateful; love-passion; free access to the cottage at all hours." Although Middleton rejects such an insinuation in the sort of righteous rebuke that convention dictates for the virtuous protagonist, he in fact falls immediately in love with Mary and rather than take her last dollars in rent, tells her to keep it for her dowry. By his quick proposal, Middleton protects himself against further moral suspicion, yet now gains access to the "jewel" he has called her—access to her body *and* her small stock of capital. Later in the play, during Edward's decline, Cribbs trots out sex again, this time to besmirch Middleton in Mary's eyes, by hinting that Edward now has plenty of prostitutes to visit in his new life in New York. This failed attempt to separate Mary from Edward leads soon to Cribbs's attempted assault on Mary—which by now we recognize as sexual at base—and gives the omnipresent William the opportunity to enter in a timely manner and repulse the attack.

Of course, this is not Cribbs's first assault on a woman. Early in the play, he physically attacks Agnes, called in the cast list *"a Maniac."* As William's sister, Agnes wanders about, speaking lines reminiscent of Shakespeare's Ophelia. She has information, however, that threatens Cribbs's position as blackmailer, and therefore he fears her Cassandra-like truth-telling. The more she babbles, the angrier he grows until, just at the moment of raising his cane, William enters to save her and prevent any harm. Ironically, Agnes has been speaking about a wedding that looks also to be a funeral, prefiguring the joy and troubles ahead for Mary and Edward, but also telling Cribbs in essence that he cannot marry, he cannot enter society, that ultimately he will be more marginalized than she, who at least has a domestic protector. Appropriately, she, and not the lawyer, is part of the tranquil scene of affirmation at the end.

Thus, while the sensation plot focuses on Middleton's exposure to drink through the tempter, Cribbs, and implies blame for the tavern keepers who ply him with booze, the domestic plots have dark twists and turns that are interconnected with the wretchedness of Middleton's decline. The audience may have been absorbed by the actor's performance during the delirium tremens scene and riveted by his quick conversion to temperance through the human angel, Rencelaw, but it may also have been bothered by the number of unresolved tensions created through various confrontations. Why is Cribbs so bad? Rencelaw follows him at the end to try to redeem him, but can we expect redemption for one who lacks Edward's essential morality when Edward himself survives only by lucky chance? Why does Middleton continue to trust Cribbs, even though Cribbs has delivered a "foul" insinuation about his sexual desires? What price does Mary pay for her continued loyalty to Edward? Is the message that all women should always forgive wayward men? If so, then how to tell apart different kinds of helplessness: for example, the stress of trying to get a husband to stop drinking or the anguish of a woman exposed to sexual or physical assault? In short, for all its seeming obviousness of plot and message, *The Drunkard,* both as play and as historicized text, has any number of troubling contradictions that remain hidden behind the sensation drama of a man wrestling with snakes.

SELECTED BIBLIOGRAPHY

Booth, Michael R. "The Drunkard's Progress: Nineteenth-Century Temperance Drama." *Dalhousie Review* 44 (1964): 205–12.

Clapp, William W., Jr. *A Record of the Boston Stage.* Boston: James Monroe, 1853. Mentions Smith throughout.

Dodd, Jill Siegel. "The Working Classes and the Temperance Movement in Ante-Bellum Boston." *Labor History* 19 (1978): 510–31.

Hixon, Don L., and Don A. Hennessee. *Nineteenth-Century American Drama: A Finding Guide,* 566–68. Metuchen, N.J.: Scarecrow, 1977. Extensive list of temperance plays.

Hodge, Francis. *Yankee Theatre: The Image of America on the Stage, 1825–1850,* 258. Austin: University of Texas Press, 1964.

Jerrold, Douglas. *Fifteen Years of a Drunkard's Life.* London, 1828. The first popular Anglo-American temperance play.

McConachie, Bruce A. *Melodramatic Formations: American Theatre and Society, 1820–1870,* 174–93 passim. Iowa City: University of Iowa Press, 1992.

Mason, Jeffrey D. "*The Drunkard* (1844) and the Temperance Movement." In *Melodrama and the Myth of America,* 61–87. Bloomington: Indiana University Press, 1993.

Meserve, Walter J. *Heralds of Promise: The Drama of the American People During the Age of Jackson, 1829–1849,* 152–54. New York: Greenwood, 1986.

Moody, Richard. Introduction to *The Drunkard. Dramas from the American Theatre, 1762–1909,* edited by Richard Moody, 277–80. Cleveland: World, 1966.

Pratt, William W. *Ten Nights in a Bar-room. A Drama in Five Acts.* Boston: W. H. Baker, [1889]. Temperance play (first staged in 1858) based on novel by T. S. Arthur.

Rahill, Frank. "The Delirium Tremens Drama." *The World of Melodrama,* 240–46. University Park: Penn State University Press, 1967.

Reynolds, David S. *Beneath the American Renaissance: The Subversive Imagination in the Age of Emerson and Melville,* 65–73, 357–59. Cambridge: Harvard University Press, 1988. Background.

Rorabaugh, W. J. *The Alcoholic Republic: An American Tradition.* New York: Oxford University Press, 1979. Background.

THE DRUNKARD;

OR,

THE FALLEN SAVED.

A Moral Domestic Drama

IN FIVE ACTS.

ADAPTED BY W. H. SMITH.

WITH THE STAGE BUSINESS, CAST OF CHARACTERS
COSTUMES, RELATIVE POSITIONS, ETC.

CAST OF CHARACTERS.

EDWARD MIDDLETON
LAWYER CRIBBS
WILLIAM DOWTON
FARMER GATES
FARMER STEVENS
OLD JOHNSON
SAM
FIRST LOAFER
SECOND LOAFER
MR. RENCELAW
LANDLORD
BAR KEEPER
WATCHMAN
MARY WILSON
AGNES DOWTON, *a Maniac*
MRS. WILSON
PATIENCE
JULIA
MISS SPINDLE

VILLAGERS, LOAFERS, WATCHMEN, &C.

AUTHOR'S PREFACE

> 'O, star of strength! I see thee stand
> And smile upon my pain;
> Thou beckonest with thy mailed hand,
> And I am strong again.'—LONGFELLOW[1]

> 'There is a tide in the affairs of men,'[2]

Right! worthy Willie Shakspeare, perfectly right—there is a tide, not only in the affairs of men, but in the casualties of the Drama also, that bears the fortunate object to success, provided the opportunity is not neglected. There could not have been a better time chosen for the production of this most successful and Domestic Drama, than the season it was first performed at the Boston Museum. No unprejudiced person will attempt to deny that it was the cause of much good, and materially aided the Temperance movement it was meant to advocate. In the representation it was a powerful and living picture, and all that saw it, felt it, for IT WAS TRUE. No one who had not seen it would feel inclined, from the mere reading, to believe the very powerful effect produced.

The action of the play located in our own city and vicinity—the scenery mostly local views, excellent—the arrangements admirable, while the acting in some instances was not to be surpassed, and throughout each character above mediocrity, all served to aid in the triumphant success that was awarded it on its first representation. Mr. Smith's personation of Edward, evidently the result of accurate and laborious study, and deep knowledge of human frailty, was at times terribly real, particularly the scene of *delirium tremens*, which though far short of the horrors of that dreadful malady, and appearing, to those unacquainted with the disease to be overstepping the bounds of nature, was true to the letter, and universally acknowledged to be the most natural, effective acting ever seen in this city. In this scene, and those depicting the distress of the family, it was no uncommon thing to see scores of men and women in the auditory weeping like children, while at the next moment their faces would radiate with smiles at the quaint humor of Bill Dowton, or the pompous peculiarities of Miss Spindle.

Many inquiries have been made as to the authorship of the Drunkard and as rumor has named a dozen or more persons, some of whom have never troubled themselves to deny their identity in regard to connexion with the subject, we give the following facts which, if of importance to any but those immediately concerned, are simply as follows. "The proprietor of the Museum, ever ready to take the tide on its flood in any matter of general interest, conceiving that a Drama might aid the cause of Temperance, and prove highly productive to his establishment, engaged a gentleman of known and appreciated literary acquirements to undertake the task. Unfortunately his production, though eminently worthy of the gentleman and scholar,[3] was from want of theatrical experience, merely a story in dialogue, entirely deficient in stage tact and dramatic effect. Under these circumstances, the manuscript was placed in the hands of Mr. W. H. Smith, with the request that he would finish and prepare it for the stage. That gentleman revised what was written, altering what he considered ineffective, and introduced the entire underplot, together with the last scene of the second act, and the entire of the third, fourth and fifth parts. No claim is laid to originality of invention in the character of Cribbs, Agnes, or any other part in the piece.

The object was not so much to prepare an original, as an effective drama.

The piece was produced under direction of Mr. Smith, in the winter of 1844, and performed that season for upwards of one hundred and forty times, and is by all acknowledged to be the most successful play ever acted in Boston.

THE DRUNKARD;

OR,

THE FALLEN SAVED.

ACT I

SCENE 1: *Interior of a pretty rural cottage.—Flowers, paintings, etc.— Everything exhibits refined taste, and elegant simplicity.—Table, with bible and arm-chair,—Table and chair with embroidery frame.—*MRS. WILSON *discovered in arm-chair,—*MARY *seated by table.*

MRS. WILSON: It was in that corner, Mary, where your poor father breathed his last—this chair is indeed dear to me for it was in this he sat the very day before he died. Oh how he loved this calm retreat, and often in his last illness he rejoiced that the companion of his youth would close his eyes in these rural shades, and be laid in yon little nook beside him; but now—

MARY: Dear mother. It is true, this sweet cottage is most dear to us. But we are not the proprietors. Old Mr. Middleton never troubled us much. But as our late worthy landlord is no more, it is generally believed that our dear cottage will be sold. We cannot censure his son for that.

MRS. WILSON: No; the young must be provided for, and willingly would I bow with resignation to that great power that loveth while it chasteneth; but when I think that you, my beloved child, will be left exposed to the thousand temptations of life a penniless orphan. [*A knock.*] Hark! who knocks? Dry your tears, my darling. Come in.

[*Enter* LAWYER CRIBBS.]

Good morning, sir. Mary, my child, a chair.

CRIBBS: [*Sitting.*] Good morning, Mrs. Wilson; good morning, my dear young lady. A sad calamity has befallen the neighborhood, my good Mrs. Wilson.

MRS. WILSON: Many a poor person, I fear, will have reason to think so, sir.

CRIBBS: Yes, yes. You are right. Ah! he was a good man, that Mr. Middleton. I knew him well. He placed great confidence in my advice.

MARY: Was he not very rich once, Mr. Cribbs?

CRIBBS: Yes, yes; when the times were good, but bad speculations, unlucky investments, false friends—alas! alas! we have all our ups and downs, my dear madam!

MRS. WILSON: Ah! Mr. Cribbs, I perceive you are a man, who—

CRIBBS: Has a heart to feel for the unfortunate. True, madam, it is the character I have attained, though I am not the man to boast. Have you any prospect of—that is—have you provided—

MARY: It is true then, too true, the cottage and garden will be sold?

CRIBBS: Why, what can the young man do, my dear? A gay young man like him. Fond of the world, given somewhat to excess, no doubt. But pardon me, my dear Miss Mary; I would not call up a blush on the cheek of modesty. But you know, the extravagance, that is, the folly—

MRS. WILSON: All, sir. I understand you—very much unlike his father I would say.

CRIBBS: I place great confidence in your prudence, Mrs. Wilson. I wish the young man well, with all my heart. Heaven knows I have cause to do so for his honored father's sake. [*Puts a handkerchief to his eyes.*]

MRS. WILSON: Come, come, Mr. Cribbs, he is better off. It is impiety to mourn a good man's death. His end was that of a Christian.

CRIBBS: Judge, then, of the interest which I take in the last remaining scion of that honored stock. But, madam, Edward Middleton. He is yet young, and—

MRS. WILSON: I think he is not more than twenty. I recollect him when a lad, a bright, blue-eyed boy, with flaxen hair, tall of his age.

CRIBBS: Twenty-three last July, madam; that is his age precisely—he is giddy, wild, and reckless. As the good man says, "when I was a child, I thought as a child." [*A pause.*—CRIBBS *looks round the room.*] Well, madam, business is business. I am a plain man, Mrs. Wilson, and sometimes called too blunt—and—and—

MARY: You mean to say that we must leave the cottage, sir.

CRIBBS: [*Pretending feeling.*] No, not *yet,* my dear young lady—I would say it is best to be prepared, and as Edward is sudden in all his movements, and as my entreaties would never change him—why, if you could find a place before he moves in the matter, it might save you from much inconvenience, that's all.

MRS. WILSON: You impose upon us a severe task, my dear sir.

CRIBBS: Bear up, my dear madam, bear up. If I may be so officious, I would try Boston—at the Intelligence Offices[4] there, any healthy young woman, like your daughter, can obtain a profitable situation—think of it, think of it, my good madam. I will see you again soon, and now heaven bless you.

[*Exit and off.*—MRS. WILSON *and* MARY *look for a moment at each other, and then embrace.*]

MRS. WILSON: Well, comfort, my daughter, comfort. It is a good thing to have a friend in the hour of trouble. This Mr. Cribbs appears to be a very feeling man; but before taking his advice, we would do well to make our proposed trial of this young man, Edward Middleton. You have the money in your purse?

MARY: It is all here, mother. Thirty dollars—the sum we have saved to purchase fuel for the winter.

MRS. WILSON: That will partially pay the rent score. When this young man finds we are disposed to deal fairly with him, he may relent. You turn pale, Mary; what ails my child?

MARY: Dear mother, it is nothing; it will soon be over—it must be done. I fear this young man. He has been described so wild, so reckless. I feel a sad foreboding—

MRS. WILSON: Fear not, Mary; call him to the door. Refuse to enter the house—give him the money, and tell him your sad story. He must, from family and association at least, have the manners of a gentleman—and however wild a youth may be, when abroad among his associates no gentleman ever insulted a friendless and unprotected woman.

MARY: You give me courage, dear mother. I should indeed be an unnatural child, if—[*Aside.*]—yet I am agitated. Oh, why do I tremble thus? [*Puts on a village bonnet, &c.*]

MRS. WILSON: [*Kisses her.*] Go forth, my child—go as the dove flew from the ark of old, and if thou shouldst fail in finding the olive branch of peace, return, and seek comfort where thou shalt surely find it—in the bosom of thy fond and widowed mother.

[*Exit <MRS. WILSON, then> MARY.*]

SCENE 2: *Front and cut woods.*

[*Enter* LAWYER CRIBBS.]

CRIBBS: Well, that interview of mock sympathy and charity is over, and I flatter myself pretty well acted too, ha! ha! Yes, the widow and her child must quit the cottage—I'm resolved. First for the wrongs I years ago endured from old Wilson; and secondly, it suits my own interests; and in all cases, between myself and others, I consider the last clause as a clincher. Ha! here comes the girl—I must watch closely here. [*Retires.*]

[MARY *enters, fearful and hesitating.*]

MARY: I have now nearly reached the old mansion house. In a few moments I shall see the young man, this dissipated collegian. Oh! my poor mother must be deceived! Such a man can have no pity for the children of poverty, misfortune's suppliants for shelter beneath the roof of his cottage—oh, my poor mother, little do you know the sufferings that—ha! a gentleman approaches. My fears tell me this is the man I seek. Shall I ever have courage to speak to him? I will pause till he has reached the house. [*Retires gathering flowers.*]

[*Enter* EDWARD MIDDLETON, *and* CRIBBS, *meeting.*]

CRIBBS: Good day, good day, son of my old friend! I have been looking for you.

EDWARD: Mr. Cribbs, your most obedient; any friends of my father are always welcome.

CRIBBS: Well said, nobly said. I see your father before me, when I look on you.

EDWARD: You were enquiring for me, Mr. Cribbs?

CRIBBS: I was. I wished to see you with regard to the cottage and lands adjoining. I have an opportunity of selling them. When last we talked upon this subject—

EDWARD: I was then ignorant that a poor widow—[MARY *at back, listening.*]—and her only daughter—

CRIBBS: Who are in arrears for rent—

EDWARD: Had lived there many years—that my father highly esteemed them—to turn them forth upon the world in the present condition of the old lady—

CRIBBS: Which old lady has a claim upon the Alms House. [MARY *shudders.*]

EDWARD: In short, Mr. Cribbs, I cannot think of depriving them of a home, dear to them as the apple of their eyes—to send them forth from the flowers which they have reared, the vines which they have trained in their course—a place endeared to them by tender domestic recollections, and past remembrances of purity and religion.

CRIBBS: Oh! all that and more—the fences which they have neglected; the garden gate off the hinges; the limbs of the old birch tree broken down for firewood; the back windows ornamented with an old hat—

EDWARD: Cease, Mr. Cribbs; all this has been explained; my foster-brother, William, has told me the whole story. The trees were broken down by idle school-boys, and with regard to an old hat in the window, why, it was the hat of a man; can as much be said of yours, Mr. Cribbs?

CRIBBS: You are pleased to be pleasant, to-day, sir. Good morning, sir; good morning.   [*Exit, muttering.*]

EDWARD: I'm sorry I offended the old man. After all he was the friend of the family; though it is strange, my poor father almost always took his advice, and was invariably unfortunate when he did so.

[*Re-enter* CRIBBS.]

CRIBBS: Good morning again; beg pardon, sir. I now understand you better. You are right; the daughter—fine girl—eh! sparkling eyes, eh! dimples, roguish glances! Ah, when I was young, eh, ha? Well, never mind; you have seen her, eh?

EDWARD: Never; explain yourself, Mr. Cribbs.

CRIBBS: If you have not seen her, you will, you know, eh! I understand. Traps for wild fowl; mother and daughter grateful; love-passion; free access to the cottage at all hours.

EDWARD: Cribbs, do you know this girl has no father?

CRIBBS: That's it; a very wild flower growing on the open heath.

EDWARD: Have you forgotten that this poor girl has not a brother?

CRIBBS: A garden without a fence, not a stake standing. You have nothing to do but to step into it.

EDWARD: Old man! I respect your grey hairs. I knew an old man once, peace to his ashes, whose hair was as grey as yours; but beneath that aged breast there beat a heart, pure as the first throbs of childhood. He was as old as you—he was more aged; his limbs tottered as yours do not—I let you go in peace. But had that old man heard you utter such foul sentences to his son: had he heard you tell me to enter, like a wolf, this fold of innocence, and tear from her mother's arms the hope of her old age, he would have forgotten the winters that have dried the pith within his aged limbs, seized you by the throat, and dashed you prostrate to the earth, as too foul a carcass to walk erect and mock the name of man.

CRIBBS: But, Mr. Middleton, sir—

EDWARD: Leave me, old man; begone; your hot lascivious breath cannot mingle with the sweet odor of these essenced wildflowers. Your raven voice will not harmonize with the warblings of these heavenly songsters, pouring forth their praises to that Almighty power, who looks with horror on your brutal crime. [MARY *rushes forward and kneels*.]

MARY: The blessings of the widow and fatherless be upon thee, may they accompany thy voice to Heaven's tribunal, not to cry for vengeance, but plead for pardon on this wretched man.

CRIBBS: Ha! The widow's daughter! Mr. Middleton you mistake me. I —I cannot endure a woman's tears. I—poor child! [*Aside*.] I'll be terribly revenged for this. [*Exit* CRIBBS.]

EDWARD: This, then, is the widow's child, nurtured in the wilderness. She knows not the cold forms of the fashionable miscalled world. Cribbs, too, gone; a tale of scandal—I'll overtake the rascal, and at least give no color to his base fabrications. [*Going*.]

MARY: Stay, sir, I pray you. I have an errand for you. This is part of the rent, which—[*Holding out money*.]

EDWARD: Nay, then, you have not overheard my discourse with the old man, who has just left us. I have told him—

MARY: That we should still remain in the cottage. Oh sir! is that a reason we should withhold from you these dues? now paid with double pleasure, since we recognize a benefactor in our creditor—take this, I entreat, 'tis but a portion of the debt; but be assured, the remainder shall be paid as soon as busy, willing hands can earn it.

EDWARD: Nay, nay, dear girl; keep it as a portion of your dowry.

MARY: Sir!

EDWARD: If you have overheard the dialogue that I just held with that old man, you must know that I sometimes speak very plain.

MARY: [*Apprehensively*.] Yes, sir.

EDWARD: I have spoken plainly to him: shall I now speak plainly to you?

MARY: Alas, sir! It is not our fault that the fences are broken down. When my poor father lived, it was not so. But since—

EDWARD: When that vile old man spoke to me of your charms, I heeded him not. There are plenty of pretty girls in this section of the country: but I have since discovered what I had before heard, something more than the ordinary beauty which he described. A charm that he is incapable of appreciating. The charm of mental excellence, noble sentiment, filial piety. These are the beauties that render you conspicuous above all the maidens I have seen. These are the charms which bind captive the hearts of men. I speak plainly, for I speak honestly, and when I ask you to keep that money as a portion of your dowry, need I say into whose hands I would like to have it fall at last.

MARY: [*Droops her head during the above.*] To affect—to affect not to understand you, sir, would be an idle return for kindness such as yours, and yet—

EDWARD: I sometimes walk down in the vicinity of your cottage, and—

MARY: Should I see you go by without stopping—why, then—

EDWARD: Then what, dear Mary?

MARY: Then I should suppose you had forgotten where we lived.

EDWARD: Thanks! [*Kisses her hand.*] Ah! little did I think when I thought of selling that dear old cottage, that it should be regarded as a casket, invaluable for the jewel it contained. [*Leads her off.*]

SCENE 3: *Interior of* MISS SPINDLE'S *dwelling house. Toilette table, looking glass, essence bottles.—All denotes vulgar wealth, devoid of elegance or taste.*—MISS SPINDLE *discovered at toilette table.*

MISS SPINDLE: The attractions of the fair sex are *synonymous*. True, old Bonus[5] is the destroyer of female charms; but as my beautiful poet, Natty P., says, in his sublime epistle to Lucinda Octavia Pauline, "Age cannot wither me, nor custom stale my infinite *vacuity*." But time is money, then money is time, and we bring back, by the aid of money, the times of youth. I value my beauty at fifty dollars a year, as that is about the sum it costs me for keeping it in repair year by year. Well, say that my beauty is repaired in this way, year by year; well, what then! I have heard a gentleman say that a pair of boots when repaired and foxed,[6] were better than they were when new. Why should it not be so with our charms? Certainly, they last longer in this way. We can have red cheeks at seventy, and, thanks to the dentist, good teeth at any time of life. Woman was made for love. They suppose that my heart is unsusceptible of the tender passion. But the heart can be regulated by money, too. I buy all the affecting novels, and all the terrible romances, and read them till my heart has become soft as maiden wax, to receive the impression of that cherished image I adore. Ah! as true as I live, there goes his foster brother, William, by the window. Hem, William! [*Taps at window.*—WILLIAM *sings without.*]

"When I was a young and roving boy
Where fancy led me I did wander,
Sweet Caroline was all my joy,
But I missed the goose and hit the gander."

[*Enter* WILLIAM DOWTON.]

WILLIAM: Good day, Miss Spindle.

MISS SPINDLE: You heard my rap, William?

WILLIAM: As much as ever, Miss Spindle. Such fingers as yours don't make a noise like the fist of a butcher.

MISS SPINDLE: My hand is small, William, but I did not suppose that you had noticed it.

WILLIAM: I only noticed it by the lightness of your tap. So I suppose you must be very light fingered.

MISS SPINDLE: Pray, sit down, William; take a chair, don't be bashful; you're too modest.

WILLIAM: It's a failing I've got, Miss Spindle. I'm so modest I always go to bed without a candle. [*Both sit.*]

MISS SPINDLE: Shall I tell you what I have thought, William?

WILLIAM: Why, that's just as you agree to with yourself. I don't care much about it, one way or t'other.

MISS SPINDLE: You were singing as you came in, William. I suppose you know I sometimes invoke the help of Polyhymnia.[7]

WILLIAM: Why, I don't know as to the help of Polyhym-nina, but if you want a good *help,* you can't do better than hire Polly Striker, old Farmer Jones's wife's daughter, by her first husband.

MISS SPINDLE: You don't understand the Heathen mythology, William.

WILLIAM: Why I hear Parson Roundtext talk sometimes of the poor benighted heathens; but I am free to say, that I can't come anything in regard to their conchology, as you call it. Will you have some shell-barks, or chestnuts, Miss Spindle?

MISS SPINDLE: No, William. But this is what I have thought. William, there are two sorts of men.

WILLIAM: Oh, yes, Miss Spindle, long ones and short ones, like cigars. Sometimes the short ones are the best smoking, too.

MISS SPINDLE: You mistake my meaning, William. Some are warm and susceptible of the charms of women.

WILLIAM: Warm, oh, yes. Florida boys, and Carolina niggers, eh?

MISS SPINDLE: While others are *cold* and apparently insensible to our beauties—

WILLIAM: Oh, yes. Newfoundlanders, Canada fellows, and Blue noses.[8]

MISS SPINDLE: Now, William, *dear* William, this is the confession I would confide in your generous secrecy. I have a trembling affection, and then, a warm, yet modest flame.

WILLIAM: Trembling affection, warm flame, why, the old girl's got the fever and ague.

MISS SPINDLE: And how to combat with this dear, yet relentless foe.

WILLIAM: Put your feet into warm water, and wood ashes, take two quarts of boiling hot arb tea. Cover yourself with four thick blankets, and six Canada comforters, take a good perspicacity, and you'll be well in the morning.

MISS SPINDLE: Sir!

WILLIAM: That's old Ma'am Brown's recipe for fever and ague, and I never yet found it fail.

MISS SPINDLE: Fever and ague! You mistake me, William, I have an ardent passion.

WILLIAM: Don't be in a passion, Miss Spindle, it's bad for your complaint.

MISS SPINDLE: You will not understand. I have a passion for one.

WILLIAM: For one! Well, it's very lucky it's only one.

MISS SPINDLE: Can you not fancy who that one is? He lives in your house.

WILLIAM: Well, I'm darned, Miss Spindle, it's either me or Mr. Middleton.

MISS SPINDLE: I never can bestow my hand without my heart, William—

WILLIAM: Why, I think myself they ought to be included in the same bill of sale.

MISS SPINDLE: Ah! William, have you ever read the "Children of the Abbey?"

WILLIAM: No, Miss Spindle, but I've read "Babes of the Wood."

MISS SPINDLE: I have read all the Romantics of the day. I have just finished Mr. Cooper's Trapper.[9]

WILLIAM: Oh! I dare say she understands trap, but she don't come the trapper over my foster brother this year.

MISS SPINDLE: He understands little of the refinements of the civilized circular. I must try something else. How do you like my new green dress? How does it become me?

WILLIAM: Beautiful! It matches very well indeed, ma'rm.

MISS SPINDLE: Matches with what, William?

WILLIAM: With your eyes, ma'rm.

MISS SPINDLE: It becomes my complexion, William.

WILLIAM: It's a beautiful match—like a span of grey horses.

MISS SPINDLE: Does your master fancy green, William?

WILLIAM: Oh, yes, ma'rm. He loves it fine, I tell you.

MISS SPINDLE: But in what respect? How did you find it out?

WILLIAM: In respect of drinking, ma'rm.

MISS SPINDLE: Drinking!

WILLIAM: Yes. He always tells the cook to make a green tea.

MISS SPINDLE: Well, William, how about the cottage? When are you going to turn out those Wilsons?

WILLIAM: The girl will be out of that place soon, depend on that, ma'rm.

MISS SPINDLE: I'm glad to hear it. I never could endure those Wilsons, and it's a duty when one knows that respectable people like your master are injured, to speak out. I know they haven't paid their rent, and do you know that girl was seen getting into a chaise with a young man when she ought to have been at work, and she did not return till nine o'clock at night, William, for I took the pains to put on my hood and cloak and look for myself—though it was raining awful.

WILLIAM: That was the time you cotched the fever, the fever and ague, ma'rm. Well, good-bye.

MISS SPINDLE: Are you going, William?

WILLIAM: Yes, ma'rm. I shall be wanted to hum. You take care of your precious health, ma'rm. Keep your feet warm, and your head cool; your mouth shut and your heart open, and you'll soon have good health, good conscience, and stand well on your pins, ma'rm. Good morning, ma'rm.

> "To reap, to sow, to plough and mow,
> And be a farmer's boy, and be a farmer's boy."

[*Exit* WILLIAM.]

MISS SPINDLE: The vulgar creature! But what could I expect? He ought to know that American ladies ought never to have any pins. But I am certain for all this, Edward, dear Edward, is dying for me —as the poet, Dr. Lardner, says: "He lets concealment, like a worm in the bud, feed on the damask curtains of—his—cheek"—damask bud. I'm quite sure it's something about bud. Yes, I am convinced, my charms as yet are undecayed, and even when old age comes on, the charm of refined education, will still remain—as the immortal Chelsea[10] Beach Poet has it:

> "You may break, you may ruin the vase, if you will,
> The scent of the roses will cling round it still."

[*Exit, affectedly.*]

SCENE 4: *Landscape View.*

[*Enter* PATIENCE BRAYTON, SAM EVANS, OLD JOHNSON, *male and female villagers.—Music.*]

PATIENCE: Come, there's young men enough, let's have a ring-play.
ALL: Yes, a ring-play. A ring-play! fall in here.
SAM: Come, darnation, who'll go inside?
PATIENCE: Go in yourself, Sam.
SAM: Well, I'm agreed. Go on.

[*They form a circle and revolve round the young man singing.*]

"I am a rich widow, I live all alone,
I have but one son, and he is my own.
Go, son, go, son, go choose you one,
Go choose a good one, or else choose none."

[SAM *chooses one of the girls.—She enters the ring. He kisses her, and the ring goes round.*]

"Now, you are married you must obey
What you have heard your parents say.
Now you are married you must prove true,
As you see others do, so do you."

[*The ring goes round.—*PATIENCE, *who is in the ring, chooses* OLD JOHNSON.]

PATIENCE: "Mercy on me, what have I done?
I've married the father instead of the son.
His legs are crooked, and ill put on.
They're all laughing at my old man." [*A general laugh.*]

SAM: Come, girls, you forget 'tis almost time for Mary Wilson's wedding.
PATIENCE: Well, now, ain't we forgetting how proud she must be, going to marry a college bred.
JOHNSON: She'll be none the better for that. Larning don't buy the child a new frock.
SAM: Well, let's have a dance, and be off at once.
ALL: Yes. Partners. A dance! a dance!   [*A village dance, and exit.*]

[*Enter* LAWYER CRIBBS.]

CRIBBS: Thus ends my prudent endeavors to get rid of those Wilsons. But, young Middleton, there is yet some hope of him. He is at present annoyed at my well-intended advice, but that shall not part us easily. I will do him some unexpected favor, worm myself into his good graces, invite him to the village bar-room, and if he falls, then, ha! ha! I shall see them begging their bread yet. The wife on her bended knees to me, praying for a morsel of food for her starving children —it will be revenge, revenge! Here comes his foster brother, William. I'll wheedle him—try the ground before I put my foot on it.

[*Enter* WILLIAM DOWTON, *whistling.*]

WILLIAM: Lawyer Cribbs, have you seen my poor, little, half-witted sister, Agnes, eh?

CRIBBS: No, William, my honest fellow, I have not. I want to speak to you a moment.

WILLIAM: [*Crossing.*] What does old Razor Chops want with me, I wonder. Well, lawyer, what is it?

CRIBBS: You seem to be in a hurry. They keep you moving, I see.

WILLIAM: These are pretty busy times, sir. Mr. Edward is going to be married—that's a dose. [*Aside.*] Senna[11] and salts.

CRIBBS: Yes, yes, ahem! Glad to hear it.

WILLIAM: Yes, I thought you seemed pleased. [*Aside.*] Looks as sour as Sam Jones, when he swallowed vinegar for sweet cider.

CRIBBS: I am a friend to early marriages, although I never was married myself. Give my best respects to Mr. Edward.

WILLIAM: Sir?

CRIBBS: William, suppose I leave it to your ingenuity to get me an invitation to the wedding, eh? And here's a half dollar to drink my health.

WILLIAM: No, I thank you, lawyer, I don't want your money.

CRIBBS: Oh, very well; no offence meant, you know. Let's step into the tavern, and take a horn[12] to the happiness of the young people.

WILLIAM: Lawyer Cribbs, or Squire, as they call you, it's my opinion, when your uncle Belzebub wants to bribe an honest fellow to do a bad action, he'd better hire a pettifogging bad lawyer to tempt him, with a counterfeit dollar in one hand, and a bottle of rum in the other.   [*Exit* WILLIAM].

CRIBBS: Ah, ah! You're a cunning scoundrel, but I'll fix you yet.

AGNES: [*Sings without.*]

> "Brake and fern and cypress dell,
> Where the slippery adder crawls."

CRIBBS: Here comes that crazy sister of his. She knows too much for my happiness. Will the creature never die? Her voice haunts me like the spectre of the youth that was engaged to her, for my own purposes I ruined, I triumphed over him—he fell—died in a drunken fit, and she went crazy. Why don't the Alms House keep such brats at home?

[*Enter* AGNES, *deranged.*]

AGNES:
> "Brake and fern and cypress dell,
> Where the slippery adder crawls.
> Where the grassy waters well,
> By the old moss-covered walls."

For the old man has his grey locks, and the young girl her fantasies.

> "Upon the heather, when the weather
> Is as wild as May,
> So they prance as they dance,
> And we'll all be gay."

But they poured too much red water in his glass. The lawyer is a fine man, ha, ha! he lives in the brick house yonder. But the will. Ah, ha, ha! the will—

CRIBBS: [*Angrily.*] Go home, Agnes, go home.

AGNES: Home! I saw a little wren yesterday. I had passed her nest often. I had counted the eggs, they were so pretty—beautiful, so beautiful—rough Robins of the mill came this morning and stole them. The little bird went to her nest, and looked in—they were gone. She chirruped mournfully and flew away. *She won't go home any more.*

CRIBBS: Agnes, who let you out? You distress the neighborhood with your muttering and singing. [*Threatening.*] I'll have you taken care of.

AGNES: There's to be a wedding in the village. I saw a coffin carried in full of bridal cake.

> "And the bride was red with weeping.
> Cypress in her hair."

Can you tell why they cry at weddings? Is it for joy? I used to weep when I was joyful. You never weep, old man. I should have been married, but my wedding dress was mildewed, so we put off the marriage till another day. They'll make a new dress for me. They say he won't come again to me and then the will, ha, ha, old man, the will.

CRIBBS: Ha, confusion! Get you gone, or thus—

[*Seizes her and raises cane,* WILLIAM *enters rapidly, and throws him round to corner.*]

WILLIAM: Why, you tarnation old black varmint! Strike my little, helpless, half-crazed sister! If it was not for your grey hairs, I'd break every bone in your black beetle body. If all I have heard be true, you'll have to account for—

CRIBBS: [*Rising.*] You'll rue this, young man, if there's any law in the land. A plain case of assault and battery. I'll put you in jail. Predicaments, premunires,[13] fifas and fieri facias.[14] I'll put you between stone walls. [*Exit, blustering.*]

WILLIAM: Put me between stone walls! If you'd have been put between two posts with a cross-beam long ago, you'd had your due, old landshark. You stay here, darling Agnes, till I come back. Fiery faces, and predicaments! If I can get you near enough to a horse-pond, I'll cool your fiery face, I'll warrant. [*Exit.*]

AGNES: [*Scattering flowers and singing.*]

"They lived down in the valley,
    Their house was painted red,
And every day the robin came
    To pick the crumbs of bread."

But the grass does not wither when they die. I will sit down till I hear the bells that are far off, for then, I think of his words. Who says he did not love me? It was a good character he wanted of the parson. A girl out of place, is like an old man out of his grave. [*Bells chime piano.*] They won't ask me to their merry-makings, now, though I washed my best calico in the brook.

"Walk up young man, there's a lady here,
    With jewels in her hair."

[*Suddenly clasps her hands and screams.*] Water, water! hear him,
oh, hear him cry for water; quick! he'll turn cold again! his lips are
blue; water, water!   [*Exit, frantically.*]

SCENE 5: *A village.—Exterior of a beautiful cottage. Vines, entwined
roses, &c.—The extreme of rural tranquil beauty.—Rustic table, with
fruit, cake, &c., &c. Rustic chairs and benches.*

[*Enter procession of villagers.—*EDWARD, MARY, MRS. WILSON.
*—Clergyman, children with baskets of flowers.—Bridesman and
bridesmaid, &c., &c.—Bells ringing.—They enter, come down,
to front, cross and up stage, singing chorus.*]

> "Hail, hail! happy pair!
>   Bells are ringing, sweet birds singing,
> All around now speaks of bliss;
>   Bright roses bringing—flowers flinging,
> Peace, purity and happiness."

EDWARD: Dearest Mary, ah, now indeed my own; words are too poor,
too weak to express the joy, the happiness that agitates my heart.
Ah, dear, dear wife, may each propitious day that dawns upon they
future life, but add another flower to the rosy garland that now en-
circles thee.

MARY: Thanks, Edward, my own loved husband, thy benison is echoed
from my inmost heart. Ah, neighbor Johnson, many thanks for your
kind remembrance of your pupils. My dear friends, your children,
too, are here.

JOHNSON: Yes, my dear Mary, your happiness sheds its genial rays
around old and young. Young man I was a witness at your father's
wedding. May your life be like his—an existence marked by probity
and honor, and your death as tranquil. Mrs. Wilson, I remember
your sweet daughter, when but a child of nine years, and that seems
only yesterday.

MARY: Dear Patience, I am glad to see you too, and who is this, your
brother? [*Points to* SAM, *corner.*]

PATIENCE: No. An acquaintance, that—

SAM: Yes. An acquaintance that—

MARY: Oh, yes, I understand.

MRS. WILSON: My dearest children, the blessing of a bereaved heart, rest, like the dews of heaven, upon you. Come neighbors, this is a festival of joy. Be happy, I entreat.

WILLIAM: Well, if there's any one here happier than Bill Dowton, I should like to know it, that's all. Come, lads and lasses, sing, dance, and be merry. [Dance—tableau.]

END OF ACT I

ACT II

SCENE 1: A chamber in MISS SPINDLE'S house.—LAWYER CRIBBS and MISS SPINDLE discovered, seated.

CRIBBS: Be explicit, my dear madam; this is a most serious affair: breach of promise, marriage promise. How my heart bleeds for you, dear young lady, suffering virtue. But tell me the particulars.

MISS SPINDLE: Oh, sir, why will you cause me to narrow up my feelings; my bleeding heart, by the recital of my afflictions. I have "let concealment like a" caterpillar on a button-wood, feed on my cambric cheek—and—[Aside.] I can't remember the rest of it.

CRIBBS: Alas, poor lady! pray go on.

MISS SPINDLE: The first of our acquaintance was down at a corn-husking. Not that I make a practice of attending such vulgar places, Squire, but—

CRIBBS: Oh, certainly not—certainly not.

MISS SPINDLE: Well, I was over-persuaded. I set up and stripped the dry coatings from the yellow-corn—only two ears—I husked no more, Squire.

CRIBBS: Indeed, indeed! two ears—you are certain it was but two ears? It is best to be particular. We shall make out a prima faciae[15] case.

MISS SPINDLE: Well, I got hold of a red ear, it was the last I husked. I think it was a red ear; so I was obliged to be kissed. Oh, Squire, think of my mortification, when I was told that such was the invariable rule—the custom at a husking.

CRIBBS: [With energy.] Your sufferings must have been intolerable.

MISS SPINDLE: Oh, sir, you know how to feel for delicate timidity. A big coarse young man, called Bill Bullus, rose up to snatch the fragrance from my unwilling cheek—

CRIBBS: [Groans.] Oh!

MISS SPINDLE: I put up my kerchief—it was a cambric, a fine cambric,

Squire Cribbs, and said I had a choice in those things—looking at Edward, whom I took to be a gentleman, you know. He took the hint immediately. Bullus fell back appalled at my manner, and Edward—oh, sir! spare my blushes.

CRIBBS: I understand—he—yes. I understand.

MISS SPINDLE: He did it, sir. I felt the pressure of his warm lip on—

CRIBBS: Your cheek, of course.

MISS SPINDLE: Oh, no, no, sir. It was said, by my friend, the Chelsea Beach Bard, that from my lips he stole ambrosical blisses.

CRIBBS: Enormous! but go on.

MISS SPINDLE: You may judge what was my confusion.

CRIBBS: Certainly, Miss Spindle.

MISS SPINDLE: The ear of corn was not more red than was my burnished cheek.

CRIBBS: I do not know, my dear young lady, but you might make out a case of assault and battery.

MISS SPINDLE: It was very rude for a college-bred. Well after that he bowed to me as we were coming out of church.

CRIBBS: Aha! the evidence comes in. Have you got proof of that, most injured fair one?

MISS SPINDLE: Oh, sir, no proof would be required. I trust that a person of my respectability need bring no proof of what they know. Well, after that I was agoing down to Mr. Simmons', and lo, a cow stood in the road. I must pass within twenty feet of the ferocious animal if I continued my route; providentially, at the very instant, Edward came down the road that turns up by Wollcott's mill. He saw my strait. He saw that I stood trembling like some fragile flower tossed by the winds of heaven. Like Sir William Wallace[16] flying to the rescue of the Greeks, he came, panting on the wings of love. He rushed like an armed castle to the side of the cow, and she wheeled about like the great leviathan of the deep, and trotted down towards the school-house.

CRIBBS: I can imagine your feelings, Miss Spindle—a delicate young lady in imminent danger. But he did no more than any man would have done.

MISS SPINDLE: Well, sir, you may judge what were the feelings of my palpitating heart, tender as it always was—

CRIBBS: Have any letters passed between you?

MISS SPINDLE: Oh, yes, yes; five or six, sir.

CRIBBS: We've got him there aha! If Miss Spindle would be so condescending as just to show me one of those letters.

MISS SPINDLE: He's got them all in his possession.

CRIBBS: Unfortunate! horrible! How did he obtain possession of those letters?

MISS SPINDLE: Oh! I sent them—sometimes by one person, sometimes by another.

CRIBBS: How, madam? *His* letters, I mean—how did he get—

MISS SPINDLE: Oh, sir, mark his ingratitude. I sent him half a dozen—

CRIBBS: [*Discouraged.*] Oh! I understand. The correspondence was all on one side, then?

MISS SPINDLE: Not one letter did he write to me. Ah! sir think of it; all my tenderness, all my devotion. Oh! my breaking heart.

CRIBBS: [*Aside.*] Oh! humbug! Well, good day, Miss Spindle. I have a pressing engagement, and—

MISS SPINDLE: Well, but lawyer Cribbs, what is your advice? How ought I to proceed?

CRIBBS: Get your friends to send you to the insane hospital, and place you among the incurable, as the most rusty, idiotic old maid that ever knit stockings.   [*Exit hastily.*]

MISS SPINDLE: Spirit of Lucretia Borgia![17] Polish pattern of purity—was there ever such a Yankee hedgehog!   [*Exit angrily.*]

SCENE 2: *A Landscape.*

[*Enter* WILLIAM DOWTON, FARMER GATES, *and* FARMER STEVENS, *meeting.*]

GATES: Good day, good day. Mr. Edward was not at church last sabbath.

STEVENS: I heard tell where he was in the afternoon.

GATES: Aye, Stevens, you told me. Well, well, I'm right sorry. We used to consider Mr. Edward a promising young man, and when we seed him get married and settle among us, we thought to have a respectable man like his father for a neighbor, and that like him, he'd go to the general court[18] one of these days. I earnestly hope he han't agoing to stick to these bad ways.

WILLIAM: I don't exactly know what you mean, Farmer Gates. Mr. Middleton is about the same free kind-hearted fellow that he ever was, it appears to me. No longer ago than this blessed morning, he says to me, Bill, says he, your birth-day comes this day week, go to Ned Grogan's, the tailor, next the post office, and get yourself measured for a new suit of clothes at my expense. Now if I that lives with him, and sees everything he does, think well of him, I don't know as other folks need be so very perpendicular about it.

STEVENS: Well, well, I'll tell you what I have heard; you know Squire Cribbs?

WILLIAM: In course I does.

STEVENS: Well, he says that if your foster brother doesn't attend a little more to his own interest—

WILLIAM: He'll do it for him, I suppose! Now, Mr. Stevens, I'll tell you what I think of that sly old fox, Squire Cribbs. He takes to wickedness just as natural as young ducks take to water. I think, really, if Mr. Edward's soul was put in a great box, that seven thousand such souls as that black beetle's wouldn't fill up the chinks—the spare room round the edges.

GATES: Give us your hand. Bill, my man, lawyer Cribbs bears but a middling character hereabout. He has got a prodigious sight of larning, and 'tis not for the likes of me to pretend to decide between you; but I'll be darned if I don't like the man that stands up for him whose bread he eats; and so, Bill, any time you want a drink of cider, just call up our way, and you shall have what you can drink, if it's a gallon.   [Exit.]

STEVENS: Well, well, William, after all neighbor Gates has said, I fear the young man's in a dangerous way—spending his Sabbaths going about the country from one tavern to another. I don't say that he does take too much liquor—but there's a great many that has began that way.   [Exit.]

WILLIAM: [Rather serious.] Well, good-bye to you, and thank'ye. I don't think Mr. Edward drinks any too much—at least I hope not. For my part I wish he'd never seen anything stronger than milk or green tea. I wish I hadn't seen them two fellers, they've just made me feel as bad as ever, when I thought I was getting well over it, and beginning to see daylight again. What, dear Mr. Edward, with such a sweet lamb of a wife, and the prettiest little girl that ever drew breath— oh, no, it's nothing. I won't borrow trouble—he just took part of a bowl of punch with a friend at the Flying Horse—but that's no more than the parson himself might do, and there's Deacon Whit-leather, he never sits down to dinner without a stiff horn of something to wash it down. Well, now, I think it's better let alone altogether—for if a man doesn't put his hand in the fire, he runs a better chance of not burning his fingers.   [Exit.]

SCENE 3: *A Country Bar-Room.—Old-fashioned gun hung up.—Cow Notices, &c. &c.—*STEVENS, *the Drover seated at table.—Several loafers.—Landlord behind Bar attending.—Decanters filled with different liquors, on bar.—Stools, benches, &c. &c.*

STEVENS: [*Seated.*] Well, I don't know, Mr. Landlord, them are 'counts we have about Queen Victory, amounts to just about as much as the frogs and mice.

LANDLORD: Oh, that's Pope; we've got the book in the house now— the battle of frogs and mice.

2D LOAFER: Landlord, will you just score up another three-center—I feel deuced bad.

LANDLORD: No, thank'ye, Sam; rub off old scores, and then—

[*Enter* EDWARD MIDDLETON, *dress rather shabby, from door.— All look at him; he walks up to the bar.*]

EDWARD: Give me some brandy. [*Drinks.*] How much, landlord!

LANDLORD: A six-pence, sir. This is something 'sperior; a bottle I keep for those who are willing to pay a little more—are you quite well, sir?

EDWARD: Well, well, quite well, I thank you—this is good, landlord, another glass.

[*Enter* CRIBBS.]

CRIBBS: Ha! Mr. Middleton, you here! He! he! he! Well, come, that's a good one. First time I was ever here except on business—dare say you can say the same. Well, this is fine. Now, my young friend, since we have met each other, we'll honor the house.

LANDLORD: Squire, how are you; glad to see you. [*Shakes hands across the bar.*] What's it to be, gentlemen. The same, Mr. Middleton?

EDWARD: Oh! I must be excused; you know I have just drank.

CRIBBS: Well, well, I'll leave it to him. Landlord, how long is it since I've seen you?

LANDLORD: Why, Squire, it must be full ten years ago; you remember the day Si Morton had his raising? the day I saw you digging in the woods.

CRIBBS: [*Starts violently.*] Go on, go on—nothing but the cramp. I'm subject to it.

LANDLORD: Well, Squire, I've never seed you since then.

CRIBBS: Well, come, let's drink; come, Edward.

LANDLORD: Oh, take a little more, Mr. Middleton—the Squire wouldn't advise you to what wasn't right.

EDWARD: Well, I—

CRIBBS: Well, come, here's whiskey—good whiskey.

EDWARD: I believe I drank—

LANDLORD: Mr. Middleton drank brandy before.

CRIBBS: Not half so healthy as good whiskey.

EDWARD: Oh, whiskey be it. It can't be stronger than the other was.

[STEVENS *looks up and shakes his head.*]

EDWARD: [*Drinks.*] Well, this is pleasant, ha! ha! this goes to the right place, eh, Cribbs. Is this Irish whiskey?

LANDLORD: Yes, sir; pure Innishowen.

EDWARD: Well, the Irish are a noble people, ain't they, Cribbs? [*Slightly intoxicated.*] Friend Cribbs, I think I may call you. I never doubted it.

CRIBBS: Never!

EDWARD: Oh! I might have suspected; but "suspicion's but at best a coward's virtue;" the sober second thought—

CRIBBS: Oh, exactly. [*Shaking his hand earnestly.*]

EDWARD: I have a heart, Cribbs—[*Getting tipsey.*] I have a heart; landlord, more whiskey; come, gentlemen, come one, come all. Landlord!

LANDLORD: In one minute, sir.

EDWARD: Landlord, give them all anything they want; come—a bumper—here's the health of my old tried friend Cribbs. [*Drinks it off.*]

CRIBBS: [*Throwing away his liquor unseen.*] Well, here goes.

EDWARD: Landlord! landlord.

LANDLORD: Sir?

EDWARD: I have a heart, Cribbs. We know how to do the handsome thing, landlord.

[CRIBBS *slyly fills* EDWARD's *glass.*]

LANDLORD: Don't we? It takes us, sir.

EDWARD: [*Drinks.*] Well, I think, landlord, a little spirit hurts no man.

LANDLORD: Oh, no, sir; no—does him good.

EDWARD: I have a heart, Squibbs—a heart, my old boy; come, let's have another horn.—[1ST LOAFER *falls asleep on bench against partition.*]—Come, boys, trot up, I'll pay.

2D LOAFER: Well, I don't want to hurt the house.

3D LOAFER: Oh, no—musn't hurt the house. [*Walking up to bar.*]

STEVENS: Come, don't you hear the news? [*Strikes* 1ST LOAFER *with whip, and he falls on ground.*]

1ST LOAFER: Hollo! what's that for?

EDWARD: Come, tread up, and drink.

1ST LOAFER: Well—[*Lazily.*]—I don't want to hurt the house. [*Tumbles against wall.*]

LANDLORD: You will hurt the house, if you butt off the plastering at that rate.

EDWARD: A bumper—well, in the absence of Burgundy, whiskey will do, eh, old Ribbs—[*Hitting* CRIBBS.]—why don't you join us, old sulky. [*To* STEVENS.]

STEVENS: I drink when I'm dry, and what I drink I pay for.

EDWARD: —You're saucy, old fellow.

STEVENS: Do you think I'm a sponge, to put my hands into another man's pocket? Go away, you make a fool of yourself.

EDWARD: A fool! say that again, and I'll knock you down—a fool!

STEVENS: [*Rising.*] I want nothing to say to you—be off—you're drunk.

EDWARD: [*Strikes him.*] Death and fury! drunk!

STEVENS: Take that, then—[CRIBBS *and others sneak off—struggle.*— STEVENS *hits him down with whip.*]—Landlord you see I was not to blame for this. [*Exit* STEVENS.]

LANDLORD: Well, he's got it any how—serve him right, quarrelsome young fool. House was quiet enough till he came in disturbing honest people. This is too bad. How to get this fellow home? He lives two miles from here, at least.

[*Enter* WILLIAM DOWTON.]

WILLIAM: Mr. Middleton—where is he? Lord ha' mercy! what is this? Speak! [*Seizes* LANDLORD.] If you have done this, I'll tear out your cursed windpipe, old heathen.

LANDLORD: In my own house? Let go my throat.

WILLIAM: Who did this?

LANDLORD: Let go; it wasn't me, it was drover Stevens.

WILLIAM: [*Throws him off, kneels by* MIDDLETON.] Blood on his forehead—Mr. Edward, speak to me, oh, speak—his poor wife—poor old sick Mrs. Wilson, too.

EDWARD: [*Reviving.*] What is this? what's been the matter here?

WILLIAM: Don't you know me, sir? It's William, sir; poor Bill, come to help you home. Sam Stanhope told me you were in a row at the tavern, sir.

EDWARD: Oh, yes, I remember; where are they all? where's Cribbs? where's Cribbs?

WILLIAM: Cribbs! was he with him?

LANDLORD: Why, yes, I guess the Squire was here a short spell. Well, you can walk, sir, can't you?

EDWARD: Walk, yes, I can walk—what's the matter with my head? Blood? I must have fallen against the corner of the bench.

LANDLORD: Don't you remember Mr. Stevens?

EDWARD: I don't know what you mean by Stevens, what the devil have I been about?

LANDLORD: Why, Stevens said you were drunk, and you hit him, and he knocked you down with his whip-handle.

WILLIAM: And if I get hold of Mr. Stevens I'll make him smell something nastier than peaches, or my name's not Bill. Come, sir, come home.

EDWARD: Drunk! fighting! Oh, shame! shame!

WILLIAM: Lean on me, Mr. Edward. You go sand your sugar, and water your bad brandy, old corkscrew! His poor wife!

EDWARD: Hush, William, hush.

WILLIAM: Pray give me your pardon, sir; oh, I wish I had died before I had seen this.

EDWARD: Drunk, fighting—my wife, my children! Oh agony! agony!
          [*Exit, leaning on* WILLIAM.—LANDLORD *retires behind bar.*]

SCENE 4: *Landscape view.*

[*Enter* CRIBBS.]

CRIBBS: So far the scheme works admirably. I know his nature well. He has tasted, and will not stop now short of madness or oblivion. I mostly fear his wife, she will have great influence over him. Ah, who's this, Bill Dowton? Where then is Middleton? [*Retires.*]

[*Enter* WILLIAM DOWTON.]

WILLIAM: Well, I don't know but he's right; poor fellow, if he were to appear before his wife, without her being warned, it might frighten her to death, poor thing, and as he says, the walk alone may do him good, and sober him a bit. The old woman takes on most cruel, too, and she so very, very ill. Here he comes. I guess he'll follow me. I'll hasten on, for if he sees me, he'll be angry, and swear I'm watching him. That old sarpent Cribbs, he'd better keep out of my track. I'd think no more of wringing his old neck, than I would twisting a tough thanksgiving turkey.   [*Exit, threatening.*]

CRIBBS: [*Advancing cautiously.*] I'm much obliged to you, most valiant Billy Dowton. I shall hold myself *non est inventus,*[19] I promise you; here comes Edward. Caution, caution. [*Retires.*]

[*Enter* EDWARD.]

EDWARD: Is this to be the issue of my life? Oh, must I ever yield to the fell tempter, and bending like a weak bulrush to the blast, still bow my manhood lower than the brute? Why, surely I have eyes to see, hands to work with, feet to walk, and brain to think, yet the best gifts of Heaven I abuse, lay aside her bounties, and with my own hand, willingly put out the light of reason. I recollect my mother said, my dear, dying mother, they were the last words I ever heard her utter,—"whoever lifts his fallen brother is greater far, than the conqueror of the world." Oh how my poor brain burns! my hand trembles! my knees shake beneath me! I cannot, will not appear before them thus; a little, a very little will revive and strengthen me. No one sees; William must be there ere *this.* Now, for my hiding place. Oh! the arch cunning of the drunkard! [*Goes to tree* R, *and from the hollow draws forth a bottle; looks round and drinks.* CRIBBS *behind exulting.*] So, so! it relieves! it strengthens! oh, glorious liquor! Why did I rail against thee? Ha, ha! [*Drinks and draws bottle.*] All gone! all! [*Throws the bottle away.*] Of what use the casket when the jewels gone? ha, ha! I can face them, now. [*Turns and meets* CRIBBS.] He here! Confusion.

CRIBBS: Why, Middleton! Edward, my dear friend, what means this?

EDWARD: Tempter! begone! Pretend not ignorance! Were you not there when that vile fray occurred? Did you not desert me?

CRIBBS: As I am a living man, I know not what you mean. Business called me out. I left you jovial and merry, with your friends.

EDWARDS: Friends! Ha! Ha! the drunkard's friends! Well, well, you may speak truth;—my brain wanders;—I'll go home!—Oh, misery! Would I were dead.

CRIBBS: Come, come; a young man like you should not think of dying. I am old enough to be your father, and I don't dream of such a thing.

EDWARD: You are a single man, Cribbs. You don't know what it is to see your little patrimony wasted away;—to feel that you are the cause of sufferings you would die to alleviate.

CRIBBS: Pooh, pooh! Suffering—your cottage is worth full five hundred dollars. It was but yesterday Farmer Amson was inquiring how much it could be bought for.

EDWARD: Bought for! Cribbs—

CRIBBS: Well, Edward, well.

EDWARD: You see you smoke curling up among the trees?

CRIBBS: Yes, Edward. It rises from your own cottage.

EDWARD: You know who built that cottage, Cribbs?

CRIBBS: Your father built it. I recollect the day. It was—

EDWARD: It was the very day I was born that yon cottage was first inhabited. You know who lives there now?

CRIBBS: Yes. You do.

EDWARD: No one else, Cribbs?

CRIBBS: Your family, to be sure—

EDWARD: And you counsel me to sell it!—to take the warm nest from that mourning bird and her young, to strip them of all that remains of hope and comfort, to make them wanderers in the wide world, and for what? To put a little pelf into my leprous hands, and then squander it for rum.

CRIBBS: You don't understand me, Edward. I am your sincere friend; believe me; come—

EDWARD: Leave me, leave me—

CRIBBS: Why, where would you go thus, Edward?

EDWARD: Home! Home!—to my sorrowing wife—her dying mother, and my poor, poor child.

CRIBBS: But not thus, Edward, not thus. Come to my house, my people are all out. We'll go in the back way,—no one will see you. Wash your face, and I'll give you a little—something to refresh you. I'll take care it shall not hurt you. Come, now, come.

EDWARD: Ought I—dare I? Oh, this deadly sickness. Is it indeed best?

CRIBBS: To be sure it is. If the neighbors see you thus—I'll take care of you. Come, come, a little brandy—good—good brandy.

EDWARD: Well, I—I—

CRIBBS: That's right—come. [*Aside.*] He's lost. Come, my dear friend, come. [*Exeunt.*]

SCENE 5: *Interior of the cottage as in Act 1st—The furniture very plain.—A want of comfort and order.—Table and two chairs.*

[*Enter* MARY *from set door.—Her dress plain and patched, but put on with neatness and care.—She is weeping.*]

MARY: Oh, Heaven, have mercy on me!—aid me!—strengthen me! Weigh not thy poor creature down with woes beyond her strength to bear. Much I fear my suffering mother never can survive the night, and Edward comes not, and when he does arrive, how will it be? Alas, alas! my dear, lost husband! I think I could nerve myself against every thing but—Oh, misery! this agony of suspense! it is too horrible.

[*Enter* JULIA *from room.—She is barefooted.—Dress clean, but very poor.*]

JULIA: Mother! dear mother, what makes you cry? I feel so sorry when you cry—don't cry any more, dear mother.

MARY: I cannot help it, dearest. Do not tell your poor father what has happened in his absence, Julia.

JULIA: No, dear mother, if you wish me not. Will it make him cry, mother? When I see you cry it makes me cry, too.

MARY: Hush, dear one, hush! Alas, he is unhappy enough already.

JULIA: Yes. Poor father! I cried last night when father came home, and was so sick. Oh, he looked so pale, and when I kissed him for good night, his face was as hot as fire. This morning he could not eat his breakfast, could he? What makes him sick so often, mother?

MARY: Hush, sweet one!

JULIA: Dear grandma so sick, too. Doctor and nurse both looked so sorry. Grandma won't die to-night, will she, mother?

MARY: Father of mercies! This is too much. [*Weeps.*] Be very quiet, Julia, I am going in to see poor grandma. [*Crossing.*] Oh, *Religion!* sweet solace of the wretched heart! Support me! aid me, in this dreadful trial.   [*Exit into room.*]

JULIA: Poor, dear mother. When grandma dies, she'll go to live in heaven, for she's good. Parson Heartall told me so, and he never tells fibs, for he is good, too.

[*Enter* WILLIAM *gently.*]

WILLIAM: Julia, where is your mother, darling?

[JULIA *puts her finger on her lip, and points to door.*]

WILLIAM: Ah, she comes.

[*Enter* MARY.]

How is poor Mrs. Wilson now, madam?

MARY: Near the end of all earthly trouble, William. She lies in broken

slumber. But where is my poor Edward? Have you not found him?
WILLIAM: Yes, ma'am, I found him in the ta— in the village—he had
fallen, and slightly hurt his forehead; he bade me come before, so as
you should not be frightened. He'll soon be here now.
MARY: Faithful friend. I wish you had not left him. Was he—Oh, what
a question for a doating wife—was he sober, William?
WILLIAM: I must not lie, dear lady. He had been taking some liquor,
but I think not much—all I hope will be well.
EDWARD: [*Sings without.*] "Wine cures the goat," &c., Ha! ha!
MARY: Oh, great Heaven!

[WILLIAM *rushes out and off, and re-enters with* EDWARD *drunk
and noisy.—*WILLIAM *trying to soothe him, he staggers as he
passes door-way.*]

EDWARD: I've had a glorious time, Bill. Old Cribbs—
MARY: Hush! dearest!
EDWARD: Why should I be silent? I am not a child. I—
MARY: My mother, Edward, my dear mother!
EDWARD: [*Sinks in chair.*] Heaven's wrath on my hard heart. I—I—
forgot. How is she? Poor woman: how is she?
MARY: Worse, Edward, worse. [*Trying to hide her tears.*]
EDWARD: And I in part the cause. Oh, horrid vice! Bill, I remember my
father's death-bed; it was a Christian's faith in his heart; hope in his
calm, blue eye; a smile upon his lip; he had never seen his Edward
drunk. Oh, had he seen it—had he seen it!
JULIA: [*Crossing to her father.*] Father, dear father? [*Striving to kiss
him.*]
EDWARD: Leave me, child, leave me. I am hot enough already. [*She
weeps, he kisses her.*] Bless you, Julia, dear, bless you. Bill, do you
remember the young elm tree by the arbor in the garden?
WILLIAM: Yes, sir.
EDWARD: Well, I slipped and fell against it, as I passed the gate. My
father planted it on the very day I saw the light. It has grown with
my growth; I seized the axe and felled it to the earth. Why should it
flourish when I am lost forever? [*Hysterically.*] Why should it lift its
head to smiling heaven while I am prostrate? Ha, ha, ha!

[A *groan is heard.—Exit* MARY.—A *pause;—a shriek.*]
    [*Enter* MARY.]

MARY: Edward, my mother—
EDWARD: Mary!—

MARY: She is dead!

EDWARD: Horror! And I the cause? Death in the house, and I without doubt the means. I cannot bear this; let me fly—

MARY: [Springing forward and clasping his neck.] Edward, dear Edward, do not leave me. I will work, I will slave, anything; we can live; but do not abandon me in misery; do not desert me, Edward! love! husband!

EDWARD: Call me not husband—curse me as your destroyer; loose your arms—leave me.

MARY: No, no! do not let him go. William, hold him.

WILLIAM: [Holding him.] Edward, dear brother!

JULIA: [Clinging to him.] Father! father!

MARY: You will be abused. No one near to aid you. Imprisoned, or something worse, Edward.

EDWARD: Loose me; leave me; why fasten me down on fire? Madness is my strength; my brain is liquid flame! [Breaks from her.—WILLIAM is obliged to catch her.] Ha! I am free. Farewell, forever. [Rushes off.]

MARY: Husband! Oh, Heaven! [Faints.]

WILLIAM: [Bursting into tears.] Edward! brother!

JULIA: Father, father! [Runs to the door and falls on the threshold.]

END OF ACT II

ACT III

SCENE 1: Broadway.

[Enter LAWYER CRIBBS.]

CRIBBS: I wonder where that drunken vagrant can have wandered? Ever since he came to New York, thanks to his ravenous appetite and my industrious agency, he has been going down hill rapidly. Could I but tempt him to some overt act, well managed, I could line my own pockets and ensure his ruin. Ha! here he comes, and two of his bright companions. He looks most wretchedly. Money gone, and no honest way to raise it. He'll be glad to speak to old Cribbs now. I must watch my time. [Retiring.]

[Enter EDWARD and two LOAFERS.]

1ST LOAFER: Cheer up, Ned; there's more money where the last came from.

EDWARD: [*Clothes torn and very shabby, hat the same.*] But I tell you my last cent is gone. I feel ill. I want more liquor.

1ST LOAFER: Well, well, you wait round here a spell. Joe and I will take a turn down to Cross street. We'll make a raise, I warrant you.

EDWARD: Well, be quick then; this burning thirst consumes me.

[*Exit* LOAFERS.]

CRIBBS: [*Advancing.*] Why! is that you, Mr. Middleton?

EDWARD: Yes, Cribbs: what there is left of me.

CRIBBS: Why I don't see that you are much altered: though you might be the better for a stitch or two in your elbows—

EDWARD: Ah, Cribbs, I have no one to care for me. I am lost; a ruined, broken-hearted man.

CRIBBS: You won't be offended, Middleton, will you? Allow me to lend you a dollar. I am not very rich you know, but you can always have a dollar or two when you want it; ask me—there! there! [*Offering it.*] Before sundown he's a few yards nearer his grave. [*Aside.*]

EDWARD: [*Slowly taking it, struggling with pride and necessity.*] Thank you, Mr. Cribbs, thank'ye; you are from the village, I hardly dare ask you if you have seen *them.*

CRIBBS: Your wife and child? Oh, they are doing charmingly. Since you left, your wife has found plenty of sewing, the gentlefolks have become interested in her pretty face, and you know she has a good education. She is as merry as a cricket, and your little girl blooming as a rose and brisk as a bee.

EDWARD: Then Mary is happy?

CRIBBS: Happy as a lark.

EDWARD: [*After a pause.*] Well, I ought to be glad of it, and since she thinks no more of me,—

CRIBBS: O yes, she thinks of you *occasionally.*

EDWARD: Does she indeed?

CRIBBS: Yes, she says she cannot but pity you. But that Heaven never sends affliction without the antidote and that, but from your brutal —hem!—your strange conduct and drunkenness—hem!—misfortune, she should never have attracted the sympathy of those kind friends, who now regard her as the pride of their circle.

EDWARD: Did she really say all that?

CRIBBS: Yes, and she *pities* you. I am sure she thinks of you, and would be glad to see you—to see you become a respectable member of society.

EDWARD: [*Musing.*] It is very kind of her—very—very kind! pities me! respectable! But, Cribbs, how can one become respectable, without a cent in his pocket, or a whole garment on his wretched carcase?

CRIBBS: [*Pause.*] There are more ways than one to remedy these casualties. If the world uses you ill, be revenged upon the world!

EDWARD: Revenged! But how, Cribbs, how?

CRIBBS: [*Cautiously.*] Do you see this paper? 'Tis a check for five thousand dollars. You are a splendid penman. Write but the name of Arden Rencelaw, and you may laugh at poverty.

EDWARD: What! forgery? and on whom? The princely merchant! the noble philanthropist! the poor man's friend! the orphan's benefactor! Out and out on you for a villain, and coward! I must be sunk indeed, when you dare propose such a baseness to my father's son. Wretch as I am, by the world despised, shunned and neglected by those who should save and succour me, I would sooner perish on the first dunghill—than that my dear child should blush for her father's crimes. Take back your base bribe, miscalled charity; the maddening drink that I should purchase with it, would be redolent of sin, and rendered still more poisonous by your foul hypocrisy. [*Throws down the money.*]

CRIBBS: [*Bursting with passion.*] Ah, you are warm, I see. You'll think better when,—when you find yourself starving.   [*Exit.*]

EDWARD: Has it then come to this?—an object of pity to my once adored wife: no longer regarded with love—respect—but cold compassion, pity; other friends have fully made up my loss. She is flourishing, too, while I am literally starving—starving—this cold-blooded fiend, too—what's to become of me? Deserted, miserable, —but one resource. I must have liquor—ha!—my handkerchief,— 'twill gain me a drink or two at all events. Brandy, aye, brandy! brandy!   [*Rushes off.*]

SCENE 2: *A Street.—Stage half dark.*

[*Enter* CRIBBS.]

CRIBBS: Plague take the fellow; who would have thought he would have been so foolishly conscientious? I will not abandon my scheme on the house of Rencelaw though; the speculation is too good to be lost. Why! as I live, here comes that old fool, Miss Spindle.

[*Enter* MISS SPINDLE, *her dress a ridiculous compound of by-gone days, and present fashions.*]

MISS SPINDLE: Why! this New York is the most awful place to find one's way I was ever in; it's all ups and downs, ins and outs. I've been trying for two hours to find Trinity Church steeple—and I can't see it, though they tell me it's six hundred yards high.

CRIBBS: Why! angelic Miss Spindle, how *do* you do? How long have you been in the commercial emporium?

MISS SPINDLE: Oh, Squire Cribbs, how d'ye do? I don't know what you mean by the uproarium, but for certain it is the noisiest place I ever did see. But, Squire, what has become of the Middletons, can you tell?

CRIBBS: I've had my eye upon them; they're down, Miss Spindle, never to rise again; as for that vagrant, Edward—

MISS SPINDLE: Ah! Squire! what an escape I had! How fortunate that I was not ruined by the nefarious influence, the malignant coruscations of his illimitable seductions. How lucky that prim Miss Mary Wilson was subjected to his hideous arts, instead of my virgin immaculate innocence!

CRIBBS: Do you know why his wife left the village and came to New York?

MISS SPINDLE: Oh, she is low, degraded! She sank so far as to take in washing, to feed herself and child. She would sooner follow her drunken husband, and endeavor to preserve him as she said, than remain where she was.

CRIBBS: Well, well, they are down low enough now. Which way are you going, towards Broadway? Why I'm going towards Broadway myself. Allow me the exquisite honor of beauing you,—this way perfection of your sex, and adoration of ours—your arm, lovely, and immaculate Miss Spindle. [*Exit together, arm in arm.*]

[*Enter* EDWARD *and* 1ST *and* 2D LOAFER.]

1ST LOAFER: To be sure I did. I swore if he didn't let me have two or three dollars, I'd tell his old man of last night's scrape, and I soon got it to get rid of me.

2D LOAFER: Hurrah for snakes! who's afraid of fire. Come, Ned, two or three glasses will soon drive away the blue devils.[20] Let's have some brandy.

EDWARD: With all my heart. Brandy, be it. Since I am thus abandoned —deserted—the sooner I drown all remembrance of my wretchedness the better come! Boys, brandy be it. Hurrah!

OMNES: [*Sing.*] "Here's a health to all good lasses!" [*Exeunt.*]

SCENE 3: *Interior of The Arbor on Broadway.—Bar with decanters, &c.—Table with Back-gammon Board at back.—Two men playing at it.—Another reading paper and smoking.—Others seated around, &c.*

[*Enter* EDWARD *and* LOAFERS, *singing.—"Here's a health," &c.*]

BAR-KEEPER: [*Behind bar.*] The same noisy fellows that were here last night. What is it to be, gentlemen?

EDWARD: Oh, brandy for me—brandy.

1ST LOAFER: Give me a gin-sling—that's what killed Goliah, ha, ha, ha!

2D LOAFER: I'll have brandy. Come, old fellows, tread up, and wet your whistles. I'll stand Sam, tread up.

[EDWARD *and others after drinking dance and sing,* "Dan Tucker," "Boatman Dance," &c.]

BAR-KEEPER: I must civilly request, gentlemen, that you will not make so much noise; you disturb others—and we wish to keep the house quiet.

EDWARD: Steady, boys, steady; don't raise a row in a decent house. More brandy, young man, if you please. Come, Bill, try it again.

1ST LOAFER: With all my heart, hurrah!

EDWARD *and* LOAFERS: "Dance, Boatman, dance," &c [*Laugh.*] More brandy, hurrah!

BAR-KEEPER: I tell you once for all, I'll not have this noise. Stop that singing.

2D LOAFER: I shan't; we'll sing as long as we please.—give me some liquor.

EDWARD: Aye, more brandy—crandy.

BAR-KEEPER: Well, will you be still, then, if I give you another drink?

EDWARD: Oh, certainly, certainly.

1ST LOAFER: In course we will—

BAR-KEEPER: Well, help yourselves. [*Hands decanters.*]

2D LOAFER: What's yours, Ned.

EDWARD: Oh, brandy—here goes. [*Fills and drinks.*]

1ST LOAFER: Here goes for the last.

OMNES: [*Singing.*] "We won't go home till morning," &c.

MAN: [*At table playing checkers.*] Look here! that's my king.

2D MAN: [*At table.*] You're a liar. I have just jumped him.

1ST MAN: [*At table.*] I tell you, you lie. [*Regular wrangle.*]

EDWARD *and* LOAFERS: Go it, you cripples. [*Singing and laughing.*]

BAR-KEEPER: Stop that noise, I tell you. Come, get out. [*Pushing man from table.—The two men fight.*]

EDWARD *and* LOAFERS: Go it, Charley. Hurrah, &c.

[*Regular scene of confusion.—Bar-room fight, &c.—Scene changes.*]

SCENE 4: *Exterior of a Bar-room on the Five Points*[21]*—Noise inside.*

[CRIBBS *enters and listens at door.*]

CRIBBS: So, a regular bar-room fight. Middleton must be secured—here's the watch.

[*Enter* 2D WATCHMAN.—*Exit* CRIBBS.]

[EDWARD, WATCHMEN *and* LOAFERS *enter struggling, singing, shouting, &c. &c. Exit fighting. Clubs are heard in all directions.* FIRST *and* SECOND LOAFERS *enter clinching each other and fighting—several knock downs: square off, recognise each other.*]

1ST LOAFER: Why, Sam, is that you?

2D LOAFER: Why, Bill, my dear fellow, is that you?

1ST LOAFER: [*Who has had his hat knocked entirely over his head, crown out.*] To be sure it is; look here, you've completely caved in my best beaver.

2D LOAFER: Well, I ask your pardon.   [*Exeunt arm in arm.*]

SCENE 5: —*A wretched garret.—Old table and chair with lamp burning dimly.—*MARY *in miserable apparel, sewing on slop-work; a wretched shawl thrown over her shoulders—Child sleeping on a straw bed on the floor, covered in part by a miserable ragged rug.—Half a loaf of bread on the table.—The ensemble of the scene indicates want and poverty.*

MARY: Alas, alas! It is very cold—faint with hunger—sick—heart weary with wretchedness, fatigue, and cold. [*Clock strikes one.*] One o'clock, and my work not near finished. I—they must be done to-night. These shirts I have promised to hand in to-morrow by the hour of eight. A miserable quarter of a dollar will repay my industry, and then my poor, poor child, thou shalt have food.

JULIA: [*Awaking.*] Oh, dear mother, I am so cold. [MARY *takes shawl from her shoulders and spreads it over the child.*] No, mother,—keep the shawl. You are cold, too. I will wait till morning, and I can warm myself at Mrs. Brien's fire; little Dennis told me I should, for the gingerbread I gave him.

[*Goes to sleep murmuring.*—MARY *puts the shawl on herself, waits till the child slumbers, and then places it over* JULIA, *and returns to work.*]

MARY: Alas! where is he on this bitter night? In vain have I made every inquiry, and cannot gain any tidings of my poor wretched husband; no one knows him by name. Perhaps already the inmate of a prison. Ah, merciful heaven, restore to me my Edward once again, and I will endure every ill that can be heaped upon me. [*Looks towards child.*] Poor Julia, she sleeps soundly, she was fortunate to-day, sweet lamb, while walking in the street in search of a few shavings, she became benumbed with cold. She sat down upon some steps, when a boy moved with compassion, took from his neck a handkerchief, and placed it upon hers, *the mother of that boy is blessed.* With the few cents he slipped into her hands, she purchased a loaf of bread, she ate a part of it. [*Taking bread from table.*] And the rest is here. [*Looks eagerly at it.*] I am hungry—horribly hungry. I shall have money in the morning. [*Pause.*] No, no, my child will wake and find her treasure gone. I will not rob my darling. [*Replaces bread on table, sinks into chair, weeping.*] That I should ever *see* his child thus! for myself, I could bear, could suffer all.

[JULIA *awakes noiselessly, perceiving shawl, rises and places it over her mother's shoulders.*]

JULIA: Dear mother, you are cold. Ah, you tried to cheat your darling.
MARY: [*On her knees.*] Now heaven be praised. I did not eat that bread.
JULIA: Why, mother, do you sit up so late? you cry so much, and look so white—mother, do not cry. Is it because father does not come to bring us bread? we shall find father bye and bye, shan't we, mother.
MARY: Yes, dearest—yes, with the kind aid of Him. [*Knock at the door.*] Who can that be? Ah, should it be Edward?

[*Enter* CRIBBS.]

CRIBBS: Your pardon, Mrs. Middleton, for my intrusion at this untimely hour, but friends are welcome at all times, and seasons, eh? So, so, you persist in remaining in these miserable quarters? when last I saw you, I advised a change.

MARY: Alas! sir, you too well know my wretched reasons for remaining. But why are you here at this strange hour; Oh, tell me, know you aught of him? Have you brought tidings of my poor Edward?

CRIBBS: [*Avoiding direct answer.*] I must say your accommodations are none of the best, and must persist in it, you would do well to shift your quarters.

MARY: Heaven help me! where would you have me go? return to the village, I will not. I must remain and find my husband.

CRIBBS: This is a strange infatuation, young woman; it is the more strange, as he has others to console him, whose soft attentions he prefers to yours.

MARY: What mean you, sir?

CRIBBS: I mean, that there are plenty of women, not of the most respectable class, who are always ready to receive presents from wild young men like him, and are not very particular in the liberties that may be taken in exchange.

MARY: Man, man, why dost thou degrade the form and sense the *great one* has bestowed on thee by falsehood? Gaze on the sharp features of that child, where famine has already set her seal, look on the hollow eyes, and the careworn form of the hapless being that brought her into life, then if you have the heart, further insult the helpless mother, and the wretched wife.

CRIBBS: These things I speak of, have been, and will be again, while there are wantons of one sex, and drunkards of the other.

MARY: Sir, you slander my husband. I know this cannot be. It is because he is poor, forsaken, reviled, and friendless, that thus I follow him, thus love him still.

CRIBBS: He would laugh in his drunken ribaldry, to hear you talk thus.

MARY: [*With proud disdain.*] Most contemptible of earth-born creatures, it is false. The only fault of my poor husband, has been intemperance, terrible, I acknowledge, but still a weakness that has assailed and prostrated the finest intellects of men who would scorn a mean and unworthy action.

CRIBBS: Tut, tut, you are very proud, considering—[*Looking round.*]—all circumstances. But come, I forgive you. You are young and beautiful, your husband is a vagabond. I am rich, I have a true affection for you, and with me—[*Attempts to take her hand.*]

MARY: Wretch! [*Throws him off.*] Have you not now proved yourself a slanderer, and to effect your own vile purposes. But know, despisable wretch, that my poor husband, clothed in rags, covered with mire, and lying drunk at my feet, is a being whose shoes, you are not worthy to unloose.

CRIBBS: Nay, then, proud beauty, you shall know my power—'tis late, you are unfriended, helpless, and thus—[*He seizes her, child screams.*]

MARY: Help! mercy!

[*She struggles, crosses,* CRIBBS *follows her.*—WILLIAM *enters hastily, seizes* CRIBBS *and throws him round, he falls.*]

WILLIAM: Well, Squire, what's the lowest you'll take for your rotten carcase? Shall I turn auctioneer, and knock you down to the highest bidder? I don't know much of pornology,[22] but I've a great notion of playing Yankee Doodle on your organ of rascality. Be off, you ugly varmint, or I'll come the steam ingine, and set your paddles going all-fired quick.

CRIBBS: I'll be revenged, if there's law or justice.

WILLIAM: Oh, get out! You're a bad case of villany versus modesty and chastity, printed in black letters, and bound in calf, off with you, or I'll serve a writ of objectment on you, a posteriori to you—I learnt that much from Mr. Middleton's law books.

CRIBBS: But I say, sir—I am a man—

WILLIAM: You a man? Nature made a blunder. She had a piece of refuse garbage, she intended to form into a *hog*, made a mistake, gave it your *shape,* and sent it into the world to be miscalled man. Get out. [*Pushes him off. Noise of falling down stairs. Re-enters.*] I did not like to hit him before you, but he's gone down these stairs, quicker than he wanted to, I guess.

MARY: Kind, generous friend, how came you here so opportunely?

WILLIAM: Why, I was just going to bed, at a boarding house close by Chatham street, when I happened to mention to the landlord, a worthy man as ever broke bread about you; he told me where you was. I thought you might be more comfortable there, and his good wife has made everything as nice and pleasant for you, as if you were her own sister. So come, Mrs. Middleton, come, Julia, dear.

MARY: But William, my poor husband. [<*Sound of*> *clubs.*]

WILLIAM: There's another row, well, if this New York isn't the awfullest place for noise. Come, Mrs. Middleton, I'll find him if he's in New York, jail or no jail, watch-house or no watch-house.

MARY: Heaven preserve my poor, dear Edward. [*Exit.*]

SCENE 6: *The Five Points—Stage dark, clubs.*

[*Enter* EDWARD MIDDLETON, *in the custody of two watchmen, he is shouting.—*WILLIAM DOWTON *enters hastily, knocks down watchmen, rescues* EDWARD, *and they exit.—Other rowdies enter, fight.—Stage clear, shouts, &c, and off.—Enter* CRIBBS, *with coat torn half off, and dancing, fighting about stage.*]

CRIBBS: Oh, my! Oh, good gracious! How can I get out of this scrape? I came here with the best intentions. Oh, my! to see the law put in force! Oh, dear! somebody has torn my coat tail—good gracious! Lord have mercy! I've lost my hat—no, here it is.

[*Picks up dreadful shabby hat and puts it on, runs from one side to another.—Enter watchmen and mob, meeting him.*]

WILLIAM: [*Pointing out* CRIBBS *to watchmen.*] That's the chap, the worst among 'em.

[*They seize* CRIBBS.]

CRIBBS: I'm a respectable man.

[*They pick him up bodily and carry him off, shouting, he exclaims, "I'm a lawyer, I'm a respectable man," &c.—*WILLIAM *follows laughing.—General confusion.*]

END OF ACT III

ACT IV

SCENE 1: *A wretched out-house or shed, supposed to be near a tavern, early morning.—Stage dark.—*EDWARD *discovered lying on ground, without hat or coat, clothes torn, eyes sunk and haggard, appearance horrible, &c., &c.*

EDWARD: [*Awakening.*] Where am I? I wonder if people dream after they are dead? hideous! hideous! I should like to be dead, if I could not dream—parched! parched! 'tis morning, is it, or coming night, which? I wanted day light, but now it has come, what shall I do in daylight! I was out of sight when it was dark—and seemed to be half-hidden from myself—early morning, the rosy hue of the coming sunshine, veiling from mortal sight the twinkling stars—what horrid dreams, will they return upon me, waking? Oh, for some brandy! rum! I am not so ashamed, so stricken with despair when I am drunk. Landlord, give me some brandy. What horrid place is this? Pain! dreadful pain! Heavens, how I tremble. Brandy! brandy? [*Sinks down in agony.*]

[*Enter* LANDLORD, *with whip.*]

LANDLORD: Where in nature can my horse be gone? Is there nobody up in this place? Hollo!

EDWARD: Hollo! Landlord, I say.

LANDLORD: What's that? Oh! I say, have you seen my horse? What— as I live, that scape-gallows, Middleton, how came he here? [*Aside.*] I thought he was in Sing-Sing.

EDWARD: Oh! I know you, you needn't draw back—we have been acquainted before now, eh! Mr.—

LANDLORD: Zounds! he knows me—yes, yes, we were acquainted once, as you say, young man; but that was in other days.

EDWARD: You are the same being still—though I am changed—miserably changed—you still sell rum don't you?

LANDLORD: I am called a respectable Inn-keeper, few words are best, young fellow. Have you seen a horse saddled and bridled near here?

EDWARD: I've seen nothing—you are respectable, you say. You speak as if you were not the common poisoner of the whole village; am not I too, respectable?

LANDLORD: [*Laughs rudely.*] Not according to present appearances. You were respectable once, and so was Lucifer—like him you have fallen past rising. You cut a pretty figure, don't you? ha! ha! what has brought you in this beastly condition, young man?

EDWARD: [*Springing up.*] You! Rum! Eternal curses on you! had it not been for your infernal poison shop in our village, I had been still a man—the foul den, where you plunder the pockets of your fellow, where you deal forth death in tumblers, and from whence goes forth the blast of ruin over the land, to mildew the bright hope of youth, to fill the widow's heart with agony, to curse the orphan, to steal the glorious mind of man, to cast them from their high estate of honest pride, and make them—such as I. How looked I when first I entered your loathsome den, and how do I look now? Where are the friends of my happy youth? where is my wife? where is my child? They have cursed me; cursed me, and forsaken me!

LANDLORD: Well, what brought you to my house? You had your senses then, I did not invite you, did I?

EDWARD: Doth hell send forth cards of invitation for its horrid orgies? Sick and faint—make me some amends, my brain is on fire. My limbs are trembling—give me some brandy—brandy. [*Seizes him.*]

LANDLORD: How can I give you brandy? my house is far from here. Let me go, vagabond!

EDWARD: Nay, I beseech you—only a glass, a single glass of brandy, rum—anything—give me liquor, or I'll—

LANDLORD: Villain! let go your hold!

EDWARD: Brandy! I have a claim on you, a deadly claim! Brandy, brandy! or I'll throttle you. [*Choking him.*]

LANDLORD: [*Struggling.*] Help, murder! I am choking! help!

[*Enter* WILLIAM DOWTON.]

WILLIAM: Good lord! what is this? Edward, Edward.

[EDWARD *releases* LANDLORD *and falls.*]

LANDLORD: You shall pay for this—villain! you shall pay for this.
                                                    [*Exit, hastily.*]

EDWARD: [*On ground in delirium.*] Here, here, friend, take it off, will you—these snakes, how they coil round me. Oh! how strong they are—there, don't kill it, no, no, don't kill it, give it brandy, poison it with rum, that will be a judicious punishment, that would be justice, ha, ha! justice! ha, ha!

WILLIAM: He does not know me.

EDWARD: Hush! gently—gently, while she's asleep. I'll kiss her. She would reject me, did she know it, hush! there, heaven bless my Mary, bless her and her child—hush! if the globe turns round once more, we shall slide from its surface into eternity. Ha, ha! great idea. A boiling sea of wine, fired by the torch of fiends! ha, ha!

WILLIAM: He's quite helpless, could I but gain assistance, he cannot move to injure himself. I must venture. [*Exit, rapidly and noiselessly.*]

EDWARD: So, so; again all's quiet—they think I cannot escape. I cheated them yesterday—'tis a sin to steal liquor—

[*Enter* MR. RENCELAW.]

But no crime to purloin sleep from a druggist's store—none—none. [*Produces phial.*] Now for the universal antidote—the powerful conquerer of all earthly care—death. [*About to drink,* RENCELAW *seizes phial and casts it from him.*] Ha! who are you, man? what would you?

RENCELAW: Nay, friend, take not your life, but mend it.

EDWARD: Friend, you know me not. I am a fiend, the ruin of those who loved me, leave me.

RENCELAW: I came not to upbraid you, or to insult you. I am aware of all your danger, and come to save you. You have been drinking.

EDWARD: That you may well know. I am dying now for liquor—and —will you give me brandy. Who are you that takes interest in an unhappy vagabond—neither my father nor my brother?

RENCELAW: I am a friend to the unfortunate. You are a man, and if a man, a brother.

EDWARD: A brother! yes, but you trouble yourself without hope. I am lost, of what use can I be to you?

RENCELAW: Perhaps I can be of use to you. Are you indeed a fallen man? [EDWARD *looks at him, sighs and hangs his head.*] There you have the greater claim upon any compassion, my attention, my utmost endeavors to raise you once more, to the station in society from which you have fallen, "for he that lifts a fallen fellow creature from the dust is greater than the hero who conquers a world."

EDWARD: [*Starts.*] Merciful heaven! My mother's dying words? Who and what are you?

RENCELAW: I am one of those whose life and labors are passed in rescuing their fellow men from the abyss into which you have fallen. I administer the pledge of sobriety to those who would once more become an ornament to society, and a blessing to themselves and to those around them.

EDWARD: That picture is too bright, it cannot be.

RENCELAW: You see before you one who for twenty years was a prey to this dreadful folly.

EDWARD: Indeed! no, no; it is too late.

RENCELAW: You mistake; it is not too late. Come with me, we will restore you to society. Reject not my prayers; strength will be given you, the Father of purity smiles upon honest endeavors. Come, my brother, enroll your name among the free, the disenthralled, and be a man again. [*Takes his hand.*]

EDWARD: Merciful heaven! grant the prayer of a poor wretch be heard.

[*Exeunt.*]

SCENE 2: *Union Square.—Lights up.—Citizens passing during the scene.—Children playing ball, hoop, &c.*

[*Enter* LAWYER CRIBBS.]

CRIBBS: Now this is a lucky escape. It's fortunate that old Sykes, the miller, was in court, who knew me, or I might have found it difficult to get out of the infernal scrape. What a dreadful night I have passed, to be sure,—what with the horrid noise of the rats, that I expected every moment would commence making a breakfast of my toes, the cold, and horrible language of my miserable and blackguard companions. I might as well have passed the crawling hours in purgatory, ugh! I'm glad it's over—catch me in such company again, that's all. Now for my design on Rencelaw and Co. I think there can be no detection, the signature is perfect. I'll get some well-dressed boy to deliver the check, receive the money, and I'm off to the far West or England, soon as possible. Would I were certain of the ruin of this drunken scoundrel, and the infamy of his tiger-like wife, I shou'd be content.

[*Enter* BOY.]

Where are you going so quickly, my lad?
BOY: On an errand, sir.

[*Enter* WILLIAM DOWTON.]

CRIBBS: Do you want to earn half a dollar?
BOY: With pleasure, sir, honestly.
CRIBBS: Oh, of course, honestly.
WILLIAM: I doubt, that, if he rows in your boat.
CRIBBS: I am obliged to meet a gentleman on business, precisely at this hour, by the Pearl St. House, call at the Mechanics' Bank for me, deliver this check, the Teller will give you the money, come back quickly, and I'll reward you with a silver dollar.
BOY: I'll be as quick as possible, sir, and thank you too. [*Exit hastily.*]
WILLIAM: I knew the old skunk had money, but I was not aware that he banked in New York. Hallo! here's Miss Spindle a-twigging the fashions; here'll be fun with the old rats. I told her half an hour ago, Cribbs was at a large party among the 'stocracy, last night.
CRIBBS: [*After putting up his wallet, sees* MISS SPINDLE.] Confound it! here's that foolish old maid, at such a time, too. Ah! there's no avoiding.

[*Enter* MISS SPINDLE.]

MISS SPINDLE: Good gracious! Mr. Cribbs, how *do* you do? I declare, how well you do look—a little dissipation improves you.

CRIBBS: What?

WILLIAM: [*Aside.*] She's beginning already. Hurrah! Go it, old gal.

MISS SPINDLE: I swow, now, I'm right glad to see you.

CRIBBS: You have all the pleasure to yourself.

WILLIAM: She'll find that out by and bye.

MISS SPINDLE: Now, don't be so snappish, Lawyer Cribbs; neighbors should be neighborly, you know. Who was it that had the pleasure to introduce you?

WILLIAM: [*Aside.*] I rather guess I went that stick of candy.

[CRIBBS *stares at* MISS SPINDLE.]

MISS SPINDLE: Now don't look so cross about it. I think you ought to feel right slick, as I do. Now do tell what kind of music had you!

WILLIAM: [*Aside.*] Plenty o' hollaring and clubs, with considerable running accompaniment.

MISS SPINDLE: Now don't look so angry and scared. Who did play the fiddle? was it Herr Noll, Young Burke,[23] or Ole Bull.[24] Don't keep my curiosity on the stretch.

CRIBBS: Belzebub stretch your curiosity! What are you yelling about Herr Noll, Young Burke, and Ole Bulls for?

WILLIAM: [*Aside.*] I calculate Captain—[*name of captain of watch*]—played first fiddle to the overture of "Lock and Key."

MISS SPINDLE: Well I swow, I never seed sich ill-temper. Why I know New York tip-tops always have somebody first chop among the fiddlers; for cousin Jemima told me when she was at the Tabernacle, her very hair stood on end when Herwig led the musicians with Heatoven's sympathy.

CRIBBS: [*Aside.*] The old fool's perfectly crazy!

WILLIAM: [*Aside.*] Well, if the old chap hadn't any music, it wasn't for want of bars and staves. I reckon he got out of his notes when they let him off.

MISS SPINDLE: Now, don't be angry, Lawyer Cribbs; you know I only ask for information. Do the 'stocracy go the hull temperance principle, and give their visitors nothing but ice water?

WILLIAM: [*Aside.*] There was a big bucket and dippers, I reckon.

CRIBBS: Miss Spindle, will you only hear me?

MISS SPINDLE: Wall, ain't I listening all the time, and you won't tell me nothin'. Were there are any real live lions there? Did Col. Johnson[25] scalp a live Indian, to amuse the ladies? Did Dr. Dodds[26] put every body into a phospheric state, when they were all dancing, and the lights went out? Did Senator D—— dance a hornpipe to please the children, and make a bowl of punch at twelve o'clock? Did—[*Out of breath.*]

WILLIAM: [*Aside.*] She'll ask him directly if the elephants played at billiards.

CRIBBS: Madam! madam! will you listen? [*Shouts out.*] In the name of confusion, what are you talking about?

MISS SPINDLE: Why, of the grand *sorrie*—the party, to be sure.

CRIBBS: I know nothing of any party; you're insane.

MISS SPINDLE: Oh, no. I ain't, neither. I was told of it by one—

CRIBBS: Told by one? who?

WILLIAM: [*Coming forward.*] Me, I calculate, watched you, I guess.

CRIBBS: Watched!

WILLIAM: Guess I did—so shut up.

CRIBBS: Confusion!

WILLIAM: I say, Squire, where did you buy your new coat?

CRIBBS: Go to the devil, both of you.

WILLIAM: Where's the tail of your old one? Ha! ha!

[*Exit* CRIBBS.—WILLIAM *follows, laughing.*]

MISS SPINDLE: Well, I swow, this is like Jedides' addle eggs. I can neither make ducks nor chickens on 'em. Well, I've got a good budget of news and scandal, any how. So I'll be off back to the village, this very day; this vile city is no safe place for romantic sensibilities and virgin purity.   [*Exit.*]

SCENE 3: *Broadway, with a view of Barnum's Museum.*

[*Enter* ARDEN RENCELAW.—BANK MESSENGER *enters after him.*]

MESSENGER: Mr. Rencelaw, Mr. Rencelaw! I beg pardon for hurridly addressing you, but our cashier desires to know if this is your signature. [*Produces check.*]

RENCELAW: My signature—good heavens, no!—five thousand dollars. Is it cashed?

MESSENGER: Not half an hour. The teller cashed it instantly.

RENCELAW: Who presented the check?

MESSENGER: A young boy, sir, whom I saw just now, recognized, and sent to the bank immediately; but the cashier Mr. Armond, arriving directly afterwards, doubted it, and I was despatched to find you.

RENCELAW: Run to the bank directly; call for a police officer as you pass. I am rather infirm, but will soon follow; do not be flurried; our measures must be prompt and I fear not for the result.

[*Exit* MESSENGER.]

[*Enter* WILLIAM DOWTON.]

Ah, honest William; I have been searching for you. Edward desired to see you.

WILLIAM: Thank and bless you, sir. How is he?—where?

RENCELAW: Comparatively well and happy, at my house. His wife and child will be here immediately; I have sent a carriage for them. Their home—their happy home—is prepared for them in the village, and I have obtained almost certain information of his grandfather's will.

WILLIAM: Thank heaven! But, sir, you appear alarmed, excited.

RENCELAW: A forgery has just been committed, in the name of our firm, upon the Mechanics' Bank.

WILLIAM: Bless me! the Mechanics' Bank? Who gave the check, sir?

RENCELAW: A boy, William.

WILLIAM: A boy; how long ago?

RENCELAW: Not half an hour! Why this eagerness?

WILLIAM: I—I'll tell you, sir. Mr. Middleton told me that Lawyer Cribbs, when the poor fellow was in poverty and drunkenness, urged him to commit a forgery. Not half an hour since, I saw Cribbs give a boy a check, and tell him to take it to the Mechanics' Bank, receive some money, and bring it to him somewhere near the Pearl Street House, where he would find him with a gentleman.

RENCELAW: So, so! I see it all. Come with me to the Tombs,[27] and secure an officer. If you should meet Middleton, do not at present mention this—come.   [*Exit.*]

WILLIAM: I'll follow you, sir, heart and hand. If I once get my grip on the old fox, he won't get easily loose, I guess.   [*Exit hastily.*]

SCENE 4: *Room in* RENCELAW'S *house; very handsome table, chairs, handsome books, &c.*

[EDWARD MIDDLETON *discovered reading—dressed, and looking well, &c.*]

EDWARD: [*Side of table.*] What gratitude do I not owe this generous, noble-hearted man, who, from the depths of wretchedness and horror, has restored me to the world, to myself, and to religion. Oh! what joy can equal the bright sensations of a thinking being, when redeemed from that degrading vice; his prisoned heart beats with rapture; his swelling veins bound with vigor; and with tremulous gratitude, he calls on the Supreme Being for blessings on his benefactor.

MARY: [*Outside.*] Where is my dear—my loved redeemed one?

[MARY *enters with* JULIA.]

Edward! my dear, dear husband. [*They embrace.*]

EDWARD: Mary, my blessed one! My child, my darling. Bounteous heaven! accept my thanks.

JULIA: Father, dear father—you look as you did the bright sunshiny morning, I first went to school. Your voice sounds as it used when I sang the evening hymn and you kissed and blessed me. You cry, father. Do not cry; but your tears are not such tears as mother shed, when she had no bread to give me.

EDWARD: [*Kisses her.*] No, my blessed child, they are not; they are tears of repentance, Julia, but of joy.

MARY: Oh! my beloved, my redeemed one, all my poor sufferings are as nothing weighed in a balance with my present joy.

[*Enter* RENCELAW.]

Respected sir, what words can express our gratification!

RENCELAW: Pay it where 'tis justly due, to heaven! I am but the humble instrument, and in your sweet content, I am rewarded.

JULIA: [*Going to* RENCELAW.] I shall not forget what mother last night taught me.

RENCELAW: What was that, sweet girl.

JULIA: In my prayers, when I have asked a blessing for my father and my mother, I pray to *Him* to bless *Arden Rencelaw* too.

RENCELAW: Dear child. [*Kisses her.*]

EDWARD: I will not wrong your generous nature, by fulsome outward gratitude, for your most noble conduct, but humbly hope, that He will give me strength to continue in the glorious path, adorned by your bright example, in the words of New England's favored poet:

> "There came a change, the cloud rolled off,
> A light fell on my brain,
> And like the passing of a dream,
> That cometh not again.

The darkness of my spirit fled,
        I saw the gulf before;
And shuddered at the waste behind,
        And am a man once more."

END OF ACT IV

ACT V

SCENE 1: *Village Landscape, as in Act I—Side Cottage.*

[*Enter* FARMER STEVENS, *and* FARMER GATES, L, *meeting.*]

STEVENS: Good afternoon, Mr. Gates. You've returned from Boston ear-
    lier than common to-day. Any news?—anything strange, eh!

GATES: Why, ye-es, I guess there is. Just by the Post Office I met William
    Dowton; how are you, says I, and was driving slowly along, when
    he hailed me to stop, and—but I forgot to ask you, has Squire Cribbs
    been here to-day?

STEVENS: I have not seen the old knave—why do you ask so particular?

GATES: Well, William, you know, is as honest as the sun, and he told
    me there were dreadful suspicions that Cribbs had committed a heavy
    forgery on the firm of Rencelaw and Co., and as I was already in
    my waggon, and had a good horse, he wished I would drive out
    pretty quick, and if old Cribbs were here, manage to detain him 'till
    Mr. Rencelaw and William arrived with the police officers—that if
    the sly old fox were guilty, he might be caught before he
    absquatulated.

STEVENS: Well, I hope, for the credit of the village, he is not guilty of
    this bad action, though I have long known his heart was blacker than
    his coat. Witness his conduct to the sweetheart of Will's poor sister,
    Agnes. Did you tell him the glad news that her senses were restored?

GATES: No, our hurry was so great; but his mind will be prepared for
    it, for good Dr. Woodworth always told him her malady was but
    temporary.

STEVENS: Well, the poor girl has got some secret, I'm sure, and she'll
    not tell it to any one but William.   [*Exit.*]

GATES: Hark! that's his voice; yes, here's William, sure enough.

[*Enter* WILLIAM.]

Well, William, every thing is just as you directed, but no signs of the old one yet.

WILLIAM: The rascal's on his way, be sure. Bill Parkins told me he saw him passing through Kings-bridge half an hour before we came through there. I guess he's taken the upper road, to lead all pursuit out of the track. Mr. Rencelaw and the police are at the cross roads, and I rather guess we can take charge of the lower part of the village; so there's no fear of our missing him; mind you're not to say anything to Edward Middleton. Mr. Rencelaw would not have him disturbed till all is secure.

GATES: Oh, I understand. How the whole village rejoiced when they saw him and his sweet wife return in peace and joy to the happy dwelling of their parents. Have you seen your sister, William?

WILLIAM: No, farmer, I haven't seen the poor girl yet. Nor do I wish it, till this business is all fixed.

GATES: Ay, but she wants to see you; she has got to tell you some secret.

WILLIAM: A secret! some of her wild fancies, I reckon, poor girl.

GATES: William, you are mistaken; your dear sister's mind is quite restored.

WILLIAM: What! how! Don't trifle with me, farmer, I could not stand it.

GATES: I tell you, William, she is sane, quite well, as Dr. Woodworth said she would be.

WILLIAM: What! will she know and call me by my name again? Shall I hear her sweet voice carolling to the sun at early morning—will she take her place among the singers at the old meeting-house again? Shall I once more at evening hear her murmur the prayers our poor old mother taught her? Thank heaven! thank heaven!

GATES: Come, William, come, rouse you, she's coming.

AGNES: [Without.]

"They called her blue-eyed Mary,
When friends and fortune smiled"

WILLIAM: Farmer, just stand back for a moment or two; all will be right in a few minutes.   [Exit FARMER.]

[Enter AGNES, plainly but neatly dressed.—Sees her brother.]

AGNES: William! brother!

WILLIAM: My darling sister! [Embrace.]

AGNES: I know you, William; I can speak to you, and hear you, dear, dear brother.

WILLIAM: May He be praised for this.

AGNES: William, I have much to tell you, and 'tis important that you should know it instantly. I know Edward Middleton is here, and it concerns him most. When I recovered my clear senses, William, when I remembered the meeting-house, and the old homestead, and the little dun cow I used to milk, and poor old Neptune, and could call them by their names—

WILLIAM: Bless you!

AGNES: Strange fancies would still keep forming in my poor brain, and remembrances flit along my memory like half-forgotten dreams. But among them, clear and distinct, was that fearful day when old Cribbs would have abused me, and you, dear brother, saved me.

WILLIAM: Darn the old varmint!

AGNES: Hush, William, the memory of that precise spot would still intrude upon me, and a vague thought that when insane I had concealed myself, and seen something hidden. Searching round carefully one day, I saw a little raised artificial hillock close beneath the hedge. I went and got a hoe from Farmer Williams' barn, and after digging near a foot below, I found—what think you, William?

WILLIAM: What, girl—what?

AGNES: Concealed in an old tin case, the will of Edward's grandfather! confirming to his dear son the full possession of all his property. The other deed under which Cribbs had acted was a forgery—

WILLIAM: Where is it now?

AGNES: In the house, safe locked up in mother's bureau till you returned.

[*Enter* RENCELAW, POLICE OFFICERS *and* BOY, *hastily.*]

RENCELAW: Friend William, Cribbs is on the upper road, coming down the hill.

[*Enter* FARMER GATES *and* FARMER STEVENS.]

WILLIAM: Farmer Gates, do you meet him here; answer any questions he may ask with seeming frankness. Sister, he is after that will, even now. Mr. Rencelaw, let us retire into the house and watch the old rascal.   [*Exeunt into house, all except* GATES.]

GATES: [*Alone.*] Well, am I to lie now, if he asks any questions? It's a new thing to me, and I'm afeared I can't do it, even in a good cause. Well, if I musn't tell truth exactly, I must do as the papers say the members do in Congress, and dodge the present question.

[*Enter* CRIBBS, *hurriedly, evidently alarmed.—Starts at seeing* FARMER, *then, familiarly.*]

CRIBBS: Good day, farmer, good day; your folks all well?

GATES: All sound and hearty.

CRIBBS: Any news, eh?

GATES: Nothing particular; corn's ris a little; sauce is lower. Potatoes hold their own, and Wilkins' cow's got a calf.

CRIBBS: Been in New York, lately, eh?

GATES: Why, yes, I was in the city this morning.

CRIBBS: Did you see William Dowton there, eh?

GATES: No, not in New York. [*Aside.*] That's dodge number one.

CRIBBS: Fine afternoon, eh?

GATES: Yes, fine day, considering.

CRIBBS: Likely to rain, eh?

GATES: If it does we shall have a shower, I guess. Come, black-coat didn't make much out of me this time.   [*Exit into house.*]

CRIBBS: He's gone. No one observes me. Now then, for the will, and instant flight! If I take the lower road I shall escape all observation. Haste—haste!   [*Exit.*]

[*Enter from house,* WILLIAM, RENCELAW, AGNES, FARMERS, POLICE OFFICERS, *and* BOY.]

WILLIAM: There he goes by the lower road. Boy, was that the man gave you the paper?

BOY: I'm sure of it, sir.

WILLIAM: Mr. Rencelaw, you know enough, sir, from what I have said, perfectly to understand our purpose?

RENCELAW: Perfectly, honest William.

WILLIAM: Now, Farmer Gates, he's gone round by the lower road, evidently to get clear of being seen if possible. Now, if we cut pretty quick across Farmer Williams' pasture we are there before him, and can keep ourselves concealed.

GATES: Certainly, William.

WILLIAM: Come along, then. Now, old Cribbs, I calculate you'll find a hornet's nest about your ears pretty almighty quick.   [*Exeunt.*]

SCENE 2: *Front and Cut Wood.*

[*Enter* WILLIAM, RENCELAW, AGNES, BOY, FARMERS, *and* POLICE OFFICERS.]

WILLIAM: All right; we're here first, now for ambuscade. All hide behind the trees. Hush! I hear a footstep; he's coming round the barn. Close, close. [*All retire.*]

[*Enter* CRIBBS *cautious and fearful.*]

CRIBBS: All's safe—I'm certain no one has observed me.
WILLIAM: [*Aside.*] What would you like to bet?
CRIBBS: Hark! 'tis nothing. Now for the will; from this fatal evidence I shall at least be secure. [*Advances to the mound, and starts.*] Powers of mischief! the earth is freshly turned. [*Searches.*] The deed is gone!

[*Enter* AGNES *hastily, and down.—In a tone of madness.*]

AGNES: The will is gone—the bird has flown,
                The rightful heir has got his own!—ha! ha!

CRIBBS: [*Paralyzed and recovering.*] Ha! betrayed! ruined! Mad devil, you shall pay for this. [*Rushes towards her.*]

[WILLIAM *enters, catches his arm, and holds up the will.*—POLICE-OFFICER, *seizes other arm, and points pistol to his head.*—RENCELAW *holds up forged check, and points to it.*—BOY, *pointing to* CRIBBS.—FARMERS.—*Picture.—Pause.*]

WILLIAM: Trapped! All day with you, Squire.
RENCELAW: Hush! William, do not oppress a poor down-fallen fellow creature. Most unfortunate of men, sincerely do I pity you.
CRIBBS: [*Recovering—bold and obdurate.*] Will your pity save me from the punishment of my misdeeds? No! when compassion is required, I'll beg it of the proud philanthropist, Arden Rencelaw.
RENCELAW: Unhappy wretch. What motives could you have? This world's goods were plenty with you—what tempted you into these double deeds of guilt?
CRIBBS: Revenge and avarice, the master passions of my nature. With my heart's deepest, blackest feelings, I hated the father of Edward Middleton. In early life he detected me in an act of vile atrocity that might have cost me my life. He would not betray, but pardoned, pitied, and despised me. From that hour I hated with a feeling of

intensity that has existed even beyond the grave, descending unim-
paired to his noble son. By cunning means, which you would call
hypocrisy, I wormed myself into the favor of the grandfather, who,
in his dying hour, delivered into my hands his papers. I and an accomplice, whom I bribed, forged the false papers; the villain left the
country. Fearful he should denounce me, should he return, I dared
not destroy the real will; but yesterday the news reached me that he
was dead. And now, one blow of evil fortune has destroyed me.

RENCELAW: Repentance may yet avail you?

CRIBBS: Nothing. I have lived a villain—a villain let me die.

[*Exit with* OFFICERS *and* FARMERS.]

RENCELAW: William, tell Middleton I shall see him in a day or two; I
must follow that poor man to New York.

WILLIAM: Oh, Mr. Rencelaw, what blessings can repay you.

RENCELAW: The blessings of my own approving conscience. "The heart
of the feeling man is like the noble tree, which, wounded itself, yet
pours forth precious balm." When the just man quits this transitory
world, the dark angel of death enshrouds him with heavenly joy, and
bears his smiling spirit to the bright regions of eternal bliss.

[*Exit* RENCELAW, *leading* BOY.]

WILLIAM: Well, if there's a happier man in all York State than Bill Dowton, I should like to see him. My brother Edward again a man,—
you, my dear sister, again restored to me—come, we'll go tell all the
news; hurrah! hurrah! [*Singing.*]

> "We'll dance all night by the bright moonlight,
> And go home with the girls in the morning."

LAST SCENE: *Interior of Cottage as in Act 1st, Scene 1st. Everything
denoting domestic peace and tranquil happiness.—The sun is setting
over the hills at back of landscape.—EDWARD discovered near music
stand.—JULIA seated on low stool.—MARY sewing at handsome work
table.—Elegant table, with astral lamp, not lighted.—Bible and other
books on it.—Two beautiful flower-stands, with roses, myrtles, &c.,
under window.—Bird-cages on wings.—Covers of tables, chairs, &c.,
all extremely neat, and in keeping.*

[EDWARD *plays on flute symphony to* "Home, Sweet Home."[28]
JULIA *sings first verse.—Flute solo accompaniment.—The burthen
is then taken up by chorus of villagers behind.—Orchestral ac-*

companiments, &c.—Gradually crescendo, forte.—Villagers enter gradually, grouping.—Action of recognition and good wishes, &c., while the melody is progressing.—The melody is repeated quicker, and all retire with the exception of EDWARD, MARY, JULIA, WILLIAM and AGNES, singing, and becoming gradually diminuendo.—Air repeated slowly.—JULIA kneels to EDWARD, who is at table, seated, in prayer.—EDWARD'S hand on Bible, and pointing up.—MARY standing, leaning upon his chair.—WILLIAM and AGNES.—Music till curtain falls.—Picture.]

THE END

FASHION *(1845)*

ANNA CORA MOWATT

Like many Americans, Anna Cora Ogden's (1819–1870) first acquaintance with the actual theater was by negation. Born in Bordeaux, France, on September 12, 1819, to Americans Samuel Gouverneur and Eliza Lewis Ogden, Anna did not even step foot on her "native" soil until 1826. Her family on their return attended the Park Theatre in New York, but Anna listened to her minister and avoided the wicked stage, much as poor Jonathan does in Tyler's *The Contrast.* Finally persuaded to attend the theater in 1831, Anna saw the great young actress of the day, Fanny Kemble, and was hooked. She wrote plays for her family of five brothers and three sisters and otherwise led the life of a precocious but sheltered young woman whose literary efforts were fostered as part of her domestic education, not encouraged as anything like a profession. But she likely retained the middle-class suspicion of professional actors shared by Americans who had not shaken off seventeenth-century strictures against the stage.

After an elopement at age fifteen with James Mowatt, a lawyer nearly twice her age, she remained under the influence of her family, traveling with her father and stepmother, Julia Fairlie Ogden, to Europe. But Anna—called Lily by her family—had by this time contracted tuberculosis, a disease that would flare up and weaken her at times for much of her adult life. By 1841, having returned to America, Mowatt learned that her husband was financially ruined. Under the guidance of her friend Epes Sargent, a Boston poet and playwright, Anna made the decision to read poems in public for money. Although her idol, Fanny Kemble, was to become famous later as a reader of Shakespeare, it was Anna Mowatt who anticipated this career path for her. And while illness prevented her from making a tour at this time, the experience gave her an opportunity to stand before an audience of strangers and speak out—and Mowatt became, perhaps, the first woman in America to earn money as a public reader.

With health a constant worry and money an even greater one, Mowatt turned to writing—novels, advice books, articles—anything to turn a dollar. At the same time, she began being hypnotized as a way of curing or ameliorating her physical pain, often going into trancelike states for days or even, in one instance, months. In 1845, her adviser and sometime hypnotist Epes Sargent pressed her to write a play for the professional stage. Although she had written plays for amateur performance, this was a big step. The result was a text that was accepted by the Park management; the premiere of *Fashion* took place on March 26, 1845.

The theater's owner, John Jacob Astor, the wealthy fur magnate whose name, as Herman Melville's narrator in "Bartleby, the Scrivener" remarks, "rings like unto bullion," ordered the third tier closed to prostitutes and filled with collegians instead. The audience was a Who's Who of literary dignitaries, including Edgar A. Poe, Mordecai M. Noah, Nathaniel Parker Willis, and William T. Porter. With a successful opening night and a twenty-performance run, Mowatt suddenly was lifted from the obscurity of a "private woman," as Mary Kelley has named the "literary domestic" of the period, to the "public stage." Her husband, whose eyesight prohibited him from engaging in full-time legal work, became her manager and wrote her contracts. But with renewed financial pressures at home, Mowatt was forced once more to put scruples aside. She decided to become not only a professional playwright but an actress as well. On June 6, 1845, she appeared with the actor W. H. Crisp (who had played Jolimaitre in *Fashion*) as Pauline Deschappelles in Edward Bulwer-Lytton's *The Lady of Lyons*. As instant a success in acting as she had been as a playwright, Anna Cora Mowatt over the next eight years became one of the best-known and best-loved of American actresses for her portrayals of virtuous young women.

Following the death of James Mowatt, Anna retired from the stage and returned to writing. Her *Autobiography* appeared in 1854, and that same year she married a Richmond newspaperman, William Foushee Ritchie. As Anna Cora Ritchie, she wrote three long stories, published together in 1856 as *Mimic Life; or, Life Behind the Curtain*. Both a defense of women who act and a trenchant critique of stage practices that exploit the theater's underclass, Mowatt's stories, along with her autobiography, serve as some of the best contemporary texts for understanding the conflict between romantic aspirations and often cruel realities of the dramatic life. In one story in particular, the somewhat autobiographical "Stella," Mowatt attacks the common prejudice that actresses are sexually promiscuous. Indeed, one of the underlying themes of her own life story is that a woman of social prominence can act and by careful choice of roles and company keep her virtue intact. As a moralist who supported the stage and criticized the exploitation of financially needy women, she must have felt the sting of irony when she learned that Ritchie was having extramarital sex with slave women in Virginia. She left him, moved to England, and died there in 1870.

Although she published and had produced one other play, *Armand*, in 1847, Mowatt's fame as an author has been sustained by *Fashion*. Like Tyler, she takes as her purview life among the elite—or as Mrs. Tiffany butchers the word, the *"ee-light."* Unlike Charlotte and Letitia, who have been raised with wealth, Mowatt's Tiffany family has just acquired it and does not know what to do with it. Following a social trend whereby men through their work become increasingly isolated—and by the evidence of this play, alienated—from the family domestic space, Mowatt shows how power to spend rests in the hands of women. This process produces an imbalanced moral universe, at least for those unaccustomed to wealth; at any rate, Mrs. Tiffany's profligate spending habits and her ludicrous purchase of culture are seen as a direct cause of the family's threatened ruin. However, the physical and moral absence of Mr. Tiffany, his ineffectual response to his wife's unconscious buying, and his willingness to commit crime in order to sustain her in her illusion show that the blame can go much further than one woman's desire to make a splash in the upper class. The moral family is a united one.

Much of the broad comedy stems from the malapropisms of Mrs. Tiffany, but the play is rife with farcical intrigue. Drawing on her own knowledge of French culture and language (as a young child, she spoke French almost exclusively), Mowatt has created in the maid Millinette the most active and interesting character in the play. Although she must dissemble in order to keep her job, Millinette is also a moral force, seeking to execute her plans in such a way that no one is humiliated. Like the scheming servants in the plays of Plautus, she pulls the strings to get the upper-class characters to act according to her will, but unlike them, she has more in mind than simply her own gain. Where the tutelary heroine, Gertrude, is a static and rather flat character, a so-called "walking lady" part—Mowatt herself disliked having to play her—Millinette is vibrant, clever, and active, a consummate actress and stage manager. As with the real stage, nothing goes quite as planned, but at the end, no one seriously blames Millinette for the errors.

Two other characters have stage antecedents. The Yankee, Trueman, has his origins in the country manners and directness of Jonathan but is no longer a buffoon. In this play, the Yankee is not only straighttalking, he is rich; this combination gives him the authority to see the pretensions of the Tiffanys as humbug. Trueman criticizes his old friend

Antony for giving in to his wife's profligacy and for allowing his clerk, Snobson, to blackmail him into selling his daughter, Seraphina, into marriage; at the same time, he makes his granddaughter, Gertrude, face up to the lies she perpetrates in a misguided effort to expose the truth of Jolimaitre's intentions. As Francis Hodge observes, this revised Yankee meets the expectations of a changing audience in the American theater; Trueman retains the country ways of his stage predecessors, just having "changed his clothes and improved his speech."

The servant Zeke clearly is a figure modeled on previous and contemporary images of blacks on stage, most notoriously on minstrel show characters who twist words and put on pretensions of intellectuality. But Mowatt also shows that Zeke shares some qualities with Millinette; while not an active schemer, Zeke, suddenly rechristened Adolph by Mrs. Tiffany, knows that his job depends on pleasing his employer. He recognizes that Mrs. Tiffany's demands are outrageous, but his efforts to satisfy her only serve to accentuate the comedy of enacted style and class. There is just a touch of the trickster figure in Zeke, not fully realized—after all, he was first played by a white actor in blackface—and some small recognition from the playwright that a servant in Zeke's situation would be at a terrible disadvantage in trying to maintain his dignity. While he may remind us uncomfortably of the "race" humor of the later *Amos 'n' Andy* radio and television series, Zeke can also be seen in the context of the 1840s as an advancement in the portrayal of African-American characters by white playwrights.

As Karen Halttunen explains, the sentimental critique in this comedy of manners returns to an ideology more popular in Tyler's time than Mowatt's, the worry over corruption by luxury. Yet she also notes the deft way Mowatt lampoons the rituals of her middle class audience without forcing them to identify with the Tiffanys. In terms of popularity on stage and continued relevance, *Fashion* is the most successful play by a female American playwright in the nineteenth century.

SELECTED BIBLIOGRAPHY

Abramson, Doris. " 'The New Path': Nineteenth-Century American Women Playwrights." In *Modern American Drama: The Female Canon*, edited by June Schlueter, 38–51. Rutherford, N.J.: Fairleigh Dickinson University Press, 1990.

Barnes, Eric Wollencott. *The Lady of Fashion: The Life and Theatre of Anna Cora Mowatt*. New York: Scribner's, 1954.

Gillespie, Patti P. "Anna Cora Ogden Mowatt Ritchie's *Fairy Fingers*: From Eugène Scribe's?" *Text and Performance Quarterly* 2 (1989): 125–34.

Halttunen, Karen. *Confidence Men and Painted Women: A Study of Middle-Class Culture in America, 1830–1870*, 153–57. New Haven: Yale University Press, 1982.

Havens, Daniel F. "Cultural Maturity and the Flowering of Native American Social Comedy: Mowatt's *Fashion* (1845)." In *The Columbian Muse of Comedy: The Development of a Native Tradition in Early American Social Comedy, 1787–1845*, 129–48. Carbondale: Southern Illinois University Press, 1973.

Hodge, Francis. *Yankee Theatre: The Image of America on the Stage, 1825–1850*, 260–61. Austin: University of Texas Press, 1964. On Trueman character.

Hutchisson, James M. "Poe, Anna Cora Mowatt, and T. Tennyson Twinkle." *Studies in the American Renaissance 1993*: 245–54.

Jefferson, Joseph. *Autobiography*, 138–39. New York: Century, 1890. Criticism of Mowatt as actress.

Johnson, Claudia. *American Actress: Perspective on the Nineteenth Century*, 120–31. Chicago: Nelson-Hall, 1984.

Kelley, Mary. *Private Woman, Public Stage: Literary Domesticity in Nineteenth-Century America*. New York: Oxford University Press, 1984.

Meserve, Walter J. *Heralds of Promise: The Drama of the American People During the Age of Jackson, 1829–1849*, 127–34. New York: Greenwood, 1986.

Moody, Richard. *America Takes the Stage: Romanticism in American Drama and Theatre, 1750–1900*, 68–69, 125–26. Bloomington: Indiana University Press.

Mowatt, Anna Cora. *Autobiography of an Actress; or, Eight Years on the Stage.* Boston: Ticknor, Reed, and Fields, 1854.

———. *Mimic Life; or, Before and Behind the Curtain. A Series of Narratives.* Boston: Ticknor and Fields, 1856. Stories published under Anna Cora Ritchie.

Poe, Edgar A. "Anna Cora Mowatt." *Essays and Reviews*, edited by G. R. Thompson, 1137–41. New York: Library of America, 1984. Part of Poe's "The Literati of New York City" series.

———. "The New Comedy by Mrs. Mowatt." *Broadway Journal* 1 (March 29, 1845): 203–5; and "Prospects of the Drama—Mrs. Mowatt's Comedy." *Broadway Journal* 1 (April 5, 1845): 219–20. Reprinted as "Mrs. Mowatt's *Fashion*" and "Mrs. Mowatt's Comedy Reconsidered." In *The American Theatre as Seen by Its Critics*, edited by Montrose J. Moses and John Mason Brown. 1934; New York: Cooper Square, 1967, 59–66.

Reviews of *Fashion*. In *The Dawning of American Drama: American Dramatic Criticism, 1746–1915*, edited by Jürgen C. Wolter, 114–18, 120. Westport, Conn.: Greenwood, 1993. Selected and abridged.

Richards, Jeffrey H. "Chastity and the Stage in Mowatt's 'Stella.'" *Studies in American Fiction* 24 (1996): 87–100.

Richardson, Gary A. "High Society: Mowatt's *Fashion*." In *American Drama from the Colonial Period through World War I: A Critical History*, 99–102. New York: Twayne, 1993.

Thompson, David W. "Early Actress-Readers: Mowatt, Kemble, and Cushman." In *Performance of Literature in Historical Perspectives*, edited by David W. Thompson, 629–50. Lanham, Md.: University Press of America, 1983.

F A S H I O N ;

OR

L I F E I N N E W Y O R K .

A Comedy,

IN FIVE ACTS.

by Anna Cora Mowatt

"Howe'er it be—it seems to me
    'Tis only noble to be good;
Kind hearts are more than coronets,
    And simple faith than Norman bloood."
               TENNYSON.[1]

PREFACE

TO THE LONDON EDITION.

The Comedy of *Fashion* was intended as a good-natured satire upon some of the follies incident to a new country, where foreign dress sometimes passes for gold, where the vanities rather than the virtues of other lands are too often imitated, and where the stamp of *fashion* gives currency even to the coinage of vice.

The reception with which the Comedy was favoured proves that the picture represented was not a highly exaggerated one.

It was first produced at the Park Theatre, New York, in March, 1845.

The splendid manner in which the play was put upon the stage, and the combined efforts of an extremely talented company, ensured it a long continued success. It was afterwards received with the same indulgence in all the principal cities of the United States, for which the authoress is doubtless indebted to the proverbial gallantry of Americans to a countrywoman.

A. C. M.

London, January, 1850.

DRAMATIS PERSONAE.

ADAM TRUEMAN, *a Farmer from Catteraugus.*
COUNT JOLIMAITRE, *a fashionable European Importation.*
COLONEL HOWARD, *an Officer in the U.S. Army.*
MR. TIFFANY, *a New York Merchant.*
T. TENNYSON TWINKLE, *a Modern Poet.*
AUGUSTUS FOGG, *a Drawing Room Appendage.*
SNOBSON, *a rare species of Confidential Clerk.*
ZEKE, *a colored Servant.*

MRS. TIFFANY, *a Lady who imagines herself fashionable.*
PRUDENCE, *a Maiden Lady of a certain age.*
MILLINETTE, *a French Lady's Maid.*
GERTRUDE, *a Governess.*
SERAPHINA TIFFANY, *a Belle.*
            Ladies and Gentlemen of the Ball Room.

COSTUMES.[2]

ADAM TRUEMAN.—First dress: A farmer's rough overcoat, coarse blue trousers, heavy boots, broad-brimmed hat, dark coloured neckerchief, stout walking stick, large bandanna tied loosely around his neck.—Second dress: Dark grey old-fashioned coat, black and yellow waistcoat, trousers as before.—Third dress: Black old-fashioned dress coat, black trousers, white vest, white cravat.

COUNT JOLIMAITRE.—First dress: Dark frock coat, light blue trousers, patent leather boots, gay coloured vest and scarf, profusion of jewellery, light overcoat.—Second dress: Full evening dress; last scene, travelling cap and cloak.

MR. TIFFANY.—First dress: Dark coat, vest, and trousers.—Second dress: Full evening dress.

MR. TWINKLE.—First dress: Green frock coat, white vest and trousers, green and white scarf.—Second dress: Full evening dress.

MR. FOGG.—First dress: Entire black suit.—Second dress: Full evening dress, same colour.

SNOBSON.—First dress: Blue Albert coat with brass buttons, yellow vest, red and black cravat, broad plaid trousers.—Second dress: Evening dress.

COL. HOWARD.—First dress: Blue undress frock coat and cap, white trousers.—Second dress: Full military uniform.

ZEKE.—Red and blue livery, cocked hat, &c.

MRS. TIFFANY.—First dress: Extravagant modern dress.—Second dress: Hat, feathers, and mantle, with the above.—Third dress: Morning dress.—Fourth dress: Rich ball dress.

SERAPHINA.—First dress: Rich modern dress, lady's tarpaulin on one side of head.—Second dress: Morning dress.—Third dress: Handsome ball dress, profusion of ornaments and flowers.—Fourth dress: Bonnet and mantle.

GERTRUDE.—First dress: White muslin.—Second dress: Ball dress, very simple.

MILLINETTE.—Lady's Maid's dress, very gay.

PRUDENCE.—Black satin, very narrow in the skirt, tight sleeves, white muslin apron, neckerchief of the same, folded over bosom, old-fashioned cap, high top and broad frill, and red ribbons.

FASHION.

ACT I

SCENE 1: *A splendid Drawing Room in the House of* MRS. TIFFANY. *Open folding doors, discovering a Conservatory. On either side glass windows down to the ground. Doors on right and left. Mirror, couches, ottomans, a table with albums, &c., beside it an arm chair.* MILLINETTE *dusting furniture, &c.* ZEKE *in a dashing livery, scarlet coat, &c.*

ZEKE: Dere's a coat to take de eyes ob all Broadway! Ah! Missy, it am de fixins dat make de natural *born* gemman. A libery for ever! Dere's a pair ob insuppressibles to 'stonish de colored population.

MILLINETTE: Oh, *oui*, Monsieur Zeke. [*Very politely.*] I not *comprend* one word he say! [*Aside.*]

ZEKE: I tell 'ee what, Missy, I'm 'stordinary glad to find dis a bery 'spectabul like situation! Now as you've made de acquaintance ob dis here family, and dere, you've had a supernumerary advantage ob me—seeing dat I only receibed my appointment dis morning. What I wants to know is your publicated opinion, privately expressed, ob de domestic circle.

MILLINETTE: You mean vat *espèce*, vat kind of personnes are Monsieur and Madame Tiffany? Ah! Monsieur is not de same ting as Madame,—not at all.

ZEKE: Well, I s'pose he ain't altogether.

MILLINETTE: Monsieur is man of business,—Madame is lady of fashion. Monsieur make de money,—Madame spend it. Monsieur nobody at all,—Madame everybody altogether. Ah! Monsieur Zeke, de money is all dat is *necessaire* in dis country to make one lady of fashion. Oh! it is quite anoder ting in *la belle France!*

ZEKE: A bery lucifer explanation. Well, now we've disposed ob de heads ob de family, who come next?

MILLINETTE: First, dere is Mademoiselle Seraphina Tiffany. Mademoiselle is not at all one proper *personne*. Mademoiselle Seraphina is one coquette. Dat is not de mode in *la belle France*; de ladies, dere, never learn *la coquetrie* until dey do get one husband.

ZEKE: I tell 'ee what, Missy, I disreprobate dat proceeding altogeder!

MILLINETTE: Vait! I have not tell you all *la famille* yet. Dere is Ma'mselle Prudence—Madame's sister, one very *bizarre* personne. Den dere is

Ma'mselle Gertrude, but she not anybody at all; she only teach Mademoiselle Seraphina *la musique*.

ZEKE: Well now, Missy, what's your own special defunctions?

MILLINETTE: I not understand, Monsieur Zeke.

ZEKE: Den I'll amplify. What's de nature ob your exclusive services?

MILLINETTE: *Ah, oui! je comprend.* I am Madame's *femme de chambre*—her lady's maid, Monsieur Zeke. I teach Madame *les modes de Paris,* and Madame set de fashion for all New York. You see, Monsieur Zeke, dat it is me, *moi-même,* dat do lead de fashion for all de American *beau monde!*

ZEKE: Yah! yah! yah! I hab de idea by de heel. Well now, p'raps you can 'lustrify my officials?

MILLINETTE: Vat you will have to do? Oh! much tings, much tings. You vait on de table,—you tend de door,—you clean de boots,—you run de errands,—you drive de carriage,—you rub de horses,—you take care of de flowers,—you carry de water,—you help cook de dinner,—you wash de dishes,—and den you always remember to do everyting I tell you to!

ZEKE: Wheugh, am dat *all?*

MILLINETTE: All I can tink of now. To-day is Madame's day of reception, and all her grand friends do make her one *petite* visit. You mind run fast ven de bell do ring.

ZEKE: Run? If it wasn't for dese superfluminous trimmings, I tell 'ee what, Missy, I'd run—

MRS. TIFFANY: [*Outside.*] Millinette!

MILLINETTE: Here comes Madame! You better go, Monsieur Zeke.

ZEKE: Look ahea, Massa Zeke, doesn't dis open rich! [*Aside.*] [*Exit.*]

[*Enter* MRS. TIFFANY, *dressed in the most extravagant height of fashion.*]

MRS. TIFFANY: Is everything in order, Millinette? Ah! very elegant, very elegant indeed! There is a *jenny-says-quoi*[3] look about this furniture,—an air of fashion and gentility perfectly bewitching. Is there not, Millinette?

MILLINETTE: Oh, oui, Madame!

MRS. TIFFANY: But where is Miss Seraphina? It is twelve o'clock; our visitors will be pouring in, and she has not made her appearance. But I hear that nothing is more fashionable than to keep people waiting.—None but vulgar persons pay any attention to punctuality. Is it not so, Millinette?

MILLINETTE: Quite *comme il faut.*⁴—Great personnes always do make little personnes wait, Madame.

MRS. TIFFANY: This mode of receiving visitors only upon one specified day of the week is a most convenient custom! It saves the trouble of keeping the house continually in order and of being always dressed. I flatter myself that I was the first to introduce it amongst the New York *ee-light.* You are quite sure that it is strictly a Parisian mode, Millinette?

MILLINETTE: Oh, *oui,* Madame; entirely *mode de Paris.*

MRS. TIFFANY: This girl is worth her weight in gold. [*Aside.*] Millinette, how do you say *arm-chair* in French?

MILLINETTE: *Fauteuil,* Madame.

MRS. TIFFANY: *Fo-tool!* That has a foreign—an out-of-the-wayish sound that is perfectly charming—and so genteel! There is something about our American words decidedly vulgar. *Fowtool!* how refined. *Fowtool! Arm-chair!* what a difference!

MILLINETTE: Madame have one charmante pronunciation. *Fowtool!* [*Mimicking aside.*] Charmante, Madame!

MRS. TIFFANY: Do you think so, Millinette? Well, I believe I have. But a woman of refinement and of fashion can always accommodate herself to everything foreign! And a week's study of that invaluable work—*"French without a Master,"* has made me quite at home in the court language of Europe! But where is the new valet? I'm rather sorry that he is black, but to obtain a white American for a domestic is almost impossible; and they call this a free country! What did you say was the name of this new servant, Millinette?

MILLINETTE: He do say his name is Monsieur Zeke.

MRS. TIFFANY: Ezekiel, I suppose. Zeke! Dear me, such a vulgar name will compromise the dignity of the whole family. Can you not suggest something more aristocratic, Millinette? Something *French!*

MILLINETTE: *Oh, oui,* Madame; *Adolph* is one very fine name.

MRS. TIFFANY: A-dolph! Charming! Ring the bell, Millinette! [MILLINETTE *rings the bell.*] I will change his name immediately, besides giving him a few directions.

[*Enter* ZEKE. MRS. TIFFANY *addresses him with great dignity.*]

Your name, I hear, is *Ezekiel.*—I consider it too plebeian an appellation to be uttered in my presence. In future you are called A-dolph. Don't reply,—never interrupt me when I am speaking. A-dolph, as my guests arrive, I desire that you will inquire the name of every person, and then announce it in a loud, clear tone. *That* is the fashion in Paris. [MILLINETTE *retires up the stage.*]

ZEKE: Consider de office discharged, Missus. [*Speaking very loudly.*]

MRS. TIFFANY: Silence! Your business is to obey and not to talk.

ZEKE: I'm dumb, Missus!

MRS. TIFFANY: [*Pointing up stage.*] A-dolph, place that *fowtool* behind me.

ZEKE: [*Looking about him.*] I hab'nt got dat far in de dictionary yet. No matter, a genus gets his learning by nature. [*Takes up the table and places it behind* MRS. TIFFANY, *then expresses in dumb show great satisfaction.* MRS. TIFFANY, *as she goes to sit, discovers the mistake.*]

MRS. TIFFANY: You dolt! Where have you lived not to know that *fowtool* is the French for *arm-chair?* What ignorance! Leave the room this instant.

[MRS. TIFFANY *draws forward an arm-chair and sits.* MILLINETTE *comes forward suppressing her merriment at* ZEKE's *mistake and removes the table.*]

ZEKE: Dem's de defects ob not having a libery education.   [*Exit.*]

[PRUDENCE *peeps in.*]

PRUDENCE: I wonder if any of the fine folks have come yet. Not a soul,—I knew they hadn't. There's Betsy all alone. [*Walks in.*] Sister Betsy!

MRS. TIFFANY: Prudence! how many times have I desired you to call me *Elizabeth? Betsy* is the height of vulgarity.

PRUDENCE: Oh! I forgot. Dear me, how spruce we do look here, to be sure,—everything in first rate style now, Betsy. [MRS. TIFFANY *looks at her angrily.*] *Elizabeth* I mean. Who would have thought, when you and I were sitting behind that little mahogany-colored counter, in Canal Street, making up flashy hats and caps—

MRS. TIFFANY: Prudence, what *do* you mean? Millinette, leave the room.

MILLINETTE: Oui, Madame.

[MILLINETTE *pretends to arrange the books upon a side table, but lingers to listen.*]

PRUDENCE: But I always predicted it,—I always told you so, Betsy,—I always said you were destined to rise above your station!

MRS. TIFFANY: Prudence! Prudence! have I not told you that—

PRUDENCE: No, Betsy, it was *I* that told *you*, when we used to buy our silks and ribbons of Mr. Antony Tiffany—*"talking Tony,"* you know we used to call him, and when you always put on the finest bonnet in our shop to go to his,—and when you staid so long smiling and chattering with him, I always told you that *something* would grow out of it—and didn't it?

MRS. TIFFANY: Millinette, send Seraphina here instantly. Leave the room.

MILLINETTE: Oui, Madame. So dis Americaine lady of fashion vas one *milliner?* Oh, vat a fine country for *les merchandes des modes!* I shall send for all my relation by de next packet! [*Aside.*]

[*Exit* MILLINETTE.]

MRS. TIFFANY: Prudence! never let me hear you mention this subject again. Forget what we *have* been, it is enough to remember that we *are* of the *upper ten thousand!*

[PRUDENCE *goes up left and sits down. Enter* SERAPHINA, *very extravagantly dressed.*]

MRS. TIFFANY: How bewitchingly you look, my dear! Does Millinette say that that head dress is strictly Parisian?

SERAPHINA: Oh yes, Mamma, all the rage! They call it a *lady's tarpaulin,* and it is the exact pattern of one worn by the Princess Clementina[5] at the last court ball.

MRS. TIFFANY: Now, Seraphina my dear, don't be too particular in your attention to gentlemen not eligible. There is Count Jolimaitre, decidedly the most fashionable foreigner in town,—and so refined,—so much accustomed to associate with the first nobility in his own country that he can hardly tolerate the vulgarity of Americans in general. You may devote yourself to him. Mrs. Proudacre is dying to become acquainted with him. By the by, if she or her daughters should happen to drop in, be sure you don't introduce them to the Count. It is not the fashion in Paris to introduce—Millinette told me so.

[*Enter* ZEKE.]

ZEKE: [*In a very loud voice.*] Mister T. Tennyson Twinkle!

MRS. TIFFANY: Show him up.   [*Exit* ZEKE.]

PRUDENCE: I must be running away! [*Going.*]

MRS. TIFFANY: Mr. T. Tennyson Twinkle—a very literary young man and a sweet poet! It is all the rage to patronize poets! Quick, Seraphina, hand me that magazine.—Mr. Twinkle writes for it.

[SERAPHINA *hands the magazine,* MRS. TIFFANY *seats herself in an arm-chair and opens the book.*]

PRUDENCE: [*Returning.*] There's Betsy trying to make out that reading without her spectacles. [*Takes a pair of spectacles out of her pocket and hands them to* MRS. TIFFANY.] There, Betsy, I knew you were going to ask for them. Ah! they're a blessing when one is growing old!

MRS. TIFFANY: What do you mean, Prudence? A woman of fashion *never* grows old! Age is always out of fashion.

PRUDENCE: Oh, dear! what a delightful thing it is to be fashionable.

[*Exit* PRUDENCE. MRS. TIFFANY *resumes her seat.*]

[*Enter* TWINKLE. *Salutes* SERAPHINA.]

TWINKLE: Fair Seraphina! the sun itself grows dim,
                Unless you aid his light and shine on him!

SERAPHINA: Ah! Mr. Twinkle, there is no such thing as answering you.

TWINKLE: [*Looks around and perceives* MRS. TIFFANY.] The "New Monthly Vernal Galaxy." Reading my verses by all that's charming! Sensible woman! I won't interrupt her. [*Aside.*]

MRS. TIFFANY: [*Rising and coming forward.*] Ah! Mr. Twinkle, is that you? I was perfectly *abimé*[6] at the perusal of your very *distingué*[7] verses.

TWINKLE: I am overwhelmed, Madam. Permit me. [*Taking the magazine.*] Yes, they do read tolerably. And you must take into consideration, ladies, the rapidity with which they were written. Four minutes and a half by the stop watch! The true test of a poet is the *velocity* with which he composes. Really they do look very prettily, and they read tolerably—*quite* tolerably—*very* tolerably,—especially the first verse. [*Reads.*] "To Seraphina T——."

SERAPHINA: Oh! Mr. Twinkle!

TWINKLE: [*Reads.*] "Around my heart"—

MRS. TIFFANY: How touching! Really, Mr. Twinkle, quite tender!

TWINKLE: [*Recommencing.*] "Around my heart"—

MRS. TIFFANY: Oh, I must tell you, Mr. Twinkle! I heard the other day that poets were the aristocrats of literature. That's one reason I like them, for I do dote on all aristocracy!

TWINKLE: Oh, Madam, how flattering! Now pray lend me your ears! [*Reads.*]

"Around my heart thou weavest"—

SERAPHINA: That is such a *sweet* commencement, Mr. Twinkle!

TWINKLE: I wish she wouldn't interrupt me! [*Aside.*] [*Reads.*] "Around my heart thou weavest a spell"—

MRS. TIFFANY: Beautiful! But excuse me one moment, while I say a word to Seraphina! Don't be too affable, my dear! Poets are very ornamental appendages to the drawing room, but they are always as poor as their own verses. They don't make eligible husbands! [*Aside to* SERAPHINA.]

TWINKLE: Confound their interruptions! [*Aside.*] My dear Madam, unless you pay the utmost attention you cannot catch the ideas. Are you ready? Well, now you shall hear it to the end! [*Reads.*]—

"Around my heart thou weavest a spell
Whose"—

[*Enter* ZEKE.]

ZEKE: Mister Augustus Fogg! A bery misty lookin young gemman! [*Aside.*]

MRS. TIFFANY: Show him up, Adolph!   [*Exit* ZEKE.]

TWINKLE: This is too much!

SERAPHINA: Exquisite verses, Mr. Twinkle,—exquisite!

TWINKLE: Ah, lovely Seraphina! your smile of approval transports me to the summit of Olympus.

SERAPHINA: Then I must frown, for I would not send you so far away.

TWINKLE: Enchantress! It's all over with her. [*Aside.*] [*Retire up and converse.*]

MRS. TIFFANY: Mr. Fogg belongs to one of our oldest families,—to be sure he is the most difficult person in the world to entertain, for he never takes the trouble to talk, and never notices anything or anybody,—but then I hear that nothing is considered so vulgar as to betray any emotion, or to attempt to render oneself agreeable!

[*Enter* MR. FOGG, *fashionably attired but in very dark clothes.*]

FOGG: [*Bowing stiffly.*] Mrs. Tiffany, your most obedient. Miss Seraphina, yours. How d'ye do, Twinkle?

MRS. TIFFANY: Mr. Fogg, how do you do? Fine weather,—delightful, isn't it?

FOGG: I am indifferent to weather, Madam.

MRS. TIFFANY: Been to the opera, Mr. Fogg? I hear that the *bow monde* make their *debutt* there every evening.

FOGG: I consider operas a bore, Madam.

SERAPHINA: [*Advancing.*] You must hear Mr. Twinkle's verses, Mr. Fogg!

FOGG: I am indifferent to verses, Miss Seraphina.

SERAPHINA: But Mr. Twinkle's verses are addressed to me!

TWINKLE: Now pay attention, Fogg! [*Reads.*]—

> "Around my heart thou weavest a spell
> Whose magic I"—

[*Enter* ZEKE.]

ZEKE: Mister—No, he say he aint no Mister—

TWINKLE:

> "Around my heart thou weavest a spell
> Whose magic I can never tell!"

MRS. TIFFANY: Speak in a loud, clear tone, A-dolph!

TWINKLE: This is terrible!

ZEKE: Mister Count Jolly-made-her!

MRS. TIFFANY: Count Jolimaitre! Good gracious! Zeke, Zeke—A-dolph I mean.—Dear me, what a mistake! [*Aside.*] Set that chair out of the way,—put that table back. Seraphina, my dear, are you all in order? Dear me! dear me! Your dress is so tumbled! [*Arranges her dress.*] What are you grinning at? [*To* ZEKE.] Beg the Count to *honor* us by walking up! [*Exit* ZEKE.] Seraphina, my dear [*aside to her*], remember now what I told you about the Count. He is a man of the highest,—good gracious! I am so flurried; and nothing is so ungenteel as agitation! what will the Count think! Mr. Twinkle, pray stand out of the way! Seraphina, my dear, place yourself on my right! Mr. Fogg, the conservatory— beautiful flowers,—pray amuse yourself in the conservatory.

FOGG: I am indifferent to flowers, Madam.

MRS. TIFFANY: Dear me! the man stands right in the way,—just where the Count must make his *entray!* [*Aside.*] Mr. Fogg,—pray—

[*Enter* COUNT JOLIMAITRE, *very dashingly dressed, wears a moustache.*]

MRS. TIFFANY: Oh, Count, this unexpected honor—

SERAPHINA: Count, this inexpressible pleasure—

COUNT: Beg you won't mention it, Madam! Miss Seraphina, your most devoted!

MRS. TIFFANY: What condescension! [*Aside.*] Count, may I take the liberty to introduce—Good gracious! I forgot. [*Aside.*] Count, I was about to remark that we never introduce in America. All our fashions are foreign, Count.

[TWINKLE, *who has stepped forward to be introduced, shows great indignation.*]

COUNT: Excuse me, Madam, our fashions have grown antediluvian before you Americans discover their existence. You are lamentably behind the age—lamentably! 'Pon my honor, a foreigner of refinement finds great difficulty in existing in this provincial atmosphere.

MRS. TIFFANY: How dreadful, Count! I am very much concerned. If there is anything which I can do, Count—

SERAPHINA: Or I, Count, to render your situation less deplorable—

COUNT: Ah! I find but one redeeming charm in America—the superlative loveliness of the feminine portion of creation—and the wealth of their obliging papas. [*Aside.*]

MRS. TIFFANY: How flattering! Ah! Count, I am afraid you will turn the head of my simple girl here. She is a perfect child of nature, Count.

COUNT: Very possibly, for though you American women are quite charming, yet, demme, there's a deal of native rust to rub off!

MRS. TIFFANY: *Rust?* Good gracious, Count! where do you find any rust? [*Looking about the room.*]

COUNT: How very unsophisticated!

MRS. TIFFANY: Count, I am so much ashamed,—pray excuse me! Although a lady of large fortune, and one, Count, who can boast of the highest connections, I blush to confess that I have never travelled,—while you, Count, I presume are at home in all the courts of Europe.

COUNT: *Courts?* Eh? Oh, yes, Madam, very true, I believe I am pretty well known in some of the courts of Europe—*police courts.* [*Aside.*] In a word, Madam, I had seen enough of civilized life—wanted to refresh myself by a sight of barbarous countries and customs—had my choice between the Sandwich Islands[8] and New York—chose New York!

MRS. TIFFANY: How complimentary to our country! And, Count, I have no doubt you speak every conceivable language? You talk English like a native.

COUNT: Eh, what? Like a native? Oh, ah, demme, yes, I am something of an Englishman. Passed one year and eight months with the Duke of Wellington, six months with Lord Brougham, two and a half with Count d'Orsay[9]—knew them all more intimately than their best friends—no heroes to me—hadn't a secret from me, I assure you,—*especially of the toilet*. [*Aside.*]

MRS. TIFFANY: Think of that, my dear! Lord Wellington and Duke Broom! [*Aside to* SERAPHINA.]

SERAPHINA: And only think of Count d'Orsay, Mamma! [*Aside to* MRS. TIFFANY.] I am so wild to see Count d'Orsay!

COUNT: Oh! a mere man milliner. Very little refinement out of Paris? Why at the very last dinner given at Lord—Lord Knowswho, would you believe it, Madam, there was an individual present who wore a *black* cravat and took *soup twice!*

MRS. TIFFANY: How shocking! the sight of him would have spoilt my appetite! Think what a great man he must be, my dear, to despise lords and counts in that way. [*Aside to* SERAPHINA.] I must leave them together. [*Aside.*] Mr. Twinkle, your arm. I have some really very *foreign exotics* to show you.

TWINKLE: I fly at your command. I wish all her exotics were blooming in their native soil! [*Aside, and glancing at the* COUNT.]

MRS. TIFFANY: Mr. Fogg, will you accompany us? My conservatory is well worthy a visit. It cost an immense sum of money.

FOGG: I am indifferent to conservatories, Madam; flowers are such a bore!

MRS. TIFFANY: I shall take no refusal. Conservatories are all the rage, —I could not exist without mine! Let me show you,—let me show you.

[*Places her arm through* MR. FOGG'S, *without his consent. Exeunt* MRS. TIFFANY, FOGG, *and* TWINKLE *into the conservatory, where they are seen walking about.*]

SERAPHINA: America, then, has no charms for you, Count?

COUNT: Excuse me,—some exceptions. I find you, for instance, particularly charming! Can't say I admire your country. Ah! if you had ever breathed the exhilarating air of Paris, ate creams at Tortoni's, dined at the Café Royale, or if you had lived in London—felt at home at St. James's, and every afternoon driven a couple of Lords and a Duchess through Hyde Park, you would find America—where you have no kings, queens, lords, nor ladies—insupportable!

SERAPHINA: Not while there was a Count in it?

[*Enter* ZEKE, *very indignant.*]

ZEKE: Where's de Missus?

[*Enter* MRS. TIFFANY, FOGG, *and* TWINKLE, *from the conservatory.*]

MRS. TIFFANY: Whom do you come to announce, A-dolph?

ZEKE: He said he wouldn't trust me—no, not eben wid so much as his name; so I wouldn't trust him up stairs, den he ups wid *his stick* and I *cuts mine.*

MRS. TIFFANY: Some of Mr. Tiffany's vulgar acquaintances. I shall die with shame. [*Aside.*] A-dolph, inform him that I am *not at home.*

[*Exit* ZEKE.]

My nerves are so shattered, I am ready to sink. Mr. Twinkle, that *fow tool,* if you please!

TWINKLE: What? What do you wish, Madam?

MRS. TIFFANY: The ignorance of these Americans! [*Aside.*] Count, may I trouble you? That *fow tool,* if you please!

COUNT: She's not talking English, nor French, but I suppose it's American. [*Aside.*]

TRUEMAN: [*Outside.*] Not at home!

ZEKE: No, Sar—Missus say she's not at home.

TRUEMAN: Out of the way you grinning nigger!

[*Enter* ADAM TRUEMAN, *dressed as a farmer, a stout cane in his hand, his boots covered with dust.* ZEKE *jumps out of his way as he enters.*] [*Exit* ZEKE.]

TRUEMAN: Where's this woman that's not *at home* in her own house? May I be shot if I wonder at it! I shouldn't think she'd ever feel *at home* in such a show-box as this! [*Looking round.*]

MRS. TIFFANY: What a plebeian looking old farmer! I wonder who he is? [*Aside.*] Sir—[*advancing very agitatedly*] what do you mean, Sir, by this *ow*dacious conduct? How dare you intrude yourself into my parlor? Do you know who I am, Sir? [*With great dignity.*] You are in the presence of Mrs. Tiffany, Sir!

TRUEMAN: Antony's wife, eh? Well now, I might have guessed that—ha! ha! ha! for I see you make it a point to carry half your husband's shop upon your back! No matter; that's being a good helpmate—

for he carried the whole of it once in a pack on his own shoulders
—now you bear a share!

MRS. TIFFANY: How dare you, you impertinent, *ow*dacious, ignorant old
man! It's all an invention. You're talking of somebody else. What
will the Count think? [*Aside.*]

TRUEMAN: Why, I thought folks had better manners in the city! This is
a civil welcome for your husband's old friend, and after my coming
all the way from Catteraugus[10] to see you and yours! First a grinning
nigger tricked out in scarlet regimentals—

MRS. TIFFANY: Let me tell you, Sir, that liveries are all the fashion!

TRUEMAN: The fashion, are they? To make men wear the *badge of
servitude* in a free land,—that's the fashion, is it? Hurrah, for re-
publican simplicity! I will venture to say now, that you have your
coat of arms too!

MRS. TIFFANY: Certainly, Sir; you can see it on the panels of my *voyture.*[11]

TRUEMAN: Oh! no need of that. I know what your escutcheon must be!
A bandbox *rampant* with a bonnet *couchant,* and a pedlar's pack
passant?[12] Ha, ha, ha! that shows both houses united!

MRS. TIFFANY: Sir! you are most profoundly ignorant.—what do you
mean by this insolence, Sir? How shall I get rid of him? [*Aside.*]

TRUEMAN: [*Looking at* SERAPHINA.] I hope that is not Gertrude!
[*Aside.*]

MRS. TIFFANY: Sir, I'd have you know that—Seraphina, my child, walk
with the gentlemen into the conservatory. [*Exeunt* SERAPHINA,
TWINKLE, FOGG *into conservatory.*] Count Jolimaitre, pray make due
allowances for the errors of this rustic! I do assure you, Count—
[*Whispers to him.*]

TRUEMAN: Count! She calls that critter with a shoe brush over his
mouth, Count! To look at him, I should have thought he was a
tailor's walking advertisement! [*Aside.*]

COUNT: [*Addressing* TRUEMAN *whom he has been inspecting through
his eye-glass.*] Where did you say you belonged, my friend? Dug out
of the ruins of Pompeii, eh?

TRUEMAN: I belong to a land in which I rejoice to find that you are a
foreigner.

COUNT: What a barbarian! He doesn't see the honor I'm doing his coun-
try! Pray, Madam, is it one of the aboriginal inhabitants of the soil?
To what tribe of Indians does he belong—the Pawnee or Choctaw?
Does he carry a tomahawk?

TRUEMAN: Something quite as useful,—do you see that? [*Shaking his
stick.* COUNT *runs behind* MRS. TIFFANY.]

MRS. TIFFANY: Oh, dear! I shall faint! Millinette! [*Approaching.*] Millinette!

[*Enter* MILLINETTE, *without advancing into the room.*]

MILLINETTE: Oui, Madame.

MRS. TIFFANY: A glass of water!   [*Exit* MILLINETTE.]
Sir, I am shocked at your plebeian conduct! This is a gentleman of the highest standing, Sir! He is a *Count*, Sir!

[*Enter* MILLINETTE, *bearing a salver with a glass of water. In advancing towards* MRS. TIFFANY, *she passes in front of the* COUNT, *starts and screams. The* COUNT, *after a start of surprise, regains his composure, plays with his eye glass, and looks perfectly unconcerned.*]

MRS. TIFFANY: What is the matter? What *is* the matter?

MILLINETTE: Noting, noting,—only—[*looks at* COUNT *and turns away her eyes again*] only—noting at all!

TRUEMAN: Don't be afraid, girl! Why, did you never see a live Count before? He's tame,—I dare say your mistress there leads him about by the ears.

MRS. TIFFANY: This is too much! Millinette, send for Mr. Tiffany instantly! [*Crosses to* MILLINETTE, *who is going.*]

MILLINETTE: He just come in, Madame!

TRUEMAN: My old friend! Where is he? Take me to him,—I long to have one more hearty shake of the hand!

MRS. TIFFANY: [*Crosses to him.*] Count, honor me by joining my daughter in the conservatory, I will return immediately.

[COUNT *bows and walks towards conservatory.* MRS. TIFFANY *following part of the way and then returning to* TRUEMAN.]

TRUEMAN: What a Jezebel! These women always play the very devil with a man, and yet I don't believe such a damaged bale of goods as *that* [*Looking at* MRS. TIFFANY.] has smothered the heart of little Antony!

MRS. TIFFANY: This way, Sir, sal vous plait.[13] [*Exit, with great dignity.*]

TRUEMAN: *Sal vous plait.* Ha, ha, ha! We'll see what Fashion has done for him.   [*Exit.*]

END OF ACT I

ACT II

SCENE 1: *Inner apartment of* MR. TIFFANY'S *Counting House*. MR. TIF-FANY, *seated at a desk looking over papers*. MR. SNOBSON, *on a high stool at another desk, with a pen behind his ear.*

SNOBSON: [*Rising, advances to the front of the stage, regards* TIFFANY *and shrugs his shoulders.*] How the old boy frets and fumes over those papers, to be sure! He's working himself into a perfect fever—ex-actly,—therefore *bleeding's* the prescription![14] So here goes! [*Aside.*] Mr. Tiffany, a word with you, if you please, Sir?

TIFFANY: [*Sitting still.*] Speak on, Mr. Snobson, I attend.

SNOBSON: What I have to say, Sir, is a matter of the first importance to the credit of the concern—the *credit* of the concern, Mr. Tiffany!

TIFFANY: Proceed, Mr. Snobson.

SNOBSON: Sir, you've a handsome house—fine carriage—nigger in livery—feed on the fat of the land—everything first rate—

TIFFANY: Well, Sir?

SNOBSON: My salary, Mr. Tiffany!

TIFFANY: It has been raised three times within the last year.

SNOBSON: Still it is insufficient for the necessities of an honest man,—mark me, an *honest* man, Mr. Tiffany.

TIFFANY: [*Crossing.*] What a weapon he has made of that word! [*Aside.*] Enough—another hundred shall be added. Does that content you?

SNOBSON: There is one other subject which I have before mentioned, Mr. Tiffany,—your daughter,—what's the reason you can't let the folks at home know at once that I'm to be *the man?*

TIFFANY: Villain! And must the only seal upon this scoundrel's lips be placed there by the hand of my daughter? [*Aside.*] Well, Sir, it shall be as you desire.

SNOBSON: And Mrs. Tiffany shall be informed of your resolution?

TIFFANY: Yes.

SNOBSON: Enough said! That's the ticket! The CREDIT *of the concern's safe,* Sir! [*Returns to his seat.*]

TIFFANY: How low have I bowed to this insolent rascal! To rise himself he mounts upon my shoulders, and unless I can shake him off he must crush me! [*Aside.*]

[*Enter* TRUEMAN.]

TRUEMAN: Here I am, Antony, man! I told you I'd pay you a visit in your money-making quarters. [*Looks around.*] But it looks as dismal here as a cell in the States' prison!

TIFFANY: [*Forcing a laugh.*] Ha, ha, ha! States' prison! You are so facetious! Ha, ha, ha!

TRUEMAN: Well, for the life of me I can't see anything so amusing in that! I should think the States' prison plaguy uncomfortable lodgings. And you laugh, man, as though you fancied yourself there already.

TIFFANY: Ha, ha, ha!

TRUEMAN: [*Imitating him.*] Ha, ha, ha! What on earth do you mean by that ill-sounding laugh, that has nothing of a laugh about it! This *fashion*-worship has made heathens and hypocrites of you all! *Deception* is your household God! A man laughs as if he were crying, and cries as if he were laughing in his sleeve. Everything is something else from what it seems to be. I have lived in your house only three days, and I've heard more lies than were ever invented during a Presidential election! First your fine lady of a wife sends me word that she's not at home—I walk up stairs, and she takes good care that *I* shall not be *at home*—wants to turn me out of doors. Then *you* come in—take your old friend by the hand—whisper, the deuce knows what, in your wife's ear, and the tables are turned in a tangent! Madam curtsies—says she's enchanted to see me—and orders her grinning nigger to show me a room.

TIFFANY: We were exceedingly happy to welcome you as our guest!

TRUEMAN: Happy? *You* happy? Ah! Antony! Antony! that hatchet face of yours, and those criss-cross furrows tell quite another story! It's many a long day since you were *happy* at anything! You look as if you'd melted down your flesh into dollars, and mortgaged your soul in the bargain! Your warm heart has grown cold over your ledger—your light spirits heavy with calculation! You have traded away your youth—your hopes—your tastes for wealth! and now you *have* the wealth you coveted, what does it profit you? Pleasure it cannot buy; for you have lost your *capacity* for enjoyment—Ease it will not bring; for the love of gain is never satisfied! It has made your counting-house a penitentiary, and your home a fashionable *museum* where there is no niche for you! You have spent so much time *ciphering* in one, that you find yourself at last a very *cipher* in the other! See me, man! seventy-two last August!—strong as a hickory and every whit as sound!

TIFFANY: I take the greatest pleasure in remarking your superiority, Sir.

TRUEMAN: Bah! no man takes pleasure in remarking the superiority of another! Why the deuce, can't you speak the truth, man? But it's not the *fashion* I suppose! I have not seen one frank, open face since— no, no, I can't say that either, though lying *is* catching! There's that girl, Gertrude, who is trying to teach your daughter music—but Gertrude was bred in the country!

TIFFANY: A good girl; my wife and daughter find her very useful.

TRUEMAN: Useful? Well I must say you have queer notions of *use!*— But come, cheer up, man! I'd rather see one of your old smiles, than know you'd realized another thousand! I hear you are making money on the true, American, high pressure system—better go slow and sure—the more steam, the greater danger of the boiler's bursting! All sound, I hope? Nothing rotten at the core?

TIFFANY: Oh, sound—quite sound!

TRUEMAN: Well that's pleasant—though I must say you don't look very pleasant about it!

TIFFANY: My good friend, although I am solvent, I may say, perfectly solvent—yet you—the fact is, you can be of some assistance to me!

TRUEMAN: That's the *fact* is it? I'm glad we've hit upon one *fact* at last! Well—

[SNOBSON, *who during this conversation has been employed in writing, but stops occasionally to listen, now gives vent to a dry, chuckling laugh.*]

TRUEMAN: Hey? What's that? Another of those deuced ill-sounding, city laughs! [*Sees* SNOBSON.] Who's that perched up on the stool of repentance—eh, Antony?

SNOBSON: The old boy has missed his text there—*that's* the stool of repentance! [*Aside and looking at* TIFFANY'S *seat.*]

TIFFANY: One of my clerks—my confidential clerk!

TRUEMAN: Confidential? Why he looks for all the world like a spy— the most inquisitorial, hang-dog face—ugh! the sight of it makes my blood run cold! Come, let us talk over matters where this critter can't give us the benefit of his opinion! Antony, the next time you choose a confidential clerk, take one that carries his credentials in his face —those in his pocket are not worth much without!

[*Exeunt* TRUEMAN *and* TIFFANY.]

SNOBSON: [*Jumping from his stool and advancing.*] The old prig has got the tin, or Tiff would never be so civil! All right—Tiff will work every shiner into the concern—all the better for me! Now I'll go and make love to Seraphina. The old woman needn't try to knock me down with any of her French lingo! Six months from to-day if I ain't

driving my two footmen tandem, down Broadway—and as fashionable as Mrs. Tiffany herself, then I ain't the trump I thought I was!
that's all. [*Looks at his watch.*] Bless me! eleven o'clock and I haven't
had my julep yet? Snobson, I'm ashamed of you!   [*Exit.*]

SCENE 2: *The interior of a beautiful conservatory; walk through the centre; stands of flower pots in bloom; a couple of rustic seats.* GERTRUDE,
attired in white, with a white rose in her hair; watering the flowers.
COLONEL HOWARD, *regarding her.*

HOWARD: I am afraid you lead a sad life here, Miss Gertrude?
GERTRUDE: [*Turning round gaily.*] What! amongst the flowers? [*Continues her occupation.*]
HOWARD: No, amongst the thistles, with which Mrs. Tiffany surrounds
you; the tempests, which her temper raises!
GERTRUDE: They never harm me. Flowers and herbs are excellent tutors.
I learn prudence from the reed, and bend until the storm has swept
over me!
HOWARD: Admirable philosophy! But still this frigid atmosphere of
fashion must be uncongenial to you? Accustomed to the pleasant
companionship of your kind friends in Geneva,[15] surely you must
regret this cold exchange?
GERTRUDE: Do you think so? Can you suppose that I could possibly
prefer a ramble in the woods to a promenade in Broadway? A wreath
of scented wild flowers to a bouquet of these sickly exotics? The
odour of new-mown hay to the heated air of this crowded conservatory? Or can you imagine that I could enjoy the quiet conversation
of my Geneva friends, more than the edifying chit-chat of a fashionable drawing room? But I see you think me totally destitute of taste!
HOWARD: You have a merry spirit to jest thus at your grievances!
GERTRUDE: I have my *mania*,—as some wise person declares that all
mankind have,—and mine is a love of independence! In Geneva, my
wants were supplied by two kind old maiden ladies, upon whom I
know not that I have any claim. I had abilities, and desired to use
them. I came here at my own request; for here I am no longer *de-
pendent! Voila tout,*[16] as Mrs. Tiffany would say.
HOWARD: Believe me, I appreciate the confidence you repose in me!
GERTRUDE: Confidence! Truly, Colonel Howard, the *confidence* is entirely on your part, in supposing that I confide that which I have no
reason to conceal! I think I informed you that Mrs. Tiffany only
received visitors on her reception day—she is therefore not prepared

to see you. Zeke—Oh! I beg his pardon—Adolph, made some mistake in admitting you.

HOWARD: Nay, Gertrude, it was not Mrs. Tiffany, nor Miss Tiffany, whom I came to see; it—it was—

GERTRUDE: The conservatory perhaps? I will leave you to examine the flowers at leisure!

HOWARD: Gertrude—listen to me. If I only dared to give utterance to what is hovering upon my lips! [*Aside.*] Gertrude!

GERTRUDE: Colonel Howard!

HOWARD: Gertrude, I must—must—

GERTRUDE: Yes, indeed you *must,* must leave me! I think I hear somebody coming—Mrs. Tiffany would not be well pleased to find you here—pray, pray leave me—that door will lead you into the street. [*Hurries him out through door; takes up her watering pot, and commences watering flowers, tying up branches, &c.*]

What a strange being is man! Why should he hesitate to say—nay, why should I prevent his saying, what I would most delight to hear? Truly man *is* strange—but woman is quite as incomprehensible! [*Walks about gathering flowers.*]

[*Enter* COUNT JOLIMAITRE.]

COUNT: There she is—the bewitching little creature! Mrs. Tiffany and her daughter are out of ear-shot. I caught a glimpse of their feathers floating down Broadway, not ten minutes ago. Just the opportunity I have been looking for! Now for an engagement with this captivating little piece of prudery! 'Pon honor, I am almost afraid she will not resist a *Count* long enough to give value to the conquest. [*Approaches her.*] *Ma belle petite,* were you gathering roses for me?

GERTRUDE: [*Starts on first perceiving him, but instantly regains her self-possession.*] The roses here, Sir, are carefully guarded with thorns—if you have the right to gather, pluck for yourself!

COUNT: Sharp as ever, little Gertrude! But now that we are alone, throw off this frigidity, and be at your ease.

GERTRUDE: Permit me to *be alone,* Sir, that I *may* be at my ease!

COUNT: Very good, *ma belle,* well said! [*Applauding her with his hands.*] Never yield too soon, even to a *title!* But, as the old girl may find her way back before long, we may as well come to particulars at once. I love you; but that you know already. [*Rubbing his eyeglass unconcernedly with his handkerchief.*] Before long I shall make Mademoiselle Seraphina my wife, and, of course, you shall remain in the family!

GERTRUDE: [*Indignantly.*] Sir—

COUNT: 'Pon my honor you shall! In France we arrange these little matters without difficulty!

GERTRUDE: But I am an *American!* Your conduct proves that you are not one! [*Going.*]

COUNT: [*Preventing her.*] Don't run away, my immaculate *petite Americaine!* Demme, you've quite overlooked my condescension—the difference of our stations—you a species of upper servant—an orphan—no friends.

[*Enter* TRUEMAN *unperceived.*]

GERTRUDE: And therefore more entitled to the respect and protection of every *true gentleman!* Had you been one, you would not have insulted me!

COUNT: My charming little orator, patriotism and declamation become you particularly! [*Approaches her.*] I feel quite tempted to taste—

TRUEMAN: [*Thrusting him aside.*] An American hickory switch! [*Strikes him.*] Well, how do you like it?

COUNT: Old matter-of-fact! [*Aside.*] Sir, how dare you?

TRUEMAN: My stick has answered that question!

GERTRUDE: Oh! now I am quite safe!

TRUEMAN: Safe! not a bit safer than before! All women would be safe, if they knew how virtue became them! As for you, Mr. Count, what have you to say for yourself? Come, speak out!

COUNT: Sir,—aw—aw—you don't understand these matters!

TRUEMAN: That's a fact! Not having had *your* experience, I don't believe I *do* understand them!

COUNT: A piece of pleasantry—a mere joke—

TRUEMAN: A joke was it? I'll show you a joke worth two of that! I'll teach you the way we natives joke with a puppy who don't respect an honest woman! [*Seizing him.*]

COUNT: Oh! oh! demme—you old ruffian! let me go. What do you mean?

TRUEMAN: Oh! a piece of pleasantry—a mere joke—very pleasant isn't it? [*Attempts to strike him again;* COUNT *struggles with him.*]

[*Enter* MRS. TIFFANY *hastily, in her bonnet and shawl.*]

MRS. TIFFANY: What is the matter? I am perfectly *abimé* with terror. Mr. Trueman, what has happened?

TRUEMAN: Oh! we have been *joking!*

MRS. TIFFANY: [*To* COUNT, *who is re-arranging his dress.*] My *dear* Count, I did not expect to find you here—how kind of you!

TRUEMAN: Your *dear* Count, has been showing his *kindness* in a very *foreign* manner. Too *foreign* I think, he found it to be relished by an *unfashionable native!* What do you think of a puppy, who insults an innocent girl all in the way of *kindness*? This Count of yours—this importation of—

COUNT: My dear Madam, demme, permit me to explain. It would be unbecoming—demme—particularly unbecoming of you—aw—aw —to pay any attention to this ignorant person. [*Crosses to* TRUEMAN.] Anything that he says concerning a man of my standing— aw—the truth is, Madam—

TRUEMAN: Let us have the truth by all means,—if it is only for the novelty's sake!

COUNT: [*Turning his back to* TRUEMAN.] You see, madam, hoping to obtain a few moments' private conversation with Miss Seraphina— with *Miss Seraphina* I say—and—aw—and knowing her passion for flowers, I found my way to your very tasteful and *recherché*[17] conservatory. [*Looks about him approvingly.*] Here I encountered this young person. She was inclined to be talkative; and I indulged her with—with a—aw—demme—a few *commonplaces!* What passed between us was mere *harmless badinage*—on *my* part. You, madam, you—so conversant with our European manners—you are aware that when a man of fashion—that is, when a woman—a man is bound—amongst noblemen, you know—

MRS. TIFFANY: I comprehend you perfectly—*parfittement*, my dear Count.

COUNT: 'Pon my honor, that's very obliging of her. [*Aside.*]

MRS. TIFFANY: I am shocked at the plebeian forwardness of this conceited girl!

TRUEMAN: [*Walking up to* COUNT.] Did you ever keep a reckoning of the lies you tell in an hour?

MRS. TIFFANY: Mr. Trueman, I blush for you! [*Crosses, to* TRUEMAN.]

TRUEMAN: Don't do that—you have no blushes to spare!

MRS. TIFFANY: It is a man of rank whom you are addressing, Sir!

TRUEMAN: A rank villain, Mrs. Antony Tiffany! A *rich one* he would be, had he as much *gold* as *brass!*

MRS. TIFFANY: Pray pardon him, Count; he knows nothing of *how ton!*[18]

COUNT: Demme, he's beneath my notice. I tell you what, old fellow— [TRUEMAN *raises his stick as* COUNT *approaches, the latter starts back.*] the sight of him discomposes me—aw—I feel quite uncomfortable—aw—let us join your charming daughter. I can't do you the honor to shoot you, Sir—[*to* TRUEMAN *you are beneath me—a nobleman can't fight a commoner! Good bye, old Truepenny! I—aw—I'm insensible to your insolence!*

[*Exeunt* COUNT *and* MRS. TIFFANY.]

TRUEMAN: You won't be insensible to a cow hide in spite of your nobility! The next time he practises any of his foreign fashions on you, Gertrude, you'll see how I'll wake up his sensibilities!

GERTRUDE: I do not know what I should have done without you, sir.

TRUEMAN: Yes, you do—you know that you would have done well enough! Never tell a lie, girl! not even for the sake of pleasing an old man! When you open your lips let your heart speak. Never tell a lie! Let your face be the looking-glass of your soul—your heart its clock—while your tongue rings the hours! But the glass must be clear, the clock true, and then there's no fear but the tongue will do its duty in a woman's head!

GERTRUDE: You are very good, Sir!

TRUEMAN: That's as it may be!—How my heart warms towards her! [*Aside.*] Gertrude, I hear that you have no mother?

GERTRUDE: Ah! no, Sir; I wish I had.

TRUEMAN: So do I! Heaven knows, so do I! [*Aside, and with emotion.*] And you have no father, Gertrude?

GERTRUDE: No, Sir—I often wish I had!

TRUEMAN: [*Hurriedly.*] Don't do that, girl! don't do that! Wish you had a mother—but never wish that you had a father again! Perhaps the one you had did not deserve such a child!

[*Enter* PRUDENCE.]

PRUDENCE: Seraphina is looking for you, Gertrude.

GERTRUDE: I will go to her. Mr. Trueman, you will not permit me to thank you, but you cannot prevent my gratitude! [*Exit.*]

TRUEMAN: [*Looking after her.*] If falsehood harbours there, I'll give up searching after truth! [*Retires up the stage musingly, and commences examining the flowers.*]

PRUDENCE: What a nice old man he is to be sure! I wish he would say something! [*Aside.*] [*Walks after him, turning when he turns—after a pause.*] Don't mind *me*, Mr. Trueman!

TRUEMAN: Mind you? Oh! no, don't be afraid.—I wasn't minding you. Nobody seems to mind you much! [*Continues walking and examining the flowers*—PRUDENCE *follows.*]

PRUDENCE: Very pretty flowers, ain't they? Gertrude takes care of them.

TRUEMAN: Gertrude? So I hear—[*Advancing.*] I suppose you can tell me now who this Gertrude—

PRUDENCE: Who she's in love with? I *knew* you were going to say that! I'll tell you all about it! Gertrude, she's in love with—Mr. Twinkle! and he's in love with her. And Seraphina she's in love with Count Jolly—what-d'ye-call-it: but Count Jolly don't take to her at all—but Colonel Howard—he's the man—he's desperate about her!

TRUEMAN: Why you feminine newspaper! Howard in love with that quintessence of affection! Howard—the only, frank, straightforward fellow that I've met since—I'll tell him my mind on the subject! And Gertrude hunting for happiness in a rhyming dictionary! The girl's a greater fool than I took her for!

PRUDENCE: So she is—you see I know all about them!

TRUEMAN: I see you do! You've a wonderful knowledge—wonderful—of *other people's concerns!* It may do here, but take my word for it, in the county of Catteraugus you'd get the name of a great *busybody*. But perhaps you know that too?

PRUDENCE: Oh! I always know what's coming. I feel it beforehand all over me. I knew something was going to happen the day you came here—and what's more I can always tell a married man from a single—I felt right off that you were a bachelor!

TRUEMAN: Felt right off I was a bachelor did you? you were sure of it —sure?—quite sure? [PRUDENCE *assents delightedly.*] Then you felt wrong!—a bachelor and a widower are not the same thing!

PRUDENCE: Oh! but it all comes to the same thing—a widower's as good as a bachelor any day! And besides I knew that you were a farmer *right off.*

TRUEMAN: On the spot, eh? I suppose you saw cabbages and green peas growing out of my hat?

PRUDENCE: No, I didn't—but I knew all about you. And I knew—[*looking down and fidgeting with her apron*] I knew you were for getting married soon! For last night I dreamt I saw your funeral going along the streets, and the mourners all dressed in white. And a funeral is a sure sign of a wedding you know! [*Nudging him with her elbow.*]

TRUEMAN: [*Imitating her voice.*] Well I can't say that I *know* any such thing! you know! [*Nudging her back.*]

PRUDENCE: Oh! it does, and there's no getting over it! For my part, I like farmers—and I know all about setting hens and turkeys, and feeding chickens, and laying eggs, and all that sort of thing!

TRUEMAN: May I be shot if mistress newspaper is not putting in an advertisement for herself! This is your city mode of courting I suppose, ha, ha, ha! [*Aside.*]

PRUDENCE: I've been west, a little; but I never was in the county of Catteraugus, myself.

TRUEMAN: Oh! you were not? And you have taken a particular fancy to go there, eh?

PRUDENCE: Perhaps I shouldn't object—

TRUEMAN: Oh!—ah!—so I suppose. Now pay attention to what I am going to say, for it is a matter of great importance to yourself.

PRUDENCE: Now it's coming—I know what he's going to say! [*Aside.*]

TRUEMAN: The next time you want to tie a man for life to your apron-strings, pick out one that don't come from the county of Catteraugus—for green horns are scarce in those parts, and modest women plenty!   [*Exit.*]

PRUDENCE: Now who'd have thought he was going to say that! But I won't give him up yet—I won't give him up.   [*Exit.*]

END OF ACT II

ACT III

SCENE 1: MRS. TIFFANY'S *Parlor.*

[*Enter* MRS. TIFFANY, *followed by* MR. TIFFANY.]

TIFFANY: Your extravagance will ruin me, Mrs. Tiffany!

MRS. TIFFANY: And your stinginess will ruin me, Mr. Tiffany! It is totally and *toot a fate*[19] impossible to convince you of the necessity of *keeping up appearances.* There is a certain display which every woman of fashion is forced to make!

TIFFANY: And pray who made *you* a woman of fashion?

MRS. TIFFANY: What a vulgar question! All women of fashion, Mr. Tiffany—

TIFFANY: In this land are *self-constituted,* like you, Madam—and *fashion* is the cloak for more sins than charity ever covered! It was for *fashion's* sake that you insisted upon my purchasing this expensive house—it was for *fashion's* sake that you ran me in debt at every exorbitant upholsterer's and extravagant furniture warehouse in the city—it was for *fashion's* sake that you built that ruinous conservatory—hired more servants than they have persons to wait upon—and dressed your footman like a harlequin!

MRS. TIFFANY: Mr. Tiffany, you are thoroughly plebeian, and insufferably *American,* in your grovelling ideas! And, pray, what was the occasion of these very *mal-ap-pro-pos*[20] remarks? Merely because I requested a paltry fifty dollars to purchase a new style of head-dress—a *bijou*[21] of an article just introduced in France.

TIFFANY: Time was, Mrs. Tiffany, when you manufactured your own French head-dresses—took off their first gloss at the public balls, and then sold them to your shortest-sighted customers. And all you knew about France, or French either, was what you spelt out at the bottom of your fashion plates—but now you have grown so fashionable, forsooth, that you have forgotten how to speak your mother tongue!

MRS. TIFFANY: Mr. Tiffany, Mr. Tiffany! Nothing is more positively vulgarian—more *unaristocratic* than any allusion to the past!

TIFFANY: Why I thought, my dear, that *aristocrats* lived principally upon the past—and traded in the market of fashion with the bones of their ancestors for capital?[22]

MRS. TIFFANY: Mr. Tiffany, such vulgar remarks are only suitable to the counting house, in my drawing room you should—

TIFFANY: Vary my sentiments with my locality, as you change your *manners* with your *dress!*

MRS. TIFFANY: Mr. Tiffany, I desire that you will purchase Count d'Orsay's "Science of Etiquette," and learn how to conduct yourself—especially before you appear at the grand ball, which I shall give on Friday!

TIFFANY: Confound your balls, Madam; they make *footballs* of my money, while you dance away all that I am worth! A pretty time to give a ball when you know that I am on the very brink of bankruptcy!

MRS. TIFFANY: So much the greater reason that nobody should suspect your circumstances, or you would lose your credit at once. Just at this crisis a ball is absolutely *necessary* to save your reputation! There is Mrs. Adolphus Dashaway—she gave the most splendid fête of the season—and I hear on very good authority that her husband has not paid his baker's bill in three months. Then there was Mrs. Honeywood—

TIFFANY: Gave a ball the night before her husband shot himself—perhaps you wish to drive me to follow his example?

MRS. TIFFANY: Good gracious! Mr. Tiffany, how you talk! I beg you won't mention anything of the kind. I consider black the most unbecoming color. I'm sure I've done all that I could to gratify you. There is that vulgar old torment, Trueman, who gives one the lie fifty times a day—haven't I been very civil to him?

TIFFANY: Civil to his *wealth*, Mrs. Tiffany! I told you that he was a rich, old farmer—the early friend of my father—my own benefactor—and that I had reason to think he might assist me in my present embarrassments. Your civility was *bought*—and like most of your *own* purchases has yet to be *paid* for.

MRS. TIFFANY: And will be, no doubt! The condescension of a woman of fashion should command any price. Mr. Trueman is insupportably indecorous—he has insulted Count Jolimaitre in the most outrageous manner. If the Count was not so deeply interested—so *abimé* with Seraphina, I am sure he would never honor us by his visits again!

TIFFANY: So much the better—he shall never marry my daughter!—I am resolved on that. Why, Madam, I am told there is in Paris a regular matrimonial stock company, who fit out indigent dandies for this market. How do I know but this fellow is one of its creatures, and that he has come here to increase its dividends by marrying a fortune?

MRS. TIFFANY: Nonsense, Mr. Tiffany. The Count, the most fashionable young man in all New York—the intimate friend of all the dukes and lords in Europe—not marry my daughter? Not permit Seraphina to become a Countess? Mr. Tiffany, you are out of your senses!

TIFFANY: That would not be very wonderful, considering how many years I have been united to you, my dear. Modern physicians pronounce lunacy infectious!

MRS. TIFFANY: Mr. Tiffany, he is a man of fashion—

TIFFANY: Fashion makes fools, but cannot *feed* them. By the bye, I have a request,—since you are bent upon ruining me by this ball, and there is no help for it,—I desire that you will send an invitation to my confidential clerk, Mr. Snobson.

MRS. TIFFANY: Mr. Snobson! Was there ever such an *you-nick* demand! Mr. Snobson would cut a pretty figure amongst my fashionable friends! I shall do no such thing, Mr. Tiffany.

TIFFANY: Then, Madam, the ball shall not take place. Have I not told you that I am in the power of this man? That there are circumstances which it is happy for you that you do not know—which you cannot comprehend,—but which render it essential that you should be civil to Mr. Snobson? Not you merely, but Seraphina also? He is a more appropriate match for her than your foreign favorite.

MRS. TIFFANY: A match for Seraphina, indeed! Mr. Tiffany, you are determined to make a *fow pas.*

TIFFANY: Mr. Snobson intends calling this morning.

MRS. TIFFANY: But, Mr. Tiffany, this is not reception day—my drawing-rooms are in the most terrible disorder—

TIFFANY: Mr. Snobson is not particular—he must be admitted.

[*Enter ZEKE.*]

ZEKE: Mr. Snobson.

[*Enter SNOBSON; exit ZEKE.*]

SNOBSON: How dye do, Marm? How are you? Mr. Tiffany, your most!—

MRS. TIFFANY: [*Formally.*] *Bung jure. Comment vow portè vow, Monsur Snobson?*[23]

SNOBSON: Oh, to be sure—very good of you—fine day.

MRS. TIFFANY: [*Pointing to a chair with great dignity.*] *Sassoyez vow,*[24] Monsur Snobson.

SNOBSON: I wonder what she's driving at? I ain't up to the fashionable lingo yet! [*Aside.*] Eh? what? Speak a little louder, Marm?

MRS. TIFFANY: What ignorance! [*Aside.*]

TIFFANY: I presume Mrs. Tiffany means that you are to take a seat.

SNOBSON: Ex-actly—very obliging of her—so I will. [*Sits.*] No ceremony amongst friends, you know—and likely to be nearer—you understand? O.K., all correct. How *is* Seraphina?

MRS. TIFFANY: Miss Tiffany is not visible this morning. [*Retires up.*]

SNOBSON: Not visible? [*Jumping up.*] I suppose that's the English for can't see her? Mr. Tiffany, Sir—[*walking up to him*] what am I to understand by this *de-fal-ca-tion,* Sir? I expected your word to be as good as your bond—beg pardon, Sir—I mean *better*—considerably better—no humbug about it, Sir.

TIFFANY: Have patience, Mr. Snobson. [*Rings bell.*]

[*Enter ZEKE.*]

Zeke, desire my daughter to come here.

MRS. TIFFANY: [*Coming down.*] Adolph—I say, Adolph—

[*ZEKE straightens himself and assumes foppish airs, as he turns to* MRS. TIFFANY.]

TIFFANY: Zeke.

ZEKE: Don't know any such nigga, Boss.

TIFFANY: Do as I bid you instantly, or off with your livery and quit the house!

ZEKE: Wheugh! I'se all dismission!   [*Exit.*]

MRS. TIFFANY: A-dolph, A-dolph! [*Calling after him.*]

SNOBSON: I brought the old boy to his bearings, didn't I though! Pull that string, and he is sure to work right. [*Aside.*] Don't make any stranger of me, Marm—I'm quite at home. If you've got any odd jobs about the house to do up, I shan't miss you. I'll amuse myself with Seraphina when she comes—we'll get along very cosily by ourselves.

MRS. TIFFANY: Permit me to inform you, Mr. Snobson, that a French mother never leaves her daughter alone with a young man—she knows your sex too well for that!

SNOBSON: Very *dis*-obliging of her—but as we're none French—

MRS. TIFFANY: You have yet to learn, Mr. Snobson, that the American *ee-light*—the aristocracy—the *how-ton*—as a matter of conscience, scrupulously follow the foreign fashions.

SNOBSON: Not when they are foreign to their interests, Marm—for instance—

[*Enter* SERAPHINA.]

There you are at last, eh, Miss? How dye do? Ma said you weren't visible. Managed to get a peep at her, eh, Mr. Tiffany?

SERAPHINA: I heard you were here, Mr. Snobson, and came without even arranging my toilette; you will excuse my negligence?

SNOBSON: Of everything but *me*, Miss.

SERAPHINA: I shall never have to ask your pardon for *that*, Mr. Snobson.

MRS. TIFFANY: Seraphina—child—really—[*As she is approaching* SER-APHINA, MR. TIFFANY *plants himself in front of his wife.*]

TIFFANY: Walk this way, Madam, if you please. To see that she fancies the surly fellow takes a weight from my heart. [*Aside.*]

MRS. TIFFANY: Mr. Tiffany, it is highly improper and not at all *distingué* to leave a young girl—

[*Enter* ZEKE.]

ZEKE: Mr. Count Jolly-made-her!

MRS. TIFFANY: Good gracious! The Count—Oh, dear!—Seraphina, run and change your dress,—no there's not time! A-dolph, admit him.
                                                              [*Exit* ZEKE]

Mr. Snobson, get out of the way, will you? Mr. Tiffany, what are you doing at home at this hour?

[*Enter* COUNT JOLIMAITRE, *ushered by* ZEKE.]

ZEKE: Dat's de genuine article ob a gemman. [*Aside.*]   [*Exit.*]
MRS. TIFFANY: My dear Count, I am overjoyed at the very sight of you.
COUNT: Flattered myself you'd be glad to see me, Madam—knew it was
    not your *jour de reception.*
MRS. TIFFANY: But for you, Count, all days—
COUNT: I thought so. Ah, Miss Tiffany, on my honor you're looking
    beautiful. [*Crosses.*]
SERAPHINA: Count, flattery from you—
SNOBSON: What? Eh? What's that you say?
SERAPHINA: Nothing but what etiquette requires. [*Aside to him.*]
COUNT: [*Regarding* MR. TIFFANY *through his eye glass.*] Your worthy
    Papa, I believe? Sir, your most obedient.

    [MR. TIFFANY *bows coldly;* COUNT *regards* SNOBSON *through his
    glass, shrugs his shoulders and turns away.*]

SNOBSON: [*To* MRS. TIFFANY.] Introduce me, will you? I never knew a
    Count in all my life—what a strange-looking animal!
MRS. TIFFANY: Mr. Snobson, it is not the fashion to introduce in France!
SNOBSON: But, Marm, we're in America. [MRS. TIFFANY *crosses to*
    COUNT.] The woman thinks she's somewhere else than where she
    is—she wants to make an *alibi?* [*Aside.*]
MRS. TIFFANY: I hope that we shall have the pleasure of seeing you on
    Friday evening, Count?
COUNT: Really, Madam, my invitations—my engagements—so numer-
    ous—I can hardly answer for myself: and you Americans take offence
    so easily—
MRS. TIFFANY: But, Count, everybody expects you at our ball—you are
    the principal attraction—
SERAPHINA: Count, you *must* come!
COUNT: Since you insist—aw—aw—there's no resisting you, Miss
    Tiffany.
MRS. TIFFANY: I am so thankful. How can I repay your condescension!
    [COUNT *and* SERAPHINA *converse.*] Mr. Snobson, will you walk this
    way?—I have *such* a cactus in full bloom—remarkable flower! Mr.
    Tiffany, pray come here—I have something particular to say.
TIFFANY: Then speak out, my dear—I thought it was highly improper
    just now to leave a girl with a young man? [*Aside to her.*]

MRS. TIFFANY: Oh, but the Count—that is different!

TIFFANY: I suppose you mean to say there's nothing of *the man* about him?

[*Enter* MILLINETTE, *with a scarf in her hand.*]

MILLINETTE: Adolph tell me he vas here. [*Aside.*] Pardon, Madame, I bring dis scarf for Mademoiselle.

MRS. TIFFANY: Very well, Millinette; you know best what is proper for her to wear.

[MR. *and* MRS. TIFFANY *and* SNOBSON *retire up; she engages the attention of both gentlemen.* MILLINETTE *crosses, towards* SERAPHINA, *gives the* COUNT *a threatening look, and commences arranging the scarf over* SERAPHINA'S *shoulders.*]

MILLINETTE: Mademoiselle, *permettez-moi.* Perfide![25] [*Aside to* COUNT. If Mademoiselle vil stand tranquille one *petit moment.* [*Turns* SERAPHINA'S *back to the* COUNT, *and pretends to arrange the scarf.*] I must speak vid you to-day, or I tell all—you find me at de foot of de stair ven you go. Prend garde![26] [*Aside to* COUNT.]

SERAPHINA: What is that you say, Millinette?

MILLINETTE: Dis scarf make you so very beautiful, Mademoiselle—*Je vous salue, mes dames.*[27] [*Curtsies.*]   [*Exit.*]

COUNT: Not a moment to lose! [*Aside.*] Miss Tiffany, I have an unpleasant—a particularly unpleasant piece of intelligence—you see, I have just received a letter from my friend—the—aw—the Earl of Airshire; the truth is, the Earl's daughter—beg you won't mention it—has distinguished me by a tender *penchant.*

SERAPHINA: I understand—and they wish you to return and marry the young lady; but surely you will not leave us, Count?

COUNT: If *you* bid me stay—I shouldn't have the conscience—I couldn't *afford* to tear myself away. I'm sure that's honest. [*Aside.*]

SERAPHINA: Oh, Count!

COUNT: Say but one word—say that you shouldn't mind being made a Countess—and I'll break with the Earl tomorrow.

SERAPHINA: Count, this surprise—but don't think of leaving the country, Count—we could not pass the time without you! I—yes—yes, Count—I do consent!

COUNT: I thought she would! [*Aside, while he embraces her.*] Enchanted, rapture, bliss, ecstasy, and all that sort of thing—words can't express it, but you understand. But it must be kept a secret—

positively it *must!* If the rumour of our engagement were whispered abroad—the Earl's daughter—the delicacy of my situation, aw—you comprehend? It is even possible that our nuptials, my charming Miss Tiffany, *our nuptials* must take place in private!

SERAPHINA: Oh, that is quite impossible!

COUNT: It's the latest fashion abroad—the very latest! Ah, I knew that would determine you. Can I depend on your secrecy?

SERAPHINA: Oh, yes! Believe me.

SNOBSON: [*Coming forward in spite of* MRS. TIFFANY'S *efforts to detain him.*] Why Seraphina, haven't you a word to throw to a dog?

TIFFANY: I shouldn't think she had after wasting so many upon a puppy. [*Aside.*]

[*Enter* ZEKE, *wearing a three-cornered hat.*]

ZEKE: Missus, de bran new carriage am below.

MRS. TIFFANY: Show it up,—I mean, Very well, A-dolph. [*Exit* ZEKE.] Count, my daughter and I are about to take an airing in our new *voyture,*—will you honor us with your company?

COUNT: Madam, I—I have a most *pressing* engagement. A letter to write to the *Earl of Airshire*—who is at present residing in the *Isle of Skye.* I must bid you good morning.

MRS. TIFFANY: Good morning, Count.   [*Exit* COUNT.]

SNOBSON: *I'm* quite at leisure, Marm. Books balanced—ledger closed —nothing to do all the afternoon,—I'm for you.

MRS. TIFFANY: [*Without noticing him.*] Come, Seraphina, come! [*As they are going* SNOBSON *follows them.*]

SNOBSON: But Marm—I was saying, Marm, I am quite at leisure—not a thing to do; have I, Mr. Tiffany?

MRS. TIFFANY: Seraphina, child—your red shawl—remember—Mr. Snobson, *bon swear!*[28]   [*Exit, leading* SERAPHINA.]

SNOBSON: Swear! Mr. Tiffany, Sir, am I to be fobbed off with a *bon swear?* D——n it, I will swear!

TIFFANY: Have patience, Mr. Snobson, if you will accompany me to the counting house—

SNOBSON: Don't count too much on me, Sir. I'll make up no more accounts until these are settled! I'll run down and jump into the carriage in spite of her *bon swear.*   [*Exit.*]

TIFFANY: You'll jump into a hornet's nest, if you do! Mr. Snobson, Mr. Snobson!   [*Exit after him.*]

SCENE 2: *Housekeeper's Room.*

[*Enter* MILLINETTE.]

MILLINETTE: I have set dat bête, Adolph, to vatch for him. He say he would come back so soon as Madame's voiture drive from de door. If he not come—but he vill—he vill—he *bien etourdi,* but he have *bon coeur.*[29]

[*Enter* COUNT.]

COUNT: Ah! Millinette, my dear, you see what a good-natured dog I am to fly at your bidding—

MILLINETTE: Fly? Ah! *trompeur!*[30] Vat for you fly from Paris? Vat for you leave me—and I love you so much? Ven you sick—you almost die—did I not stay by you—take care of you—and you have no else friend? Vat for you leave Paris?

COUNT: Never allude to disagreeable subjects, *mon enfant!* I was forced by uncontrollable circumstances to fly to the land of liberty—

MILLINETTE: Vat you do vid all the money I give you? The last sou I had—did I not give you?

COUNT: I dare say you did, ma petite—wish you'd been better supplied! [*Aside.*] Don't ask any questions here—can't explain now—the next time we meet—

MILLINETTE: But, ah! ven shall ve meet—ven? You not deceive me, not any more.

COUNT: Deceive you! I'd rather deceive myself—I wish I could! I'd persuade myself you were once more washing linen in the Seine! [*Aside.*]

MILLICENT: I vil tell you ven ve shall meet—On Friday night Madame give one grand ball—you come *sans doute*[31]—den ven de supper is served—de Americans tink of noting else ven de supper come—den you steal out of de room, and you find me here—and you give me one grand *explanation!*

[*Enter* GERTRUDE, *unperceived.*]

COUNT: Friday night—while supper is serving—*parole d'honneur*[32] I will be here—I will explain every thing—my sudden departure from Paris—my—demme, my countship—everything! Now let me go—if any of the family should discover us—

GERTRUDE: [*Who during the last speech has gradually advanced.*] They might discover more than you think it advisable for them to know!

COUNT: The devil!

MILLINETTE: *Mon Dieu!* Mademoiselle Gertrude!

COUNT: [*Recovering himself.*] My dear Miss Gertrude, let me explain
—aw—aw—nothing is more natural than the situation in which you
find me—

GERTRUDE: I am inclined to believe that, Sir.

COUNT: Now,—'pon my honor, that's not fair. Here is Millinette will
bear witness to what I am about to say—

GERTRUDE: Oh, I have not the slightest doubt of that, Sir.

COUNT: You see, Millinette happened to be lady's-maid in the family
of—of—the Duchess Chateau D'Espague—and I chanced to be a
particular friend of the Duchess—*very particular* I assure you! Of
course I saw Millinette, and she, demme, she saw me! Didn't you,
Millinette?

MILLINETTE: Oh! oui—Mademoiselle, I knew him ver vell.

COUNT: Well, it is a remarkable fact that—being in correspondence with
this very Duchess—at this very time—

GERTRUDE: That is sufficient, Sir—I am already so well acquainted with
your extraordinary talents for improvisation, that I will not further
tax your invention—

MILLINETTE: Ah! Mademoiselle Gertrude do not betray us—have pity!

COUNT: [*Assuming an air of dignity.*] Silence, Millinette! My word has
been doubted—the word of a nobleman! I will inform my friend,
Mrs. Tiffany, of this young person's audacity. [*Going.*]

GERTRUDE: His own weapons alone can foil this villain! [*Aside.*] Sir—
Sir—Count! [*At the last word the* COUNT *turns.*] Perhaps, Sir, the
least said about this matter the better!

COUNT: [*Delightedly.*] The least said? We won't say anything at all.
She's coming round—couldn't resist me! [*Aside.*] Charming Gertrude—

MILLINETTE: Quoi? Vat that you say?

COUNT: My sweet, adorable Millinette, hold your tongue, will you?
[*Aside to her.*]

MILLINETTE: [*Aloud.*] No, I vill not! If you do look so from out your
eyes at her again, I vill tell all!

COUNT: Oh, I never could manage two women at once,—jealousy
makes the dear creatures so spiteful. The only valor is in flight!
[*Aside.*] Miss Gertrude, I wish you good morning. Millinette, *mon
enfant,* adieu.   [*Exit.*]

MILLINETTE: But I have one word more to say. Stop, Stop!

                                                    [*Exit after him.*]

GERTRUDE: [*Musingly.*] Friday night, while supper is serving, he is to meet Millinette here and explain—what? This man is an impostor! His insulting me—his familiarity with Millinette—his whole conduct—prove it. If I tell Mrs. Tiffany this she will disbelieve me, and one word may place this so-called Count on his guard. To convince Seraphina would be equally difficult, and her rashness and infatuation may render her miserable for life. No—she shall be saved! I must devise some plan for opening their eyes. Truly, if I *cannot* invent one, I shall be the first woman who was ever at a loss for a stratagem—especially to punish a villain or to shield a friend.

[*Exit.*]

END OF ACT III

ACT IV

SCENE 1: *Ball Room splendidly illuminated. A curtain hung at the further end.* MR. *and* MRS. TIFFANY, SERAPHINA, GERTRUDE, FOGG, TWINKLE, COUNT, SNOBSON, COLONEL HOWARD, *a number of guests—some seated, some standing. As the curtain rises, a cotillion is danced;* GERTRUDE *dancing with* HOWARD, SERAPHINA *with* COUNT.

COUNT: [*Advancing with* SERAPHINA *to the front of the stage.*] To-morrow then—to-morrow—I may salute you as my bride—demme, my Countess!

[*Enter* ZEKE, *with refreshments.*]

SERAPHINA: Yes, to-morrow.

[*As the* COUNT *is about to reply,* SNOBSON *thrusts himself in front of* SERAPHINA.]

SNOBSON: You said you'd dance with me, Miss—now take my fin, and we'll walk about and see what's going on.

[COUNT *raises his eye-glass, regards* SNOBSON, *and leads* SERAPHINA *away;* SNOBSON *follows, endeavoring to attract her attention, but encounters* ZEKE, *bearing a waiter of refreshments; stops, helps himself, and puts some in his pockets.*]

Here's the treat! get my to-morrow's luncheon out of Tiff.

[*Enter* TRUEMAN, *yawning and rubbing his eyes.*]

TRUEMAN: What a nap I've had, to be sure! [*Looks at his watch.*] Eleven o'clock, as I'm alive! Just the time when country folks are comfortably *turned in,* and here your grand *turn-out* has hardly begun yet! [*To* TIFFANY, *who approaches.*]

GERTRUDE: [*Advancing.*] I was just coming to look for you, Mr. Trueman. I began to fancy that you were paying a visit to dream-land.

TRUEMAN: So I was, child—so I was—and I saw a face—like yours—but brighter!—even brighter. [*To* TIFFANY.] There's a smile for you, man! It makes one feel that the world has something worth living for in it yet! Do you remember a smile like that, Antony? Ah! I see you don't—but I do—I do! [*Much moved.*]

HOWARD: [*Advancing.*] Good evening, Mr. Trueman. [*Offers his hand.*]

TRUEMAN: That's right man; give me your whole hand! When a man offers me the tips of his fingers, I know at once there's nothing in him worth seeking beyond his fingers' ends.

[TRUEMAN *and* HOWARD, GERTRUDE *and* TIFFANY *converse.*]

MRS. TIFFANY: [*Advancing.*] I'm in such a fidget lest that vulgar old fellow should disgrace us by some of his plebeian remarks! What it is to give a ball, when one is forced to invite vulgar people!

[MRS. TIFFANY *advances towards* TRUEMAN; SERAPHINA *stands conversing flippantly with the gentlemen who surround her; amongst them is* TWINKLE, *who having taken a magazine from his pocket, is reading to her, much to the undisguised annoyance of* SNOBSON.]

Dear me, Mr. Trueman, you are very late—quite in the fashion I declare!

TRUEMAN: Fashion! And pray what is *fashion,* madam? An agreement between certain persons to live without using their souls! to substitute etiquette for virtue—decorum for purity—manners for morals! to affect a shame for the works of their Creator! and expend all their rapture upon the works of their tailors and dressmakers!

MRS. TIFFANY: You have the most *ow-tray* ideas, Mr. Trueman—quite rustic, and deplorably *American!* But pray walk this way. [MRS. TIFFANY *and* TRUEMAN *go up.*]

COUNT: [*Advancing to* GERTRUDE; HOWARD, *a short distance behind her.*] Miss Gertrude—no opportunity of speaking to you before—in demand you know!

GERTRUDE: I have no choice, I must be civil to him. [*Aside.*] What were you remarking, Sir?

COUNT: Miss Gertrude—charming Ger—aw—aw—I never found it so difficult to speak to a woman before. [*Aside.*]

GERTRUDE: Yes, a very charming ball—many beautiful faces here.

COUNT: Only one!—aw—aw—one—the fact is—[*Talks to her in dumb show.*]

HOWARD: What could old Trueman have meant by saying she fancied that puppy of a Count—that paste jewel thrust upon the little finger of society.

COUNT: Miss Gertrude—aw—'pon my honor—you don't understand —really—aw—aw—will you dance the polka with me?

[GERTRUDE *bows and gives him her hand; he leads her to the set forming;* HOWARD *remains looking after them.*]

HOWARD: Going to dance with him too! A few days ago she would hardly bow to him civilly—could old Trueman have had reasons for what he said? [*Retires up.*]

[*Dance, the polka;* SERAPHINA, *after having distributed her bouquet, vinaigrette and fan amongst the gentlemen, dances with* SNOBSON.]

PRUDENCE: [*Peeping in, as dance concludes.*] I don't like dancing on Friday; something strange is always sure to happen! I'll be on the look out. [*Remains peeping and concealing herself when any of the company approach.*]

GERTRUDE: [*Advancing hastily.*] They are preparing the supper—now if I can only dispose of Millinette while I unmask this insolent pretender!   [*Exit.*]

PRUDENCE: [*Peeping.*] What's that she said? It's coming!

[*Re-enter* GERTRUDE, *bearing a small basket filled with bouquets; approaches* MRS. TIFFANY; *they walk to the front of the stage.*]

GERTRUDE: Excuse me, Madam—I believe this is just the hour at which you ordered supper?

MRS. TIFFANY: Well, what's that to you! So you've been dancing with the Count—how dare you dance with a nobleman—*you?*

GERTRUDE: I will answer that question half an hour hence. At present I have something to propose, which I think will gratify you and please your guests. I have heard that at the most elegant balls in Paris, it is customary—

MRS. TIFFANY: What? what?

GERTRUDE: To station a servant at the door with a basket of flowers.

A bouquet is then presented to every lady as she passes in—I prepared this basket a short time ago. As the company walk in to supper, might not the flowers be distributed to advantage?

MRS. TIFFANY: How *distingué!* You are a good creature, Gertrude—there, run and hand the *bokettes* to them yourself! You shall have the whole credit of the thing.

GERTRUDE: Caught in my own net! [*Aside.*] But, madam, I know so little of fashion—Millinette, being French, herself will do it with so much more grace. I am sure Millinette—

MRS. TIFFANY: So am I. She will do it a thousand times better than you—there go call her.

GERTRUDE: [*Giving basket.*] But madam, pray order Millinette not to leave her station till supper is ended—as the company pass out of the supper room she may find that some of the ladies have been overlooked.

MRS. TIFFANY: That is true—very thoughtful of you, Gertrude.

[*Exit* GERTRUDE.]

What a *recherché* idea!

[*Enter* MILLINETTE.]

Here Millinette, take this basket. Place yourself there, and distribute these *bokettes* as the company pass in to supper; but remember not to stir from the spot until supper is over. It is a French fashion you know, Millinette. I am so delighted to be the first to introduce it—it will be all the rage in the *bow-monde!*

MILLINETTE: Mon Dieu! dis vill ruin all! [*Aside.*] Madame, Madame, let me tell you, Madame, dat in France, in Paris, it is de custom to present *les* bouquets ven everybody first come—long before de supper. Dis vould be *outré! barbare!* not at all la mode! Ven dey do come in dat is de fashion in Paris!

MRS. TIFFANY: Dear me! Millinette, what is the difference? besides I'd have you to know that Americans always improve upon French fashions! here, take the basket, and let me see that you do it in the most *you-nick* and genteel manner.

[MILLINETTE *poutingly takes the basket and retires up stage. A march. Curtain hung at the further end of the room is drawn back, and discloses a room, in the centre of which stands a supper table, beautifully decorated and illuminated; the company promenade two by two into the supper room;* MILLINETTE *presents bouquets as they pass;* COUNT *leads* MRS. TIFFANY.]

TRUEMAN: [*Encountering* FOGG, *who is hurrying alone to the supper room.*] Mr. Fogg, never mind the supper, man! Ha, ha, ha! Of course you are indifferent to suppers!

FOGG: Indifferent! suppers—oh, ah—no, Sir—suppers? no—no—I'm not indifferent to suppers! [*Hurries away towards table.*]

TRUEMAN: Ha, ha, ha! Here's a new discovery I've made in the fashionable world! Fashion don't permit the critters to have *heads* or *hearts,* but it allows them stomachs! [*To* TIFFANY, *who advances.*] So it's not fashionable to *feel,* but it's fashionable to *feed,* eh, Antony? ha, ha, ha!

[TRUEMAN *and* TIFFANY *retire towards supper room. Enter* GERTRUDE, *followed by* ZEKE.]

GERTRUDE: Zeke, go to the supper room instantly,—whisper to Count Jolimaitre that all is ready, and that he must keep his appointment without delay,—then watch him, and as he passes out of the room, place yourself in front of Millinette in such a manner, that the Count cannot see her nor she him. Be sure that they do not see each other—everything depends upon that.

ZEKE: Missey, consider dat business brought to a scientific conclusion.
[*Exit into supper room. Exit* GERTRUDE.]

PRUDENCE: [*Who has been listening.*] What can she want of the Count? I always suspected that Gertrude, because she is so merry and busy! Mr. Trueman thinks so much of her too—I'll tell him this! There's something wrong—but it all comes of giving a ball on a Friday! How astonished the dear old man will be when he finds out how much I know! [*Advances timidly towards the supper room.*]

SCENE 2: *Housekeeper's room; dark stage; table, two chairs.*

[*Enter* GERTRUDE, *with a lighted candle in her hand.*]

GERTRUDE: So far the scheme prospers! and yet this imprudence—if I fail? Fail! to lack courage in a difficulty, or ingenuity in a dilemma, are not woman's failings!

[*Enter* ZEKE, *with a napkin over his arm, and a bottle of champagne in his hand.*]

Well Zeke—Adolph!

ZEKE: Dat's right, Missey; I feels just now as if dat was my legitimate title; dis here's de stuff to make a nigger feel like a gemman!

GERTRUDE: But is he coming?

ZEKE: He's coming! [*Sound of a champagne cork heard.*] Do you hear dat, Missey? Don't it put you all in a froth, and make you feel as light as a cork? Dere's nothing like the *union brand,* to wake up de harmonies ob de heart. [*Drinks from bottle.*]

GERTRUDE: Remember to keep watch upon the outside—do not stir from the spot; when I call you, come in quickly with a light—now, will you be gone!

ZEKE: I'm off, Missey, like a champagne cork wid de strings cut.

GERTRUDE: I think I hear the Count's step. [*Stage dark; she blows out candle.*] Now if I can but disguise my voice, and make the best of my French.

[*Enter* COUNT.]

COUNT: Millinette, where are you? How am I to see you in the dark?

GERTRUDE: [*Imitating* MILLINETTE'S *voice in a whisper.*] Hush! *parle bas.*[33]

COUNT: Come here and give me a kiss.

GERTRUDE: Non—non—[*retreating alarmed,* COUNT *follows*] make haste, I must know all.

COUNT: You did not use to be so deuced particular.

ZEKE: [*Without.*] No admission, gemman! Box office closed, tickets stopped!

TRUEMAN: [*Without.*] Out of my way; do you want me to try if your head is as hard as my stick?

GERTRUDE: What shall I do? Ruined, ruined! [*She stands with her hand clasped in speechless despair.*]

COUNT: Halloa! they are coming here, Millinette! Millinette, why don't you speak? Where can I hide myself? [*Running about stage, feeling for a door.*] Where are all your closets? If I could only get out—or get in somewhere; may I be smothered in a clothes basket, if you ever catch me in such a scrape again! [*His hand accidentally touches the knob of a door opening into a closet.*] Fortune's favorite yet! I'm safe! [*Gets into closet and closes door.*]

[*Enter* PRUDENCE, TRUEMAN, MRS. TIFFANY, *and* COLONEL HOWARD, *followed by* ZEKE, *bearing a light; lights up.*]

PRUDENCE: Here they are, the Count and Gertrude! I told you so! [*Stops in surprise on seeing only* GERTRUDE.]

TRUEMAN: And you see what a lie you told!

MRS. TIFFANY: Prudence, how dare you create this disturbance in my house? To suspect the Count too—a nobleman!

HOWARD: My sweet Gertrude, this foolish old woman would—

PRUDENCE: Oh! you needn't talk—I heard her make the appointment —I know he's here—or he's been here. I wonder if she hasn't hid him away! [*Runs peeping about the room.*]

TRUEMAN: [*Following her angrily.*] You're what I call a confounded— troublesome—meddling—old—prying—[*As he says the last word,* PRUDENCE *opens closet where the* COUNT *is concealed.*] Thunder and lightning!

PRUDENCE: I told you so!

> [*They all stand aghast;* MRS. TIFFANY, *with her hands lifted in surprise and anger;* TRUEMAN, *clutching his stick;* HOWARD, *looking with an expression of bewildered horror from the* COUNT *to* GERTRUDE.]

MRS. TIFFANY: [*Shaking her fist at* GERTRUDE.] You depraved little minx! this is the meaning of your dancing with the Count!

COUNT: [*Stepping from the closet and advancing.*] I don't know what to make of it! Millinette not here! Miss Gertrude—oh! I see—a disguise—the girl's desperate about me—the way with them all. [*Aside.*]

TRUEMAN: I'm choking—I can't speak—Gertrude—no—no—it is some horrid mistake! [*Partly aside, changes his tone suddenly*]. The villain! I'll hunt the truth out of him, if there's any in—[*approaches* COUNT *threateningly*] do you see this stick? You made its first acquaintance a few days ago; it is time you were better known to each other.

> [*As* TRUEMAN *attempts to seize him,* COUNT *escapes, and shields himself behind* MRS. TIFFANY, TRUEMAN *following.*]

COUNT: You ruffian! would you strike a woman?—Madam—my dear Madam—keep off that barbarous old man, and I will explain! Madam, with—aw—your natural *bon gout*[34]—aw—your fashionable refinement—aw—your—aw—your knowledge of *foreign customs*—

MRS. TIFFANY: Oh! Count, I hope it ain't a *foreign custom* for the nobility to shut themselves up in the dark with young women? We think such things *dreadful* in *America*.

COUNT: Demme—aw—hear what I have to say, Madam—I'll satisfy all sides—I am perfectly innocent in this affair—'pon my honor I am! That young lady shall inform you that I am so herself!—can't

help it, sorry for her. Old matter-of-fact won't be convinced any
other way,—that club of his is so particularly unpleasant! [*Aside.*]
Madam, I was summoned here *malgré moi*,[35] and not knowing whom
I was to meet—Miss Gertrude, favor this company by saying whether
or not you directed—that—aw—aw—that colored individual to
conduct me here?

GERTRUDE: Sir, you well know—

COUNT: A simple yes or no will suffice.

MRS. TIFFANY: Answer the Count's question instantly, Miss.

GERTRUDE: I did—but—

COUNT: You hear, Madam—

TRUEMAN: I won't believe it—I can't! Here you nigger, stop rolling up
your eyes, and let us know whether she told you to bring that critter
here?

ZEKE: I'se refuse to gib ebidence; dat's de device ob de skilfullest counsels ob de day! Can't answer, Boss—neber git a word out ob dis
child—Yah! yah!   [*Exit.*]

GERTRUDE: Mrs. Tiffany,—Mr. Trueman, if you will but have
patience—

TRUEMAN: Patience! Oh, Gertrude, you've taken from an old man something better and dearer than his patience—the one bright hope of
nineteen years of self-denial—of nineteen years of—[*Throws himself
upon a chair, his head leaning on table.*]

MRS. TIFFANY: Get out of my house, you *ow*dacious—you ruined—you
abimé[36] young woman! You will corrupt all my family. Good gracious! don't touch me—don't come near me. Never let me see your
face after to-morrow. Pack. [*Goes up.*]

HOWARD: Gertrude, I have striven to find some excuse for you—to
doubt—to disbelieve—but this is beyond all endurance!   [*Exit.*]

[*Enter* MILLINETTE *in haste.*]

MILLINETTE: I could not come before—[*Stops in surprise at seeing the
persons assembled.*] Mon Dieu! vat does dis mean?

COUNT: Hold your tongue, fool! You will ruin everything. I will explain
to-morrow. [*Aside to her.*] Mrs. Tiffany—Madam—my dear
Madam, let me conduct you back to the ball-room. [*She takes his
arm.*] You see I am quite innocent in this matter; a man of my standing, you know,—aw, aw—you comprehend the whole affair.
                          [*Exit* COUNT *leading* MRS. TIFFANY.]

MILLINETTE: I vill say to him von vord, I will!   [*Exit.*]

GERTRUDE: Mr. Trueman, I beseech you—I insist upon being heard,—
I claim it as a right!

TRUEMAN: Right? How dare you have the face, girl, to talk of rights!
[*Comes down.*] You had more rights than you thought for, but you
have forfeited them all! All right to love, respect, protection, and to
not a little else that you don't dream of. Go, go! I'll start for Catteraugus to-morrow,—I've seen enough of what fashion can do!
[*Exit.*]

PRUDENCE: [*Wiping her eyes.*] Dear old man, how he takes on! I'll go
and console him!   [*Exit.*]

GERTRUDE: This is too much! How heavy a penalty has my imprudence
cost me!—his esteem, and that of one dearer—my home—my—
[*Burst of lively music from ball-room.*] They are dancing, and I—I
should be weeping, if pride had not sealed up my tears.

[*She sinks into a chair. Band plays the polka behind till curtain
falls.*]

END OF ACT IV

ACT V

SCENE 1: MRS. TIFFANY'S *Drawing Room—same Scene as Act 1st.* GER-
TRUDE *seated, at a table, with her head leaning on her hand; in the
other hand she holds a pen. A sheet of paper and an inkstand before
her.*

GERTRUDE: How shall I write to them? What shall I say? Prevaricate I
cannot—[*rises and comes forward*] and yet if I write the truth—
simple souls! how can they comprehend the motives for my conduct?
Nay—the truly pure see no imaginary evil in others! It is only vice,
that reflecting its own image, suspects even the innocent. I have no
time to lose—I must prepare them for my return. [*Resumes her seat
and writes.*] What a true pleasure there is in daring to be frank! [*After
writing a few lines more pauses.*] Not so frank either,—there is one
name that I cannot mention. Ah! that he should suspect—should
despise me. [*Writes.*]

[*Enter TRUEMAN.*]

TRUEMAN: There she is! If this girl's soul had only been as fair as her face,—yet she dared to speak the truth,—I'll not forget that! A woman who refuses to tell a lie has one spark of heaven in her still. [*Approaches her.*] Gertrude, [GERTRUDE *starts and looks up*] what are you writing there? Plotting more mischief, eh, girl?

GERTRUDE: I was writing a few lines, to some friends in Geneva.

TRUEMAN: The Wilsons, eh?

GERTRUDE: [*Surprised, rising.*] Are you acquainted with them, Sir?

TRUEMAN: I shouldn't wonder if I was. I suppose you have taken good care not to mention the dark room—that foreign puppy in the closet—the pleasant surprise—and all that sort of thing, eh?

GERTRUDE: I have no reason for concealment, Sir! for I have done nothing of which I am ashamed!

TRUEMAN: Then I can't say much for your modesty.

GERTRUDE: I should not wish you to say more than I deserve.

TRUEMAN: There's a bold minx! [*Aside.*]

GERTRUDE: Since my affairs seem to have excited your interest—I will not say *curiosity*—perhaps you even feel a desire to inspect my correspondence? There, [*handing the letter*] I pride myself upon my good nature,—you may like to take advantage of it?

TRUEMAN: With what an air she carries it off! [*Aside.*] Take advantage of it? So I will. [*Reads.*] What's this? "French chambermaid—Count—impostor—infatuation—Seraphina—Millinette—disguised myself—expose him." Thunder and lightning! I see it all! Come and kiss me, girl! [GERTRUDE *evinces surprise.*] No, no—I forgot—it won't do to come to that yet! She's a rare girl! I'm out of my senses with joy! I don't know what to do with myself! Tol, de rol, de rol, de ra! [*Capers and sings.*]

GERTRUDE: What a remarkable old man! [*Aside.*] Then you do me justice, Mr. Trueman?

TRUEMAN: I say I don't! Justice? You're above all dependence upon justice! Hurrah! I've found one true woman at last! *True?* [*Pauses thoughtfully.*] Humph! I didn't think of that flaw! Plotting and manoeuvering—not much truth in that! An honest girl should be above stratagems!

GERTRUDE: But my *motive*, Sir, was good.

TRUEMAN: That's not enough—your *actions* must be *good* as well as your *motives!* Why could you not tell the silly girl that the man was an impostor?

GERTRUDE: I did inform her of my suspicions—she ridiculed them; the plan I chose was an imprudent one, but I could not devise—

TRUEMAN: I hate devising! Give me a woman with the *firmness* to be *frank!* But no matter—I had no right to look for an angel out of Paradise; and I am as happy—as happy as a Lord! that is, ten times happier than any Lord ever was! tol, de rol, de rol! Oh! you—you —I'll thrash every fellow that says a word against you!

GERTRUDE: You will have plenty of employment then, Sir, for I do not know of one just now who would speak in my favor!

TRUEMAN: Not *one,* eh? Why, where's your dear Mr. Twinkle? I know all about it—can't say that I admire your choice of a husband! But there's no accounting for a girl's taste.

GERTRUDE: Mr. Twinkle! Indeed you are quite mistaken!

TRUEMAN: No—really? Then you're not taken with him, eh?

GERTRUDE: Not even with his rhymes.

TRUEMAN: Hang that old mother meddle-much! What a fool she has made of me. And so you're quite free, and I may choose a husband for you myself? Heart-whole, eh?

GERTRUDE: I—I—I trust there is nothing *unsound* about my heart.

TRUEMAN: There it is again. Don't prevaricate, girl! I tell you an *evasion* is a *lie in contemplation,* and I hate lying! Out with the truth! Is your heart *free* or not?

GERTRUDE: Nay, Sir, since you *demand* an answer, permit *me* to demand by what right you ask the question?

[*Enter* HOWARD.]

Colonel Howard here!

TRUEMAN: I'm out again! What's the Colonel to her? [*Retires up.*]

HOWARD: [*Crosses to her.*] I have come, Gertrude, to bid you farewell. To-morrow I resign my commission and leave this city, perhaps for ever. You, Gertrude, it is you who have exiled me! After last evening—

TRUEMAN: [*Coming forward to* HOWARD.] What the plague have you got to say about last evening?

HOWARD: Mr. Trueman!

TRUEMAN: What have you got to say about last evening? and what have you to say to that little girl at all? It's Tiffany's precious daughter you're in love with.

HOWARD: Miss Tiffany? Never! I never had the slightest pretension—

TRUEMAN: That lying old woman! But I'm glad of it! Oh! Ah! Um! [*Looking significantly at* GERTRUDE *and then at* HOWARD.] I see how it is. So you don't choose to marry Seraphina, eh? Well now, whom do you choose to marry? [*Glancing at* GERTRUDE.]

HOWARD: I shall not marry at all!

TRUEMAN: You won't? [*Looking at them both again.*] Why you don't mean to say that you don't like—[*Points with his thumb to* GERTRUDE.]

GERTRUDE: Mr. Trueman, I may have been wrong to boast of my good nature, but do not presume too far upon it.

HOWARD: You like frankness, Mr. Trueman, therefore I will speak plainly. I have long cherished a dream from which I was last night rudely awakened.

TRUEMAN: And that's what you call speaking plainly? Well, I differ with you! But I can guess what you mean. Last night you suspected Gertrude there of—[*Angrily.*] of what no man shall ever suspect her again while I'm above ground! You did her injustice,—it was a mistake! There, now that matter's settled. Go, and ask her to forgive you,—she's woman enough to do it! Go, go!

HOWARD: Mr. Trueman, you have forgotten to whom you dictate.

TRUEMAN: Then you won't do it? you won't ask her pardon?

HOWARD: Most undoubtedly I will not—not at any man's bidding. I must first know—

TRUEMAN: You won't do it? Then if I don't give you a lesson in politeness—

HOWARD: I will be because you find me your *tutor* in the same science. I am not a man to brook an insult, Mr. Trueman! but we'll not quarrel in presence of the lady.

TRUEMAN: Won't we? I don't know that—

GERTRUDE: Pray, Mr. Trueman—Colonel Howard, pray desist, Mr. Trueman, for my sake! [*Taking hold of his arm to hold him back.*] Colonel Howard, if you will read this letter it will explain everything. [*Hands letter to* HOWARD, *who reads.*]

TRUEMAN: He don't deserve an explanation! Didn't I tell him that it was a mistake? Refuse to beg your pardon! I'll teach him, I'll teach him!

HOWARD: [*After reading.*] Gertrude, how have I wronged you!

TRUEMAN: Oh, you'll beg her pardon now? [*Between them.*]

HOWARD: Hers, Sir, and yours! Gertrude, I fear—

TRUEMAN: You needn't,—she'll forgive you. You don't know these women as well as I do,—they're always ready to pardon; it's their nature, and they can't help it. Come along, I left Antony and his wife in the dining room; we'll go and find them. I've a story of my own to tell! As for you, Colonel, you may follow. Come along, Come along! [*Leads out* GERTRUDE, *followed by* HOWARD.]

[*Enter* MR. *and* MRS. TIFFANY, MR. TIFFANY *with a bundle of bills in his hand.*]

MRS. TIFFANY: I beg you won't mention the subject again, Mr. Tiffany. Nothing is more plebeian than a discussion upon economy—nothing more *ungenteel* than looking over and fretting over one's bills!

TIFFANY: Then I suppose, my dear, it is quite as ungenteel to *pay* one's bills?

MRS. TIFFANY: Certainly! I hear the *ee*-light never condescend to do anything of the kind. The honor of their invaluable patronage is sufficient for the persons they employ!

TIFFANY: *Patronage* then is a newly invented food upon which the working classes fatten? What convenient appetites poor people must have! Now listen to what I am going to say. As soon as my daughter marries Mr. Snobson—

[*Enter* PRUDENCE, *a three-cornered note in her hand.*]

PRUDENCE: Oh, dear! oh, dear! what shall we do! Such a misfortune! Such a disaster! Oh, dear! oh, dear!

MRS. TIFFANY: Prudence, you are the most tiresome creature! What *is* the matter?

PRUDENCE: [*Pacing up and down the stage.*] Such a disgrace to the whole family! But I always expected it. Oh, dear! oh, dear!

MRS. TIFFANY: [*Following her up and down the stage.*] What are you talking about, Prudence? Will you tell me what has happened?

PRUDENCE: [*Still pacing,* MRS. TIFFANY *following.*] Oh! I can't, I can't! You'll feel so dreadfully! How could she do such a thing! But I expected nothing else! I never did, I never did!

MRS. TIFFANY: [*Still following.*] Good gracious! what do you mean, Prudence? Tell me, will you tell me? I shall get into such a passion! What *is* the matter?

PRUDENCE: [*Still pacing.*] Oh, Betsy, Betsy! That your daughter should have come to that! Dear me, dear me!

TIFFANY: Seraphina? Did you say Seraphina? What has happened to her? what has she done? [*Following* PRUDENCE *up and down the stage on the opposite side from* MRS. TIFFANY.]

MRS. TIFFANY: [*Still following.*] What *has* she done? what *has* she done?

PRUDENCE: Oh! something dreadful—dreadful—shocking!

TIFFANY: [*Still following.*] Speak quickly and plainly—you torture me by this delay,—Prudence, be calm, and speak! What is it?

PRUDENCE: [*Stopping.*] Zeke just told me—he carried her travelling trunk himself—she gave him a whole dollar! Oh, my!

TIFFANY: Her trunk? where? where?

PRUDENCE: Round the corner!

MRS. TIFFANY: What did she want with her trunk? You are the most vexatious creature, Prudence! There is no bearing your ridiculous conduct!

PRUDENCE: Oh, you will have worse to bear—worse! Seraphina's gone!

TIFFANY: Gone! where?

PRUDENCE: Off!—eloped—eloped with the Count! Dear me, dear me! I always told you she would!

TIFFANY: Then I am ruined! [*Stands with his face buried in his hands.*]

MRS. TIFFANY: Oh, what a ridiculous girl! And she might have had such a splendid wedding! What could have possessed her?

TIFFANY: The devil himself possessed her, for she has ruined me past all redemption! Gone, Prudence, did you say gone? Are you *sure* they are gone?

PRUDENCE: Didn't I tell you so! Just look at this note—one might know by the very fold of it—

TIFFANY: [*Snatching the note.*] Let me see it! [*Opens the note and reads.*] "My dear Ma,—When you receive this I shall be a *countess!* Isn't it a sweet title? The Count and I were forced to be married privately, for reasons which I will explain in my next. You must pacify Pa, and put him in a good humor before I come back, though now I'm to be a countess I suppose I shouldn't care!" Undutiful huzzy! "We are going to make a little excursion and will be back in a week

"Your dutiful daughter—Seraphina."

A man's curse is sure to spring up at his own hearth,—here is mine! The sole curb upon that villain gone, I am wholly in his power! Oh! the first downward step from honor—he who take it cannot pause in his mad descent and is sure to be hurried on to ruin!

MRS. TIFFANY: Why, Mr. Tiffany, how you do take on! And I dare say to elope was the most fashionable way after all!

[*Enter* TRUEMAN, *leading* GERTRUDE, *and followed by* HOWARD.]

TRUEMAN: Where are all the folks? Here, Antony, you are the man I want. We've been hunting for you all over the house. Why—what's the matter? There's a face for a thriving city merchant! Ah! Antony, you never wore such a hang-dog look as that when you trotted about the country with your pack upon your back! Your shoulders are no broader now—but they've a heavier load to carry—that's plain!

MRS. TIFFANY: Mr. Trueman, such allusions are highly improper! What would my daughter, *the Countess,* say!

GERTRUDE: The Countess? Oh! Madam!

MRS. TIFFANY: Yes, the Countess! My daughter Seraphina, the Countess *dee* Jolimaitre! What have you to say to that? No wonder you are surprised after your *recherché, abimé* conduct! I have told you already, Miss Gertrude, that you were not a proper person to enjoy the inestimable advantages of my patronage. You are dismissed—do you understand? Discharged!

TRUEMAN: Have you done? Very well, it's my turn now. Antony, perhaps what I have to say don't concern you as much as some others —but I want you to listen to me. You remember, Antony, [*his tone becomes serious*], a blue-eyed, smiling girl—

TIFFANY: Your daughter, Sir? I remember her well.

TRUEMAN: None ever saw her to forget her! Give me your hand, man. There—that will do! Now let me go on. I never coveted wealth— yet twenty years ago I found myself the richest farmer in Catteraugus. This cursed money made my girl an object of speculation. Every idle fellow that wanted to feather his nest was sure to come courting Ruth. There was one—my heart misgave me the instant I laid eyes on him—for he was a city chap, and not over fond of the truth. But Ruth—ah! she was too pure herself to look for guile! His fine words and his fair looks—the old story—she was taken with him—I said, "no"—but the girl liked her own way better than her old father's— girls always do! and one morning—the rascal robbed me—not of my money, he would have been welcome to that—but of the only treasure I cherished—my daughter!

TIFFANY: But you forgave her!

TRUEMAN: I did! I knew she would never forgive herself—that was punishment enough! The scoundrel thought he was marrying my gold with my daughter—he was mistaken! I took care that they should never want; but that was all. She loved him—what will not woman love? The villain broke her heart—mine was tougher, or it wouldn't have stood what it did. A year after they were married, he forsook her! She came back to her old home—her old father! It couldn't last long—she pined—and pined—and—then—she died! Don't think me an old fool—though I am one—for grieving won't bring her back. [*Bursts into tears.*]

TIFFANY: It was a heavy loss!

TRUEMAN: So heavy, that I should not have cared how soon I followed her, but for the child she left! As I pressed that child in my arms, I swore that my unlucky wealth should never curse it, as it had cursed its mother! It was all I had to love—but I sent it away—and the neighbors thought it was dead. The girl was brought up tenderly but humbly by my wife's relatives in Geneva. I had her taught true independence—she had hands—capacities—and should use them! Money should never buy her a husband! for I resolved not to claim her until she had made her choice, and found the man who was willing to take her for herself alone. She turned out a rare girl! and it's time her old grandfather claimed her. Here he is to do it! And there stands Ruth's child! Old Adam's heiress! Gertrude, Gertrude! —my child!

[GERTRUDE *rushes into his arms.*]

PRUDENCE: [*After a pause.*] Do tell; I want to know! But I knew it! I always said Gertrude would turn out somebody, after all!

MRS. TIFFANY: Dear me! Gertrude an heiress! My dear Gertrude, I always thought you a very charming girl—quite YOU-NICK—an heiress! I must give her a ball! I'll introduce her into society myself—of course an heiress must make a sensation! [*Aside.*]

HOWARD: I am too bewildered even to wish her joy. Ah! there will be plenty to do that now—but the gulf between us is wider than ever. [*Aside.*]

TRUEMAN: Step forward, young man, and let us know what you are muttering about. I said I would never claim her until she had found the man who loved her for herself. I *have* claimed her—yet I never break my word—I think I *have* found that man! and here he is. [*Strikes* HOWARD *on the shoulder.*] Gertrude's yours! There—never say a word, man—don't bore me with your thanks—you can cancel all obligations by making that child happy! There—take her!—Well, girl, and what do you say?

GERTRUDE: That I rejoice too much at having found a parent for my first act to be one of disobedience! [*Gives her hand to* HOWARD.]

TRUEMAN: How very dutiful! and how disinterested!

[TIFFANY *retires up—and paces the stage, exhibiting great agitation.*]

PRUDENCE: [*To* TRUEMAN.] All the *single folks* are getting married!

TRUEMAN: No they are not. You and I are single folks, and we're not likely to get married.

MRS. TIFFANY: My dear Mr. Trueman—my sweet Gertrude, when my daughter, the Countess, returns, she will be delighted to hear of this *deenooment!* I assure you that the Countess will be quite charmed!

GERTRUDE: The Countess? Pray Madam where *is* Seraphina?

MRS. TIFFANY: The Countess *dee* Jolimaitre, my dear, is at this moment on her way to—to Washington! Where after visiting all the fashionable curiosities of the day—including the President—she will return to grace her native city!

GERTRUDE: I hope you are only jesting, Madam? Seraphina is not married?

MRS. TIFFANY: Excuse me, my dear, my daughter had this morning the honor of being united to the Count *dee* Jolimaitre!

GERTRUDE: Madam! He is an impostor!

MRS. TIFFANY: Good gracious! Gertrude, how can you talk in that disrespectful way of a man of rank? An heiress, my dear, should have better manners! The Count—

[*Enter* MILLINETTE, *crying.*]

MILLINETTE: Oh! Madame! I will tell everyting—oh! dat monstre! He break my heart!

MRS. TIFFANY: Millinette, what is the matter?

MILLINETTE: Oh! he promise to marry me—I love him much—and now Zeke say he run away vid Mademoiselle Seraphina!

MRS. TIFFANY: What insolence! The girl is mad! Count Jolimaitre marry my *femmy de chamber!*

MILLINETTE: Oh! Madame, he is not one Count, not at all! Dat is only de title he go by in dis country. De foreigners always take de large title ven dey do come here. His name *à Paris* vas Gustave Tread-mill. But he not one Frenchman at all, but he do live one long time *à Paris.* First he live vid Monsieur Vermicelle—dere he vas de head cook! Den he live vid Monsieur Tire-nez, de barber! After dat he live vid Monsieur le Comte Frippon-fin—and dere he vas le Comte's valet! Dere, now I tell everyting I feel one great deal better!

MRS. TIFFANY: Oh! good gracious! I shall faint! Not a Count! What will everybody say? It's no such thing! I say he *is* a Count! One can see the foreign *jenny says quoi* in his face! Don't you think I can tell a Count when I see one? I say he *is* a Count!

[*Enter* SNOBSON, *his hat on—his hands thrust in his pocket—evidently a little intoxicated.*]

SNOBSON: I won't stand it! I say I won't!

TIFFANY: [*Rushing up to him.*] Mr. Snobson, for heaven's sake—[*Aside.*]

SNOBSON: Keep off! I'm a hard customer to get the better of! You'll see if I don't come out strong!

TRUEMAN: [*Quietly knocking off* SNOBSON'S *hat with his stick.*] Where are your manners, man?

SNOBSON: My business ain't with you, Catteraugus; you've waked up the wrong passenger!—Now the way I'll put it into Tiff will be a caution. I'll make him wince! That extra mint julep has put the true pluck in me. Now for it! [*Aside.*] Mr. Tiffany, Sir—you needn't think to come over me, Sir—you'll have to get up a little earlier in the morning before you do *that*, Sir! I'd like to know, Sir, how you came to assist your daughter in running away with that foreign loafer? It was a downright swindle, Sir. After the conversation I and you had on that subject she wasn't your property, Sir.

TRUEMAN: What, Antony, is that the way your city clerk bullies his boss?

SNOBSON: You're drunk, Catteraugus—don't expose yourself—you're drunk! Taken a little too much toddy, my old boy! Be quiet! I'll look after you, and they won't find it out. If you want to be busy, you may take care of my *hat*—I feel so deuced weak in the chest, I don't think I *could* pick it up myself.—Now to put the screws to Tiff. [*Aside.*] Mr. Tiffany, Sir—you have broken your word, as no virtuous individual—no honorable member—of—the—com—mu—ni—ty—

TIFFANY: Have some pity, Mr. Snobson, I beseech you! I had nothing to do with my daughter's elopement! I will agree to anything you desire—your salary shall be doubled—trebled—[*Aside to him.*]

SNOBSON: [*Aloud.*] No you don't. No bribery and corruption.

TIFFANY: I implore you to be silent. You shall become partner of the concern, if you please—only do not speak. You are not yourself at this moment. [*Aside to him.*]

SNOBSON: Ain't I though. I feel *twice* myself. I feel like two Snobsons rolled into one, and I'm chock full of the spunk of a dozen! Now Mr. Tiffany, Sir—

TIFFANY: I shall go distracted! Mr. Snobson, if you have one spark of manly feeling—[*Aside to him.*]

TRUEMAN: Antony, why do you stand disputing with that drunken jackass? Where's your nigger? Let him kick the critter out, and be of use for once in his life.

SNOBSON: Better be quiet, Catteraugus. This ain't your hash, so keep your spoon out of the dish. Don't expose yourself, old boy.

TRUEMAN: Turn him out, Antony!

SNOBSON: He daren't do it! Ain't I up to him? Ain't he in my power? Can't I knock him into a cocked hat with a word? And now he's got my steam up—I *will* do it!

TIFFANY: [*Beseechingly.*] Mr. Snobson—my friend—

SNOBSON: It's no go—steam's up—and I don't stand at anything!

TRUEMAN: You won't *stand* here long unless you mend your manners —you're not the first man I've *upset* because he didn't know his place.

SNOBSON: I know where Tiff's place is, and that's in the *States' Prison!* It's bespoke already. He would have it! He wouldn't take pattern of me, and behave like a gentleman! He's a *forger,* Sir!

[TIFFANY *throws himself into a chair in an attitude of despair; the others stand transfixed with astonishment.*]

He's been forging Dick Anderson's endorsements of his notes these ten months. He's got a couple in the bank that will send him to the wall any how—if he can't make a raise. I took them there myself! Now you know what he's worth. I said I'd expose him, and I have done it!

MRS. TIFFANY: Get out of the house! You ugly, little, drunken brute, get out! It's not true. Mr. Trueman, put him out; you have got a stick —put him out!

[*Enter* SERAPHINA, *in her bonnet and shawl—a parasol in her hand.*]

SERAPHINA: I hope Zeke hasn't delivered my note. [*Stops in surprise at seeing the persons assembled.*]

MRS. TIFFANY: Oh, here is the Countess! [*Advances to embrace her.*]

TIFFANY: [*Starting from his seat, and seizing* SERAPHINA *violently by the arm.*] Are—you—married?

SERAPHINA: Goodness, Pa, how you frighten me! No, I'm not married, *quite.*

TIFFANY: Thank heaven.

MRS. TIFFANY: [*Drawing* SERAPHINA *aside.*] What's the matter? Why did you come back?

SERAPHINA: The clergyman wasn't at home—I came back for my jewels—the Count said nobility couldn't get on without them.

TIFFANY: I may be saved yet! Seraphina, my child, you will not see me disgraced—ruined! I have been a kind father to you—at least I have tried to be one—although your mother's extravagance made a *mad-man* of me! The Count is an impostor—you seemed to like him—

[*Pointing to* SNOBSON.] Heaven forgive me! [*Aside.*] Marry *him* and save *me*. You, Mr. Trueman, you will be my friend in this hour of extreme need—you will advance the sum which I require—I pledge myself to return it. My wife—my child—who will support them were I—the thought makes me frantic! You will aid me? You had a child yourself.

TRUEMAN: But I did not *sell* her—it was her own doings. Shame on you, Antony! Put a price on your own flesh and blood! Shame on such foul traffic!

TIFFANY: Save me—I conjure you—for my father's sake.

TRUEMAN: For your *father's* SON's sake I will *not* aid you in becoming a greater villain than you are!

GERTRUDE: Mr. Trueman—Father, I should say—save him—do not embitter our happiness by permitting this calamity to fall upon another—

TRUEMAN: Enough—I did not need your voice, child. I am going to settle this matter my own way. [*Goes up to* SNOBSON—*who has seated himself and fallen asleep—tilts him out of the chair.*]

SNOBSON: [*Waking up.*] Eh? Where's the fire? Oh! it's you, Catteraugus.

TRUEMAN: If I comprehend aright, you have been for some time aware of your principal's forgeries? [*As he says this, he beckons to* HOWARD, *who advances as witness.*]

SNOBSON: You've hit the nail, Catteraugus! Old chap saw that I was up to him six months ago; left off throwing dust into my eyes—

TRUEMAN: Oh, he did!

SNOBSON: Made no bones of forging Anderson's name at my elbow.

TRUEMAN: Forged at your elbow? You saw him do it?

SNOBSON: I did.

TRUEMAN: Repeatedly?

SNOBSON: Re—pea—ted—ly.

TRUEMAN: Then you, Rattlesnake, if he goes to the States' Prison, you'll take up your quarters there too. You are an accomplice, an *accessory!*

[TRUEMAN *walks away and seats himself,* HOWARD *rejoins* GERTRUDE. SNOBSON *stands for some time bewildered.*]

SNOBSON: The deuce, so I am! I never thought of that! I must make myself scarce. I'll be off! Tiff, I say Tiff! [*going up to him and speaking confidentially*] that drunken old rip has got us in his power. Let's give him the slip and be off. They want men of genius at the West, —we're sure to get on! You—you can set up for a writing master,

and teach copying *signatures;* and I—I'll give lectures on *temperance!*
You won't come, eh? Then I'm off without you. Good bye, Catteraugus! Which is the way to California? [*Steals off.*]

TRUEMAN: There's one debt your city owes me. And now let us see
what other nuisances we can abate. Antony, I'm not given to preaching, therefore I shall not say much about what you have done. Your
face speaks for itself,—the crime has brought its punishment along
with it.

TIFFANY: Indeed it has, Sir! In *one year* I have lived a *century* of misery.

TRUEMAN: I believe you, and upon one condition I will assist you—

TIFFANY: My friend—my first, ever kind friend,—only name it!

TRUEMAN: You must sell your house and all these gew gaws, and bundle
your wife and daughter off to the country. There let them learn economy, true independence, and home virtues, instead of foreign follies.
As for yourself, continue your business—but let moderation, in future, be your counsellor, and let *honesty* be your confidential clerk.

TIFFANY: Mr. Trueman, you have made existence once more precious
to me! My wife and daughter shall quit the city to-morrow, and—

PRUDENCE: It's all coming right! It's all coming right! We'll go to the
county of Catteraugus. [*Walking up to* TRUEMAN.]

TRUEMAN: No you won't,—I make that a stipulation, Antony; keep
clear of Catteraugus. None of your fashionable examples there!

[JOLIMAITRE *appears in the conservatory and peeps into the room
unperceived.*]

COUNT: What can detain Seraphina? We ought to be off!

MILLINETTE: [*Turns round, perceives him, runs and forces him into the
room.*] Here he is! Ah, Gustave, mon cher Gustave! I have you now
and we never part no more. Don't frown, Gustave, don't frown—

TRUEMAN: Come forward, Mr. Count! and for the edification of fashionable society confess that you're an impostor.

COUNT: An impostor? Why, you abominable old—

TRUEMAN: Oh, your feminine friend has told us all about it, the cook
—the valet—barber and all that sort of thing. Come, confess, and
something may be done for you.

COUNT: Well then, I do confess I am no count; but really, ladies and
gentlemen, I may recommend myself as the most capital cook.

MRS. TIFFANY: Oh, Seraphina!

SERAPHINA: Oh, Ma! [*They embrace and retire up.*]

TRUEMAN: Promise me to call upon the whole circle of your fashionable acquaintances with your own advertisements and in your cook's attire, and I will set you up in business to-morrow. Better turn stomachs than turn heads!

MILLINETTE: But you will marry me?

COUNT: Give us your hand, Millinette! Sir, command me for the most delicate *paté*—the daintiest *croquette à la royale*—the most transcendent *omelette soufflée* that ever issued from a French pastry-cook's oven. I hope you will pardon my conduct, but I heard that in America, where you pay homage to titles while you profess to scorn them—where *Fashion* makes the basest coin current—where you have no kings, no princes, no *nobility*—

TRUEMAN: Stop there! I object to your use of that word. When justice is found only among lawyers—health among physicians—and patriotism among politicians, *then* may you say that there is no *nobility* where there are no titles! But we *have* kings, princes, and nobles in abundance—of *Nature's stamp*, if not of *Fashion's*,—we have honest men, warm-hearted and brave, and we have women—gentle, fair, and true, to whom no *title* could add *nobility*.

EPILOGUE

PRUDENCE: I told you so! And now you hear and see. I told you *Fashion* would the fashion be!

TRUEMAN: Then both its point and moral I distrust.

COUNT: Sir, is that liberal?

HOWARD: Or is it just?

TRUEMAN: The guilty have escaped!

TIFFANY: Is, therefore, sin
Made charming? Ah! there's punishment within!
Guilt ever carries his own scourge along.

GERTRUDE: Virtue her own reward!

TRUEMAN: You're right, I'm wrong.

MRS. TIFFANY: How we have been deceived!

PRUDENCE: I told you so.

SERAPHINA: To lose at once a title and a beau!

COUNT JOLIMAITRE: A count no more, I'm no more of *account*.

TRUEMAN: But to a nobler title you may mount,
And be in time—who knows?—an honest man!

COUNT JOLIMAITRE: Eh, Millinette?

MILLINETTE: Oh, oui,—I know you can!

GERTRUDE: [To audience.] But, ere we close the scene, a word with
    you,—
  We charge you answer,—Is this picture true?
  Some little mercy to our efforts show,
  Then let the world your honest verdict know.
  Here let it see portrayed its ruling passion,
  And learn to prize at its just value—Fashion.

THE END

UNCLE TOM'S CABIN *(1852)*

George L. Aiken

The success of *The Drunkard* and other temperance plays indicated that
American audiences were ready for sensation plays that at least acknowledged topical issues. At the same time as Smith's vehicle for dis-
playing delirium tremens was drawing crowds, however, another form
of stage performance was growing rapidly in popularity: the minstrel
show. Often credited to the actor Thomas Dartmouth Rice, who first
"jumped Jim Crow" on stage in the 1830s, minstrelsy soon evolved into
a variety show featuring white men in blackface doing songs, skits, and
jokes for mass audiences. One of the ironies of the period of the 1840s
and 1850s is that at the very time when the crisis over slavery was
coming to a head, American theatergoers were flocking to see escapist
shows about carefree blacks. It was almost as if the abolitionist demand
to end slavery pushed uncommitted citizens into pretending that the
"Negro Problem" was nothing more than an evening's light entertainment.

Mowatt's *Fashion*, which can also be seen in the context of the
minstrel-show craze of the mid-1840s, in its small way challenged some
of the stereotypes in black portrayal. A more radical challenge would
come from the novelist Harriet Beecher Stowe, whose book *Uncle Tom's
Cabin; or, Life Among the Lowly* began appearing serially in 1851. The
greatest best-seller of the time, *Uncle Tom's Cabin* created an excitement few books in publishing history have ever matched. Here was a
novel with all the elements of midcentury popular fiction—parallel
plots, a sentimental heroine, and good pitched against evil—that not
only grappled with a great political theme, slavery, but also dared to
portray black characters who, instead of being comic background, took
center page and sympathy. The handsome, articulate, and fearless
George Harris; the daring mother, Eliza Harris; and the Christlike Uncle
Tom resisted the usual depiction of blacks in books and on stage. To
put this story in the theater would involve either major changes or risks.

Stowe's novel has had a major reinterpretation in recent years, helped
along by Jane Tompkins's query into the place of the novel in the formation of the literary canon. Indeed, the biography of Stowe by Joan
Hedrick has continued the push to bring the "crusader in crinoline," as

she was called by an earlier biographer, into the spotlight. But the play of *Uncle Tom* has another and, to some extent, a divergent history from the novel. Stowe's first installment appeared in the *National Era* on June 5, 1851, and continued until April 1, 1852. On March 20, 1852, *Uncle Tom* appeared in book form. Some of the early attempts to dramatize were based on the serial version, without knowledge of the ending. And as the nineteenth-century stage was the equivalent to today's television movie industry, such a book would naturally attract opportunist playwrights and managers who thought to make a profit from Stowe's popularity. Since there was not yet a uniform copyright law, no one needed to ask the author's permission or pay royalties to her for transforming her novel into a play.

The first important version brought to the stage was that of Charles Western Taylor, appearing at New York's National Theatre in late August and early September 1852; this one, like others, had a happy ending. Other attempts include Clifton Tayleure's, opening in Detroit in October 1852, and Henry J. Conway's, eventually staged by P. T. Barnum in New York in November 1853. Barnum, who had earlier brought *The Drunkard* to his multimedia museum in order to make money from the appearance of moral reform, exploited racial prejudice in attracting patrons and dropped reform like a hot horseshoe. The entrepreneur wanted no white person to feel threatened by the slavery issue and consequently advertised the happy ending. Others, Southerners and pro-slavery writers in particular, created novels and plays that ridiculed Stowe's book and attempted to show an Uncle Tom–like character "as he really is"—a darky buffoon, not a human being. In large measure, what Stowe intended—to encourage Christian feeling for the downtrodden of real life—was largely lost in many of the versions that made it to the stage.

After Taylor's *Tom* had already died in New York, another was just catching on in upstate Troy. On September 27, 1852, George C. Howard mounted a production scripted by his cousin, George L. Aiken (1830–1876)—about whom little has been written—and starring Mrs. Howard (Caroline Emily Fox, whom Howard had met while playing in *The Drunkard*) as Topsy; Howard as St. Clare; and his daughter, Cordelia, then four years old, as Eva. This play, in four acts, covered the novel only as far as the death of Eva; another play, up to the death of Tom, also four acts, was performed in November. Finally, Aiken—who played George Harris and George Shelby in Troy—combined his two plays into one six-act version. On December 1, after one hundred performances of the various Uncle Tom plays, Howard closed out his Troy run, one of the most remarkable for a provincial playhouse in the history of the American theater.

A. H. Purdy, who had staged the failed Taylor script, encouraged the Howards to bring the Troy show to New York. The rest is history—or at least an important part of it. Purdy's production of Aiken's text, which successfully resisted the competition from Barnum's Conway version, ran for 325 performances from July 18, 1853, to May 13, 1854. Meanwhile, other versions popped up everywhere, including translated plays throughout Europe. After the Civil War, Uncle Tom did not lose his appeal; traveling troupes turned "Tom shows" into an industry. Harry Birdoff chronicles the appearance of humble performances of just a few actors—and "double mammoth" versions in which two Topsys or two Toms would appear on stage at the same time. These postwar stagings were popular everywhere, including the South. The literary historian C. Hugh Holman used to tell his students of his boyhood in South Carolina in the early twentieth century when the coming of the Tom show to town was the big excitement of the year. Despite the popularity of Stowe's novel, most Americans probably got their Uncle Tom experience from one of the myriad performances on stage.

Of all the stage versions, Aiken's comes closest to matching the novel. All the major characters are present: Eliza, George Harris (whose violent self-defense outraged many proponents of the passive Negro stereotype), St. Clare, Eva, Ophelia, Cassy, Legree, and, of course, Uncle Tom himself. The scenes that became best known on stage were Eliza crossing the ice floe, the death of little Eva, and the death of Uncle Tom. But Aiken, for all his fidelity to Stowe's text and his ability to recognize the theatricality of some of her material, also knew that he was writing for a different medium. The humor in Stowe, some of it at Ophelia's expense, is broadened by Aiken to include the added character of Gumption Cute, a laughable loser, and Ophelia herself, who becomes a one-joke character muttering "shiftless!" One of the biggest transformations is Topsy; while some of the dialogue is quite like that in the novel, Aiken's character also dances a breakdown and becomes a thoroughly theatrical character—one very near a minstrel "darky." "In like Topsy" became a phrase for the stage figure—played by an adult white woman in burned cork—not the abused child of Stowe's book. As Jeffrey Mason observes, the net effect of Aiken's changes is to cancel out the serious material, so as to minimize the political controversy generated by pro- and antiabolitionist responses to book and play.

Nevertheless, despite the compromises necessary to put on anything like a portrayal of reality for the midcentury stage, Aiken's dramatization provides a significant advance in the representation of blacks on stage. It offers, in essence, a new set of types to replace the minstrel-show caricatures of the time. In fact, the actor who played Uncle Tom first, Greenbury Germon, had to be encouraged to take the role as something new because he did not want to play yet another minstrel figure. Harris and Eliza are both light-skinned blacks who speak not in dialect but in the stage diction familiar to middle-class whites. Thus, one of Stowe's objects—to get her white audience to identify with the thoughts and feelings of blacks—is accomplished through this mediating strategy of turning slaves into middle-class strivers. Tom and Topsy, though very different characters, are both portrayed as dark and dialect-speaking; thus, they are close enough to earlier representations to require only a small leap to accept them on some sympathetic grounds.

This mediation between audience prejudice and complication of character on stage continues with another clever Stowe device, the use of the New Englander in the Deep South. By having the worst slaveholder be a transplanted Yankee, Stowe and Aiken appease (or attempt to appease) those who might see Uncle Tom as a sectional attack. Like other stage plays about the subject, notably The Octoroon, Uncle Tom's Cabin seeks amelioration by promising sensation and delivering comforting entertainment. Sobbing over the staged death of the little white girl was an easy enough thing to do at a time when grieving families (like the Stowes) routinely brought in daguerreotypists to photograph their just-dead infants. Feeling sorry for the enterprising young black couple was also easy when their makeup was light and their mode of speech familiar. Aiken's adaptation of Stowe may seem itself to perpetuate racial stereotypes, but in its time, it gave to audiences something new to feel: sympathy for enacted African Americans on stage.

SELECTED BIBLIOGRAPHY

Birdoff, Harry. The World's Greatest Hit: Uncle Tom's Cabin. New York: Vanni, 1947.

Dormon, James H., Jr. Theater in the Ante-Bellum South, 1815–1861, 278–80. Chapel Hill: University of North Carolina Press, 1967.

Disher, Maurice Willson. Blood and Thunder: Mid-Victorian Melodrama and Its Origins, 244–47. 1949; New York: Haskell House, 1974.

Drummond, A. M., and Richard Moody. "The Hit of the Century: Uncle Tom's Cabin—1852–1952." Educational Theatre Journal 4 (1952): 315–22.

Grimsted, David A. "Uncle Tom from Page to Stage: Limitations of Nineteenth-Century Drama." *Quarterly Journal of Speech* 56 (1970): 235–44.

Hedrick, Joan D. *Harriet Beecher Stowe: A Life*. New York: Oxford University Press, 1994.

Hodge, Francis. *Yankee Theatre: The Image of America on the Stage, 1825–1850*, 259. Austin: University of Texas Press, 1964.

McConachie, Bruce A. "Out of the Kitchen and into the Marketplace: Normalizing *Uncle Tom's Cabin* for the Antebellum Stage." *Journal of American Drama and Theatre* 3 (1991): 5–28.

McDowell, John H. " 'I'm Going There, Uncle Tom': Original Scenery, Documents, and a Promptbook Production of *Uncle Tom's Cabin*." *Theatre Studies* 24–25 (1977–1979): 119–38.

Mason, Jeffrey. "*Uncle Tom's Cabin* (1852) and the Politics of Race." In *Melodrama and the Myth of America*, 89–126. Bloomington: Indiana University Press, 1993. New historicist.

Moody, Richard. *America Takes the Stage: Romanticism in American Drama and Theatre, 1750–1900*, 69–78, 127–28. Bloomington: Indiana University Press, 1955.

"Places of Public Amusement. Theatres and Concert Rooms." *Putnam's Monthly Magazine* 3 (1854): 141–52; reprinted in *The Dawning of American Drama: American Dramatic Criticism, 1746–1915*, edited by Jürgen C. Wolter, 143–46. Westport, Conn.: Greenwood, 1993. Contemporary comment.

Rahill, Frank. *The World of Melodrama*, 247–53. University Park: Pennsylvania State University Press, 1967.

Richardson, Gary A. *American Drama from the Colonial Period through World War I: A Critical History*, 103–6. New York: Twayne, 1993.

Robson, Mark. "Aiken's Dramatic Version of *Uncle Tom's Cabin*: A Success Story for the Negro Characters." *Publications of the Arkansas Philological Association* 10 (1984): 69–78.

Toll, Robert C. *Blacking Up: The Minstrel Show in Nineteenth-Century America*, 88–97. New York: Oxford University Press, 1974.

Tompkins, Jane. "Sentimental Power: *Uncle Tom's Cabin* and the Politics of Literary History." In *Sensational Designs: The Cultural Work of American Fiction, 1790–1860*, 122–46. New York: Oxford University Press, 1985. Influential essay on Stowe's novel whose insights are also useful for play.

UNCLE TOM'S CABIN;

OR,

LIFE AMONG THE LOWLY.

A Domestic Drama in Six Acts.

DRAMATIZED BY GEORGE L. AIKEN.

TO WHICH ARE ADDED

A Description of the Costumes—Cast of the Characters—
Entrances and Exits—
Relative Positions of the Performers on the Stage, and
the whole of the Stage Business

AS PERFORMED AT THE

PRINCIPAL ENGLISH AND AMERICAN THEATERS.

CAST OF CHARACTERS

UNCLE TOM
GEORGE HARRIS
GEORGE SHELBY
ST. CLARE
PHINEAS FLETCHER
GUMPTION CUTE
MR. WILSON
DEACON PERRY
SHELBY
HALEY
LEGREE
TOM LOKER
MARKS
SKEGGS
MANN
ADOLF
SAMBO
QUIMBO
DOCTOR
WAITER
HARRY, a Child
EVA
ELIZA
CASSY
MARIE
OPHELIA
CHLOE
TOPSY
EMMELINE

UNCLE TOM'S CABIN

ACT I

SCENE 1: *Plain Chamber.*

[*Enter* ELIZA, *meeting* GEORGE.]

ELIZA: Ah! George, is it you? Well, I am so glad you've come! [GEORGE *regards her mournfully.*] Why don't you smile, and ask after Harry?

GEORGE: [*Bitterly.*] I wish he'd never been born! I wish I'd never been born myself!

ELIZA: [*Sinking her head upon his breast and weeping.*] Oh, George!

GEROGE: There, now, Eliza; it's too bad for me to make you feel so. Oh! how I wish you had never seen me—you might have been happy!

ELIZA: George! George! how can you talk so? What dreadful thing has happened, or is going to happen? I'm sure we've been very happy till lately.

GEORGE: So we have, dear. But oh! I wish I'd never seen you, nor you me.

ELIZA: Oh, George! how can you?

GEORGE: Yes, Eliza, it's all misery! misery! The very life is burning out of me! I'm a poor, miserable, forlorn drudge! I shall only drag you down with me, that's all! What's the use of our trying to do anything—trying to know anything—trying to be anything? I wish I was dead!

ELIZA: Oh! now, dear George, that is really wicked. I know how you feel about losing your place in the factory, and you have a hard master; but pray be patient—

GEORGE: Patient! Haven't I been patient? Did I say a word when he came and took me away—for no earthly reason—from the place where everybody was kind to me? I'd paid him truly every cent of my earnings, and they all say I worked well.

ELIZA: Well, it *is* dreadful; but, after all, he is your master, you know.

GEORGE: My master! And who made him my master? That's what I think of! What right has he to me? I'm as much of a man as he is! What right has he to make a dray-horse of me?—to take me from things I can do better than he can, and put me to work that any horse can do? He tries to do it; he says he'll bring me down and humble me, and he puts me to just the hardest, meanest and dirtiest work, on purpose.

ELIZA: Oh, George! George! you frighten me. Why, I never heard you talk so. I'm afraid you'll do something dreadful. I don't wonder at your feelings at all; but oh, do be careful—for my sake, for Harry's.

GEORGE: I have been careful, and I have been patient, but it's growing worse and worse—flesh and blood can't bear it any longer. Every chance he can get to insult and torment me he takes. He says that though I don't say anything, he sees that I've got the devil in me, and he means to bring it out; and one of these days it will come out, in a way that he won't like, or I'm mistaken.

ELIZA: Well, I always thought that I must obey my master and mistress, or I couldn't be a Christian.

GEORGE: There is some sense in it in your case. They have brought you up like a child—fed you, clothed you and taught you, so that you have a good education—that is some reason why they should claim you. But I have been kicked and cuffed and sworn at, and what do I owe? I've paid for all my keeping a hundred times over. I won't bear it!—no, I *won't!* Master will find out that I'm one whipping won't tame. My day will come yet, if he don't look out!

ELIZA: What are you doing to do? Oh! George, don't do anything wicked; if you only trust in heaven and try to do right, it will deliver you.

GEORGE: Eliza, my heart's full of bitterness. I can't trust in heaven. Why does it let things be so?

ELIZA: Oh George! we must all have faith. Mistress says that when all things go wrong to us, we must believe that heaven is doing the very best.

GEORGE: That's easy for people to say who are sitting on their sofas and riding in their carriages; but let them be where I am—I guess it would come some harder. I wish I could be good; but my heart burns and can't be reconciled. You couldn't, in my place, you can't now, if I tell you all I've got to say; you don't know the whole yet.

ELIZA: What do you mean?

GEORGE: Well, lately my master has been saying that he was a fool to let me marry off the place—that he hates Mr. Shelby and all his tribe—and he says he won't let me come here any more, and that I shall take a wife and settle down on his place.

ELIZA: But you were married to *me* by the minister, as much as if you had been a white man.

GEORGE: Don't you know I can't hold you for my wife if he chooses to part us? That is why I wish I'd never seen you—it would have been better for us both—it would have been better for our poor child if he had never been born.

ELIZA: Oh! but my master is so kind.

GEORGE: Yes, but who knows?—he may die, and then Harry may be sold to nobody knows who. What pleasure is it that he is handsome and smart and bright? I tell you, Eliza, that a sword will pierce through your soul for every good and pleasant thing your child is or has. It will make him worth too much for you to keep.

ELIZA: Heaven forbid!

GEORGE: So, Eliza, my girl, bear up now, and good-by, for I'm going.

ELIZA: Going, George! Going where?

GEORGE: To Canada;[1] and when I'm there I'll buy you—that's all the hope that's left us. You have a kind master, that won't refuse to sell you. I'll buy you and the boy—heaven helping me, I will!

ELIZA: Oh, dreadful! If you should be taken?

GEORGE: I won't be taken, Eliza—I'll *die* first! I'll be free, or I'll die!

ELIZA: You will not kill yourself?

GEORGE: No need for that; they will kill me, fast enough. I will never go down the river alive.

ELIZA: Oh, George! for my sake, do be careful. Don't lay hands on yourself, or anybody else. You are tempted too much, but don't. Go, if you must, but go carefully, prudently, and pray heaven to help you!

GEORGE: Well, then, Eliza, hear my plan. I'm going home quite resigned, you understand, as if all was over. I've got some preparations made, and there are those that will help me; and in the course of a few days I shall be among the missing. Well, now, good-by.

ELIZA: A moment—our boy.

GEORGE: [*Choked with emotion.*] True, I had forgotten him; one last look, and then farewell!

ELIZA: And heaven grant it be not forever! [*Exeunt.*]

SCENE 2: *A dining-room.—Table and chairs.—Dessert, wine, &c., on table.*—SHELBY *and* HALEY *discovered at table.*

SHELBY: That is the way I should arrange the matter.

HALEY: I can't make trade that way—I positively can't, Mr. Shelby. [*Drinks.*]

SHELBY: Why, the fact is, Haley, Tom is an uncommon fellow! He is

certainly worth that sum anywhere—steady, honest, capable, man-
ages my whole farm like a clock!

HALEY: You mean honest, as niggers go. [*Fills glass.*]

SHELBY: No; I mean, really, Tom is a good, steady, sensible, pious fellow. He got religion at a camp-meeting, four years ago, and I believe
he really *did* get it. I've trusted him since then, with everything I
have—money, house, horses, and let him come and go round the
country, and I always found him true and square in everything!

HALEY: Some folks don't believe there is pious niggers, Shelby, but *I do.*
I had a fellow, now, in this yer last lot I took to Orleans—'twas as
good as a meetin' now, really, to hear that critter pray; and he was
quite gentle and quiet like. He fetched me a good sum, too, for I
bought him cheap of a man that was 'bliged to sell out, so I realized
six hundred on him. Yes, I consider religion a valeyable thing in a
nigger, when it's the genuine article and no mistake.

SHELBY: Well, Tom's got the real article, if ever a fellow had. Why, last
fall I let him go to Cincinnati alone, to do business for me and bring
home five hundred dollars. "Tom," says I to him, "I trust you, because I think you are a Christian—I know you wouldn't cheat." Tom
comes back sure enough; I knew he would. Some low fellows, they
say, said to him—"Tom, why don't you make tracks for Canada?"
"Ah, master trusted me, and I couldn't," was his answer. They told
me all about it. I am sorry to part with Tom, I must say. You ought
to let him cover the whole balance of the debt, and you would, Haley,
if you had any conscience.

HALEY: Well, I've got just as much conscience as any man in business
can afford to keep, just a little, you know, to swear by, as 'twere;
and then I'm ready to do anything in reason to 'blige friends, but
this yer, you see, is a leetle too hard on a fellow—a leetle too hard!
[*Fills glass again.*]

SHELBY: Well, then, Haley, how will you trade?

HALEY: Well, haven't you a boy or a girl that you could throw in with
Tom?

SHELBY: Hum! none that I could well spare; to tell the truth, it's only
hard necessity makes me willing to sell at all. I don't like parting
with any of my hands, that's a fact.

[HARRY *runs in.*]

Hulloa! Jim Crow! [*Throws a bunch of raisins towards him.*] Pick
that up now. [HARRY *does so.*]

HALEY: Bravo, little 'un! [*Throws an orange, which* HARRY *catches. He sings and dances around the stage.*] Hurrah! Bravo! What a young 'un! That chap's a case, I'll promise. Tell you what, Shelby, fling in that chap, and I'll settle the business. Come, now, if that ain't doing the thing up about the rightest!

[ELIZA *enters.—Starts on beholding* HALEY, *and gazes fearfully at* HARRY, *who runs and clings to her dress, showing the orange, &c.*]

SHELBY: Well, Eliza?

ELIZA: I was looking for Harry, please, sir.

SHELBY: Well, take him away, then.

[ELIZA *grasps the child eagerly in her arms, and casting another glance of apprehension at* HALEY, *exits hastily.*]

HALEY: By Jupiter! there's an article, now. You might make your fortune on that ar gal in Orleans any day. I've seen over a thousand in my day, paid down for gals not a bit handsomer.

SHELBY: I don't want to make my fortune on her. Another glass of wine. [*Fills the glasses.*]

HALEY: [*Drinks and smacks his lips.*] Capital wine—first chop! Come, how will you trade about the gal? What shall I say for her? What'll you take?

SHELBY: Mr. Haley, she is not to be sold. My wife wouldn't part with her for her weight in gold.

HALEY: Ay, ay! women always say such things, 'cause they hain't no sort of calculation. Just show 'em how many watches, feathers and trinkets one's weight in gold would buy, and that alters the case, I reckon.

SHELBY: I tell you, Haley, this must not be spoken of—I say no, and I mean no.

HALEY: Well, you'll let me have the boy tho'; you must own that I have come down pretty handsomely for him.

SHELBY: What on earth can you want with the child?

HALEY: Why, I've got a friend that's going into this yer branch of the business—wants to buy up handsome boys to raise for the market. Well, what do you say?

SHELBY: I'll think the matter over and talk with my wife.

HALEY: Oh, certainly, by all means; but I'm in a devil of a hurry, and shall want to know as soon as possible, what I may depend on. [*Rises and puts on his overcoat, which hangs on a chair.—Takes hat and whip.*]

SHELBY: Well, call up this evening, between six and seven, and you shall
    have my answer.

HALEY: All right. Take care of yourself, old boy!   [*Exit.*]

SHELBY: If anybody had ever told me that I should sell Tom to those
    rascally traders, I should never have believed it. Now it must come
    for aught I see, and Eliza's child too. So much for being in debt,
    heigho! The fellow sees his advantage and means to push it.

SCENE 3: *Snowy landscape.*—UNCLE TOM'S *Cabin.*—*Snow on roof.*—
Praticable door and window.—*Dark Stage.*—*Music.*

    [*Enter* ELIZA *hastily, with* HARRY *in her arms.*]

ELIZA: My poor boy; they have sold you, but your mother will save you
    yet!

    [*Goes to Cabin and taps on window.*—AUNT CHLOE *appears at
    window with a large white night-cap on.*]

CHLOE: Good Lord! what's that? My sakes alive if it ain't Lizy! Get on
    your clothes, old man, quick! I'm gwine to open the door.

    [*The door opens and* CHLOE *enters, followed by* UNCLE TOM *in
    his shirt sleeves, holding a tallow candle.*]

TOM: [*Holding the light towards* ELIZA.] Lord bless you! I'm skeered to
    look at ye, Lizy! Are ye tuck sick, or what's come over ye?

ELIZA: I'm running away, Uncle Tom and Aunt Chloe, carrying off my
    child! Master sold him!

TOM and CHLOE: Sold him!

ELIZA: Yes, sold him! I crept into the closet by mistress' door to-night,
    and heard master tell mistress that he had sold my Harry, and you,
    Uncle Tom, both, to a trader, and that the man was to take posses-
    sion to-morrow.

CHLOE: The good Lord have pity on us! Oh! it don't seem as if it was
    true. What has he done that master should sell *him?*

ELIZA: He hasn't done anything—it isn't for that. Master don't want to
    sell, and mistress—she's always good. I heard her plead and beg for
    us, but he told her 'twas no use—that he was in this man's debt, and
    he had got the power over him, and that if he did not pay him off
    clear, it would end in his having to sell the place and all the people
    and move off.

CHLOE: Well, old man, why don't you run away, too? Will you wait to be toted down the river, where they kill niggers with hard work and starving? I'd a heap rather die than go there, any day! There's time for ye, be off with Lizy—you've got a pass to come and go any time. Come, bustle up, and I'll get your things together.

TOM: No, no—I ain't going. Let Eliza go—it's her right. I wouldn't be the one to say no—'tain't in natur for her to stay; but you heard what she said? If I must be sold, or all the people on the place, and everything go to rack, why, let me be sold. I s'pose I can bar it as well as any one. Mas'r always found me on the spot—he always will. I never have broken trust, nor used my pass no ways contrary to my word, and I never will. It's better for me to go alone, than to break up the place and sell all. Mas'r ain't to blame, and he'll take care of you and the poor little 'uns! [Overcome.]

CHLOE: Now, old man, what is you gwine to cry for? Does you want to break this old woman's heart? [Crying.]

ELIZA: I saw my husband only this afternoon, and I little knew then what was to come. He told me he was going to run away. Do try, if you can, to get word to him. Tell him how I went and why I went, and tell him I'm going to try and find Canada. You must give my love to him, and tell him if I never see him again on earth, I trust we shall meet in heaven!

TOM: Dat is right, Lizy, trust in the Lord—he is our best friend—our only comforter.

ELIZA: You won't go with me, Uncle Tom?

TOM: No; time was when I would, but the Lord's given me a work among these yer poor souls, and I'll stay with 'em and bear my cross with 'em till the end. It's different with you—it's more'n you could stand, and you'd better go if you can.

ELIZA: Uncle Tom, I'll try it!

TOM: Amen! The Lord help ye!   [Exit ELIZA and HARRY.]

CHLOE: What is you gwine to do, old man? What's to become of you?

TOM: [Solemnly.] Him that saved Daniel in the den of lions—that saved the children in the fiery furnace—Him that walked on the sea and bade the winds to be still—He's alive yet! and I've faith to believe He can deliver me!

CHLOE: You is right, old man.

TOM: The Lord is good unto all that trust him, Chloe.

[Exeunt into Cabin.]

SCENE 4: *Room in Tavern by the river side.—A large window, through which the river is seen, filled with floating ice.—Moonlight.—Table and chairs brought on.*

[*Enter* PHINEAS.]

PHINEAS: Chaw me up into tobaccy ends! how in the name of all that's onpossible am I to get across that yer pesky river? It's a reg'lar blockade of ice! I promised Ruth to meet her to-night, and she'll be into my har if I don't come. [*Goes to window.*] That's a conglomerated prospect for a loveyer! What in creation's to be done? That thar river looks like a permiscuous ice-cream shop come to an awful state of friz. If I war on the adjacent bank, I wouldn't care a teetotal atom. Rile up, you old varmint, and shake the ice off your back!

[*Enter* ELIZA *and* HARRY.]

ELIZA: Courage, my boy—we have reached the river. Let it but roll between us and our pursuers, and we are safe! [*Goes to window.*] Gracious powers! the river is choked with cakes of ice!

PHINEAS: Holloa, gal!—what's the matter? You look kind of streaked.

ELIZA: Is there any ferry or boat that takes people over now?

PHINEAS: Well, I guess not; the boats have stopped running.

ELIZA: [*In dismay.*] Stopped running?

PHINEAS: Maybe you're wanting to get over—anybody sick? Ye seem mighty anxious.

ELIZA: I—I—I've got a child that's very dangerous. I never heard of it till last night, and I've walked quite a distance to-day, in hopes to get to the ferry.

PHINEAS: Well, now, that's onlucky; I'm re'lly consarned for ye. Thar's a man, a piece down here, that's going over with some truck this evening, if he duss to; he'll be in here to supper to-night, so you'd better set down and wait. That's a smart little chap. Say, young 'un, have a chaw tobaccy? [*Takes out a large plug and a bowie-knife.*]

ELIZA: No, no! not any for him.

PHINEAS: Oh! he don't use it, eh? Hain't come to it yet? Well, I have. [*Cuts off a large piece, and returns the plug and knife to pocket.*] What's the matter with the young 'un? He looks kind of white in the gills!

ELIZA: Poor fellow! he is not used to walking, and I've hurried him on so.

PHINEAS: Tuckered, eh? Well, there's a little room there, with a fire in it. Take the babby in there, make yourself comfortable till that thar ferryman shows his countenance—I'll stand the damage.

ELIZA: How shall I thank you for such kindness to a stranger?

PHINEAS: Well, if you don't know how, why, don't try; that's the tee-total. Come, vamoose!   [*Exit* ELIZA *and* HARRY.]
Chaw me into sassage meat, if that ain't a perpendicular fine gal! she's a reg'lar A No. 1 sort of female! How'n thunder am I to get across this refrigerated stream of water? I can't wait for that ferryman.

[*Enter* MARKS.]

Halloa! what sort of a critter's this? [*Advances.*] Say, stranger, will you have something to drink?

MARKS: You are excessively kind: I don't care if I do.

PHINEAS: Ah! he's a human. Holloa, thar! bring us a jug of whisky instantaneously, or expect to be teetotally chawed up! Squat yourself, stranger, and go in for enjoyment. [*They sit at table.*] Who are you, and what's your name?

MARKS: I am a lawyer, and my name is Marks.

PHINEAS: A land shark, eh? Well, I don't think no worse on you for that. The law is a kind of necessary evil; and it breeds lawyers just as an old stump does fungus. Ah! here's the whisky.

[*Enter* WAITER, *with jug and tumblers. Places them on table.*]

Here, you—take that shin-plaster. [*Gives bill.*] I don't want any change—thar's a gal stopping in that room—the balance will pay for her—d'ye hear?—vamoose! [*Exit* WAITER.—*Fills glass.*] Take hold, neighbor Marks—don't shirk the critter. Here's hoping your path of true love may never have an ice-choked river to cross! [*They drink.*]

MARKS: Want to cross the river, eh?

PHINEAS: Well, I do, stranger. Fact is, I'm in love with the teetotalist pretty girl, over on the Ohio side, that ever wore a Quaker bonnet. Take another swig, neighbor. [*Fills glasses, and they drink.*]

MARKS: A Quaker, eh?

PHINEAS: Yes—kind of strange, ain't it? The way of it was this:—I used to own a grist of niggers—had 'em to work on my plantation, just below here. Well, stranger, do you know I fell in with that gal—of course I was considerably smashed—knocked into a pretty conglomerated heap—and I told her so. She said she wouldn't hear a word from me so long as I owned a nigger!

MARKS: You sold them, I suppose?

PHINEAS: You're teetotally wrong, neighbor. I gave them all their freedom, and told 'em to vamoose!

MARKS: Ah! yes—very noble, I dare say; but rather expensive. This act
won you your lady-love, eh?

PHINEAS: You're off the track again, neighbor. She felt kind of pleased
about it, and smiled, and all that; but she said she could never be
mine unless I turned Quaker! Thunder and earth! what do you think
of that? You're a lawyer—come, now, what's your opinion? Don't
you call it a knotty point?

MARKS: Most decidedly. Of course you refused.

PHINEAS: Teetotally; but she told me to think better of it, and come to-
night and give her my final conclusion. Chaw me into mince-meat,
if I haven't made up my mind to do it!

MARKS: You astonish me!

PHINEAS: Well, you see, I can't get along without that gal;—she's sort
of fixed my flint, and I'm sure to hang fire without her. I know I
shall make a queer sort of Quaker, because you see, neighbor, I ain't
precisely the kind of material to make a Quaker out of.

MARKS: No, not exactly.

PHINEAS: Well, I can't stop no longer. I must try to get across that
candaverous river some way. It's getting late—take care of yourself,
neighbor lawyer. I'm a teetotal victim to a pair of black eyes. Chaw
me up to feed hogs if I'm not in a ruinatious state!   [Exit.]

MARKS: Queer genius, that, very!

     [Enter TOM LOKER.]

So you've come at last.

LOKER: Yes. [Looks into jug.] Empty! Waiter! more whisky!

     [WAITER enters with jug, and removes the empty one.—Enter
     HALEY.]

HALEY: By the land! if this yer ain't the nearest, now, to what I've heard
people call Providence! Why, Loker, how are ye?

LOKER: The devil! What brought you here, Haley?

HALEY: [Sitting at table.] I say, Tom, this yer's the luckiest thing in the
world. I'm in a devil of a hobble, and you must help me out!

LOKER: Ugh! aw! like enough. A body may be pretty sure of that when
you're glad to see 'em, or can make something off of 'em. What's
the blow now?

HALEY: You've got a friend here—partner, perhaps?

LOKER: Yes, I have. Here, Marks—here's that ar fellow that I was with in Natchez.

MARKS: [*Grasping* HALEY's *hand.*] Shall be pleased with his acquaintance. Mr. Haley, I believe?

HALEY: The same, sir. The fact is, gentlemen, this morning I bought a young 'un of Shelby up above here. His mother got wind of it, and what does she do but cut her lucky with him; and I'm afraid by this time that she has crossed the river, for I tracked her to this very place.

MARKS: So, then, ye're fairly sewed up, ain't ye? He! he! he! it's neatly done, too.

HALEY: This young 'un business makes lots of trouble in the trade.

MARKS: Now, Mr. Haley, what is it? Do you want us to undertake to catch this gal?

HALEY: The gal's no matter of mine—she's Shelby's—it's only the boy. I was a fool for buying the monkey.

LOKER: You're generally a fool!

MARKS: Come now, Loker, none of your huffs; you see, Mr. Haley's a-puttin' us in a way of a good job, I reckon; just hold still—these yer arrangements are my forte. This yer gal, Mr. Haley—how is she?—what is she?

[ELIZA *appears, with* HARRY, *listening.*]

HALEY: Well, white and handsome—well brought up. I'd have given Shelby eight hundred or a thousand, and then made well on her.

MARKS: White and handsome—well brought up! Look here, now, Loker, a beautiful opening. We'll do a business here on our own account. We does the catchin'; the boy, of course, goes to Mr. Haley—we takes the gal to Orleans to speculate on. Ain't it beautiful? [*They confer together.*]

ELIZA: Powers of mercy, protect me! How shall I escape these human bloodhounds?[2] Ah! the window—the river of ice! That dark stream lies between me and liberty! Surely the ice will bear my trifling weight. It is my only chance of escape—better sink beneath the cold waters, with my child locked in my arms, than have him torn from me and sold into bondage. He sleeps upon my breast—Heaven, I put my trust in thee! [*Gets out of window.*]

MARKS: Well, Tom Loker, what do you say?

LOKER: It'll do!

[*Strikes his hand violently on the table.*—ELIZA *screams.*—*They all start to their feet.*—ELIZA *disappears.*—*Music, chord.*]

HALEY: By the land, there she is now! [*They all rush to the window.*]

MARKS: She's making for the river!

LOKER: Let's after her!

[*Music.—They all leap through the window.—Change.*]

SCENE 5: *Snowy Landscape.—Music.*

[*Enter* ELIZA, *with* HARRY, *hurriedly.*]

ELIZA: They press upon my footsteps—the river is my only hope! Heaven grant me strength to reach it, ere they overtake me! Courage, my child!—we will be free—or perish!   [*Rushes off.*]

[*Enter* LOKER, HALEY *and* MARKS.]

HALEY: We'll catch her yet; the river will stop her!

MARKS: No, it won't, for look! she has jumped upon the ice! She's a brave gal, anyhow!

LOKER: She'll be drowned!

HALEY: Curse that young 'un! I shall lose him, after all.

LOKER: Come on, Marks, to the ferry!

MARKS: Aye, to the ferry!—a hundred dollars for a boat!

[*Music.—They rush off.*]

SCENE 6: *The entire depth of stage, representing the Ohio River filled with Floating Ice. Bank on right and in front.*

[ELIZA *appears, with* HARRY, *on a cake of ice, and floats slowly across.—*HALEY, LOKER *and* MARKS, *on bank, right hand, observing.—*PHINEAS *on opposite shore.*]

END OF ACT I

ACT II

SCENE 1: *A Handsome Parlor.* MARIE *discovered reclining on a sofa.*

MARIE: [*Looking at a note.*] What can possibly detain St. Clare? According to this note, he should have been here a fortnight ago. [*Noise of carriage without.*] I do believe he has come at last.

[EVA *runs in.*]

EVA: Mamma! [*Throws her arms around* MARIE'S *neck, and kisses her.*]

MARIE: That will do—take care, child—don't you make my head ache! [*Kisses her languidly.*]

[*Enter* ST. CLARE, OPHELIA, *and* TOM, *nicely dressed.*]

ST. CLARE: Well, my dear Marie, here we are at last. The wanderers have arrived, you see. Allow me to present my cousin, Miss Ophelia, who is about to undertake the office of our housekeeper.

MARIE: [*Rising to a sitting posture.*] I am delighted to see you. How do you like the appearance of our city?

EVA: [*Running to* OPHELIA.] Oh! is it not beautiful? My own darling home!—is it not beautiful?

OPHELIA: Yes, it is a pretty place, though it looks rather old and heathenish to me.

ST. CLARE: Tom, my boy, this seems to suit you?

TOM: Yes, mas'r, it looks about the right thing.

ST. CLARE: See here, Marie, I've brought you a coachman, at last, to order. I tell you, he's a regular hearse for blackness and sobriety, and will drive you like a funeral, if you wish. Open your eyes, now, and look at him. Now, don't say I never think about you when I'm gone.

MARIE: I know he'll get drunk.

ST. CLARE: Oh! no he won't. He's warranted a pious and sober article.

MARIE: Well, I hope he may turn out well; it's more than I expect, though.

ST. CLARE: Have you no curiosity to learn how and where I picked up Tom?

EVA: *Uncle* Tom, papa; that's his name.

ST. CLARE: Right, my little sunbeam!

TOM: Please, mas'r, that ain't no 'casion to say nothing 'bout me.

ST. CLARE: You are too modest, my modern Hannibal.[3] Do you know, Marie, that our little Eva took a fancy to Uncle Tom—whom we met on board the steamboat—and persuaded me to buy him?

MARIE: Ah! she is so odd!

ST. CLARE: As we approached the landing, a sudden rush of the passengers precipitated Eva into the water—

MARIE: Gracious heavens!

ST. CLARE: A man leaped into the river, and, as she rose to the surface of the water, grasped her in his arms, and held her up until she could be drawn on the boat again. Who was that man, Eva?

EVA: Uncle Tom! [*Runs to him.—He lifts her in his arms.—She kisses him.*]

TOM: The dear soul!

OPHELIA: [*Astonished.*] How shiftless!

ST. CLARE: [*Overhearing her.*] What's the matter now, pray?

OPHELIA: Well, I want to be kind to everybody, and I wouldn't have anything hurt, but as to kissing—

ST. CLARE: Niggers! that you're not up to, hey?

OPHELIA: Yes, that's it—how can she?

ST. CLARE: Oh! bless you, it's nothing when you are used to it!

OPHELIA: I could never be so shiftless!

EVA: Come with me, Uncle Tom, and I will show you about the house. [*Crosses with* TOM.]

TOM: Can I go, mas'r?

ST. CLARE: Yes, Tom; she is your little mistress—your only duty will be to attend to her! [TOM *bows and exits.*]

MARIE: Eva, my dear!

EVA: Well, mamma?

MARIE: Do not exert yourself too much

EVA: No, mamma! [*Runs out.*]

OPHELIA: [*Lifting up her hands.*] How shiftless!

[ST. CLARE *sits next to* MARIE *on sofa.*—OPHELIA *next to* ST. CLARE.]

ST. CLARE: Well, what do you think of Uncle Tom, Marie?

MARIE: He is a perfect behemoth!

ST. CLARE: Come, now, Marie, be gracious, and say something pretty to a fellow!

MARIE: You've been gone a fortnight beyond the time!

ST. CLARE: Well, you know I wrote you the reason.

MARIE: Such a short, cold letter!

ST. CLARE: Dear me! the mail was just going, and it had to be that or nothing.

MARIE: That's just the way; always something to make your journeys long and letters short!

ST. CLARE: Look at this. [*Takes an elegant velvet case from his pocket.*] Here's a present I got for you in New York—a daguerreotype⁴ of Eva and myself.

MARIE: [*Looks at it with a dissatisfied air.*] What made you sit in such an awkward position?

ST. CLARE: Well, the position may be a matter of opinion, but what do you think of the likeness?

MARIE: [*Closing the case snappishly.*] If you don't think anything of my opinion in one case, I suppose you wouldn't in another.

OPHELIA: [*Sententiously, aside.*] How shiftless!

ST. CLARE: Hang the woman! Come, Marie, what do you think of the likeness? Don't be nonsensical now.

MARIE: It's very inconsiderate of you, St. Clare, to insist on my talking and looking at things. You know I've been lying all day with the sick headache, and there's been such a tumult made ever since you came, I'm half dead!

OPHELIA: You're subject to the sick headache, ma'am?

MARIE: Yes, I'm a perfect martyr to it!

OPHELIA: Juniper-berry tea is good for sick headache; at least, Molly, Deacon Abraham Perry's wife, used to say so; and she was a great nurse.

ST. CLARE: I'll have the first juniper-berries that get ripe in our garden by the lake brought in for that especial purpose. Come, cousin, let us take a stroll in the garden. Will you join us, Marie?

MARIE: I wonder how you can ask such a question, when you know how fragile I am. I shall retire to my chamber, and repose till dinner time.   [*Exit.*]

OPHELIA: [*Looking after her.*] How shiftless!

ST. CLARE: Come, cousin! [*As he goes out.*] Look out for the babies! If I step upon anybody, let them mention it.

OPHELIA: Babies under foot! How shiftless!   [*Exeunt.*]

SCENE 2: *A Garden.* TOM *discovered, seated on a bank, with* EVA *on his knee—his button-holes are filled with flowers, and* EVA *is hanging a wreath around his neck.*

[*Enter* ST. CLARE *and* OPHELIA, *observing.*]

EVA: Oh, Tom; you look so funny.

TOM: [*Sees* ST. CLARE *and puts* EVA *down.*] I begs pardon, mas'r, but the young missis would do it. Look yer, I'm like the ox, mentioned in the good book, dressed for the sacrifice.

ST. CLARE: I say, what do you think, Pussy? Which do you like the best—to live as they do at your uncle's, up in Vermont, or to have a house full of servants, as we do?

EVA: Oh! of course our way is the pleasantest.

ST. CLARE: [*Patting her head.*] Why so?

EVA: Because it makes so many more round you to love, you know.

OPHELIA: Now, that's just like Eva—just one of her odd speeches.

EVA: Is it an odd speech, papa?

ST. CLARE: Rather, as this world goes, Pussy. But where has my little Eva been?

EVA: Oh! I've been up in Tom's room, hearing him sing.

ST. CLARE: Hearing Tom sing, hey?

EVA: Oh, yes! he sings such beautiful things, about the new Jerusalem, and bright angels, and the land of Canaan.

ST. CLARE: I dare say; it's better than the opera, isn't it?

EVA: Yes; and he's going to teach them to me.

ST. CLARE: Singing lessons, hey? You are coming on.

EVA: Yes, he sings for me, and I read to him in my Bible, and he explains what it means. Come, Tom.   [She takes his hand and they exit.]

ST. CLARE: [Aside.] Oh, Evangeline! Rightly named; hath not heaven made thee an evangel to me?

OPHELIA: How shiftless! How can you let her?

ST. CLARE: Why not?

OPHELIA: Why, I don't know; it seems so dreadful.

ST. CLARE: You would think no harm in a child's caressing a large dog, even if he was black; but a creature that can think, reason and feel, and is immortal, you shudder at. Confess it, cousin. I know the feeling among some of you Northerners well enough. Not that there is a particle of virtue in our not having it, but custom with us does what Christianity ought to do: obliterates the feeling of personal prejudice. You loathe them as you would a snake or a toad, yet you are indignant at their wrongs. You would not have them abused, but you don't want to have anything to do with them yourselves. Isn't that it?

OPHELIA: Well, cousin, there may be some truth in this.

ST. CLARE: What would the poor and lowly do without children? Your little child is your only true democrat. Tom, now, is a hero to Eva; his stories are wonders in her eyes; his songs and Methodist hymns are better than an opera, and the traps[5] and little bits of trash in his pockets a mine of jewels, and he the most wonderful Tom that ever wore a black skin. This is one of the roses of Eden that the Lord has dropped down expressly for the poor and lowly, who get few enough of any other kind.

OPHELIA: It's strange, cousin; one might almost think you was a *professor*,[6] to hear you talk.

ST. CLARE: A professor?

OPHELIA: Yes, a professor of religion.

ST. CLARE: Not at all; not a professor as you town folks have it, and what is worse, I'm afraid, not a *practicer,* either.

OPHELIA: What makes you talk so, then?

ST. CLARE: Nothing is easier than talking. My forte lies in talking, and yours, cousin, lies in doing. And speaking of that puts me in mind that I have made a purchase for your department. There's the article now. Here, Topsy! [*Whistles.*]

[TOPSY *runs on.*]

OPHELIA: Good gracious! what a heathenish, shiftless looking object! St. Clare, what in the world have you brought that thing here for?

ST. CLARE: For you to educate, to be sure, and train in the way she should go. I thought she was rather a funny specimen in the Jim Crow[7] line. Here, Topsy, give us a song, and show us some of your dancing.

[TOPSY *sings a verse and dances a breakdown.*]

OPHELIA: [*Paralyzed.*] Well, of all things! If I ever saw the like!

ST. CLARE: [*Smothering a laugh.*] Topsy, this is your new mistress—I'm going to give you up to her. See now that you behave yourself.

TOPSY: Yes, mas'r.

ST. CLARE: You're going to be good, Topsy, you understand?

TOPSY: Oh, yes, mas'r.

OPHELIA: Now, St. Clare, what upon earth is this for? Your house is so full of these plagues now, that a body can't set down their foot without treading on 'em. I get up in the morning and find one asleep behind the door, and see one black head poking out from under the table—one lying on the door mat, and they are moping and mowing and grinning between all the railings, and tumbling over the kitchen floor! What on earth did you want to bring this one for?

ST. CLARE: For you to educate—din't I tell you? You're always preaching about educating; I thought I would make you a present of a fresh caught specimen, and let you try your hand on her and bring her up in the way she should go.

OPHELIA: I don't want her, I am sure; I have more to do with 'em now than I want to.

ST. CLARE: That's you Christians, all over. You'll get up a society, and get some poor missionary to spend all his days among just such heathens; but let me see one of you that would take one into your house with you, and take the labor of their conversion upon yourselves.

OPHELIA: Well, I didn't think of it in that light. It might be a real missionary work. Well, I'll do what I can. [*Advances to* TOPSY.] She's dreadful dirty and shiftless! How old are you, Topsy?

TOPSY: Dunno, missis.

OPHELIA: How shiftless! Don't know how old you are? Didn't anybody ever tell you? Who was your mother?

TOPSY: [*Grinning.*] Never had none.

OPHELIA: Never had any mother? What do you mean? Where was you born?

TOPSY: Never was born.

OPHELIA: You mustn't answer me in that way. I'm not playing with you. Tell me where you was born, and who your father and mother were.

TOPSY: Never was born, tell you; never had no father, nor mother, nor nothin'. I war raised by a speculator, with lots of others. Old Aunt Sue used to take car' on us.

ST. CLARE: She speaks the truth, cousin. Speculators buy them up cheap, when they are little, and get them raised for the market.

OPHELIA: How long have you lived with your master and mistress?

TOPSY: Dunno, missis.

OPHELIA: How shiftless! Is it a year, or more, or less?

TOPSY: Dunno, missis.

ST. CLARE: She does not know what a year is; she don't even know her own age.

OPHELIA: Have you ever heard anything about heaven, Topsy? [TOPSY *looks bewildered and grins.*] Do you know who made you?

TOPSY: Nobody, as I knows on, he, he, he! I 'spect I growed. Don't think nobody never made me.

OPHELIA: The shiftless heathen! What can you do? What did you do for your master and mistress?

TOPSY: Fetch water—and wash dishes—and rub knives—and wait on folks—and dance breakdowns.

OPHELIA: I shall break down, I'm afraid, in trying to make anything of you, you shiftless mortal!

ST. CLARE: You find virgin soil, there, cousin; put in your own ideas— you won't find many to pull up. [*Exit laughing.*]

OPHELIA: [*Takes out her handkerchief.—A pair of gloves falls.—*TOPSY *picks them up slyly and puts them in her sleeve.*] Follow me, you benighted innocent!

TOPSY: Yes, missis.

[*As* OPHELIA *turns her back to her, she seizes the end of the ribbon she wears around her waist, and twitches it off.*—OPHELIA *turns and sees her as she is putting it in her other sleeve.*—OPHELIA *takes ribbon from her.*]

OPHELIA: What's this? You naughty, wicked girl, you've been stealing this?

TOPSY: Laws! why, that ar's missis' ribbon, an't it? How could it got caught in my sleeve?

OPHELIA: Topsy, you naughty girl, don't you tell me a lie—you stole that ribbon!

TOPSY: Missis, I declare for't, I didn't—never seed it till dis yer blessed minnit.

OPHELIA: Topsy, don't you know it's wicked to tell lies?

TOPSY: I never tells no lies, missis; it's just de truth I've been telling now, and nothin' else.

OPHELIA: Topsy, I shall have to whip you, if you tell lies so.

TOPSY: Laws, missis, if you's to whip all day, couldn't say no other way. I never seed dat ar—it must a got caught in my sleeve. [*Blubbers.*]

OPHELIA: [*Seizes her by the shoulders.*] Don't you tell me that again, you barefaced fibber! [*Shakes her.—The gloves fall on stage.*] There you, my gloves too—you outrageous young heathen! [*Picks them up.*] Will you tell me, now, you didn't steal the ribbon?

TOPSY: No, missis; stole de gloves, but didn't steal de ribbon. It was permiskus.

OPHELIA: Why, you young reprobate!

TOPSY: Yes—I's knows I's wicked.

OPHELIA: Then you know you ought to be punished. [*Boxes her ears.*] What do you think of that?

TOPSY: He, he, he! De Lord, missis; dat wouldn't kill a 'skeeter! [*Runs off laughing.*—OPHELIA *follows indignantly.*]

SCENE 3: *The Tavern by the River.—Table and chairs.—Jug and glasses on table.—On flat is a printed placard, headed:*—"Four Hundred Dollars Reward—Runaway—George Harris!"

[PHINEAS *is discovered, seated at table.*]

PHINEAS: So yer I am; and a pretty business I've undertook to do. Find the husband of the gal that crossed the river on the ice two or three days ago. Ruth said I must do it, and I'll be teetotally chewed up if

I don't do it. I see they've offered a reward for him, dead or alive. How in creation am I to find the varmint? He isn't likely to go round looking natural, with a full description of his hide and figure staring him in the face.

[*Enter* MR. WILSON.]

I say, stranger, how are ye? [*Rises and comes forward.*]

WILSON: Well, I reckon.

PHINEAS: Any news? [*Takes out plug and knife.*]

WILSON: Not that I know of.

PHINEAS: [*Cutting a piece of tobacco and offering it.*] Chaw?

WILSON: No, thank ye—it don't agree with me.

PHINEAS: Don't, eh? [*Putting it in his own mouth.*] I never felt any the worse for it.

WILSON: [*Sees placard.*] What's that?

PHINEAS: Nigger advertised. [*Advances towards it and spits on it.*] There's my mind upon that.

WILSON: Why, now stranger, what's that for?

PHINEAS: I'd do it all the same to the writer of that ar paper, if he was here. Any man that owns a boy like that, and can't find any better way of treating him than branding him on the hand with the letter H, as that paper states, *deserves* to lose him. Such papers as this ar' a shame to old Kaintuck! that's my mind right out, if anybody wants to know.

WILSON: Well, now, that's a fact.

PHINEAS: I used to have a gang of boys, sir—that was before I fell in love—and I just told 'em:—"Boys," says I, "run now! Dig! put! jest when you want to. I never shall come to look after you!" That's the way I kept mine. Let 'em know they are free to run any time, and it jest stops their wanting to. It stands to reason it should. Treat 'em like men, and you'll have men's work.

WILSON: I think you are altogether right, friend, and this man described here is a fine fellow—no mistake about that. He worked for me some half dozen years in my bagging factory, and he was my best hand, sir. He is an ingenious fellow, too; he invented a machine for the cleaning of hemp—a really valuable affair; it's gone into use in several factories. His master holds the patent of it.

PHINEAS: I'll warrant ye; holds it, and makes money out of it, and then turns round and brands the boy in his right hand! If I had a fair chance, I'd mark him, I reckon, so that he'd carry it *one* while!

[*Enter* GEORGE HARRIS, *disguised.*]

GEORGE [*Speaking as he enters.*] Jim, see to the trunks. [*Sees* WILSON.] Ah! Mr. Wilson here?

WILSON: Bless my soul, can it be?

GEORGE: [*Advances and grasps his hand.*] Mr. Wilson, I see you remember me, Mr. Butler, of Oaklands, Shelby county.

WILSON: Ye—yes—yes—sir.

PHINEAS: Holloa! there's a screw loose here somewhere. That old gentleman seems to be struck into a pretty considerable heap of astonishment. May I be teetotally chawed up! if I don't believe that's the identical man I'm arter. [*Crosses to* GEORGE.] How are ye, George Harris?

GEORGE: [*Starting back and thrusting his hands into his breast.*] You know me?

PHINEAS: Ha, ha, ha! I rather conclude I do; but don't get riled, I ain't a bloodhound in disguise.

GEORGE: How did you discover me?

PHINEAS: By a teetotal smart guess. You're the very man I want to see. Do you know I was sent after you?

GEORGE: Ah! by my master?

PHINEAS: No; by your wife.

GEORGE: My wife! Where is she?

PHINEAS: She's stopping with a Quaker family over on the Ohio side.

GEORGE: Then she is safe?

PHINEAS: Teetotally!

GEORGE: Conduct me to her.

PHINEAS: Just wait a brace of shakes[8] and I'll do it. I've got to go and get the boat ready. 'Twon't take me but a minute—make yourself comfortable till I get back. Chaw me up! but this is what I call doing things in short order.   [*Exit.*]

WILSON: George!

GEORGE: Yes, George!

WILSON: I couldn't have thought it!

GEORGE: I am pretty well disguised, I fancy; you see I don't answer to the advertisement at all.

WILSON: George, this is a dangerous game you are playing; I could not have advised you to it.

GEORGE: I can do it on my own responsibility.

WILSON: Well, George, I suppose you're running away—leaving your lawful master, George (I don't wonder at it), at the same time, I'm sorry, George, yes, decidedly. I think I must say that it's my duty to tell you so.

GEORGE: Why are you sorry, sir?

WILSON: Why, to see you, as it were, setting yourself in opposition to the laws of your country.

GEORGE: *My* country! What country have *I*, but the grave? And I would to heaven that I was laid there!

WILSON: George, you've got a hard master, in fact he is—well, he conducts himself reprehensibly—I can't pretend to defend him. I'm sorry for you, now; it's a bad case—very bad; but we must all submit to the indications of Providence, George, don't you see?

GEORGE: I wonder, Mr. Wilson, if the Indians should come and take you a prisoner away from your wife and children, and want to keep you all your life hoeing corn for them, if you'd think it your duty to abide in the condition in which you were called? I rather imagine that you'd think the first stray horse you could find an indication of Providence, shouldn't you?

WILSON: Really, George, putting the case in that somewhat peculiar light—I don't know—under those circumstances—but what I might. But it seems to me you are running an awful risk. You can't hope to carry it out. If you're taken it will be worse with you than ever; they'll only abuse you, and half kill you, and sell you down the river.

GEORGE: Mr. Wilson, I know all this. I *do* run a risk, but—[*Throws open coat and shows pistols and knife in his belt.*] There! I'm ready for them. Down South I never *will* go! no, if it comes to that, I can earn myself at least six feet of free soil—the first and last I shall ever own in Kentucky!

WILSON: Why, George, this state of mind is awful—it's getting really desperate. I'm concerned. Going to break the laws of your country?

GEORGE: My country again! Sir, I haven't any country any more than I have any father. I don't want anything of *your* country, except to be left alone—to go peaceably out of it; but if any man tries to stop me, let him take care, for I am desperate. I'll fight for my liberty, to the last breath I breathe! You say your fathers did it; if it was right for them, it is right for me!

WILSON: [*Walking up and down and fanning his face with a large yellow silk handkerchief.*] Blast 'em all! Haven't I always said so—the infernal old cusses! Bless me! I hope I an't swearing now! Well, go ahead, George, go ahead. But be careful, my boy; don't shoot anybody, unless—well, you'd *better* not shoot—at least I wouldn't *hit* anybody, you know.

GEORGE: Only in self-defense.

WILSON: Well, well. [*Fumbling in his pocket.*] I suppose, perhaps, I an't following my judgment—hang it, I won't follow my judgment. So here, George. [*Takes out a pocket-book and offers* GEORGE *a roll of bills.*]

GEORGE: No, my kind, good sir, you've done a great deal for me, and this might get you into trouble. I have money enough, I hope, to take me as far as I need it.

WILSON: No; but you must, George. Money is a great help everywhere; can't have too much, if you get it honestly. Take it, *do* take it, *now* do, my boy!

GEORGE: [*Taking the money.*] On condition, sir, that I may repay it at some future time, I will.

WILSON: And now, George, how long are you going to travel in this way? Not long or far, I hope? It's well carried on, but too bold.

GEORGE: Mr. Wilson, it is *so bold*, and this tavern is so near, that they will never think of it; they will look for me on ahead, and you yourself wouldn't know me.

WILSON: But the mark on your hand?

GEORGE: [*Draws off his glove and shows scar.*] That is a parting mark of Mr. Harris' regard. Looks interesting, doesn't it? [*Puts on glove again.*]

WILSON: I declare, my very blood runs cold when I think of it—your condition and your risks!

GEORGE: Mine has run cold a good many years; at present, it's about up to the boiling point.

WILSON: George, something has brought you out wonderfully. You hold up your head, and move and speak like another man.

GEORGE: [*Proudly.*] Because I'm a *freeman!* Yes, sir; I've said "master" for the last time to any man: *I'm free!*

WILSON: Take care! You are not sure; you may be taken.

GEORGE: All men are free and equal *in the grave,* if it comes to that, Mr. Wilson.

[*Enter* PHINEAS.]

PHINEAS: Them's my sentiment, to a teetotal atom, and I don't care who knows it! Neighbor, the boat is ready, and the sooner we make tracks the better. I've seen some mysterious strangers lurking about these diggings, so we'd better put.

GEORGE: Farewell, Mr. Wilson, and heaven reward you for the many kindnesses you have shown the poor fugitive!

WILSON: [*Grasping his hand.*] You're a brave fellow, George. I wish in my heart you were safe through, though—that's what I do.

PHINEAS: And ain't I the man of all creation to put him through, stranger? Chaw me up if I don't take him to his dear little wife, in the smallest possible quantity of time. Come, neighbor, let's vamoose.

GEORGE: Farewell, Mr. Wilson. [*Crosses.*]

WILSON: My best wishes go with you, George.   [*Exit.*]

PHINEAS: You're a trump, old Slow-and-Easy.

GEORGE: [*Looking off.*] Look! look!

PHINEAS: Consarn their picters, here they come! We can't get out of the house without their seeing us. We're teetotally treed!

GEORGE: Let us fight our way through them!

PHINEAS: No, that won't do; there are too many of them for a fair fight—we should be chawed up in no time. [*Looks round and sees trap door.*] Holloa! here's a cellar door. Just you step down here a few minutes, while I parley with them. [*Lifts trap.*]

GEORGE: I am resolved to perish sooner than surrender! [*Goes down trap.*]

PHINEAS: That's your sort! [*Closes trap and stands on it.*] Here they are!

[*Enter* HALEY, MARKS, LOKER *and three* MEN.]

HALEY: Say, stranger, you haven't seen a runaway darkey about these parts, eh?

PHINEAS: What kind of a darkey?

HALEY: A mulatto chap, almost as light-complexioned as a white man.

PHINEAS: Was he a pretty good-looking chap?

HALEY: Yes.

PHINEAS: Kind of tall?

HALEY: Yes.

PHINEAS: With brown hair?

HALEY: Yes.

PHINEAS: And dark eyes?

HALEY: Yes.

PHINEAS: Pretty well dressed?

HALEY: Yes.

PHINEAS: Scar on his right hand?

HALEY: Yes, yes.

PHINEAS: Well, I ain't seen him.

HALEY: Oh, bother! Come, boys, let's search the house.   [*Exeunt.*]

PHINEAS: [*Raises trap.*] Now, then, neighbor George.

[GEORGE *enters, up trap.*]

Now's the time to cut your lucky.

GEORGE: Follow me, Phineas.

PHINEAS: In a brace of shakes. [*Is closing trap as* HALEY, MARKS, LOKER, &C., *re-enter.*]

HALEY: Ah! he's down in the cellar. Follow me boys!

[*Thrusts Phineas aside, and rushes down trap, followed by the others. Phineas closes trap and stands on it.*]

PHINEAS: Chaw me up! but I've got 'em all in a trap. [*Knocking below.*] Be quiet, you pesky varmints! [*Knocking.*] They're getting mighty oneasy. [*Knocking.*] Will you be quiet, you savagerous critters! [*The trap is forced open.* HALEY *and* MARKS *appear.* PHINEAS *seizes a chair and stands over trap—picture.*] Down with you or I'll smash you into apple-fritters! [*Tableau.*]

SCENE 4: *A Plain Chamber.*

TOPSY: [*Without.*] You go 'long. No more nigger dan you be! [*Enters —shouts and laughter without—looks off.*] You seem to think yourself white folks. You ain't nerry one—black *nor* white. I'd like to be one or turrer. Law! you niggers, does you know you's all sinners? Well, you is—everybody is. White folks is sinners too—Miss Feely says so—but I 'spects niggers is the biggest ones. But Lor'! ye ain't any on ye up to me. I's so awful wicked there can't nobody do nothin' with me. I used to keep old missis a-swarin' at me half de time. I 'spects I's de wickedest critter in de world. [*Song and dance introduced.*]

[*Enter* EVA.]

EVA: Oh, Topsy! Topsy! you have been very wrong again.

TOPSY: Well, I 'spects I have.

EVA: What makes you do so?

TOPSY: I dunno; I 'spects it's cause I's so wicked.

EVA: Why did you spoil Jane's earrings?

TOPSY: 'Cause she's so proud. She called me a little black imp, and turned up her pretty nose at me 'cause she is whiter than I am. I was gwine by her room, and I seed her coral earrings lying on de table, so I threw dem on de floor, and put my foot on 'em, and scrunched 'em all to little bits—he! he! he! I's so wicked.

EVA: Don't you know that was very wrong?

TOPSY: I don't car'. I despises dem what sets up for fine ladies, when dey ain't nothin' but cream-colored niggers! Dere's Miss Rosa—she gives me lots of 'pertinent remarks. T'other night she was gwine to ball. She put on a beau'ful dress that missis give her—wid her har curled, all nice and pretty. She hab to go down de back stairs—dey am dark—and I puts a pail of hot water on dem, and she put her foot into it, and den she go tumblin' to de bottom of de stairs, and de water go all ober her, and spile her dress, and scald her dreadful bad! He! he! he! I's so wicked!

EVA: Oh! how could you!

TOPSY: Don't dey despise me 'cause I don't know nothing? Don't dey laugh at me 'cause I'm brack, and dey ain't?

EVA: But you shouldn't mind them.

TOPSY: Well, I don't mind dem; but when dey are passing under my winder, I trows dirty water on 'em, and dat spiles der complexions.

EVA: What does make you so bad, Topsy? Why won't you try and be good? Don't you love anybody, Topsy?

TOPSY: Can't recommember.

EVA: But you love your father and mother?

TOPSY: Never had none; ye know, I telled ye that, Miss Eva.

EVA: Oh! I know; but hadn't you any brother, or sister, or aunt, or—

TOPSY: No, none on 'em—never had nothin' nor nobody. I's brack—no one loves me!

EVA: Oh! Topsy, I love you! [*Laying her hand on* TOPSY'S *shoulder.*] I love you because you haven't had any father, or mother, or friends. I love you, and I want you to be good. I wish you would try to be good for my sake.

[TOPSY *looks astonished for a moment, and then bursts into tears.*]

Only think of it, Topsy—*you* can be one of those spirits bright Uncle Tom sings about!

TOPSY: Oh! dear Miss Eva—dear Miss Eva! I will try—I will try! I never did care nothin' about it before.

EVA: If you try, you will succeed. Come with me. [*Crosses and takes* TOPSY'S *hand.*]

TOPSY: I will try; but den, I's so wicked!

[*Exit* EVA, *followed by* TOPSY, *crying.*]

SCENE 5: *Chamber*.

[*Enter* GEORGE, ELIZA *and* HARRY.]

GEORGE: At length, Eliza, after many wanderings, we are again united.

ELIZA: Thanks to these generous Quakers, who have so kindly sheltered us.

GEORGE: Not forgetting our friend Phineas.

ELIZA: I do indeed owe him much. 'Twas he I met upon the icy river's bank, after that fearful, but successful attempt, when I fled from the slave-trader with my child in my arms.

GEORGE: It seems almost incredible that you could have crossed the river on the ice.

ELIZA: Yes, I did. Heaven helping me, I crossed on the ice, for they were behind me—right behind—and there was no other way.

GEORGE: But the ice was all in broken-up blocks, swinging and heaving up and down in the water.

ELIZA: I know it was—I know it; I did not think I should get over, but I did not care—I could but die if I did not! I leaped on the ice, but how I got across I don't know; the first I remember, a man was helping me up the bank—that man was Phineas.

GEORGE: My brave girl! you deserve your freedom—you have richly earned it!

ELIZA: And when we get to Canada I can help you to work, and between us we can find something to live on.

GEORGE: Yes, Eliza, so long as we have each other, and our boy. Oh, Eliza, if these people only knew what a blessing it is for a man to feel that his wife and child belong to *him!* I've often wondered to see men that could call their wives and children *their own*, fretting and worrying about anything else. Why, I feel rich and strong, though we have nothing but our bare hands. If they will only let me alone now, I will be satisfied—thankful!

ELIZA: But we are not quite out of danger; we are not yet in Canada.

GEORGE: True; but it seems as if I smelt the free air, and it makes me strong!

[*Enter* PHINEAS, *dressed as a Quaker*.]

PHINEAS: [*With a snuffle*.] Verily, friends, how is it with thee?—hum!

GEORGE: Why, Phineas, what means this metamorphosis!

PHINEAS: I've become a Quaker! that's the meaning on't.

GEORGE: What—you?

PHINEAS: Teetotally! I was driven to it by a strong argument, composed of a pair of sparkling eyes, rosy cheeks, and pouting lips. Them lips would persuade a man to assassinate his grandmother! [*Assumes the Quaker tone again.*] Verily, George, I have discovered something of importance to the interests of thee and thy party, and it were well for thee to hear it.

GEORGE: Keep us not in suspense!

PHINEAS: Well, after I left you on the road, I stopped at a little, lone tavern, just below here. Well, I was tired with hard driving, and, after my supper, I stretched myself down on a pile of bags in the corner, and pulled a buffalo hide over me—and what does I do but get fast asleep.

GEORGE: With one ear open, Phineas?

PHINEAS: No, I slept ears and all for an hour or two, for I was pretty well tired; but when I came to myself a little, I found that there were some men in the room, sitting round a table, drinking and talking; and I thought, before I made much muster, I'd just see what they were up to, especially as I heard them say something about the Quakers. Then I listened with both ears and found they were talking about you. So I kept quiet, and heard them lay off all their plans. They've got a right notion of the track we are going to-night, and they'll be down after us, six or eight strong. So, now, what's to be done?

ELIZA: What *shall* we do, George?

GEORGE: I know what I shall do! [*Takes out pistols.*]

PHINEAS: Ay—ay, thou seest, Eliza, how it will work—pistols—phitz —poppers!

ELIZA: I see; but I pray it come not to that!

GEORGE: I don't want to involve any one with or for me. If you will lend me your vehicle, and direct me, I will drive alone to the next stand.

PHINEAS: Ah! well, friend, but thee'll need a driver for all that. Thee's quite welcome to do all the fighting thee knows; but I know a thing or two about the road that thee doesn't.

GEORGE: But I don't want to involve you.

PHINEAS: Involve me! Why, chaw me—that is to say—when thee does involve me, please to let me know.

ELIZA: Phineas is a wise and skillful man. You will do well, George, to abide by his judgment. And, oh! George, be not hasty with these— young blood is hot! [*Laying her hand on pistols.*]

GEORGE: I will attack no man. All I ask of this country is to be left alone, and I will go out peaceably. But I'll fight to the last breath before they shall take from me my wife and son! Can you blame me?

PHINEAS: Mortal man cannot blame thee, neighbor George! Flesh and blood could not do otherwise. Woe unto the world because of offenses, but woe unto them through whom the offense cometh! That's gospel, teetotally!

GEORGE: Would not even you, sir, do the same, in my place?

PHINEAS: I pray that I be not tried; the flesh is weak—but I think my flesh would be pretty tolerably strong in such a case; I ain't sure, friend George, that I shouldn't hold a fellow for thee, if thee had any accounts to settle with him.

ELIZA: Heaven grant we be not tempted.

PHINEAS: But if we are tempted too much, why, consarn 'em! let them look out, that's all.

GEORGE: It's quite plain you was not born for a Quaker. The old nature has its way in you pretty strong yet.

PHINEAS: Well, I reckon you are pretty teetotally right.

GEORGE: Had we not better hasten our flight?

PHINEAS: Well, I rather conclude we had; we're full two hours ahead of them, if they start at the time they planned; so let's vamoose.

[*Exeunt.*]

SCENE 6: *A Rocky Pass in the Hills.—Large set rock and platform.*

PHINEAS: [*Without.*] Out with you in a twinkling, every one, and up into these rocks with me! run *now*, if you *ever* did run! [*Music.*]

[PHINEAS *enters, with* HARRY *in his arms.—*GEORGE *supporting* ELIZA.]

Come up here; this is one of our old hunting dens. Come up. [*They ascend the rock.*] Well, here we are. Let 'em get us if they can. Whoever comes here has to walk single file between those two rocks, in fair range of your pistols—d'ye see?

GEORGE: I do see. And now, as this affair is mine, let me take all the risk, and do all the fighting.

PHINEAS: Thee's quite welcome to do the fighting, George; but I may have the fun of looking on, I suppose. But see, these fellows are kind of debating down there, and looking up, like hens when they are going to fly up onto the roost. Hadn't thee better give 'em a word of advice, before they come up, jest to tell 'em handsomely they'll be shot if they do.

[LOKER, MARKS, *and three* MEN *enter.*]

MARKS: Well, Tom, your coons are fairly treed.

LOKER: Yes, I see 'em go up right here; and here's a path—I'm for going right up. They can't jump down in a hurry, and it won't take long to ferret 'em out.

MARKS: But, Tom, they might fire at us from behind the rocks. That would be ugly, you know.

LOKER: Ugh! always for saving your skin, Marks. No danger; niggers are too plaguy scared!

MARKS: I don't know why I shouldn't save my skin; it's the best I've got; and niggers do fight like the devil sometimes.

GEORGE: [*Rising on the rock.*] Gentlemen, who are you down there, and what do you want?

LOKER: We want a party of runaway niggers. One George and Eliza Harris, and their son. We've got the officers here, and a warrant to take 'em too. D'ye hear? An't you George Harris, that belonged to Mr. Harris, of Shelby county, Kentucky?

GEORGE: I am George Harris. A Mr. Harris, of Kentucky, did call me his property. But now I'm a freeman, standing on heaven's free soil! My wife and child I claim as mine. We have arms to defend ourselves, and we mean to do it. You can come up if you like; but the first one that comes within range of our bullets is a dead man!

MARKS: Oh, come—come, young man, this an't no kind of talk at all for you. You see we're officers of justice. We've got the law on our side, and the power and so forth; so you'd better give up peaceably, you see—for you'll certainly have to give up at last.

GEORGE: I know very well that you've got the law on your side, and the power; but you haven't got us. We are standing here as free as you are, and by the great power that made us, we'll fight for our liberty till we die!

[*During this,* MARKS *draws a pistol, and when he concludes fires at him.*—ELIZA *screams.*]

GEORGE: It's nothing, Eliza; I am unhurt.

PHINEAS: [*Drawing* GEORGE *down.*] Thee'd better keep out of sight with thy speechifying; they're teetotal mean scamps.

LOKER: What did you do that for, Marks?

MARKS: You see, you get jist as much for him dead as alive in Kentucky.

GEORGE: Now, Phineas, the first man that advances I fire at; you take the second, and so on. It won't do to waste two shots on one.

PHINEAS: But what if you don't hit?

GEORGE: I'll try my best.

PHINEAS: Creation! Chaw me up if there an't stuff in you!

MARKS: I think I must have hit some on 'em. I heard a squeal.

LOKER: I'm going right up for one. I never was afraid of niggers, and I an't a going to be now. Who goes after me?

[*Music.—*LOKER *dashes up the rock.—*GEORGE *fires.—He staggers for a moment, then springs to the top.—*PHINEAS *seizes him.—A struggle.*]

PHINEAS: Friend, thee is not wanted here! [*Throws* LOKER *over the rock.*]

MARKS: [*Retreating.*] Lord help us—they're perfect devils!

[*Music.—*MARKS *and Party run off.* GEORGE *and* ELIZA *kneel in an attitude of thanksgiving, with the* CHILD *between them.—* PHINEAS *stands over them exulting.—Tableau.*]

END OF ACT II

ACT III

SCENE 1: *Chamber.*

[*Enter* ST. CLARE, *followed by* TOM.]

ST. CLARE: [*Giving money and papers to* TOM.] There, Tom, are the bills, and the money to liquidate them.

TOM: Yes, mas'r.

ST. CLARE: Well, Tom, what are you waiting for? Isn't all right there?

TOM: I'm 'fraid not, mas'r.

ST. CLARE: Why, Tom, what's the matter? You look as solemn as a coffin.

TOM: I feel very bad, mas'r. I allays have thought that mas'r would be good to everybody.

ST. CLARE: Well, Tom, haven't I been? Come, now, what do you want? There's something you haven't got, I suppose, and this is the preface.

TOM: Mas'r allays been good to me. I haven't nothing to complain of on that head; but there is one that mas'r isn't good to.

ST. CLARE: Why, Tom, what's got into you? Speak out—what do you mean?

TOM: Last night, between one and two, I thought so. I studied upon the matter then—mas'r isn't good to *himself*.

ST. CLARE: Ah! now I understand; you allude to the state in which I came home last night. Well, to tell the truth, I *was* slightly elevated —a little more champagne on board than I could comfortably carry. That's all, isn't it?

TOM: [*Deeply affected—clasping his hands and weeping.*] All! Oh! my dear young mas'r, I'm 'fraid it will be *loss of all—all*, body and soul. The good book says, "It biteth like a serpent and stingeth like an adder," my dear mas'r.

ST. CLARE: You poor, silly fool! I'm not worth crying over.

TOM: Oh, mas'r! I implore you to think of it before it gets too late.

ST. CLARE: Well, I won't go to any more of their cursed nonsense, Tom—on my honor, I won't. I don't know why I haven't stopped long ago; I've always despised *it*, and myself for it. So now, Tom, wipe up your eyes and go about your errands.

TOM: Bless you, mas'r. I feel much better now. You have taken a load from poor Tom's heart. Bless you!

ST. CLARE: Come, come, no blessing! I'm not so wonderfully good, now. There, I'll pledge my honor to you, Tom, you don't see me so again.

[*Exit* TOM.]

I'll keep my faith with him, too.

OPHELIA: [*Without.*] Come along, you shiftless mortal!

ST. CLARE: What new witchcraft has Topsy been brewing? That commotion is of her raising, I'll be bound.

[*Enter* OPHELIA, *dragging in* TOPSY.]

OPHELIA: Come here now; I will tell your master.

ST. CLARE: What's the matter now?

OPHELIA: The matter is that I cannot be plagued with this girl any longer. It's past all bearing; flesh and blood cannot endure it. Here I locked her up and gave her a hymn to study; and what does she do but spy out where I put my key, and has gone to my bureau, and got a bonnet-trimming and cut it all to pieces to make dolls' jackets! I never saw anything like it in my life!

ST. CLARE: What have you done to her?

OPHELIA: What have I done? What haven't I done? Your wife says I ought to have her whipped till she couldn't stand.

ST. CLARE: I don't doubt it. Tell me of the lovely rule of woman. I never saw above a dozen women that wouldn't half kill a horse, or a servant, either, if they had their own way with them—let alone a man.

OPHELIA: I am sure, St. Clare, I don't know what to do. I've taught and taught—I've talked till I'm tired; I've whipped her, I've punished her in every way I could think of, and still she's just what she was at first.

ST. CLARE: Come here, Tops, you monkey! [TOPSY *crosses to* ST. CLARE, *grinning.*] What makes you behave so?

TOPSY: 'Spects it's my wicked heart—Miss Feely says so.

ST. CLARE: Don't you see how much Miss Ophelia has done for you? She says she has done everything she can think of.

TOPSY: Lor', yes, mas'r! old missis used to say so, too. She whipped me a heap harder, and used to pull my ha'r, and knock my head agin the door; but it didn't do me no good. I 'spects if they's to pull every spear of ha'r out o' my head, it wouldn't do no good neither—I's so wicked! Laws! I's nothin' but a nigger, no ways! [*Goes up.*]

OPHELIA: Well, I shall have to give her up; I can't have that trouble any longer.

ST. CLARE: I'd like to ask you one question.

OPHELIA: What is it?

ST. CLARE: Why, if your doctrine is not strong enough to save one heathen child, that you can have at home here, all to yourself, what's the use of sending one or two poor missionaries off with it among thousands of just such? I suppose this girl is a fair sample of what thousands of your heathen are.

OPHELIA: I'm sure I don't know; I never saw such a girl as this.

ST. CLARE: What makes you so bad, Tops? Why won't you try and be good? Don't you love any one, Topsy?

TOPSY: Dunno nothin' 'bout love; I loves candy and sich, that's all.

OPHELIA: But, Topsy, if you'd only try to be good, you might.

TOPSY: Couldn't never be nothin' but a nigger, if I was ever so good. If I could be skinned and come white, I'd try then.

ST. CLARE: People can love you, if you are black, Topsy. Miss Ophelia would love you, if you were good. [TOPSY *laughs.*] Don't you think so?

TOPSY: No, she can't b'ar me, 'cause I'm a nigger—she'd's soon have a toad touch her. There can't nobody love niggers, and niggers can't do nothin'. I don't car'! [*Whistles.*]

ST. CLARE: Silence, you incorrigible imp, and begone!

TOPSY: He! he! he! didn't get much out of dis chile!   [*Exit.*]

OPHELIA: I've always had a prejudice against negroes, and it's a fact—

I never could bear to have that child touch me, but I didn't think she knew it.

ST. CLARE: Trust any child to find that out; there's no keeping it from them. But I believe all the trying in the world to benefit a child, and all the substantial favors you can do them, will never excite one emotion of gratitude, while that feeling of repugnance remains in the heart. It's a queer kind of fact, but so it is.

OPHELIA: I don't know how I can help it—they are disagreeable to me, this girl in particular. How can I help feeling so?

ST. CLARE: Eva does, it seems.

OPHELIA: Well, she's so loving. I wish I was like her. She might teach me a lesson.

ST. CLARE: It would not be the first time a little child had been used to instruct an old disciple, if it were so. Come, let us seek Eva, in her favorite bower by the lake.

OPHELIA: Why, the dew is falling; she mustn't be out there. She is unwell, I know.

ST. CLARE: Don't be croaking, cousin—I hate it.

OPHELIA: But she has that cough.

ST. CLARE: Oh, nonsense, of that cough—it is not anything. She has taken a little cold, perhaps.

OPHELIA: Well, that was just the way Eliza Jane was taken—and Ellen—

ST. CLARE: Oh, stop these hobgoblin, nurse legends. You old hands get so wise, that a child cannot cough or sneeze, but you see desperation and ruin at hand. Only take care of the child, keep her from the night air, and don't let her play too hard, and she'll do well enough.

[*Exeunt.*]

SCENE 2: *The flat represents the lake. The rays of the setting sun tinge the waters with gold.—A large tree.—Beneath this is a grassy bank, on which* EVA *and* TOM *are seated side by side.—*EVA *has a Bible open on her lap.*

TOM: Read dat passage again, please, Miss Eva?

EVA: [*Reading.*] "And I saw a sea of glass, mingled with fire."[9] [*Stopping suddenly and pointing to lake.*] Tom, there it is!

TOM: What, Miss Eva?

EVA: Don't you see there? There's a "sea of glass, mingled with fire."

TOM: True enough, Miss Eva. [*Sings.*]

> Oh, had I the wings of the morning,
> I'd fly away to Canaan's shore;

> Bright angels should convey me home,
> To the New Jerusalem.

EVA: Where do you suppose New Jerusalem is, Uncle Tom?

TOM: Oh, up in the clouds, Miss Eva.

EVA: Then I think I see it. Look in those clouds; they look like great gates of pearl; and you can see beyond them—far, far off—it's all gold! Tom, sing about "spirits bright."

TOM [*Sings.*]

> I see a band of spirits bright,
> That taste the glories there;
> They are all robed in spotless white,
> And conquering palms they bear.

EVA: Uncle Tom, I've seen *them.*

TOM: To be sure you have; you are one of them yourself. You are the brightest spirit I ever saw.

EVA: They come to me sometimes in my sleep—those spirits bright—

> They are all robed in spotless white,
> And conquering palms they bear.

Uncle Tom, I'm going there.

TOM: Where, Miss Eva?

EVA: [*Pointing to the sky.*] I'm going *there,* to the spirits bright, Tom; I'm going before long.

TOM: It's jest no use tryin' to keep Miss Eva here; I've allays said so. She's got the Lord's mark in her forehead. She wasn't never like a child that's to live—there was always something deep in her eyes. [*Rises and comes forward.—*EVA *also comes forward, leaving Bible on bank.*]

[*Enter* ST. CLARE.]

ST. CLARE: Ah! my little pussy, you look as blooming as a rose! You are better now-a-days, are you not?

EVA: Papa, I've had things I wanted to say to you a great while. I want to say them now, before I get weaker.

ST. CLARE: Nay, this is an idle fear, Eva; you know you grow stronger every day.

EVA: It's all no use, papa, to keep it to myself any longer. The time is coming that I am going to leave you; I am going, and never to come back.

ST. CLARE: Oh, now, my dear little Eva! you've got nervous and low-spirited; you mustn't indulge such gloomy thoughts.

EVA: No, papa, don't deceive yourself, I am *not* any better; I know it perfectly well, and I am going before long. I am not nervous—I am not low-spirited. If it were not for you, papa, and my friends, I should be perfectly happy. I want to go—I long to go!

ST. CLARE: Why, dear child, what has made your poor little heart so sad? You have everything to make you happy that could be given you.

EVA: I had rather be in heaven! There are a great many things here that make me sad—that seem dreadful to me; I had rather be there; but I don't want to leave you—it almost breaks my heart!

ST. CLARE: What makes you sad, and what seems dreadful, Eva?

EVA: I feel sad for our poor people, they love me dearly, and they are good and kind to me. I wish, papa, they were all *free!*

ST. CLARE: Why, Eva, child, don't you think they are well enough off, now?

EVA: [*Not heeding the question.*] Papa, isn't there a way to have slaves made free? When I am dead, papa, then you will think of me, and do it for my sake?

ST. CLARE: When you are dead, Eva? Oh, child, don't talk to me so! You are all I have on earth!

EVA: Papa, these poor creatures love their children as much as you do me. Tom loves his children. Oh, do something for them!

ST. CLARE: There, there darling; only don't distress yourself, and don't talk of dying, and I will do anything you wish.

EVA: And promise me, dear father, that Tom shall have his freedom as soon as—[*hesitating*]—I am gone!

ST. CLARE: Yes, dear, I will do anything in the world—anything you ask me to. There, Tom, take her to her chamber; this evening air is too chill for her. [*Music.—Kisses her.*]

[TOM *takes* EVA *in his arms, and exits.*]

ST. CLARE: [*Gazing mournfully after* EVA.] Has there ever been a child like Eva? Yes, there has been; but their names are always on gravestones, and their sweet smiles, their heavenly eyes, their singular words and ways, are among the buried treasures of yearning hearts. It is as if heaven had an especial band of angels, whose office it is to sojourn for a season here, and endear to them the wayward human heart, that they might bear it upward with them in their homeward flight. When you see that deep, spiritual light in the eye, when the little soul reveals itself in words sweeter and wiser than the ordinary words of children, hope not to retain that child; for the seal of heaven is on it, and the light of immortality looks out from its eyes!

[*Music.—Exit.*]

SCENE 3: *A corridor.*

[*Enter* TOM; *he listens at door and then lies down. Enter* OPHELIA, *with candle.*]

OPHELIA: Uncle Tom, what alive have you taken to sleeping anywhere and everywhere, like a dog, for? I thought you were one of the orderly sort, that liked to lie in bed in a Christian way.

TOM: [*Rises.—Mysteriously.*] I do, Miss Feely, I do, but now—

OPHELIA: Well, what now?

TOM: We mustn't speak loud; Mas'r St. Clare won't hear on't; but Miss Feely, you know there must be somebody watchin' for the bridegroom.

OPHELIA: What do you mean, Tom?

TOM: You know it says in Scripture, "At midnight there was a great cry made, behold the bridegroom cometh!"[10] That's what I'm 'spectin' now, every night, Miss Feely, and I couldn't sleep out of hearing, noways.

OPHELIA: Why, Uncle Tom, what makes you think so?

TOM: Miss Eva, she talks to me. The Lord, he sends his messenger in the soul. I must be thar, Miss Feely; for when that ar blessed child goes into the kingdom, they'll open the door so wide, we'll all get a look in at the glory!

OPHELIA: Uncle Tom, did Miss Eva say she felt more unwell than usual to-night?

TOM: No; but she told me she was coming nearer—thar's them that tells it to the child, Miss Feely. It's the angels—it's the trumpet sound afore the break o' day!

OPHELIA: Heaven grant your fears be vain! Come in, Tom.   [*Exeunt.*]

SCENE 4: EVA'S *chamber.* EVA *discovered on a couch.—A table stands near the couch, with a lamp on it. The light shines upon* EVA'S *face, which is very pale.—Scene half dark.—*UNCLE TOM *is kneeling near the foot of the couch.—*OPHELIA *stands at the head.—*ST. CLARE *at back. —Scene opens to plaintive music.*

[*After a strain, enter* MARIE, *hastily.*]

MARIE: St. Clare! Cousin! Oh! what is the matter now?

ST. CLARE: [*Hoarsely.*] Hush! she is dying!

MARIE: [*Sinking on her knees, beside* TOM.] Dying!

ST. CLARE: Oh! if she would only wake and speak once more. [*Bending over* EVA.] Eva, darling!

EVA: [*Uncloses her eyes, smiles, raises her head and tries to speak.*]

ST. CLARE: Do you know me, Eva?

EVA: [*Throwing her arms feebly about his neck.*] Dear papa! [*Her arms drop and she sinks back.*]

ST. CLARE: Oh, heaven! this is dreadful! Oh! Tom, my boy, it is killing me!

TOM: Look at her, mas'r. [*Points to* EVA.]

ST. CLARE: Eva! [*A pause.*] She does not hear. Oh, Eva! tell us what you see. What is it?

EVA: [*Feebly smiling.*] Oh! love! joy! peace! [*Dies.*]

TOM: Oh! bless the Lord! it's over, dear mas'r, it's over.

ST. CLARE: [*Sinking on his knees.*] Farewell, beloved child! the bright eternal doors have closed after thee. We shall see thy sweet face no more. Oh! woe for them who watched thy entrance into heaven, when they shall wake and find only the cold, gray sky of daily life, and thou gone forever! [*Solemn music, slow curtain.*]

END OF ACT III

ACT IV

SCENE 1: *A Street in New Orleans.*

[*Enter* GUMPTION CUTE, *meeting* MARKS.]

CUTE: How do ye dew?

MARKS: How are you?

CUTE: Well, now, squire, it's a fact that I am dead broke and busted up.

MARKS: You have been speculating, I suppose?

CUTE: That's just it and nothing shorter.

MARKS: You have had poor success, you say?

CUTE: Tarnation bad, now I tell you. You see I came to this part of the country to make my fortune.

MARKS: And you did not do it?

CUTE: Scarcely. The first thing I tried my hand at was keeping school. I opened an academy for the instruction of youth in the various branches of orthography, geography, and other graphies.

MARKS: Did you succeed in getting any pupils?

CUTE: Oh, lots on 'em! and a pretty set of dunces they were, too. After the first quarter, I called on the respectable parents of the juveniles, and requested them to fork over. To which they politely answered —don't you wish you may get it?

MARKS: What did you do then?

CUTE: Well, I kind of pulled up stakes and left those diggin's. Well, then I went into Spiritual Rappings[11] for a living. That paid pretty well for a short time, till I met with an accident.

MARKS: An accident?

CUTE: Yes; a tall Yahoo[12] called on me one day, and wanted me to summon the spirit of his mother—which, of course, I did. He asked me about a dozen questions which I answered to his satisfaction. At last he wanted to know what she died of—I said, Cholera. You never did see a critter so riled as he was. "Look yere, stranger," said he, "it's my opinion that you're a pesky humbug! for my mother was blown up in a *Steamboat!*" With that he left the premises. The next day the people furnished me with a conveyance, and I rode out of town.

MARKS: Rode out of town?

CUTE: Yes; on a rail!

MARKS: I suppose you gave up the spirits, after that?

CUTE: Well, I reckon I did; it had such an effect on my spirits.

MARKS: It's a wonder they didn't tar and feather you.

CUTE: There was some mention made of that, but when they said *feathers*, I felt as if I had wings, and flew away.

MARKS: You cut and run?

CUTE: Yes; I didn't like their company and I cut it. Well, after that I let myself out as an overseer on a cotton plantation. I made a pretty good thing of that, though it was dreadful trying to my feelings to flog the darkies; but I got used to it after a while, and then I used to lather 'em like Jehu.[13] Well, the proprietor got the fever and ague and shook himself out of town. The place and all the fixings were sold at auction, and I found myself adrift once more.

MARKS: What are you doing at present?

CUTE: I'm in search of a rich relation of mine.

MARKS: A rich relation?

CUTE: Yes, a Miss Ophelia St. Clare. You see, a niece of hers married one of my second cousins—that's how I came to be a relation of hers. She came on here from Vermont to be housekeeper to a cousin of hers, of the same name.

MARKS: I know him well.

CUTE: The deuce you do!—well, that's lucky.

MARKS: Yes, he lives in this city.

CUTE: Say, you just point out the locality, and I'll give him a call.

MARKS: Stop a bit. Suppose you shouldn't be able to raise the wind in that quarter, what have you thought of doing?

CUTE: Well, nothing particular.

MARKS: How should you like to enter into a nice, profitable business— one that pays well?

CUTE: That's just about my measure—it would suit me to a hair. What is it?

MARKS: Nigger catching.

CUTE: Catching niggers! What on airth do you mean?

MARKS: Why, when there's a large reward offered for a runaway darkey, we goes after him, catches him, and gest the reward.

CUTE: Yes, that's all right so far—but s'pose there ain't no reward offered?

MARKS: Why, then we catches the darkey on our own account, sells him, and pockets the proceeds.

CUTE: By chowder, that ain't a bad speculation!

MARKS: What do you say? I want a partner. You see, I lost my partner last year, up in Ohio—he was a powerful fellow.

CUTE: Lost him! How did you lose him!

MARKS: Well, you see, Tom and I—his name was Tom Loker—Tom and I were after a mulatto chap, called George Harris, that run away from Kentucky. We traced him through the greater part of Ohio, and came up with him near the Pennsylvania line. He took refuge among some rocks, and showed fight.

CUTE: Oh! then runaway darkies show fight, do they?

MARKS: Sometimes. Well, Tom—like a headstrong fool as he was— rushed up the rocks, and a Quaker chap, who was helping this George Harris, threw him over the cliff.

CUTE: Was he killed?

MARKS: Well, I didn't stop to find out. Seeing that the darkies were stronger than I thought, I made tracks for a safe place.

CUTE: And what became of this George Harris?

MARKS: Oh! he and his wife and child got away safe into Canada. You see, they will get away sometimes, though it isn't very often. Now what do you say? You are just the figure for a fighting partner. Is it a bargain?

CUTE: Well, I rather calculate our teams won't hitch, no how. By chowder, I haint' no idea of setting myself up, as a target for darkies to fire at—that's a speculation that don't suit my constitution.

MARKS: You're afraid, then?

CUTE: No, I ain't; it's against my principles.

MARKS: Your principles—how so?

CUTE: Because my principles are to keep a sharp lookout for No. 1. I shouldn't feel wholesome if a darkey was to throw me over that cliff to look after Tom Loker.   [*Exeunt, arm-in-arm.*]

SCENE 2: *Gothic Chamber. Slow music.* ST. CLARE *discovered, seated on sofa.* TOM *to the left.*

ST. CLARE: Oh! Tom, my boy, the whole world is as empty as an egg shell.

TOM: I know it, mas'r, I know it. But oh! if mas'r could look up—up where our dear Miss Eva is—

ST. CLARE: Ah, Tom! I do look up; but the trouble is, I don't see anything when I do. I wish I could. It seems to be given to children and poor, honest fellows like you, to see what we cannot. How comes it?

TOM: "Thou hast hid from the wise and prudent, and revealed unto babes; even so, Father, for so it seemed good in thy sight."[14]

ST. CLARE: Tom, I don't believe—I've got the habit of doubting—I want to believe and I cannot.

TOM: Dear mas'r, pray to the good Lord: "Lord, I believe; help thou my unbelief."[15]

ST. CLARE: Who knows anything about anything? Was all that beautiful love and faith only one of the ever-shifting phases of human feeling, having nothing real to rest on, passing away with the little breath? And is there no more Eva—nothing?

TOM: Oh! dear mas'r, there is. I know it; I'm sure of it. Do, do, dear mas'r, believe it!

ST. CLARE: How do you know there is, Tom? You never saw the Lord.

TOM: Felt Him in my soul, mas'r—feel Him now! Oh! mas'r, when I was sold away from my old woman and the children, I was jest a'most broken up—I felt as if there warn't nothing left—and then the Lord stood by me, and He says, "Fear not, Tom," and He brings light and joy into a poor fellow's soul—makes all peace; and I's so happy, and loves everybody, and feels willin' to be jest where the Lord wants to put me. I know it couldn't come from me, 'cause I's a poor, complaining creature—it comes from above, and I know He's willin' to do for mas'r.

ST. CLARE: [*Grasping* TOM'S *hand.*] Tom, you love me!

TOM: I's willin' to lay down my life this blessed day for you.

ST. CLARE: [*Sadly.*] Poor, foolish fellow! I'm not worth the love of one good, honest heart like yours.

TOM: Oh, mas'r! there's more than me loves you—the blessed Savior loves you.

ST. CLARE: How do you know that, Tom?

TOM: The love of the Savior passeth knowledge.

ST. CLARE: [*Turns away.*] Singular! that the story of a man who lived and died eighteen hundred years ago, can affect people so yet. But He was no man. [*Rises.*] No man ever had such long and living power. Oh! that I could believe what my mother taught me, and pray as I did when I was a boy. But, Tom, all this time I have forgotten why I sent for you. I'm going to make a freeman of you; so have your trunk packed, and get ready to set out for Kentuck.

TOM: [*Joyfully.*] Bless the Lord!

ST. CLARE: [*Dryly.*] You haven't had such very bad times here, that you need be in such a rapture, Tom.

TOM: No, no, mas'r, 'tain't that; it's being a *freeman*—that's what I'm joyin' for.

ST. CLARE: Why, Tom, don't you think, for your own part, you've been better off than to be free?

TOM: No, *indeed,* Mas'r St. Clare—no, indeed!

ST. CLARE: Why, Tom, you couldn't possibly have earned, by your work, such clothes and such living as I have given you.

TOM: I know all that, Mas'r St. Clare—mas'r's been too good; but I'd rather have poor clothes, poor house, poor everything, and have 'em *mine,* than have the best, if they belonged to somebody else. I had *so,* mas'r; I think it's natur', mas'r.

ST. CLARE: I suppose so, Tom; and you'll be going off and leaving me in a month or so—though why you shouldn't no mortal knows.

TOM: Not while mas'r is in trouble. I'll stay with mas'r as long as he wants me, so as I can be any use.

ST. CLARE: [*Sadly.*] Not while I'm in trouble, Tom? And when will my trouble be over?

TOM: When you are a believer.

ST. CLARE: And you really mean to stay by me till that day comes? [*Smiling and laying his hand on* TOM's *shoulder.*] Ah, Tom! I won't keep you till that day. Go home to your wife and children, and give my love to all.

TOM: I's faith to think that day will come—the Lord has a work for mas'r.

ST. CLARE: A work, hey? Well, now, Tom, give me your views on what sort of a work it is—let's hear.

TOM: Why, even a poor fellow like me has a work; and Mas'r St. Clare, that has larnin', and riches, and friends, how much he might do for the Lord.

ST. CLARE: Tom, you seem to think the Lord needs a great deal done for him.

TOM: We does for him when we does for his creatures.

ST. CLARE: Good theology, Tom. Thank you, my boy; I like to hear you talk. But go now, Tom, and leave me alone.   [*Exit* TOM.] That faithful fellow's words have excited a train of thoughts that almost bear me, on the strong tide of faith and feeling, to the gates of that heaven I so vividly conceive. They seem to bring me nearer to Eva.

OPHELIA: [*Outside.*] What are you doing there, you limb of Satan? You've been stealing something, I'll be bound.

[OPHELIA *drags in* TOPSY.]

TOPSY: You go 'long, Miss Feely, 'tain't none o' your business.

ST. CLARE: Heyday! what is all this commotion?

OPHELIA: She's been stealing.

TOPSY: [*Sobbing.*] I hain't neither.

OPHELIA: What have you got in your bosom?

TOPSY: I've got my hand dar.

OPHELIA: But what have you got in your hand?

TOPSY: Nuffin'.

OPHELIA: That's a fib, Topsy.

TOPSY: Well, I 'spects it is.

OPHELIA: Give it to me, whatever it is.

TOPSY: It's mine—I hope I may die this bressed minute, if it don't b'long to me.

OPHELIA: Topsy, I order you to give me that article; don't let me have to ask you again. [TOPSY *reluctantly takes the foot of an old stocking from her bosom and hands it to* OPHELIA.] Sakes alive! what is all this? [*Takes from it a lock of hair, and a small book, with a bit of crape twisted around it.*]

TOPSY: Dat's a lock of ha'r dat Miss Eva give me—she cut it from her own beau'ful head herself.

ST. CLARE: [*Takes book.*] Why did you wrap *this* [*pointing to crape*] around the book?

TOPSY: 'Cause—'cause—'cause 'twas Miss Eva's. Oh! don't take 'em away, please! [*Sits down on stage, and putting her apron over her head, begins to sob vehemently.*]

OPHELIA: Come, come, don't cry; you shall have them.

TOPSY: [*Jumps up joyfully and takes them.*] I wants to keep 'em, 'cause dey makes me good; I ain't half so wicked as I used to was.

[*Runs off.*]

ST. CLARE: I really think you can make something of that girl. Any mind that is capable of a *real sorrow* is capable of good. You must try and do something with her.

OPHELIA: The child has improved very much; I have great hopes of her.

ST. CLARE: I believe I'll go down the street, a few moments, and hear the news.

OPHELIA: Shall I call Tom to attend you?

ST. CLARE: No, I shall be back in an hour.   [*Exit.*]

OPHELIA: He's got an excellent heart, but then he's so dreadful shiftless!

[*Exit.*]

SCENE 3:[16] *Front Chamber.*

[*Enter* TOPSY.]

TOPSY: Dar's something de matter wid me—I isn't a bit like myself. I haven't done anything wrong since poor Miss Eva went up in de skies and left us. When I's gwine to do anything wicked, I tinks of her, and somehow I can't do it. I's getting to be good, dat's a fact. I 'spects when I's dead I shall be turned into a little brack angel.

[*Enter* OPHELIA.]

OPHELIA: Topsy, I've been looking for you; I've got something very particular to say to you.

TOPSY: Does you want me to say the catechism?

OPHELIA: No, not now.

TOPSY: [*Aside.*] Golly! dat's one comfort.

OPHELIA: Now, Topsy, I want you to try and understand what I am
   going to say to you.

TOPSY: Yes, missis, I'll open my ears dreful wide.

OPHELIA: Mr. St. Clare has given you to me, Topsy.

TOPSY: Den I b'longs to you, don't I? Golly! I thought I always belonged
   to you.

OPHELIA: Not till to-day have I received any authority to call you my
   property.

TOPSY: I's your property, am I? Well, if you say so, I 'spects I am.

OPHELIA: Topsy, I can give you your liberty.

TOPSY: My liberty?

OPHELIA: Yes, Topsy.

TOPSY: Has you got 'um with you?

OPHELIA: I have, Topsy.

TOPSY: Is it clothes or wittles?

OPHELIA: How shiftless! Don't you know what your liberty is, Topsy?

TOPSY: How should I know when I never seed 'um?

OPHELIA: Topsy, I am going to leave this place; I am going many miles
   away—to my own home in Vermont.

TOPSY: Den what's to become of dis chile?

OPHELIA: If you wish to go, I will take you with me.

TOPSY: Miss Feely, I doesn't want to leave you no how, I loves you, I
   does.

OPHELIA: Then you shall share my home for the rest of your days.
   Come, Topsy.

TOPSY: Stop, Miss Feely; does dey hab any oberseers in Varmount?

OPHELIA: No, Topsy.

TOPSY: Nor cotton plantations, nor sugar factories, nor darkies, nor
   whipping, nor nothin'?

OPHELIA: No, Topsy.

TOPSY: By golly! de quicker you is gwine de better den.

   [*Enter* TOM, *hastily.*]

TOM: Oh, Miss Feely! Miss Feely!

OPHELIA: Gracious me, Tom! what's the matter?

TOM: Oh, Mas'r St. Clare, Mas'r St. Clare!

OPHELIA: Well, Tom, well?

TOM: They've just brought him home and I do believe he's killed.

OPHELIA: Killed?

TOPSY: Oh, dear! what's to become of de poor darkies now?

TOM: He's dreadful weak. It's just as much as he can do to speak. He wanted me to call you.

OPHELIA: My poor cousin! Who would have thought of it? Don't say a word to his wife, Tom; the danger may not be so great as you think; it would only distress her. Come with me; you may be able to afford some assistance.   [*Exeunt.*]

SCENE 4: *Handsome Chamber.* ST. CLARE *discovered seated on sofa.* OPHELIA, TOM *and* TOPSY *are clustered around him.* DOCTOR *back of sofa, feeling his pulse. Slow music.*

ST. CLARE: [*Raising himself feebly.*] Tom—poor fellow!

TOM: Well, mas'r?

ST. CLARE: I have received my death wound.

TOM: Oh, no, no, mas'r!

ST. CLARE: I feel that I am dying—Tom, pray!

TOM: [*Sinking on his knees.*] I do pray, mas'r! I do pray!

ST. CLARE: [*After a pause.*] Tom, one thing preys upon my mind—I have forgotten to sign your freedom papers. What will become of you when I am gone?

TOM: Don't think of that, mas'r.

ST. CLARE: I was wrong, Tom, very wrong, to neglect it. I may be the cause of much suffering to you hereafter. Marie, my wife—she—oh!—

OPHELIA: His mind is wandering.

ST. CLARE: [*Energetically.*] No! it is coming *home* at last! [*sinks back*] at last! at last! Eva, I come! [*Dies.*] [*Music.—Slow curtain.*]

END OF ACT IV

ACT V

SCENE 1: *An Auction Mart.* UNCLE TOM *and* EMMELINE *at back—* ADOLF, SKEGGS, MARKS, MANN *and various spectators discovered.*

[MARKS *and* MANN *come forward.*]

MARKS: Hulloa, Alf! What brings you here?

MANN: Well, I was wanting a valet, and I heard that St. Clare's lot was going; I thought I'd just look at them.

MARKS: Catch me ever buying any of St. Clare's people. Spoilt niggers, every one—impudent as the devil.

MANN: Never fear that; if I get 'em, I'll soon have their airs out of them—they'll soon find that they've another kind of master to deal with than St. Clare. 'Pon my word, I'll buy that fellow—I like the shape of him. [*Pointing to* ADOLF.]

MARKS: You'll find it'll take all you've got to keep him—he's deucedly extravagant.

MANN: Yes, but my lord will find that he *can't* be extravagant with *me*. Just let him be sent to the calaboose a few times, and thoroughly dressed down, I'll tell you if it don't bring him to a sense of his ways. Oh! I'll reform him, up hill and down, you'll see. I'll buy him, that's flat.

[*Enter* LEGREE—*he goes up and looks at* ADOLF, *whose boots are nicely blacked.*]

LEGREE: A nigger with his boots blacked—bah! [*Spits on them.*] Holloa, you! [*To* TOM.] Let's see your teeth. [*Seizes* TOM *by the jaw and opens his mouth.*] Strip up your sleeve and show your muscle. [TOM *does so.*] Where was you raised?

TOM: In Kentuck, mas'r.

LEGREE: What have you done?

TOM: Had care of mas'r's farm.

LEGREE: That's a likely story. [*Turns to* EMMELINE.] You're a nice looking girl enough. How old are you? [*Grasps her arm.*]

EMMELINE: [*Shrieking.*] Ah! you hurt me.

SKEGGS: Stop that, you minx! No whimpering here. The sale is going to begin. [*Mounts the rostrum.*] Gentlemen, the next article I shall offer you to-day is Adolf, late valet to Mr. St. Clare. How much am I offered? [*Various bids are made.* ADOLF *is knocked down to* MANN *for eight hundred dollars.*] Gentlemen, I now offer a prime article— the quadroon girl, Emmeline, only fifteen years of age, warranted in every respect. [*Business as before.* EMMELINE *is sold to* LEGREE *for one thousand dollars.*] Now, I shall close to-day's sale by offering you the valuable article known as Uncle Tom, the most useful nigger ever raised. Gentlemen in want of an overseer, now is the time to bid. [*Business as before.* TOM *is sold to* LEGREE *for twelve hundred dollars.*]

LEGREE: Now look here, you two belong to me.

[TOM *and* EMMELINE *sink on their knees.*]

TOM: Heaven help us, then! [*Music.*—LEGREE *stands over them exulting. Picture.*]

SCENE 2: *The Garden of* MISS OPHELIA'S *House in Vermont.*

[*Enter* OPHELIA *and* DEACON PERRY.]

DEACON: Miss Ophelia, allow me to offer you my congratulations upon your safe arrival in your native place. I hope it is your intention to pass the remainder of your days with us?

OPHELIA: Well, Deacon, I have come here with that express purpose.

DEACON: I presume you were not over-pleased with the South?

OPHELIA: Well, to tell the truth, Deacon, I wasn't; I liked the country very well, but the people there are so dreadful shiftless.

DEACON: The result, I presume, of living in a warm climate.

OPHELIA: Well, Deacon, what is the news among you all here?

DEACON: Well, we live on in the same even jog-trot pace. Nothing of any consequence has happened.—Oh! I forgot. [*Takes out his handkerchief.*] I've lost my wife; my Molly has left me. [*Wipes his eyes.*]

OPHELIA: Poor soul! I pity you, Deacon.

DEACON: Thank you. You perceive I bear my loss with resignation.

OPHELIA: How you must miss her tongue!

DEACON: Molly certainly was fond of talking. She always would have the last word—heigho!

OPHELIA: What was her complaint, Deacon?

DEACON: A very mild and soothing one, Miss Ophelia; she had a severe attack of the lockjaw.

OPHELIA: Dreadful!

DEACON: Wasn't it? When she found she couldn't use her tongue, she took it so much to heart that it struck to her stomach and killed her. Poor dear! Excuse my handkerchief; she's been dead only eighteen months.

OPHELIA: Why, Deacon, by this time you ought to be setting your cap for another wife.

DEACON: Do you think so, Miss Ophelia?

OPHELIA: I don't see why you shouldn't—you are still a good-looking man, Deacon.

DEACON: Ah! well, I think I do wear well—in fact, I may say remarkably well. It has been observed to me before.

OPHELIA: And you are not much over fifty?

DEACON: Just turned of forty, I assure you.

OPHELIA: Hale and hearty?

DEACON: Health excellent—look at my eye! Strong as a lion—look at my arm! A No. 1 constitution—look at my leg!!!

OPHELIA: Have you no thoughts of choosing another partner?

DEACON: Well, to tell you the truth, I have.

OPHELIA: Who is she?

DEACON: She is not far distant. [*Looks at* OPHELIA *in a languishing manner.*] I have her in my eye at this present moment.

OPHELIA: [*Aside.*] Really, I believe he's going to pop. Why, surely, Deacon, you don't mean to—

DEACON: Yes, Miss Ophelia, I do mean; and believe me, when I say— [*Looking off.*] The Lord be good to us, but I believe there is the devil coming!

[TOPSY *runs on with bouquet. She is now dressed very neatly.*]

TOPSY: Miss Feely, here is some flowers dat I hab been gathering for you. [*Gives bouquet.*]

OPHELIA: That's a good child.

DEACON: Miss Ophelia, who is this young person?

OPHELIA: She is my daughter.

DEACON: [*Aside.*] Her daughter! Then she must have married a colored man off South. I was not aware that you had been married, Miss Ophelia?

OPHELIA: Married? Sakes alive! What made you think I had been married?

DEACON: Good gracious! I'm getting confused. Didn't I understand you to say that this—somewhat tanned—young lady was your daughter?

OPHELIA: Only by adoption. She is my adopted daughter.

DEACON: O—oh! [*Aside.*] I breathe again.

TOPSY: [*Aside.*] By golly! Dat old man's eyes stick out of 'um head dre'ful. Guess he never seed anything like me afore.

OPHELIA: Deacon, won't you step into the house and refresh yourself after your walk?

DEACON: I accept your polite invitation. [*Offers his arm.*] Allow me.

OPHELIA: As gallant as ever, Deacon. I declare, you grow younger every day.

DEACON: You can never grow old, madam.

OPHELIA: Ah, you flatterer!   [*Exeunt.*]

TOPSY: Dar dey go, like an old goose and gander. Guess dat ole gemblemun feels kind of confectionary—rather sweet on my old missis. By golly! She's been dre'ful kind to me ever since I come away from de South; and I loves her, I does, 'cause she takes such car' on me and gives me dese fine clothes. I tries to be good too, and I's getting 'long 'mazin' fast. I's not so wicked as I used to was. [*Looks out.*] Holloa! dar's some one comin' here. I wonder what he wants now. [*Retires, observing.*]

[*Enter* GUMPTION CUTE, *very shabby—a small bundle, on a stick, over his shoulder.*]

CUTE: By chowder, here I am again. Phew! it's a pretty considerable tall piece of walking between here and New Orleans, not to mention the wear of shoe-leather. I guess I'm about done up. If this streak of bad luck lasts much longer, I'll borrow sixpence to buy a rope, and hang myself right straight up! When I went to call on Miss Ophelia, I swow if I didn't find out that she had left for Varmount; so I kind of concluded to make tracks in that direction myself, and as I didn't have any money left, why I had to foot it, and here I am in old Varmount once more. They told me Miss Ophelia lived up here. I wonder if she will remember the relationship. [*Sees* TOPSY.] By chowder, there's a darkey. Look here, Charcoal!

TOPSY: [*Comes forward.*] My name isn't Charcoal—it's Topsy.

CUTE: Oh! Your name is Topsy, is it, you juvenile specimen of Day & Martin?[17]

TOPSY: Tell you I don't know nothin' 'bout Day & Martin. I's Topsy and I belong to Miss Feely St. Clare.

CUTE: I'm much obleeged to you, you small extract of Japan,[18] for your information. So Miss Ophelia lives up there in the white house, does she?

TOPSY: Well, she don't do nothin' else.

CUTE: Well, then, just locomote your pins.

TOPSY: What—what's dat?

CUTE: Walk your chalks!

TOPSY: By golly! dere ain't no chalk 'bout me.

CUTE: Move your trotters.

TOPSY: How you does spoke! What you mean by trotters?

CUTE: Why, your feet, Stove Polish.

TOPSY: What does you want me to move my feet for?

CUTE: To tell your mistress, you ebony angel, that a gentleman wishes to see her.

TOPSY: Does you call yourself a gentleman? By golly! you look more like a scar'-crow.

CUTE: Now look here, you Charcoal, don't you be sassy. I'm a gentle-

man in distress; a done-up speculator; one that has seen better days
—long time ago—and better clothes too, by chowder! My creditors
are like my boots—they've no soles. I'm a victim to circumstances.
I've been through much and survived it. I've taken walking exercise
for the benefit of my heath; but as I was trying to live on air at the
same time, it was a losing speculation, 'cause it gave me such a dreadful appetite.

TOPSY: Golly! you look as if you could eat an ox, horns and all.

CUTE: Well, I calculate I could, if he was roasted—it's a speculation I
should like to engage in. I have returned like the fellow that run away
in Scripture; and if anybody's got a fatted calf they want to kill, all
they got to do is to fetch him along. Do you know, Charcoal, that
your mistress is a relation of mine?

TOPSY: Is she your uncle?

CUTE: No, no, not quite so near as that. My second cousin married her
niece.

TOPSY: And does you want to see Miss Feely?

CUTE: I do. I have come to seek a home beneath her roof, and take care
of all the spare change she don't want to use.

TOPSY: Den just you follow me, mas'r.

CUTE: Stop! By chowder, I've got a great idee. Say, you Day & Martin,
how should you like to enter into a speculation?

TOPSY: Golly! I doesn't know what a spec—spec—cu—what-do-you-
call-'um am.

CUTE: Well, now, I calculate I've hit upon about the right thing. Why
should I degrade the manly dignity of the Cutes by becoming a
beggar—expose myself to the chance of receiving the cold shoulder
as a poor relation? By chowder, my blood biles as I think of it!
Topsy, you can make my fortune, and your own, too. I've an idee
in my head that is worth a million of dollars.

TOPSY: Golly! is your head worth dat? Guess you wouldn't bring dat
out South for de whole of you.

CUTE: Don't you be too severe now, Charcoal; I'm a man of genius. Did
you ever hear of Barnum?[19]

TOPSY: Barnum! Barnum! Does he live out South?

CUTE: No, he lives in New York. Do you know how he made his
fortune?

TOPSY: What is him fortin, hey? Is it something he wears?

CUTE: Chowder, how green you are!

TOPSY: [*Indignantly.*] Sar, I hab you to know I's not green; I's brack.

CUTE: To be sure you are, Day & Martin. I calculate, when a person says another has a fortune, he means he's got plenty of money, Charcoal.

TOPSY: And did he make the money?

CUTE: Sartin sure, and no mistake.

TOPSY: Golly! now I thought money always growed.

CUTE: Oh, git out! You are too cute—you are cuterer than I am; and I'm Cute by name and cute by nature. Well, as I was saying, Barnum made his money by exhibiting a *woolly* horse; now wouldn't it be an all-fired speculation to show you as the woolly gal?

TOPSY: You want to make a sight of me?

CUTE: I'll give you half the receipts, by chowder!

TOPSY: Should I have to leave Miss Feely?

CUTE: To be sure you would.

TOPSY: Den you hab to get a woolly gal somewhere else, Mas'r Cute.

[*Runs off.*]

CUTE: There's another speculation gone to smash, by chowder! [*Exit.*]

SCENE 3: *A Rude Chamber.* TOM *is discovered, in old clothes, seated on a stool; he holds in his hand a paper containing a curl of* EVA'S *hair. The scene opens to the symphony of "Old Folks at Home."*

TOM: I have come to de dark places; I's going through the vale of shadows. My heart sinks at times and feels just like a big lump of lead. Den it gits up in my throat and chokes me till de tears roll out of my eyes; den I take out dis curl of little Miss Eva's hair, and the sight of it brings calm to my mind and I feels strong again. [*Kisses the curl and puts it in his breast—takes out a silver dollar, which is suspended around his neck by a string.*] Dere's de bright silver dollar dat Mas'r George Shelby gave me the day I was sold away from old Kentuck, and I've kept it ever since. Mas'r George must have grown to be a man by this time. I wonder if I shall ever see him again.

SONG.—*"Old Folks at Home"*

[*Enter* LEGREE, EMMELINE, SAMBO *and* QUIMBO.]

LEGREE: Shut up, you black cuss! Did you think I wanted any of your infernal howling? [*Turns to* EMMELINE.] We're home. [EMMELINE *shrinks from him. He takes hold of her ear.*] You didn't ever wear earrings?

EMMELINE: [*Trembling.*] No, master.

LEGREE: Well, I'll give you a pair, if you're a good girl. You needn't be so frightened; I don't mean to make you work very hard. You'll have fine times with me and live like a lady; only be a good girl.

EMMELINE: My soul sickens as his eyes gaze upon me. His touch makes my very flesh creep.

LEGREE: [*Turns to* TOM, *and points to* SAMBO *and* QUIMBO.] Ye see what ye'd get if ye'd try to run off. These yer boys have been raised to track niggers, and they'd just as soon chaw one on ye up as eat their suppers; so mind yourself. [*To* EMMELINE.] Come, mistress, you go in here with me. [*Taking* EMMELINE'S *hand, and leading her away.*]

EMMELINE: [*Withdrawing her hand, and shrinking back.*] No, no! let me work in the fields; I don't want to be a lady.

LEGREE: Oh! you're going to be contrary, are you? I'll soon take all that out of you.

EMMELINE: Kill me, if you will.

LEGREE: Oh! you want to be killed, do you? Now, come here, you Tom, you see I told you I didn't buy you jest for the common work; I mean to promote you and make a driver of you, and to-night ye may jest as well be gin to get yer hand in. Now, ye just take this yer gal, and flog her; ye've seen enough on't to know how.

TOM: I beg mas'r's pardon—hopes mas'r won't set me at that. It's what I an't used to—never did, and can't do—no way possible.

LEGREE: Ye'll larn a pretty smart chance of things ye never did know before I've done with ye. [*Strikes* TOM *with whip, three blows.— Music chord each blow.*] There! now will ye tell me ye can't do it?

TOM: Yes, mas'r! I'm willing to work night and day, and work while there's life and breath in me; but this yer thing I can't feel it right to do, and, mas'r I *never* shall do it, *never!*

LEGREE: What! ye black beast! tell *me* ye don't think it right to do what I tell ye! What have any of you cussed cattle to do with thinking what's right? I'll put a stop to it. Why, what do ye think ye are? Maybe ye think yer a gentleman, master Tom, to be telling your master what's right and what an't! So you pretend it's wrong to flog the gal?

TOM: I think so, mas'r; 'twould be downright cruel, and it's what I never will do, mas'r. If you mean to kill me, kill me; but as to raising my hand agin any one here, I never shall—I'll die first!

LEGREE: Well, here's a pious dog at last, let down among us sinners— powerful holy critter he must be. Here, you rascal! you make believe to be so pious, didn't you never read out of your Bible, "Servants, obey your masters?" An't I your master? Didn't I pay twelve hundred dollars, cash, for all there is inside your cussed old black shell? An't you mine, body and soul?

TOM: No, no! My soul an't yours, mas'r; you haven't bought it—ye can't buy it; it's been bought and paid for by one that is able to keep it, and you can't harm it!

LEGREE: I can't? we'll see, we'll see! Here, Sambo! Quimbo! give this dog such a breaking in as he won't get over this month!

EMMELINE: Oh, no! you will not be so cruel—have some mercy! [*Clings to* TOM.]

LEGREE: Mercy? you won't find any in this shop! Away with the black cuss! Flog him within an inch of his life?

[*Music.*—SAMBO *and* QUIMBO *seize* TOM *and drag him up stage.* LEGREE *seizes* EMMELINE, *and throws her.*—*She falls on her knees, with her hands lifted in supplication.*—LEGREE *raises his whip, as if to strike* TOM.—*Picture.*]

SCENE 4: *Plain Chamber.*

[*Enter* OPHELIA, *followed by* TOPSY.]

OPHELIA: A person inquiring for me, did you say, Topsy?

TOPSY: Yes, missis.

OPHELIA: What kind of a looking man is he?

TOPSY: By golly! he's very queer looking man, anyway; and den he talks to dre'ful funny. What does you think?—yah! yah! he wanted to 'zibite me as de woolly gal! yah! yah!

OPHELIA: Oh! I understand. Some cute Yankee, who wants to purchase you, to make a show of—the heartless wretch!

TOPSY: Dat's just him, missis; dat's just his name. He tole me dat it was Cute—Mr. Cute Speculashum—dat's him.

OPHELIA: What did you say to him, Topsy?

TOPSY: Well, I didn't say much; it was brief and to the point—I tole him I wouldn't leave you, Miss Feely, no how.

OPHELIA: That's right, Topsy; you know you are very comfortable here—you wouldn't fare quite so well if you went away among strangers.

TOPSY: By golly! I know dat; you takes care on me, and makes me good. I don't steal any now, and I don't swar, and I don't dance break-downs. Oh! I isn't so wicked as I used to was.

OPHELIA: That's right, Topsy; now show the gentleman, or whatever he is, up.

TOPSY: By golly! I guess he won't make much out of Miss Feely. [*Exit.*]

OPHELIA: I wonder who this person can be? Perhaps it is some old acquaintance, who has heard of my arrival, and who comes on a social visit.

[*Enter* CUTE.]

CUTE: Aunt, how do ye do? Well, I swan, the sight of you is good for weak eyes. [*Offers his hand.*]

OPHELIA: [*Coldly drawing back.*] Really, sir, I can't say that I ever had the pleasure of seeing you before.

CUTE: Well, it's a fact that you never did. You see I never happened to be in your neighborhood afore now. Of course you've heard of me? I'm one of the Cutes—Gumption Cute, the first and only son of Josiah and Maria Cute, of Oniontown, on the Onion river, in the north part of this ere State of Varmount.

OPHELIA: Can't say I ever heard the name before.

CUTE: Well, then, I calculate your memory must be a little ricketty. I'm a relation of yours.

OPHELIA: A relation of mine! Why, I never heard of any Cutes in our family.

CUTE: Well, I shouldn't wonder if you never did. Don't you remember your niece, Mary?

OPHELIA: Of course I do. What a shiftless question!

CUTE: Well, you see, my second cousin, Abijah Blake, married her; so you see that makes me a relation of yours.

OPHELIA: Rather a distant one, I should say.

CUTE: By chowder! I'm *near* enough, just at present.

OPHELIA: Well, you certainly are a sort of connection of mine.

CUTE: Yes, kind of sort of.

OPHELIA: And of course you are welcome to my house, as long as you choose to make it your home.

CUTE: By chowder! I'm booked for the next six months—this isn't a bad speculation.

OPHELIA: I hope you left all your folks well at home?

CUTE: Well, yes, they're pretty comfortably disposed of. Father and mother's dead, and Uncle Josh has gone to California. I am the only representative of the Cutes left.

OPHELIA: There doesn't seem to be a great deal of *you* left. I declare, you are positively in rags.

CUTE: Well, you see, the fact is, I've been speculating—trying to get bank-notes—specie-rags, as they say—but I calculate I've turned out rags of another sort.

OPHELIA: I'm sorry for your ill luck, but I am afraid you have been shiftless.

CUTE: By chowder! I've done all that a fellow could do. You see, somehow, everything I take hold of kind of bursts up.

OPHELIA: Well, well, perhaps you'll do better for the future; make yourself at home. I have got to see to some household matters, so excuse me for a short time. [*Aside.*] Impudent and shiftless!   [*Exit.*]

CUTE: By chowder! I rather guess that this speculation will hitch. She's a good-natured old critter; I reckon I'll be a son to her while she lives, and take care of her valuables arter she's a defunct departed. I wonder if they keep the vittles in this ere room? Guess not. I've got extensive accommodations for all sorts of eatables. I'm a regular vacuum, throughout—pockets and all. I'm chuck full of emptiness. [*Looks out.*] Holloa! who's this elderly individual coming upstairs? He looks like a compound essence of starch and dignity. I wonder if he isn't another relation of mine. I should like a rich old fellow now for an uncle.

[*Enter* DEACON PERRY.]

DEACON: Ha! a stranger here!

CUTE: How d'ye do?

DEACON: You are a friend to Miss Ophelia, I presume?

CUTE: Well, I rather calculate that I am a leetle more than a friend.

DEACON: [*Aside.*] Bless me! what can he mean by those mysterious words? Can he be her—no, I don't think he can. She said she wasn't—well, at all events, it's very suspicious.

CUTE: The old fellow seems kind of stuck up.

DEACON: You are a particular friend to Miss Ophelia, you say?

CUTE: Well, I calculate I am.

DEACON: Bound to her by any tender tie?

CUTE: It's something more than a tie—it's a regular double-twisted knot.

DEACON: Ah! just as I suspected. [*Aside.*] Might I inquire the nature of that tie?

CUTE: Well, it's the natural tie of relationship.

DEACON: A relation—what relation!

CUTE: Why, you see, my second cousin, Abijah Blake, married her niece, Mary.

DEACON: Oh! is that all?

CUTE: By chowder, ain't that enough?

DEACON: Then you are not her husband?

CUTE: To be sure I ain't. What put that ere idea into your cranium?

DEACON: [*Shaking him vigorously by the hand.*] My dear sir, I'm delighted to see you.

CUTE: Holloa! you ain't going slightly insane, are you?

DEACON: No, no fear of that; I'm only happy, that's all.

CUTE: I wonder if he's been taking a nipper?

DEACON: As you are a relation of Miss Ophelia's, I think it proper that I should make you my confidant; in fact, let you into a little scheme that I have lately conceived.

CUTE: Is it a speculation?

DEACON: Well, it is, just at present; but I trust before many hours to make it a surety.

CUTE: By chowder! I hope it won't serve you the way my speculations have served me. But fire away, old boy, and give us the prospectus.

DEACON: Well, then, my young friend, I have been thinking, ever since Miss Ophelia returned to Vermont, that she was just the person to fill the place of my lamented Molly.

CUTE: Say, you couldn't tell us who your lamented Molly was, could you?

DEACON: Why, the late Mrs. Perry, to be sure.

CUTE: Oh! then the lamented Polly was your wife?

DEACON: She was.

CUTE: And now you wish to marry Miss Ophelia?

DEACON: Exactly.

CUTE: [*Aside.*] Consarn this old porpoise! if I let him do that he'll Jew me out of my living. By chowder! I'll put a spoke in his wheel.

DEACON: Well, what do you say? will you intercede for me with your aunt?

CUTE: No! bust me up if I do!

DEACON: No?

CUTE: No, I tell you. I forbid the bans. Now, ain't you a purty individual, to talk about getting married, you old superannuated Methuselah specimen of humanity! Why, you've got one foot in etarnity already, and t'other ain't fit to stand on. Go home and go to bed! have your head shaved, and send for a lawyer to make your will, leave your property to your heirs—if you hain't got any, why leave it to me—I'll take care of it, and charge nothing for the trouble.

DEACON: Really, sir, this language, to one of my standing, is highly indecorous—it's more, sir, than I feel willing to endure, sir. I shall expect an explanation, sir.

CUTE: Now, you see, old gouty toes, you're losing your temper.

DEACON: Sir, I'm a deacon; I never lost my temper in all my life, sir.

CUTE: Now, you see, you're getting excited; you had better go; we can't have a disturbance here!

DEACON: No, sir! I shall not go, sir! I shall not go until I have seen Miss Ophelia. I wish to know if she will countenance this insult.

CUTE: Now keep cool, old stick-in-the-mud! Draw it mild, old timber-toes!

DEACON: Damn it all, sir, what—

CUTE: Oh! Only think, now, what would people say to hear a deacon swearing like a trooper?

DEACON: Sir—I—you—this is too much, sir.

CUTE: Well, now, I calculate that's just about my opinion, so we'll have no more of it. Get out of this! start your boots, or by chowder! I'll pitch you from one end of the stairs to the other.

[*Enter* OPHELIA.]

OPHELIA: Hoity toity! What's the meaning of all these loud words?

CUTE: ⎱ Well, you see, Aunt—

DEACON: ⎰ Miss Ophelia, I beg—

CUTE: Now, look here, you just hush your yap! How can I fix up matters if you keep jabbering?

OPHELIA: Silence! for shame, Mr. Cute. Is that the way you speak to the deacon?

CUTE: Darn the deacon!

OPHELIA: Deacon Perry, what is all this?

DEACON: Madam, a few words will explain everything. Hearing from this person that he was your nephew, I ventured to tell him that I cherished hopes of making you my wife, whereupon he flew into a violent passion, and ordered me out of the house.

OPHELIA: Does this house belong to you or me, Mr. Cute?

CUTE: Well, to you, I reckon.

OPHELIA: Then how dare you give orders in it?

CUTE: Well, I calculated you wouldn't care about marrying old half-a-century there.

OPHELIA: That's enough; I will marry him; and as for you [*points to the right*], get out.

CUTE: Get out?

OPHELIA: Yes; the sooner the better.

CUTE: Darned if I don't serve him out first though.

[*Music.*—CUTE *makes a dash at* DEACON, *who gets behind* OPHE-
LIA. TOPSY *enters with a broom and beats* CUTE *around stage.*—
OPHELIA *faints in* DEACON'S *arms.*—CUTE *falls, and* TOPSY *butts
him, kneeling over him.*—*Quick drop.*]

END OF ACT V

ACT VI

SCENE 1: *Dark Landscape.*—*An old, roofless shed.* TOM *is discovered in
shed, lying on some old cotton bagging.* CASSY *kneels by his side, holding a cup to his lips.*

CASSY: Drink all ye want. I knew how it would be. It isn't the first time
I've been out in the night, carrying water to such as you.

TOM [*Returning cup*]. Thank you, missis.

CASSY: Don't call me missis. I'm a miserable slave like yourself—a lower
one than you can ever be! It's no use, my poor fellow, this you've
been trying to do. You were a brave fellow. You had the right on
your side; but it's all in vain for you to struggle. You are in the Devil's
hands: he is the strongest, and you must give up.

TOM: Oh! how can I give up?

CASSY: You see *you* don't know anything about it; I do. Here you are,
on a lone plantation, ten miles from any other, in the swamps; not
a white person here who could testify, if you were burned alive.
There's no law here that can do you, or any of us, the least good;
and this man! there's no earthly thing that he is not bad enough to
do. I could make one's hair rise, and their teeth chatter, if I should
only tell what I've seen and been knowing to here; and it's no use
resisting! Did I *want* to live with him? Wasn't I a woman delicately
bred? And he!—Father in Heaven! what was he and is he? And yet
I've lived with him these five years, and cursed every moment of my
life night and day.

TOM: Oh heaven! have you quite forgot us poor critters?

CASSY: And what are these miserable low dogs you work with, that you
should suffer on their account? Every one of them would turn against
you the first time they get a chance. They are all of them as low and
cruel to each other as they can be; there's no use in your suffering
to keep from hurting them!

TOM: What made 'em cruel? If I give out, I shall get used to it, and grow, little by little, just like 'em. No, no, missis, I've lost everything, wife, and children, and home, and a kind master, and he would have set me free if he'd only lived a day longer—I've lost everything in *this* world, and now I can't lose heaven, too; no, I can't get to be wicked besides all.

CASSY: But it can't be that He will lay sin to our account; He won't charge it to us when we are forced to it; He'll charge it to them that drove us to it. Can I do anything more for you? Shall I give you some more water?

TOM: Oh missis! I wish you'd go to Him who can give you living waters!

CASSY: Go to him! Where is he? Who is he?

TOM: Our Heavenly Father!

CASSY: I used to see the picture of Him, over the altar, when I was a girl; but *He isn't here!* There's nothing here but sin, and long, long despair! There, there, don't talk any more, my poor fellow. Try to sleep, if you can. I must hasten back, lest my absence be noted. Think of me when I am gone, Uncle Tom, and pray, pray for me.

[*Music.—Exit* CASSY.—TOM *sinks back to sleep.*]

SCENE 2: *Street in New Orleans.*

[*Enter* GEORGE SHELBY.]

GEORGE: At length my mission of mercy is nearly finished; I have reached my journey's end. I have now but to find the house of Mr. St. Clare, re-purchase old Uncle Tom, and convey him back to his wife and children, in old Kentucky. Some one approaches; he may, perhaps, be able to give me the information I require. I will accost him.

[*Enter* MARKS.]

Pray, sir, can you tell me where Mr. St. Clare dwells?

MARKS: Where I don't think you'll be in a hurry to seek him.

GEORGE: And where is that?

MARKS: In the grave!

GEORGE: Stay, sir! you may be able to give me some information concerning Mr. St. Clare.

MARKS: I beg pardon, sir. I am a lawyer; I can't afford to *give* anything.

GEORGE: But you would have no objections to selling it?

MARKS: Not the slightest.

GEORGE: What do you value it at?

MARKS: Well, say five dollars, that's reasonable.

GEORGE: There they are. [*Gives money.*] Now answer me to the best of your ability. Has the death of St. Clare caused his slaves to be sold?

MARKS: It has.

GEORGE: How were they sold?

MARKS: At auction—they went dirt cheap.

GEORGE: How were they bought—all in one lot?

MARKS: No, they went to different bidders.

GEORGE: Was you present at the sale?

MARKS: I was.

GEORGE: Do you remember seeing a negro among them called Tom?

MARKS: What, Uncle Tom?

GEORGE: The same—who bought him?

MARKS: A Mr. Legree.

GEORGE: Where is his plantation?

MARKS: Up in Louisiana, on the Red River; but a man never could find it unless he had been there before.

GEORGE: Who could I get to direct me there?

MARKS: Well, stranger, I don't know of any one just at present, 'cept myself, could find it for you; it's such an out-of-the-way sort of hole; and if you are a mind to come down handsomely, why, I'll do it.

GEORGE: The reward shall be ample.

MARKS: Enough said, stranger; let's take the steamboat at once.

[*Exeunt.*]

SCENE 3: *A Rough Chamber.*

[*Enter* LEGREE.—*Sits.*]

LEGREE: Plague on that Sambo, to kick up this yer row between me and the new hands.

[CASSY *steals on, and stands behind him.*]

The fellow won't be fit to work for a week now, right in the press of the season.

CASSY: Yes, just like you.

LEGREE: Hah! you she-devil! you've come back, have you? [*Rises.*]

CASSY: Yes, I have; come to have my own way, too.

LEGREE: You lie, you jade! I'll be up to my word. Either you behave yourself, or stay down in the quarters and fare and work with the rest.

CASSY: I'd rather, ten thousand times, live in the dirtiest hole in the quarters, than be under your hoof!

LEGREE: But you are under my hoof, for all that, that's one comfort; so sit down here and listen to reason. [*Grasps her wrist.*]

CASSY: Simon Legree, take care! [LEGREE *lets go his hold.*] You're afraid of me, Simon, and you've reason to be; for I've got the Devil in me!

LEGREE: I believe to my soul you have. After all, Cassy, why can't you be friends with me, as you used to?

CASSY: [*Bitterly.*] Used to!

LEGREE: I wish, Cassy, you'd behave yourself decently.

CASSY: *You* talk about behaving decently! and what have you been doing? You haven't even sense enough to keep from spoiling one of your best hands, right in the most pressing season, just for your devilish temper.

LEGREE: I was a fool, it's a fact, to let any such brangle[20] come up; but when Tom set up his will he had to be broke in.

CASSY: You'll never break *him* in.

LEGREE: Won't I? I'd like to know if I won't! He'll be the first nigger that ever come it round me! I'll break every bone in his body but he shall give up.

[*Enter* SAMBO, *with a paper in his hand, stands bowing.*]

LEGREE: What's that, you dog?

SAMBO: It's a witch thing, mas'r.

LEGREE: A what?

SAMBO: Something that niggers gits from witches. Keep 'em from feeling when they's flogged. He had it tied round his neck with a black string.

[LEGREE *takes the paper and opens it.—A silver dollar drops on the stage, and a long curl of light hair twines around his finger.*]

LEGREE: Damnation. [*Stamping and writhing, as if the hair burned him.*] Where did this come from? Take it off! burn it up! burn it up! [*Throws the curl away.*] What did you bring it to me for?

SAMBO: [*Trembling.*] I beg pardon, mas'r; I thought you would like to see 'um.

LEGREE: Don't you bring me any more of your devilish things. [*Shakes his fist at* SAMBO *who runs off.—*LEGREE *kicks the dollar after him.*] Blast it! where did he get that? If it didn't look just like—whoo! I thought I'd forgot that. Curse me if I think there's any such thing as forgetting anything, any how.

CASSY: What is the matter with you, Legree? What is there in a simple curl of fair hair to appall a man like you—you who are familiar with every form of cruelty.

LEGREE: Cassy, to-night the past has been recalled to me—the past that I have so long and vainly striven to forget.

CASSY: Hast aught on this earth power to move a soul like thine?

LEGREE: Yes, for hard and reprobate as I now seem, there has been a time when I have been rocked on the bosom of a mother, cradled with prayers and pious hymns, my now seared brow bedewed with the waters of holy baptism.

CASSY: [*Aside.*] What sweet memories of childhood can thus soften down that heart of iron?

LEGREE: In early childhood, a fair-haired woman has led me, at the sound of Sabbath bells, to worship and to pray. Born of a hard-tempered sire, on whom that gentle woman had wasted a world of unvalued love, I followed in the steps of my father. Boisterous, unruly and tyrannical, I despised all her counsel, and would have none of her reproof, and, at an early age, broke from her to seek my fortunes on the sea. I never came home but once after that; and then my mother, with the yearning of a heart that must love something, and had nothing else to love, clung to me, and sought with passionate prayers and entreaties to win me from a life of sin.

CASSY: That was your day of grace, Legree; then good angels called you, and mercy held you by the hand.

LEGREE: My heart inly relented; there was a conflict, but sin got the victory, and I set all the force of my rough nature against the conviction of my conscience. I drank and swore, was wilder and more brutal than ever. And one night, when my mother, in the last agony of her despair, knelt at my feet, I spurned her from me, threw her senseless on the floor, and with brutal curses fled to my ship.

CASSY: Then the fiend took thee for his own.

LEGREE: The next I heard of my mother was one night while I was carousing among drunken companions. A letter was put in my hands. I opened it, and a lock of long, curling hair fell from it, and twined about my fingers, even as that locked twined but now. The letter told me that my mother was dead, and that dying she blest and forgave me! [*Buries his face in his hands.*]

CASSY: Why did you not even then renounce your evil ways?

LEGREE: There is a dread, unhallowed necromancy of evil, that turns things sweetest and holiest to phantoms of horror and affright. That pale, loving mother,—her dying prayers, her forgiving love,—

wrought in my demoniac heart of sin only as a damning sentence, bringing with it a fearful looking for of judgment and fiery indignation.

CASSY: And yet you would not strive to avert the doom that threatened you.

LEGREE: I burned the lock of hair and I burned the letter; and when I saw them hissing and crackling in the flame, inly shuddered as I thought of everlasting fires! I tried to drink and revel, and swear away the memory; but often in the deep night, whose solemn stillness arraigns the soul in forced communion with itself, I have seen that pale mother rising by my bed-side, and felt the soft twining of that hair around my fingers, 'till the cold sweat would roll down my face, and I would spring from my bed in horror—horror! [*Falls in chair. —After a pause.*] What the devil ails me? Large drops of sweat stand on my forehead, and my heart beats heavy and thick with fear. I thought I saw something white rising and glimmering in the gloom before me, and it seemed to bear my mother's face! I know one thing; I'll let that fellow Tom alone, after this. What did I want with his cussed paper? I believe I am bewitched sure enough! I've been shivering and sweating ever since! Where did he get that hair? I couldn't have been that! I *burn'd* that up, I know I did! I would be a joke if hair could rise from the dead! I'll have Sambo and Quimbo up here to sing and dance one of their dances, and keep off these horrid notions. Here, Sambo! Quimbo!   [*Exit.*]

CASSY: Yes, Legree, that golden tress was charmed; each hair had in it a spell of terror and remorse for thee, and was used by a mightier power to bind thy cruel hands from inflicting uttermost evil on the helpless!   [*Exit.*]

SCENE 4: *Street.*

[*Enter* MARKS, *meeting* CUTE, *who enters, dressed in an old faded uniform.*]

MARKS: By the land, stranger, but it strikes me that I've seen you somewhere before.

CUTE: By chowder! do you know now, that's just what I was a going to say?

MARKS: Isn't your name Cute?

CUTE: You're right, I calculate. Yours is Marks, I reckon.

MARKS: Just so.

CUTE: Well, I swow, I'm glad to see you. [*They shake hands.*] How's your wholesome?

MARKS: Hearty as ever. Well, who would have thought of ever seeing you again. Why, I thought you was in Vermont?

CUTE: Well, so I was. You see I went there after that rich relation of mine—but the speculation didn't turn out well.

MARKS: How so?

CUTE: Why, you see, she took a shine to an old fellow—Deacon Abraham Perry—and married him.

MARKS: Oh, that rather put your nose out of joint in that quarter.

CUTE: Busted me right up, I tell you. The deacon did the handsome thing, though; he said if I would leave the neighborhood and go out South again, he'd stand the damage. I calculate I didn't give him much time to change his mind, and so, you see, here I am again.

MARKS: What are you doing in that soldier rig?

CUTE: Oh, this is my sign.

MARKS: Your sign?

CUTE: Yes; you see, I'm engaged just at present in an all-fired good speculation; I'm a Fillibusterow.[21]

MARKS: A what?

CUTE: A fillibusterow! Don't you know what that is? It's Spanish for Cuban Volunteer; and means a chap that goes the whole porker for glory and all that ere sort of thing.

MARKS: Oh! you've joined the order of the Lone Star!

CUTE: You've hit it. You see I bought this uniform at a second-hand clothing store; I puts it on and goes to a benevolent individual and I says to him—appealing to his feelings—I'm one of the fellows that went to Cuba and got massacred by the bloody Spaniards. I'm in a destitute condition—give me a trifle to pay my passage back, so I can whop the tyrannical cusses and avenge my brave fellow sogers what got slewed there.

MARKS: How pathetic!

CUTE: I tell you it works up the feelings of benevolent individuals dreadfully. It draws tears from their eyes and money from their pockets. By chowder! One old chap gave me a hundred dollars to help on the cause.

MARKS: I admire a genius like yours.

CUTE: But I say, what are you up to?

MARKS: I am the travelling companion of a young gentleman by the name of Shelby, who is going to the plantation of a Mr. Legree, on the Red River, to buy an old darkey who used to belong to his father.

CUTE: Legree—Legree? Well, now, I calculate I've heard that ere name afore.

MARKS: Do you remember that man who drew a bowie knife on you in New Orleans?

CUTE: By chowder! I remember the circumstance just as well as if it was yesterday; but I can't say that I recollect much about the man, for you see I was in something of a hurry about that time and didn't stop to take a good look at him.

MARKS: Well, that man was this same Mr. Legree.

CUTE: Do you know, now, I should like to pay that critter off?

MARKS: Then I'll give you an opportunity.

CUTE: Chowder! how will you do that?

MARKS: Do you remember the gentleman that interfered between you and Legree?

CUTE: Yes—well?

MARKS: He received the blow that was intended for you, and died from the effects of it. So, you see, Legree is a murderer, and we are the only witnesses of the deed. His life is in our hands.

CUTE: Let's have him right up and make him dance on nothing to the tune of Yankee Doodle!

MARKS: Stop a bit. Don't you see a chance for a profitable speculation?

CUTE: A speculation! Fire away, don't be bashful; I'm the man for a speculation.

MARKS: I have made a deposition to the Governor of the State of all the particulars of that affair at Orleans.

CUTE: What did you do that for?

MARKS: To get a warrant for his arrest.

CUTE: Oh! and have you got it?

MARKS: Yes; here it is. [*Takes out paper.*]

CUTE: Well, now, I don't see how you are going to make anything by that bit of paper?

MARKS: But I do. I shall say to Legree, I have got a warrant against you for murder; my friend, Mr. Cute, and myself are the only witnesses who can appear against you. Give us a thousand dollars, and we will tear the warrant and be silent.

CUTE: Then Mr. Legree forks over a thousand dollars, and your friend Cute pockets five hundred of it. Is that the calculation?

MARKS: If you will join me in the undertaking.

CUTE: I'll do it, by chowder!

MARKS: Your hand to bind the bargain.

CUTE: I'll stick by you thro' thick and thin.

MARKS: Enough said.

CUTE: Then shake. [*They shake hands.*]

MARKS: But I say, Cute, he may be contrary and show fight.

CUTE: Never mind, we've got the law on our side, and we're bound to stir him up. If he don't come down handsomely, we'll present him with a neck-tie made of hemp!

MARKS: I declare you're getting spunky.

CUTE: Well, I reckon I am. Let's go and have something to drink. Tell you what, Marks, if we don't get *him*, we'll have his hide, by chowder! [*Exeunt, arm in arm.*]

SCENE 5: *Rough Chamber.*

[*Enter* LEGREE, *followed by* SAMBO.]

LEGREE: Go and send Cassy to me.

SAMBO: Yes, mas'r. [*Exit.*]

LEGREE: Curse the woman! she's got a temper worse than the devil! I shall do her an injury one of these days, if she isn't careful.

[*Re-enter* SAMBO, *frightened.*]

What's the matter with you, you black scoundrel?

SAMBO: S'help me, mas'r, she isn't dere.

LEGREE: I suppose she's about the house somewhere?

SAMBO: No, she isn't, mas'r; I's been all over de house and I can't find nothing of her nor Emmeline.

LEGREE: Bolted, by the Lord! Call out the dogs! Saddle my horse! Stop! are you sure they really have gone?

SAMBO: Yes, mas'r; I's been in every room 'cept the haunted garret, and dey wouldn't go dere.

LEGREE: I have it! Now, Sambo, you jest go and walk that Tom up here, right away! [*Exit* SAMBO.]

The old cuss is at the bottom of this yer whole matter; and I'll have it out of his infernal black hide, or I'll know the reason why! I *hate* him—I *hate* him! And isn't he *mine?* Can't I do what I like with him? Who's to hinder, I wonder?

[TOM *is dragged on by* SAMBO *and* QUIMBO.]

LEGREE: [*Grimly confronting* TOM.] Well, Tom, do you know I've made up my mind to *kill* you?

TOM: It's very likely, Mas'r.

LEGREE: *I—have—done—just—that—thing*, Tom, unless you tell me what do you know about these yer gals? [TOM *is silent*.] D'ye hear? Speak!

TOM: I hain't got anything to tell, mas'r.

LEGREE: Do you dare to tell me, you old black rascal, you don't know? Speak! Do you know anything?

TOM: I know, mas'r; but I can't tell anything. *I can die!*

LEGREE: Hark ye, Tom! ye think, 'cause I have let you off before, I don't mean what I say; but, this time, I have made *up my mind*, and counted the cost. You've always stood it out agin me; now, I'll *conquer ye or kill ye!* one or t'other. I'll count every drop of blood there is in you, and take 'em, one by one, 'till ye give up!

TOM: Mas'r, if you was sick, or in trouble, or dying, and I could save, I'd *give* you my heart's blood; and, if taking every drop of blood in this poor old body would save your precious soul, I'd give 'em freely. Do the worst you can, my troubles will be over soon; but if you don't repent, yours won't never end.

[LEGREE *strikes* TOM *down with the butt of his whip*.]

LEGREE: How do you like that?

SAMBO: He's most gone, mas'r!

TOM: [*Rises feebly on his hands*.] There an't no more you can do! I forgive you with all my soul. [*Sinks back, and is carried off by* SAMBO *and* QUIMBO.]

LEGREE: I believe he's done for finally. Well, his mouth is shut up at last—that's one comfort.

[*Enter* GEORGE SHELBY, MARKS *and* CUTE.]

Strangers! Well, what do you want?

GEORGE: I understand that you bought in New Orleans a negro named Tom?

LEGREE: Yes, I did buy such a fellow, and a devil of a bargain I had of it, too! I believe he's trying to die, but I don't know as he'll make it out.

GEORGE: Where is he? Let me see him!

SAMBO: Dere he is! [*Points to* TOM.]

LEGREE: How dare you speak? [*Drives* SAMBO *and* QUIMBO *off*.]

[GEORGE *exits*.]

CUTE: Now's the time to nab him.

MARKS: How are you, Mr. Legree?

LEGREE: What the devil brought you here?

MARKS: This little bit of paper. I arrest you for the murder of Mr. St. Clare. What do you say to that?

LEGREE: This is my answer! [*Makes a blow at* MARKS, *who dodges, and* CUTE *receives the blow—he cries out and runs off.* MARKS *fires at* LEGREE, *and follows* CUTE.] I am hit!—the game's up! [*Falls dead.* QUIMBO *and* SAMBO *return and carry him off laughing.*]

[GEORGE SHELBY *enters, supporting* TOM.—*Music. They advance and* TOM *falls, center.*]

GEORGE: Oh! dear Uncle Tom! do wake—do speak once more! look up! Here's Master George—your own little Master George. Don't you know me?

TOM: [*Opening his eyes and speaking in a feeble tone.*] Mas'r George! Bless de Lord! it's all I wanted! They hav'n't forgot me! It warms my soul; it does my old heart good! Now I shall die content!

GEORGE: You sha'n't die! you mustn't die, nor think of it. I have come to buy you, and take you home.

TOM: Oh, Mas'r George, you're too late. The Lord has bought me, and is going to take me home.

GEORGE: Oh! don't die. It will kill me—it will break my heart to think what you have suffered, poor, poor fellow!

TOM: Don't call me poor fellow. I *have* been poor fellow; but that's all past and gone now. I'm right in the door, going into glory! Oh, Mas'r George! *Heaven has come!* I've got the victory! the Lord has given it to me! Glory be to His name! [*Dies.*]

[*Solemn music.*—GEORGE *covers* UNCLE TOM *with his cloak, and kneels over him. Clouds work on and conceal them, and then work off.*]

SCENE 6: *Gorgeous clouds, tinted with sunlight.* EVA, *robed in white, is discovered on the back of a milk-white dove, with expanded wings, as if just soaring upward. Her hands are extended in benediction over* ST. CLARE *and* UNCLE TOM, *who are kneeling and gazing up to her. Impressive music.—Slow curtain.*

THE END

THE OCTOROON *(1859)*

Dion Boucicault

Of all playwrights working in America before the Civil War, Dion Bou-cicault (1820–1890) cast the longest shadow. Called variously "the greatest of the classical dramatists, certainly in English" (Frank Rahill) and "the greatest dramatist of the Victorian age" (Richard Fawkes), Boucicault dominated the stage in both London and New York, turning out original melodramas, adaptations, and translations from the French in profusion. Promulgator of sensation plays, action melodramas, and various stage techniques that enhanced illusion, Boucicault saw the stage as an enchanted space, an arena for the artist to concoct whatever it took to please an audience. Even though his style of drama was sup-planted by the new realism of the 1880s and 1890s, his work influenced such modern dramatists as George Bernard Shaw.

In the year of his death, Boucicault articulated the kind of theater he had been promoting since his first hit, *London Assurance,* of 1841. "I deny that the drama is, or ever was intended to be, a copy of Nature," he claimed in an essay for *Arena* in 1890. For Boucicault, the plays of Ibsen pointed in the wrong direction, toward an aesthetic to be judged by an elite audience on some standard of fidelity to the real. For him, as for most playwrights of the midcentury theater, there was another standard: "Public opinion is the highest and sole court of jurisdiction in literary and artistic matters . . . and the drama is, therefore, made by the collaboration of the people and the poet." Thus, success is measured in popularity: please the crowd, meet their desires, and the playwright will find a place in the pantheon of the great.

During much of his life, Boucicault seemed surrounded by, and thrived upon, controversy. Even today, there are a number of mysteries concerning his birth. Detective work by Albert Johnson and Robert Ho-gan suggests that he was most likely born in December (probably the 27th) of 1820 to Anna Maria Darley Boursiquot and her husband, Sam-uel, a Dublin merchant. However, his name—Dionysius Lardner Boursiquot—and the separation of his parents in the 1830s gave to the public the idea that young Dion was the natural son of a neighbor, Dionysius Lardner, a young physician nearly half the age of the play-wright's legal father. When his first play was being mounted in London, the press already was broaching his possible illegitimacy (which Johnson, using various court records, mostly discounts). A few years later, when his first wife, Anne Guiot, died under mysterious circumstances, rumors suggested that either he did not care or that he had pushed her off a cliff. After his 1868 train-rescue melodrama, *After Dark,* proved a hit in London, he became embroiled in a lawsuit with American dramatist Augustin Daly, who claimed that the use of any scene in which someone is saved from an oncoming locomotive was under copyright to his own play, *Under the Gaslight.* And, in 1885, Boucicault appeared to commit bigamy when he married an American actress, Louise Thorndyke, while his second wife, British actress Agnes Robertson, claimed they were still married.

No play of his occasioned more controversy than *The Octoroon.* Boucicault had first come to New York in 1853, fresh from his London hit from the year before, *The Corsican Brothers* (one of Queen Victoria's favorite plays), when the American city was buzzing with competing *Uncle Tom's Cabins.* Successfully launching Agnes's career in New York, Boucicault produced vehicles for her and at the same time threw himself into the life of an American writer. Teaming up with Robert Montgomery Bird and another dramatist, George Henry Boker, Boucicault managed to help secure passage of the first major copyright law in the United States in 1856. The following year, his adaptation of a French melodrama, *Les Pauvres de Paris,* drew crowds at Wallack's theater as *The Poor of New York.* By the time *The Octoroon* was produced in December 1859, Boucicault was well known as a writer, actor, and producer. Starring Joseph Jefferson as Salem Scudder, Agnes Robertson as Zoe, and himself as Wahnotee, Boucicault's melodrama of "life in Louisiana" was attended by crowds divided hotly by the issue of slavery.

Despite its topicality, *The Octoroon* had been written by a master of playing to mass taste. Boucicault handles what in its time was sensational material. The central female character, Zoe, is the product of miscegenation between Mrs. Peyton's late husband and a slave mistress. She is beautiful, light-skinned, accomplished—and in love with the white hero, George Peyton, the nephew of her biological father and thus, technically, her cousin. Sympathies for her are aroused when we learn of a plot by the Simon Legree–like overseer, M'Closky, another transplanted New Englander with a heart of flint. Threats to her freedom and to her love for George seem to show the arbitrary cruelties of slavery and might be seen as playing into the sentiments of abolitionists.

But as Jefferson himself later wrote, the playwright probably had no such intentions. "The dialogue and characters of the play made one feel for the South, but the action proclaimed against slavery and called loudly for its abolition." In other words, Jefferson remarked, the play "was non-committal." Boucicault himself, in a letter to the *Times* of London that has been reprinted by Richard Fawkes, shows that he thought "the delineations in *Uncle Tom's Cabin* of the conditions of the slaves, their lives, and feelings were not faithful. I found the slaves, as a race, a happy, gentle, kindly treated population." Whether Boucicault believed his own screed is hard to say. But he was savvy enough to know that New York, as a trading center, had a large number of citizens and visitors who were sympathetic to the South. To be popular—his guiding desire—he had to appeal to more than one political group. Adding to his need for a mass audience was the fact that he had recently purchased and refurbished the Winter Garden Theater and was losing money. His strategy, then, was to portray the majority of slaveholders as decent, caring people who were prevented by law from going farther to help Zoe than they do.

Another strategy was to divide overseers between the evil M'Closky and the good, if somewhat inept, Salem Scudder. Like his rival, Scudder is also a New Englander, but the enterprising, comic Yankee of long stage tradition. He loves Zoe with a restrained affection that can never be articulated; he must yield to George's more conventionally romantic feelings and distinguish his admiration from M'Closky's lust. More importantly, Scudder is a tinkerer, and keeps a photographic apparatus, a daguerreotype camera. Boucicault, always on the lookout for the new prop or gimmick, was one of the first playwrights to use a camera as a plot device. Scudder's friendship with the boy Paul and the Indian Wahnotee is fixed in the object of the camera. Because the daguerreotype relied on sunlight and created a picture directly on a plate, it became possible to appeal to the picture-crazy audience—by the 1850s, everyone with a quarter could afford a daguerreotype portrait—with a telltale artifact that was plausible and spoke to their everyday life. Thus, Scudder is more detective than wooer and the plot more centered on whodunit than on the political implications of slavery. Even so, it is Scudder who enunciates the doctrine of white dominance that underlies all the action.

The focus of attention in the play is Zoe. Like Eliza Harris from *Uncle Tom's Cabin*, Zoe is made to seem white in all but arbitrary racial designation. She is one of a series of figures who would be labeled "the tragic mulatta," the beautiful young woman "tainted" by a drop of African blood and thus doomed to a premature mortality. Boucicault based much of his plot on a novel by Mayne Reid, *The Quadroon,* of 1856, but he may have also gotten ideas both from *Uncle Tom's Cabin* and an earlier British play, *The Creole* (1847), by Shirley Brooks. Brooks, like fellow London dramatist Douglas Jerrold, later became famous as a writer for *Punch,* the British humor periodical, but he had also taken a balloon ride with Boucicault in the same year his play came out. In *The Creole,* the beloved slave woman, Louise, like the later Zoe, sees death as her way out; but a telltale artifact, a decree freeing slaves, ends this as a possibility, and she marries the young white man who has been her suitor. That play ends with a plea—clearly directed at Americans—to remember that there are still young women in bondage. The British audience, smug in knowing that slavery had already been outlawed in their own country and possessions, could roundly cheer the antislavery sentiment without being threatened.

But Boucicault knew that Zoe was, in 1859 America, a threatening figure, for if she is allowed to act completely on her desires for George, then the play would proclaim that miscegenation is no longer a taboo and that blacks are not "tainted" after all. While not unusual in London, such an ending and proclamation would have had a radicalizing effect and turned the stage into a forum for political statements. Conservative to the core, the American theater could not make that leap. It is perhaps not surprising to learn, then, that when Boucicault took his play to London in 1861, he rewrote the ending of *The Octoroon,* curtailing the action of acts 4 and 5 into one and omitting Zoe's suicide. In the final tableau, George enters carrying Zoe in his arms—alive and presumably his future bride. For all its dallying with controversy, Boucicault's American *Octoroon* could not push past the racism that still gripped theater audiences in the United States.

SELECTED BIBLIOGRAPHY

Boucicault, Dion. "The Art of Dramatic Composition." *North American Review* 126 (January 1878): 40–52.
———. "The Debut of a Dramatist." *North American Review* 148 (April 1889): 454–63.
———. "The Decline of the Drama." *North American Review* 125 (September 1877): 235–45.
———. "Early Days of a Dramatist." *North American Review* 148 (May 1889): 584–93.

———. "The Future American Drama." *Arena* 2 (November 1890): 641–52.

———. "Leaves from a Dramatist's Diary." *North American Review* 149 (August 1889): 228–36.

———. *Plays,* edited by Allardyce Nicoll and F. Theodore Cloak. *America's Lost Plays.* Vol. 1. 1940; Bloomington: Indiana University Press, 1965.

———. "Theatres, Halls and Audiences." *North American Review* 149 (October 1889): 429–36.

Degan, John A. "How to End *The Octoroon.*" *Educational Theatre Journal* 27 (1975): 170–78.

Fawkes, Richard. *Dion Boucicault.* London: Quartet, 1979.

Hogan, Robert. *Dion Boucicault.* New York: Twayne, 1969.

Jefferson, Joseph. *Autobiography.* New York: Century, 1890.

Johnson, Albert E. "The Birth of Dion Boucicault." *Modern Drama* 11 (1968): 157–63.

———. "Dion Boucicault Learns to Act." *Players* 48.2 (1973): 78–85.

———. "Dion Boucicault: Man and Fable." *Educational Theatre Journal* 6 (1954): 311–16.

———. "Fabulous Boucicault." *Theatre Arts* 37 (March 1953): 26–30, 90–93.

Kaplan, Sidney. "*The Octoroon*: Early History of the Drama of Miscegenation." *Journal of Negro History* 20 (1951): 547–57.

Kosok, Heinz. "Dion Boucicault's 'American' Plays: Considerations on Defining National Literatures in English." In *Literature and the Art of Creation,* edited by Robert Welch and Suheil Badi Bushrui, 81–97. Totowa, N.J.: Barnes & Noble, 1988.

Krause, David. "The Theatre of Dion Boucicault: A Short View of His Life and Art." In *The Dolmen Boucicault,* edited by David Krause, 9–47. Dublin: Dolmen Press, 1964.

Parkin, Andrew. Introduction. *Selected Plays of Dion Boucicault,* 7–22. Washington: Catholic University of America Press, 1987.

Rahill, Frank. *The World of Melodrama,* 182–94. University Park: Pennsylvania State University Press, 1967.

Reid, [Thomas] Mayne. *The Quadroon, or A Lover's Adventures in Louisiana.* 3 vols. London: G. W. Hyde, 1856.

Richardson, Gary A. *American Drama from the Colonial Period through World War I: A Critical History,* 106–13. New York: Twayne, 1993.

———. "Boucicault's *The Octoroon* and American Law." *Theatre Journal* 34 (1982): 155–64.

Roach, Joseph R. "Slave Spectacles and Tragic Octoroons: A Cultural Genealogy of Antebellum Performance." *Theatre Survey* 33 (1992): 167–87.

Walsh, Townsend. *The Career of Dion Boucicault.* New York: Dunlap Society, 1915.

THE

O C T O R O O N ;

OR,

LIFE IN LOUISIANA.

A Play,

IN FIVE ACTS.

BY

DION BOUCICAULT, ESQ.,

AUTHOR OF

"The Colleen Bawn," "West End," etc.

———

PRINTED, NOT PUBLISHED.

CHARACTERS

GEORGE PEYTON
SALEM SCUDDER,
MR. SUNNYSIDE
JACOB M'CLOSKY
WAHNOTEE
CAPTAIN RATTS
COLONEL POINTDEXTER
JULES THIBODEAUX
JUDGE CAILLOU
LAFOUCHE
JACKSON
OLD PETE
PAUL, *a boy slave*
SOLON

MRS. PEYTON
ZOE
DORA SUNNYSIDE
GRACE
MINNIE
DIDO

COSTUMES.

GEORGE PEYTON.—*Light travelling suit.*
JACOB M'CLOSKY.—*Dark coat, light waistcoat, brown trousers.*
SCUDDER.—*Light plantation suit.*
PETE AND NEGROES.—*Canvas trousers, shoes, striped calico shirts.*
SUNNYSIDE.—*Planter's nankeen suit, broad-brimmed straw hat.*
RATTS.—*(Captain of a steamer.) Black coat, waistcoat, and trousers.*
INDIAN.—*Deer-skin trousers and body, blanket, moccasins, Indian knot and feathers for the hair.*
MRS. PEYTON.—*Black silk dress.*
ZOE.—*White muslin dress.*
DORA.—*Fashionable morning dress, hat and feather.*
FEMALE SLAVES.—*Striped skirts and calico jackets, some with kerchiefs round the head.*

THE OCTOROON

ACT I

SCENE 1: *A view of the Plantation Terrebonne, in Louisiana.—A branch of the Mississippi is seen winding through the Estate.—A low built, but extensive Planter's Dwelling, surrounded with a veranda, and raised a few feet from the ground, occupies the left side.—A table and chairs.* GRACE *discovered sitting at breakfast-table with* CHILDREN.

[*Enter* SOLON, *from house.*]

SOLON: Yah! you bomn'ble fry—git out—a gen'leman can't pass for you.

GRACE: [*Seizing a fly whisk.*] Hee! ha—git out! [*Drives* CHILDREN *away; in escaping they tumble against and trip up* SOLON, *who falls with tray; the* CHILDREN *steal the bananas and rolls that fall about.*]

[*Enter* PETE *(he is lame); he carries a mop and pail.*]

PETE: Hey! laws a massey! why, clar out! drop dat banana! I'll murder this yer crowd. [*He chases* CHILDREN *about; they leap over railing at back.*] [*Exit* SOLON.]
Dem little niggers is a judgment upon dis generation.

[*Enter* GEORGE, *from house.*]

GEORGE: What's the matter, Pete?

PETE: It's dem black trash, Mas'r George; dis ere property wants claring; dem's getting too numerous round: when I gets time I'll kill some on 'em, sure!

GEORGE: They don't seem to be scared by the threat.

PETE: Top, you varmin! top till I get enough of you in one place!

GEORGE: Were they all born on this estate?

PETE: Guess they nebber was born—dem tings? what, dem?—get away! Born here—dem darkies? What, on Terrebonne? Don't b'lieve it, Mas'r George; dem black tings never was born at all; dey swarmed one mornin' on a sassafras tree in the swamp; I cotched 'em; dey ain't no 'count. Don't b'lieve dey'll turn out niggers when dey're growed; dey'll come out sunthin else.

GRACE: Yes, Mas'r George, dey was born here; and old Pete is fonder on 'em dan he is of his fiddle on a Sunday.

PETE: What? dem tings—dem?—get away. [*Makes blow at the* CHIL-

451

DREN.] Born here! dem darkies! What, on Terrebonne? Don't b'lieve it, Mas'r George,—no. One morning dey swarmed on a sassafras tree in de swamp, and I cotched 'em all in a sieve,—dat's how dey come on top of dis yearth—git out, you.—ya, ya! [*Laughs*].

[*Exit* GRACE.]

[*Enter* MRS. PEYTON, *from house.*]

MRS. PEYTON: So, Pete, you are spoiling those children as usual!

PETE: Dat's right, missus! gib it to ole Pete! he's allers in for it. Git away dere! Ya! if dey ain't all lighted, like coons, on dat snake fence, just out of shot. Look dar! Ya! ya! Dem debils. Ya!

MRS. PEYTON: Pete, do you hear?

PETE: Git down dar! I'm arter you! [*Hobbles off.*]

MRS. PEYTON: You are out early this morning, George.

GEORGE: I was up before daylight. We got the horses saddled, and galloped down the shell road over the Piney Patch; then coasting the Bayou Lake, we crossed the long swamps, by Paul's Path, and so came home again.

MRS. PEYTON: [*Laughing.*] You seem already familiar with the names of every spot on the estate.

[*Enter* PETE.—*Arranges breakfast, &c.*]

GEORGE: Just one month ago I quitted Paris. I left that siren city as I would have left a beloved woman.

MRS. PEYTON: No wonder! I dare say you left at least a dozen beloved women there, at the same time.

GEORGE: I feel that I departed amid universal and sincere regret. I left my loves and my creditors equally inconsolable.

MRS. PEYTON: George, you are incorrigible. Ah! you remind me so much of your uncle, the judge.

GEORGE: Bless his dear old handwriting, it's all I ever saw of him. For ten years his letters came every quarter-day,[1] with a remittance and a word of advice in his formal cavalier style; and then a joke in the postscript, that upset the dignity of the foregoing. Aunt, when he died, two years ago, I read over those letters of his, and if I didn't cry like a baby——

MRS. PEYTON: No, George; say you wept like a man. And so you really kept those foolish letters?

GEORGE: Yes; I kept the letters, and squandered the money.

MRS. PEYTON: [*Embracing him.*] Ah! why were you not my son—you are so like my dear husband.

[*Enter* SALEM SCUDDER.]

SCUDDER: Ain't he! Yes—when I saw him and Miss Zoe galloping through the green sugar crop, and doing ten dollars' worth of damage at every stride, says I, how like his old uncle he do make the dirt fly.

GEORGE: O, aunt! what a bright, gay creature she is!

SCUDDER: What, Zoe! Guess that you didn't leave anything female in Europe that can lift an eyelash beside that gal. When she goes along, she just leaves a streak of love behind her. It's a good drink to see her come into the cotton fields—the niggers get fresh on the sight of her. If she ain't worth her weight in sunshine you may take one of my fingers off, and choose which you like.

MRS. PEYTON: She need not keep us waiting breakfast, though. Pete, tell Miss Zoe that we are waiting.

PETE: Yes, missus. Why, Minnie, why don't you run when you hear, you lazy crittur? [MINNIE *runs off.*] Dat's de laziest nigger on dis yere property. [*Sits down.*] Don't do nuffin.

MRS. PEYTON: My dear George, you are left in your uncle's will heir to this estate.

GEORGE: Subject to your life interest and an annuity to Zoe, it is not so?

MRS. PEYTON: I fear that the property is so involved that the strictest economy will scarcely recover it. My dear husband never kept any accounts, and we scarcely know in what condition the estate really is.

SCUDDER: Yes, we do, ma'am; it's in a darned bad condition. Ten years ago the judge took as overseer a bit of Connecticut hardware called M'Closky. The judge didn't understand accounts—the overseer did. For a year or two all went fine. The judge drew money like Bourbon whiskey from a barrel, and never turned off the tap. But out it flew, free for everybody or anybody to beg, borrow, or steal. So it went, till one day the judge found the tap wouldn't run. He looked in to see what stopped it, and pulled out a big mortgage. "Sign that," says the overseer; "it's only a formality." "All right," says the judge, and away went a thousand acres; so at the end of eight years, Jacob M'Closky, Esquire, finds himself proprietor of the richest half of Terrebonne—

GEORGE: But the other half is free.

SCUDDER: No, it ain't; because, just then, what does the judge do, but hire another overseer—a Yankee—a Yankee named Salem Scudder.

MRS. PEYTON: O, no, it was—

SCUDDER: Hold on, now! I'm going to straighten this account clear out. What was this here Scudder? Well, he lived in New York by sittin' with his heels up in front of French's Hotel, and inventin'—

GEORGE: Inventing what?

SCUDDER: Improvements—anything, from a stay-lace to a fire-engine. Well, he cut that for the photographing line. He and his apparatus arrived here, took the judge's likeness and his fancy, who made him overseer right off. Well, sir, what does this Scudder do but introduces his inventions and improvements on this estate. His new cotton gins broke down, the steam sugar-mills burst up, until he finished off with his folly what Mr. M'Closky with his knavery began.

MRS. PEYTON: O, Salem! how can you say so? Haven't you worked like a horse?

SCUDDER: No, ma'am, I worked like an ass—an honest one, and that's all. Now, Mr. George, between the two overseers, you and that good old lady have come to the ground; that is the state of things, just as near as I can fix it. [ZOE *sings without.*]

GEORGE: 'Tis Zoe.

SCUDDER: O, I have not spoiled that anyhow. I can't introduce any darned improvement there. Ain't that a cure for old age; it kinder lifts the heart up, don't it?

MRS. PEYTON: Poor child! what will become of her when I am gone? If you haven't spoiled her, I fear I have. She has had the education of a lady.

GEORGE: I have remarked that she is treated by the neighbors with a kind of familiar condescension that annoyed me.

SCUDDER: Don't you know that she is the natural daughter of the judge, your uncle, and that old lady thar just adored anything her husband cared for; and this girl, that another woman would a hated, she loves as if she'd been her own child.

GEORGE: Aunt, I am prouder and happier to be your nephew and heir to the ruins of Terrebonne, than I would have been to have had half Louisiana without you.

[*Enter* ZOE, *from house.*]

ZOE: Am I late? Ah! Mr. Scudder, good morning.

SCUDDER: Thank'ye. I'm from fair to middlin', like a bamboo cane, much the same all year round.

ZOE: No; like a sugar cane; so dry outside, one would never think there was so much sweetness within.

SCUDDER: Look here; I can't stand that gal! If I stop here, I shall hug her right off. [*Sees* PETE, *who has set his pail down, up stage, and goes to sleep on it.*] If that old nigger ain't asleep, I'm blamed. Hillo! [*Kicks pail out from under* PETE, *and lets him down.*]   [*Exit.*]

PETE: Hi! Debbel's in de pail! What's breakfass?

[*Enter* SOLON *and* DIDO *with coffee-pot, dishes, &c.*]

DIDO: Bless'ee, Missey Zoe, here it be. Dere's a dish of penpans²—jess taste, Mas'r George—and here's fried bananas; smell 'em, do, sa glosh.

PETE: Hole yer tongue, Dido. Whar's de coffee? [*Pours out.*] If it don't stain de cup, your wicked ole life's in danger, sure! dat right! black as nigger; clar as ice. You may drink dat, Mas'r George. [*Looks off.*] Yah! here's Mas'r Sunnyside, and Missey Dora, jist drove up. Some of you niggers run and hole de hosses; and take dis, Dido. [*Gives her coffee-pot to hold, and hobbles off, followed by* SOLON *and* DIDO.]

[*Enter* SUNNYSIDE *and* DORA.]

SUNNYSIDE: Good day, ma'am. [*Shakes hands with* GEORGE.] I see we are just in time for breakfast. [*Sits.*]

DORA: O, none for me; I never eat. [*Sits.*]

GEORGE: [*Aside.*] They do not notice Zoe.—[*Aloud.*] You don't see Zoe, Mr. Sunnyside.

SUNNYSIDE: Ah! Zoe, girl; are you there?

DORA: Take my shawl, Zoe. [ZOE *helps her.*] What a good creature she is.

SUNNYSIDE: I dare say, now, that in Europe you have never met any lady more beautiful in person, or more polished in manners, than that girl.

GEORGE: You are right, sir; though I shrank from expressing that opinion in her presence, so bluntly.

SUNNYSIDE: Why so?

GEORGE: It may be considered offensive.

SUNNYSIDE: [*Astonished.*] What? I say, Zoe, do you hear that?

DORA: Mr. Peyton is joking.

MRS. PEYTON: My nephew is not acquainted with our customs in Louisiana, but he will soon understand.

GEORGE: Never, aunt! I shall never understand how to wound the feelings of any lady; and, if that is the custom here, I shall never acquire it.

DORA: Zoe, my dear, what does he mean?

ZOE: I don't know.

GEORGE: Excuse me, I'll light a cigar. [*Goes up.*]

DORA: [*Aside to* ZOE.] Isn't he sweet! O, dear Zoe, is he in love with anybody?

ZOE: How can I tell?

DORA: Ask him, I want to know; don't say I told you to inquire, but find out. Minnie, fan me, it is so nice—and his clothes are French, ain't they?

ZOE: I think so; shall I ask him that too?

DORA: No, dear. I wish he would make love to me. When he speaks to one he does it so easy, so gentle; it isn't bar-room style; love lined with drinks, sighs tinged with tobacco—and they say all the women in Paris were in love with him, which I feel *I* shall be: stop fanning me; what nice boots he wears.

SUNNYSIDE: [*To* MRS. PEYTON.] Yes, ma'am, I hold a mortgage over Terrebonne; mine's a ninth, and pretty near covers all the property, except the slaves. I believe Mr. M'Closky has a bill of sale on them. O, here he is.

[*Enter* M'CLOSKY.]

SUNNYSIDE: Good morning. Mr. M'Closky.

M'CLOSKY: Good morning, Mr. Sunnyside; Miss Dora, your servant.

DORA: [*Seated.*] Fan me, Minnie,—[*Aside.*] I don't like that man.

M'CLOSKY: [*Aside.*] Insolent as usual.—[*Aloud.*] You begged me to call this morning. I hope I'm not intruding.

MRS. PEYTON: My nephew, Mr. Peyton.

M'CLOSKY: O, how d'ye do, sir? [*Offers hand,* GEORGE *bows coldly, aside.*] A puppy, if he brings any of his European airs here we'll fix him.—[*Aloud.*] Zoe, tell Pete to give my mare a feed, will ye?

GEORGE: [*Angrily.*] Sir.

M'CLOSKY: Hillo! did I tread on ye?

MRS. PEYTON: What is the matter with George?

ZOE: [*Takes fan from* MINNIE.] Go, Minnie, tell Pete; run!

[*Exit* MINNIE.]

MRS. PEYTON: Grace, attend to Mr. M'Closky.

M'CLOSKY: A julep, gal, that's my breakfast, and a bit of cheese.

GEORGE: [*Aside to* MRS. PEYTON.] How can you ask that vulgar ruffian to your table?

MRS. PEYTON: Hospitality in Europe is a courtesy; here, it is an obligation. We tender food to a stranger, not because he is a gentleman, but because he is hungry.

GEORGE: Aunt, I will take my rifle down to the Atchafalaya.[3] Paul has promised me a bear and a deer or two. I see my little Nimrod yonder, with his Indian companion. Excuse me ladies. Ho! Paul! [*Enters house.*]

PAUL: [*Outside.*] I'ss, Mas'r George.

[*Enter* PAUL, *with* INDIAN, *who goes up.*]

SUNNYSIDE: It's a shame to allow that young cub to run over the swamps and woods, hunting and fishing his life away instead of hoeing cane.

MRS. PEYTON: The child was a favorite of the judge, who encouraged his gambols. I couldn't bear to see him put to work.

GEORGE: [*Returning with rifle.*] Come, Paul, are you ready?

PAUL: I'ss, Mas'r George. O, golly! ain't that a pooty gun.

M'CLOSKY: See here, you imps; if I catch you, and your red skin yonder, gunning in my swamps, I'll give you rats, mind; them vagabonds, when the game's about, shoot my pigs. [*Exit* GEORGE *into house.*]

PAUL: You gib me rattan, Mas'r Clostry, but I guess you take a berry long stick to Wahnotee; ugh, he make bacon of you.

M'CLOSKY: Make bacon of me, you young whelp. Do you mean that I'm a pig? Hold on a bit. [*Seizes whip, and holds* PAUL.]

ZOE: O, sir! don't, pray, don't.

M'CLOSKY: [*Slowly lowering his whip.*] Darn you, red skin, I'll pay you off some day, both of ye. [*Returns to table and drinks.*]

SUNNYSIDE: That Indian is a nuisance. Why don't he return to his nation out West?

M'CLOSKY: He's too fond of thieving and whiskey.

ZOE: No; Wahnotee is a gentle, honest creature, and remains here because he loves that boy with the tenderness of a woman. When Paul was taken down with the swamp fever the Indian sat outside the hut, and neither ate, slept, or spoke for five days, till the child could recognize and call him to his bedside. He who can love so well is honest—don't speak ill of poor Wahnotee.

MRS. PEYTON: Wahnotee, will you go back to your people?

WAHNOTEE: Sleugh.

PAUL: He don't understand; he speaks a mash-up of Indian and Mexican. Wahnotee Patira na sepau assa wigiran.

WAHNOTEE: Weal Omenee.

PAUL: Says he'll go if I'll go with him. He calls me Omenee, the Pigeon, and Miss Zoe is Ninemoosha, the Sweetheart.

WAHNOTEE: [*Pointing to* ZOE.] Ninemoosha.

PAUL: If Omenee remains, Wahnotee will die in Terrebonne. [*During the dialogue* WAHNOTEE *has taken* GEORGE'S *gun.*]

GEORGE: Now I'm ready. [GEORGE *tries to regain his gun;* WAHNOTEE *refuses to give it up;* PAUL *quietly takes it from him, and remonstrates with him.*]

DORA: Zoe, he's going; I want him to stay and make love to me: that's what I came for to-day.

MRS. PEYTON: George, I can't spare Paul for an hour or two; he must run over to the landing; the steamer from New Orleans passed up the river last night, and if there's a mail they have thrown it ashore.

SUNNYSIDE: I saw the mail-bags lying in the shed this morning.

MRS. PEYTON: I expect an important letter from Liverpool; away with you, Paul; bring the mail-bags here.

PAUL: I'm 'most afraid to take Wahnotee to the shed, there's rum there.

WAHNOTEE: Rum!

PAUL: Come, then, but if I catch you drinkin', O, laws a mussey, you'll get snakes! I'll gib it you! now mind.   [*Exit with* INDIAN.]

GEORGE: Come, Miss Dora, let me offer you my arm.

DORA: Mr. George, I am afraid, if all we hear is true, you have led a dreadful life in Europe.

GEORGE: That's a challenge to begin a description of my feminine adventures.

DORA: You have been in love, then?

GEORGE: Two hundred and forty-nine times! Let me relate you the worst cases.

DORA: No! no!

GEORGE: I'll put the naughty parts in French.

DORA: I won't hear a word! O, you horrible man! go on.

[*Exit* GEORGE *and* DORA *to house.*]

M'CLOSKY: Now, ma'am, I'd like a little business, if agreeable. I bring you news: your banker, old La Fouche, of New Orleans, is dead; the executors are winding up his affairs, and have foreclosed on all over-due mortgages, so Terrebonne is for sale. Here's the Picayune [*producing paper*] with the advertisement.

ZOE: Terrebonne for sale!

MRS. PEYTON: Terrebonne for sale, and you, sir, will doubtless become its purchaser.

M'CLOSKY: Well, ma'am, I spose there's no law agin my bidding for it. The more bidders, the better for you. You'll take care, I guess, it don't go too cheap.

MRS. PEYTON: O, sir, I don't value the place for its price, but for the many happy days I've spent here: that landscape, flat and uninteresting though it may be, is full of charm for me; those poor people, born around me, growing up about my heart, have bounded my view of life; and now to lose that homely scene, lose their black, ungainly faces: O, sir, perhaps you should be as old as I am, to feel as I do, when my past life is torn away from me.

M'CLOSKY: I'd be darned glad if somebody would tear my past life away from *me*. Sorry I can't help you, but the fact is, you're in such an all-fired mess that you couldn't be pulled out without a derrick.

MRS. PEYTON: Yes, there is a hope left yet, and I cling to it. The house of Mason Brothers, of Liverpool, failed some twenty years ago in my husband's debt.

M'CLOSKY: They owed him over fifty thousand dollars.

MRS. PEYTON: I cannot find the entry in my husband's accounts; but you, Mr. M'Closky, can doubtless detect it. Zoe, bring here the judge's old desk; it is in the library.   [*Exit* ZOE *to house.*]

M'CLOSKY: You don't expect to recover any of this old debt, do you?

MRS. PEYTON: Yes; the firm has recovered itself, and I received a notice two months ago that some settlement might be anticipated.

SUNNYSIDE: Why, with principal and interest this debt has been more than doubled in twenty years.

MRS. PEYTON: But it may be years yet before it will be paid off, if ever.

SUNNYSIDE: If there's a chance of it, there's not a planter round here who wouldn't lend you the whole cash, to keep your name and blood amongst us. Come, cheer up, old friend.

MRS. PEYTON: Ah! Sunnyside, how good you are; so like my poor Peyton.   [*Exit* MRS. PEYTON *and* SUNNYSIDE *to house.*]

M'CLOSKY: Curse their old families—they cut me—a bilious, conceited, thin lot of dried up aristocracy. I hate 'em. Just because my grandfather wasn't some broken-down Virginia transplant, or a stingy old Creole, I ain't fit to sit down with the same meat with them. It makes my blood so hot I feel my heart hiss. I'll sweep these Peytons from this section of the country. Their presence keeps alive the reproach against me that I ruined them; yet, if this money should come. Bah! There's no chance of it. Then, if they go, they'll take Zoe—she'll follow them. Darn that girl; she makes me quiver when I think of her; she's took me for all I'm worth.

[*Enter* ZOE *from house, with the desk.*]

O, here, do you know what [the] annuity the old judge left you is worth to-day? Not a picayune.

ZOE: It's surely worth the love that dictated it; here are the papers and accounts. [*Putting it on the table.*]

M'CLOSKY: Stop, Zoe; come here! How would you like to rule the house of the richest planter on Atchafalaya—eh? or say the word, and I'll buy this old barrack, and you shall be mistress of Terrebonne.

ZOE: O, sir, do not speak so to me!

M'CLOSKY: Why not! look here, these Peytons are bust; out 'em; I am rich, jine me; I'll set you up grand, and we'll give these first families here our dust, until you'll see their white skins shrivel up with hate and rage: what d'ye say?

ZOE: Let me pass! O, pray, let me go!

M'CLOSKY: What, you won't, won't ye? If young George Peyton was to make you the same offer, you'd jump at it, pretty darned quick, I guess. Come, Zoe, don't be a fool; I'd marry you if I could, but you know I can't; so just say what you want. Here, then, I'll put back these Peytons in Terrebonne, and they shall know you done it; yes, they'll have you to thank for saving them from ruin.

ZOE: Do you think they would live here on such terms?

M'CLOSKY: Why not? We'll hire out our slaves, and live on their wages.

ZOE: But I'm not a slave.

M'CLOSKY: No; if you were I'd buy you, if you cost all I'm worth.

ZOE: Let me pass!

M'CLOSKY: Stop.

[*Enter* SCUDDER.]

SCUDDER: Let her pass.

M'CLOSKY: Eh?

SCUDDER: Let her pass! [*Takes out his knife.*]　　　[*Exit* ZOE *to house.*]

M'CLOSKY: Is that you, Mr. Overseer? [*Examines paper.*]

SCUDDER: Yes, I'm here, somewhere, interferin'.

M'CLOSKY: [*Sitting.*] A pretty mess you've got this estate into—

SCUDDER: Yes—me and Co.—we done it; but, as you were senior partner in the concern, I reckon you got the big lick.

M'CLOSKY: What d'ye mean?

SCUDDER: Let me proceed by illustration. [*Sits.*] Look thar! [*Points with knife.*] D'ye see that tree?—It's called a live oak, and is a native here; beside it grows a creeper; year after year that creeper twines its long arms round and round the tree—packing the earth dry all about its roots—living on its life—overspanning its branches, until at last the live oak withers and dies out. Do you know what the niggers round here call that sight? they call it the Yankee hugging the Creole. [*Sits.*]

M'CLOSKY: Mr. Scudder, I've listened to a great many of your insinuations, and now I'd like to come to an understanding of what they mean. If you want a quarrel—

SCUDDER: No, I'm the skurriest crittur at a fight you ever see; my legs have been too well brought up to stand and see my body abused; I take good care of myself, I can tell you.

M'CLOSKY: Because I heard that you had traduced my character.

SCUDDER: Traduced! Whoever said so lied. I always said you were the darndest thief that ever escaped a white jail to mispresent the North to the South.

M'CLOSKY: [Raises hand to back of his neck.] What!

SCUDDER: Take your hand down—take it down. [M'CLOSKY lowers his hand.] Whenever I gets into company like yours, I always start with the advantage on my side.

M'CLOSKY: What d'ye mean?

SCUDDER: I mean that before you could draw that bowie-knife you wear down your back, I'd cut you into shingles. Keep quiet, and let's talk sense. You wanted to come to an understanding, and I'm coming thar as quick as I can. Now, Jacob M'Closky, you despise me because you think I'm a fool; I despise you because I know you to be a knave. Between us we've ruined these Peytons; you fired the judge, and I finished off the widow. Now, I feel bad about my share in the business. I'd give half the balance of my life to wipe out my part of the work. Many a night I've laid awake and thought how to pull them through, till I've cried like a child over the sum I couldn't do; and you know how darned hard 'tis to make a Yankee cry.

M'CLOSKY: Well, what's that to me?

SCUDDER: Hold on, Jacob, I'm coming to that—I tell ye, I'm such a fool—I can't bear the feeling, it keeps at me like a skin complaint and if this family is sold up—

M'CLOSKY: What then?

SCUDDER: [Rising.] I'd cut my throat—or yours—yours I'd prefer.

M'CLOSKY: Would you now? why don't you do it?

SCUDDER: 'Cos I's skeered to try! I never killed a man in my life—and civilization is so strong in me I guess I couldn't do it—I'd like to, though!

M'CLOSKY: And all for the sake of that old woman and that young puppy—eh? No other cause to hate—to envy me—to be jealous of me—eh?

SCUDDER: Jealous! what for?

M'CLOSKY: Ask the color in your face: d'ye think I can't read you, like a book? With your New England hypocrisy, you would persuade yourself it was this family alone you cared for: it ain't—you know it ain't—'tis the "Octoroon;" and you love her as I do, and you hate me because I'm your rival—that's where the tears come from, Salem Scudder, if you ever shed any—that's where the shoe pinches.

SCUDDER: Wal, I do like the gal; she's a—

M'CLOSKY: She's in love with young Peyton; it made me curse whar it made you cry, as it does now; I see the tears on your cheeks now.

SCUDDER: Look at 'em, Jacob, for they are honest water from the well of truth. I ain't ashamed of it—I do love the gal; but I ain't jealous of you, because I believe the only sincere feeling about you is your love for Zoe, and it does your heart good to have her image thar; but I believe you put it thar to spile. By fair means I don't think you can get her, and don't you try foul with her, 'cause if you do, Jacob, civilization be darned. I'm on you like a painter,[4] and when I'm drawed out I'm pizin. [*Exit* SCUDDER *to house.*]

M'CLOSKY: Fair or foul, I'll have her—take that home with you. [*Opens desk.*] What's here—judgments? yes, plenty of 'em; bill of costs; account with Citizens' Bank—what's this? "Judgment, 40,000 'Thibodeaux against Peyton,'"—surely, that is the judgment under which this estate is now advertised for sale—[*takes up paper and examines it*] yes, "Thibodeaux against Peyton, 1838." Hold on! whew! this is worth taking to—in this desk the judge used to keep one paper I want—this should be it. [*Reads.*] "The free papers of my daughter, Zoe, registered February 4th, 1841." Why, judge, wasn't you lawyer enough to know that while a judgment stood against you it was a lien on your slaves? Zoe is your child by a quadroon slave, and you didn't free her; blood! if this is so, she's mine! this old Liverpool debt—that may cross me—if it only arrive too late—if it don't come by this mail— Hold on! this letter the old lady expects —that's it; let me only head off that letter, and Terrebonne will be sold before they can recover it. That boy and the Indian have gone down to the landing for the post-bags; they'll idle on the way as usual; my mare will take me across the swamp, and before they can reach the shed, I'll have purified them bags—ne'er a letter shall show this mail. Ha, ha!—[*Calls.*] Pete, you old turkey-buzzard, saddle my mare. Then, if I sink every dollar I'm worth in her purchase, I'll own that Octoroon. [*Stands with his hand extended towards the house, and tableau.*]

END OF ACT I

ACT II

[*The Wharf—goods, boxes, and bales scattered about—a camera on stand.*]

[SCUDDER, DORA, GEORGE, *and* PAUL *discovered;* DORA *being photographed by* SCUDDER, *who is arranging photographic apparatus,* GEORGE *and* PAUL *looking on at back.*]

SCUDDER: Just turn your face a leetle this way—fix your—let's see—look here.

DORA: So?

SCUDDER: That's right. [*Puts his head under the darkening apron.*] It's such a long time since I did this sort of thing, and this old machine has got so dirty and stiff, I'm afraid it won't operate. That's about right. Now don't stir.

PAUL: Ugh! she look as though she war gwine to have a tooth drawed!

SCUDDER: I've got four plates ready, in case we miss the first shot. One of them is prepared with a self-developing liquid that I've invented. I hope it will turn out better than most of my notions. Now fix yourself. Are you ready?

DORA: Ready!

SCUDDER: Fire!—one, two, three. [SCUDDER *takes out watch.*]

PAUL: Now it's cooking, laws mussey, I feel it all inside, as if it was at a lottery.

SCUDDER: So! [*Throws down apron.*] That's enough. [*Withdraws slide, turns and sees* PAUL.] What! what are you doing there, you young varmint! Ain't you took them bags to the house yet?

PAUL: Now, it ain't no use trying to get mad, Mas'r Scudder. I'm gwine! I only come back to find Wahnotee; whar is dat ign'ant Injiun?

SCUDDER: You'll find him scenting round the rum store, hitched up by the nose. [*Exit into room.*]

PAUL: [*Calling at door.*] Say, Mas'r Scudder, take me in dat telescope?

SCUDDER: [*Inside room.*] Get out, you cub! clar out!

PAUL: You got four of dem dishes ready. Gosh, wouldn't I like to hab myself took! What's de charge, Mas'r Scudder? [*Runs off.*]

[*Enter* SCUDDER, *from room.*]

SCUDDER: Job had none of them critters on his plantation, else he'd never ha' stood through so many chapters. Well, that has come out clear, ain't it? [*Shows plate.*]

DORA: O, beautiful! Look, Mr. Peyton.

GEORGE: [*Looking.*] Yes, very fine!

SCUDDER: The apparatus can't mistake. When I travelled round with this machine, the homely folks used to sing out, "Hillo, mister, this ain't like me!" "Ma'am," says I, "the apparatus can't mistake." "But mister, that ain't my nose." "Ma'am, your nose drawed it. The machine can't err—you may mistake your phiz, but the apparatus don't." "But, sir, it ain't agreeable." "No, ma'am, the truth seldom is."

[*Enter* PETE, *puffing.*]

PETE: Mas'r Scudder! Mas'r Scudder!

SCUDDER: Hillo! what are you blowing about like a steamboat with one wheel for?

PETE: *You* blow, Mas'r Scudder, when I tole you: dere's a man from Noo Aleens just arriv' at de house, and he's stuck up two papers on de gates: "For sale—dis yer property," and a heap of oder tings—and he seen misses, and arter he shown some papers she burst out crying—I yelled; den de corious of little niggers dey set up, den de hull plantation children—de live stock reared up and created a purpiration of lamentation as did de ole heart good to har.

DORA: What's the matter?

SCUDDER: He's come.

PETE: Dass it—I saw'm!

SCUDDER: The sheriff from New Orleans has taken possession—Terrebonne is in the hands of the law.

[*Enter* ZOE.]

ZOE: O, Mr. Scudder! Dora! Mr. Peyton! come home—there are strangers in the house.

DORA: Stay, Mr. Peyton: Zoe, a word! [*Leads her forward—aside.*] Zoe, the more I see of George Peyton the better I like him; but he is too modest—that is a very impertinent virtue in a man.

ZOE: I'm no judge, dear.

DORA: Of course not, you little fool; no one ever made love to you, and you can't understand; I mean, that George knows I am an heiress; my fortune would release this estate from debt.

ZOE: O, I see!

DORA: If he would only propose to marry me I would accept him, but he don't know that, and he will go on fooling, in his slow European way, until it is too late.

ZOE: What's to be done?

DORA: You tell him.

ZOE: What? that he isn't to go on fooling in his slow—

DORA: No, you goose! twit him on his silence and abstraction—I'm sure it's plain enough, for he has not spoken two words to me all the day; then joke round the subject, and at last speak out.

SCUDDER: Pete, as you came here, did you pass Paul and the Indian with the letter-bags?

PETE: No, sar; but dem vagabonds neber take de 'specable straight road, dey goes by de swamp. [*Exit up path.*]

SCUDDER: Come, sir!

DORA: [*To* ZOE.] Now's your time.—[*Aloud.*] Mr. Scudder, take us with you—Mr. Peyton is so slow, there's no getting him on.

[*Exit* DORA *and* SCUDDER.]

ZOE: They are gone!—[*Glancing at* GEORGE.] Poor fellow, he has lost all.

GEORGE: Poor child! how sad she looks now she has no resource.

ZOE: How shall I ask him to stay?

GEORGE: Zoe, will you remain here? I wish to speak to you.

ZOE: [*Aside.*] Well, that saves trouble.

GEORGE: By our ruin, you lose all.

ZOE: O, I'm nothing; think of yourself.

GEORGE: I can think of nothing but the image that remains face to face with me: so beautiful, so simple, so confiding, that I dare not express the feelings that have grown up so rapidly in my heart.

ZOE: [*Aside.*] He means Dora.

GEORGE: If I dared to speak!

ZOE: That's just what you must do, and do it at once, or it will be too late.

GEORGE: Has my love been divined?

ZOE: It has been more than suspected.

GEORGE: Zoe, listen to me, then. I shall see this estate pass from me without a sigh, for it possesses no charm for me; the wealth I covet is the love of those around me—eyes that are rich in fond looks, lips that breathe endearing words; the only estate I value is the heart of one true woman, and the slaves I'd have are her thoughts.

ZOE: George, George, your words take away my breath!

GEORGE: The world, Zoe, the free struggle of minds and hands, is before me; the education bestowed on me by my dear uncle is a noble heritage which no sheriff can seize; with that I can build up a fortune, spread a roof over the heads I love, and place before them the food I have earned; I will work—

ZOE: Work! I thought none but colored people worked.

GEORGE: Work, Zoe, is the salt that gives savor to life.

ZOE: Dora said you were slow: if she could hear you now—

GEORGE: Zoe, you are young; your mirror must have told you that you are beautiful. Is your heart free?

ZOE: Free? of course it is!

GEORGE: We have known each other but a few days, but to me those days have been worth all the rest of my life. Zoe, you have suspected the feeling that now commands an utterance—you have seen that I love you.

ZOE: Me! you love *me*?

GEORGE: As my wife,—the sharer of my hopes, my ambitions, and my sorrows: under the shelter of your love I could watch the storms of fortune pass unheeded by.

ZOE: *My* love! *My* love? George, you know not what you say. *I* the sharer of your sorrows—your wife. Do you know what I am?

GEORGE: Your birth—I know it. Has not my dear aunt forgotten it— she who had the most right to remember it? You are illegitimate, but love knows no prejudice.

ZOE: [*Aside.*] Alas! he does not know, he does not know! and will despise me, spurn me, loathe me, when he learns who, what, he has so loved.—[*Aloud.*] George, O, forgive me! Yes, I love you—I did not know it until your words showed me what has been in my heart; each of them awoke a new sense, and now I know how unhappy— how very unhappy I am.

GEORGE: Zoe, what have I said to wound you?

ZOE: Nothing; but you must learn what I thought you already knew. George, you cannot marry me; the laws forbid it!

GEORGE: Forbid it?

ZOE: There is a gulf between us, as wide as your love, as deep as my despair; but, O, tell me, say you will pity me! that you will not throw me from you like a poisoned thing!

GEORGE: Zoe, explain yourself—your language fills me with shapeless fears.

ZOE: And what shall I say? I—my mother was—no, no—not her! Why should I refer the blame to her? George, do you see that hand you hold? look at these fingers; do you see the nails are of a bluish tinge?

GEORGE: Yes, near the quick there is a faint blue mark.

ZOE: Look in my eyes; is not the same color in the white?

GEORGE: It is their beauty.

ZOE: Could you see the roots of my hair you would see the same dark, fatal mark. Do you know what that is?

GEORGE: No.

ZOE: That is the ineffaceable curse of Cain. Of the blood that feeds my heart, one drop in eight is black—bright red as the rest may be, that one drop poisons all the flood; those seven bright drops give me love like yours—hope like yours—ambition like yours—life hung with passions like dew-drops on the morning flowers; but the one black drop gives me despair, for I'm an unclean thing—forbidden by the laws—I'm an Octoroon!

GEORGE: Zoe, I love you none the less; this knowledge brings no revolt to my heart, and I can overcome the obstacle.

ZOE: But *I* cannot.

GEORGE: We can leave this country, and go far away where none can know.

ZOE: And our mother, she who from infancy treated me with such fondness, she who, as you said, had most reason to spurn me, can she forget what I am? Will she gladly see you wedded to the child of her husband's slave? No! she would revolt from it, as all but you would; and if I consented to hear the cries of my heart, if I did not crush out my infant love, what would she say to the poor girl on whom she had bestowed so much? No, no!

GEORGE: Zoe, must we immolate our lives on her prejudice?

ZOE: Yes, for I'd rather be black than ungrateful! Ah, George, our race has at least one virtue—it knows how to suffer!

GEORGE: Each word you utter makes my love sink deeper into my heart.

ZOE: And I remained here to induce you to offer that heart to Dora!

GEORGE: If you bid me do so I will obey you—

ZOE: No, no! if you cannot be mine, O, let me not blush when I think of you.

GEORGE: Dearest Zoe!   [*Exit* GEORGE *and* ZOE.]

[*As they exit,* M'CLOSKY *rises from behind rock, and looks after them.*]

M'CLOSKY: She loves him! I felt it—and how she can love! [*Advances.*] That one black drop of blood burns in her veins and lights up her heart like a foggy sun. O, how I lapped up her words, like a thirsty bloodhound! I'll have her, if it costs me my life! Yonder the boy still lurks with those mail-bags; the devil still keeps him here to tempt me, darn his yellow skin. I arrived just too late; he had grabbed the prize as I came up. Hillo! he's coming this way, fighting with his Injiun. [*Conceals himself.*]

[*Enter* PAUL, *wrestling with* WAHNOTEE.]

PAUL: It ain't no use now: you got to gib it up!

WAHNOTEE: Ugh!

PAUL: It won't do! You got dat bottle of rum hid under your blanket—gib it up now, you—. Yar! [*Wrenches it from him.*] You nasty, lying Injiun! It's no use you putting on airs; I ain't gwine to sit up wid you all night and you drunk. Hillo! war's de crowd gone? And dar's de 'paratus—O, gosh, if I could take a likeness ob dis child! Uh—uh, let's have a peep. [*Looks through camera.*] O, golly! yar, you Wahnotee? you stan' dar, I see you. Ta demine usti. [*Goes and looks at* WAHNOTEE *through the camera;* WAHNOTEE *springs back with an expression of alarm.*]

WAHNOTEE: No tue Wahnotee.

PAUL: Ha, ha! he tinks it's a gun. You ign'ant Injiun, it can't hurt you! Stop, here's dem dishes—plates—dat's what he call 'em, all fix: I see Mas'r Scudder do it often—tink I can take likeness—stay dere, Wahnotee.

WAHNOTEE: No, carabine tue.

PAUL: I must operate and take my own likeness too—how debbel I do dat? Can't be ober dar an' here too—I ain't twins. Ugh! ach! 'Top; you look, you Wahnotee; you see dis rag, eh? Well, when I say go, den lift dis rag like dis, see! den run to dat pine tree up dar [*points*] and back agin, and den pull down de rag so, d'ye see?

WAHNOTEE: Hugh!

PAUL: Den you hab glass ob rum.

WAHNOTEE: Rum!

PAUL: Dat wakes him up. Coute Wahnotee in omenee dit go Wahnotee, poina la fa, comb a pine tree, la revieut sala, la fa.

WAHNOTEE: Fire-water!

PAUL: Yes, den a glass ob fire-water; now den. [*Throws mail-bags down and sits on them.*] Pret, now den go. [WAHNOTEE *raises apron and runs off,* PAUL *sits for his picture*—M'CLOSKY *appears.*]

M'CLOSKY: Where are they? Ah, yonder goes the Indian!

PAUL: De time he gone just 'bout enough to cook dat dish plate.

M'CLOSKY: Yonder is the boy—now is my time! What's he doing; is he asleep? [*Advances.*] He is sitting on my prize! darn his carcass! I'll clear him off there—he'll never know what stunned him. [*Takes* INDIAN's *tomahawk and steals to* PAUL.]

PAUL: Dam dat Injiun! is dat him creeping dar? I daren't move fear to spile myself. [M'CLOSKY *strikes him on the head—he falls dead.*]

M'CLOSKY: Hooraw! the bags are mine—now for it!—[*Opens mailbags.*] What's here? Sunnyside, Pointdexter, Jackson, Peyton; here it is—the Liverpool post-mark, sure enough!—[*Opens letter—reads.*] "Madam, we are instructed by the firm of Mason and Co., to inform you that a dividend of forty per cent, is payable on the 1st proximo,[5] this amount in consideration of position, they send herewith, and you will find enclosed by draft to your order, on the Bank of Louisiana, which please acknowledge—the balance will be paid in full, with interest, in three, six, and nine months—your drafts on Mason Brothers at those dates will be accepted by La Palisse and Compagnie, N.O., so that you may command immediate use of the whole amount at once, if required. Yours, &c., James Brown." What a find! this infernal letter would have saved all. [*During the reading of letter he remains nearly motionless under the focus of the camera.*] But now I guess it will arrive too late—these darned U.S. mails are to blame. The Injiun! he must not see me.   [*Exit rapidly.*]

[WAHNOTEE *runs on, pulls down apron—sees* PAUL *lying on ground—speaks to him—thinks he's shamming sleep—gesticulates and jabbers—goes to him—moves him with feet, then kneels down to rouse him—to his horror finds him dead—expresses great grief—raises his eyes—they fall upon the camera—rises with savage growl, seizes tomahawk and smashes camera to pieces, then goes to* PAUL—*expresses grief, sorrow, and fondness, and takes him in his arms to carry him away.—Tableau.*]

END OF ACT II

ACT III

SCENE : *A Room in* MRS. PEYTON's *house; entrances.—An Auction Bill stuck up,—chairs and tables.*

[SOLON *and* GRACE *discovered.*]

PETE: [*Outside.*] Dis way—dis way.

[*Enter* PETE, POINTDEXTER, JACKSON, LAFOUCHE, *and* CAILLOU.]

PETE: Dis way, gen'l'men; now Solon—Grace—dey's hot and tirsty—
   sangaree,⁶ brandy, rum.
JACKSON: Well, what d'ye say, Lafouche—d'ye smile?

   [*Enter* THIBODEAUX *and* SUNNYSIDE.]

THIBODEAUX: I hope we don't intrude on the family.
PETE: You see dat hole in dar, sar. I was raised on dis yar plantation—
   neber see no door in it—always open, sar, for stranger to walk in.
SUNNYSIDE: And for substance to walk out.

   [*Enter* RATTS.]

RATTS: Fine southern style that, eh!
LAFOUCHE: [*Reading bill.*] "A fine, well-built old family mansion, re-
   plete with every comfort."
RATTS: There's one name on the list of slaves scratched, I see.
LAFOUCHE: Yes; No. 49, Paul, a quadroon boy, aged thirteen.
SUNNYSIDE: He's missing.
POINTDEXTER: Run away, I suppose.
PETE: [*Indignantly.*] No, sar; nigger nebber cut stick on Terrebonne; dat
   boy's dead, sure.
RATTS: What, Picayune Paul, as we called him, that used to come aboard
   my boat?—poor little darkey, I hope not; many a picayune he picked
   up for his dance and nigger songs, and he supplied our table with
   fish and game from the Bayous.
PETE: Nebber supply no more, sar—nebber dance again. Mas'r Ratts,
   you hard him sing about de place where de good niggers go, de last
   time.
RATTS: Well!
PETE: Well, he gone dar hisself; why, I tink so—'cause we missed Paul
   for some days, but nebber tout nothin' till one night dat Injiun Wahnotee suddenly stood right dar 'mongst us—was in his war paint,
   and mighty cold and grave—he sit down by de fire. "Whar's Paul?"
   I say—he smoke and smoke, but nebber look out ob de fire; well,
   knowing dem critters, I wait a long time—den he say, "Wahnotee,
   great chief"; den I say nothing—smoke anoder time—last, rising to
   go, he turn round at door, and say berry low—O, like a woman's
   voice, he say, "Omenee Pangeuk,"—dat is, Paul is dead—nebber see
   him since.
RATTS: That red-skin killed him.
SUNNYSIDE: So we believe; and so mad are the folks around, if they
   catch the red-skin they'll lynch him sure.

RATTS: Lynch him! Darn his copper carcass, I've got a set of Irish deck-hands aboard that just loved that child; and after I tell them this, let them get a sight of the red-skin, I believe they would eat him, tomahawk and all. Poor little Paul!

THIBODEAUX: What was he worth?

RATTS: Well, near on five hundred dollars.

PETE: [Scandalized.] What, sar! You p'tend to be sorry for Paul, and prize him like dat. Five hundred dollars!—[To THIBODEAUX.] Tousand dollars, Massa Thibodeaux.

[Enter SCUDDER.]

SCUDDER: Gentlemen, the sale takes place at three. Good morning, Colonel. It's near that now, and there's still the sugar-houses to be inspected. Good day, Mr. Thibodeaux—shall we drive down that way? Mr. Lafouche, why, how do you do, sir? you're looking well.

LAFOUCHE: Sorry I can't return the compliment.

RATTS: Salem's looking a kinder hollowed out.

SCUDDER: What, Mr. Ratts, are you going to invest in swamps?

RATTS: No; I want a nigger.

SCUDDER: Hush.

PETE: Eh! wass dat?

SCUDDER: Mr. Sunnyside, I can't do this job of showin' round the folks; my stomach goes agin it. I want Pete here a minute.

SUNNYSIDE: I'll accompany them certainly.

SCUDDER: [Eagerly.] Will ye? Thank ye; thank ye.

SUNNYSIDE: We must excuse Scudder, friends. I'll see you round the estate.

[Enter GEORGE and MRS. PEYTON.]

LAFOUCHE: Good morning, Mrs. Peyton. [All salute.]

SUNNYSIDE: This way, gentlemen.

RATTS: [Aside to SUNNYSIDE.] I say, I'd like to say summit soft to the old woman; perhaps it wouldn't go well, would it?

THIBODEAUX: No; leave it alone.

RATTS: Darn it, when I see a woman in trouble, I feel like selling the skin off my back.

[Exit THIBODEAUX, SUNNYSIDE, RATTS, POINTDEXTER, GRACE, JACKSON, LAFOUCHE, CAILLOU, SOLON.]

SCUDDER: [Aside to PETE.] Go outside, there; listen to what you hear, then go down to the quarters and tell the boys, for I can't do it. O, get out.

PETE: He said I wan't[7] a nigger. Laws, mussey! What am goin' to cum ob us! [Exit slowly, as if concealing himself.]

GEORGE: My dear aunt, why do you not move from this painful scene? Go with Dora to Sunnyside.

MRS. PEYTON: No, George; your uncle said to me with his dying breath, "Nellie, never leave Terrebonne," and I never will leave it, till the law compels me.

SCUDDER: Mr. George, I'm going to say somethin' that has been chokin' me for some time. I know you'll excuse it. Thar's Miss Dora—that girl's in love with you; yes, sir, her eyes are startin' out of her head with it: now her fortune would redeem a good part of this estate.

MRS. PEYTON: Why, George, I never suspected this!

GEORGE: I did, aunt, I confess, but—

MRS. PEYTON: And you hesitated from motives of delicacy?

SCUDDER: No, ma'am; here's the plan of it. Mr. George is in love with Zoe.

GEORGE: Scudder!

MRS. PEYTON: George!

SCUDDER: Hold on now! things have got so jammed in on top of us, we ain't got time to put kid gloves on to handle them. He loves Zoe, and has found out that she loves him. [Sighing.] Well, that's all right; but as he can't marry her, and as Miss Dora would jump at him—

MRS. PEYTON: Why didn't you mention this before?

SCUDDER: Why, because I love Zoe, too, and I couldn't take that young feller from her; and she's jist living on the sight of him, as I saw her do; and they so happy in spite of this yer misery around them, and they reproachin' themselves with not feeling as they ought. I've seen it, I tell you; and darn it, ma'am, can't you see that's what's been a hollowing me out so—I beg your pardon.

MRS. PEYTON: O, George,—my son, let me call you,—I do not speak for my own sake, nor for the loss of the estate, but for the poor people here: they will be sold, divided, and taken away—they have been born here. Heaven has denied me children; so all the strings of my heart have grown around and amongst them, like the fibres and roots of an old tree in its native earth. O, let all go, but save them! With them around us, if we have not wealth, we shall at least have the home that they alone can make—

GEORGE: My dear mother—Mr. Scudder—you teach me what I ought to do; if Miss Sunnyside will accept me as I am, Terrebonne shall be saved: I will sell myself, but the slaves shall be protected.

MRS. PEYTON: Sell yourself, George! Is not Dora worth any man's—

SCUDDER: Don't say that, ma'am; don't say that to a man that loves another gal. He's going to do an heroic act; don't spile it.

MRS. PEYTON: But Zoe is only an Octoroon.

SCUDDER: She's won this race agin the white, anyhow; it's too late now to start her pedigree.

[*Enter* DORA.]

SCUDDER: [*Seeing* DORA.] Come, Mrs. Peyton, take my arm. Hush! here's the other one: she's a little too thoroughbred—too much of the greyhound; but the heart's there, I believe.

[*Exit* SCUDDER *and* MRS. PEYTON.]

DORA: Poor Mrs. Peyton.

GEORGE: Miss Sunnyside, permit me a word: a feeling of delicacy has suspended upon my lips an avowal, which—

DORA: [*Aside.*] O, dear, has he suddenly come to his senses?

[*Enter* ZOE, *she stops at back.*]

GEORGE: In a word, I have seen and admired you!

DORA: [*Aside.*] He has a strange way of showing it. European, I suppose.

GEORGE: If you would pardon the abruptness of the question, I would ask you. Do you think the sincere devotion of my life to make yours happy would succeed?

DORA: [*Aside.*] Well, he has the oddest way of making love.

GEORGE: You are silent?

DORA: Mr. Peyton, I presume you have hesitated to make this avowal because you feared, in the present condition of affairs here, your object might be misconstrued, and that your attention was rather to my fortune than myself. [*A pause.*] Why don't he speak?—I mean, you feared I might not give you credit for sincere and pure feelings. Well, you wrong me. I don't think you capable of anything else than—

GEORGE: No, I hesitated because an attachment I had formed before I had the pleasure of seeing you had not altogether died out.

DORA: [*Smiling.*] Some of those sirens of Paris, I presume. [*Pause.*] I shall endeavor not to be jealous of the past; perhaps I have no right to be. [*Pause.*] But now that vagrant love is—eh? faded—is it not? Why don't you speak, sir?

GEORGE: Because, Miss Sunnyside, I have not learned to lie.

DORA: Good gracious—who wants you to?

GEORGE: I do, but I can't do it. No, the love I speak of is not such as

you suppose,—it is a passion that has grown up here since I arrived;
but it is a hopeless, mad, wild feeling, that must perish.

DORA: Here! since you arrived! Impossible: you have seen no one; whom
can you mean?

ZOE: [*Advancing.*] Me.

GEORGE: Zoe!

DORA: You!

ZOE: Forgive him, Dora; for he knew no better until I told him. Dora,
you are right. He is incapable of any but sincere and pure feelings—
so are you. He loves me—what of that? You know you can't be
jealous of a poor creature like me. If he caught the fever, were stung
by a snake, or possessed of any other poisonous or unclean thing,
you could pity, tend, love him through it, and for your gentle care
he would love you in return. Well, is he not thus afflicted now? I am
his love—he loves an Octoroon.

GEORGE: O, Zoe, you break my heart!

DORA: At college they said I was a fool—I must be. At New Orleans,
they said, "She's pretty, very pretty, but no brains." I'm afraid they
must be right; I can't understand a word of all this.

ZOE: Dear Dora, try to understand it with your heart. You love George;
you love him dearly; I know it: and you deserve to be loved by him.
He will love you—he must. His love for me will pass away—it shall.
You heard him say it was hopeless. O, forgive him and me!

DORA: [*Weeping.*] O, why did he speak to me at all then? You've made
me cry, then, and I hate you both!   [*Exit, through room.*]

> [*Enter* MRS. PEYTON *and* SCUDDER, M'CLOSKY *and* POINT-
> DEXTER.]

M'CLOSKY: I'm sorry to intrude, but the business I came upon will excuse me.

MRS. PEYTON: Here is my nephew, sir.

ZOE: Perhaps I had better go.

M'CLOSKY: Wal, as it consarns you, perhaps you better had.

SCUDDER: Consarns Zoe?

M'CLOSKY: I don't know; she may as well hear the hull of it. Go on,
Colonel—Colonel Pointdexter, ma'am—the mortgagee, auctioneer,
and general agent.

POINTDEXTER: Pardon me, madam, but do you know these papers?
[*Hands papers to* MRS. PEYTON.]

MRS. PEYTON: [*Takes them.*] Yes, sir; they were the free papers of the girl Zoe; but they were in my husband's secretary. How came they in your possession?

M'CLOSKY: I—I found them.

GEORGE: And you purloined them?

M'CLOSKY: Hold on, you'll see. Go on, Colonel.

POINTDEXTER: The list of your slaves is incomplete—it wants one.

SCUDDER: The boy Paul—we know it.

POINTDEXTER: No, sir; you have omitted the Octoroon girl, Zoe.

MRS. PEYTON:⎫ Zoe!
ZOE: ⎬ Me!

POINTDEXTER: At the time the judge executed those free papers to his infant slave, a judgment stood recorded against him; while that was on record he had no right to make away with his property. That judgment still exists: under it and others this estate is sold to-day. Those free papers ain't worth the sand that's on 'em.

MRS. PEYTON: Zoe a slave! It is impossible!

POINTDEXTER: It is certain, madam: the judge was negligent, and doubt-less forgot this small formality.

SCUDDER: But the creditors will not claim the gal?

M'CLOSKY: Excuse me; one of the principal mortgagees has made the demand.   [*Exit* M'CLOSKY *and* POINTDEXTER.]

SCUDDER: Hold on yere, George Peyton; you sit down there. You're trembling so, you'll fall down directly. This blow has staggered me some.

MRS. PEYTON: O, Zoe, my child! don't think too hardly of your poor father.

ZOE: I shall do so if you weep. See, I'm calm.

SCUDDER: Calm as a tombstone, and with about as much life. I see it in your face.

GEORGE: It cannot be! It shall not be!

SCUDDER: Hold your tongue—it must. Be calm—darn the things; the proceeds of this sale won't cover the debts of the estate. Consarn those Liverpool English fellers, why couldn't they send something by the last mail? Even a letter, promising something—such is the feeling round amongst the planters. Darn me, if I couldn't raise thirty thousand on the envelope alone, and ten thousand more on the postmark.

GEORGE: Zoe, they shall not take you from us while I live.

SCUDDER: Don't be a fool; they'd kill you, and then take her, just as soon as—stop: Old Sunnyside, he'll buy her! that'll save her.

ZOE: No, it won't; we have confessed to Dora that we love each other. How can she then ask her father to free me?

SCUDDER: What in thunder made you do that?

ZOE: Because it was the truth; and I had rather be a slave with a free soul, than remain free with a slavish, deceitful heart. My father gives me freedom—at least he thought so. May Heaven bless him for the thought, bless him for the happiness he spread around my life. You say the proceeds of the sale will not cover his debts. Let me be sold then, that I may free his name. I give him back the liberty he bestowed upon me; for I can never repay him the love he bore his poor Octoroon child, on whose breast his last sigh was drawn, into whose eyes he looked with the last gaze of affection.

MRS. PEYTON: O, my husband! I thank Heaven you have not lived to see this day.

ZOE: George, leave me! I would be alone a little while.

GEORGE: Zoe! [*Turns away overpowered.*]

ZOE: Do not weep, George. Dear George, you now see what a miserable thing I am.

GEORGE: Zoe!

SCUDDER: I wish they could sell *me!* I brought half this ruin on this family, with my all-fired improvements. I deserve to be a nigger this day—I feel like one, inside.   [*Exit* SCUDDER.]

ZOE: Go now, George—leave me—take her with you.

[*Exit* MRS. PEYTON *and* GEORGE.]

A slave! a slave! Is this a dream?—for my brain reels with the blow. He said so. What! then I shall be sold!—sold! and my master—O! [*falls on her knees, with her face in her hands*] no—no master, but one. George—George—hush—they come! save me! No, [*looks off*] 'tis Pete and the servants—they come this way. [*Enters inner room.*]

[*Enter* PETE, GRACE, MINNIE, SOLON, DIDO, *and all* NEGROES.]

PETE: Cum yer now—stand round, cause I've got to talk to you darkies—keep dem chil'n quiet—don't make no noise, de missus up dar har us.

SOLON: Go on, Pete.

PETE: Gen'l'men, my colored frens and ladies, dar's mighty bad news gone round. Dis yer prop'ty to be sold—old Terrebonne—whar we all been raised, is gwine—dey's gwine to tak it away—can't stop here no how.

OMNES: O-o!—O-o!

PETE: Hold quiet, you trash o'niggers! tink anybody wants you to cry?

Who's you to set up screeching?—be quiet! But dis ain't all. Now, my culled brethren, gird up your lines, and listen—hold on yer bref —it's a comin. We tought dat de niggers would belong to de ole missus, and if she lost Terrebonne, we must live dere allers, and we would hire out, and bring our wages to ole Missus Peyton.

OMNES: Ya! ya! Well—

PETE: Hush! I tell ye, 't'ain't so—we can't do it—we've got to be sold—

OMNES: Sold!

PETE: Will you hush? she will har you. Yes! I listen dar jess now—dar was ole lady cryin'—Mas'r George—ah! you seen dem big tears in his eyes. O, Mas'r Scudder, he didn't cry zackly; both ob his eyes and cheek look like de bad Bayou in low season—so dry dat I cry for him. [*Raising his voice.*] Den say de missus, "Tain't for de land I keer, but for dem poor niggers—dey'll be sold—dat wot stagger me." "No," say Mas'r George, "I'd rather sell myself fuss; but dey shan't suffer, nohow,—I see 'em dam fuss."

OMNES: O, bless um! Bless, Mas'r George.

PETE: Hole yer tongues. Yes, for you, for me, for dem little ones, dem folks cried. Now, den, if Grace dere wid her chil'n were all sold, she'll begin screechin' like a cat. She didn't mind how kind old judge was to her; and Solon, too, he'll holler, and break de ole lady's heart.

GRACE: No, Pete; no, I won't. I'll bear it.

PETE: I don't tink you will any more, but dis here will; 'cause de family spile Dido, de has. She nebber was worth much 'a dat nigger.

DIDO: How dar you say dat, you black nigger, you? I fetch as much as any odder cook in Louisiana.

PETE: What's de use of your takin' it kind, and comfortin' de missus heart, if Minnie dere, and Louise, and Marie, and Julie is to spile it?

MINNIE: We won't, Pete; we won't.

PETE: [*To the men.*] Dar, do ye hear dat, ye mis'able darkies; dem gals is worth a boat load of kinder men dem is. Cum, for de pride of de family, let every darky look his best for the judge's sake—dat ole man so good to us, and dat ole woman—so dem strangers from New Orleans shall say, Dem's happy darkies, dem's a fine set of niggers; every one say when he's sold, "Lor' bless dis yer family I'm gwine out of, and send me as good a home."

OMNES: We'll do it, Pete; we'll do it.

PETE: Hush! hark! I tell ye dar's somebody in dar. Who is it?

GRACE: It's Missy Zoe, See! see!

PETE: Come along; she har what we say, and she's cryin' for us. None

o' ye ign'rant niggers could cry for yerselves like dat. Come here
quite: now quite.   [*Exeunt* PETE *and all the* NEGROES, *slowly.*]

[*Enter* ZOE *(supposed to have overheard the last scene).*]

ZOE: O! must I learn from these poor wretches how much I owe, and
how I ought to pay the debt? Have I slept upon the benefits I received, and never saw, never felt, never knew that I was forgetful
and ungrateful? O, my father! my dear, dear father! forgive your
poor child. You made her life too happy, and now these tears will
flow. Let me hide them till I teach my heart. O, my—my heart!
                           [*Exit, with a low, wailing, suffocating cry.*]

[*Enter* M'CLOSKY, LAFOUCHE, JACKSON, SUNNYSIDE, *and* POINT-
DEXTER.]

POINTDEXTER: [*Looking at watch.*] Come, the hour is past. I think we
may begin business. Where is Mr. Scudder?
JACKSON: I want to get to Ophelensis to-night.

[*Enter* DORA.]

DORA: Father, come here.
SUNNYSIDE: Why, Dora, what's the matter? Your eyes are red.
DORA: Are they? thank you. I don't care, they were blue this morning,
but it don't signify now.
SUNNYSIDE: My darling! who has been teasing you?
DORA: Never mind. I want you to buy Terrebonne.
SUNNYSIDE: Buy Terrebonne! What for?
DORA: No matter—buy it!
SUNNYSIDE: It will cost me all I'm worth. This is folly, Dora.
DORA: Is my plantation at Comptableau worth this?
SUNNYSIDE: Nearly—perhaps.
DORA: Sell it, then, and buy this.
SUNNYSIDE: Are you mad, my love?
DORA: Do you want *me* to stop here and *bid* for it?
SUNNYSIDE: Good gracious! no.
DORA: Then I'll do it, if you don't.
SUNNYSIDE: I will! I will! But for Heaven's sake go—here comes the
crowd.   [*Exit* DORA.]
What on earth does that child mean or want?

[*Enter* SCUDDER, GEORGE, RATTS, CAILLOU, PETE, GRACE, MIN-
NIE, *and all the* NEGROES. *A large table is at back.* POINTDEXTER

mounts the table with his hammer, his CLERK *sits at his feet. A* NEGRO *mounts the table from behind. The* COMPANY *sit.*]

POINTDEXTER: Now, gentlemen, we shall proceed to business. It ain't necessary for me to dilate, describe, or enumerate; Terrebonne is known to you as one of the richest bits of sile in Louisiana, and its condition reflects credit on them as had to keep it. I'll trouble you for that piece of baccy, Judge—thank you—so, gentlemen, as life is short, we'll start right off. The first lot on here is the estate in block, with its sugar-houses, stock, machines, implements, good dwelling-houses and furniture. If there is no bid for the estate and stuff, we'll sell it in smaller lots. Come, Mr. Thibodeaux, a man has a chance once in his life—here's yours.

THIBODEAUX: Go on. What's the reserve bid?

POINTDEXTER: The first mortgagee bids forty thousand dollars.

THIBODEAUX: Forty-five thousand.

SUNNYSIDE: Fifty thousand.

POINTDEXTER: When you have done joking, gentlemen, you'll say one hundred and twenty thousand. It carried that easy on mortgage.

LAFOUCHE: Then why don't you buy it yourself, Colonel?

POINTDEXTER: I'm waiting on your fifty thousand bid.

CAILLOU: Eighty thousand.

POINTDEXTER: Don't be afraid: it ain't going for that, Judge.

SUNNYSIDE: Ninety thousand.

POINTDEXTER: We're getting on.

THIBODEAUX: One hundred—

POINTDEXTER: One hundred thousand bid for this mag—

CAILLOU: One hundred and ten thousand—

POINTDEXTER: Good again—one hundred and—

SUNNYSIDE: Twenty.

POINTDEXTER: And twenty thousand bid. Squire Sunnyside is going to sell this at fifty thousand advance to-morrow.—[*Looks round.*] Where's that man from Mobile that wanted to give one hundred and eighty thousand?

THIBODEAUX: I guess he ain't left home yet, Colonel.

POINTDEXTER: I shall knock it down to the Squire—going—gone—for one hundred and twenty thousand dollars. [*Raises hammer.*] Judge, you can raise the hull on mortgage—going for half its value. [*Knocks.*] Squire Sunnyside, you've got a pretty bit o' land, Squire. Hillo, darkey, hand me a smash dar.

SUNNYSIDE: I got more than I can work now.

POINTDEXTER: Then buy the hands along with the property. Now, gentlemen, I'm proud to submit to you the finest lot of field hands and
house servants that was ever offered for competition: they speak for
themselves, and do credit to their owners.—[*Reads.*] "No. 1, Solon,
a guest boy, and good waiter."

PETE: That's my son—buy him, Mas'r Ratts; he's sure to sarve you well.

POINTDEXTER: Hold your tongue!

RATTS: Let the old darkey alone—eight hundred for that boy.

CAILLOU: Nine.

RATTS: A thousand.

SOLON: Thank you, Mas'r Ratts: I die for you, sar; hold up for one,
sar.

RATTS: Look here, the boy knows and likes me, Judge; let him come my
way?

CAILLOU: Go on—I'm dumb.

POINTDEXTER: One thousand bid. [*Knocks.*] He's yours, Captain Ratts,
Magnolia steamer. [SOLON *goes down and stands behind* RATTS.]
"No. 2, the yellow girl Grace, with two children—Saul, aged four,
and Victoria five." [*They get on table.*]

SCUDDER: That's Solon's wife and children, Judge.

GRACE: [*To* RATTS.] Buy me, Mas'r Ratts, do buy me, sar?

RATTS: What in thunder should I do with you and those devils on board
my boat?

GRACE: Wash, sar—cook, sar—anything.

RATTS: Eight hundred agin, then—I'll go it.

JACKSON: Nine.

RATTS: I'm broke, Solon—I can't stop the Judge.

THIBODEAUX: What's the matter, Ratts? I'll lend you all you want. Go
it, if you're a mind to.

RATTS: Eleven.

JACKSON: Twelve.

SUNNYSIDE: O, O!

SCUDDER: [*To* JACKSON.] Judge, my friend. The Judge is a little deaf.
Hello! [*Speaking in his ear-trumpet.*] This gal and them children belong to that boy Solon there. You're bidding to separate them, Judge.

JACKSON: The devil I am! [*Rises.*] I'll take back my bid, Colonel.

POINTDEXTER: All right, Judge; I thought there was a mistake. I must
keep you, Captain, to the eleven hundred.

RATTS: Go it.

POINTDEXTER: Eleven hundred—going—going—sold! "No. 3, Pete, a
house servant."

PETE: Dat's me—yer, I'm comin'—stand round dar. [*Tumbles upon the table.*]

POINTDEXTER: Aged seventy-two.

PETE: What's dat? A mistake, sar—forty-six.

POINTDEXTER: Lame.

PETE: But don't mount to nuffin—kin work cannel. Come, Judge, pick up. Now's your time, sar.

JACKSON: One hundred dollars.

PETE: What, sar? me! for me—look ye here! [*Dances.*]

GEORGE: Five hundred.

PETE: Mas'r George—ah, no, sar—don't buy me—keep your money for some udder dat is to be sold. I ain't no count, sar.

POINTDEXTER: Five hundred bid—it's a good price. [*Knocks.*] He's yours, Mr. George Peyton. [PETE *goes down.*] "No. 4, the Octoroon girl, Zoe."

[*Enter* ZOE, *very pale, and stands on table.*—M'CLOSKY *hitherto has taken no interest in the sale, now turns his chair.*]

SUNNYSIDE: [*Rising.*] Gentlemen, we are all acquainted with the circumstances of this girl's position, and I feel sure that no one here will oppose the family who desires to redeem the child of our esteemed and noble friend, the late Judge Peyton.

OMNES: Hear! bravo! hear!

POINTDEXTER: While the proceeds of this sale promises to realize less than the debts upon it, it is my duty to prevent any collusion for the depreciation of the property.

RATTS: Darn ye! You're a man as well as an auctioneer, ain't ye?

POINTDEXTER: What is offered for this slave?

SUNNYSIDE: One thousand dollars.

M'CLOSKY: Two thousand.

SUNNYSIDE: Three thousand.

M'CLOSKY: Five thousand.

GEORGE: Demon!

SUNNYSIDE: I bid seven thousand, which is the last dollar this family possesses.

M'CLOSKY: Eight.

THIBODEAUX: Nine.

OMNES: Bravo!

M'CLOSKY: Ten. It's no use, Squire.

SCUDDER: Jacob M'Closky, you shan't have that girl. Now, take care what you do. Twelve thousand.

M'CLOSKY: Shan't I? Fifteen thousand. Best that any of ye.

POINTDEXTER: Fifteen thousand bid for the Octoroon.

[*Enter* DORA.]

DORA: Twenty thousand.

OMNES: Bravo!

M'CLOSKY: Twenty-five thousand.

OMNES: [*Groan.*] O! O!

GEORGE: Yelping hound—take that. [*Rushes on* M'CLOSKY—M'CLOSKY *draws his knife.*]

SCUDDER: [*Darts between them.*] Hold on, George Peyton—stand back. This is your own house; we are under your uncle's roof; recollect yourself. And, strangers, ain't we forgetting there's a lady present. [*The knives disappear.*] If we can't behave like Christians, let's try and act like gentlemen. Go on, Colonel.

LAFOUCHE: He didn't ought to bid against a lady.

M'CLOSKY: O, that's it, is it? Then I'd like to hire a lady to go to auction and buy my hands.

POINTDEXTER: Gentlemen, I believe none of us have two feelings about the conduct of that man; but he has the law on his side—we may regret, but we must respect it. Mr. M'Closky has bid twenty-five thousand dollars for the Octoroon. Is there any other bid? For the first time, twenty-five thousand—last time! [*Brings hammer down.*] To Jacob M'Closky, the Octoroon girl, Zoe, twenty-five thousand dollars. [*Tableaux.*]

END OF ACT III

ACT IV

SCENE : *The Wharf. The Steamer "Magnolia," alongside; a bluff rock.* RATTS *discovered, superintending the loading of ship.*

[*Enter* LAFOUCHE *and* JACKSON.]

JACKSON: How long before we start, captain?

RATTS: Just as soon as we put this cotton on board.

[*Enter* PETE, *with lantern, and* SCUDDER, *with notebook.*]

SCUDDER: One hundred and forty-nine bales. Can you take any more?

RATTS: Not a bale. I've got engaged eight hundred bales at the next

landing, and one hundred hogsheads of sugar at Patten's Slide—
that'll take my guards under—hurry up thar.

VOICE: [*Outside.*] Wood's aboard.

RATTS: All aboard then.

[*Enter* M'CLOSKY.]

SCUDDER: Sign that receipt, captain, and save me going up to the clerk.

M'CLOSKY: See here—there's a small freight of turpentine in the fore
hold there, and one of the barrels leaks; a spark from your engines
might set the ship on fire, and you'd go with it.

RATTS: You be darned! Go and try it, if you've a mind to.

LAFOUCHE: Captain, you've loaded up here until the boat is sunk so
deep in the mud she won't float.

RATTS: [*Calls off.*] Wood up thar, you Pollo—hang on to the safety
valve—guess she'll crawl off on her paddies. [*Shouts heard.*]

JACKSON: What's the matter?

[*Enter* SOLON.]

SOLON: We got him!

SCUDDER: Who?

SOLON: The Injiun!

SCUDDER: Wahnotee? Where is he? D'ye call running away from a fellow catching him?

RATTS: Here he comes.

OMNES: Where? Where?

[*Enter* WAHNOTEE; *they are all about to rush on him.*]

SCUDDER: Hold on! stan' round thar! no violence—the critter don't
know what we mean.

JACKSON: Let him answer for the boy, then.

M'CLOSKY: Down with him—lynch him.

OMNES: Lynch him!   [*Exit* LAFOUCHE.]

SCUDDER: Stan' back, I say! I'll nip the first that lays a finger on him.
Pete, speak to the red-skin.

PETE: Whar's Paul, Wahnotee? What's come ob de child?

WAHNOTEE: Paul wunce—Paul pangeuk.

PETE: Pangeuk—dead.

WAHNOTEE: Mort!

M'CLOSKY: And you killed him? [*They approach again.*]

SCUDDER: Hold on!

PETE: Um, Paul reste?

WAHNOTEE: Hugh vieu. [*Goes.*] Paul reste ci!

SCUDDER: Here, stay! [*Examines the ground.*] The earth has been stirred here lately.

WAHNOTEE: Weenee Paul. [*Points down, and shows by pantomime how he buried* PAUL.]

SCUDDER: The Injiun means that he buried him there! Stop! here's a bit of leather; [*draws out mail-bags*] the mail-bags that were lost! [*Sees tomahawk in* WAHNOTEE's *belt—draws it out and examines it.*] Look! here are marks of blood—look thar, red-skin, what's that?

WAHNOTEE: Paul! [*Makes sign that* PAUL *was killed by a blow on the head.*]

M'CLOSKY: He confesses it; the Indian got drunk, quarreled with him, and killed him.

[*Re-enter* LAFOUCHE, *with smashed apparatus.*]

LAFOUCHE: Here are evidences of the crime: this rum-bottle half emptied—this photographic apparatus smashed—and there are marks of blood and footsteps around the shed.

M'CLOSKY: What more d'ye want—ain't that proof enough? Lynch him!

OMNES: Lynch him! Lynch him!

SCUDDER: Stan' back, boys! He's an Injiun—fair play.

JACKSON: Try him, then—try him on the spot of his crime.

OMNES: Try him! Try him!

LAFOUCHE: Don't let him escape!

RATTS: I'll see to that. [*Draws revolver.*] If he stirs, I'll put a bullet through his skull, mighty quick.

M'CLOSKY: Come, form a court then, choose a jury—we'll fix this varmin.

[*Enter* THIBODEAUX *and* CAILLOU.]

THIBODEAUX: What's the matter?

LAFOUCHE: We've caught this murdering Injiun, and are going to try him. [WAHNOTEE *sits, rolled in blanket.*]

PETE: Poor little Paul—poor little nigger!

SCUDDER: This business goes agin me, Ratts—'tain't right.

LAFOUCHE: We're ready; the jury's impanelled—go ahead—who'll be accuser?

RATTS: M'Closky.

M'CLOSKY: Me?

RATTS: Yes; you was the first to hail Judge Lynch.

M'CLOSKY: Well, what's the use of argument whar guilt sticks out so plain; the boy and Injiun were alone when last seen.

SCUDDER: Who says that?

M'CLOSKY: Everybody—that is, I heard so.

SCUDDER: Say what you know—not what you heard.

M'CLOSKY: I know then that the boy was killed with that tomahawk—the red-skin owns it—the signs of violence are all round the shed—this apparatus smashed—ain't it plain that in a drunken fit he slew the boy, and when sober concealed the body yonder?

OMNES: That's it—that's it.

RATTS: Who defends the Injiun?

SCUDDER: I will; for it is agin my natur' to b'lieve him guilty; and if he be, this ain't the place, nor you the authority to try him. How are we sure the boy is dead at all? There are no witnesses but a rum bottle and an old machine. Is it on such evidence you'd hang a human being?

RATTS: His own confession.

SCUDDER: I appeal against your usurped authority. This lynch law is a wild and lawless proceeding. Here's a pictur' for a civilized community to afford: yonder, a poor, ignorant savage, and round him a circle of hearts, white with revenge and hate, thirsting for his blood: you call yourselves judges—you ain't—you're a jury of executioners. It is such scenes as these that bring disgrace upon our Western life.

M'CLOSKY: Evidence! Evidence! Give us evidence. We've had talk enough; now for proof.

OMNES: Yes, yes! Proof, proof.

SCUDDER: Where am I to get it? The proof is here, in my heart.

PETE: [*Who has been looking about the camera.*] Top, sar! Top a big! O, laws-a-mussey, see dis; here's a pictur' I found stickin' in that yar telescope machine, sar! look sar!

SCUDDER: A photographic plate. [PETE *holds lantern up.*] What's this, eh? two forms! The child—'tis he! dead—and above him—Ah! ah! Jacob M'Closky, 'twas you murdered that boy!

M'CLOSKY: Me?

SCUDDER: You! You slew him with that tomahawk; and as you stood over his body with the letter in your hand, you thought that no witness saw the deed, that no eye was on you—but there was, Jacob M'Closky, there was. The eye of the Eternal was on you—the blessed sun in heaven, that, looking down, struck upon this plate the image of the dead. Here you are, in the very attitude of your crime!

M'CLOSKY: 'Tis false!

SCUDDER: 'Tis true! the apparatus can't lie. Look there, jurymen. [*Shows plate to jury.*] Look there. O, you wanted evidence—you called for proof—Heaven has answered and convicted you.

M'CLOSKY: What court of law would receive such evidence? [*Going.*]

RATTS: Stop; *this* would. You called it yourself; you wanted to make us murder that Injiun; and since we've got our hands in for justice, we'll try it on *you*. What say ye? shall we have one law for the red-skin and another for the white?

OMNES: Try him! Try him!

RATTS: Who'll be accuser?

SCUDDER: I will! Fellow-citizens, you are convened and assembled here under a higher power than the law. What's the law? When the ship's abroad on the ocean, when the army is before the enemy, where in thunder's the law? It is in the hearts of brave men, who can tell right from wrong, and from whom justice can't be bought. So it is here, in the wilds of the West, where our hatred of crime is measured by the speed of our executions—where necessity is law! I say, then, air you honest men? air you true? Put your hands on your naked breasts, and let every man as don't feel a real American heart there, bustin' up with freedom, truth, and right, let that man step out—that's the oath I put to ye—and then say, Darn ye, go it!

OMNES: Go on. Go on.

SCUDDER: No! I won't go on; that man's down. I won't strike him, even with words. Jacob, your accuser is that picter of the crime—let that speak—defend yourself.

M'CLOSKY: [*Draws knife.*] I will, quicker than lightning.

RATTS: Seize him, then! [*They rush on* M'CLOSKY, *and disarm him.*] He can fight though he's a painter: claws all over.

SCUDDER: Stop! Search him, we may find more evidence.

M'CLOSKY: Would you rob me first, and murder me afterwards?

RATTS: [*Searching him.*] That's his programme—here's a pocketbook.

SCUDDER: [*Opens it.*] What's here? Letters! Hello! To "Mrs. Peyton, Terrebonne, Louisiana, United States." Liverpool post mark. Ho! I've got hold of the tail of a rat—come out. [*Reads.*] What's this? A draft for eighty-five thousand dollars, and credit on Palisse and Co., of New Orleans, for the balance. Hi! the rat's out. You killed the boy to steal this letter from the mail-bags—you stole this letter, that the money should not arrive in time to save the Octoroon; had it done so, the lien on the estate would have ceased, and Zoe be free.

OMNES: Lynch him! Lynch him! Down with him!

SCUDDER: Silence in the court: stand back, let the gentlemen of the jury retire, consult, and return their verdict.

RATTS: I'm responsible for the crittur—go on.

PETE: [To WAHNOTEE.] See Injiun; look dar [shows him plate], see dat innocent: look, dar's de murderer of poor Paul.

WAHNOTEE: Ugh! [Examines plate.]

PETE: Ya! as he? Closky tue Paul—kill de child with your tomahawk dar: 'twasn't you, no—ole Pete allus say so. Poor Injiun lub our little Paul. [WAHNOTEE rises and looks at M'CLOSKY—he is in his war paint and fully armed.]

SCUDDER: What say ye, gentlemen? Is the prisoner guilty, or is he not guilty?

OMNES: Guilty!

SCUDDER: And what is to be his punishment?

OMNES: Death! [All advance.]

WAHNOTEE: [Crosses to M'CLOSKY.] Ugh!

SCUDDER: No, Injiun; we deal out justice here, not revenge. 'Tain't you he has injured, 'tis the white man, whose laws he has offended.

RATTS: Away with him—put him down the aft hatch, till we rig his funeral.

M'CLOSKY: Fifty against one! O! if I had you one by one, alone in the swamp, I'd rip ye all. [He is borne off in boat, struggling.]

SCUDDER: Now then to business.

PETE: [Re-enters from boat.] O, law, sir, dat debil Closky, he tore hisself from de gen'lam, knock me down, take my light, and trows it on de turpentine barrels, and de shed's all afire! [Fire seen.]

JACKSON: [Re-entering.] We are catching fire forward: quick, cut free from the shore.

RATTS: All hands aboard there—cut the starn ropes—give her headway!

ALL: Ay, ay! [Cry of "fire" heard—engine bells heard—steam whistle noise.]

RATTS: Cut all away for'ard—overboard with every bale afire.

[The Steamer moves off—fire kept up—M'CLOSKY re-enters, swimming on.]

M'CLOSKY: Ha! have I fixed ye? Burn! burn! that's right. You thought you had cornered me, did ye? As I swam down, I thought I heard something in the water, as if pursuing me—one of them darned alligators, I suppose—they swarm hereabout—may they crunch every limb of ye! [Exit.]

[WAHNOTEE *swims on—finds trail—follows him. The Steamer floats on at back, burning. Tableaux.*]

CURTAIN

END OF ACT IV

ACT V

SCENE 1.: —*Negroes' Quarters.*

[*Enter* ZOE.]

ZOE: It wants an hour yet to daylight—here is Pete's hut—[*Knocks.*] He sleeps—no; I see a light.

DIDO: [*Enters from hut.*] Who dat?

ZOE: Hush, aunty! 'Tis I—Zoe.

DIDO: Missey Zoe! Why you out in de swamp dis time ob night—you catch de fever sure—you is all wet.

ZOE: Where's Pete?

DIDO: He gone down to de landing last night wid Mas'r Scudder: not come back since—kint make it out.

ZOE: Aunty, there is sickness up at the house: I have been up all night beside one who suffers, and I remembered that when I had the fever you gave me a drink, a bitter drink, that made me sleep—do you remember it?

DIDO: Didn't I? Dem doctors ain't no 'count; dey don't know nuffin.

ZOE: No; but you, aunty, you are wise—you know every plant, don't you, and what it is good for?

DIDO: Dat you drink is fust rate for red fever. Is de folks' head bad?

ZOE: Very bad, aunty; and the heart aches worse, so they can get no rest.

DIDO: Hold on a bit, I get you de bottle.   [*Exit.*]

ZOE: In a few hours that man, my master, will come for me: he has paid my price, and he only consented to let me remain here this one night, because Mrs. Peyton promised to give me up to him to-day.

DIDO: [*Re-enters with phial.*] Here 'tis—now you give one timble-full —dat's nuff.

ZOE: All there is there would kill one, wouldn't it?

DIDO: Guess it kill a dozen—nebber try.

ZOE: It's not a painful death, aunty, is it? You told me it produced a
long, long sleep.

DIDO: Why you tremble so? Why you speak so wild? What you's gwine
to do, missey?

ZOE: Give me the drink.

DIDO: No. Who dat sick at de house?

ZOE: Give it to me.

DIDO: No. You want to hurt yourself. O, Miss Zoe, why you ask ole
Dido for dis pizen?

ZOE: Listen to me. I love one who is here, and he loves me—George. I
sat outside his door all night—I heard his sighs—his agony—torn
from him by my coming fate; and he said, "I'd rather see her dead
than this!"

DIDO: Dead!

ZOE: He said so—then I rose up, and stole from the house, and ran
down to the bayou; but its cold, black, silent stream terrified me—
drowning must be so horrible a death. I could not do it. Then, as I
knelt there, weeping for courage, a snake rattled beside me. I shrunk
from it and fled. Death was there beside me, and I dared not take it.
O! I'm afraid to die; yet I am more afraid to live.

DIDO: Die!

ZOE: So I came here to you; to you, my own dear nurse; to you, who
so often hushed me to sleep when I was a child; who dried my eyes
and put your little Zoe to rest. Ah! give me the rest that no master
but One can disturb—the sleep from which I shall awake free! You
can protect me from that man—do let me die without pain. [Music.]

DIDO: No, no—life is good for young ting like you.

ZOE: O! good, good nurse: you will, you will.

DIDO: No—g'way.

ZOE: Then I shall never leave Terrebonne—the drink, nurse; the drink;
that I may never leave my home—my dear, dear home. You will not
give me to that man? Your own Zoe, that loves you, aunty, so much,
so much.—[Gets phial.] Ah! I have it.

DIDO: No, missey. O! no—don't.

ZOE: Hush!   [Runs off.]

DIDO: Here, Solon, Minnie, Grace.

[They enter.]

ALL: Was de matter?

DIDO: Miss Zoe got de pizen.   [Exit.]

ALL: O! O!   [Exeunt.]

SCENE 2: *Cane-brake Bayou.—Bank—Triangle Fire—Canoe—*
M'CLOSKY *discovered asleep.*

M'CLOSKY: Burn, burn! blaze away! How the flames crack. I'm not guilty: would ye murder me? Cut, cut the rope—I choke—choke!—Ah! [*Wakes.*] Hello! where am I? Why, I was dreaming—curse it! I can never sleep now without dreaming. Hush! I thought I heard the sound of a paddle in the water. All night, as I fled through the cane-brake, I heard footsteps behind me. I lost them in the cedar swamp —again they haunted my path down the bayou, moving as I moved, resting when I rested—hush! there again!—no; it was only the wind over the canes. The sun is rising. I must launch my dug-out, and put for the bay, and in a few hours I shall be safe from pursuit on board of one of the coasting schooners that run from Galveston to Mata-gorda.[8] In a little time this darned business will blow over, and I can show again. Hark! there's that noise again! If it was the ghost of that murdered boy haunting me! Well—I didn't mean to kill him, did I? Well, then, what has my all-cowardly heart got to skeer me so for? [*Music. Gets in canoe and rows off,—*WAHNOTEE *paddles canoe on,—gets out and finds trail—paddles off after him.*]

SCENE 3: *Cedar Swamp.*

[*Enter* SCUDDER *and* PETE.]

SCUDDER: Come on, Pete, we shan't reach the house before mid-day.
PETE: Nebber mind, sa, we bring good news—it won't spile for de keeping.
SCUDDER: Ten miles we've had to walk, because some blamed varmin onhitched our dug-out. I left it last night all safe.
PETE: P'r'aps it floated away itself.
SCUDDER: No; the hitching line was cut with a knife.
PETE: Say, Mas'r Scudder, s'pose we go in round by de quarters and raise the darkies, den dey cum long wid us, and we 'proach dat ole house like Gin'ral Jackson when he took London[9] out dar.
SCUDDER: Hello, Pete, I never heard of that affair.
PETE: I tell you, sa—hush!
SCUDDER: What? [*Music.*]
PETE: Was dat?—a cry out dar in de swamp—dar agin!
SCUDDER: So it is. Something forcing its way through the undergrowth—it comes this way—it's either a bear or a runaway

nigger. [*Draws pistol*—M'CLOSKY *rushes on, and falls at* SCUDDER'S *feet.*]

SCUDDER: Stand off—what are ye?

PETE: Mas'r Clusky.

M'CLOSKY: Save me—save me! I can go no farther. I heard voices.

SCUDDER: Who's after you?

M'CLOSKY: I don't know, but I feel it's death! In some form, human, or wild beast, or ghost, it has tracked me through the night. I fled; it followed. Hark! there it comes—it comes—don't you hear a footstep on the dry leaves?

SCUDDER: Your crime has driven you mad.

M'CLOSKY: D'ye hear it—nearer—nearer—ah! [WAHNOTEE *rushes on, and at* M'CLOSKY.]

SCUDDER: The Injiun! by thunder.

PETE: You're a dead man, Mas'r Clusky—you got to b'lieve dat.

M'CLOSKY: No—no. If I must die, give me up to the law; but save me from the tomahawk. You are a white man; you'll not leave one of your own blood to be butchered by the red-skin?

SCUDDER: Hold on now, Jacob; we've got to figure on that—let us look straight at the thing. Here we are on the selvage of civilization. It ain't our side, I believe, rightly; but Nature has said that where the white man sets his foot, the red man and the black man shall up sticks and stand around. But what do we pay for that possession? In cash? No—in kind—that is, in protection, forbearance, gentleness, in all them goods that show the critters the difference between the Christian and the savage. Now, what have you done to show them the distinction? for, darn me, if I can find out.

M'CLOSKY: For what I have done, let me be tried.

SCUDDER: You have been tried—honestly tried and convicted. Providence has chosen your executioner. I shan't interfere.

PETE: O, no; Mas'r Scudder, don't leave Mas'r Closky like dat—don't sa—'tain't what good Christian should do.

SCUDDER: D'ye hear that, Jacob? This old nigger, the grandfather of the boy you murdered, speaks for you—don't that go through you? D'ye feel it? Go on, Pete, you've waked up the Christian here, and the old hoss responds. [*Throws bowie-knife to* M'CLOSKY.] Take that and defend yourself.

[*Exit* SCUDDER *and* PETE,—WAHNOTEE *faces him.—Fight—buss.*—M'CLOSKY *runs off,*—WAHNOTEE *follows him.—Screams outside.*]

SCENE 4: *Parlor at Terrebonne.*

[*Enter* ZOE. *Music.*]

ZOE: My home, my home! I must see you no more. Those little flowers can live, but I cannot. To-morrow they'll bloom the same—all will be here as now, and I shall be cold. O! my life, my happy life: why has it been so bright?

[*Enter* MRS. PEYTON *and* DORA.]

DORA: Zoe, where have you been?

MRS. PEYTON: We felt quite uneasy about you.

ZOE: I've been to the Negro quarters. I suppose I shall go before long, and I wished to visit all the places, once again, to see the poor people.

MRS. PEYTON: Zoe, dear, I'm glad to see you more calm this morning.

DORA: But how pale she looks, and she trembles so.

ZOE: Do I?

[*Enter* GEORGE.]

Ah! he is here.

DORA: George, here she is!

ZOE: I have come to say good-bye, sir; two hard words—so hard, they might break many a heart; mightn't they?

GEORGE: O, Zoe! can you smile at this moment?

ZOE: You see how easily I have become reconciled to my fate—so it will be with you. You will not forget poor Zoe! but her image will pass away like a little cloud that obscured your happiness a while— you will love each other; you are both too good not to join your hearts. Brightness will return amongst you. Dora, I once made you weep; those were the only tears I caused anybody. Will you forgive me?

DORA: Forgive you—[*Kisses her.*]

ZOE: I feel you do, George.

GEORGE: Zoe, you are pale. Zoe!—she faints!

ZOE: No; a weakness, that's all—a little water. [DORA *gets water.*] I have a restorative here—will you pour it in the glass? [DORA *attempts to take it.*] No; not you—George. [GEORGE *pours contents of phial in glass.*] Now, give it to me. George, dear George, do you love me?

GEORGE: Do you doubt it, Zoe?

ZOE: No! [*Drinks.*]

DORA: Zoe, if all I possess would buy your freedom, I would gladly give it.

ZOE: I am free! I had but one Master on earth, and he has given me my freedom!

DORA: Alas! but the deed that freed you was not lawful.

ZOE: Not lawful—no—but I am going to where there is no law—where there is only justice.

GEORGE: Zoe, you are suffering—your lips are white—your cheeks are flushed.

ZOE: I must be going—it is late. Farewell, Dora. [*Retires.*]

PETE: [*Outside.*] What's Missus—whar's Mas'r George?

GEORGE: They come.

[*Enter* SCUDDER.]

SCUDDER: Stand around and let me pass—room thar! I feel so big with joy, creation ain't wide enough to hold me. Mrs. Peyton, George Peyton, Terrebonne is yours. It was that rascal M'Closky—but he got rats, I swow—he killed the boy, Paul to rob this letter from the mail-bags—the letter from Liverpool you know—he sot fire to the shed—that was how the steamboat got burned up.

MRS. PEYTON: What d'ye mean?

SCUDDER: Read—read that. [*Gives letter.*]

GEORGE: Explain yourself.

[*Enter* SUNNYSIDE.]

SUNNYSIDE: Is it true?

SCUDDER: Every word of it, Squire. Here, you tell it, since you know it. If I was to try, I'd bust.

MRS. PEYTON: Read, George. Terrebonne is yours.

[*Enter* PETE, DIDO, SOLON, MINNIE, *and* GRACE.]

PETE: Whar is she—whar is Miss Zoe?

SCUDDER: What's the matter?

PETE: Don't ax me. Whar's de gal? I say.

SCUDDER: Here she is—Zoe!—water—she faints.

PETE: No—no. 'Tain't no faint—she's a dying, sa: she got pison from old Dido here, this mornin'.

GEORGE: Zoe.

SCUDDER: Zoe! is this true?—no, it ain't—darn it, say it ain't. Look here, you're free, you know; nary a master to hurt you now: you will stop here as long as you're a mind to, only don't look so.

DORA: Her eyes have changed color.

PETE: Dat's what her soul's gwine to do. It's going up dar, whar dere's no line atween folks.

GEORGE: She revives.

ZOE: [*On sofa.*] George—where—where—

GEORGE: O, Zoe! what have you done?

ZOE: Last night I overheard you weeping in your room, and you said, "I'd rather see her dead than so!"

GEORGE: Have I then prompted you to this?

ZOE: No; but I loved you so, I could not bear my fate; and then I stood between your heart and hers. When I am dead she will not be jealous of your love for me, no laws will stand between us. Lift me; so— [GEORGE *raises her head*]—let me look at you, that your face may be the last I see of this world. O! George, you may, without a blush, confess your love for the Octoroon! [*Dies*—GEORGE *lowers her head gently.—Kneels.—Others form picture.*]

[*Darken front of house and stage.*]

[*Light fires.—Draw flats and discover* PAUL'S *grave.—*M'CLOSKY *dead on it.—*WAHNOTEE *standing triumphantly over him.*]

SLOW CURTAIN

EXPLANATORY AND TEXTUAL NOTES

The Contrast, by Royall Tyler

1. *Prologue.* Probably by Tyler. It appeared originally in the New York *Daily Advertiser*, April 20, 1787.
2. *Wignell.* See introduction to Tyler.
3. *Mall, battery.* Areas of New York City, then confined to the southern tip of Manhattan.
4. *friseur.* Hairdresser, literally, one who curls hair (French).
5. *Buffon.* Georges-Louis Leclerc de Buffon (1707–1788), French biologist.
6. *Spectator.* The advice columnist in influential London paper *The Spectator*, edited by Joseph Addison (1672–1719) and Richard Steele (1672–1729).
7. *Sir Charles Grandison, Clarissa Harlow, Shenstone, and the Sentimental Journey.* All refer to British epistolary or sentimental writers of the period: novels *Sir Charles Grandison* and *Clarissa Harlowe* by Samuel Richardson (1689–1761); *A Sentimental Journey through France and Italy* by Laurence Sterne (1713–1768); William Shenstone (1714–1763), poet.
8. *Lovelace.* The seducer villain in *Clarissa*.
9. *Chesterfield.* Philip Dormer Stanhope (1694–1773), fourth earl of Chesterfield. Author of notorious *Letters to His Son* (1774), advice on how to enjoy life without becoming entangled by relationships. Book was especially controversial in postwar America, admired for its elegance of style but denounced by high-minded patriots as reflecting the moral corruption of Europe.
10. *Song.* A popular song of the day, "Alknomook" first appeared in England in 1783; the most probable author is Anne Home Hunter, a British writer. See Tanselle, 58–59.
11. *cockade.* Knotted ribbon worn by patriot soldiers; see also *André*.
12. *quit-rent.* In medieval practice, the sum paid by a freeman to the feudal lord in order to remove himself from any obligatory service. While Van Rough may be using the term simply to indicate the income generated by a large piece of land, it should be noted that wealthy Dutch

landholders, or patroons, perpetuated a medieval-type landholding system in the New York colony well into the eighteenth century.

13. *pipe of Madeira.* Large barrel (126 gallons) of Spanish wine.

14. *Harlem Heights.* High ground in northern Manhattan, scene of minor patriot victory on September 16, 1776, before Washington's forces were driven from New York.

15. *pensorosos.* People of thoughtful, grave demeanor (from Italian *pensieroso*).

16. *commutation notes.* Maturing notes given to Revolutionary War officers in lieu of immediate severance pay. If cashed in early, the amount of money realized was much reduced from the notes' full value.

17. *en-bon-point.* Plumpness (from French *embonpoint*).

18. *cits.* Citizens, with implication of low, unworthy.

19. *Ranelagh, Vauxhall,* Public gardens in London and vicinity.

20. *Votre . . .* Your very humble servant, Sir (French).

21. *sans ceremonie.* Without ceremony (French).

22. *Shays.* Daniel Shays (1747?–1825), leader of rebels against state government in western Massachusetts during 1786–87. Tyler was part of an expeditionary force sent to subdue rebels and capture Shays. He was in New York to enlist that state's cooperation in helping Massachusetts in putting down Shays's Rebellion when *The Contrast* was first played.

23. *Shin.* Reference to the Cincinnati (and probably pronounced Shinshinnati), an honorary society composed of Revolutionary War officers, including Washington, but thought by anti-Federalists to be a quasi-aristocracy in the making.

24. *lignum vitae.* Literally, wood of life (Latin), used to refer to certain tropical trees and their wood. Jonathan may mean something like ornamental or rare, i.e., "fancy."

25. *Governor Hutchinson . . .* Thomas Hutchinson (1711–1780), last royal governor of Massachusetts, was often pilloried in effigy with Frederick North (1732–1792), second earl of Guilford and called Lord North, who was prime minister of Great Britain during the American Revolution; carts featuring their likenesses and that of the devil were used as patriot propaganda weapons.

26. *Blueskin.* Through various associations in Britain connected to the color blue, including Presbyterians who would sit in their services until they burned blue with cold, blueskin came to signify a patriotic American and strict Calvinist, sometimes used derogatorily.

27. *sugar-dram.* Small amount of sugar; in apothecary weight, equivalent to 0.125 ounce.

28. *Lady Wortley Montagu.* Mary Pierrepont (1689–1762), poet, some-

time friend of Pope, wife to Edward Wortley Montagu, and writer of advice letters to her daughter. Dimple, of course, is quoting Chesterfield throughout his speech.

29. *Milton.* John Milton (1608–1674), whose poem *Paradise Lost* is cited.

30. *sang-froid.* Literally, cold blood (French); used to indicate composure.

31. *outré.* Exaggerated; here, outrageous (French).

32. *Madame Rambouillet.* Catherine d'Angennes (1588–1665), marquise de Rambouillet, was a literary hostess in Paris, but who died long before Chesterfield, let alone his son, was born.

33. *un amiable petit Jonathan.* A polite little Jonathan (French).

34. *long entry . . .* In this scene, Jonathan describes successively the John Street Theatre, where *The Contrast* was first played; a production of Sheridan's *The School for Scandal,* with its character Joseph Surface, by the Old American Company; and O'Keeffe's comic opera *The Poor Soldier,* starring Thomas Wignell as Darby. Since Wignell played Jonathan in the first performance of Tyler's play, the joke is that he is describing himself. See introduction to Tyler.

35. *Roslin Castle, the Maid of the Mill.* "Roslin Castle," the most popular funeral tune played by military bands during the Revolution; "The Maid of the Mill," title song to English opera by Samuel Arnold (1740–1802) that was first performed in New York in 1769.

36. *bundling.* Reference to practice in New England of allowing engaged couples to cuddle in bed while they are fully clothed.

37. *Montagu.* Edward Montagu (1713–1775), British writer whose *Reflections on the Rise and Fall of Ancient Republics* influences Manly's speech.

38. *Mandeville.* Bernard Mandeville (1670–1733), Dutch-born British satirist and author of *The Fable of the Bees, or, Private Vices, Public Benefits.*

39. *Amphictyons.* Literally, neighbors (Greek); refers to a Panhellenic council of ancient Greece that looked for common bonds among city states.

40. *gamut.* Full range of musical notes; here, a guidebook to the full range of appropriate sounds and expressions for all social occasions.

41. *affettuoso, piano, fortissimo.* Musical terms; literally, affectionate, slowly or softly, extremely loud (Italian).

42. *Handel's.* George Frideric Handel (1685–1759), German-born English composer who wrote many musical pieces, especially oratorios, for formal occasions, including performances at Westminster Abbey.

43. *Ben Jonson.* British poet, songwriter, and playwright (1572–1637).

44. *caudle.* Sweet alcoholic drink administered to the sick. Cake and caudle suggests obligatory, not for pleasure.

45. *"Love . . ."* From poem by Alexander Pope (1688–1744), "Eloisa to Abelard."

46. *Marquis.* Marie-Joseph-Paul-Yves-Roch-Gilbert du Motier de Lafayette (1757–1834), French-born general in Continental army, closely connected to Washington.

André, by William Dunlap

1. *represented.* Dunlap refers to the page in the 1798 version; see page 102 in this collection.

2. *Old American Company.* The same company that put on *The Contrast* in 1787. The only actor to play in both Tyler's and Dunlap's plays was Lewis Hallam, Jr., who was cast here as the General.

3. *Martin.* Actor who played Seward.

4. *Tappan.* Village in New York, on west side of Hudson and just north of New Jersey line.

5. *South.* Most of the major battles in the Revolutionary War by 1780 were being fought in the South; the concluding battle, at Yorktown, Virginia, was conducted in October 1781.

6. *Arnold.* Benedict Arnold (1741–1801), in the early phase of the war, had earned a reputation as a fierce fighter for the patriot side and took part in several important battles. Discontent with his status in the Continental army, among other things, General Arnold arranged to turn over to the British the American fortress at West Point, on the west side of the Hudson and upriver from the scene of action in the play. Major John André, a British officer stationed in New York City, sixty miles to the south, was selected as the contact for Arnold's treason. After a false start, André and Arnold met near Haverstraw, on the west side of the Hudson, on September 20, for negotiations. Disguised as John Anderson, André was arrested on September 23 by three American militiamen near Tarrytown (on the eastern side of the Hudson) as he rode on horse to the British lines. Arnold escaped to New York in a British vessel in the Hudson.

7. *rough farmer.* André's captors, John Paulding, Isaac Van Wart, and David Williams, who indeed did refuse bribes before conducting him to an American position at North Castle.

8. *General.* Obviously intended to be Washington, who faced one of his most personally difficult moments of the war. He took much criticism for the proceedings against André, but for reasons of army morale and discipline felt execution was required.

9. *Leonidas.* King of Sparta who resisted to the death a huge Persian force at Thermopylae in 480 B.C.

10. *Scotia.* Scotland.

11. *spy.* The debate over André was whether, as the British maintained, he was under a flag of truce and therefore innocent; or whether he was to be considered a spy. The case turned on the deception; André sought to disguise the fact that he was a British officer in American territory, and he carried incriminating papers about West Point. Arnold issued passes, but for "John Anderson," further contributing to the deception.

12. *gibbet.* Once convinced his fate was inescapable, André requested to be shot as a soldier rather than be hanged. For Washington, there was no question: according to the rules of war, spies are hanged, in a mode of punishment, like crucifixion among the Romans, designed to humiliate the criminal. To do otherwise would be to call his crime into question.

13. *manes.* Revered spirit of the dead.

14. *Sir Henry.* Clinton (1738–1795), supreme British commander in North America, 1778–81.

15. *Hills of Moab.* Probably refers to incident in Numbers 22–24, where the king of Moab, Balak, asks Balaam to curse the Israelites, who have entered his territory on their return from Egypt. But God appears to Balaam, and Balaam delivers praises of Israel rather than the expected curses. Other Old Testament prophets routinely denounce and prophesy against Moab.

16. *Coeur de Lion.* King Richard I (1157–1199) of England, "the Lion-Hearted."

17. *Honora.* Honora Sneyd, André's mistress, who did in fact marry another but had died in England before André was arrested.

18. *How.* The lines from here until the end of the scene are Dunlap's originals. After the first performance in 1798, he replaced them with the lines he includes in his Preface.

19. *hand.* Washington, who was famously controlled in his emotions, did, apparently, weep in the presence of Lafayette over the André business.

20. *Otway, Pierre.* Pierre, in Thomas Otway's play *Venice Preserved* (1682), enlists his friend Jaffeir in a rebellion against Venetian tyranny, is caught, and just before his execution is stabbed by Jaffeir, who then stabs himself.

The Indian Princess, by James Nelson Barker

1. *Jean Jacques, Mademoiselle Lambercier.* In the *Confessions* of Jean-Jacques Rousseau (1712–1778), Mademoiselle Lambercier is mentioned as his governess, with hints of his heightened erotic interest when she was at her harshest.

2. *Smith.* Captain John Smith (1580–1631) was one of the original Jamestown settlers, arriving in 1607, becoming president of the colony in 1608, but departing for England in 1609 after being injured in a gunpowder explosion. The time period here, by Barker's references to his main source, Smith's *The Generall Historie of Virginia, New England, and the Summer Isles* (1624), coincides roughly with Smith's tenure, but the playwright has taken considerable poetic license by having later episodes overlap with Smith's presence in Virginia. For many of the notes that follow, I am indebted to the notes and the texts in *The Complete Works of Captain John Smith,* edited by Philip L. Barbour, 3 vols. (Chapel Hill: University of North Carolina Press, 1986).

3. *music.* "The music is now published and sold by Mr. G. E. Blake, No. 1, South Third-street, Philadelphia." (Barker's note.)

4. *Powhatan River.* Smith's name for James River.

5. *Percy, Rolfe, Raleigh.* George Percy (1580–1632) was an original Jamestown colonist from 1607 and deputy governor from 1609 to 1610 and again in 1611. As the brother of the ninth earl of Northumberland, Percy, unlike the son of a yeoman Captain Smith, would have been considered a gentleman. John Rolfe (1585–1622), legendary husband of Pocahontas, did not arrive in Virginia until 1610, the year after Smith had returned to England. Sir Walter Raleigh (1554–1618) sponsored the expedition that led to the first English colony on Roanoke Island (1584), now in North Carolina, but then considered as "Virginia."

6. *Walter and Larry.* Neither of these, nor Robin, nor any of the women, except for Pocahontas, is historical.

7. *Turkey and Tartary.* Walter here and later in the play refers to episodes in Smith's life before he became an adventurer in Virginia. As described in his *The True Travels, Adventures, and Observations of Captaine John Smith* (1630), the young soldier of fortune late in the year 1600 joined Austrian forces fighting against the Ottoman Turks in Central Europe. In 1602, during a siege, Smith engaged in ritual combat with three Turkish soldiers (presumably in turbans), killed, then beheaded them. Smith's crest, entered in 1625, shows the heads of three Turks. Later, Smith was captured by Turks, sold into slavery,

escaped, and traveled through Turkey and Tartary (the area that includes the current republics in the Caucasus region) into Russia and back into Central Europe before eventually and circuitously returning to England.

8. *mussulmans.* Moslem Turks.

9. *en passant.* By the way (French).

10. *Och! . . .* Various Irish ejaculations or lamentations. Hubbaboo is a savage war cry; hone, or ohone, is something like "alas!"

11. *Werocomoco, Powhatan.* Spelled variously by Smith, Werowocomoco, located on the York River, was the seat of power of Powhatan (154?–1618). By the time of Smith's arrival in Virginia, Powhatan had become the supreme Algonkian chieftain in an area that includes Tidewater and eastern Virginia up to the top of Chesapeake Bay.

12. *Pocahontas.* A girl of only eleven or twelve when Smith first met her, Pocahontas (1595?–1617) was a daughter of Powhatan, who often aided the Jamestown colonists. After marrying John Rolfe in 1614, she moved to London in 1616, where she died.

13. *flamingo.* Obviously, not a bird native to Virginia.

14. *Susquehannocks, Miami.* The Susquehannocks were a tribe who lived north of Powhatan's dominion and spoke an Iroquoian language. Although described by Smith as a large and frightening-looking people, he also notes that they were quite friendly and that they looked upon the English as gods. Miami is not historical, although the name would have conjured up for Barker's audience the Ohio region tribe that engaged an expeditionary force of United States soldiers in 1791 and routed them, killing hundreds.

15. *carcajou.* Wolverine.

16. *Nantaquas.* Sometimes spelled Naukquawis, a son of Powhatan and minor figure in Smith's accounts. However, in a letter to Queen Anne, reprinted in the *Generall Historie,* Smith describes Nantaquas as "the most manliest, comeliest, boldest spirit, I ever saw in a Salvage" (*Complete Works,* 2:258) and like his sister, Pocahontas, of great help to Smith during his captivity by Powhatan.

17. *Aresqui.* Not a word encountered in Smith. Barker may be playing on Ares, god of war in ancient Greece; see also *Okee* below, note 26.

18. *spalpeen.* Irish expression for laborer, but used derogatorily to mean rascal.

19. *Cassen, Emery, and Robinson.* In the episode leading up to the famous scene with Smith and Pocahontas, Smith describes an exploratory trip he took up the Chickahominy River. Leaving a larger boat in the wide part of the river, Smith and four others, two Natives and two whites, Thomas Emry and Jehu Robinson, explored a narrower portion by

canoe. Meanwhile, the barge with the main body of English had drifted toward shore. Unbeknownst to Smith, a large group of Indians, probably a hunting party, surprised them and killed George Cassen before the barge was able to get back out to open water. Smith himself left the canoe and the two Englishmen to go hunting for food. On returning, he discovered Robinson and Emry dead and himself surrounded by a number he gives as two hundred or three hundred warriors. After firing at the Algonkians, killing at least one, Smith was captured and eventually taken to Werowocomoco.

20. *ducks.* In the 1808 edition, the word *ducks* was inserted after "plunged in" in what was probably a printer's error. I have restored it to what seems to be its logical place.

21. *Grimosco.* Not a name in Smith; probably a coinage of grim with Mosco, the name of a Native from Wighcocomoco. Barker has taken the harsher qualities that Smith assigns to Powhatan and spread them to Miami and Grimosco, leaving the Powhatan of the play to appear as the doting and somewhat foolish father, a stage type of the period.

22. *free.* This episode is based on Smith's one-sentence account of being saved from clubbing by Pocahontas. Barker, like many to follow him, elaborates on and romanticizes the scene.

23. *love-lim'd.* Refers to English method of catching birds by placing sticky lime in a tree from which birds cannot escape.

24. *sarbacan.* Blow-gun.

25. *discovery.* Smith's travels throughout the region of the Chesapeake Bay in the late spring and summer of 1608.

26. *Okee.* Also called Okeus, an idol and possibly god. Smith's men did seize an Okee at one point.

27. *fillip.* Finger snap.

28. *mascardo.* One of several words used by Smith with a Spanish ending. The Virginian masquerade refers to a ritual dance of Algonkian women witnessed and described by Smith.

29. *Bacchantes.* Female followers of Bacchus, ancient Greek god of wine, notorious for their frenzied dancing.

30. *Philomel.* The nightingale, a bird native to England but not America.

31. *praties.* Potatoes (Anglo-Irish dialect).

32. *Orlando.* Lovesick character in Shakespeare's *As You Like It,* a play that has strong influences on this one.

33. *Sigismund.* Zsigmond Báthory (1572–1613), prince of Transylvania, for whom Smith engaged as a soldier of fortune. It was during the siege of Regall that Smith fought his combat with three Turks.

34. *Turbisha, Grualdo, Bonamolgro.* Names (the spellings vary) given by Smith for the three Turks he killed.

35. *Tragabizandy*. Charatza Trabigzanda (literally, "the girl from Trebizond"), Greek lover of the Turkish captain who purchased Smith after his enslavement. Sent to the young woman as a present, Smith describes her kindness to him (see *Complete Works,* 3:186, n.2).

36. *bashaw*. Officer (Turkish).

37. *Calamata*. Woman in Russia who, after Smith's escape from slavery, "largely supplied all his wants" (*Complete Works,* 3:201).

38. *faulchion*. Falchion, medieval-era broadsword.

39. *Delawar*. Thomas West (1577–1618), Lord De La Warr, first governor of Virginia, 1610–1611. West arrived in Virginia after Smith had departed.

40. *Camilla*. Literally, a virgin without fault (Latin), Camilla appears in Virgil's *Aeneid,* Books 8 and 11, as a Volscian girl who becomes a warrior in the service of Diana, fighting for Turnus, but is killed by Arruns, an Etruscan.

The Gladiator, by Robert Montgomery Bird

1. *Pompey . . . Sylla rotting*. See Introduction. Cheius Pompeius Magnus (106–48 B.C.), Roman consul and general; Quintus Caecilius Metellus Pius (?–c. 63 B.C.), Roman consul and leader of private army; Quintus Sertorius (c. 123–72 B.C.), Roman general and politician, allied with Mithridates, ruler of Spain, and subject of play by American writer David Paul Brown, *Sertorius: or, The Roman Patriot* (1830); Lucius Licinius Lucullus (c. 117–58 or 56 B.C.), Roman general, consul, and victor over Mithridates; Mithridates VI (120–63 B.C.), king of Pontus in Asia Minor and implacable foe of Rome; Marcus Terentius Varro Lucullus (?–50s B.C.), brother to Lucius, Roman proconsul in Macedonia and conqueror in Thrace; Julius Caesar (100–44 B.C.), Roman politician, military figure, writer, and later emperor; Gaius Marius (c. 157–86 B.C.), rival of Sulla, expeller of aristocratic party from Rome, and subject of play by American writer Richard Penn Smith, *Caius Marius* (1831); Lucius Cornelius Sulla (138–78 B.C.), Roman dictator and dominant political figure. For other notes below, in addition to standard reference works, I am indebted to Keith R. Bradley, "The Slave War of Spartacus," in his *Slavery and Rebellion in the Roman World, 140 B.C.–70 B.C.* (Bloomington: Indiana University Press, 1989), 83–101.

2. *praetor, Crassus*. In the time of Sulla, praetor was a title reserved for a military magistrate with the powers of judge, normally subordinate

to consul. Marcus Licinius Crassus (115–53 B.C.), ally of Sulla, praetor, then commander against Spartacus.

3. *quœtor*. Lowest level of magistrate in Rome, with financial responsibilities.

4. *gladiator*. Fighters whose purpose was entertainment, gladiators were owned by private individuals and exhibited with imperial permission. They were, as the play suggests, slaves, war prisoners, and other "bondmen," but included volunteers who needed the money. The word comes from *gladius*, a double-edged sword.

5. *Capuan*. Resident of Capua, city in western Italy known for its gladiatorial exhibitions. Cneius Lentulus Batiatus was a *lanista*, or trainer of gladiators, known to history only for running the school from which Spartacus escaped.

6. *crucified*. Crucifixion was a common punishment among the Romans, often seen as a humiliation and thus reserved for those of low status. As indicated later in the play, the Romans used mass crucifixions as punishment for the rebellious gladiators.

7. *Saturnalia*. Holiday in Rome in which normal social roles are reversed.

8. *Thrace*. Area bordered by contemporary Macedonia, Bulgaria, Turkey, and the Strymon River in Greece, Thrace was the scene of Roman military campaigns against Thracian raiders from the second century B.C. on. Its inhabitants were an Indo-European people, thought by the Greeks and Romans to be savage.

9. *Clypeus*. A clipeus is a circular shield.

10. *Strymon*. River in eastern Greece (ancient Macedonia) that was the ancient western border of Thrace.

11. *Spartacus*. A Thracian gladiator whose revolt against his bondage actually began in Capua in 73 B.C. with his escape from the gladiatorial school there. The play follows the progress of the uprising, the gathering of as many as ninety thousand men, and his eventual defeat by Crassus in 71 B.C.

12. *drachmas, sesterces*. A drachma is silver coin of ancient Greece, also used as a Roman denomination. Here it means a coin of high value. A sestertius is one-quarter of a silver denarius, the basic Roman coin of the period.

13. *Cerberus*. Three-headed guardian dog of the underworld.

14. *vine-branch*. "The MS. contains the following note, written in Bird's hand: 'This (the vine branch) was the badge of a centurion's office, and he should carry it—at least in camp and in his embassies'" (Foust's note).

15. *Campania*. Region in southern Italy, where Capua was located.

16. *Aqua Sextia*. Roman troops under Gaius Marius defeated a force of

Germanic tribes, Ambrones and Teutones, at Aquae Sextiae in Transalpine Gaul (the location of modern Aix-en-Provence in southern France), in 102 B.C.

17. *Crixus.* A gladiator from Gaul who led rebel forces with Spartacus but left to fight under his own command and was killed in 72 B.C.

18. *Praetorian Guards.* The *cohors praetoria*, bodyguards to generals and thought of as elite troops.

19. *Lictors, Aediles, Conquistitores.* Various titles for minor officials in Roman system. Lictors were attendants, often accompanying men of higher rank at public games. Aediles had responsibility for public entertainments.

20. *African.* Hannibal (247–183? B.C.), the leader of armies from Carthage in North Africa against Rome in the Punic Wars.

21. *Brennus.* Leader of a Galatian-Gallic invasion of Greece in 279 B.C., wounded at Delphi, eventually committed suicide.

22. *obolus.* Ancient Greek coin worth one-sixth of a drachma; here, a coin of little value.

23. *Vindicta.* Literally, revenge, with implications of reversal (Latin); here, sign of praetor's power to overturn a prior judgment or status.

24. *Ciconian, Hebrus.* The Cicones were a people attacked by Odysseus on his way home from the Trojan Wars; Hebrus, the river forming the eastern boundary of the Cicones' territory in Thrace. Spartacus here claims the Cicones as his Thracian ancestors.

25. *cogging.* Cheating.

26. *Act III, Scene 1.* "There is a query in Bird's handwriting 'whether to restore the beginning of this scene or some part of it?' It seems that Dr. Bird submitted the MS. of *The Gladiator* to Edwin Forrest for revision, who no doubt suggested many of the cuts indicated" (Foust's note).

27. *Gellius.* Lucius Gellius Poplicola, consul appointed in 72 B.C., who defeated band of slaves under Crixus, but was himself defeated by Spartacus and forced to yield his command of legions to Crassus. Survived another fifteen or so years.

28. *Lentulus.* Not the Lentulus of the play, but the consul Gnaeus Cornelius Lentulus Clodianus, appointed with Gellius in 72 B.C., also defeated by Spartacus.

29. *maw.* "The original reading, struck out in the MS., was '—a thing to rot/In a hyena's paunch.' The reading I have adopted is written in a hand resembling Forrest's, in pencil, and is probably his suggestion" (Foust's note).

30. *cot.* Cottage.

31. *runagates.* Renegades.

32. *face.* "There are the following notes in Bird's hand, evidently in answer to Forrest's suggested cuts.

'Think you had better keep these expressions particularly the *flourishing fool* and *straw*. They express, in a very lofty and furious style, the contempt which such a man as Spartacus would feel at finding himself resisted by a younker.

"The term *boy's* was meant as a substitute for boyish; not, as if asking the question of others, *the face of this boy*' " (Foust's note).

33. *Velabrum.* Busy area alongside Tiber in Rome, near Forum and Capitol.

34. *Scropha.* Gnaeus Tremellius Scrofa, quaestor in 71 B.C. and cavalry commander, seriously wounded in battle and defeated by Spartacus.

35. *conqueror.* According to Foust, the original lines of this passage read: "I have found ye, wife, and in a noble hour. / When we met last, I was a slave; and now, / In a consul's camp, I stand a conqueror!"

36. *scene.* "This scene is struck out in the MS. and, according to a note in Bird's handwriting, was 'omitted in the representation' " (Foust's note).

37. *Mummius.* Subordinate commander under Crassus who disobeyed orders and was defeated by Spartacus.

38. *decimated, duplates, tithes.* In the Roman army, mutinies or other failures were punished by decimation, a process where every tenth (tithed) soldier was picked out by a commander to be killed. *Duplate* is double, so the sense of the speech is that the soldiers from the armies of the defeated consuls should be rounded up and subject to double decimation, or every two in ten killed. In fact, the defeated Roman armies do appear to have been decimated by order of Crassus to restore discipline.

39. *hair-brained.* Old spelling for hare-brained.

40. *Brundisium.* City in Calabria, in the heel of the boot in southern Italy. The war eventually shifted to the south as Spartacus contemplated going to Sicily.

41. *Ostia.* City close to Rome.

42. *slavish.* "There is a query in Bird's hand,—'Shall I substitute vile, odious, degrading, or some other word?' " (Foust's note).

43. *brock.* Badger, often in conjunction with "stinking" (OED).

44. *dinging.* Here, give violence to.

45. *Rhegium.* City at tip of toe in extreme southern Italy, across from Sicily.

46. *Haemus, Euxine, Adria, Tartarus.* Respectively, mountain in Thrace, Black Sea, Adriatic Sea, hell.

47. *Phlegethon.* River of fire in Hades.

13. *Jehu.* Notorious Hebrew soldier who became king (d. 815 B.C.), fought many battles, and killed several rivals.
14. *in thy sight.* Words of Jesus in Matthew 11:25–26 and Luke 10:21.
15. *unbelief.* Mark 9:24, father of an afflicted child speaking to Jesus.
16. *Scene 3.* In a promptbook of the play at the New York Public Library, an additional scene occurs between this scene and act 4, scene 2. The text is not complete, but it shows Marks and Cute in a New Orleans barroom; Legree coming in, then St. Clare; Cute antagonizing Legree, and the latter wounding St. Clare in his rush with a knife to get at Cute. See the version reprinted in Richard Moody, ed. *Dramas from the American Theatre, 1762–1909* (Cleveland: World, 1966), 383. St. Clare's injury is only reported in Stowe, not realized; the business of Marks and Cute as witnesses is Aiken's invention.
17. *Day & Martin.* Blackface minstrel act of the period.
18. *extract of Japan.* Refers to process of japanning, the application of black lacquer to decorative ware.
19. *Barnum.* Phineas Taylor Barnum (1810–1891), the New York entertainment entrepreneur, who exhibited both faked and real prodigies of nature at his museum, as well as hosted rival versions of *Uncle Tom's Cabin* at the museum theater.
20. *brangle.* Violent disagreement, row.
21. *Fillibusterow. Filibustero* (Spanish), adventurer, freebooter; one who joins a private army for service in a foreign land. Cute refers to an abortive effort by Southerners—working against United States government policy—to invade Cuba in support of the potential revolutionary Narciso López, in August 1850. Fifty-two Americans in vessels off-shore were captured by Spanish authorities, brought to Havana, and executed.

The Octoroon, by Dion Boucicault

1. *quarter-day.* Regular payment day in each of the four quarters of the year.
2. *penpans.* I have not been able to identify this word. Myron Matlaw in this collated edition of *The Octoroon* prints "pompano," a kind of fish. See *Nineteenth-Century American Plays,* edited by Myron Matlaw (New York: Applause, 1985), 106.
3. *Atchafalaya.* Bay off southwest coast of Terrebonne Parish, in southern Louisiana. The plantation of Terrebonne is presumably located in this bayou region near the Gulf of Mexico. Many of the planters'

        names—Caillou, Thibodeaux, Lafouche—are also borrowed from place names in that section of Louisiana.

4. *painter.* Panther, that is, American cougar.

5. *proximo.* Of the next month.

6. *sangaree.* Cold alcoholic beverage flavored with nutmeg.

7. *won't.* Was not; Pete is responding to previous uses of "want" by Ratts and Scudder.

8. *Matagorda.* Town, county, and peninsula along Gulf Coast just south of Galveston, Texas. M'Closky might feel safer in Matamoros, Mexico, just across the Rio Grande from Brownsville, Texas.

9. *London.* Pete is probably referring to General Andrew Jackson's decisive victory over the British at the Battle of New Orleans at the end of the War of 1812.

FOR THE BEST IN PAPERBACKS, LOOK FOR THE

In every corner of the world, on every subject under the sun, Penguin represents quality and variety—the very best in publishing today.

For complete information about books available from Penguin—including Puffins, Penguin Classics, and Arkana—and how to order them, write to us at the appropriate address below. Please note that for copyright reasons the selection of books varies from country to country.

In the United Kingdom: Please write to *Dept. JC, Penguin Books Ltd, FREEPOST, West Drayton, Middlesex UB7 0BR.*

If you have any difficulty in obtaining a title, please send your order with the correct money, plus ten percent for postage and packaging, to *P.O. Box No. 11, West Drayton, Middlesex UB7 0BR*

In the United States: Please write to *Consumer Sales, Penguin USA, P.O. Box 999, Dept. 17109, Bergenfield, New Jersey 07621-0120.* Visa and MasterCard holders call 1-800-253-6476 to order all Penguin titles

In Canada: Please write to *Penguin Books Canada Ltd, 10 Alcorn Avenue, Suite 300, Toronto, Ontario M4V 3B2*

In Australia: Please write to *Penguin Books Australia Ltd, P.O. Box 257, Ringwood, Victoria 3134*

In New Zealand: Please write to *Penguin Books (NZ) Ltd, Private Bag 102902, North Shore Mail Centre, Auckland 10*

In India: Please write to *Penguin Books India Pvt Ltd, 706 Eros Apartments, 56 Nehru Place, New Delhi 110 019*

In the Netherlands: Please write to *Penguin Books Netherlands bv, Postbus 3507, NL-1001 AH Amsterdam*

In Germany: Please write to *Penguin Books Deutschland GmbH, Metzlerstrasse 26, 60594 Frankfurt am Main*

In Spain: Please write to *Penguin Books S. A., Bravo Murillo 19, 1° B, 28015 Madrid*

In Italy: Please write to *Penguin Italia s.r.l., Via Felice Casati 20, I-20124 Milano*

In France: Please write to *Penguin France S. A., 17 rue Lejeune, F–31000 Toulouse*

In Japan: Please write to *Penguin Books Japan, Ishikiribashi Building, 2–5–4, Suido, Bunkyo-ku, Tokyo 112*

In Greece: Please write to *Penguin Hellas Ltd, Dimocritou 3, GR–106 71 Athens*

In South Africa: Please write to *Longman Penguin Southern Africa (Pty) Ltd, Private Bag X08, Bertsham 2013*